DIGITAL LABOUR
AND KARL MARX

How is labour changing in the age of computers, the Internet, and social media such as Facebook, Google, YouTube and Twitter? In *Digital Labour and Karl Marx*, Christian Fuchs attempts to answer that question, crafting a systematic critical theorisation of labour as performed in the capitalist ICT industry. Relying on a range of global case studies—from unpaid social media prosumers or Chinese hardware assemblers at Foxconn to miners in the Democratic Republic of Congo—Fuchs sheds light on the labour costs of digital media, examining the way ICT corporations exploit human labour and the impact of this exploitation on the lives, bodies, and minds of workers.

Christian Fuchs is professor of social media at the University of Westminster in London. He is the author of more than 200 academic publications in the fields of Internet studies, social media studies, critical social theory and information society studies. He is the editor of the open access online journal *tripleC: Communication, Capitalism & Critique.* Among his publications are the books *Internet and Society, Foundations of Critical Media and Information Studies,* and the collected volumes *Internet and Surveillance: The Challenges of Web 2.0 and Social Media* and *Critique, Social Media, and the Information Society.*

DIGITAL LABOUR AND KARL MARX

Christian Fuchs

Routledge
Taylor & Francis Group

NEW YORK AND LONDON

First published 2014
by Routledge
711 Third Avenue, New York, NY 10017

and by Routledge
2 Park Square, Milton Park, Abingdon, Oxon OX14 4RN

Routledge is an imprint of the Taylor & Francis Group, an informa business

Library of Congress Cataloging-in-Publication Data
Fuchs, Christian, 1976-
Digital labor and Karl Marx / Christian Fuchs.
    pages cm
  Includes bibliographical references and index.
 1. Knowledge workers. 2. Information technology—Economic aspects. 3. Information technology—Social aspects. 4. Industrial sociology. I. Title.
HD8039.K59F83   2013
335.4'12—dc23   2013017800

ISBN: 978-0-415-71615-4 (hbk)
ISBN: 978-1-315-88007-5 (ebk)

Typeset in Bembo
by Apex CoVantage, LLC

This book is dedicated to Marisol and the singularity
of our non-labour of love

El amor
me dará aire, espacio,
alimento para crecer y ser mejor,
como una Revolución
que hace de cada día
el comienzo de una nueva victoria

—Gioconda Belli

CONTENTS

FIGURES AND TABLES

FIGURES

TABLES

1

INTRODUCTION

1.1. The Need for Studying Digital Labour

Muhanga Kawaya, an enslaved miner in North Kivu (Democratic Republic of Congo) who extracts minerals that are needed for the manufacturing of laptops and mobile phones, describes his work in the following way: "As you crawl through the tiny hole, using your arms and fingers to scratch, there's not enough space to dig properly and you get badly grazed all over. And then, when you do finally come back out with the cassiterite, the soldiers are waiting to grab it at gunpoint. Which means you have nothing to buy food with. So we're always hungry" (Finnwatch 2007, 20). A Chinese engineer at Foxconn Shenzhen, where computers and mobile phones that are sold by Western companies are assembled, says, "We produced the first generation iPad. We were busy throughout a 6-month period and had to work on Sundays. We only had a rest day every 13 days. And there was no overtime premium for weekends. Working for 12 hours a day really made me exhausted" (SACOM 2010, 7). In Silicon Valley, a Cambodian ICT (information and communications technology) assembler exposed to toxic substances reports, "I talked to my co-workers who felt the same way [that I did] but they never brought it up, out of fear of losing their job" (Pellow and Park 2002, 139). Mohan, a project manager in the Indian software industry who is in his mid-30s, explains, "Work takes a priority. [. . .] The area occupied by family and others keeps reducing" (D'Mello and Sahay 2007, 179). Another software engineer argues, "Sometimes you start at 8 am and then finish at 10–11 pm, five days a week. And anytime you can be called. [. . .] Also you don't develop any hobbies" (ibid.). A software engineer at Google describes the working situation there: "Cons—Because of the large amounts of benefits (such as free foods) there seems to be an unsaid rule that employees are expected to work longer hours. Many people work more than 8 hours a day and then will be on email or work for a couple hours at home, at night as well (or on the weekends). It may be hard to perform extremely well with a good work/life balance. Advice to Senior Management—Give engineers more freedom to use 20% time to work on cool projects without the stress of having to do 120% work" (www.glassdoor. com). The Amazon Mechanical Turk is a "marketplace for work" that "gives businesses and developers access to an on-demand, scalable workforce. Workers select from thousands of tasks and work whenever it is convenient" (www.mturk.com). Clients can advertise on the platform that they look for certain services for a certain wage, to which those who want to perform them can respond online. If the deal comes about, then the worker performs the task and submits the result to the client online. The work tasks almost exclusively involve informational work. A search for speech transcription tasks (conducted on November 20, 2012) resulted in three tasks that had (if one assumes that it takes on average six hours of work time to transcribe one hour of interview time) an hourly wage of (a) US$4, (b) US$4 and (c) US$3. In contrast, typical professional transcription services (e.g. www.fingertipstyping.co.uk/prices_and_turnaround.htm, www.franklin-square. com/transcription_per_line.htm) charge approximately US$15–$25 per hour.

In February 2013, the German public service station broadcaster ARD aired the documentary *Ausgeliefert! Leiharbeiter bei Amazon* (At mercy[1]! Contract workers at Amazon). The investigative reporters Diana Löbl and Peter Onneken documented that Amazon Germany employs 5,000 immigrants (from e.g. Poland, Romania, Spain, Hungary and other countries) as contract workers in its warehouse. They showed that these workers are extremely low-paid, live in groups of six or seven workers who do not know each other in small cottages, where two people share tiny bedrooms. They only get temporary contracts and are employed by temp agencies. The contracts are written in German, although many workers do not understand this language. On one day, the warehouse workers often run up to 17 kilometres, which can negatively impact their feet and skin. The workers do not see and sign the contract before they come to Germany and then often have to find out that they earn less than initially promised. One contract shown in the documentary specifies €8.52 per hour, although the worker was initially promised €9.68, which is 12% more. These workers can be hired and fired as Amazon wishes. Trade union secretary Heiner Reimann (with trade union ver. di) describes these Amazon workers as "workers without rights" (10:41–10:46). A driver said, "Temp work. [...] I am not in favour of this slave trade. [...] They earn so little money, partly they have to beg for coffee in the canteen" (14:20–14:35). Selvina, a Spanish contract worker, said, "It is like a machine. We are a cog in this machine" (17:12–17:16). The documentary presented footage that indicated Amazon's supposed evasion of paying social security taxes for their employees. The workers have to commute long distances to their workplace in overcrowded buses supplied by Amazon. Often they wait and commute for hours. If the bus arrives late, they face wage deductions. The workers can be controlled any time, even outside of the workplace, and there are security guards patrolling the housing estates, their dining rooms, and the factory premises. The ARD investigative journalists show that there are security forces from the H.E.S.S. company and that security guards act and look like a paramilitary force, entering workers' homes while they are not there to control them by taking pictures. One worker says, "When we eat, they are always there. [. . .] They enter the houses while the people are not there and also when the people sleep or take a shower" (19:09–19:25). Another one reports that the guards argue, "This is our house. [. . .] You must do what we say. And here we are like the police" (19:25–19:38). The reporters show that some security guards wear clothes from Thor Steinar, a neo-Nazi brand. H.E.S.S. stands for Hensel European Security Services. (Rudolf Hess was Hitler's deputy.) H.E.S.S. sells, according to the ARD documentary, clothes that are considered to be right-wing extremist brands in Germany (Commando Industries). The documentary shows that some of the H.E.S.S. employees and management personnel are part of the hooligan scene or have circles of right-wing extremist friends. In the days after the documentary was aired on ARD (February 13), almost every minute somebody posted a protest message on Amazon's Facebook page. Some example comments are: "Nazis, conditions like in a modern labour camp, unlimited greed for profits. BE ASHAMED!"[2] "Modern slavery, but the main thing for you is that your profits are doing well"[3] "Shame on you, bloody bastards! you'll never have my and my friends' money! i hope you'll go on default veeeery quickly!" "Profits that are based on a new form of slavery should be confiscated just like profits from drug trafficking!"[4]

Work.Shop.Play is an online platform owned by CBS Outdoor Limited. It describes its purpose in the following way:

> We are interested in your ideas, opinions, behaviour and general feedback on a variety of topics. One week we may send you surveys asking how you feel about topics in the news at the moment. The next, we might ask you how often you drink coffee, what brands you buy and which coffee shop you prefer. The week after that, it might be a survey about new technology, which gadgets you own and why you bought them. [. . .] CBS Outdoor work with lots of big brands, telling them how to best advertise and market their products and services to consumers. [. . .] Sometimes, the research team at CBS Outdoor will use survey results to create material for our sales teams to present to these brands. Other times we'll be using the results internally, to better inform our company about urban audiences. Occasionally we may post survey results on Twitter or Facebook. [. . .] When we were setting up work.shop.play. we thought long and hard about how to reward our members. We developed a list of prizes that we think will appeal to everyone—such as cinema and theatre tickets, shopping vouchers, magazine subscriptions and guidebooks to UK cities. From time to time there will also be bigger prizes up for grabs, such as nights away at a top hotel—and

> sometimes there may be one prize, while others there may be 10 or more. (workshopplay.co.uk, accessed February 17, 2013)

Facebook has asked users to translate its site into other languages without payment. Translation is crowdsourced to users. Javier Olivan, head of Growth, Engagement, Mobile Adoption at Facebook, sees user-generated platform translation as "cool" because Facebook's goal is to "have one day everybody on the planet on Facebook" (MSNBC 2008).

> Valentin Macias, 29, a Californian who teaches English in Seoul, South Korea, has volunteered in the past to translate for the nonprofit Internet encyclopedia Wikipedia but said he won't do it for Facebook. "[Wikipedia is] an altruistic, charitable, information-sharing, donation-supported cause", Macias told The Associated Press in a Facebook message. "Facebook is not. Therefore, people should not be tricked into donating their time and energy to a multimillion-dollar company so that the company can make millions more—at least not without some type of compensation." (ibid.)

These examples outline various forms of labour associated with the ICT industry. They differ in amount in regard to the levels of payment; health risks; physical, ideological and social violence; stress; free time; overtime; and the forms of coercion and control the workers are experiencing, but all have in common that human labour-power is exploited in a way that monetarily benefits ICT corporations and has negative impacts on the lives, bodies or minds of workers. The forms of labour described in this book are all types of digital labour because they are part of a collective work force that is required for the existence, usage and application of digital media. What defines them is not a common type of occupation, but rather the industry they contribute to and in which capital exploits them. The kind of definition one chooses of categories such as digital labour or virtual work, their degree of inclusivity or exclusivity, are first and foremost political choices. The approach taken in this book advocates a broad understanding of digital labour based on an industry rather than an occupation definition in order to stress the commonality of exploitation, capital as the common enemy of a broad range of workers and the need to globalize and network struggles in order to overcome the rule of capitalism. Some of the workers described in this book are not just exploited by digital media capital, but also and sometimes simultaneously by other forms of capital. It is then a matter of degree to which extent these forms of labour are digital labour and simultaneously other forms of labour. If we imagine a company with job rotation so that each worker on average assembles laptops for 50% of his/her work time and cars for the other half of the time, a worker in this factory is a digital worker for 50%. S/he is however an industrial worker for 100% because the content of both manufacturing activities is the industrial assemblage of components into commodities. The different forms of digital labour are connected in an international division of digital labour (IDDL), in which all labour necessary for the existence, usage and application of digital media is "disconnected, isolated [...], carried on side by side" and ossified "into a systematic division" (Marx 1867c, 456). Studies of the information economy, or what some term the creative or cultural industries, have been dominated by the capital side of the analysis, whereas the labour side has been rather missing. In this context, Nicholas Garnham already asserted in 1990 that "the bibliography on the producers of culture is scandalously empty" (Garnham 1990, 12) and that there is a focus on the analysis of media barons and their companies. Ten years later, he saw this problem as persisting: "The problem of media producers has been neglected in recent media and Cultural Studies—indeed in social theory generally—because of the general linguistic turn and the supposed death of the author that has accompanied it. If the author does not exist or has no intentional power, why study her or him?" (Garnham 2000a, 84). Again ten years later, Vincent Mosco (2011, 230) argued that "labour remains the blind spot of communication and Cultural Studies" and that therefore "labour needs to be placed high on the agenda or projects for the renewal of Cultural Studies". A particular problem of contemporary media and communication studies is the strong focus on the capital side of the creative and cultural economy and the neglect of the labour side. Richard Maxwell and Toby Miller make a similar assessment: "Most writings in media studies constrict the ambit of media labor such that the industry mavens [...] define production. This mirrors the growth ideology and apolitical enchantment with media technologies found in most trade publications, entertainment news outlets, and fan culture" (Maxwell and Miller 2012, 16). They argue for "critical scholarship into media labor" that considers "the physical nature of work and what it does to people and the environment" (ibid.). Vicki Mayer, Miranda J. Banks and John Thornton Caldwell (2009, 4) speak in this context of the need for media production studies that "take the lived realities of people involved in in media production as the subjects for theorizing production as culture". Juliet Webster (2011, 2) observes that the study of ICT's role in society has often been

> guided by pragmatism rather than by social critique. In many countries, there is and has been for some twenty or more years, a discernible body of work which is concerned primarily with interpreting technological innovations as socially neutral processes or with the practicalities of ICT implementation. There are strong pressures on researchers, particularly in a context of economic crisis and restructuring, to retreat into this type of work. In this context, critical social research often becomes displaced by research which is driven by an over-optimistic technological agenda. Researchers find they have to survive in a world where economic growth and constant innovation are the leitmotifs underlying not only economic but social policy.

She calls for resisting these tendencies and for engaged ICTs and society research that is doing research and doing politics and is a form of activism. The task of this book is to develop a critical theorization of some of the labour performed in the capitalist ICT industry. The overall question of the book is: What is digital labour and how can its working conditions best be understood? For providing answers, more fundamental questions need to be asked: What is labour? What is economic value? How does labour create value? How is labour changing in the age of computers, the Internet and "social media" such as Facebook, Google, YouTube and Twitter? Labour and economic value are inherently connected. Labour takes place in certain spaces and is spent during certain time periods. Time and space are crucial dimensions of labour. Discussions about the spatial changes and spatial disembedding of labour have been discussed with concepts such as globalization (see Fuchs 2003, Ritzer and Atalay 2010), outsourcing, offshoring and global/international division of labour (Grossman 1980, Mies 1986). Globalization has been theorized as time-space-compression (Harvey 1989, timeless time and spaceless space (Castells 1996) and as time-space distanciation (Giddens 1990). This shows that time and space are crucial dimensions of societal changes. Given that labour is at the heart of the economy, both time and space are crucial for understanding labour. The labour needed for the production of a certain commodity is in many cases not confined to single places, but takes place in many interconnected spaces that are diffused around the globe so that capital tries to minimise investment costs for labour and resources and to maximise profits. But labour not only has spatial aspects, it also takes place in time, which is obvious when talking about working time, free time, spare time, working hours, production time, circulation time, distribution time, the turnover time of capital, the acceleration of production or the intensification of work.

Labour time is so crucial for capitalism because labour-power is organized as a commodity and therefore every second of labour costs money. This is the reason why capital has the interest to make workers work as long as possible for as little wages as possible and to make them labour as intensively as possible so that the highest possible profit (which is the outcome of unpaid labour time) can be achieved. Value in a Marxist approach (Marx's labour theory of value) is the amount of performed labour hours that are needed for the production of a certain commodity. There is an individual labour time for the production of every single commodity that is difficult to measure. What matters economically is therefore the average labour time that is spent during a certain time period (such as one year) for producing a commodity. Average labour values can be calculated for commodity production in one company, a group of companies, an entire industry in a country or internationally. Capital strives to reduce the value of a commodity in order to increase profits. A decrease of the value of a commodity means a speed-up of production (i.e. the same labour time that costs a certain amount of money will suddenly produce a higher number of the same commodity, although the labour costs have not increased, which allows accumulating more profit per time unit).

The outlined examples show the importance of labour time for the ICT industry: Slave mineral workers like Muhanga Kawaya work at gunpoint with the threat of being killed, which makes them work long hours for low or no wages so that a maximum of labour time remains unpaid. The workers at Foxconn are working long hours and unpaid overtime so that Apple and other ICT companies reduce labour costs. Foxconn workers have relatively low wages and work very long hours. Foxconn tries to lengthen the working day in order to increase the sum of hours that is unpaid. ICT assemblers in Silicon Valley, who are predominantly female immigrants, have quite comparable labour conditions, and many of them are exposed during working hours to toxic substances. In the Indian software industry and at Google, software engineers are overworked. They work very long hours and do not have much time for hobbies, relaxing, friends and family. Software developers at Google, in India and in other countries are highly stressed because they work in project-based software engineering with high time pressure. Their lifetime tends to become labour time. The Amazon Mechanical Turk is a method of getting work done in the same time as in the case of regular employment by irregular forms of labour that are cheaper. It helps companies to find workers who work for the time a regular employee would take for a certain task, but for a lower payment. The idea is to crowdsource work over the Internet in order to reduce costs, that is, to pay less for the same labour time as under regular working conditions. The temporary workers at Amazon Germany have temporary limited contracts, which put them under pressure to accept and not to resist the poor working conditions because they are afraid of losing their jobs. Many of them come from countries that were hard hit by the economic crisis, where they are facing unemployment. Crisis drives them into accepting work under early industrial conditions. Paramilitary control should make the employees work more and faster during the work time. It aims at an intensification of work. Low wages for temp workers who are facing economic hardship means that Amazon can make more profit than in employment relations that have collective bargaining, collective wage agreements and unionization. Time plays an important role in this example in the form of insecure temporary employment, work time intensification and the lowering of hourly wages.

In return for their efforts to participate in surveys whose results are sold as commodities, users of Work.Shop.Play can win prizes such as cinema and theatre tickets, shopping vouchers and special offers. Of course only a few win; most of the work is completely unremunerated. The idea of the Work.Shop.Play platform is that users work in their free time and thereby have the chance to win vouchers and goods that enable shopping, entertainment and play. Playing on social media becomes actual work and the promise is that users in return get opportunities for shopping and more play. Work.Shop.Play extends the capitalist logic of commodities and consumption to the home and play time. The boundaries between work and play as well as between work time and free/play time are liquid on Work. Shop.Play. Facebook translations are outsourced user work. The users are expected to perform the translation without remuneration. The idea is to transform usage time into work time. The lengthening of working day, unpaid working times, the intensification of work time by fascist security forces, overwork, spare time as labour time, overtime—the examples show that labour time is a crucial aspect of the capitalist ICT industry.

The task of this book is to better understand labour and value generation in the context of digital media. Chapters 3 and 4 contextualize digital labour in the academic landscape: Chapter 3 shows how the field of contemporary Cultural Studies is positioning itself towards Karl Marx's works and studying labour and capitalism. Chapter 4 deals with the relevance of Dallas Smythe's work for understanding digital labour. Smythe was the founding figure of the field of critical political economy of media and communication, and he elaborated a labour theory of the media that sees viewing/reading/listening time on commercial media as audience labour that creates value. He coined in this context the notion of the audience commodity. This approach has in the context of the digital labour debate gained new relevance. Chapter 5 contextualizes digital labour in the debate on the concept of the information society. It asks whether we live in capitalism or an information society. Chapters 6–11 analyse various forms of labour in the international division of digital labour (IDDL) in order to introduce concepts for a digital labour theory-toolbox and show examples of how to apply such theoretical categories. Chapter 6 deals with slave workers in Africa who extract minerals that form the physical foundation of laptops, computers, mobile phones and other ICTs. Chapter 7 looks at the working conditions in Chinese hardware assemblage, specifically the situation in Foxconn factories. Chapter 8 discusses the labour conditions of Indian software engineers. Chapter 9 analyses work in Silicon Valley, especially software engineering at Google. Chapter 10 looks at precarious service work with the help of the example of call centre work. Chapter 11 focuses on the unpaid digital labour of Internet prosumers using the example of Facebook. In order to avoid misunderstandings, I want to make clear that each of the chapters 6–11 does not define concepts that are specific for only one form of digital labour. The task is rather to introduce a multifaceted conceptual digital labour theory-toolbox with theoretical notions such as absolute and relative surplus-value production, commodity fetishism, formal and real subsumption, housewifization, labour aristocracy, modes of production, play labour, productive forces, prosumers commodification, slavery, the new imperialism, primitive accumulation, etc. Chapters 6–11 show examples of how to apply these categories. These chapters do not claim that a specific concept is only applicable to one of the specifically discussed forms of labour. I give examples of how to apply these concepts with the help of case studies. The point is that Marx's writings and Marxist theory provide a rich category system that can be applied for critically understanding digital labour and other forms of labour. Specific working conditions of specific types of digital labour are historical and dynamic, they do not stay fixed, but change with the development and crises of capitalism. The first task for developing a digital labour theory-toolbox that needs to be undertaken and to which this book contributes is therefore to introduce concepts and to show examples of how to apply them. Chapter 12 draws conclusions from the preceding analysis and points out aspects of resistance against the exploitation of digital labour. It discusses in this context especially the Occupy movement as a new working-class movement and its use of the Internet and social media.

The approach taken in this book for critically theorizing and explaining social media and digital labour is grounded in the works of Karl Marx. Chapter 2 outlines as theoretical framework important concepts of Marx's theory. But why is Marx's theory a suitable framework? This question requires further discussion.

1.2. The Disappearance and Return of Karl Marx

- "Marx makes a comeback" (*Svenska Dagbladet,* October 17, 2008).
- "Crunch resurrects Marx" (*The Independent,* October 17, 2008).
- "Crisis allows us to reconsider left-wing ideas" (*The Irish Times,* October 18, 2008).
- "Marx exhumed, capitalism buried" (*Sydney Morning Herald,* October 23, 2008).
- "Marx Renaissance" (*Korea Times,* January 1, 2009).
- "Was Marx Right All Along?" (*The Evening Standard,* March 30, 2009).
- "'Marx is fashionable again', declares Jorn Schutrumpf, head of the Berlin publishing house Dietz, which brings out the works of Marx and his collaborator Friedrich Engels. Sales have trebled—albeit from a pretty low level—since 2005 and have soared since the summer. [. . .] The Archbishop of Canterbury, Rowan Williams, gave him a decent review last month: 'Marx long ago observed the way in which unbridled capitalism became a kind of mythology, ascribing reality, power and agency to things that had no life in themselves'. Even the Pope has put in a good word for the old atheist— praising his 'great analytical skill'" (*The Times,* "Financial Crisis Gives Added Capital to Marx's Writings", October 20, 2008).
- "No one claims that we're all Marxists now but I do think the old boy deserves some credit for noticing that 'it's the economy, stupid' and that many of the apparently omniscient titans who ascend the commanding heights of the economy are not so much stupid as downright imbecilic, driven by a mad exploitative greed that threatens us all. Marx's work is not holy writ, despite the strivings of some disciples to present it as such" (*The Evening Standard,* "Was Marx Right All Along?", March 30, 2009).
- "Karl Marx is back. That, at least, is the verdict of publishers and bookshops in Germany who say that his works are flying off the shelves" (*The Guardian,* "Booklovers Turn to Karl Marx as Financial Crisis Bites in Germany", October 15, 2008).

- "Policy makers struggling to understand the barrage of financial panics, protests and other ills afflicting the world would do well to study the works of a long-dead economist: Karl Marx. The sooner they recognize we're facing a once-in-a-lifetime crisis of capitalism, the better equipped they will be to manage a way out of it" (*Bloomberg Business Week,* "Give Karl Marx a Chance to Save the World Economy", August 28, 2011).
- *Time* magazine showed Marx on its cover on February 2, 2009, and asked in respect to the crisis: "What would Marx think?" In the cover story, Marx was presented as the saviour of capitalism and was thereby mutilated beyond recognition: "Rethinking Marx. As we work out how to save capitalism, it's worth studying the system's greatest critic" (*Time Magazine Europe,* February 2, 2009).

These news clippings indicate that with the new global crisis of capitalism, we seem to have entered new Marxian times. That there is suddenly a surging interest in Karl Marx's work is an indication for the persistence of capitalism, class conflicts and crisis. At the same time, the bourgeois press tries to limit Marx and to stifle his theory by interpreting Marx as the new saviour of capitalism. One should remember that he was not only a brilliant analyst of capitalism, he was also the strongest critic of capitalism in his time:

> In short, the Communists everywhere support every revolutionary movement against the existing social and political order of things. In all these movements, they bring to the front, as the leading question in each, the property question, no matter what its degree of development at the time. Finally, they labour everywhere for the union and agreement of the democratic parties of all countries. The Communists disdain to conceal their views and aims. They openly declare that their ends can be attained only by the forcible overthrow of all existing social conditions. Let the ruling classes tremble at a Communistic revolution. The proletarians have nothing to lose but their chains. They have a world to win. Proletarians of all lands unite! (Marx and Engels 1848/2004, 94)

In 1977, Dallas Smythe published his seminal article "Communications: Blindspot of Western Marxism" (Smythe 1977a), in which he argued that Western Marxism had not given enough attention to the complex role of communications in capitalism. Thirty-five years have passed and the rise of neoliberalism resulted in a turn away from an interest in social class and capitalism. Instead, it became fashionable to speak of globalization, postmodernism and, with the fall of Communism, even the end of history. In essence, Marxism became the blind spot of all social science. Marxist academics were marginalized and it was increasingly career threatening for a young academic to take an explicitly Marxist approach to social analysis.

The declining interest in Marx and Marxism is visualized in figures 1.1 and 1.2, which show the number of articles in the Social Sciences Citation Index that contain one of the keywords "Marx", "Marxist" or "Marxism" in the article topic description and were published in the five time periods 1968–1977, 1978–1987, 1988–1997, 1998–2007 and 2008–2012. Choosing these periods allows one to determine if there has been a change since the start of the new capitalist crisis in 2008 and also makes sense because social upheavals in 1968 marked a break that also transformed academia.

Figure 1.1 shows that there was a relatively large academic article output about Marx in the period 1978–1987 (2,574). Given that the number of articles published increases historically, interest in the period 1968–1977 also seems to have been high. One can observe a clear contraction of the output about articles focusing on Marx in the periods 1988–1997 (1,713) and 1998–2007 (1,127). Given the earlier increase of published articles, this contraction is even more pronounced. This period has also been the time of the intensification of neoliberalism, the commodification of everything (including public service communication in many countries) and a strong turn towards postmodernism and culturalism in the social sciences.

There are multiple reasons for the disappearance of Marx:

- The rise of neoliberal class struggle from above.
- The commodification of everything, including the commons and public universities.
- The rise of postmodernism.
- The lack of trust in alternatives.

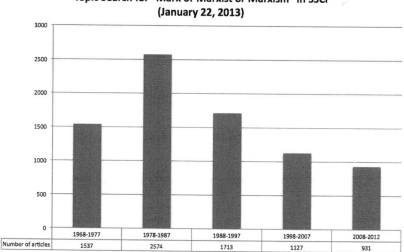

FIGURE 1.1 Number of articles published about Marx and Marxism that are listed in the Social Sciences Citation Index in ten-year intervals

- The low presence and intensity of struggles.
- In a climate of conservative backlash and commodification of academia, it was not opportune and conducive for an academic career and for academic reputation to conduct Marxist studies.

In figure 1.2, one can see that the annual average number of articles published about Marxism in the period 2008–2012 (186) has increased in comparisons to the periods 1998–2007 (113 per year) and 1988–1997 (171 per year). This circumstance is an empirical indicator of a renewed interest in Marx and Marxism in the social sciences, most likely an effect of the new capitalist crisis. The question is whether and how this interest can be sustained and materialized in institutional transformations.

Due to the rising income gap between the rich and the poor, widespread precarious labour and the new global capitalist crisis, neoliberalism is no longer seen as common sense. The dark side of capitalism, with its rising levels of class conflict, is now recognized worldwide. Eagleton (2011) notes that never has a thinker been so travestied as Marx and demonstrates that the core of Marx's work runs contrary to common prejudices about his work. But since the start of the global capitalist crisis in 2008, a considerable scholarly interest in the works of Marx has taken root. Žižek argues that the antagonisms of contemporary capitalism in the context of the ecological crisis, intellectual property, biogenetics, new forms of apartheid and slums show that we still need the Marxian notion of class and that there is a need to renew Marxism and to defend its lost causes in order to

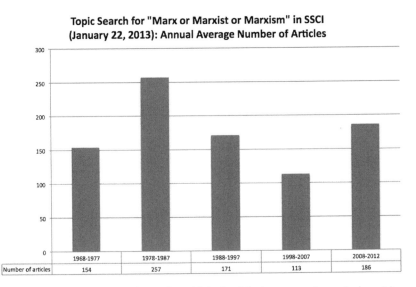

Topic Search for "Marx or Marxist or Marxism" in SSCI (January 22, 2013): Annual Average Number of Articles

	1968-1977	1978-1987	1988-1997	1998-2007	2008-2012
Number of articles	154	257	171	113	186

FIGURE 1.2 Average number of annually published articles in ten-year intervals about Marx and Marxism that are listed in the Social Sciences Citation Index

"render problematic the all-too-easy liberal-democratic alternative" that is posed by the new forms of a soft capitalism that promises but fails to realize ideals like participation, self-organization, and cooperation (Žižek 2008, 6). Moreover, Žižek (2010b) argues that the recent world economic crisis has resulted in a renewed interest in the Marxian critique of political economy. Hobsbawm (2011, 12–13) argues that for understanding the global dimension of contemporary capitalism, capitalism's contradictions and crises and the existence of socio-economic inequality we "must ask Marx's questions" (13). "Economic and political liberalism, singly or in combination, cannot provide the solution to the problems of the twenty-first century. Once again the time has come to take Marx seriously" (ibid., 419). Jameson argues that global capitalism, "its crises and the catastrophes appropriate to this present" and global unemployment show that "Marx remains as inexhaustible as capital itself" (Jameson 2011, 1) and make *Capital, Volume 1* (Marx 1867c) a most timely book.

"Monetary crises, independent of real crises or as an intensification of them, are unavoidable" in capitalism (Marx 1894, 649). For Marx, financial crises are not avoidable by regulated financial markets or moral rules that limit greed because greed is for him a necessary structural feature of capitalism that derives from the necessity of capitalists to accumulate ever more capital and to increase profit rates or to perish. Competition between capitals and the need to expand accumulation result in attempts to create "financial innovations" that have a high risk but allow very high short-time revenue rates. The fictitious value of commercial papers stands in no direct relation with the actual value created in the companies that is signified by the fictitious value. Financial bubbles are the effect (i.e. share prices that do not reflect the actual profitability and which fall heavily once a burst of the financial bubble is triggered by events that destroy the investors' expectations for high future returns). The new world economic crisis that started in 2008 is the most obvious reason for the return of the interest in Marx.

This shift is, however, multidimensional and has multiple causes:

- The new world economic crisis has resulted in an increasing interest in the dynamics and contradictions of capitalism and the notion of crisis.
- Neoliberalism and the precarization of work and life can best be analysed as phenomenon class, exploitation and commodification.
- New social movements (the anti-corporate movement, global justice movement, Occupy movement) have an interest in questions of class.
- The financialization of the economy can be analysed with categories such as the new imperialism or fictitious capital.
- New global wars bring about an interest in the category of imperialism.
- Contemporary revolutions and rebellions (such as the Arab Spring) give attention to the relevance of revolution, emancipation and liberation.
- The globalization discourse has been accompanied by discussions about global capitalism.

- The role of mediatization, ICTs and knowledge work in contemporary capitalism was anticipated by Marx's focus on the general intellect.
- A whole generation of precariously working university scholars and students

Indicative of an increased interest in capitalism as an object of study in media and communication studies is the circumstance that several special issues have focused on the role of communication, media and culture in the capitalist crisis:

tripleC: Communication, Capitalism & Critique (www.triple-c.at)-Journal for a Global Sustainable Information Society

tripleC—Journal for a Global Sustainable Information Society: "Capitalist Crisis, Communication & Culture" 8 (2), (2009): 193–309, edited by Christian Fuchs, Matthias Schafranek, David Hakken and Marcus Breen.

International Journal of Communication: "Global Financial Crisis" 4 (2010), edited by Paula Chakravartty and John D.H. Downing.

Cultural Studies: "The Economic Crisis and After" 24 (3), (2010): 283–444.

İrfan Erdogan (2012) has analysed 210 articles that mentioned Marx and that were published in 77 selected media and communication journals between January 2007 and June 2011. He found that "Mainstream studies ignore and liberal-democrats generally appreciate Marx", whereas the main criticisms of Marx come from "so-called 'critical' or 'alternative' approaches", whose "'alternatives' are 'alternatives to Marx'" and critical in the sense of a "criticism directed against Marx" (382). At the same time as there are sustained attempts to downplay the importance of Marx for the study of society, media and communication, there are indicators of a certain degree of new engagement with Marx. One of them is the special issue of *tripleC* (www.triple-c.at) "Marx Is Back—The Importance of Marxist Theory and Research for Critical Communication Studies Today" (Fuchs and Mosco 2012), which features 29 articles on more than 500 pages. Another one was the conference "Critique, Democracy and Philosophy in 21st Century Information Society: Towards Critical Theories of Social Media", at which a sustained engagement with Marx and communication today took place, especially by and among PhD students (see Fuchs 2012a, 2012d).

Whereas Marx was always relevant, this relevance has not been much acknowledged in media and communication studies in recent years. It has rather been common, as Erdogan (2012) shows, to misinterpret and misunderstand Marx, which partly came also from a misreading of his works or from outright ignorance of his works. Terry Eagleton (2011) discusses ten common prejudices against Marx and Marxism and shows why Marx was right and why these prejudices are wrong. We have added to the following overview a media and communication dimension to each prejudice. These communication dimensions point towards common prejudices against Marx within media and communication studies.

I want to counter each of the anti-Marxian prejudices with a counter-claim that is grounded in the analyses presented in this book which show the importance of Marx for understanding society and the media critically.

(1a) *Marxist Outdatedness!*
Marxism is old-fashioned and not suited for a post-industrial society.

(1b) *Marxist Topicality!*
In order to adequately and critically understand communication in society, we need Marx.

(2a) *Marxist Repression!*
Marxism may sound good in theory, but in practice it can only result in terror, tyranny and mass murder. The feasibility of a socialist society and socialist media are illusionary.

(2b) *Capitalist Repression!*
Capitalism neither sounds like a good idea/theory nor does it work in practice, as the reality of large-scale inequality, global war and environmental devastation shows. The feasibility of socialism and socialist media arises out of the crises of capitalism.

(3a) *Marxism = Determinism!*
Marx believed in deterministic laws of history and the automatic end of capitalism that would also entail the automatic end of capitalist media.

(3b) *Marxism = Dialectics and Complexity!*
Marxian and Hegelian dialectics allow us to see the history of society and the media as being shaped by structural conditioning, open-ended struggles and a dialectic of structure and agency.

(4a) *Marxist Do-Goodism!*
Marx had a naïve picture of humanity's goodness and ignored that humans are naturally selfish, acquisitive, aggressive and competitive. The media industry is therefore necessarily based on profit and competition; otherwise it cannot work.

(4b) *Capitalist Wickedness!*
The logic of individualism, egoism, profit maximization and competition has been tried and tested under neoliberal capitalism, which has also transformed the media landscape and made it more unequal.

(5a) *Marxist Reductionism!*
Marx and Marxism reduce all cultural and political phenomena to the economy. They do not have an understanding of non-economic aspects of the media and communication.

(5b) *Marxist Complexity!*
Contemporary developments show that the economy in capitalism is not determining but a special system that results in the circumstance that all phenomena under capitalism, which includes all media phenomena, have class aspects and are dialectically related to class. Class is a necessary, although certainly not sufficient, condition for explaining phenomena of contemporary society.

(6a)   *Marxist Anti-Humanism!*
Marx had no interests in religion and ethics and reduced consciousness to matter. He therefore paved the way for the anti-humanism of Stalin and others. Marxism cannot ground media ethics.

(6b)   *Marxist Humanism!*
Marx was a deep humanist and communism was for him practical humanism, class struggle practical ethics. His theory was deeply ethical and normative. Critical Political Economy of the Media necessarily includes a critical ethics of the media.

(7a)   *The Outdatedness of Class!*
Marxism's obsession with class is outdated. Today, the expansion of knowledge work is removing all class barriers.

(7b)   *The Importance of Class!*
High socio-economic inequality at all levels of societal organization is indicative of the circumstance that contemporary society is first and foremost a multilevelled class society. Knowledge work is no homogenous category but rather a class-structured space that includes internal class relations and stratification patterns (both a manager and a precariously employed call centre agent or data entry clerk are knowledge workers).

(8a)   *Marxists Oppose Democracy!*
Marxists favour violent revolution and oppose peaceful reform and democracy. They do not accept the important role of the media for democracy.

(8b)   *Socialism = Democracy!*
Capitalism has a history of human rights violations, structural violence and warfare. In the realm of the media, there is a capitalist history of media support for anti-democratic goals. Marxism is a demand for peace, democracy and democratic media. Marx in his own journalistic writings and practice struggled for free speech, democratic journalism and democratic media, and to end to censorship.

(9a)   *Marxist Dictatorship!*
Marxism's logic is the logic of the party that results in the logic of the state and the installation of monstrous dictators that control, monitor, manipulate and censor the media.

(9b)   *Capitalist Dictatorship!*
Capitalism installs a monstrous economic dictatorship that controls, monitors, manipulates and censors the media by economic and ideological means. Marxism's logic is one of a well-rounded humanity fostering conditions that enable people to be active in many pursuits and includes the view that everyone can become a journalist.

(10a) *Non-Class-Oriented New Social Movements!*
New social movements (feminism, environmentalism, gay rights, peace movement, youth movement, etc.) have left class and Marxism behind. Struggles for alternative media are related to the new social movements, not to class struggles.

(10b) *Class-Oriented New Social Movements!*
   The new movements resulting from the current crisis (such as the Occupy
   movement) as well as recent movements for democratic globalization are
   movements that are bound together by deep concern for inequality and
   class. Contemporary struggles are class struggles that make use of a multitude of alternative media.

A Marxist theory of communication should "demonstrate how communication
and culture are material practices, how labor and language are mutually constituted,
and how communication and information are dialectical instances of the same social activity, the social construction of meaning. Situating these tasks within a larger
framework of understanding power and resistance would place communication
directly into the flow of a Marxian tradition that remains alive and relevant today"
(Mosco 2009, 44). A Marxist theory of communication sees communication in relation to capitalism, "placing in the foreground the analysis of capitalism, including
the development of the forces and relations of production, commodification and
the production of surplus value, social class divisions and struggles, contradictions
and oppositional movements" (ibid., 94). Marxist media and communication studies are not only relevant now, but have been so for a long time because communication has always been embedded into structures of inequality in class societies. With
the rise of neoliberalism, Marxist communication theory has suffered a setback
because it had become common to marginalize and discriminate against Marxist
scholarship (see Erdogan 2012) and to replace Marxism with postmodernism. So
Marx was always relevant, but being Marxist and practising Marxism were always
difficult, in part because Marxist studies lacked a solid institutional base. What we
can see today is a rising interest in Marx's work. The question is whether it will
be possible to channel this interest into institutional transformations that challenge
the predominant administrative character of media institutions and strengthen the
institutionalization of critical studies of media and communication.

   Some scholars have said that Marx never commented on networked media
(McLuhan 2001, 41), which is refuted by not only Marx's discussions of the telegraph, but also the one in which Marx describes a global information network,
in which "everyone attempts to inform himself" on others and "connections are
introduced" (Marx 1857/1858b, 161). Such a description not only sounds like
an anticipation of the concept of the Internet, it is also an indication that Marx's
thought is relevant for media/communication studies and Internet studies. This
passage in the *Grundrisse* is an indication that although the Internet as technology
was a product of the Cold War and Californian counter-culture, its concept was
already anticipated by Marx in the 19th century—*Karl Marx invented the Internet!*

   Christian Fuchs and Nick Dyer-Witheford (2013) have argued that ten concepts
especially make Marx's works crucial for understanding the Internet and social media:

(1)   dialectics
(2)   capitalism

(3)   commodity/commodification
(4)   surplus value, exploitation, alienation, class
(5)   globalization
(6)   ideology/ideology critique
(7)   class struggle
(8)   commons
(9)   public sphere
(10) communism

The outlined concepts allow one to formulate an incomplete research agenda for critical Internet studies that includes the following questions:

(1)   How can the creation, the development and the contradictions of the Internet be understood within a dialectically informed historical perspective?
(2)   What exactly is the role of the Internet in capitalism? How can this role be theorized and empirically measured? Which Internet-based capital accumulation models are there?
(3)   Which forms of commodification do we find on the Internet and how do they work?
(4)   Which different forms of surplus value creation are there on the Internet? How do they work? What do users think about them?
(5)   How does the Internet interact with globalization processes?
(6)   Which myths and ideologies are there about the Internet? How can they be uncovered, analysed and criticized?
(7)   What is the role of the Internet in class struggles? What are the potentials, realities and limits of struggles for an alternative Internet?
(8)   What are Internet commons? How does the commodification of the Internet commons work? Which models for strengthening the Internet commons are there?
(9)   What are the potentials and limits of the Internet for bringing about a public sphere?
(10) What is a commons-based Internet in a commons-based society? Which germ forms and models of a commons-based Internet are there? How can the establishment of a commons-based Internet and corresponding struggles be strengthened?

A number of scholars have conducted important work for trying to overcome the labour blind spot of media and communication studies. Vincent Mosco and Catherine McKercher have edited a series of collections about communicative labour (McKercher and Mosco 2006, 2007; Mosco, McKercher and Huws 2010) as well as a monograph (Mosco and McKercher 2008). Ursula Huws' editing of the journal *Work Organisation Labour and Globalisation* (see www. analyticapublications.co.uk) has resulted in the establishment of an important platform for the publication of critical studies of labour in the context of knowledge, ICTs and the media. A number of conferences have contributed to the emergence of a discourse on digital labour: "Digital Labour: Workers, Authors, Citizens" (Western University, London, Ontario, Canada, October 16–18, 2009; see ir.lib.uwo.ca/digitallabour, Burston, Dyer-Witheford and Hearn 2010); "The Internet as Playground and Factory" (New York, New School, November 12–14, 2009; see digitallabor.org, Scholz 2013), and "The 4th ICTs and Society Conference: Critique, Democracy and Philosophy in 21st Century Information Society: Towards Critical Theories of Social Media" (Uppsala University, Uppsala, Sweden, May 2–4, 2012; see www.icts-and-society.net/events/uppsala2012, Fuchs and Sandoval 2014, Fuchs 2012a, 2012d). The journal *tripleC* has increasingly moved towards publishing Marxist works on digital media and informational capitalism, as with the special issue "Marx Is Back—The Importance of Marxist Theory and Research for Critical Communication Studies Today" (Fuchs and Mosco 2012). The EU COST Action IS1202 "Dynamics of Virtual Work" (2012–2016, dynamicsofvirtualwork.com) points out the need to refocus the study of the creative and cultural economy on issues such as the global division of labour in this industry, the working conditions involved in the international division of digital labour (IDDL), precarious cultural labour, the problem of "free" digital labour and challenges to theorizing digital labour's value creation, the challenge of prosumption (productive consumption) and playbour (play labour) for knowledge work, policy perspectives on virtual work (the role of trade unions, watchdog and civil society projects such as MakeIT Fair, policy problems and challenges for the regulation of virtual work, etc.) and occupational identities in knowledge work. Marx, capitalism, labour and digital labour have become more important in media and communication studies, although the mainstream is still dominated by administrative research. The task is to further institutionalize these studies so that a new generation of Marxist media and communication scholars can emerge, blossom and rise to become the new mainstream.

Notes

1 "Ausgeliefert!" is a play on words. It on the one hand means that something (like an Amazon parcel) gets delivered and on the other hand that one is at the mercy of somebody.
2 "Nazis, Bedingungen wie in einem modernen Arbeitslager und grenzenlose Profitgier. SCHÄMT EUCH!"
3 "Modernes Sklaventum, aber Hauptsache der Profit stimmt".
4 "Gewinne, die auf einer neuen Spielart von Sklaverei beruhen, sollten genaso [sic] eingezogen warden, wie etwa Gewinne aus Drogenhandel!" (All comments are from the Amazon.de Facebook page, February 16–17, 2013.)

PART I

Theoretical Foundations of Studying Digital Labour

2

AN INTRODUCTION TO KARL MARX'S THEORY

This chapter introduces basic theoretical categories that are used throughout the book. As the basic theoretical framework is Marx's theory, the chapter explains some of the categories that Marx used. After an introduction (2.1), the terms "labour" and "work" are discussed and I explain how Marx uses these terms (2.2). This exposition is followed by an explanation of basic concepts of Marx's labour theory of value (2.3): use-value, value, exchange-value, money, price, value and price of labour-power, surplus value. The categories developed in this chapter will help the reader in later chapters to understand how concrete cases of digital labour, such as Facebook usage, slave mineral workers, hardware assembly, software engineering and call centre work, can be theoretically explained in a critical manner.

For understanding digital labour, one needs to understand what labour and work are. Karl Marx has established the most influential modern theory of labour. It therefore makes sense to engage with his theory. If we want to answer the question "What is digital labour?", then reading Marx can be very helpful. In this chapter, I make the argument that we need to ask related questions: What is work? What is labour? What is digital work? What is digital labour?

2.1. Introduction

A question that has thus not been given much focus in the digital labour debate is how to best define digital labour. This chapter makes a contribution to finding answers. For doing so, it is necessary to engage with two related questions: What is labour? What is work? If answers to these questions can be given, then based on them one can think about how to define digital labour/work. This chapter is structured in such a way that it first gives a systematic overview of Marx's discussion of the terms "labour" and "work" (section 2.2) and then explains the labour theory of value (section 2.3). First a more agency-based/subjective approach is taken, which is then connected to a more structural view that connects labour to value-generation in the form of the labour theory of value. This book uses Marxist political economy as a theoretical approach. This means that it grounds the notions of work and labour in a systematic reading of Karl Marx's works. But why should one use Karl Marx's theory for better understanding what labour and work are and not any other theory? Aristotle made a distinction between poíesis (the creation of works from nature) and praxis (self-determined action). This philosophical distinction certainly reflects the class structures of ancient Greek society at the time of Aristotle, where slave work (poíesis) enabled the idle activity, politics and philosophical thinking of Greek citizens (praxis, theoría). In the philosophy of Christian religion, work was seen as a virtue, as expressed in Paulus' ethics of labour: "The one who is unwilling to work shall not eat" (2 Thessalonians 3:10, NIV). Thomas Aquinas took up these ethics of labour in his concept of the vita activa but added a dual pole, the vita contemplativa, as religious element. In Protestant ethics, the dualism between vita activa and vita contemplativa was challenged by Martin Luther and others who saw labour itself as a religious practice and the vita contemplativa not as a higher religious form of existence detached from labour. John Locke considered labour as unpleasant necessity that is opposed to art and thought and argued that the poor should be forced to work. For Adam Smith, the poverty of labour and the wealth of capital are connected; they are for him not God-given as assumed in earlier Christian philosophy, but a social relation that is a necessary condition for progress. Hegel described work in the context of an estate-based society, in which peasants, citizens and civil servants have different forms of work that are structured in the form of a hierarchy of recognition and a division of labour. In contrast to this conception, in which the modern class relation between capitalists and workers is invisible, Hegel also described the dialectic of master and slave that reflects the contours of capitalist class relations. In Christian philosophy, the existence of alienated labour and class relations was always considered God-given. In classical political economy, the idea of the God-given nature of toil and poverty was given up and class relations were conceived as social relations. This relation was however considered necessary for progress; its potential sublation was not seen as a historical potential enabled by the development of the productive forces. Classical political economy refused to clarify its claim that the current state of the capitalist mode of production is eternal. As a consequence, it saw the form of labour that exists in capitalism and that is characterized by a division of labour, private property and class relations as eternal and naturalized it thereby. In contrast, Marx was critical of such views. Therefore, his approach is a critique of political economy and not only a contribution to political economy. Marx was the first author who described the historical character of work as a crucial point for understanding political economy (Marx 1867c, 131–132). When discussing what work and labour are, Marx offers the most thorough analysis that is available. In encyclopaedias and dictionaries of economics, entries such as labour, labour-power, labour process or labour theory are therefore often predominantly associated with Marx and Marxist theory (see e.g. the corresponding entries in Eatwell, Milgate and Newman 1987).

2.2. Marx on Work and Labour

One can distinguish three levels of Marx's works, on which we analyse how he conceives the concepts of work and labour: society in general (2.2.1), class societies and capitalism (2.2.2) and communism (2.2.3).

2.2.1. Work and Labour in Society

Marx gave an anthropological characterisation of work. In *The German Ideology*, Marx and Engels (1845/1846, 37) argue that work is a conscious productive activity that transforms and organizes nature so that humans "*produce* their means of subsistence" in order to satisfy human needs, which constitutes "the production of material life itself" (ibid., 47). "Real labour is purposeful activity aimed at the creation of a use value, at the appropriation of natural material in a manner which corresponds to particular needs" (Marx 1861–1863). Humans are producing beings that produce both physical resources and ideas. For organizing production and society, humans enter "definite social and political relations" (Marx and Engels 1845/1846, 41). In the *Introduction to the Critique of Political Economy* (ibid., 1–23), Marx explains that the economy involves in all societies processes of production, distribution and consumption and that work is an activity embedded into this system. In *Capital, Volume 1,* Marx begins the discussion of capitalism with an exposition of the commodity form. After defining two aspects of a commodity, namely use-value and exchange-value, he switches from the analysis of objective structures in section 1.1 to the analysis of subjectivity (i.e. the world of work) in section 1.2, "The dual character of the labour embodied in commodities". In this chapter, Marx argues that work has both an anthropological and a historical character: In all societies, it is an activity that produces goods that satisfy human needs. In concrete societies, work takes on specific historical characteristics, such as slave work, house work, wage work and so on. In the *Contribution to the critique of political economy*, Marx says: "As useful activity directed to the appropriation of natural factors in one form or another, labour is a natural condition of human existence, a condition of material interchange between man and nature, quite independent of the form of society. On the other hand, the labour which posits exchange-value is a specific social form of labour" (Marx 1859).

A basic question that we have to pose when discussing the concepts of work and labour is whether work/labour is an essence of human society or a specific expression of economic domination. Let us for this purpose compare two quotes from Marx, in which he talks about work and which show the importance of clearly defining the anthropological and historical dimension of work:

(1) "Labour, then, as the creator, of use-values, is useful labour, is a condition of human existence which is independent of all forms of society; it is an eternal natural necessity which mediates the metabolism between man and nature, and therefore human life itself" (Marx 1867c, 133).[1]

(2) "The realm of freedom really begins only where labour determined by necessity and external expediency ends; it lies by its very nature beyond the sphere of material production proper" (Marx 1894, 958–959)[2]

In the first quotation, Marx sees work as a necessary element of all societies. The second quotation is more ambiguous: It can on the one hand mean that in a communist society alienation ceases to exist and that therefore work no longer exists because it is always alienated. Or it can mean that labour as an alienated form of work comes to an end and work takes on a humane character. In *The German Ideology,* Marx and Engels (1845/1846) argue that communism abolishes the division of labour and enables the "transformation of labour into self-activity" (97) and that the "communist revolution [. . .] does away with *labour*" (60). After the word "labour" (*Arbeit* in the German original) Marx crossed out the words "the modern form of activity under the rule of" (ibid.), which shows that he was not so sure if he should use the formulation that communism does away with *Arbeit* or does away with the modern form of the organization of *Arbeit*. So given these different passages from various works, it is not clear if Marx thought that work/labour exists in a communist society or not. The problem is further complicated by the fact that he wrote in German, where there is one common word for work and labour—*Arbeit,* although there is also the term *Werktätigkeit* (the activity of creating works) that is a much more general concept but tends to be hardly used in German. The term *Arbeit* was translated sometimes as "work" and sometimes as "labour". Engels has pointed out in a footnote to Marx's *Capital* that the English language allows one to make a semantic differentiation: "The English language has the advantage of possessing two separate words for these two different aspects of labour. Labour which creates use-values and is qualitatively determined is called 'work' as opposed to 'labour'; labour which creates value and is only measured quantitatively is called 'labour', as opposed to 'work'" (Marx 1867c, 138). In this book, I will use this distinction for discerning digital labour from digital work.

Adopting this terminology allows one to avoid confusion. Labour is a necessarily alienated form of work, in which humans do not control and own the means and results of production. It is a historic form of the organization of work in class societies. Work in contrast is a much more general concept common to all societies. It is a process, in which humans make use of technologies for transforming nature and society in such a way that goods and services are created that satisfy human needs. Given this distinction, the translation of the passage in *The German Ideology*—where Marx and Engels say that communism does away with labour—is feasible, whereas the other cited passages should better be translated as communism enabling the transformation of work organized as labour into work as self-activity. The passage in *Capital, Volume 3,* is especially ambiguous (both in the German original and the English translation), and this ambiguity could best be resolved by translating the sentence the following way: The realm of freedom really begins only where labour, which is a form of work that is determined by necessity and external expediency, ends.

Raymond Williams (1983, 176–179) argues that the word "labour" comes from the French word *labor* and the Latin term *laborem* and appeared in the English language first around 1300. It was associated with hard work, pain and trouble. In the 18th century, it would have attained the meaning of work under capitalist conditions that stands in a class relationship with capital. The term "work" comes from the Old English word *weorc* and is the "most general word for doing something" (ibid., 334). In capitalism the term on the one hand has, according to Williams (ibid., 334–337), acquired the same meaning as labour—a paid job—but would have in contrast also kept its original broader meaning. In order to be able to differentiate the dual historical and essential character of work, it is feasible to make a semantic differentiation between labour and work.

Herbert Marcuse (1933, 123) argues that the modern economic concept of labour as wage labour has influenced the general understanding of work and has resulted in "the narrowing of the concept". Marcuse distinguishes between a general form of labour (work) that is an essential and foundational category that describes productive human activities in all societies and the economic concept of labour as it is typical for modern societies. Work has for Marcuse three dimensions: *Arbeiten* (working as a process), *das Gearbeitete* (the object of work) and *das zu-Arbeitende* (the goal of work). Marcuse argues that work has three important characteristics: duration, permanence and burden. The essential duration of work means that it is never finished, work is an "enduring being-at and being-in-work" (ibid., 129). Work is permanent because an object as the result of production is "worked into the 'world'" (ibid., 130). That work involves a burden does not necessarily mean for Marcuse that it is toil, but the abstinence from individual pleasure: in work "man is always taken away from his self-being and toward something else: he is always with an other and for an other" (ibid.). Marcuse stresses that work is not just producing a world of goods, but it organizes the "economics of life" (ibid., 134). The "first and final purpose" of work is to "bring about the being of Dasein itself, in order to 'secure' its duration and permanence" (ibid., 135). Work involves the production of physical use-values (such as food, housing, clothes) and non-physical use-values (such as social relations, communications, happiness) that satisfy human life. In the *Economic Manuscripts of 1861–1863,* Marx (1861–1863) argues that the means of labour contain the material of labour and the means of labour. This formulation is still somewhat inept because it uses the term "means of labour" twice. In the *Grundrisse,* Marx (1857/1858b, 300) makes clear that the labour activity, the labour material, the labour instrument and the labour product are inherently connected aspects of production. Labour is a "sublation of sublation" (Marx 1857/1858a, 222)[3]: labour is a "form-giving activity" (Marx 1857/1858b, 301) that sublates itself in the production process and sublates the material. Thereby it creates "a new objective form" (ibid.), a new product. This means that labour is a process of productive consumption: it consumes natural products and labour-power and in this process creates a new product. "Labour uses up its material elements, its objects and its instruments. It consumes them, and is therefore a process of consumption. [. . .] Thus the product of individual consumption is the consumer himself; the result of productive consumption is a product distinct from the consumer" (Marx 1867c, 290). The outcome of this process are use-values (Marx 1857/1858b, 301). This shows that here Marx uses the term "use-value" in a general anthropological sense. In *Capital,* Marx (1867c) makes a threefold distinction between labour-power, the object of labour and the instruments of labour: "The simple elements of the labour process are (1) purposeful activity, (2) the object on which that work is performed, and (3) the instruments of that work" (284). Marx's discussion of the production process can be presented in a systematic way by using Hegel's concept of the dialectic of subject and object. Hegel (1991) has spoken of a dialectical relation of subject and object: the existence of a producing subject is based on an external objective environment that enables and constrains (i.e. conditions) human existence. Human activities can transform the external (social, cultural, economic, political, natural) environment. As a result of the interaction of subject and object, new reality is created—Hegel terms the result of this interaction "subject-object". Figure 2.1 shows that Hegel's notion of subject, object, and subject-object form a dialectical triangle.

Hegel (1991) characterizes the "subjective concept" as formal notion (§162), a finite determination of understanding, a general notion (§162), "altogether concrete" (§164). He defines "the subject" as "the posited unseparatedness of the moments in their distinction" (§164). Hegel characterizes objectivity as totality (§193), "external objectivity" (§208), "external to an other" (§193), "the objective world in general" that "falls apart inwardly into [an] undetermined manifoldness" (§193), "immediate being" (§194), "indifference vis-à-vis the distinction" (§194), "realisation of purpose" (§194), "purposive activity" (§206) and "the means" (§206). The Idea is "the Subject-Object" (§162), absolute Truth (§162), the unity of the subjective and the objective (§212), "the absolute unity of Concept and objectivity" (§213), "the Subject-Object" understood as "the unity of the ideal and the real, of the finite and the infinite, of the soul and the body" (§214). Hegel also says that the "Idea is essentially process" (§215). Marx applied Hegel's dialectic of subject and object on a more concrete level to the economy in order to explain how the process of economic production works. There is the purposeful activity of human subjects—labour-power: "We mean by labour-power, or

Hegel, logic of the concept (third subdivision of the logic, Encyclopaedia I, §§ 160-244)

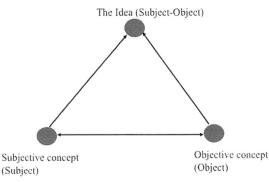

FIGURE 2.1 The dialectical triangle of subject-object-subject/object

labour-capacity, the aggregate of those mental and physical capabilities existing in the physical form, the living personality, of a human being, capabilities which he sets in motion whenever he produces a use-value of any kind" (Marx 1867c, 270). Labour is the use of labour-power: "The use of labour-power is labour itself. [. . .] Labour is, first of all, a process by which man, through his own actions, mediates, regulates and controls the metabolism between himself and nature" (ibid., 283). Labour-power is used on an object—the object of labour *(Arbeitsgegenstand)*: The land is "the universal material for human labour" (ibid., 284), and "the object of labour counts as raw material only when it has already undergone some alteration by means of labour" (ibid., 284–285). For transforming nature by labour, instruments of labour (technologies) are needed: "An instrument of labour is a thing, or a complex of things, which the worker interposes between himself and the object of his labour and which serves as a conductor, directing his activity onto that object. He makes use of the mechanical, physical and chemical properties of some substances in order to set them to work on other substances as instruments of his power, and in accordance with his purposes" (ibid., 285). The result of the labour process is the labour product: "In the labour process, therefore, man's activity via the instruments of labour, effects an alteration in the object of labour which was intended from the outset. The process is extinguished in the product. The product of the process is a use-value, a piece of natural material adapted to human needs by means of a change in its form. Labour has become bound up in its object: labour has been objectified, the object has been worked on" (ibid., 287). "All 3 moments of the process, whose subject is labour and whose factors are the material on which and the means of labour with which it operates, come together in a neutral result—the *product*" (Marx 1861–1863). In the *Economic-Philosophic Manuscripts,* Marx argues that the relationship of subject and object results in the objectification of labour in a new product: "The product of labour is labour which has been congealed in an object, which has become material: it is the objectification of labour" (Marx 1844, 71). Marx terms this whole system the productive forces (see what I term the "dialectical triangle of the work process" in figure 2.2): human subjects have labour-power that in the labour process interacts with the means of production (object). The means of production consist of the object of labour (natural resources, raw materials) and the instruments of labour (technology). In the labour process, humans transform the object of labour (nature) by making use of their labour-power with the help of instruments of labour. The result is a product of labour, which is a Hegelian subject-object, or, as Marx says, a product, in which labour has become bound up in its object: labour is objectified in the product and the object is as a result transformed into a use-value that serves human needs. The next figure summarizes the dialectical subject-object process in the economy. The productive forces are a system in which subjective productive forces (human labour-power) make use of technical productive forces (part of the objective productive forces) in order to transform parts of the natural productive forces (which are also part of the objective productive forces) so that a labour product emerges. One goal of the development of the system of productive forces is to increase the productivity of labour, that is, the output (amount of products) that labour generates per unit of time. Marx therefore defined the concept of the development of the productive forces (= the increase of the productivity of labour) as "an alteration in the labour process of such a kind as to shorten the labour-time socially necessary for the production of a [. . . good], and to endow a given quantity of labour with the power of producing a greater quantity of use-value" (Marx 1867c, 431). Another goal of the development of the productive forces can be the enhancement of human self-development by reducing necessary labour time and hard work (toil).

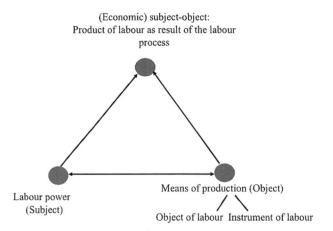

FIGURE 2.2 The dialectical triangle of the work process: The system of productive forces—the labour process as dialectical subject-object

2.2.2. Labour in Capitalism and Other Class Societies

Work in class societies (= labour) is organized in such a way that the products of labour and surplus labour (i.e. labour that goes beyond the time necessary for satisfying basic human needs) are appropriated and owned by a dominant class that exploits the producers of surplus: "Capital did not invent surplus labour. Wherever a part of society possesses the monopoly of the means of production, the worker, free or unfree, must add to the labour-time necessary for his own maintenance an extra quantity of labour-time in order to produce the means of subsistence for the owner of the means of production, whether this proprietor be an Athenian *kaloz k'agadoz* ['aristocrat'], an Etruscan theocrat, a *civis romanus,* a Norman baron, an American slave-owner, a Wallachian boyar, a modern land-lord or a capitalist" (Marx 1867c, 334–335). Marx (1857/1858b, 238) says that in class society, "labour will create alien property and property will command alien labour".

Marx focused much of his intellectual efforts on the analysis of capitalism and the role that labour plays therein. The *Grundrisse*'s first part, the "Chapter on money", does not have any specific focus on labour. The term is used here and there, but not in a systematic way and mainly in such a way that it is subsumed to the terms "money" and "commodity". The first real appearance of labour is in the *Grundrisse*'s second part, the "Chapter on capital", namely in a section titled "Exchange value emerging from circulation, a presupposition of circulation, pre-serving and multiplying itself in it by means of labour" (ibid., 264–265). Marx here makes clear that capital and labour stand in a contradictory dialectical relation-ship in capitalism, a class relationship: "The labour which stands opposite capital is *alien* labour, and the capital which stands opposite labour is *alien* capital" (ibid., 266). The existence of capital depends on the existence of and "connection with *not-capital,* the negation of capital", that is, labour. Therefore the "real *not-capital* is *labour*" (ibid., 274). The effect of this class relation is that labour faces a dialectic of poverty and wealth: it "is absolute poverty as object" (labour does not own what it produces) and at the same time "the general possibility of wealth" (only labour, not capital, produces and is a necessary condition of wealth) (ibid., 296). The wealth that labour creates is the wealth of capital and therefore the poverty of labour. Marx points out that in capitalism the worker sells his/her labour-power as commodity to the capitalist and thereby works during one part of the day (necessary labour time) for creating the "value of his labour-power, i.e. the value of his means of subsistence" (Marx 1867c, 324), and another part of the day not "for himself" but for the capitalist. During this time, he "creates surplus-value" (ibid., 325). Marx calls this part of the day "surplus labour-time, and to the labour expended during that time I give the name of surplus labour" (ibid., 325). The specific characteristic of capitalism is that labour-power becomes a commodity that does not own the means and results of production and is compelled to work a certain share of the day without payment (i.e. to conduct surplus labour) so that surplus value is created that is transformed into capital and monetary profit in the moment the commodity, in which this labour is objectified, is sold on the market. Labour is therefore alienated in a manifold sense.

Marx (1844, 69–84) has for the first time used the notion of alienation in a detailed manner in the *Economic-Philosophic Manuscripts*' section "On estranged labour". He there identifies four forms of alienation: (a) alienation from the product, (b) alienation from the labour process in the form of forced labour (ibid., 74), (c) alienation from himself/herself—"Estranged labour turns thus: (3) Man's species being, both nature and his spiritual species property, into a being alien to him, into a means to his individual existence. It estranges man's own body from him, as it does external nature and his spiritual essence, his human being" (ibid., 77–78)—and (d) the alienation from other humans and society. On the one hand, the exposition of alienation in the *Economic-Philosophic Manuscripts* is not as systematic as in the *Grundrisse* and *Capital*. On the other hand, Marx focuses more on the anthropological consequences of alienation for the human being and thereby employs the notion of the species-being in his early work. He formulated the foundations of the concept of alienation in the *Economic-Philosophic Manuscripts* and elaborated later systematically and in more detail the economic foundations of alienation. For Althusser (1969, 249), Marx's notion of alienation is an "ideological concept" used in "his Early Works". "In his later works, however, the term appears very rarely" (Althusser 1969, 249). Althusser speaks of an "epistemological break" that "divides Marx's thought into two long essential periods: the 'ideological' period before, and the scientific period after, the break in 1845" (ibid., 34). This means that Althusser considers the notion of alienation and works such as the *Economic-Philosophic Manuscripts* as esoteric. In contrast, we will show that Marx did not give up the notion of alienation, but rather that it is a concept that he first created in his early works and that is present also in his major writings.

In a passage in the *Grundrisse,* Marx makes clear which elements of alienation there are in capitalism: the worker is alienated from (a) herself/himself because labour is controlled by capital, (b) the material of labour, (c) the object of labour and (d) the product of labour. "The material on which it [labour] works is alien material; the instrument is likewise an alien instrument; its labour appears as a mere accessory to their substance and hence objectifies itself in things not belonging to it. Indeed, living labour itself appears as alien vis-à-vis living labour capacity, whose labour it is, whose own life's expression it is, for it has been surrendered to capital in exchange for objectified labour, for the product of labour itself. [. . .] labour capacity's own labour is as alien to it—and it really is, as regards its direction etc.—as are material and instrument. Which is why the product then appears to it as a combination of alien material, alien instrument and alien labour—as alien property" (Marx 1857/1858b, 462). These four elements of alienation can be related to the labour process that consists in a Hegelian sense of a subject, an object and a subject-object, as shown in figure 2.2. Alienation is alienation of the subject from itself (labour-power is put to use for and is controlled by capital), alienation from the object (the objects of labour and the instruments of labour) and alienation from the subject-object (the products of labour). The alienation process is visualized in figure 2.3. Alienation in capitalism means that workers do not control their labour-power, the means of production and the results of production and are compelled to work part of the day for capital in order to survive. The four forms of alienation constitute together the system of the exploitation of labour: labour-power because of its manifold alienations is compelled to work without payment for capital, which results in the production of surplus value and monetary profit. Exploitation takes place within specific relations of production—class relations.

Production and the development of the productive forces do not form an abstract process. Although production is a common process in the economy of all societies, it can in reality only take place within concrete historical conditions, in which humans enter certain social relations with each other. Marx speaks in this context of the relations of production. He says that in societies that are based on a division of labour, the relations of production develop into class relations: a dominant class exploits the labour-power of a dominated class, which works to a certain extent for free, produces a surplus for others and does not own the fruits of its own labour. The system is enabled by the circumstance that the dominant class privately owns the means of production and has means of violence (physical force, the state and laws, the dull economic compression that forces workers to work for others in order to be able to obtain in return products or money that allow them to consume and to survive) at hand that force the dominated class into being exploited.

Alienation in capitalism makes the worker "double free"—forced to sell his/her labour-power on the labour market and property-less: "the confrontation

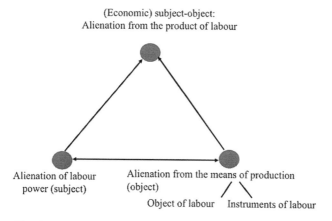

FIGURE 2.3 The alienation process in capitalism

of, and the contact between, two very different kinds of commodity owners; on the one hand, the owners of money, means of production, means of subsistence, who are eager to valorize the sum of values they have appropriated by buying the labour-power of others; on the other hand, free workers, the sellers of their own labour-power, and therefore the sellers of labour. Free workers, in the double sense that they neither form part of the means of production themselves, as would be the case with slaves, serfs, etc., nor do they own the means of production, as would be the case with self-employed peasant proprietors. [. . .] The process, therefore, which creates the capital-relation can be nothing other than the process which divorces the worker from the ownership of the conditions of his own labour; it is a process which operates two transformations, whereby the social means of subsistence and production are turned into capital, and the immediate producers are turned into wage-labourers" (Marx 1867c, 874). In capitalism, the capitalist class owns the means of production and holds the power to exploit the labour of the proletariat. The latter is forced to sell its labour-power as commodity to the capitalists. The proletariat cannot survive without selling its labour-power to the capitalists in order to obtain wages. Capitalists need the labour-power of the proletariat in order to produce commodities that are sold on markets and contain unpaid surplus value (unpaid labour time) that is transformed into profit so that capital is accumulated. Marx characterizes the capitalist class relation of production as constituting the "antagonistic character of capitalist accumulation", which means that class relations "produce bourgeois wealth, i.e. the wealth of the bourgeois class, only by continually annihilating the wealth" of the proletariat (ibid., 799). Proletarians and capitalists are dialectically connected. The relative "deprivation" of the proletariat and the "plentitude" of capital "match each other exactly" (ibid., 1062). The proletariat is "a machine for the production of surplus-value", and capitalists are "a machine for the transformation of this surplus-value into surplus capital" (ibid., 742). For Marx, capitalism is based on the capitalists' permanent theft of unpaid labour from workers. This is the reason why he characterizes capital as vampire and werewolf. "Capital is dead labour which, vampire-like, lives only by sucking living labour, and lives the more, the more labour it sucks" (ibid., 342). The production of surplus value "forms the specific content and purpose of capitalist production" (ibid., 411); it is "the *differentia specifica* of capitalist production", "the absolute law of this mode of production" (769), the "driving force and the final result of the capitalist process of production" (976). In capitalism, labour is subsumed under the power of capital: "This natural power of labour appears as a power incorporated into capital for the latter's own self-preservation, just as the productive forces of social labour appear as inherent characteristics of capital, and just as the constant appropriation of surplus labour by the capitalists appears as the constant self-valorization of capital. All the powers of labour project themselves as powers of capital, just as all the value-forms of the commodity do as forms of money" (ibid., 755–756). Marx speaks in this context also of the formal subsumption of labour under capital, which means that the "labour process becomes the instrument of the valorization process" so that "the capitalist intervenes in the process as its director, manager", and engages in the "direct exploitation of the labour of others" (ibid., 1019). Based on this formal subsumption, there is also the real subsumption of labour under capital, where command and coercion are built into machines and the application of science (ibid., 1023–1015) so that productivity increases and labour is indirectly commanded by capital and directly faces the speed and speed-up of production caused by machinery.

Within capitalist relations of production, the productive forces are not just means for producing human wealth and use-values, they are means for the exploitation of the labour of the proletariat and for intensifying this exploitation so that more labour is exploited per unit of time, which results in the production of more commodities in the same time period and in the creation of more surplus value and more profit. Marx therefore speaks of the capitalist antagonism between the productive forces and the relations of production. Within "the capitalist system all methods for raising the social productivity of labour are put into effect at the cost of the individual worker; [. . .] all means for the development of production undergo a dialectical inversion so that they become means of domination and exploitation of the producers" (ibid., 799).

In capitalism, dead labour (capital) dominates living labour: "The sole antithesis to objectified labour is non-objectified, *living labour*. The one is present in space, the other in time, the one is in the past, the other in the present, the one is already embodied in a use value, the other, as human activity-in-process, is currently engaged in the process of self-objectification, the one is value, the other is value-creating" (Marx 1861–1863).

In section 1.2 of *Capital, Volume 1,* Marx introduces the distinction between abstract and concrete labour. This distinction reflects the fact that Marx wrote both a critique of capitalism and an economic theory in the same book and that these two levels have resulted in two series of categories that are both constituents of capitalism, but they represent on the one hand that which is specific for capitalism and on the other hand that which forms the essence of all economies and therefore also exists in capitalism and interacts dialectically with capitalism's historic reality. These categories are shown in table 2.1 and constitute for Marx the dual character of capitalism.

Marx explains that concrete labour is the use-value generating aspect of labour (work) and that abstract labour creates value. "While, therefore, with reference to use-value, the labour contained in a commodity counts only qualitatively, with reference to value it counts only quantitatively, once it has been reduced to human labour pure and simple. In the former case it was a matter of the 'how' and the 'what' of labour, in the latter of the 'how much', of the temporal duration of labour. Since the magnitude of the value of a commodity represents nothing but the quantity of labour embodied in it, it follows that all commodities, when taken in certain proportions, must be equal in value" (Marx 1867c, 136).

TABLE 2.1 Marx's description of the dual character of capitalism

Essential categories	Historic categories
Work	Labour
Use-value	Exchange-value
Concrete labour	Abstract labour
Work process	Valorization process
Necessary labour	Surplus labour

Abstract labour is that kind of labour which makes the privately spent use-value producing work comparable. Abstract labour describes a specific quality of a capitalist mode of production. Marx says, "Equality in the full sense between different kinds of labour can be arrived at only if we abstract from their real inequality, if we reduce them to the characteristic they have in common, that of being the expenditure of human labour-power, of human labour in the abstract" (ibid., 166). In the concept of abstract labour, several abstractions from the concrete are involved. These abstractions mirror real social relations that are established by commodity exchanges in capitalism. By exchanging commodities, producers abstract their activities from the specific quality of the work that was involved to produce a commodity. This means that there is (a) an abstraction from the physical properties of goods (their use-values), (b) an abstraction from single products so that social relations between commodities in exchange are established, (c) an abstraction from simple labour activities to more complex tasks, and (d) an abstraction from specific qualities under which specific labour processes took place (such as bad working conditions, low payment, etc.) so that common properties of commodities are foregrounded by the value concept.

Abstract human labour is the substance of value; it is a common characteristic of commodities. Abstract human labour creates the value of a commodity, that is, it is the performance of the (average) labour in a certain time span that is needed for producing a commodity. "A use-value, or useful article, therefore, has value only because abstract human labour is objectified [*vergegenständlicht*] or materialized in it" (ibid., 129). The values of commodities are "determined by their cost of production, in other words by the labour time required to produce them" (ibid., 137). The magnitude of value is measured "by means of the quantity of the 'value-forming substance', the labour, contained in the article. This quantity is measured by its duration, and the labour-time is itself measured on the particular scale of hours, days, etc." (ibid., 129). The value of commodities as determined by labour time is only their *average value*" (Marx 1857/1858b, 137). "If we consider *commodities as values*, we consider them exclusively under the single aspect of *realized, fixed, or, if you like, crystallized social labour*" (Marx 1865).

Marx distinguishes between productive and unproductive labour: "*Productive labour* is only that which produces *capital*. [. . .] *Labour becomes productive only by producing its own opposite"* (Marx 1857/1858b, 305). "The only worker who is productive is one who produces surplus-value for the capitalist, or in other words contributes towards the self-valorization of capital" (Marx 1867c, 644). In this context, the question arises if only wage labour is productive or if also non-wage labour can be productive. Marx gave an answer in the *Grundrisse*. In the section "Exchange value emerging from circulation, a presupposition of circulation, preserving and multiplying itself in it by means of labour" (Marx 1857/1858b, 264ff) in the *Grundrisse*'s "Chapter on money", Marx argues that capital and labour confront each other in an exchange relationship, in which the use-value of labour—labour-power—is exchanged with money. It thereby becomes clear that Marx's main focus in the *Grundrisse* is on *wage* labour. Antonio Negri (1979/1988, 165) argues in this context that in the *Grundrisse*, "labour can only be defined in terms of the relations of exchange and the capitalist structure of production. The only concept of labour that we find in Marx is that of wage labour". Work would therefore be nothing "to be reformed, reinstated, liberated, or sublimated; it exists only as a concept and a reality to be abolished" (ibid.). Negri does not distinguish between work and labour, but conceives both as necessarily alienated. Negri (1979/1988) also sees that Marx focused his attention in the *Grundrisse* on wage labour, but does not further problematize this circumstance, although the *Grundrisse* is Marx's work that Negri most cherishes. The German language, just like English, allows in principle one to make a distinction, namely between *Werktätigkeit* (work as the activity of bringing about works) and *Arbeit* (labour).

But there is also a formulation in the *Grundrisse* where Marx sees labour as communal or combined labour (Marx 1857/1858b, 470), as collective worker *(Gesamtarbeiter)*. This idea was also taken up in *Capital, Volume 1,* where he defines the collective worker as "a collective labourer, i.e. a combination of workers" (Marx 1867c, 644), and argues that labour is productive if it is part of the combined labour force: "In order to work productively, it is no longer necessary for the individual himself to put his hand to the object; it is sufficient for him to be an organ of the collective labourer, and to perform any one of its subordinate functions" (ibid.). The collective worker is an "aggregate *worker*" whose "*combined activity*" results materially in an *aggregate* product" (ibid., 1040). The "activity of this aggregate labour-power" is "the immediate production of surplus-value, the *immediate conversion of this latter into capital*" (ibid.). This means that in capitalism, the collective worker is a productive worker that creates value, surplus value and capital. The notion of the collective worker allows an interpretation of Marx that is not wage-labour-centric because the collective worker as combined work force also contains all those activities that are unpaid but directly or indirectly serve capital's needs. Labour-power needs to be reproduced: in other words, there are certain activities during a certain time period of the day that help the worker recreate and sustain his/her labour capacity. "The value of labour-power is determined, as in the case of every other commodity, by the labour-time necessary for the production, and consequently also the reproduction, of this specific article" (ibid., 274). This includes means of subsistence for workers and their families, practice, training, education and so on (Marx 1861–1863). This means that there are activities that need to be performed by someone and that reproduce labour-power. One can in this context speak of reproductive labour, which is a form of labour that is mostly unpaid. Non-wage labour "ensures the reproduction of labour power and living conditions" (Mies, Bennholdt-Thomsen and Werlhof 1988, 18). It is labour spent "in the production of life, or subsistence production" (ibid., 70).

2.2.3. Work in Communism

Based on the distinction between work and labour, one can say that for Marx communism is a society without labour because alienation ceases to exist. There are passages in his works where he points out what the conditions of non-alienated work look like. The main condition of communism is that the means of production are collectively owned: "Let us finally imagine, for a change, an association of free men, working with the means of production held in common, and expending their many different forms of labour-power in full self-awareness as one single social labour force" (Marx 1867c, 171–172).

In the *Grundrisse*'s "Fragment on Machines" (Marx 1857/1858b, 690–712), Marx argues that the development of capitalism's productive forces results in an increased role of technology (fixed constant capital) and thereby historically increases the importance of science and knowledge work in the economy and society. One can read this section of the *Grundrisse* as an early forecasting of the emergence of what is nowadays called information society. Marx also points out the transformation of work in a communist society: It would not be based on the "theft of alien labour time" (ibid., 705), but on the "free development of individualities" enabled by the "general reduction of the necessary labour of society to a minimum, which then corresponds to the artistic, scientific etc. development of the individuals in the time set free, and with the means created for all of them" (ibid., 706). If technology reduces necessary labour time to a minimum and class relations are abolished, a new source of wealth would emerge: "The measure of wealth is then not any longer, in any way, labour time, but rather disposable time" (ibid., 604).

The *Grundrisse* make clear the importance of technology and science for raising productivity to levels that enable communism. In *The German Ideology*, Marx and Engels stress that high productivity allows overcoming the division of labour and the transformation of work in such a way that it becomes well-rounded manifold activity: "in communist society, where nobody has one exclusive sphere of activity but each can become accomplished in any branch he wishes, society regulates the general production and thus makes it possible for me to do one thing today and another tomorrow, to hunt in the morning, fish in the afternoon, rear cattle in the evening, criticise after dinner, just as I have a mind, without ever becoming hunter, fisherman, shepherd or critic" (Marx and Engels 1845/1846, 53).

Once "the productive forces have also increased with the all-around development of the individual, and all the springs of co-operative wealth flow more abundantly" (Marx 1875), a communist society that is based on the principle "From each according to his ability, to each according to his needs!" (ibid.) can be established.

In another passage in the *Grundrisse,* Marx introduces the idea that work becomes general in communism and speaks of general work. This includes "the participation of the individual in the communal world of products" (Marx 1857/1858b, 171), "communal production" (172), "an organization of labour whose consequence would be the participation of the individual in communal consumption" (172). This means that in a communist society, workers control the production process together and collectively own the instruments and products of labour. In communism, work is general and universal because ownership and control of the conditions, instruments, objects and products of work have been generalized so that there is universal control and ownership of production. As in *The German Ideology,* Marx employs the notion of well-rounded development (Marx 1857/1858a, 105; Marx 1857/1858b, 172[4]) that "depends on economization of time" so that "[e]conomy of time" is that to which "all economy ultimately reduces itself" (Marx 1857/1858a, 173). Communism requires a labour-saving economy achieved with the help of highly productive technologies. General labour operates in the context of such an economy. Common ownership and high productivity give a new character to work in a communist society. Work is no longer labour and no longer alienated, the labour process and all its elements are rather commonly controlled (foreign ownership is eliminated), self-determined time is maximized, work can become manifold and an expression of manifold creative activities that do not primarily satisfy human necessities, but rather human pleasures that go beyond necessity and do not know the phenomenon of scarcity. Labour is transformed into work.

Herbert Marcuse (1955) argues that the performance principle means that Thanatos governs humans and society and that alienation unleashes aggressive drives within humans (repressive desublimation) which result in an overall violent and aggressive society. Due to the high productivity reached in late-modern society, a historical alternative would be possible: the elimination of the repressive reality principle, the reduction of necessary working time to a minimum and the maximization of free time, an eroticization of society and the body, the shaping of society and humans by Eros and the emergence of libidinous social relations. Such a development would be a historical possibility—but one incompatible with capitalism and patriarchy. In a communist society, work (and society as a whole) could become libidinous and pleasurable; labour would not rule the pleasure principle but the pleasure principle would shape work, the economy and all of society. In a communist society, work no longer has to organize the necessities of life, but rather productivity is so high that human survival is guaranteed by very little necessary work, which enables a maximum of free time for creative activities. The realm of necessity turns into a realm of freedom: "The realm of freedom really begins only where labour determined by necessity and external expediency ends; it lies by its very nature beyond the sphere of material production proper"[5] (Marx 1894, 958–959). The realm of freedom is "the specific mode of Dasein's praxis beyond material production and reproduction" (Marcuse 1933, 144). Freed from the necessity of production, the character of labour has changed: "It no longer serves the purpose of making mere Dasein happen; it is no longer a constant effort to establish and secure life-space. Its course has altered as it were. Labor no longer aims at the formation and fulfilment of Dasein as something that it first has to bring about and secure; instead, it proceeds from the form and plentitude of Dasein as its realization" (Marcuse 1933, 144). The realm of freedom abolishes the division of labour that "severs the essential union" of freedom and necessity (ibid., 149). Given this overview of the concepts of work and labour, we can next have a look at Marx's labour theory of value.

2.3. Marx's Labour Theory of Value

Section 2.3.1 presents an entry point into the debate on the labour theory of value, namely an overview of the contemporary German debate on this approach. In section 2.3.2, I provide my own conceptualization of the value concept that is based on a Hegelian-dialectical interpretation of Marx's works (2.3.2.1: use-value and value, 2.3.2.2: exchange-value, 2.3.2.3: money and price, 2.3.2.4: the value and price of labour-power, 2.3.2.5: surplus value).

2.3.1. The German Debate on Marx's Labour Theory of Value

There has been a profound and controversial debate on Marx's concept of value in the German-speaking world. The reason why I have chosen this debate as an entry point into discussing Marx's concept of value is not only that the involved scholars have profound knowledge of Marx's works, but also that most of the contributions are only available in German so that such a discussion opens up this debate to an international audience. The German political economist Michael Heinrich (2012, 55) argues that only "with the act of exchange does value obtain an objective value form". He is a representative of a school of Marxist thought known as the "New Reading of Marx" (Neue Marx-Lektüre) that formed in Germany and is grounded in the works of Hans-Georg Backhaus (2011) and Helmut Reichelt (2001, 2008), who interpret Marx's value form analysis in a logical way, oppose a historical interpretation and have argued for a monetary value theory. Their main works have not been translated to English. The authors prefer to publish in German, so this discourse has stayed very Germanic in character. This *Deutschtümelei* (German jingoism) also has to do with the circumstance that these authors think that the widely read edition of *Capital, Volume 1* (Marx 1867a, c)— which is grounded in Marx's second German edition from 1872 and Engels' third and fourth editions—is undialectical and a regression behind the status of the first German edition and that it contains a popularized and wrong version of the value form analysis. They therefore think that studies of Marx's critique of the political economy should be limited to the first German edition of *Capital* (Marx 1867b), the *Grundrisse* and a fragment known as the Urtext (original text) that Marx (1858) wrote at the time when he put together *A Contribution to the Critique of Political Economy* in 1858. Backhaus and Reichelt have advanced a monetary theory of value that Heinrich has taken up and further elaborated: "Marx's value theory is rather a *monetary theory of value*: without the value form, commodities cannot be related to one another as values, and only with the money form does an adequate form of value exist. 'Substantialist' conceptions of value, which attempt to establish the existence of value within individual objects, are *pre-monetary theories of value*. [...] The usual 'Marxist' value theory that alleges that value is already completely determined by 'socially necessary labor-time' is also a pre-monetary value theory" (Heinrich 2012, 63–64). Heinrich's (1999) main book is *Die Wissenschaft vom Wert* (The science of value). It was first published in 1991 and in a second edition in 1999 and was (unsurprisingly) written in German. He argues that an interpretation of Marx's labour theory of value as a "quantitative theory of labour quantities" reduces Marx to the level of a "socialist Ricardian" (Heinrich 1999, 208; translation from German). Heinrich's basic point is that value does not exist in the individual commodity, but only in exchange, and therefore is dependent on the money form. The labour products' "objective form of value exists only as the *common* objectivity of value in exchange, and the all-sided exchange of *commodities* (in contrast to the exchange of isolated products) exists only as reference of commodities to *money*" (ibid., 250, translation from German[6]). Commodities would not have value before they are exchanged (ibid., 216). Money is "not simply a formal translation of an immanent magnitude of value that has already measured the quantity of value. It is rather the necessary and above all the *only possible* form of the appearance of the commodity value, there can be no form of appearance of value that is independent of exchange" (ibid., 242, translation from German[7]). Heinrich (1999, 280) argues that in his approach the transformation problem of how prices are related to values does not exist.

Also Slavoj Žižek propagates a concept of value that is similar to Heinrich's. He argues that abstract labour "is a value-relationship which constitutes itself only in exchange, it is not the substantial property of a commodity independently of its relations with other commodities" (Žižek 2010b, 213). Value would not exist as essence, but only as "appearance in exchange" (ibid., 214).

Heinrich (1999) argues that this exchange- and money-concept of value correctly conceptualizes value as a social relationship. "Private labour transforms itself into social labour only in exchange, it becomes value-creating labour. But then it also follows, as already mentioned above, that the commodities only obtain value and the magnitude of value *within* exchange" (ibid., 232, translation from German[8]). In the first German edition of *Capital, Volume 1*, money is not part of the value form analysis; Marx introduced the money form as part of the value form analysis in the second German edition. Heinrich (1999, 228) agrees with Gerhard Göhler (1980) that this resulted in a "reduced dialectic". Backhaus and Reichelt (1995) have written a discussion of Heinrich's (1999) *Science of Value,* in which they say that Heinrich assumes logical difference and temporal identity of value and price (Backhaus and Reichelt 1995, 68) and repeat their opinion that the widely read edition of *Capital, Volume 1,* contains a popularization and reduction of the value form analysis.

In Marx's (1867b, 15–44) original value form analysis in the first edition of *Capital* that Heinrich, Reichelt, Backhaus and their followers foreground, there are four forms of value:

I.   The simple form of value: x commodity A = y commodity B
II. The expanded form of value: z commodity A = u commodity B = v commodity C = w commodity D = x commodity E = y commodity F = etc.
III. The inverted or reflexive form of value: u commodity B = z commodity A, v commodity C = z commodity A, w commodity D = z commodity A, x commodity E = z commodity A, y commodity F = z commodity A, etc.
IV. The general equivalent form of value:

   z commodity A = u commodity B = v commodity C = w commodity D = x commodity E = y commodity F = etc.
   u commodity B = z commodity A = v commodity C = w commodity D = x commodity E = y commodity F = etc.
   v commodity C = z commodity A = u commodity B = w commodity D = x commodity E = y commodity F = etc.
   w commodity D = z commodity A = u commodity B = v commodity C = x commodity E = y commodity F = etc.
   x commodity E = z commodity A = u commodity B = v commodity C = w commodity D = y commodity F = etc.
   y commodity F = z commodity A = u commodity B = v commodity C = w commodity D = x commodity E = etc.

Starting with the second edition of *Capital* (Marx 1872) and in subsequent editions, the first version of the value form analysis was replaced by the following one (Marx 1867a, 62–85; Marx 1867c, 138–163; Marx 1872, 81–113):

A.   Simple/isolated/accidental form of value:
   x commodity A = y commodity B
B.   Total/expanded form of value:
   z commodity A = u commodity B = v commodity C = w commodity D = x commodity E = etc.
C.   General form of value:
   u commodity B = z commodity A, v commodity C = z commodity A, w commodity D = z commodity A, x commodity E = z commodity A, etc.

D. Money form:

a ounces of gold = z commodity A, a ounces of gold = u commodity B,
a ounces of gold = v commodity C, a ounces of gold = w commodity D,
a ounces of gold = x commodity E, etc.

Dieter Wolf (2008, 94) argues that Heinrich's thesis that there is a break in the presentation of the value form between the first and the second edition of *Capital, Volume 1,* is incorrect because the general equivalent form is almost identical with the money form (although it is also different because money is a monopolized form of the general equivalent, ibid., 98) and Marx included the general form already in the first edition in the value form analysis. One can add that the original German edition contains a contradictory presentation of the value form because Marx added an annex called "Die Werthform" (The value form; Marx 1867b, 764–784), in which the money form is presented as the fourth form of value (I. Simple form of value, II. Expanded form of value, III. General form of value, IV. Money form), which is already the form of presentation that Marx later chose to move in the second edition from the annex into chapter 1.1.

Dieter Wolf (2004, 46) argues that Reichelt and Backhaus only select specific passages from the *Grundrisse* and the Urtext, based on which they claim that Marx later in *Capital* regressed behind a certain status of knowledge. They would ignore the shortcomings of both works and thereby constitute a new dogmatism that presents itself as non-dogmatic criticism of *Capital.*

Marx's value form analysis can be interpreted with the help of Hegel's dialectic of the One and the Many and of Attraction and Repulsion (see figures 2.4 and 2.5). Repulsion means "a distinguishing of the One from itself, the repulsion of the One", it "makes Many Ones" (Hegel 1830, §97). The "One manifests an utter incompatibility with itself, a self-repulsion: and what makes itself explicitly be, is the Many" (ibid.). But repulsion turns into Attraction: "The One, as already remarked, just is self-exclusion and explicit putting itself as the Many. Each of the Many however is itself a One, and in virtue of its so behaving, this all rounded repulsion is by one stroke converted into its opposite—Attraction" (ibid.). "But the Many are one the same as another: each is One, or even one of the Many; they are consequently one and the same. Or when we study all that Repulsion involves, we see that as a negative attitude of many Ones to one another, it is just as essentially a connective reference of them to each other; and as those to which the One is related in its act of repulsion are ones, it is in them thrown into relation with itself. The repulsion therefore has an equal right to be called Attraction; and the exclusive One, or Being-for-self, suppresses itself" (ibid., §98).

Marx shows in the value form analysis that commodities attract and repulse each other. They repulse each other because they have different natural forms, qualities, materials and use-values. They are many different commodities. But abstract labour equalizes them in the production process, and money (or another

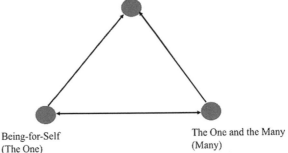

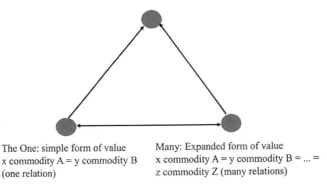

FIGURE 2.4 The dialectic of the One and the Many, Repulsion and Attraction

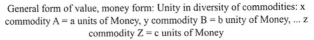

FIGURE 2.5 The dialectic of the forms of value as the dialectic of the One and the Many

general equivalent) equalizes them in the exchange process: They all contain quanta of human labour and are therefore objectifications of value that is in the exchange process assessed as representation of equal human labour. Qualitative different commodities that repulse each other attract each other via a general equivalent in the exchange process. The general form of value constructs a unity of the diversity of commodities. Marx describes it as the form of value that is "common to all" commodities and that therefore is general in character (Marx 1867c, 157).

Wolfgang Fritz Haug (2003b, 2007) argues that the "New Reading of Capital" assumption—that Marx "popularized" the presentation of the value form analysis because of the political influence of the labour movement on his thinking and that a non-scientific analysis resulted from it—results in a Marx interpretation that is distant from political praxis and has no grounding in actual reality, and that Marx (1867c, 105) himself described later versions of *Capital* as epistemological progress that has "scientific value". The problem of Heinrich, Backhaus, Reichelt and their followers for Haug is that they assume there is an "abiogenesis of the commodity characters in the moment of sale" (Haug 2007, 562, translation from German[9]) and that "Marx's value form-analytical theory of money is inverted into a money-theoretical ('monetary') theory of value" that is ahistorical (ibid., 563, translation from German[10]).

Heinrich's exchange- and money-theory of value is circulation-oriented and decentres the value concept from the realm of production. It cannot account for the fact that capitalists may not be able to sell commodities because of market problems, are therefore not able to realize profit, but nonetheless have exploited their employee's labour in the production process. From Heinrich's (1999, 232) formulation that commodities "only obtain value and the magnitude of value *within* exchange", it follows that a commodity that is not successfully exchanged with money (sold) does not have value and therefore also has no surplus value, which logically implies that the workers who produced it have not been exploited. The logical consequence is that Heinrich considers work only as being exploited if (a) it is remunerated and (b) the produced goods are successfully sold on the market. In contrast, it is feasible to assume that if humans contribute to the production of a commodity that shall be sold in order to accumulate capital and realize profit, they create value and are exploited if their remuneration lies below the price that *can* be achieved for the produced commodities on average on the market. This does not presuppose that commodities are actually sold, but that they are produced with the intention to be sold in order to accumulate capital. Value is created in the production process. If the commodity is sold, value changes its form in the circulation process from the commodity form to the money form. There can be realization problems (e.g. a drop in wages that results in less demand, different production conditions that allow one company to sell its commodities cheaper than other companies in the same industry, etc.), so there is never a guarantee that value changes from the commodity form to the money form. Heinrich ignores the dynamic and crisis-prone character of capitalism and underestimates the role of the production process in the exploitation of labour and class relations. Robert Kurz (2012) has provided the most extensive critique thus far of Heinrich's approach. He argues that Heinrich and the New Reading of Capital approach, by denying that value is a substance constituted in production, advance a "circulation-ideological and exchange-ideological" (ibid., 9) approach that is compatible with both neoclassical economics and postmodern thinking (155–156, 171, 185). As one consequence of his approach, Heinrich would assume an automatic regeneration capacity of capitalism in crises (Kurz 2012, chapters 13, 15) and postulate an "automatic washing machine of capital" (ibid., 306).

Based on this discussion, I next want to provide my own thoughts about Marx's labour theory of value that will in a further step be connected to the realm of the media.

2.3.2. A Reconstruction of Marx's Labour Theory of Value

Dieter Wolf (2008, 70) argues that Marx focuses in *Capital, Volume 1*'s chapter 1.1 on the analysis of commodity structures with abstraction from human practices and introduces the practical labour process that is mediated with the level of commodity structures in chapter 1.2. One can say that chapter 1 follows a dialectical structure (see figure 2.6): First an objective view is taken (the commodity), then a subjective one (labour), which is then combined in the value form analysis that shows how subjects exchange objects that represent objectified subjectivity (human labour).

2.3.2.1. Use-Value and Value

Marx argues in chapter 1.1 of *Capital, Volume 1* (Marx 1867c, 125–131) that a commodity—the "elementary form" of capitalism (ibid., 125)—has two factors: use-value and value. "The usefulness of a thing makes it a use-value" (ibid., 126).

Abstract human labour is the substance of value; it is a common characteristic of commodities. The value of a commodity is the average labour time that is needed for producing it. Labour time is the measure of value. Value has both a substance and a magnitude and is in these characteristics connected to human labour and labour time. *The substance of value*: Value is a "social system, which is common" to all commodities, "the common factor" in the exchange relation (ibid., 128). "A use-value, or useful article, therefore, has value only because abstract human labour is objectified [*vergegenständlicht*] or materialized in it" (ibid., 129). The

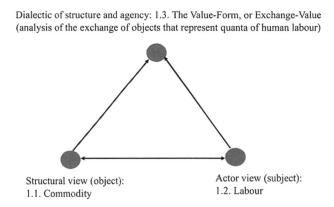

Dialectic of structure and agency: 1.3. The Value-Form, or Exchange-Value
(analysis of the exchange of objects that represent quanta of human labour)

Structural view (object):
1.1. Commodity

Actor view (subject):
1.2. Labour

FIGURE 2.6 The dialectic of structure and agency in chapter 1 of Marx's *Capital, Volume 1*

values of commodities are "determined by their cost of production, in other words by the labour time required to produce them" (ibid., 137). *The measure or magnitude of value:* The magnitude of value is measured "by means of the quantity of the 'value-forming substance', the labour, contained in the article. This quantity is measured by its duration, and the labour-time is itself measured on the particular scale of hours, days, etc." (ibid., 129). To be precise, socially necessary labour is the substance of value: "Socially necessary labour-time is the labour-time required to produce any use-value under the conditions of production normal for a given society and with the average degree of skill and intensity of labour prevalent in that society. [. . .] What exclusively determines the magnitude of the value of any article is therefore the amount of labour socially necessary, or the labour-time socially necessary for its production" (ibid.). "The value of commodities as determined by labour time is only their *average value*" (Marx 1857/1858b, 137). "If we consider *commodities as values,* we consider them exclusively under the single aspect of *realized, fixed,* or, if you like, *crystallized social labour*" (Marx 1865). Socially necessary labour determines an average commodity value that "is to be viewed on the one hand as the average value of the commodities produced in a particular sphere" (Marx 1894, 279). Every commodity has an individual value (production time). What counts on the market and in the industry is however the average production time. On the market in one industry, average labour times needed for producing similar commodities compete with each other. Socially necessary labour time is the average labour time that is needed in the entire economy for producing a commodity based on average skills and an average level of productivity. An individual capital has its own productivity, its workforce has a specific skill level and so forth. So the average value of a commodity produced may deviate from the socially necessary labour required to produce the commodity on average in the entire industry. The law of value has to do with the speed of production and the level of productivity: The higher the productivity used to create a commodity, the lower its value: "In general, the greater the productivity of labour, the less the labour-time required to produce an article, the less the mass of labour crystallized in that article, and the less its value. Inversely, the less the productivity of labour, the greater the labour-time necessary to produce an article, and the greater its value. The value of a commodity, therefore, varies directly as the quantity, and inversely as the productivity, of the labour which finds its realization within the commodity" (Marx 1867c, 131). Value is the essence of a commodity. Expressing it in another way, one can also say that abstract labour is the essence of value (Cleaver 2000, 111). Exchange value is the form of the appearance of value (Wolf 2002, 157; Cleaver 2000, 111). "In other words, work for capital only has meaning and only appears as a social relation when it is embodied in a product that is exchanged (and, ultimately, that earns surplus value)" (Cleaver 2000, 111). Money is a specific form of the appearance of value, the highest form of value. Christopher J. Arthur (2004, 108–109) argues in this context by applying Hegel's dialectical logic to Marx's *Capital* that value is the commodity's essence (value-in-itself), the value-forms the form of the appearance of value (value-for-itself) and money the actuality of value (value-in-and-for-itself).

Harry Cleaver (2000) argues that the distinction of the two factors of the commodity—use-value and value—in chapter 1.1 of Marx's *Capital, Volume 1,* should be read as being connected to the class relation between capital and labour: The "view of the commodity as use-value is the perspective of the working class. It sees commodities (e.g. food or energy) primarily as objects of appropriation and consumption, things to be used to satisfy its needs. Capital sees these same commodities primarily as exchange-values—mere means toward the end of increasing itself and its social control via the realization of surplus value and profit" (99). But in order to survive in capitalism, humans must sell their labour-power and thereby become interested in exchange value, whereas capitalists in order to achieve profit need the use-value of labour-power. Whereas labour is first interested in the qualitative side and capital in the quantitative side of the commodity, in order to obtain these goals each side has to turn into the other. Marx described this connectedness of value and the class relationship between capital and labour in the following way: "The separation of property from labour" (Marx 1857/1858b, 295) includes also a separation from the ownership of value: labour time is not the workers' time, but time under the command of capital. Labour is therefore "not-value", "not-capital", "not-raw-material", "not-instrument of labour", "not-raw-product" (ibid.): it is "absolute poverty", which means an "exclusion from objective wealth" (ibid., 296). But at the same time, private owners require labour in order to possess capital, value, raw materials and wealth: they require them as subjects that produce capital and value. So labour is not-value and at the same time value, not-capital and at the same time capital: it is the "living source of value", the "general possibility" of wealth (ibid.). Labour "is absolute poverty as object, on one side, and is, on the other side, the general possibility of wealth as subject and as activity" (ibid.). Labour and value have contradictory existences that are related to each other. Wolf (2008, 106) argues against Heinrich that all commodities and their values have a societal and social character before they are exchanged because they all have the same general characteristic, that they are products of human labour that is organized in society. Marx sees value and labour as social categories in a threefold sense. (1) Individual labour produces value that all economic producers in society create: In "the form of commodity-values, all labour is expressed as equal human labour" (Marx 1867c, 152). Therefore the "labour of different individuals is equal" (Marx 1859). (2) Labour-time is a characteristic of all production processes in society: "the labour-time of a particular individual is directly represented as *labour-time in general*". "It is the labour-time of an individual, *his* labour-time, but only as labour-time common to all" (ibid.). (3) The outcome of value-generating labour performed in society is a product that is traded based on a universal equivalent of exchange (in capitalism: money) that all use in the exchange process: "universal labour-time finds its expression in a universal product, a *universal equivalent,* a definite amount of materialised labour-time, for which the distinct form of the use-value in which it is manifested as the direct product of one person is a matter of complete indifference" (ibid.). In modern society, human labour is in most cases not an individual process but a social process—many workers act together as a combined worker. This is another reason why modern labour and value production is always a social process. Wolf (2002, 151–165) criticizes that Backhaus conceives price and money as the third thing that commodities have in common. In contrast, Wolf stresses that price and money are expressions of value and that value itself is the third concept the two commodities have in common.

2.3.2.2. Exchange-Value

In exchange, humans set values of commodities as something equal, and different use-values get a common denominator in the form of money (or another general equivalent of exchange): many things are getting united as a unity of diversity of commodities is created by the general form of value. "Exchange-value appears first of all as the quantitative relation, the proportion, in which use-values of one kind exchange for use-values of another kind" (Marx 1867c, 126). Exchange-value is "the necessary mode of expression, or form of appearance, of value" (ibid., 128). In exchange, concrete use-values that satisfy human needs are set as equals. They are all different in that they satisfy different human needs, but setting them as equals (x commodity A = y commodity B; or: x commodity = a units of money; y commodity B = a units of money) abstracts from this difference and constructs an equality by establishing an exchange relationship between two quantities of different commodities. The equalized commodities are considered to represent the same amount of value. The exchange relationship that in capitalism is organized with the help of money, which acts as a general equivalent of exchange, constructs a unity in diversity, a unity of the different use-values of commodities. In the exchange process, commodities are reduced to that which they have in common—value. Value is the third commonality of commodities (Wolf 2008, 104). Commodities "possess an objective character as values only in so far as they are all expressions of an identical social substance, human labour [. . .] their objective character as values is therefore purely social" (Marx 1867c, 138–139).

Value has an objective form in the sense that certain quanta of abstract human labour are objectified in it on average. This objectivity is social and societal because all commodities are products of human labour that is organized in society and the production process is itself a social process. But value is not only objective and in this objectivity societal, but it is also social as an exchange relationship itself: In the exchange relationship x commodity A = y commodity B, the value of commodity A is expressed in the use-value of commodity B and the value of commodity B in the use-value of commodity A (Wolf 2002, 131). "By means of the value-relation, therefore, the natural form of commodity B becomes the value-form of commodity A, in other words the physical body of commodity B becomes a mirror for the value of commodity A. Commodity A, then, in entering into a relation with commodity B as an object of value [*Wertkörper*], as a materialization of human labour, makes the use-value B into the material through which its own value is expressed. The value of commodity A, thus expressed in the use-value of commodity B, has the form of relative value" (Marx 1867c, 144). "If one says, for instance, one yard of linen is worth two pounds of coffee, then the exchange-value of linen is expressed in the use-value of coffee, and it is moreover expressed in a definite quantity of this use-value" (Marx 1859). The contradiction between value and use-value of a commodity (the double character of a commodity as use-value and value that is created by concrete labour and abstract labour) is sublated in the form of the exchange value, that is, by the fact that the value of the commodity is expressed in the use-value of another commodity via the exchange relationship. Value has at the same time an objective and social form. Therefore Heinrich's attempt to ridicule those who argue that value exists in production and prior to exchange and the money form, as substantialists and Ricardians that neglect the social form of value, is one-sided and does not see the double character of value. For Hegel (1830, §90), quality means "Being with a character or mode. [. . .] And as reflected into itself in this its character or mode, Determinate Being is a somewhat, as existent". Quantity is "the exclusive unit, and the identification or equalisation of these units" (ibid., §100). "Quantity, essentially invested with the exclusionist character which it involves, is Quantum (or How Much): i.e. limited quantity" (ibid., §101). The dialectical unity of Quantity and Quality is called the Measure. "Measure is the qualitative quantum, in the first place as immediate—a quantum, to which a determinate being or a quality is attached" (ibid., §107). "We measure, e.g. the length of different chords that have been put into a state of vibration, with an eye to the qualitative difference of the tones caused by their vibration, corresponding to this difference of length. Similarly, in chemistry, we try to ascertain the quantity of the matters brought into combination, in order to find out the measures or proportions conditioning such combinations, that is to say, those quantities which give rise to definite qualities. In statistics, too, the numbers with which the study is engaged are important only from the qualitative results conditioned by them" (ibid., §106). In the equation 1 computer = 500 €, we have qualities of the economy (computer, money) that are present in certain quantities (1 computer, 500 units of money). In their exchange, we measure a relationship between the two commodities: a certain quantity (value) of one commodity is expressed in the use-value of the other. The next figure shows Hegel's dialectic of quality, quantity and measure. It is followed by a figure that applies this dialectic to Marx's notions of use-value, value and exchange-value.

Hegel, Encyclopaedia I, The Doctrine of Being, §§ 84-111

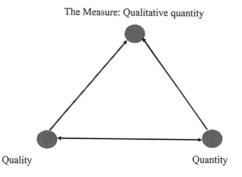

FIGURE 2.7 The dialectic of quality, quantity and the measure

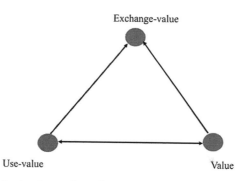

FIGURE 2.8 The dialectic of use-value, value and exchange-value

2.3.2.3. Money and Price

"Price is the money-name of the labour objectified in a commodity" (Marx 1867c, 195–196). A commodity expresses its value in the money price. Money is a measure of the value of a commodity. It is the most developed form of value. The money price is a specific monopolized form of the appearance of value that shapes exchange in capitalist society by acting as generalized medium of exchange in (almost) all market relations in which commodities are exchanged. Money has a "social monopoly [. . .] to play the part of universal equivalent within the world of commodities" (ibid., 162). Money is related to the class conflict between labour and capital (Cleaver 2000, 156–158): Capital aims at lowering the price of wage labour (wages) and increasing the price of commodities in order to increase profits. Workers can refuse work in the form of strikes and thereby attack the wage mediation and money profit, and they can refuse or eliminate prices by trying to obtain use-values below market prices or for free (e.g. by refusing to buy certain products and producing them together with others). So money is not only a medium of circulation, but also a "mediator between the classes" (ibid., 158) and an object of class struggle.

That two commodities have the same price does not mean that they necessarily have the same value, only that they are assessed as having the same value. Marx argues that value and price do not necessarily coincide. There can be incongruences and oscillations: "The magnitude of the value of a commodity therefore expresses a necessary relation to social labour-time which is inherent in the process by which its value is created. With the transformation of the magnitude of value into the price this necessary relation appears as the exchange-ratio between a single commodity and the money commodity which exists outside it. This relation, however, may express both the magnitude of value of the commodity and the greater or lesser quantity of money for which it can be sold under the given circumstances. The possibility, therefore, of a quantitative incongruity between price and magnitude of value, i.e. the possibility that the price may diverge from the magnitude of value, is inherent in the price-form itself" (Marx 1867c, 196).

Socially necessary labour time is "the centre of gravity around which price turns" (Marx 1894, 279). Value is "'the centre of gravity' of market prices, the axis round which these fluctuate" (Bidet 2009, 81). The commodities "whose individual value stands below the market price will realize an extra surplus-value or surplus profit, while those whose individual value stands above the market price will be unable to realize a part of the surplus-value which they contain" (Marx 1894, 279). "The market value is always different, is always below or above this average value of a commodity. [. . .] The price of a commodity constantly stands above or below the value of the commodity, and the value of the commodity itself exists only in this up-and-down movement of commodity prices" (Marx 1857/1858, 137). In Hegelian dialectical language, one can say that the price is a "constant negation of the negation, i.e. of itself as negation of real value" (ibid.).

Robert Kurz (2012, 184) argues that prices cannot be read off commodity-values, but that values and prices are also not independent. For example, the price of a toothbrush would always be much lower than the one of a car because the socially necessary labour to produce a toothbrush would necessarily be much lower than the one required for a car. At the same time, there would be no guarantee that the desired price can be achieved on the market because heavy competition could force capitalists to sell their commodities below the commodities' value (ibid., 185).

The transformation problem deals with the question of how values are transformed into prices. Based on Moishe Postone (1993), one can argue that the engagement with this problem is based on the assumption that Marx's theory can be used for deriving a price theory and on the assumption that this was also Marx's intention. Postone (1993, 134) in contrast argues that the "divergence of prices from values" is "integral to [. . .] Marx's analysis". Marx's "intention is not to formulate a price theory but to show how value induces a level of appearance that disguises it" (ibid.). The price form veils the specificities of value.

2.3.2.4. The Value and Price of Labour-Power

Imagine two situations:

(1) There is only one company in the world producing computers and there is a significant demand for this type of good. There is almost unlimited supply of the workforce and a securitization of work by military means: Workers who resist working are shot. There is no labour legislation, i.e. the owners of the computer company are free to choose the standard work time, wages, rest times, etc. It takes on average 15 minutes to assemble one computer and the price of one computer is 500 Euros. There are fixed constant capital costs of 100 Euros. The price depends on the investment costs. Given that the labour supply is limited, capitalists will try to reduce the labour costs to a minimum in order to maximize profits. In the example, they can, as a result of the fascist conditions of production, enslave the workers, pay no wages, and thereby maximize the profit to the possible maximum of 400 Euros.

(2) There is a regime change and labour legislation is introduced. There is now a minimum wage that requires the capitalist in the first example to pay 200 Euros in wage costs for the production of one computer. The production conditions remain unchanged, the constant capital costs are still 100 Euros. The capitalist is used to making 400 Euros profit per computer; based on the calculation that he makes a profit of 400% per computer he has acquired a luxurious lifestyle that he does not want to give up. If he demands the same price for each computer, the profit per commodity will halve from 400 Euros to 200 Euros. Given that there is no competition but a high demand for computers, he decides to increase the price of one computer from 500 to 700 Euros, which allows him to continue to achieve a profit of 400 Euros.

The examples aim to show that prices cannot simply be derived and calculated from labour values, but depend on the politics of class struggle. Jacques Bidet (2009) therefore speaks of the sociopolitical concept of value that is coupled to the political-economic concept of value. In capitalism, labour as the substance of value is coupled to "the social compulsion" for the expenditure of labour that is "exercised over the workers by the capitalist class" (ibid., 51). Labour is therefore a class concept and value is connected to labour's class relation to capital. Capital has to secure the command over labour, which is a political task. Labour can try to resist this command, which would be a political answer to this command. If "the substance of value is abstract labour, expenditure, it is coupled in the mode of production with its correlative, the social compulsion for this expenditure (a market compulsion exercised over the workers by the capitalist class), with which it forms, in the unity of the concept, a social and class relationship" (ibid.).

The concepts of value and abstract labour are therefore simultaneously an expression of political economy and sociopolitical class struggle. Also Marx stressed this connection in relation to the value and price of labour: "During the time of the anti-Jacobin war, undertaken, as the incorrigible tax-eater and sinecurist, old George Rose, used to say, to save the comforts of our holy religion from the inroads of the French infidels, the honest English farmers, so tenderly handled in a former chapter of ours, depressed the wages of the agricultural labourers even beneath that *mere physical minimum,* but made up by Poor Laws the remainder necessary for the physical perpetuation of the race. This was a glorious way to convert the wages labourer into a slave, and Shakespeare's proud yeoman into a pauper" (Marx 1865).

The sociopolitical concept of class has led Bidet (2007) to stress that capitalism "really poses the market *and the organization,* the two mediations, the two forms of rational-reasonable coordination at social scale, as its logical presuppositions. It poses them while turning them into the two *class factors* which are combined in the modern *class relation*". Although coming from another background, namely Autonomous Marxism, Harry Cleaver (2000) argues like Bidet for a political reading of Marx's *Capital*. Like Bidet, Cleaver also sees class relations as an important aspect of value: "The exchange-value of labour-power is, as we have seen, the money which the working class receives for its sale. Yet for the working class this exchange-value is at once income and a source of power in its struggle with capital, while for the latter it is a cost and a deduction from total value produced, a threat to surplus value and thus to capital's power. Because of these differences there is often a struggle over the form in which the working class will receive the exchange-value of its labour-power: money wages, wages in kind, social services, welfare, unemployment benefits, pensions, and so forth" (Cleaver 2000, 101).

What is the value of labour-power? "The value of labour-power is determined, as in the case of every other commodity, by the labour-time necessary for the production, and consequently also the reproduction, of this specific article. [. . .] the value of labour-power is the value of the means of subsistence necessary for the maintenance of its owner" (Marx 1867c, 274). The means of reproduction of a worker include his/her own subsistence costs and the ones of her/his family, education for obtaining skills, and health care for maintaining in a physical and mental status that allows the continuance of work. Harry Cleaver stresses in this concept the Autonomous-Marxist concept of the social worker and the social factory: "Both housework and schoolwork are intended to contribute to keeping the value of labour-power low" (Cleaver 2000, 123). The more unpaid labour time is available in the reproduction of labour-power, the more the "amount of variable capital necessary for the reproduction of the working class" decreases, so that the social worker in the social factory contributes "to the expansion of surplus value" (ibid.). The technical changes of capitalism (i.e. the technical increase of productivity or what Marx termed relative surplus-value production) result, as Mario Tronti (1962) argues, in the emergence of a social factory. The factory extends its boundaries into all areas of society: "The more capitalist development proceeds, i.e. the more the production of relative surplus value asserts and extends itself, the more the cycle production—distribution—exchange—consumption closes itself inevitably, the societal relation between capitalist production and bourgeois society, between factory and society, between society and the state become more and more organic. At the highest level of capitalist development the societal relation becomes a moment of the relations of production, and the whole of society becomes cause and expression of production, i.e. the whole society lives as a function of the factory and the factory extends its exclusive domination to the whole of society. [...] When the factory raises itself to the master of the whole of society—the entire societal production becomes industrial production—then the specific characteristics of the factory get lost inside of the general characteristics of society" (Tronti 1962, 30–31, translation from German). As the example has tried to show, the price of labour (wages) depends on the politically set working conditions, which are the actual, temporal and dynamically changing result of the class struggle between capital and labour. Organizations of the working class, such as the trade unions, "aim at nothing less than to prevent the *reduction of wages* below the level that is traditionally maintained in the various branches of industry. That is to say, they wish to prevent the *price* of labour-power from falling below its *value*" (Marx 1867c, 1069). In the first example, the wages are driven by the power of capital in class struggle to an absolute minimum, below the subsistence level of wage labour (i.e. below the value of labour-power). In the second example, class struggle empowers worker organizations and allows them to raise the price of labour-power. The examples show that "value is established in a class struggle defined by the question of the price of labour-power" (Bidet 2009, 101). "By comparing the standard wages or values of labour in different countries, and by comparing them in different historical epochs of the same country, you will find that the *value of labour* itself is not a fixed but a variable magnitude, even supposing the values of all other commodities to remain constant" (Marx 1865).

2.3.2.5. Surplus Value

Workers are forced to enter class relations and to produce profit in order to survive, which enables capital to appropriate surplus. The notion of exploited surplus value is the main concept of Marx's theory, by which he intends to show that capitalism is a class society. "The theory of surplus value is in consequence immediately the theory of exploitation" (Negri 1991, 74) and, one can add, the theory of class and as a consequence the political demand for a classless society.

Enrique Dussel argues that in his work on the *Grundrisse,* Marx had "for the first time in his work [...] discovered the category of surplus value" (Dussel 2008, 77) in December 1857: "if the worker needs only half a working day in order to live a whole day, then, in order to keep alive as a worker, he needs to work only half a day. The second half of the day is forced labour; surplus labour" (Marx 1857/1858b, 324). Surplus value means that workers are compelled to work more than necessary for satisfying their immediate needs; they produce an excess for free that is appropriated by capitalists: "What appears as surplus value on capital's side appears identically on the worker's side as surplus labour in excess of his requirements as worker, hence in excess of his immediate requirements for keeping himself alive" (ibid., 324–325). "The surplus value which capital obtains through the production process consists only of the excess of surplus labour over necessary labour. The increase in productive force can increase surplus labour—i.e. the excess of labour objectified in capital as product over the labour objectified in the exchange value of the working day—only to the extent that it diminishes the relation of necessary labour to surplus labour, and only in the proportion in which it diminishes this relation. Surplus value is exactly equal to surplus labour; the increase of one [is] exactly measured by the diminution of necessary labour" (ibid., 339).

In *Capital, Volume 1,* Marx defines surplus value in the following way: The capitalist "wants to produce a commodity greater in value than the sum of the values of the commodities used to produce it, namely the means of production and the labour-power he purchased with his good money on the open market. His aim is to produce not only a use-value, but a commodity; not only use-value, but value; and not just value, but also surplus value [. . .] The cotton originally bought for £100 is for example re-sold at £100 + £10, i.e. £110. The complete form of this process is therefore M-C-M', where M' = M + ΔM, i.e. the original sum advanced plus an increment. This increment or excess over the original value I call 'surplus-value'" (Marx 1867c, 293, 251).

Capital is not money but money that is increased through accumulation, "money which begets money" (ibid., 256). Marx argued that the value of labour-power is the average amount of time that is needed for the production of goods that are necessary for survival (necessary labour time), which in capitalism is paid for by workers with their wages. Surplus labour time is all of labour time that exceeds necessary labour time, remains unpaid, is appropriated for free by capitalists and is transformed into money profit. Surplus value "is in substance the materialization of unpaid labour-time. The secret of the self-valorization of capital resolves itself into the fact that it has at its disposal a definite quantity of the unpaid labour of other people" (ibid., 672). Surplus value "costs the worker labour but the capitalist nothing", but "none the less becomes the legitimate property of the capitalist" (ibid.). "Capital also developed into a coercive relation, and this compels the working class to do more work than would be required by the narrow circle of its own needs. As an agent in producing the activity of others, as an extractor of surplus labour and an exploiter of labour-power, it surpasses all earlier systems of production, which were based on directly compulsory labour, in its energy and its quality of unbounded and ruthless activity" (ibid., 425).

For Marx, capitalism is based on the permanent theft of unpaid labour from workers by capitalists. This is the reason why he characterizes capital as vampire and werewolf (ibid., 342, 411).

2.4. Conclusion

For theorizing digital labour, a labour theory of value is needed. Based on Marx's theory, we can distinguish between work and labour as anthropological and historical forms of human activity. This distinction is reflected in capitalism in the dual character of the commodity that is both use-value and (exchange) value at the same time. The notion of alienated labour is grounded in a general model of the work process that has been conceptualized based on a dialectic of subject and object in the economy that has been presented in the form of a model, the Hegelian-Marxist dialectical triangle of the work process. This model is based on Hegel's dialectic of the subject and the object that Marx used for theorizing the labour process as dialectical process. Various aspects of a Marxist theory of work and labour—such as the notions of abstract and concrete labour, double-free labour, productive labour, the collective worker and general work—have been presented. Work is a dialectical interconnection of human subjects (labour-power) that use instruments on objects so that products emerge that satisfy human needs. Labour is based on a fourfold alienation of the human being from labour-power, the objects of labour and the tools of labour as well as the results of labour. Alienation in capitalist societies is alienation of workers from all poles of this dialectic and from the whole process itself that constitutes class relations and exploitation. This chapter has also discussed Marx's concept of value by introducing the contemporary German debate on Marx's labour theory of value (Michael Heinrich, Hans-Georg Backhaus, Helmut Reichelt, Wolfgang Fritz Haug, Dieter Wolf, Robert Kurz). In a reconstruction of Marx's labour theory of value, a Hegelian interpretation of the concepts of use-value, value, exchange-value, money, price, the value and price of labour-power and surplus value has been given. I have stressed the role of politics and class struggle in the relationship of wages and prices and thereby argue, like Harry Cleaver and Jacques Bidet, for a political interpretation of the value concept. Value is an objective concept determined by the amount of working hours needed on average for the production of a commodity. The transition from the level of value to the level of commodity prices and the degree of profits is established in and through class struggle. This struggle is focused on the capitalist class's attempt to reduce wage costs, that is, to make the proletariat work a larger part of the working day without pay, and potential resistance against wage reductions and the intensification and extension of work. The price of labour (wages) depends on the politically set working conditions, which are the actual, temporal and dynamically changing result of the class struggle between capital and labour. The purpose of chapter 2 was to set out foundations of Marx's labour theory of value as context for the discussion of digital labour. The next two chapters will focus on the academic context, namely on the question how media and communication studies is positioning itself towards Marx and Marx's topics. This is achieved by first having a look at Marx in Cultural Studies and then at contemporary discussions on the relevance of Dallas Smythe's works.

Notes

1 "Als Bildnerin von Gebrauchswerten, als nützliche Arbeit, ist die Arbeit daher eine von allen Gesellschaftsformen unabhängige Existenzbedingung des Menschen, ewige Naturnotwendigkeit, um den Stoffwechsel zwischen Mensch und Natur, also das menschliche Leben zu vermitteln" (MEW 23, 192).

2 "Das Reich der Freiheit beginnt in der Tat erst da, wo das Arbeiten, das durch Not und äußere Zweckmäßigkeit bestimmt ist, aufhört; es liegt also der Natur der Sache nach jenseits der Sphäre der eigentlichen materiellen Produktion" (MEW 25, 828).

3 I have provided here my own translation because the English translation of "Aufheben dieses Aufhebens" (Marx 1857/1858a, 222) as "suspension of this suspension" (Marx 1857/1858b, 301) does not capture the Hegelian-dialectical meaning of the term *Aufhebung* that is correctly translated with the term "sublation".

4 "Allseitigkeit ihrer Entwicklung" has here been translated as "multiplicity of its development". But in order to be consistent with the terminology in *The German Ideology*, a more adequate translation would be to speak of the "well-roundedness of its [society's] development".

5 "Das Reich der Freiheit beginnt in der Tat erst da, wo das Arbeiten, das durch Not und äußere Zweckmäßigkeit bestimmt ist, aufhört; es liegt also der Natur der Sache nach jenseits der Sphäre der eigentlichen materiellen Produktion" (MEW 25, 828).

6 "Ihre Wertgegenständlichkeit existiert nur als *gemeinsame* Wertgegenständlichkeit im Austausch, und der allseitige Austausch von Waren (im Unterschied zum Tausch vereinzelter Produkte) existiert nur als Bezug der Waren auf *Geld*".

7 "[. . .] ist Geld als Wertmaß nicht einfach eine formale Übersetzung eines immanenten Wertmaßes, welches die Wertgröße bereits gemessen hat. Es ist vielmehr die notwendige und vor allem *einzig mögliche* Erscheinungsform des Warenwerts, eine vom Tausch unabhängige Erscheinungsform des Werts kann es nicht geben".

8 "Erst innerhalb des Austausches verwandelt sich die Privatarbeit wirklich in gesellschaftliche Arbeit, wird sie zu wertbildender Arbeit. Dann folgt aber auch, wovon bereits oben die Rede war, daß den Waren erst *innerhalb* des Austausches Wert und Wertgröße zukommt".

9 "Es ist, als fände eine Urzeugung der Warencharaktere im Moment des Verkaufs statt".

10 "Die wertformanalytische Geldtheorie von Marx wird in eine geldtheoretische ('monetäre') Werttheorie verkehrt; dem dialektischen Totalitätsdenken wird die Geschichte ausgetrieben".

3

CONTEMPORARY CULTURAL STUDIES AND KARL MARX

Cultural Studies is a field that analyses culture and has its origins in the works of thinkers such as Richard Hoggart, Raymond Williams and Edward P. Thompson who were influenced by Marxist thinking. This chapter takes a look at what role Marx plays in contemporary Cultural Studies, which means that it discusses what role is assigned to capitalism, class, labour and value in specific approaches.

The introduction (3.1) discusses the role of Marx for early Cultural Studies, Stuart Hall and the controversy between Nicholas Garnham and Lawrence Grossberg in the mid-1990s. The subsequent sections discuss three contemporary Cultural Studies books: Lawrence Grossberg's *Cultural Studies in the Future Tense* (3.2), John Hartley's *Digital Futures for Cultural and Media Studies* (3.3) and the collected volume *The Renewal of Cultural Studies* (3.4) which was edited by Paul Smith. All three approaches argue for the importance of giving attention to the economy in Cultural Studies but differ widely in what role Marx should have in such a refocusing.

3.1. Introduction

The works of Karl Marx had an important influence on early Cultural Studies. So for example, Raymond Williams stated in one of his earliest books, *Culture & Society: 1780–1950,* that he is "interested in Marxist theory because socialism and communism are now important" (Williams 1958, 284). Williams argued for and worked on a "Marxist theory of culture" that recognizes "diversity and complexity", takes |account of continuity within change|, allows "for chance and certain limited autonomies", but takes "the facts of the economic structure and the consequent social relations as the guiding string on which a culture is woven, and by following which a culture is to be understood" (ibid., 269).

Edward P. Thompson argued for a Marxism that stresses human experience and culture. He defended such a Marxism politically against Stalinism (Thompson 1957), theoretically on the left against Althusserian structuralism (Thompson 1978a) and against the right-wing reactions against Marx led by thinkers like Leszek Kolakowski (Thompson 1973). Thompson argued that this form of Marxist thinking was present, first, in Marx's "writings on alienation, commodity fetishism, and reification; and, second, in his notion of man, in history, continuously making over his own nature" (Thompson 1978a, 165). The political perspective underlying Thompson's political and theoretical interventions is socialist humanism, a position that "is humanist because it places once again real men and women at the centre of socialist theory and aspiration, instead of the resounding abstractions—the Party, Marxism-Leninism-Stalinism, the Two Camps, the Vanguard of the Working-Class—so dear to Stalinism. It is socialist because it re-affirms the revolutionary perspectives of Communism, faith in the revolutionary potentialities not only of the Human Race or of the Dictatorship of the Proletariat but of real men and women" (Thompson 1957, 109).

In the 1990s, a controversy between Cultural Studies and Critical Political Economy developed that culminated in an exchange between Nicholas Garnham (1995a, b) and Lawrence Grossberg (1995). The basic points of criticism are summarized in table 3.1. Garnham (1995a, 64) summarizes the criticism of Cultural Studies by saying that the latter refuses "to think through the implications of its own claim that the forms of subordination and their attendant cultural practices—to which Cultural Studies gives analytical priority—are grounded within a capitalist mode of production". The discussion between Garnham and Grossberg is an indication that something fundamentally changed in Cultural Studies since the time Williams and Thompson had written their major works, namely a profound move away from Marx, Marxism and the analysis of culture in the context of class and capitalism.

The contemporary return of Marx was preceded by a disappearance of Marx. In 1990, it was announced that Stuart Hall's keynote talk at the conference "Cultural Studies: Now and in the Future" would have the title "The Marxist Element in Cultural Studies" (Sparks 1996, 72). The programme finally announced him as talking about "Cultural Studies and Its Theoretical Legacies", which is also the title of the published version of the presentation (Hall 1992/1996). Hall describes the troubled relationship of his version of Cultural Studies to Marx. He says that there was never a moment "when Cultural Studies and marxism represented a perfect theoretical fit" because Marx's work has "great inadequacies": According to Hall, Marx "did not talk about [. . .] culture, ideology, language, the

TABLE 3.1 The controversy between Nicholas Garnham and Lawrence Grossberg

Topic	Nicholas Garnham	Lawrence Grossberg
The basic difference between Cultural Studies and Critical Political Economy	Political Economy sees class as the key to the structure of domination: in capitalism, non-class domination is always related to class domination. Cultural Studies sees class and gender, race, etc. as independent; it ignores the economy and class.	Political Economy is a form of class/economic reductionism and determinism. Cultural Studies sees a plurality of articulated differences.
Assessment of classical Cultural Studies works	Williams, Hoggart and Thompson stressed working-class culture and the struggle against capitalism.	Williams, Hoggart and Thompson focused on practices, by which people represent themselves and the world.
The analysis of production	Cultural Studies gives priority to cultural practices and ignores that they are grounded in the capitalist mode of production.	Political Economy equates production with the cultural industries.
The analysis of consumption	Cultural Studies focuses on cultural consumption/leisure instead of production/work/institutions. Cultural Studies sees the interpretation of culture as arbitrary and always resistant, authentic, progressive.	Political Economy ignores studying consumption and everyday life. Some but not all work in Cultural Studies celebrates popular culture as resistant. Political Economy sees people as passively manipulated cultural dupes and culture only as commodity and ideological tool. Cultural Studies says that institutions cannot control how people interpret culture. Cultural Studies sees consumers as active.
Truth and ethics	Cultural Studies rejects the notion of truth and therefore ethics and the quest for a just society.	Notions like truth and false consciousness are elitist.

symbolic". A certain "reductionism and economism" and "Eurocentrism" would be "intrinsic to marxism" (ibid., 265). Therefore "the encounter between British Cultural Studies and marxism has first to be understood as the engagement with a problem" (ibid.). The 1990s and 2000s were decades of the disappearance of Marx in the humanities and social sciences in general. Hall generalizes and constructs a homogeneity of British Cultural Studies that never existed. Whereas his own encounter with Marx may always have been troubled and at the time, when he felt more attracted by Marx's works, was mainly an encounter with Althusser's structuralism, other representatives of Cultural Studies, namely Edward P. Thompson and Raymond Williams, were much attracted by humanist Marxism. Whereas Hall took up Althusser's work, Edward P. Thompson at the same time employed his theoretical and literary skills for writing a bitter satirical critique of Althusser from a Marxist-humanist standpoint (Thompson 1978a) and for writing a defence of Marx and Marxism against Leszek Kolakowski, a former humanist Marxist who published a book against Marx and Marxism (Kolakowski 2005). So the identification and depth of engagement with Marxism has definitely been different in various strands of Cultural Studies. Stuart Hall gives (against his own epistemology) a quite non-complex, non-contextualized and reductionistic reading of Cultural Studies and Marxism that too much generalizes his own experiences and worldview.

Vincent Mosco (2009) argues that Hoggart, Williams, Thompson, Willis and Hall "maintained a strong commitment to an engaged class analysis" (Mosco 2009, 233), but that later Cultural Studies became "less than clear about its commitment to political projects and purposes" (229) and that it is "hard to make the case that Cultural Studies has devoted much attention to labor, the activity that occupies most people's waking hours" (214). Colin Sparks describes the relationship between Stuart Hall's version of Cultural Studies and Marxism as a "move towards marxism and move away from marxism" (Sparks 1996, 71). He argues that Hall in the 1970s engaged with structural Marxism, which culminated in the *Policing the Crisis* book (Hall et al. 1978), and that then there was a "slow movement away from any self-identification with marxism" (Sparks 1996, 88) in the 1980s that was influenced by the uptake of Ernesto Laclau's approach. The resulting "distance between Cultural Studies and marxism" is for Sparks a "retrograde move" (ibid., 98). "Marrying" Marxism and Cultural Studies would remain "an important and fruitful project" (ibid., 99). Ernesto Laclau has in a trialogue with Judith Butler and Slavoj Žižek admitted that in postmodern approaches it is a common language game to "transform 'class' into one more link in an enumerative chain [. . .] 'race, gender, ethnicity, etc.—*and* class" (Butler, Laclau and Žižek 2000, 297) and to put class deliberately as the last element in the chain in order to stress its unimportance—Laclau speaks of "deconstructing classes" (ibid., 296). Žižek has in this context in my opinion correctly said that postmodernism, Cultural Studies and post-Marxism have, by assuming an "irreducible plurality of struggles", accepted "capitalism as 'the only game in town'" and have renounced "any real attempt to overcome the existing capitalist liberal regime" (ibid., 95). Colin Sparks (1996, 92) holds that the Laclauian move in Cultural Studies was to "give equal weight to each of the members of the 'holy trinity' of race, class and gender". According to Laclau himself, the task of his approach was to deliberately ignore and downplay the importance of class in favour of other forms of power. Given that we today live in times where the interest in Marx's works and the economic in general has returned, the question arises as to which role Marx should play in the analysis of media, communication and culture and which role his works actually do play in such studies. In order to contribute to the discussion of this question, this chapter addresses the role of Marx in current works of selected representatives of Cultural Studies and argues for a renewed reading and interpretation of Marx's works in the context of studying the media, communication and culture.

I discuss the role of Marx's theory in three books published by prominent representatives of Cultural Studies: Lawrence Grossberg's *Cultural Studies in the Future Tense* (section 3.2), John Hartley's *Digital Futures for Cultural and Media Studies* (section 3.3) and the collected volume *The Renewal of Cultural Studies,* which features 27 contributions and was edited by Paul Smith (section 3.4). Many approaches in contemporary Cultural Studies agree that the economic has to be taken more into account, although there is no agreement on how this engagement with the economy should look. The position taken in this chapter is that the analysis of media, communication and culture requires a profound engagement with, discussion of and interpretation of Karl Marx's works (section 3.5).

I have taken a look at how the three selected books have discussed the relationship of Cultural Studies to Marx and Marxist theory. The books were published in the past three years, so all are relatively recent, and have set themselves the task to reflect on the future of Cultural Studies. This is already indicated in the titles of the three works: *Cultural Studies in the Future Tense* (Grossberg 2010), *Digital Futures for Cultural and Media Studies* (Hartley 2012), and *The Renewal of Cultural Studies* (Smith 2011b). Grossberg's title choice indicates that the book sets the stage for the future of Cultural Studies. Hartley goes one step further and includes a specific statement on what the future of Cultural Studies should look like in the title: he wants this field to focus on the analysis of digital media. Paul Smith's book title is also oriented on the future of Cultural Studies, but unlike Grossberg and Hartley it makes a quite normative statement, namely that something is wrong with Cultural Studies and therefore it needs to be renewed.

I conducted a book title search covering the years 2010–2013 for the keyword "Cultural Studies" in the British Library's catalogue (date: February 2, 2013). It produced 47 results that have both words in their title and refer to the academic field named Cultural Studies. Many of these books are introductions and have titles such as *Introducing Cultural Studies, Introduction to Cognitive Cultural Studies, Cultural Studies: A Practical Introduction,* or *American Cultural Studies: An Introduction to American Culture.* So most of these books are oriented on documenting specific aspects of the history of Cultural Studies, whereas only a few are concerned with assessing the current status and the potential futures of Cultural Studies. In contrast, the three selected books have exactly the purpose of critically assessing the present and helping to construct the future of Cultural Studies and are therefore suited for further analysis.

The three books have in common that they see a problem in contemporary Cultural Studies and a task for the future. For Grossberg, the problem is that "too much of the work that takes place under the sign of Cultural Studies has simply become too lazy" (Grossberg 2010, 2). For Hartley, the problem is that media and Cultural Studies was founded on and would stick to a broadcasting model of the media that sees "everyday cultural practices [. . .] beset on all sides by darker forces that seemed to be exploiting the pleasure-seeking consumer for quite different ends, both political and corporate" (Hartley 2012, 1). For Smith, the problem is that Cultural Studies on the one hand has always had "this kind of residual desire for some form of political efficacy" (Ross and Smith 2011, 245), but on the other hand by its institutionalization this desire would have "turned into something like a phantom limb" (ibid., 246). So all three books have in common that they perceive a crisis of Cultural Studies and the need to change something in this field of studies. The profound crisis of contemporary society is on the academic level accompanied by a profound crisis of Cultural Studies. This is at least the impression that one gets from reading the books of these authors, who can all be considered among the most influential contemporary figures in Cultural Studies.

All three books identify a future task for Cultural Studies. For Grossberg, the task is to "construct a vision for Cultural Studies out of its own intellectual and political history" (Grossberg 2010, 3). His book is "an attempt to set an agenda for Cultural Studies work in the present and into the future" and to "produce a Cultural Studies capable of responding to the contemporary worlds and the struggle constituting them" (ibid.). For Hartley, the task is to reform Cultural Studies so that it takes into account digital media and the "dialogic model of communication" (Hartley 2012, 2). The task for Paul Smith's collected volume is to "help define a new kind of identity for Cultural Studies" (Smith 2011a, 2) and to give answers to the question, "What can and should Cultural Studies be doing right now?" (ibid., 3). These tasks vary in the way they want to transform Cultural Studies but have in common that in the situation of the crisis of Cultural Studies they want to contribute to its reconstruction.

I discuss the books in chronological order of publication and therefore start with Lawrence Grossberg.

3.2. Lawrence Grossberg: *Cultural Studies in the Future Tense*

Grossberg (2010, 16) argues that Cultural Studies focuses on complexity by refusing "to reduce the complexity of reality to any single plane or domain of existence". It would be "decidedly antireductionist" (ibid., 17), contextual and opposed to universalism and completeness (ibid.). "Radical contextualism is the heart of Cultural Studies" (ibid., 20). This contextuality is expressed in the use of Stuart Hall's concept of articulation, the "transformative practice or work of making, unmaking, and remaking relations and contexts, of establishing new relations out of old relations or non-relations" (ibid., 21). It focuses on "discovering the heterogeneity, the differences, the fractures, in the wholes" (ibid., 22). Power has "multiple axes and dimensions that cannot be reduced to one another" (ibid., 29). "Contexts are always in relations to other contexts, producing complex sets of multidimensional relations and connections" (ibid., 31). The "commitment to complexity, contingency, contestation, and multiplicity" is "a hallmark of Cultural Studies" (ibid., 54).

Grossberg sees an important role for economics in Cultural Studies today. He argues that Cultural Studies should "take on and take up economic questions without falling back into forms of reductionism and essentialism" (ibid., 101), which logically implies that previously there was a neglect and ignorance of economic questions. Grossberg argues that Cultural Studies "does need to take questions of economics more seriously" (ibid., 105). He says that it should do so in a way "which would not reproduce the reductionism of many forms of political economy" (ibid.). Looking back on the debate between Cultural Studies and Marxist/Critical Political Economy of the Media, he says that Cultural Studies opposes "economic and class reductionism" and refuses "to believe that the economy could define the bottom line of every account of social realities" (ibid.). Paul Smith argues in this context from within the Cultural Studies field that the claim by certain Cultural Studies scholars that Marxism is "reductive" and "economically determinist" is a rhetoric used "to eschew the economic" (Smith 2006, 337). The result would be an "anarchist or nihilistic stance in relation to the object" (ibid., 338). As a result, Cultural Studies would have followed "numerous dead ends and crises" and would have been held back from "realizing its best intellectual and political aspirations" (ibid., 339).

Grossberg's own approach of reconciling economics and Cultural Studies starts with a discussion of Marx's labour theory of value (Grossberg 2010, 151–165). He argues for "a radically contextual theory of value and, hence, a radically contextual reading of Marx's labor theory of value" (ibid., 156). Grossberg aims at decentring the value concept from the labour concept and therefore interprets it in its broader meaning as representation, desire, measure of a degree of singularity and what is good and desirable (ibid., 158–159). He suggests a "general theory of value" (ibid., 159) that is based on the assumption of a "multiplicity, dispersion, and contingency of values" (122). Value would involve the production of all types of surplus so that "the real" is "always greater than, in excess of, the actual" (ibid., 160). The contemporary crisis would be constituted by manifold "crises of commensuration" (ibid.) and the inability to measure/value various differences, which would have resulted in religious, political, economic, intellectual and financial fundamentalisms (167–168) that demand "the extermination of the other" (168). The financial crisis would have been caused "by the existence of an enormous set of financial ('toxic') assets that cannot be commensurated—that is to say, their value cannot be calculated" (ibid., 167), but it would just form one of many simultaneous crises of commensuration. The Research Assessment Exercise (RAE) is an assessment of research conducted in the United Kingdom that aims at producing "quality profiles for each submission of research activity" (www.rae.ac.uk). It tries to measure the quality of research and to thereby compare and rank higher education institutions and departments. The results have implications for budget allocation. In the 2008 RAE, 45% of the submissions of Middlesex University in the "unit of assessment" area of philosophy were classified as 3★ (internationally excellent) and 20% as 4★ (world-leading), which makes a total of 65% excellent (4★ + 3★) research. Seven institutions received better, 8 the same (including the Universities of Cambridge and Oxford) and 26 worse results. According to this assessment, philosophy at Middlesex University was very good. In April 2010, Middlesex University announced that it would close all philosophy programmes and terminate further recruitments in this area for "simply financial" reasons and "based on the fact that the University believes that it may be able to generate more revenue if it shifts its resources to other subjects".[1] The announcement was followed by protests, an occupation, the suspension of staff members and students, many protest letters to the university's administration—signed by such leading intellectuals as Étienne Balibar, Judith Butler, David Harvey, Martha Nussbaum or Jacques Rancière—and the institutional relocation of the Centre for Research in Modern European Philosophy from Middlesex University to Kingston University. In 2012, no courses and research in the area of philosophy were indicated on Middlesex University's website (see www.mdx.ac.uk, accessed August 30, 2012)—philosophy had formally ceased to exist at the university. In 2011, philosophy at London Metropolitan University and the University of Greenwich was facing similar debates as at Middlesex University. Modern universities are based on an enlightenment ideal—they accumulate systematic knowledge that aims at advancing the status of human knowledge about the world as well as society. In this accumulation, universities compete with each other. Capitalist industry and governments apply the accumulated scientific knowledge, whereas the workforce and management in the modern economy apply the accumulated educational skills created by higher education. The Nobel Prize, established in 1895, is characteristic for the modern competitive assessment of knowledge and universities in the areas of chemistry, economics, literature, medicine, peace and physics. Modern universities are inherently shaped by an economic logic of accumulation, competition and ranking. At the same time, the university has also been a locus and space for the formation of counterculture, critical ideas, and political protests that question the very logic of accumulation and resulting inequalities in society at large. An important step in the institutionalization of quality assessment was the establishment of the Science Citation Index in 1960 that is today owned by a commercial publishing company—Thomson Reuters. The index originated in the natural sciences but was later extended to cover the humanities (Arts and Humanities Index) and the social sciences (Social Sciences Citation Index). Nationwide research assessments (such as the RAE) and global university rankings are more recent developments. The first RAE was conducted in 1986 under the Thatcher government. The first Times Higher Education World University

Ranking was published in 2004. The Academic Ranking of World Universities has been conducted since 2003.

These phenomena are indications that economic logic is one immanent feature of the modern university system and that in neo-liberal times, the economization of higher education and research has become an even stronger feature of universities. The closing of philosophy at Middlesex University is an indication that fields, programmes, and people engaged in areas that are difficult to subsume under the logic of revenue generation and industry are prone to being dropped. In this example, the contradictions of economization became fully apparent: Although receiving very good results in one form of economization (research assessment), philosophy at Middlesex University was closed because of another form of economization (monetary revenue): the university management thought that the department does not generate enough monetary revenue. I have chosen this example because it shows how modern culture and contemporary modern culture in particular are shaped by economic logic. It shows that the central (moral) value of modern society is (economic) value. The "radical contextuality" that Lawrence Grossberg propagates does not allow grasping the particular role that the economic logic of accumulation and money plays in modern society. It advances a peculiar kind of relativism disguised under headlines such as contextuality, multidimensionality, heterogeneity and difference. Modern society definitely is complex in that it is made up of many interacting and interdependent spheres (the economy, politics, everyday life, private life, the public sphere, the media, higher education, health and care, nature, arts, entertainment, sports, etc.), but there is a need for a conceptual apparatus that allows one to analyse the power relations between these spheres. It is unlikely that all spheres and actors in a state, phase or "conjuncture" of society have the same power. There are indications that the economic sphere has in capitalism always been the dominant (although not determining) sphere. A "radical contextualism" results in a dualistic relativism that cannot adequately analyse power *relations* and power *distributions* (and as a consequence power struggles) and sees power as independently constituted in multiple spheres. Rejecting such a position does not mean that struggles against capitalism and domination are impossible, but it does mean that in modern society all struggles necessarily have an economic dimension that is of particular importance. It is important not only that there are multiple spheres of power, but that these spheres are *related* to each other in variable dimensions that are determined in struggles. Radical contextualism risks conceiving and analysing power as independent containers, not as power relations. Grossberg propagates the equal importance of all societal spheres, which results in a concept of multiple values that dissolves Marxian theory into a "general theory of value" and classifies all attempts to stress a particular importance and shaping role of the economic—which has in media and Cultural Studies especially been stressed by Marxist Political Economy—as "economic and class reductionism", economism, capitalocentrism, essentialism and so forth. Grossberg calls for respecting "each other as allies" (Grossberg 2010,

201) but at the same time continues to uphold old prejudices against Marxist Political Economy that were most fiercely expressed in the debate between him and Nicholas Garnham, in which he concluded that he "must decline the invitation to reconcile" Cultural Studies and the Political Economy of Culture and the Media, stating, "we don't need a divorce because we were never married" (Grossberg 1995, 80; see also Garnham 1995a, b).

Grossberg calls for giving more attention to the economy in Cultural Studies. He does so himself by engaging with economics, including Marx's labour theory of value, which he introduces and dismisses with the argument that the value concept needs to be broadened in order to avoid economic reductionism and to conceive, based on Marx's dialectic, the economy as contradictory. So he sets up a Marxist camouflage argument (the importance of contradictions) in order to dismiss Marx and the labour theory of value and instead use a relativist approach on cultural economy. Toby Miller argues in this context that Grossberg caricatures the political economy approach and asks him to "rethink the anti-Marxism" because it is the "wrong target" (Miller 2011, 322).

A recent book by John Hartley represents another prominent approach that advances the idea of connecting Cultural Studies to economics.

3.3. John Hartley: *Digital Futures for Cultural and Media Studies*

John Hartley (2012) describes the emergence of a "dialogical model of communication" (2), in which "everyone is a producer" (3), and discusses the implications of this model for media and Cultural Studies. His general argument is that with the rise of online platforms that support social networking and user-generated content production and diffusion, journalism, the public sphere, universities, the mass media, citizenship, archives and other institutions have become more democratic because "people have more say in producing as well as consuming" (ibid., 14). These developments would be advanced by the emergence of "consumer entrepreneurship" (ibid., 25), social network markets (48) and microproductivity (52). Hartley shares with Grossberg the assessment that Cultural Studies is in crisis. It would have lost steam and adventurousness and would have gotten lost in "infinitely extensible micro-level" analyses that do not "pay enough attention to the macro level" (ibid., 28). Like Grossberg, Hartley ascertains that Cultural Studies "has not enjoyed a sustained dialogue with economics" and has "remained aloof from the turbulent changes *within* economics" (ibid., 35). Hartley acknowledges that Marxist Political Economy has given attention to the economics of culture (he mentions Chomsky, Garnham, Miller and Schiller; ibid.), but claims that this approach "was too challenging, knowing what was wrong in advance" (46), and assumes "single-cause determinations of entire systems" (55).

Hartley's version of introducing economics into Cultural Studies is called "Cultural Science 2.0" and wants to achieve this aim by using evolutionary economics. It stresses that value in the cultural industries today emerges dynamically from the co-creativity of citizens and users in social networks. Hartley metaphorically uses the language of evolutionary systems theory, complexity theory and self-organization theory, but fails to systematically apply concepts of this theory approach (such as control parameters, critical values, fluctuations, feedback loops, circular causality, nonlinearity, bifurcation, autopoiesis, order out of chaos, emergence, openness, symmetry braking, synergism, unpredictability, etc.) to the Internet. (For a different approach that is critical in intention see Fuchs 2008.) Hartley also does not seriously engage with the fact that thinkers like Friedrich August Hayek (the concept of spontaneous order) and Niklas Luhmann (the concepts of functional differentiation and self-reference) have used the language of self-organization and complexity for ideologically legitimatizing neo-liberalism (see Fuchs 2008, chapters 2 and 3). Hartley (2012, 57) only briefly asks if his approach is "stalking horses for neo-liberalism". He has a negative answer to this question, grounded in the fact that *Adbusters* magazine once also referred positively to evolutionary economics. Just like with one of Hartley's (2005) earlier works, one gets the impression that *Digital Futures for Cultural and Media Studies* is "a Powerpoint presentation by a management consultant" that has the goal "to nourish the entrepreneurial self" (McGuigan 2006, 373). Hartley says that cultural analysis has been shaped on the one hand by an approach that is "'critical' in the Williams/Hall tradition" and on the other a romantic approach represented by the "Fiske/Hartley" tradition that propagates "as widely as possible the emancipationist potential of participatory media" (Hartley 2012, 182). The opposition of critical and romantic logically implies that Hartley considers his own approach as being uncritical. Consequently, he propagates staying in the romantic tradition and the thought that Cultural Studies turns "from 'critique' as a method to *evolution* as a methodological goal" (ibid., 183). The focus of theory shall, according to Hartley, shift from critical studies to evolution. He argues for what one could term uncritical evolutionary Cultural Studies.

Hartley's bottom line is that the Internet is a self-organizing network, in which "everyone is networked with everyone else" (ibid., 196), and that this system constitutes a new source of democracy and dialogic communication. He does not take into account the simple counter-argument that not everybody has access to this "democratic self-organizing network": 32.7% of the world population and only 13.5% of all Africans had access to the Internet in August 2012 (www.internetworldstats.com/stats.htm, accessed August 30, 2012). Nor does he take into account the argument that on Twitter, Facebook, YouTube and so on, some—especially large companies, established political actors and celebrities—are "more equal" than others, have more views, clicks, friends, connections, which reflects the actual power inequalities of society (for a detailed form of this argument, see Fuchs 2011a, chapter 7; Fuchs 2013). Hartley (2012, 56) mentions that social network markets may have hubs and be dominated by elites, but this analysis is not systematically connected to power inequalities in society. It rather seems that Hartley assumes that such markets are nonetheless a realm of democracy because many have communicative tools available that can, if they are lucky and hard-working, enable them to become part of this elite, at least for a short time. This logic is at the heart of neo-liberalism's stress on performance, individualism and personal responsibility for success, failures and downfall. Hartley shows no sympathy with the outcasts and exploits of the social media age, people like Tian Yu, a Foxconn worker, who in 2010 at the age of 17 attempted suicide by jumping from a building because he could no longer stand the bad working conditions in the factory that produces among other gadgets iPods and iPads and as a result is now paralysed from the waist down, or the children, who as slaves extract "conflict minerals" such as cassiterite, wolframite, coltan, gold, tungsten, tantalum or tin in countries like the Democratic Republic of Congo that are used as raw materials for the production of ICTs. Not only are such stories missing in Hartley's account of contemporary digital media, he rather speaks the language and conveys the same messages as business manifestos that claim that we see the emergence of "a new economic democracy" (Tapscott and Williams 2007, 15) in times of high socio-economic inequality and youth unemployment. Hartley represents the interests of the owners of the likes of Facebook and Google.

Paul Smith has edited a collected volume that also discusses, among other things, the relationship of Cultural Studies and economics.

3.4. Paul Smith: *The Renewal of Cultural Studies*

The Renewal of Cultural Studies is a collection edited by Paul Smith (2011b) that features 27 contributions. Most of the contributors share with Grossberg and Hartley the conviction that the economic needs to be taken serious by Cultural Studies and has in the past too often been neglected. But there is a profound difference between this volume and the books by Grossberg and Hartley, namely the relationship to Marx and Critical Political Economy. Smith holds that "British Cultural Studies is a narrative of ever-increasing suspicion of Marxist thinking" (Smith 2011a, 5). Cultural Studies has "an extreme desire not to be seen as Marxist" (Ross and Smith 2011, 252). The result would have been an "increasing irrelevance of Cultural Studies' practice" (Couldry 2011, 10). Paul Smith argues that Cultural Studies has become politically irrelevant and is therefore like a "phantom limb" (Ross and Smith 2011, 246). In the introduction, Smith (2011a) asks the question what Cultural Studies should be doing right now. An answer that he suggests and that many of the contributors in the volume agree on is that "an increased attention to political economy is a sine qua non for a revived Cultural Studies" (ibid., 6).

Almost all the authors in Smith's collected volume share the insight that Cultural Studies has ignored labour and the economic and has to take them seriously. So for example, Andrew Ross says, "Whether or not this is a reductive narrative, it's clear that labor, work, and the politics of the workplace have been constantly neglected" in Cultural Studies (Ross and Smith 2011, 252). Nick Couldry supports this view: "After three decades of neoliberal discourse and a particular version of globalization based on inequality, exclusion, and market fundamentalism, the issue of labor foregrounded by [Andrew] Ross is clearly central. It is difficult to imagine any meaningful 'project' of Cultural Studies—understood politically and socially—that does not address the broader questions of how people experience the economy and society in which they work (or seek work), perhaps vote, and certainly consume" (Couldry 2011, 10–11). Vincent Mosco (2011, 230) argues that "labor remains the blind spot of communication and Cultural Studies" and that therefore "labor needs to be placed high on the agenda or projects for the renewal of Cultural Studies". S. Charusheela (2011, 177) says that it "is a perennial claim that Cultural Studies does not pay enough attention to economy". Given this analysis, many contributors in Smith's (2011) volume hold that Cultural Studies should explicitly reorient itself as Marxist Cultural Studies that works based on Marxist theory, the analysis of labour and class and Critical Political Economy. So, for example, Max Gulias (2011) argues that Cultural Studies needs a Marxist methodology, which would require one "to revisit Marxist labor theory", but much "non-Marxist Cultural Studies" would stay preoccupied with the sign systems constituted by consumer-spectators and disregard the labour of humans in capitalism (ibid., 149). Randy Martin (2011) argues that financialization is a key topic for renewing Cultural Studies and grounding it in Marxism. Marcus Breen says that in the era of neo-liberalism and capitalist crisis, for Cultural Studies "the time has come to reassert the primacy of political economy, by rearticulating economy with culture instead of pretending that some sort of indeterminacy will magically give Cultural Studies credibility" (Breen 2011, 208).

The impression that one gets from the books by Grossberg, Hartley and Smith is that paradoxically the crisis of capitalism is accompanied by a crisis of Cultural Studies. At the same time, there are indications for a renewal of Marxism. The implication is that the time is ripe for taking Marx seriously, reading Marx, using Marx for thinking about media, communication, and culture, introducing Marx and Marxism to our students, and especially institutionalizing Marx and Marxist studies in the courses about media, communication and culture taught at universities as well as in the research we conduct and the projects we apply for and help fund. It is time to no longer introduce students to small excerpts from Marx and Engels as (alleged) examples of economic reductionism, but to rather read together with them full works of Marx and Engels, such as *Capital, The Economic & Philosophic Manuscripts,* the *Grundrisse, The German Ideology, The Communist Manifesto, The Condition of the Working Class in England, The Poverty of Philosophy, The Holy Family, The Class Struggle in France, The 18th Brumaire of Louis Bonaparte, The Civil War in France, The Dialectics of Nature,* the articles published in *Rheinische Zeitung,* and so on. Marx is too often seen and treated as the outside and outsider of the study of media, communication and culture. It is time that he takes centre stage, which requires resources, institutions, positions—and therefore the struggle to change academia. Smith's (2011b) book shows that besides the class/labour-relativist approach of Grossberg and the celebratory approach of Hartley, there is also a true interest in Marx and the notions of class and labour in Cultural Studies. Speaking about Cultural Studies, Toby Miller (2010, 99) notes that although labour "is central to humanity", it is overall "largely absent from our field". He argues that in the cultural industries, a cognitariat has emerged that has "high levels of educational attainment, and great facility with cultural technologies and genres" and is facing conditions of "flexible production and ideologies of 'freedom'" (ibid., 98). He therefore suggests this equation: culture + labour = precariat. Andrew Ross (2008, 2009) in a similar vein stresses the role of precarious labour in the cultural industries. Creativity would for many come "at a heavy sacrificial cost—longer hours in pursuit of the satisfying finish, price discounts in return for aesthetic recognition, self-exploitation in response to the gift of autonomy, and dispensability in exchange for flexibility" (Ross 2008, 34). Employees in the IT industry would often describe their workplaces as "high-tech sweatshops" (ibid., 43). Related work has in the field of Cultural Studies, for example, been advanced by Maxwell (2001a) and Maxwell and Miller (2005/2006). Hesmondhalgh and Baker (2011) show the ambivalence of much creative industry work that is precarious but cherished because of the fun, contacts, reputation, creativity and self-determination that it may involve. Such engagement with labour and class within Cultural Studies complements the concern within the Political Economy of the Media and Communication with issues relating to class, exploitation, value and labour in the context of the media, culture and communication that have been strongly inspired by Karl Marx's works (see Burston, Dyer-Witheford and Hearn 2010; Fuchs and Mosco 2012; Huws 2003, McKercher and Mosco 2006, 2007; Mosco and McKercher 2008; Mosco, McKercher and Huws 2010). The problem of Cultural Studies is, as Robert Babe says, that its "poststructuralist turn [. . .] instigated the separation" (Babe 2009, 9) from economics. A reintegration requires first and foremost "setting aside poststructuralist Cultural Studies" (ibid., 196) and seriously engaging with Marx and Marxism. Various entry points into the discussion of Marx today can be taken. One of them is via the concept of value. One can equally choose other concepts such as labour, commodity or capital as entry points because all of these notions are dialectically connected: commodities have value and are produced by labour in order to produce capital that enables the production of more commodities.

3.5. Conclusion

Graeme Turner (2012, 158) in providing answers to the question "What's become of Cultural Studies?" argues that this field has lost power as a political project and turned into a "genre of academic performance" that is "merely self-serving". One of my arguments in this chapter has been that one cause of this circumstance is that Cultural Studies has had a troubled relationship with Karl Marx's works. Early representatives like Raymond Williams and Edward P. Thompson were strongly influenced by and contributed to humanist Marxism, whereas Stuart Hall at times was influenced by structural Marxism and at times moved away from Marxism. The move away from Marx occurred especially in the past three decades under the influence of postmodern thinking. The analysis of three contemporary Cultural Studies works showed that there is a broad agreement that Cultural Studies needs to engage more with the economic today. How such an engagement shall look and how it relates to the works of Karl Marx are contested. John Hartley argues for the replacement of a critical and Marxian approach in Cultural Studies by evolutionary economics. Lawrence Grossberg uses Marx against Marx in order to argue for a radically contextualist interpretation of the value concept and a theory of crisis that is based on a general theory of value. Paul Smith and others make a point for the renewal of a genuine Marxist Cultural Studies.

My own position is that not only do we today need to take seriously how the economic interacts with culture and the media, but that we can gain much from reading, discussing and interpreting the multitude of Karl Marx's original works. I argue for an institutional revolution that buries prejudices against Karl Marx (see Eagleton 2011 for a brilliant invalidation of the ten most common prejudices against Marx) and starts to take him seriously in the study of the media and culture. There is a generation of students and young scholars today who have been growing up under post-welfarist conditions and know the reality of precarious labour and precarious life. At the same time, we are living in a world with multidimensional global inequalities. Interpreting and changing this world requires us to think about class, crisis, critique and capitalism. If we are in this context interested in critically studying the role of communication in the context of crisis, class and capitalism, the engagement with the ideas of the thinker who has had the largest intellectual and practical influence on the study of these phenomena is an absolute necessity. Only an engagement with Marx can create a cultural and media studies that is topical, politically relevant, practical and critical, in the current times of global crisis and resurgent critique. Such an engagement requires not just interested scholars and students (that anyway already exist), but also institutional changes of universities, funding agencies, journals, conferences, academic associations and entire research fields. Academia has experienced an administrative and neo-liberal turn. Marxism is not just the resulting answer to these changes, but also the solution to the resulting problems. A step forward in taking Marx serious again is to engage with the works of the founding figure of the Critical Political Economy of Media and Communication—Dallas Smythe, whose work has recently been revitalized in the context of the digital labour debate.

Note

1 http://savemdxphil.com/2010/04/28/middlesex-university-announces-the-closure-of-its-top-rated-department-philosophy/. (accessed August 8, 2013).

4

DALLAS SMYTHE AND AUDIENCE LABOUR TODAY

Dallas Smythe was the founder of the approach of Critical Political Economy of the Media and Communication. He argued for a Marxist theory of communication and introduced the notions of audience labour and audience commodification that show how commercial mass media that use advertising work. In recent years, Smythe's works have again become quite influential because corporate Internet platforms such as Facebook and Google make use of the unpaid labour of users. This chapter first gives an introduction (4.1), then argues why Dallas Smythe is important today (4.2), discusses the renewal of the audience commodity category (4.3) and argues that Internet prosumer commodification is a new form of audience commodification on social media (4.4) and that play is a specific form of ideology on social media (4.5). It also presents criticisms of critics of the application of Dallas Smythe's works to digital labour (4.6) and draws some conclusions (4.7). The chapter overall argues that Dallas Smythe's works in combination with Karl Marx's theory are a helpful tool for critically understanding digital labour.

4.1. Introduction

In 1977, Dallas Smythe published his seminal article "Communications: Blindspot of Western Marxism" (Smythe 1977a), in which he argued that Western Marxism has not given enough attention to the complex role of communications in capitalism. The article's publication was followed by an important foundational debate of media sociology that came to be known as "the Blindspot Debate" (Murdock 1978, Livant 1979; Smythe answered with a rejoinder to Murdock: Smythe 1994, 292–299) and by another article of Smythe's on the same topic

("On the Audience Commodity and Its Work" in: Smythe 1981, 22–51). More than 30 years have passed and the rise of neo-liberalism resulted in a turn away from the interest in class and capitalism and brought about the rise of postmodernism and the logic of the commodification of everything: Marxism became the blind spot of the social sciences.

The task of this chapter is to explore perspectives for the Marxist study of media and communication today. First, I discuss the importance of taking a Marxist approach for studying media and communication (section 4.2). Second, I give a short overview of the audience commodity, its audience labour debate and its renewal (section 4.3). Dallas Smythe made important contributions to a labour theory of the audience that can today be used for grounding a digital labour theory of value. In section 4.4, I analyse social media capital accumulation with the help of the notion of Internet prosumer commodification. Section 4.5 provides an overview of ideological changes that relate to digital media, perceived changes and the relationship between play and labour in contemporary capitalism (playbour). Section 4.6 presents a critique of criticisms of the digital labour debate. Finally, I draw some conclusions.

4.2. The Importance of Critical Political Economy, Critical Theory and Dallas Smythe

Dallas Smythe was a founding figure in the establishment of Critical/Marxist Political Economy of Communication and taught the first course in the field (Mosco 2009, 82). He stressed the importance of studying media and communication in a critical and non-administrative way: "By 'critical' researchable problems we mean how to reshape or invent institutions to meet the collective needs of the relevant social community. [. . .] By 'critical' tools, we refer to historical, materialist analysis of the contradictory process in the real world. By 'administrative' ideology, we mean the linking of administrative-type problems and tools, with interpretation of results that supports, or does not seriously disturb, the status quo. By 'critical' ideology, we refer to the linking of 'critical' researchable problems and critical tools with interpretations that involve radical changes in the established order" (Smythe and Dinh 1983, 118).

In the article "On the Political Economy of Communications", Smythe defined the "central purpose of the study of the political economy of communications" as the evaluation of "the effects of communication agencies in terms of the policies by which they are organised and operated" and the analysis of "the structure and policies of these communication agencies in their social settings" (Smythe 1960, 564). He identified various communications policy areas in this article. Whereas there are foundations of a general political economy in this chapter, there are no traces of Marx in it. Janet Wasko (2004, 311) argues that although "Smythe's discussion at this point did not employ radical or Marxist terminology, it was a major departure from the kind of research that dominated the study of mass communications at that time". Wasko points out that it was in the "1970s that the political economy of media and communications (PE/C) was explicitly defined again but this time within a more explicitly Marxist framework" (ibid., 312). She mentions in this context the works of Nicholas Garnham, Peter Golding, Armand Mattelart, Graham Murdock and Dallas Smythe as well as the Blindspot Debate (ibid., 312–313).

Later, Smythe (1981) formulated explicitly the need for a Marxist Political Economy of Communications. He spoke of a "Marxist theory of communication" (Smythe 1994, 258) and that critical theory means "Marxist or quasi-Marxist" theory (ibid., 256). He identified eight core aspects of a Marxist political economy of communications (Smythe 1981, xvi–xviii):

(1) materiality,
(2) monopoly capitalism,
(3) audience commodification and advertising,
(4) media communication as part of the base of capitalism,
(5) labour-power,
(6) critique of technological determinism,
(7) the dialectic of consciousness, ideology and hegemony on the one side and material practices on the other side, and
(8) the dialectics of arts and science.

Smythe reminds us of the importance of the engagement with Marx's works for studying the media in capitalism critically. He argued that Gramsci and the Frankfurt School advanced the concepts of ideology, consciousness and hegemony as areas "saturated with subjectivism and positivism" (ibid., xvii). These Marxist thinkers would have advanced an "idealist theory of the communications commodity" (Smythe 1994, 268) that situates the media only on the superstructure of capitalism and forgets to ask what economic functions they serve in capitalism.

In a review of Hans Magnus Enzensberger's (1974) book *The Consciousness Industry,* Smythe on the one hand agreed with Enzensberger that the "mind industry" wants to "'sell the existing order", but on the other hand disagreed with the assumption that its "main business and concern is not to sell its product" (Enzensberger 1974, 10): "Enzensberger's theory that every social system's communications policy serves the controlling class interest in perpetuating that system is of course correct", but to say that "the mass media and consciousness industry have no product" would mean to identify commodity production with "crude physical production" (Smythe 1977b, 200). Smythe (1977b) characterizes Enzensberger's views as bourgeois, idealistic and anarcho-liberal. For Smythe (1994, 266–291), the material aspect of communications is that audiences work, are exploited and are sold as commodity to advertisers. He was more interested in aspects of surplus value generation of the media than their ideological effects.

So Smythe called for analysing the media more in terms of surplus value and exploitation and less in terms of manipulation. Nicholas Garnham (1990, 30) shares with Smythe the insight that the Political Economy of Communications should "shift attention away from the conception of the mass media as ideological apparatuses" and focus on the analysis of their "economic role" in surplus value generation and advertising. The analysis of media as "vehicles for ideological domination" is for Garnham (2004, 94) "a busted flush" that is not needed for explaining "the relatively smooth reproduction of capitalism".

Given the analyses of Smythe and Garnham, the impression can be created that Frankfurt School critical theory focuses on ideology critique and the Political Economy of Media/Communications on the analysis of capital accumulation by and with the help of the media. This is however a misunderstanding. Although widely read works of the Frankfurt School focused on ideology (Adorno, Frenkel-Brunswik, Levinson and Sanford 1950; Horkheimer and Adorno 2002; Marcuse 1964), other books in its book series *Frankfurter Beiträge zur Soziologie* dealt with the changes of accumulation in what was termed late capitalism or monopoly capitalism (for example, Pollock 1956, Friedmann 1959). The Marxist political economist Henryk Grossmann was one of the most important members of the Institut für Sozialforschung in the 1920s and wrote his main work at the institute (Grossmann 1929). Although only few will today agree with Grossmann's theory of capitalist breakdown, it remains a fact that Marxist political economy was an element of the Institut für Sozialforschung right from its beginning and had in Pollock and Grossmann two important representatives. After Max Horkheimer became director of the institute in 1930, he formulated an interdisciplinary research programme that aimed at bringing together philosophers and scholars from a broad range of disciplines, including economics (Horkheimer 1931). When formulating their general concepts of critical theory, both Horkheimer (2002, 244) and Marcuse (1941) had a combination of philosophy and Marx's critique of the political economy in mind.

Just like Critical Political Economy was not alien to the Frankfurt School, ideology critique has also not been alien to the approach of the Critical Political Economy of the Media and Communication. For Graham Murdock and Peter Golding (1974, 4), the media are organizations that "produce and distribute commodities", are means for distributing advertisements and also have an "ideological dimension" by disseminating "ideas about economic and political structures". Murdock (1978, 469) stressed in the Blindspot Debate that there are non-advertising-based culture industries (like popular culture) that sell "explanations of social order and structured inequality" and "work with and through ideology—selling the system" (see also Artz 2008, 64). Murdock (1978) argued in the Blindspot Debate that Smythe did not enough acknowledge Western Marxism in Europe and that one needs a balance between ideology critique and political economy for analysing the media in capitalism.

Smythe himself acknowledged the importance of ideology when talking about the "consciousness industry" (Smythe 1981, 4–9, 270–299). Although critical of Hans Magnus Enzensberger's works (Smythe 1977b), Smythe took up Enzensberger's concept of the consciousness industry and interpreted it in his own way. In contrast to the Frankfurt School, Smythe does not understand ideology as false consciousness but as a "system of beliefs, attitudes, and ideas" (Smythe 1981, 171). The task of the consciousness industry is for Smythe to make people buy commodities and pay taxes (Smythe 1994, 250). Its further task is to promote values that favour capitalism and the private property system (ibid., 251–253). One role of the capitalist media would be the "pervasive reinforcement of the ideological basis of the capitalist system", assumptions like "human nature is necessarily selfish and possessive. It has always been this way: You can't change human nature" (Smythe 1994, 251). So while Smythe criticized the Frankfurt School, he advanced and confirmed the importance of ideology critique himself. Robert Babe (2000) argues in this context that although Smythe stressed the need for a materialist theory of culture that sees audience power "as the media's main output", his concept of the consciousness industry "is 'idealist' in Smythe's sense of the term" (133–134). The circumstance that Smythe took up Enzensberger's terminology and gave space to discussing the attempts of the media to ideologically distort reality shows that although he used fierce words against some representatives of the Frankfurt School (idealist, bourgeois, etc.), he did not altogether dismiss ideology critique; rather, he wanted to open up the debate for also giving attention to the media's capital accumulation strategies that are coupled to its role as mind manager.

A difference between the Critical Political Economy of Media and Communications and critical theory is that the first is strongly rooted in economic theory and the second in philosophy and social theory. Dallas Smythe acknowledged this difference: "While the cutting edge of critical theory lies in political economy, critical theory in communications has the transdisciplinary scope of the social sciences, humanities, and arts" (Smythe 1984, 211). Smythe defined critical theory broadly as "criticism of the contradictory aspects of the phenomena in their systemic context" (Smythe and Dinh 1983, 123) and therefore concluded that critical theory is not necessarily Marxist. The historical critical theory of the Frankfurt School has its roots in Marxist political philosophy, so the question is if one should really have a broad definition of the term "critical" that does not focus on systemic critique.

The approaches of the Frankfurt School and of Critical/Marxist Political Economy of Media and Communication should be understood as being complementary. There has been a stronger focus on ideology critique in the Frankfurt School approach for historical reasons. For Horkheimer and Theodor Adorno, the rise of German fascism, the Stalinist praxis and American consumer capitalism showed the defeat of the revolutionary potentials of the working class (Habermas 1984, 366–367). They wanted to explain why the revolutionary

German working class followed Hitler, which brought up the interest in the analysis of the authoritarian personality and media propaganda. As Communists and coming from Jewish families, Horkheimer and Adorno (as well as their colleagues) were directly threatened by the violence of National Socialism and therefore had to escape from Germany. The violent consequences of Nazi ideology may partly explain the relevance that the notion of ideology had throughout their lives in their works. The Anglo-American approach of the Political Economy of the Media and Communications was developed by people such as Dallas Smythe and Herbert Schiller in countries that during the Second World War fought against fascism. Whereas North American capitalism was after 1945 based on liberal ideology, anti-communism and a strong consumer culture that certainly also had fascist potentials, German post-war capitalism was built on the legacy of National Socialism and a strong persistence of fascist thinking in everyday life and politics.

The lives of Smythe and Schiller themselves were not, as in the case of Horkheimer and Adorno, directly threatened by fascist regimes. But both showed a lot of concern about fascism, which shaped their thought. Vincent Mosco (2009, 83) writes in this context that contacts with anti-fascists who fought in the Spanish civil war had profound political effects on Smythe's thinking. Serving in the US Army in World War II and working for the US government in Germany after the war had "substantial formative influence" (ibid., 85) on Herbert Schiller. The works of the American economist Robert A. Brady influenced both Smythe's and Schiller's thinking (Schiller 1999). Brady had contacts with Franz Neumann, a representative of the Frankfurt School who was in exile in the United States and just like Brady (1937) wrote an analysis of National Socialism (Neumann 1942). Brady was especially concerned with fascist potentials of capitalism, as in the form of media propaganda and public relations. Neumann (1942) stressed that National Socialism was a form of monopoly capitalism that was based on a leadership cult. Dan Schiller (1999, 100) argues that "Brady endowed the study of the political economy of communications with a critical intellectual legacy". The fascist threat was a concern for both German critical theorists and North American critical political economists.

Horkheimer's (1947) notion of instrumental reason and Marcuse's (1964) notion of technological rationality open up connections between the two approaches. Horkheimer and Marcuse stressed that in capitalism there is a tendency that freedom of action is replaced by instrumental decision-making on the part of capital and the state so that the individual is expected only to react and not to act. The two concepts are grounded in Georg Lukács' (1923/1972) notion of reification that is a reformulation of Marx's (1867c) concept of fetishism. Reification means "that a relation between people takes on the character of a thing and thus acquires 'phantom objectivity', an autonomy that seems so strictly rational and all-embracing as to conceal every trace of its fundamental nature: the relation between people" (Lukács 1923/1972, 83).

The media in capitalism are modes of reification in a multiple sense:

- First, commercial media reduce humans to the status of consumers of advertisements.
- Second, culture is in capitalism to a large degree connected to the commodity form. There are cultural commodities that are bought by consumers and audience and user commodities that media consumers and Internet prosumers become themselves.
- Third, in order to reproduce its existence, capitalism has to present itself as the best possible (or only possible) system and makes use of the media in order to try to keep this message (in all its differentiated forms) hegemonic.

The first and the second dimension constitute the economic dimension of instrumental reason, the third dimension the ideological form of instrumental reason. Capitalist media are necessarily means of advertising and commodification and spaces of ideology. Advertisement and cultural commodification make humans an instrument for economic profit accumulation. Ideology aims at instilling the belief in the system of capital and commodities into humans' subjectivity. The goal is that human thoughts and actions do not go beyond capitalism, do not question and revolt against this system and thereby play the role of instruments for the perpetuation of capitalism. It is of course an important question to what extent ideology is always successful and to what degree it is questioned and resisted, but the crucial aspect about ideology is that it encompasses strategies and attempts to make human subjects instrumental in the reproduction of domination and exploitation.

For Marx, the analysis of capitalism starts with the analysis of the commodity: "The wealth of societies in which the capitalist mode of production prevails appears as an 'immense collection of commodities'; the individual commodity appears as its elementary form" (Marx 1867c, 125). Marx therefore begins the analysis of capitalism with the analysis of the commodity: its use-value, exchange-value, value, the labour embodied in it, the value forms of the commodity, including the money form (x commodity A = y amount of money). After this analysis, Marx turns in chapter 1.4 (*The Fetishism of the Commodity and Its Secret*) of *Capital, Volume 1*, to the analysis of ideology as an immanent feature of the commodity. The "mysterious character of the commodity-form" is that human social relations that create commodities are not visible in the commodity, but appear as "the socio-natural properties of these things". "The definite social relation between men themselves [take in ideologies] [. . .] the fantastic form of a relation between things" (Marx 1867c, 165). Ideologies legitimatize various phenomena by creating the impression that the latter exist always and naturally and by ignoring the historical and social character of things. So for Marx, ideology and commodification are interconnected aspects of capitalism. A Marxist theory of communication should therefore, besides the focus on struggles and alternatives, have a double focus on the role of media and communication in the context of ideology and commodification.

Smythe said that the "starting point for a general Marxist theory of communications is [. . .] the theory of commodity exchange" (Smythe 1994, 259). Adorno acknowledged that "the concept of exchange is [. . .] the hinge connecting the conception of a critical theory of society to the construction of the concept of society as a totality" (Adorno 2000, 32). Commodity and commodity exchange are crucial concepts for Critical Political Economy and critical theory. As the commodity concept is connected to both capital accumulation and ideology, both approaches should start simultaneously with the value aspects and the ideology aspects of media commodities.

Accumulation and ideology go hand in hand. An example: "social media". After the dot.com crisis in 2000, there was a need to establish new capital accumulation strategies for the capitalist Internet economy. Investors were reluctant to invest finance capital as venture capital into digital media companies after the crisis. So the discourse on "social media" became focused on new capital accumulation models for the Internet economy. Nobody knew if the users were interested in microblogs, social networking sites and the like. The rise of "social media" as a new capital accumulation model was accompanied by a social media ideology: that "social media" are new ("Web 2.0"), pose new opportunities for participation, will bring about an "economic democracy" and enable new forms of political struggle ("Twitter revolution") and more democracy ("participatory culture"). The rise of new media was accompanied by a techno-deterministic and techno-optimistic ideology. This ideology was necessary for convincing investors and users to support the social media capital accumulation model. The political economy of surplus value generation on "social media" and ideology heavily interacted here in order to enable the economic and discursive rise of "social media".

Some scholars tends to say that Frankfurt School and the Critical Political Economy of Media and Communication are pessimistic and elitist and neglect audiences (see for example Hall 1986, 1988; Grossberg 1995). They say that the concept of ideology as false consciousness makes "both the masses and the capitalists look like judgemental dopes" (Hall 1986, 33). Hall (1988, 44) criticizes Lukács (whose works have been one of the main influences on the Frankfurt School) by saying that the false consciousness theorem is simplistic (it assumes that "vast numbers of ordinary people, mentally equipped in much the same way as you or I, can simply be thoroughly and systematically duped into misrecognising entirely where their real interests lie") and elitist ("Even less acceptable is the position that, whereas 'they'—the masses—are the dupes of history, 'we'—the privileged—[. . .] can see, transitively, right through into the truth, the essence, of a situation").

In other works, Hall advocated a different concept of ideology that is not completely unrelated to the one of the Frankfurt School. In their work *Policing the Crisis,* Hall et al. (1978) showed how the state and the media use moral panics about crime as "the principal ideological consciousness by means of which a 'silent majority' is won over to the support of increasingly coercive measures" (221) and the establishment of a law-and-order society. If both the mainstream media and the police argue for increasing law-and-order policies in the course of a moral panic, then they both legitimate the control process, and a mutual enforcement of the "control culture" and a "signification culture" emerges (ibid., 76) so that "the mutual articulation" of the two "create an *effective ideological and control closure* around the issue" (ibid.). The media, just like the police, then act as "an apparatus of the control process itself—an 'ideological state apparatus'" (ibid.).

Hall, in his criticism of the Frankfurt School that can be read as self-criticism of his own earlier works, misrecognizes that not all people are equally educated because in a class society basic and higher education are to a certain extent also shaped by class differences so that left-wing intellectuals tend to have more time and resources than white- and blue-collar workers for engaging in studying how capitalism works. Recognizing this circumstance means that ideology critique gives organic intellectuals a role in struggles because they have the potential of "providing a map of the structure of domination and the terrain of struggle" (Garnham 1995a, 68). For Hall, the assumption that ordinary people are active and critical follows from the rejection of the manipulation thesis: "Since ordinary people are not cultural dopes, they are perfectly capable of recognising the way the realities of working-class life are reorganised, reconstructed, and reshaped by the way they are represented (i.e. re-presented) in, say, Coronation Street" (Hall 1981/1998, 447). Lawrence Grossberg (1995) argued that both the Frankfurt School and Political Economy have a simple "model of domination in which people are seen as passively manipulated 'cultural dupes'" (75) and that for them "culture matters only as a commodity and an ideological tool of manipulation" (76).

In contrast to such claims, Dallas Smythe had a very balanced view of the audience: capital would attempt to control audiences, but they would have the potential to resist: "People are subject to relentless pressures from Consciousness Industry; they are besieged with an avalanche of consumer goods and services; they are themselves produced as (audience) commodities; they reproduce their own lives and energies as damaged and in commodity form. But people are by no means passive or powerless. People do resist the powerful and manifold pressures of capital as best they can" (Smythe 1981, 270).

Adorno, who is vilified by many scholars as the prototypical cultural pessimist and elitist, had a positive vision for a medium like TV. For television (in German *Fernsehen,* literally, "to watch into the distance") "to keep the promise still resonating within the word, it must emancipate itself from everything within which it—reckless wish-fulfilment—refutes its own principle and betrays the idea of Good Fortune for the smaller fortunes of the department store" (Adorno 2005, 57). Adorno frequently acknowledges the need and potentials of emancipation. In the case of TV, he points out that enabling watching into the distance beyond capitalism is a good fortune. This is indirectly a call for the creation of alternative media that question the status quo. Adorno also did not, as falsely claimed by many, despise popular culture. He was for example a fan of Charlie Chaplin and pointed out the critical role of the clown in popular culture (Adorno 1996). Even in the "Culture Industry" chapter of *Dialectic of the Enlightenment,* the positive elements of popular culture are visible: for example, when Adorno writes that "traces of something better persist in those features of the culture industry by which it resembles the circus" (Horkheimer and Adorno 2002, 114). Adorno (1977, 680) in his *Erziehung nach Auschwitz* (*Education after Auschwitz*) wrote about the positive role that TV could play in anti-fascist education in Germany after Auschwitz. If one goes beyond a superficial and selective reading of Adorno, then one will find his deep belief in the possibility of emancipation and in the role that culture can play in it. English translations of Horkheimer's and Adorno's works are imprecise because the language of the two philosophers is complex and not easily translatable. But besides the problem non-German-speakers are facing when reading Horkheimer and Adorno, there seems to be a certain non-willingness to engage thoroughly with the Frankfurt School's and Critical Political Economy's origins in order to set up a straw man.

Karl Marx (1867c) titled his magnum opus not *Capital: A Political Economy* but rather *Capital: A Critique of Political Economy.* Political economy is a broad field, incorporating also traditions of thinking grounded in classical liberal economic thought and thinkers such as Malthus, Mill, Petty, Ricardo, Say, Smith and Ure that Marx studied, sublated and was highly critical of in his works. His main point of criticism of political economy is that it fetishizes capitalism. Its thinkers "confine themselves to systematising in a pedantic way, and proclaiming for everlasting truths, the banal and complacent notions held by the bourgeois agents of production about their own world, which is to them the best possible one" (Marx 1867c, 175). They postulate that categories like commodities, money, exchange-value, capital, markets or competition are anthropological features of all society, thereby ignoring the categories' historical character and enmeshment into class struggles. Marx showed the contradictions of political economy's thought and took classical political economy as a starting point for a critique of capitalism that considers "every historically developed form as being in a fluid state, in motion", and analyses how "the movement of capitalist society is full of contradictions" (ibid., 103), which calls for the "development of the contradictions of a given historical form" by political practice (619) and means that Marx's approach is "in its very essence critical and revolutionary" (103).

Marx developed a critique of the political economy of capitalism, which sees critique as threefold process:

(a)   an analysis and critique of capitalism,
(b)   a critique of liberal ideology, thought and academia,
(c)   transformative practice.

To be precise, one should not speak of Political Economy of Media/ Communications, but of the Critique of the Political Economy of Communication, Culture, Information and the Media. Some authors realized this circumstance and stressed that what is needed is a "Marxist theory of communication" (Smythe 1994, 258), that critical theory means "Marxist or quasi-Marxist" theory (ibid., 256) and that "Critical Political Economy of Communications" is critical in the sense of being "broadly marxisant" (Murdock and Golding 2005, 61).

Robin Mansell argues that Smythe engaged in establishing a critical media and communication studies which "had at its core the need to interrogate the systemic character of capitalism as it was expressed through the means of structures of communication" (Mansell 1995, 51) and that his focus was on exposing "through critical research the articulation of political and economic power relations as they were expressed in the institutional relations embedded in technology and the content of communication in all its forms" (ibid., 47). Robin Mansell points out the importance of a critical methodology in Smythe's approach. As already shown, Smythe was interested in developing a Marxist theory of communication (Smythe 1994, 258) and argued that critical theory is a Marxist theory (256). It is therefore consequent and important to characterize Smythe's approach not just as critical communication research—which it certainly also but not exclusively was—but as Marxist communication studies, which means a unity of theoretical/philosophical, empirical and ethical studies of media and communication that is focused on the analysis of contradictions, structures and practices of domination, exploitation, struggles, ideologies and alternatives to capitalism in relation to media and communication. One should not split off the importance of Marx and Marxism from Smythe's approach and reduce him to having established a critical empirical research methodology. Janet Wasko stresses in this context that Marx's 11th Feuerbach thesis ("The philosophers have only interpreted the world, in various ways; the point is to change it") applied to the work and life of Dallas Smythe: "Analyzing and understanding the role of communications in the modern world might be enough for most communication scholars. But Dallas Smythe also sought to change the world, not only by his extensive research and teaching in academia, but in his work in the public sector, and through his life as a social activist" (Wasko 1993, 1).

In the German discussions about the Critique of the Political Economy of the Media, Horst Holzer (1973, 131; 1994, 202ff) and Manfred Knoche (2005) have distinguished four functions of the media in capitalism that are relevant for the Marxist Critique of the Political Economy of the Media and Communication:

(1) capital accumulation in the media industry;
(2) advertising, public relations and sales promotion for other industries;
(3) legitimization of domination and ideological manipulation;
(4) reproduction, regeneration and qualification of labour-power.

Holzer and Knoche have provided a good framework that is, however, too structuralistic and lacks the aspect of struggles and alternative. So building on and at the same time going beyond Holzer and Knoche, one can say that the task of a critical theory and the Critique of the Political Economy of Communications, Culture, Information and the Media is to focus on the critique and analysis of the role of communication, culture, information and the media in capitalism in the context of:

(a) processes of capital accumulation (including the analysis of capital, markets, commodity logic, competition, exchange-value, the antagonisms of the mode of production, productive forces, crises, advertising, etc.),

(b) class relations (with a focus on work, labour, the mode of the exploitation of surplus value, etc.),

(c) domination in general and the relationship of forms of domination to exploitation,

(d) ideology (both in academia and everyday life) as well as the analysis of and engagement in

(e) struggles against the dominant order, which includes the analysis and support of

(f) social movement struggles and

(g) social movement media that

(h) aim at the establishment of a democratic-socialist society that is based on communication commons as part of structures of commonly owned means of production (Fuchs 2011a).

The approach thereby realizes that in capitalism all forms of domination are connected to forms of exploitation (Fuchs 2008, 2011a). So I am arguing for a combination of critical theory and Critical Political Economy. However, such an approach does not have to stay pure in terms of its theory connections; it is open for theoretical links, as my own drawing on certain concepts by authors such as Sigmund Freud, Pierre Bourdieu or Gilles Deleuze in this chapter shall show. My basic contention is that in establishing such links, it is important to maintain an analytical framework that stresses the importance of capitalism and class (i.e. that is guided by Marxist theory). In the next section, I will give a brief overview of one foundational debate in critical media and communication studies that has gained new relevance today: the "Blindspot Debate", in which Dallas Smythe introduced the notion of the audience commodity.

4.3. The Renewal of the Audience Labour and Audience Commodity Debate

According to Dallas Smythe, he first formulated the "'blind spot' argument about audience members' work for advertisers" (Lent 1995, 34) in 1951 in the article "The Consumer's Stake in Radio and Television" (Smythe 1951). In this chapter,

Smythe asks what "the nature of the 'product'" (ibid., 109) of radio and television actually is. First, there would be a market for receivers. Second, "there is that product known as station time, and sometimes as audience loyalty (measured by ratings) which stations sell to advertisers. What is sold is a program for the audience (in whose continuing loyalty the station management has a vital interest), and the probability of developing audience loyalty to the advertiser. [...] In commercial radio and television, our Janus-like product is paid for twice. It is paid for once, as a producer's good, if you please, when the sponsor pays for its production. And it is paid for again, as a consumer's good, when the more or less predictable audience response results in the ringing of cash registers where the sponsor's product is sold to ultimate consumers" (ibid., 119). It would therefore be a myth that "radio and television programs are 'free'" (ibid., 110). Smythe here shows a clear concern for the role of advertising in commercial radio and television and the audience as a product. The notion of the audience commodity is already present in the 1951 article in an implicit manner, whereas Smythe formulated it more explicitly in the 1970s.

In 1977, Dallas Smythe argued that the "material reality under monopoly capitalism is that all non-sleeping time of most of the population is work time. [...] Of the off-the-job work time, the largest single block is time of the audiences, which is sold to advertisers. [...] In 'their' time which is sold to advertisers workers (a) perform essential marketing functions for the producers of consumers' goods, and (b) work at the production and reproduction of labour power" (Smythe 1977a, 3). David Hesmondhalgh (2010) remarks that also sleeping time can be seen as reproductive work time that re-creates labour-power. Smythe stressed this circumstance (not in the "Blindspot" article, but later) when writing, "For the great majority of the population [...] 24 hours a day is work time" (Smythe 1981, 47).

Media content would be "an inducement (gift, bribe or 'Free lunch') to recruit potential members of the audience and to maintain their loyal attention" (Smythe 1977a, 5). Smythe (1977a; 1981, 22–51) introduced the notion of the audience commodity for analysing media advertisement models, in which the audience is sold as a commodity to advertisers: "Because audience power is produced, sold, purchased and consumed, it commands a price and is a commodity. [...] You audience members contribute your unpaid work time and in exchange you receive the program material and the explicit advertisements" (Smythe 1981, 26, 233). Audiences "work to market [...] things to themselves" (ibid., 4). The "main function of the mass media [...] is to produce audiences prepared to be dutiful consumers" (Smythe 1994, 250). Work would not necessarily be wage labour but a general category—"doing something creative" (Smythe 1981, 26).

Eileen Meehan (1984) argues that commercial media not only have a commodity message and an audience commodity, but also commodity ratings. She stresses the importance of the question "how do ratings and the ratings industry fit into the production of the commodity message?" (ibid., 217) for answering the question "what commodity is produced by mass communications industries?" (216). Meehan (1993) says that ratings serve "to set the price that networks" can demand and that advertisers have "to pay for access to the commodity audience" (ibid., 387). It would depend on the used measurement technique how strongly the audience measurement industry over- or underestimated the audience size. The ratings industry would be highly monopolized, and monopoly capitalists (like A.C. Nielsen) would set the standards of measurement. The ratings industry would have a preference for measuring a particular audience that is likely to buy and consume a lot of commodities; therefore, "the commodity audience and commodity ratings are entirely artificial and manufactured" (ibid., 389). Chen (2003) has coined in this context the notion of the fictitious audience commodity. Meehan (2007, 164) stresses that "all television viewers are not in television's commodity audience and [. . .] some parts of the commodity audience are more valuable than others". Richard Maxwell makes an argument comparable to Meehan: "Where then is the human labor that produces the value reflected in the audience commodity form? I argue that it can be located in the ratings industry, advertising and broadcast marketing firms, and other areas of the image and information industries" (Maxwell 1991, 32). Smythe would be right that in the case of communications productive labour is not only located in the sphere of production, but also the sphere of circulation. Commodity fetishism would create the illusion that the fact that audiences are sold means that they create value. Göran Bolin concludes based on Meehan's arguments that there is an "empiric fallacy of Smythe, Jhally and Livant, and Andrejevic, who see statistics as representative of reality" and says that "it is not the viewers who work, but rather the statisticians" (Bolin 2009, 357; see also Bolin 2011, 37, 84). This claim might be too strong because it implies that the audience cannot be exploited by capital. But there is no doubt that the audience commodity is connected to the rise of the ratings industry that engages in setting prices for audiences. If the audience produces the value of the audience commodity, then the ratings industry sets the price of this commodity and thereby is central in the transformation of audience commodity values into prices. With the rise of commercial Internet platforms, audience ratings no longer need to be approximated, but permanent surveillance of user activities and user content allows the definition of precisely defined consumer groups with specific interests. It is exactly known to which group a consumer belongs, and advertising is targeted to these groups.

Eileen Meehan (2002) points out that the audience commodity is gendered:

(a) Employees who sell ads tend to be female and low-paid.
(b) Advertisers and the advertising industry tend to base assumptions about the audience commodity on sexist values and so "discriminate against anyone outside the commodity audience of white, 18- to 34-year-old, heterosexual, English-speaking, upscale men" (Meehan 2002, 220). Focusing on the connection of gender and class, patriarchy and capitalism, sex and money in the

media is an important task that has faced both neglect and mutual interest on the side of feminists and political economists (Meehan and Riordan 2002). Valerie Steeves and Janet Wasko (2002) point out that socialist/Marxist feminism and Marxist political economy are natural allies, but that there has been a turn away from socialism and the interest in the connection of patriarchy and capitalism in feminism. They stress that it is an important task both for feminism and political economy not just to focus on words, symbols and discourses of gender and the media, but to realize that "words, symbols, and discourses are important in shaping structures of inequality" (Steeves and Wasko 2002, 26).

Sut Jhally (1987, chapter 2) argues that Dallas Smythe's notion of the audience commodity is too imprecise. Jhally says that advertisers buy the watching time of the audience as a commodity. His central assumption is that one should see "watching time as the media commodity" (ibid., 73). "When the audience watches commercial television it is working for the media, producing both value and surplus value" (ibid., 83). He says that the networks buy the watching-power of the audience (ibid., 75). Jhally argues that the audience watching time is the programme time and that advertising watching time is surplus time (ibid., 76). The audience's wage would be the programming (ibid., 85). "The programming, the value of watching-power, is the wage of the audience, the variable capital of the communications industry" (Jhally and Livant 1986/2006, 36). The question that arises is if watching time can be considered to be a wage equivalent in a society whose main structures are money and capital.

So I disagree with Jhally's argument that the wage that TV viewers receive is the TV programme, that the necessary labour time is the watching of non-advertising programmes and that the surplus labour time is the watching of advertisements. You cannot live by watching TV, so watching TV is not an equivalent to a wage. Göran Bolin argues in this context, "It might be argued that what audiences get is television programmes, but if audiences are working, and if their salary is entertainment shows, how can they further convert this salary? The average viewer cannot buy food for the experience earned in watching an entertainment or any other television show" (Bolin 2005, 297; Bolin 2011, 37).

Rather, all watching time of commercial TV is surplus labour time. In the "digital labour" debate, some people employ an argument that is related to the one by Jhally. They argue that Facebook does not exploit users because they receive free access to the platform as a "wage". There is a difference to Jhally because he maintains the notion of exploitation and surplus value, but both arguments ignore that money is the most important structure in capitalism and is privileged over all other structures and relations in terms of the power that it gives to its owners. Therefore, Marx argues that in capitalism, money has a "social monopoly [. . .] to play the part of universal equivalent within the world of commodities" (Marx 1867c, 162).

The human is, as Marx (1844) knew, a natural and a social being that needs to eat and to communicate in order to survive. In capitalism, the access to many means of human survival is organized through the commodity and money form: you can only get access to many of the necessary means of survival if you are able to buy commodities. And to do so, you need to get hold of money. And for the largest share of people, this circumstance compels them to sell their labour-power as a commodity in order to earn a wage that they can use to buy means of survival. The means of communication are part of the means of survival. If they are organized as public or common goods, then means of communication can escape the money form and people do not have to pay in order to get access to them. Some means of communication, as for example most movies and popular culture, are organized as commodities that are sold. One can only get access by paying for them or by trying to undercut the commodity form (e.g. by downloading them without payment on the Internet). Internet platforms like Facebook and Twitter provide access to means of communication without selling access or content as commodity, yet they do not stand outside the commodity form, but rather commodify users' data. In return for the commodification of data, Facebook and Twitter provide a means of communication to their users. These means could be considered as being in-kind goods provided as return for the users granting the companies the possibility to access and commodify personal data. If the relationship between users and platform were organized in the form of a modern wage relationship, then the users would receive money in return for the commodification of their digital labour-power. They could use this money for buying various means of survival. The difference from such monetary payments is that users on Facebook and Twitter do not receive a universal medium of exchange, but rather one specific means of communication. By giving users access to their platforms, Facebook and Twitter do not provide general means of survival, but instead access to a particular means of communication whose use serves their own profit interests. This is not to say that I argue for payments to users of corporate Internet platforms that are advertising-financed. I rather argue for the creation of non-commercial non-profit alternatives that altogether escape, sublate and struggle against the commodity form.

The point I want to make is that the means of communication that Facebook and Twitter provide to its users are not simple means of survival and should not be analytically treated as such, but are rather also means of production for the creation of value and profit. This circumstance arises from the simultaneous character of social media users as consumers of technological services and producers of data, commodities, value and profit. The circumstance that the means of consumption/communication provided by Facebook are not simple means of survival, but that in this consumption all users during the full consumption time produce value for Facebook and Twitter, makes the argument inappropriate that service access is a form of a wage. If one buys a can of Coke from parts of the wage one earns and drinks it, one does not produce value (and as a consequence profit for Coca-Cola) during the drinking/consumption process; rather, for being able to drink the Coke one has to pay money so that Coca-Cola realizes monetary profit. The consumption does not directly create value for the company. On Facebook and Twitter, the consumption process of the service entails all online communication and usage time. All of this time is not only reproduction time (i.e. time for the reproduction of labour-power), but at the same time labour time that produces data commodities that are offered by Facebook and Twitter for sale to advertising clients. In the consumption process, the users do not just reproduce their labour-power but produce commodities. So on Facebook, YouTube and Twitter, all consumption time is commodity production time.

The analytical problem in relation to TV, radio and newspapers that Smythe and Jhally had to cope with was that consuming these media is a rather passive activity. Therefore, they had to find a way to argue that this behaviour also produces surplus value. Jhally's analysis that, in the case of television, watching time is sold as a commodity equals saying that the more watchers there are, the higher advertising profits are generated. This part of the analysis is feasible, but in the world of the Internet, the situation is different. Here users are not passive watchers, but to a certain degree active creators of content. Advertisers are not only interested in the time that users spend online, but also in the products that are created during this time—user-generated digital content and online behaviour. The users' data—information about their uploaded data, social networks, their interests, demographic data, their browsing and interaction behaviour—is sold to the advertisers as a commodity. Contrary to the world of television that Jhally analyses, on the Internet the users' subjective creations are commodified. Therefore, Smythe's original formulation holds here that the audience itself—its subjectivity and the results of its subjective creative activity—is sold as a commodity. The Internet is an active medium, where consumers of information are as a tendency also producers of information. Therefore, in the case of Facebook and other corporate social media, it is better to speak of Internet prosumer commodification (Fuchs 2010b). However, television has today also become digital and more interactive so that audience commodification can take place in real-time and make use of consumer profiles and new forms of commerce (T-commerce, U-commerce, etc.) that further advance commodification (Andrejevic 2009, McGuigan 2012).

Brett Caraway (2011) claims that the audience is no commodity because "the activities of the audience are not under the direct control of the capitalist. Nor is it clear that the product of the labor of the audience (whatever that may be) is alienated from the audience" (Caraway 2011, 697). Capitalism uses the force of markets to coerce workers to sell their labour-power: if you do not work for a wage, you are unlikely to survive. Whereas wage labour is coerced by the threat of physical violence (the threat is death because of the lack of being able to purchase and consume goods), audience labour is coerced by ideological violence (the threat is to have fewer social contacts because of missing information from the media and missing communication capacities that are needed for sustaining social relations). Audiences are under the ideological control of capitalists who possess control over the means of communication. If for example people stop using Facebook and social networking sites, they may miss certain social contact opportunities. They can refuse to become a Facebook worker, just like an employee can refuse to work for a wage, but they may as a consequence suffer social disadvantages in society. Commercial media coerce individuals to use them. The more monopoly power they possess, the easier it gets to exert this coercion over media consumers and users.

The product of the working audience is the attention given to programmes that feature advertising breaks. Access to audience attention is exchanged with money paid by advertisers to commercial media operators. The audience cannot control its attention itself because it does not own, create and control the commercial media; instead, their labour and attention is alienated—others, namely the corporate media and their advertising clients, define and control the programme time. The same is true for Facebook and other commercial user-generated content Internet sites, on which user labour generates content and transaction data are surveilled and sold to advertising clients, which get access to the attention of specifically targeted groups. Users of commercial social media platforms do not control and own their data; they are alienated from it. The labour that generates audience commodity is exploited because it generates value and products that are owned by others, which constitutes at the same time an alienation process. Digital labour is ideologically coerced. Being coerced, exploited and alienated makes audience labour a class in itself.

David Hesmondhalgh (2010, 280) claims that "Smythe's account is crude, reductionist and functionalist, totally underestimating contradiction and struggle in capitalism", and that it "has totally lost its connection to pragmatic political struggle". Similarly, in a contemporary critique of Smythe's audience commodity theory and its application to digital media, Caraway (2011) argues that "Smythe's theory represents a one-sided class analysis which devalues working-class subjectivity" (696), gives "no discussion of wage struggles, product boycotts, or consumer safety" (700), and thereby conducts "audience commodity fetishism", in which "we are all now merely cogs in the capitalist machine" (700). Caraway's criticism of Critical Political Economy coincides with his celebration of the "creative energy residing in the new media environment" (706), which sets his analysis on par with social media determinists like Henry Jenkins, who argue that "the Web has become a site of consumer participation" (Jenkins 2008, 137) and that media are today a locus of "participatory culture" (Jenkins 2008). These criticisms are based on uninformed or deliberately selective readings of Smythe that ignore his focus on alternative media as counterpart to audience commodification. Smythe does not celebrate audiences as always rebelling and does not argue for social-democratic reformism that tolerates exploitation and misery. His analysis rather implies the need for the overthrow of capitalism in order to humanize society and the overthrow of the capitalist media system in order to humanize the media.

Dallas Smythe did not ignore the ability of humans to create alternative futures, which is shown by the fact that he engaged with the idea of an alternative communication system. For Smythe, political subjectivity is revolutionary subjectivity that aims at fundamentally transforming society and establishing an alternative media system. Critics such as Hesmondhalgh and Caraway overlook this aspect of Smythe's approach. Mao wrote in 1957 about big-character posters (Dazibao, Tatsepao): "We should put up big-character posters and hold forums".[1] In 1958, he said, "The Tatsepao, or big-character poster, is [a] powerful new weapon, a means of criticism and self-criticism which was created by the masses during the rectification movement; at the same time it is used to expose and attack the enemy. It is also a powerful weapon for conducting debate and education in accordance with the broadest mass democracy. People write down their views, suggestions or exposures and criticisms of others in big characters on large sheets of paper and put them up in conspicuous places for people to read".[2]

When Dallas Smythe wrote in the early 1970s about communication in China in his article "After Bicycles, What?" (Smythe 1994, 230–244), he took up Mao's idea of the big-character posters for thinking about how to democratically organize the broadcasting system. He spoke of a "two-way system in which each receiver would have the capability to provide either a voice or voice-and-picture response. [. . .] a two-way TV system would be like an electronic tatzupao system" (ibid., 231–232). These thoughts paralleled the ideas of Hans Magnus Enzensberger's (1970) concept of emancipatory media use, Walter Benjamin's (1934, 1936/1939) idea of the reader/writer and Bertolt Brecht's (1932/2000) notion of an alternative radio in his radio theory.

Mao had the idea of a media system that is controlled by the people in grassroots processes, and Smythe applied this idea to electronic media for formulating a concept of alternative electronic media. Yuezhi Zhao (2011) points out the relevance of Smythe's article and his ideas of an alternative non-capitalist communication system for China. Given a world dominated by the logic of neoliberal capitalism (both in the West and China), she stresses, inspired by Smythe, the importance of establishing communications and societies that are based on non-capitalist logic. Zhao (2007a, 92) argues that Smythe raised the question "After bicycles, what?" "in the context of China's search for a socialist alternative to capitalist modernity, with the hope that China would avoid the capitalist path of development". She says that although Smythe misjudged the political situation in China in the 1970s in a number of points, his intervention would continue to "offer a useful point of departure in analyzing not only the deployment and development of ICTs in China during the reform era, but also the broad path of China's post-Mao development strategy and its sustainability" (ibid., 96). The question one would have today to ask about Chinese media in Dallas Smythe's manner would be: After mobile phones, what? (Zhao 2007a). Whereas to the question "After bicycles, what?", Smythe answered that China should create a media structure that favours "public goods and services [. . .] against goods and services for individual, private use" (Smythe 1994, 243), ICTs would not only serve capitalist purposes but would "by their very nature" be social and allow "alternative uses", including collective political action (Zhao 2007a, 96). The reality of ICTs in China would show the antagonistic character of these technologies as means of both domination and protest.

Dallas Smythe was fundamentally concerned with processes of commodification and audience labour, which is reflected in his creation of the audience commodity category. Although he was critical of some other Marxist theories of culture, important elements of ideology critique and alternative media accompany his focus on the audience commodity. He was furthermore deeply concerned about social struggles for a better world and democratic communications. Smythe's work was connected to politics: for example, he worked with unions to improve the working conditions of communications workers; gave testimonies and conducted studies in favour of public ownership of satellites, public service broadcasting and affordable universal access to telecommunications; and spoke out against corporate media control and monopolization (Yao 2010). He also was involved in debates about the establishment of a New World Information and Communication Order and acted as a public intellectual (ibid.). The claim that Smythe had no connection to political struggles, pragmatic or not, is therefore not feasible.

Janet Wasko (2005, 29) argues that "with the increasing spread of privatised, advertiser-supported media, the audience commodity concept has been accepted by many political economists, as well as other communication theorists". In recent years, this tendency has grown and there has been a revival of the interest in Dallas Smythe's works, especially in relation to the question of whether the users of commercial "social media" are workers and are exploited. Tiziana Terranova made an early contribution to the digital labour debate by introducing the notion of free Internet labour: "Simultaneously voluntarily given and unwaged, enjoyed and exploited, free labor on the Net includes the activity of building Web sites, modifying software packages, reading and participating in mailing lists, and building virtual spaces on MUDs and MOOs" (Terranova 2000, 33). Terranova connected the concept of free labour to the Autonomist Marxist concept of immaterial labour, but did not think of the connectedness to Dallas Smythe's notion of the audience commodity.

I have stressed in my works that Smythe's concept of the audience commodity is very well suited for describing the exploitation of user activities by corporate platforms on the contemporary Internet, and I have in this context coined the notion of the Internet prosumer commodity (Fuchs 2012a, 2011a, 2011b, 2010b, 2009). Vince Manzerolle (2010) builds on this analysis and on Smythe's works for analysing prosumer commodification on the mobile Internet, for which he uses the concept of the mobile audience commodity. Marisol Sandoval (2012) empirically analysed the reality of Internet prosumer commodification and found that more than 90% of all analysed web platforms used targeted advertising and the surveillance and commodification of users' data. A qualitative analysis of the terms and policies that legally guarantee Internet prosumer commodification show that they are "confusing, misleading, ideological, or even manipulative. [. . .] They try to create the impression that the only aim of these platforms is to provide to its users an attractive high-quality service and experience that allows them to produce their own media content and to connect with friends. The fact that these platforms are owned by commercial companies that aim at increasing their profits by selling user information and space for advertisements remains hidden" (Sandoval 2012, 164–165).

Vincent Mosco (2009) argues in a discussion of Smythe's audience commodity concept that digital "systems which measure and monitor precisely each information transaction are now used to refine the process of delivering audiences of viewers, listeners, readers, movie fans, telephone and computer users, to advertisers. [. . .] This is a major refinement in the commodification of viewers over the earlier system of delivering mass audiences and it has been applied to practically every communication medium today, including the Internet, where social networking sites like Facebook provide detailed information on users" (ibid., 137). Graham Murdock (2011) points out that Internet gifting organized by commercial platforms like Google "points to a more general incorporation of gift relations into the economy of commodities" that signifies "the intensification of exploitation" (ibid., 30–31). One "of the major tasks now facing a critical political economy of culture and communication" would be to argue the case "for a public cultural commons for the digital age" (ibid., 37).

Nick Dyer-Witheford argues that Smythe's analysis has today gained credibility because the "level of surveillance in the home tends toward that already experienced in the workplace, and the activity of the waged 'watchman' in the automatic factory, described by Marx, becomes integrally linked with the unpaid 'watching time' that he or she passes in front of the television" (Dyer-Witheford 1999, 119). Interactive systems would enable "the compilation of comprehensive profiles of consumer behavior" that allows the "ever more precise targeting of consumers differentiated by taste and income" (ibid., 118). He is critical that Smythe would too "often assume that capital's intended exploitation of audience power is fully successful" (ibid., 119) and says that activities like online piracy and alternative media are attempts to break capital's dominance.

Mark Andrejevic (2002, 2004, 2009) has applied Sut Jhally's (1987) analysis to reality TV, the Internet, social networking sites and interactive media in general. He says that there the accumulation strategy is based on exploiting not the work of watching, but the work of being watched. Andrejevic (2012) argues that the Marxian concept of exploitation needs to be updated for the online world ("exploitation 2.0") by realizing that on platforms like Google or Facebook, "monitoring becomes an integral component of the online value chain both for sites that rely upon direct payment and for user-generated content sties that rely upon indirect payment (advertising)" so that "user activity is redoubled on commercial platforms in the form of productive information about user activity" (Andrejevic 2012, 84). "It is important to understand that the capture and sale of TGI [= transaction generated information] generates harm by supporting discrimination in markets in ways that capture consumer surplus" (Gandy 2011, 451). Lauer (2008) offers an analysis that is related to the one by Andrejevic.

Cohen (2008, 8) argues based on Smythe that the "labour involved in the production of Web 2.0 content" is the production of "information, social networks, relationships, and affect". Coté and Pybus (2010) stress that one cannot speak of audience labour on the Internet; therefore, they use the term "immaterial labour 2.0". Bermejo (2009), Couvering (2004, 2011), Kang and McAllister (2011) and Lee (2011) apply the notion of audience commodification to Google and search engines. McStay (2011) uses the audience commodity concept for the analysis of online advertising. Napoli (2010) stresses that audience commodification is being taken one step further online so that users even engage in taking over the work of advertisers by spreading advertising messages online to their contacts or by co-creating advertising content.

The more than 500-page-long *tripleC* special issue *Marx Is Back—The Importance of Marxist Theory and Research for Critical Communication Studies Today,* which was edited by Christian Fuchs and Vincent Mosco (2012), shows the importance of Marx's works for critically understanding the media and communication today. It also shows a sustained interest in and relevance of Dallas Smythe's work, especially in the context of the digital labour debate. Several contributors stress that Smythe's audience commodity theory is very well applicable to digital labour on platforms like Facebook or YouTube (Ekman 2012, Fisher 2012, Hebblewhite 2012, Nixon 2012, Prey 2012, Prodnik 2012).

The discussion shows that Smythe's Marxist/Critical Political Economy of the Media and Communication has had a crucial influence on the digital labour debate. What the discussed approaches share is the analysis that digital labour is exploited by capital. The exploitation of digital labour involves three elements:

- Coercion: Users are ideologically coerced to use commercial platforms in order to be able to engage in communication, sharing and the creation and maintenance of social relations, without which their lives would be less meaningful.
- Alienation: Companies, not the users, own the platforms and the created profit.
- Appropriation: Users spend time on corporate Internet platforms that are funded by targeted advertising capital accumulation models. The time spent on corporate platforms is the value created by their unpaid digital labour. Their digital labour creates social relations, profile data, user-generated content and transaction data (browsing behaviour)—a data commodity that is offered for sale by Internet corporations to advertising clients that can select

certain user groups they want to target. The act of exploitation is already created by the circumstance that users create a data commodity, in which their online work time is objectified, and that they do not own this data themselves, but rather corporate Internet platforms with the help of terms of use and privacy policies acquire ownership of this data. Corporate Internet platforms offer the data commodity that is the result of Internet prosumption activity for sale to advertisers. The value realization process, the transformation of value into profit, takes place when targeted users view the advertisement (pay per view) or click on it (pay per click). Not all data commodities are sold all of the time and specific groups of data commodities are more popular than others, but exploitation always takes place at the point of the production and appropriation of the commodity and prior to a commodity's sale.

In section 4.4, I will provide an analysis of how commodification works on corporate social media platforms. Section 4.5 will then analyse ideological structures that are associated with digital media. Analysing digital media thereby makes both use of the unity of the critical analysis of commodification and ideology critique that I argued for in section 4.2.

4.4. Digital Labour: Capital Accumulation and Commodification on Social Media

For a deeper analysis of how the notion of the audience commodity can be applied for analysing digital labour on "social media", we need to engage with Marx's analysis of capitalism. In the three volumes of *Capital,* Marx analyses the accumulation process of capital. This process, as described by Marx, is visualized in figure 4.1.

In the accumulation of capital, capitalists buy labour-power and means of production (raw materials, technologies, etc.) in order to organize the production of new commodities that are sold with the expectation to make money profit that is partly reinvested. Marx distinguishes two spheres of capital accumulation: the circulation sphere and the sphere of production. In the circulation sphere, capital transforms its value form. First money, M, is transformed into commodities (from the standpoint of the capitalist as buyer)—the capitalist purchases the commodities labour-power, L, and means of production, Mp. The process, M-C, is based on the two purchases, M-L and M-Mp. This means that due to private property structures, workers do not own the means of production, the products they produce or the profit they generate. Capitalists own these resources. In the sphere of production, a new good is produced: the value of labour-power and the value of the means of production are added to the product. Value takes on the form of productive capital, P. The value form of labour is variable capital, v (which can be observed as wages), the value form of the means of production constant capital, c (which can be observed as the total price of the means of production/producer goods).

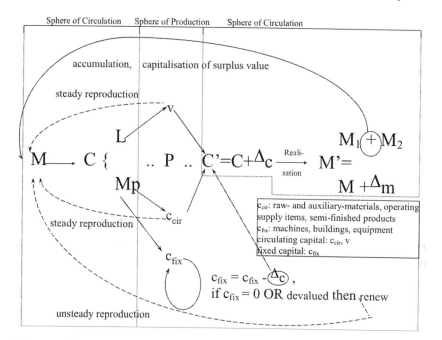

FIGURE 4.1 The accumulation/expanded reproduction of capital

In the sphere of production, capital stops its metamorphosis so that capital circulation comes to a halt. There is the production of new value, V', of the commodity. V' contains the value of the necessary constant and variable capital and surplus value Δs of the surplus product. Unpaid labour generates surplus value and profit. Surplus value is the part of the working day that is unpaid. It is the part of the workday (measured in hours) that is used for producing profit. Profit does not belong to workers but to capitalists. Capitalists do not pay for the production of surplus. Therefore, the production of surplus value is a process of exploitation. The value, V', of the new commodity after production is V' = c + v + s. The commodity then leaves the sphere of production and again enters the circulation sphere, in which capital conducts its next metamorphosis: it is transformed from the commodity form back into the money form by being sold on the market. Surplus value is realized in the form of money. The initial money capital, M, now takes on the form M' = M + Δm, it has been increased by an increment Δm that is called profit. Accumulation of capital means that the produced surplus value/profit is (partly) reinvested/capitalized. The end point of one process, M', becomes the starting point of a new accumulation process. One part of M', M_1, is reinvested. Accumulation means the aggregation of capital by investment and the exploitation of labour in the capital circuit M-C .. P .. C'-M', in which the end product M' becomes a new starting point M. The total process makes up the dynamic character of capital. Capital is money that is permanently increasing because of the exploitation of surplus value.

Commodities are sold at prices that are higher than the investment costs so that money profit is generated. Marx argues that one decisive quality of capital accumulation is that profit is an emergent property of production that is produced by labour but owned by capitalists. Without labour, no profit could be made. Workers are forced to enter class relations and to produce profit in order to survive, which enables capital to appropriate surplus. The notion of surplus value is the main concept of Marx's theory, by which he intends to show that capitalism is a class society. "The theory of surplus value is in consequence immediately the theory of exploitation" (Negri 1991, 74). One can add: The theory of surplus value is the theory of class and as a consequence the political demand for a classless society.

Capital is not money but money that is increased through accumulation, "money which begets money" (Marx 1867c, 256). Marx argues that the value of labour-power is the average amount of time that is needed for the production of goods that are necessary for survival (necessary labour time). Wages represent the value of necessary labour time at the level of prices. Surplus labour time is labour time that exceeds necessary labour time, remains unpaid, is appropriated for free by capitalists and is transformed into money profit. Surplus value "is in substance the materialisation of unpaid labour-time. The secret of the self-valorisation of capital resolves itself into the fact that it has at its disposal a definite quantity of the unpaid labour of other people" (ibid., 672). The production of surplus value is "the *differentia specifica* of capitalist production" (ibid., 769) and the "driving force and the final result of the capitalist process of production" (976).

Many corporate social media platforms (Facebook, YouTube, etc.) accumulate capital with the help of targeted advertising that is tailored to individual user data and behaviour. Capitalism is based on the imperative to accumulate ever more capital. To achieve this, capitalists either have to prolong the working day (absolute surplus value production) or to increase the productivity of labour (relative surplus value production). (On relative surplus value, see Marx 1867c, chapter 12.) Relative surplus value production means that productivity is increased so that more commodities and more surplus value can be produced in the same time period as before. "For example, suppose a cobbler, with a given set of tools, makes one pair of boots in one working day of 12 hours. If he is to make two pairs in the same time, the productivity of his labour must be doubled; and this cannot be done except by an alteration in his tools or in his mode of working, or both. Hence the conditions of production of his labour, i.e. his mode of production, and the labour process itself, must be revolutionised. By an increase in the productivity of labour, we mean an alteration in the labour process of such a kind as to shorten the labour-time socially necessary for the production of a commodity, and to endow a given quantity of labour with the power of producing a greater quantity of use-value. [. . .] I call that surplus-value which is produced by lengthening of the working day, *absolute surplus-value*. In contrast to this, I call that surplus-value which arises from the curtailment of the necessary labour-time, and from the corresponding alteration in the respective lengths of the two components of the working day, *relative surplus-value*" (Marx 1867c, 431–432).

Sut Jhally (1987, 78) argues that "reorganising the watching audience in terms of demographics" is a form of relative surplus value production. One can interpret targeted Internet advertising as a form of relative surplus value production: At one point in time, the advertisers not only show one advertisement to the audience as in non-targeted advertising, but they show different advertisements to different user groups depending on the monitoring, assessment and comparison of the users' interests and online behaviour. With traditional forms of television, all watchers see the same advertisements at the same time. In targeted online advertising, advertising companies can present different ads at the same time. The efficiency of advertising is increased: the advertisers can show more advertisements that are likely to fit the interests of consumers in the same time period as in non-targeted advertising. Partly the advertising company's wage labourers and partly the Internet users, whose user-generated data and transaction data are utilized, produce the profit generated from these advertisements. The more targeted advertisements there are, the more likely it is that users recognize ads and click on them.

The users' click-and-buy process is the surplus value realization process of the advertising company. This process transforms surplus value into money profit. Targeted advertising allows Internet companies to present not just one advertisement at one point in time to users, but rather numerous advertisements, so that there is the production of more total advertising time that presents commodities to users. Relative surplus value production means that more surplus value is generated in the same time period as earlier. Targeted online advertising is more productive than non-targeted online advertising because it allows presenting more ads in the same time period. These ads contain more surplus value than the non-targeted ads (i.e. more unpaid labour time of the advertising company's paid employees and of users, who generate user-generated content and transaction data).

Alvin Toffler (1980) introduced the notion of the prosumer in the early 1980s. It means the "progressive blurring of the line that separates producer from consumer" (Toffler 1980, 267). Toffler describes the age of prosumption as the arrival of a new form of economic and political democracy, self-determined work, labour autonomy, local production and autonomous self-production. But he overlooks that prosumption is used for outsourcing work to users and consumers, who work without payment. Thereby corporations reduce their investment and labour costs, jobs are destroyed and consumers who work for free are extremely exploited. They produce surplus value that is appropriated and turned into profit by corporations which do not pay wages. Notwithstanding Toffler's uncritical optimism, his notion of the "prosumer" describes important changes of media structures and practices and can therefore also be adopted for critical studies.

Ritzer and Jurgenson (2010) argue that Web 2.0 facilitates the emergence of "prosumer capitalism", that the capitalist economy "has always been dominated by prosumption" (14) and that prosumption is an inherent feature of Mc-Donaldization. The two authors' analysis ignores that prosumption is only one of many tendencies of capitalism, but neither its only nor its dominant quality. Capitalism is multidimensional and has multiple interlinked dimensions. It is at the same time finance capitalism, imperialistic capitalism, informational capitalism, hyper-industrial capitalism (oil, gas), crisis capitalism and so on. Not all of these dimensions are equally important (Fuchs 2011a, chapter 5).

We have seen that Dallas Smythe's (1977a, 1981) analysis of the audience commodity has gained new relevance today in the digital labour debate. With the rise of user-generated content, free access social networking platforms and other free access platforms that yield profit by online advertisement—a development subsumed under categories such as Web 2.0, social software and social networking sites—the web seems to come close to accumulation strategies employed by capital on traditional mass media like TV or radio. Users who upload photos and other images, write wall postings and comments, send mail to their contacts, accumulate friends or browse other profiles on Facebook constitute an audience commodity that is sold to advertisers. The difference between the audience commodity on traditional mass media and on the Internet is that in the latter case the users are also content producers, there is user-generated content and the users engage in permanent creative activity, communication, community building and content-production. That the users are more active on the Internet than in the reception of TV or radio content is due to the decentralized structure of the Internet that allows many-to-many communication. Because of the permanent activity of the recipients and their status as prosumers, we can say that in the case of corporate social media the audience commodity is an Internet prosumer commodity (Fuchs 2010b). The conflict between Cultural Studies and Critical Political Economy of the Media (see Ferguson and Golding 1997; Garnham 1995a, b; Grossberg 1995) about the question of the activity and creativity of the audience has been resolved in relation to the Internet today: On Facebook, Twitter and blogs, users are fairly active and creative, which reflects Cultural Studies' insights about the active character of recipients, but this active and creative user character is the very source of exploitation, which reflects Critical Political Economy's stress on class and exploitation.

Economic surveillance on corporate social media is surveillance of prosumers, who dynamically and permanently create and share user-generated content; browse profiles and data; interact with others; join, create and build communities; and co-create information. The corporate web platform operators and their third-party advertising clients continuously monitor and record personal data and online activities. They store, merge and analyse collected data. This allows them to create detailed user profiles and to know a lot about the users' personal interests and online behaviours. Surveillance is an inherent feature of corporate social media's capital accumulation model (Fuchs 2012a, Sandoval 2012). Social media that are based on targeted advertising sell prosumers as a commodity to advertising clients.

There is an exchange of money for the access to user data that allows economic user surveillance. The exchange value of the social media prosumer commodity is the money value that the operators obtain from their clients. Its use value is the multitude of personal data and usage behaviour that is dominated by the commodity and exchange value form. The corporations' surveillance of the prosumers' permanently produced use-values (i.e. personal data and interactions) enables targeted advertising that aims at luring the prosumers into consumption and shopping. It also aims at manipulating prosumers' desires and needs in the interest of corporations and the commodities they offer. Whereas audience commodification in newspapers and traditional broadcasting was always based on statistical assessments of audience rates and characteristics (Bolin 2011), Internet surveillance gives social media corporations an exact picture of the interests and activities of users. The characteristics (interests and usage behaviour) and the size (the number of users in a specific interest group) of the Internet prosumer commodity can therefore be exactly determined, and it can also be exactly determined who is part of a consumer group that should be targeted by specific ads and who is not.

In grounding the approach of a critical political economy of personal information, Oscar Gandy has introduced the notion of the panoptic sort: "The panoptic sort is a difference machine that sorts individuals into categories and classes on the basis of routine measurements. It is a discriminatory technology that allocates options and opportunities on the basis of those measures and the administrative models that they inform" (Gandy 1993, 15). It is a system of power and disciplinary surveillance that identifies, classifies and assesses (ibid.). The mechanism of targeted advertising on social media is the form of surveillance that Gandy has characterized as panoptic sorting: it *identifies* the interests of users by closely surveilling their personal data and usage behaviour, it *classifies* them into consumer groups and it *assesses* their interests in comparison to other consumers and to available advertisements, which are then targeted at the users.

Social media users are double objects of commodification: they are commodities themselves and through this commodification their consciousness becomes, while online, permanently exposed to commodity logic in the form of advertisements. Most online time is advertising time. On corporate social media, targeted advertising makes use of the users' personal data, interests, interactions, information behaviour and also the interactions with other websites. So while you are using Facebook, Twitter, YouTube and the like, it is not just you interacting with others and browsing profiles; all of these activities are framed by advertisements presented to you. These advertisements come about by permanent surveillance of your online activities. Such advertisements do not necessarily represent consumers' real needs and desires because the ads are based on calculated assumptions, whereas needs are much more complex and spontaneous. The ads mainly reflect marketing decisions and economic power relations. They do not simply provide information about products as offers to buy, but present information about products of powerful companies.

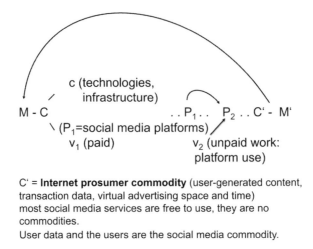

C' = **Internet prosumer commodity** (user-generated content, transaction data, virtual advertising space and time)
most social media services are free to use, they are no commodities.
User data and the users are the social media commodity.

FIGURE 4.2 Capital accumulation on corporate social media platforms that are based on targeted advertising

Figure 4.2 shows the process of capital accumulation on corporate social media platforms that are funded by targeted advertising. Social media corporations invest money (M) for buying capital: technologies (server space, computers, organizational infrastructure, etc.) and labour-power (paid employees). These are the constant capital (c) and the variable capital v1 outlays. The outcome of the production process, P1, is not a commodity that is directly sold, but rather a social media service (the specific platforms) that is made available without payment to users. As a consequence of this circumstance, management literature has focused on identifying how to make profit from free Internet services. Chris Anderson (2009) has identified 50 models of how an Internet service is given for free in order to boost the selling of other services or where an Internet service is given for free for one type of customers and sold to others. The waged employees, who create social media online environments that are accessed by users, produce part of the surplus value. The users employ the platform for generating content that they upload (user-generated data). The constant and variable capital invested by social media companies (c, v1) that is objectified in the online environment is the prerequisite for their activities in the production process, P2. Their products are user-generated data, personal data, social networks and transaction data about their browsing behaviour and communication behaviour on corporate social media. They invest a certain labour time, v2, in this process.

Corporate social media sell the users' data commodity to advertising clients at a price that is larger than the invested constant and variable capital. Partly the users and partly the corporations' employees create the surplus value contained in this commodity. The difference is that the users are unpaid and therefore—in monetary terms—infinitely exploited. Once the Internet prosumer commodity that contains the user-generated content, transaction data and the right to access virtual advertising space and time is sold to advertising clients, the commodity is transformed into money capital, and surplus value is transformed into money capital. A counter-argument to the insight that commercial social media companies exploit Internet prosumers is that the latter in exchange for their work receive access to a service. One can here however interpose that service access cannot be seen as a salary because users cannot "further convert this salary [...] [They] cannot buy food" (Bolin 2011, 37) with it.

For Marx (1867c), the rate of profit rp is the relation of profit to investment costs:

$$rp = p / (c + v) = profit / (constant\ capital\ (= fixed\ costs) + variable\ capital\ (= wages)).$$

If Internet users become productive prosumers, then in terms of Marxian class theory this means that they become productive labourers who produce surplus value and are exploited by capital, because for Marx productive labour generates surplus value (Fuchs 2010b). Therefore, exploited surplus value producers are not merely those who are employed by Internet corporations for programming, updating and maintaining the software and hardware, performing marketing activities, and so forth, but also the users and prosumers, who engage in the production of user-generated content. New media corporations do not (or hardly) pay the users for the production of content. One accumulation strategy is to give them free access to services and platforms and let them produce content and to accumulate a large number of prosumers that are sold as a commodity to third-party advertisers. A product is not sold to the users, but the users are sold as a commodity to advertisers. The more users a platform has, the higher the advertising rates can be set. The productive labour time that capital exploits involves on the one hand the labour time of the paid employees and on the other hand all of the time that is spent online by the users. Digital media corporations pay salaries for the first type of knowledge labour. Users produce data that is used and sold by the platforms without payment. They work for free. There are neither variable nor constant investment costs. The formula for the rate of profit needs to be transformed for this accumulation strategy:

$$rp = p / (c + v1 + v2)$$

where p: profit, c: constant capital, v1: wages paid to fixed employees and v2: wages paid to users.

The typical situation is that $v2 = > 0$ and that v2 substitutes v1 ($v1 = > v2 = 0$). If the production of content and the time spent online were carried out by paid employees, the variable costs (wages) would rise and profits would therefore decrease. This shows that Internet prosumer activity in a capitalist society can be interpreted as the outsourcing of productive labour to users (in management literature the term "crowdsourcing" has been established, see Howe 2008), who work completely for free and help maximize the rate of exploitation e:

e = s / v = surplus value / variable capital

The rate of exploitation (also called the rate of surplus value) measures the relationship of workers' unpaid work time and paid work time. The higher the rate of exploitation, the more work time is unpaid. Users of commercial social media platforms have no wages (v = 0). None of their usage time is remunerated in order to fund subsistence. Therefore the rate of surplus value converges towards infinity. Internet prosumer labour is infinitely exploited by capital. This means that capitalist prosumption is an extreme form of exploitation in which the pro-sumers work completely for free. Infinite exploitation means that all or nearly all online activity and time becomes part of commodities and no share of this time is paid. Smythe (1994, 297) spoke of the commercial audience as "mind slaves", so we may speak of commercial social media users as online slaves. Marx (1867c) dis-tinguishes between necessary labour time and surplus labour time. The first is the time a person needs to work in order to create the money equivalent for a wage that is required for buying goods needed for survival. The second is all additional labour time. Users are not paid on corporate social media (or for consuming other types of corporate media); therefore they cannot generate money for buying food or other goods needed for survival. Therefore all online time on corporate social media like Google, Facebook, YouTube or Twitter is surplus labour time.

So one line of argument is that on the monetary level, users are infinitely exploited because they do not receive a wage, although platforms like Facebook make monetary profits. There is also a second line of argument: The Facebook platform is a means of communicative survival for users and a means of the capi-talist production of value, commodities and profit. It is at the same time means of consumption and means of production. If the platform is considered as in-kind good provided to the users as means of communicative survival, then all costs that Facebook has for providing the platform can be considered as de facto value of an in-kind good "paid" as means of consumption to its value producers. According to Marx, the value of a good is the sum of constant capital, variable capital and profit: V' = c + v + p. In the case of the Facebook platform as good, there is no profit because it is not sold as a commodity. Rather, user data is sold as a com-modity. Therefore the value of the Facebook platform is the sum of the invested constant and variable capital. This implies that one can consider Facebook's in-vestment costs as constituting the "wages" of its users. In 2011, Facebook's total costs and expenses were US$1.955 billion and its revenue was US$3.711 bil-lion (Facebook SEC Filings: Form S-1 Registration Statement). So Facebook made a profit of US$1.756 billion in 2011. If one accepts the argument that the Facebook platform is an in-kind good provided to the users and that therefore Facebook's investment costs form a wage-equivalent for means of consumption, then the rate of exploitation of the total Facebook workforce consisting of paid employees and users is e = profits / investment costs = 1.955 / 1.756 = 1.113 = 111.3%. This means that the profits that Facebook makes are 111% times the monetary value of the investments it makes for services that are consumed by users as "wage-equivalent".

There are, however, some limitations of this second line of argument. In capitalism, money forms a monopolized generalized means of exchange. With the term "wages", Marx means the price of wage labour expressed in monetary terms, i.e. money as the general equivalent of exchange. Marx considers the emergence of wage labour as a specific feature of capitalism. Wage labour is "double free":

(1)   Workers are not physically owned by capitalists like slaves; they are rather compelled to sell their labour-power in exchange for a wage in order to survive.

(2)   This compulsion is based on the circumstance that they are "free" from/not in control of the ownership of the means of production and capital.

So the notion of the wage in a capitalist society presupposes access to a general equivalent of exchange that can be spent for purchasing various commodities that have different use-values. Therefore Marx (1849) says that "wages are the amount of money which the capitalist pays for a certain period of work or for a certain amount of work. [. . .] The exchange value of a commodity estimated in money is called its price. Wages therefore are only a special name for the price of labour-power, and are usually called the price of labour; it is the special name for the price of this peculiar commodity, which has no other repository than human flesh and blood". Money is in capitalism the monopolized general equivalent of exchange. It has special relevance because it can be used for getting hold of most use-values. It is therefore not a straightforward argument to treat in-kind goods as wage-equivalents. The specific structures of capitalism privilege money as a specific and general equivalent of exchange. The money logic therefore has special relevance. I nonetheless want to offer both interpretations of the "wage" of Facebook users for interpretation and discussion. No matter which interpretation one chooses, both versions imply that Facebook users are workers that are exploited.

Users spent 10.5 billion minutes on Facebook per day in January 2011 (Facebook, SEC Filings, Amendment No. 3 to Form S-1 Registration Statement). We can therefore make the following estimates about the value generated on Facebook:

Value generated on Facebook in 2011: 10.5 billion * 365 = 3832.5 billion minutes = 63.875 billion working hours per year

Average working hours per year of a full-time worker: 1,800

Value generated on Facebook in 2011: 35,486,111 full-time equivalents of work

The rate of exploitation is calculated as the ratio e = surplus labour time / necessary labour time = unpaid labour time / paid labour time. In the case of Facebook, all 64.99 billion working hours were unpaid, so the surplus labour time amounts to the full amount of labour time. Given that Facebook exploits more than 35 billion full-time equivalents of free labour or more than 60 billion hours of unpaid work time, it becomes clear that Facebook's business model is based on the outsourcing/crowdsourcing of paid work time to unpaid work time. Given that Facebook's profits were US$1 billion in 2011 (Facebook, SEC Filings, Amendment No. 3 to Form S-1 Registration Statement), it becomes clear that free user labour is at the heart of Facebook's business model. That the rate of exploitation is infinite means that no wages are paid, that all user labour is unremunerated and creates value. Free user labour is what Marx (1867c) termed abstract labour, labour that creates value.

By abstract human labour, Marx means that aspect of labour in a commodity-producing society that makes commodities comparable and exchangeable: "Whether 20 yards of linen = 1 coat or = 20 coats or = x coats, i.e. whether a given quantity of linen is worth few or many coats, it is always implied, whatever the proportion, that the linen and the coat, as magnitudes of value, are expressions of the same unit, things of the same nature. Linen = coat is the basis of the equation. [...] By equating, for example, the coat as a thing of value to the linen, we equate the labour embedded in the coat with the labour embedded in the linen. Now it is true that the tailoring which makes the coat is concrete labour of a different sort from the weaving which makes the linen. But the act of equating tailoring with weaving reduces the former in fact to what is really equal in the two kinds of labour, to the characteristic they have in common of being human labour. This is a roundabout way of saying that weaving too, in so far as it weaves value, has nothing to distinguish it from tailoring, and, consequently, is abstract human labour. It is only the expression of equivalence between different sorts of commodities which brings to view the specific character of value-creating labour, by actually reducing the different kinds of labour embedded in the different kinds of commodity to their common quality of being human labour in general" (Marx 1867c, 141–142).

Abstract labour is "abstract" because it is a dimension of labour, for which we have to abstract from the qualitative differences of commodities (their use-values) and see what they have in common, that is, that they are all products of human labour and objectifications of a certain amount of labour, which makes them comparable and exchangeable in certain relations (x commodity A = y commodity B = ...): "If then we disregard the use-value of commodities, only one property remains, that of being products of labour. But even the product of labour has already been transformed in our hands. If we make abstraction from its use-value, we abstract also from the material constituents and forms which make it a use-value" (ibid., 128). "A use-value, or useful article, therefore, has value only because abstract human labour is objectified or materialised in it. How, then, is the magnitude of this value to be measured? By means of the quantity of the 'value-forming substance', the labour, contained in the article. This quantity is measured by its duration, and the labour-time is itself measured on the particular scale of hours, days etc." (ibid., 129).

At the level of values, we can say that the collective Facebook worker works almost 64 billion hours per year. The surplus hours and surplus work amount to 64 billion hours per year. Personal and social data is the product that is created in this work time. The more hours users work on Facebook, the more data they generate. The more hours users spend on Facebook, the more ads are generated and presented to them. So productive time is also advertising time (although not all advertising time is turned into money profit, only a portion of it).

From Facebook's balance sheet that was published at its stock market registration, we know that its profit rate in 2011 = total profit/total costs and expenses = 1 billion / 1.955 billion = 51.2% (Facebook Inc., SEC Filings Facebook, Form S-1 Registration Statement). This is a very high profit rate, especially in times of global economic crisis. Such a rate can mainly be achieved by the circumstance that Facebook has a low number of employees, 3,976 at the end of June 2012,[3] but can without costs valorize the entire work time of its users for generating its commodity—data commodities. Infinite exploitation of the users (= no wage) allowed Facebook a profit rate of > 50% in 2011. The secret of Facebook's profits is that it mobilizes billions of hours of users' work time (at the level of values) that is unpaid (at the level of prices).

Unpaid labour extends to different realms, such as Google, Twitter, YouTube, Baidu, LinkedIn, knowledge creation and reproduction, "reproductive labour" such as housework, care work, educational work, affective work and sexual work so that the human being in contemporary capitalism spends a lot of working hours every day in creating value for capital by abstract labour that is unpaid. We can therefore say that life has become a factory, factory life. The factory is not limited to the space of wage labour but extends into everyday life. The secret of corporate social media's capital accumulation is that it mobilizes a huge number of unpaid workers, who engage in a tremendous amount of fully unpaid working hours which generate data commodities that are sold as targeted advertisements. There is a need to mobilize value production and to make it free labour at the same time in order for this capital accumulation to function.

Marx described a contradiction between value and labour time: the development of technological productivity reduces the labour time needed for producing a commodity, but at the same time labour time is the only measure and source of wealth in capitalism: "Capital itself is the moving contradiction, [in] that it presses to reduce labour time to a minimum, while it posits labour time, on the other side, as sole measure and source of wealth. Hence it diminishes labour time in the necessary form so as to increase it in the superfluous form; hence posits the superfluous in growing measure as a condition—question of life or death—for the necessary" (Marx 1857/1858b, 706). The result of this contradiction is, as contemporary capitalism shows, unemployment and precarious labour.

In contemporary capitalism, this contradiction takes on a second meaning and reality that is at the heart of corporate social media's capital accumulation model: Corporate social media capital tries to push down the costs of necessary labour (wages) to a minimum, but at the same time increases superfluous labour that is unpaid as productive labour that creates surplus value. The contradiction between necessary and superfluous labour takes on its specific form on corporate social media: paid labour is reduced, unpaid labour is increased, value generation is outsourced from paid to unpaid labour. The contradiction between superfluous and necessary labour is sublated so that a new quality emerges: value-creation is transferred to unpaid labour. At the same time, the contradiction is set at a new level and intensified because the property-lessness, poverty, and precariousness of labour on the one hand and the wealth of capital are intensified.

Michael A. Lebowitz (1986, 165) argues that Smythe's approach is only a "Marxist-sounding communications theory". Marxism would assume that "surplus value in capitalism is generated in the direct process of production, the process where workers (having surrendered the property rights over the disposition of their labour-power) are *compelled* to work longer than is necessary to produce the equivalent of their wage. Perhaps it is for this reason that there is hesitation in accepting the conception that audiences work, are exploited, and produce surplus value—in that it is a paradigm quite different to the Marxist paradigm" (ibid., 167). Media capitalists would compete "for the expenditures of competing industrial capitalists" and would help to "increase the commodity sales of industrial capitalists", and their profits would be "a share of the surplus value of industrial capital" (ibid., 169). Smythe's audience commodity approach would advance an "entirely un-Marxian argument with un-Marxian conclusions" (ibid., 170).

Lebowitz bases his argument on three specific assumptions that he claims to be inherent to Marx's works:

(1)   that industrial capital is the central form of capital,
(2)   that only work performed under the command of industrial capital is productive labour and creates surplus value,
(3)   that only wage labour can be exploited.

The immediate theoretical and political consequences of this logic of argumentation are the following ones:

(1)   Commercial media are subsumed to industrial capital.
(2)   Slaves, house workers and other unpaid workers are not exploited.
(3)   The wage and non-wage work performed under the command of media capital is unproductive work. Media companies cannot exploit workers because they create products and services that are part of the circulation sphere of capitalism.

The political question that Lebowitz's argument poses is if one wants to share the implications of a wage-centric theory of exploitation that unpaid workers cannot be exploited. Productive labour (i.e. labour that generates surplus value) is a complex, contradictory and inconsistent topic within Marx's works. In *Capital, Volume 1,* Marx distinguishes different concepts of productive labour. In the narrower sense, the "only worker who is productive is one who produces surplus-value for the capitalist, or in other words contributes towards the self-valorization of capital" (Marx 1867c, 644). This formulation does not imply that only a wage-worker can be a producer of surplus value, because there can be workers that produce for capital but are unpaid (i.e. surplus labour time makes up 100% of their work time). In a second definition, Marx argues that for being considered a productive worker, "it is no longer necessary for the individual himself to put his hand to the object; it is sufficient for him to be an organ of the collective labourer, and to perform any one of its subordinate functions" (ibid., 643–644). This means that productive labour understood this way implies that a worker who contributes to a "social product" that is controlled by a capitalist and is the "joint product of a collective labourer" (ibid., 643) is an exploited worker, no matter if s/he receives a wage for it or not. S/he is part of a collective or social worker. In a third approach, Marx abstracts from the capitalist production process and argues in chapter 5 in the German edition and chapter 7 of the English edition of *Capital, Volume 1,* that all work is productive because it creates products that are conditions and results of work.

Given the first two understandings, there is no necessity to assume that Marx saw non-wage workers that contribute to capitalist production processes as "unproductive" and non-exploited. Lebowitz gives one interpretation of Marx's works and claims that this is the only possible interpretation and that one is not a Marxist if one does not share this interpretation. The common name for this logical procedure is dogmatism. Representatives of wage-labour dogmatism can certainly counter my argument by citing passages from the *Theories of Surplus Value* or *Capital, Volume 3,* where Marx argues that circulation workers, commercial workers in trade or servants are unproductive workers. But it remains a fact that in his most thought-out book, namely *Capital, Volume 1*—which, in contrast to *Volume 2* and *Volume 3* (which were edited by Engels after Marx's death) and the *Theories of Surplus Value* (which were unpublished notes), he authorized for publication and subsequently revised several times—Marx wrote passages that allow a non-wage-labour-fetishistic interpretation of the concept of productive labour.

In contrast to wage fetishism, Marx argued that surplus labour—and therefore the concept of exploitation—is not specific to capitalism: "Capital did not invent surplus labour. Wherever a part of society possesses the monopoly of the means of production, the worker, free or unfree, must add to the labour-time necessary for his own maintenance an extra quantity of labour-time in order to produce the means of subsistence for the owner of the means of production, whether this proprietor be an Athenian kalos kagathon [aristocrat], an Etruscan theocrat, a *civis romanus,* a Norman baron, an American slave-owner, a Wallachian boyar, a modern landlord or a capitalist" (Marx 1867c, 344–345). Marx argued that the slave performs 100% of his work as unpaid work: "With the *slave,* on the contrary, even that part of his labour which is paid appears to be unpaid. Of course, in order to work the slave must live, and one part of his working day goes to replace the value of his own maintenance. But since no bargain is struck between him and his master, and no acts of selling and buying are going on between the two parties, all his labour seems to be given away for nothing" (Marx 1865).

Although having different origins, contexts and theoretical implications, the works of Dallas Smythe and Autonomous Marxism share the criticism of wage-labour fetishism as well as the concept of a collective workforce that contributes to the production of surplus value, is exploited by capital and is constituted in various spaces of capitalism, including the factory, the household, colonies of primitive accumulation and leisure.

In the context of a digital labour theory of value, it is not so easy to fix advertising in the realm of capital circulation and to reduce it to a relationship that is determined by industrial capital. Within the overall capitalist economy, the commercial media and advertising industries certainly take the role that they help other capitalists realize their profits; that is, they spread messages about why specific commodities should be bought. But they form a capitalist industry in itself that accumulates capital based on the exploitation of work. For Marx, the notion of productive labour is primarily oriented on criticizing the exploitation process. And given that the media and advertising industry is oriented on profit-making and makes use of the work of paid employees and unpaid users/media consumers, it follows that this industry makes use of unpaid labour time for creating profit; that is, the involved work "produces surplus-value for the capitalist" and "contributes towards the self-valorisation of capital" (Marx 1867c, 644)—which is Marx's definition of productive labour. In addition, in the digital labour context it is not so easy to say that media audiences are just media consumers and therefore located in the consumption and circulation realm because the consumption of digital media to a certain extent produces content, behavioural data, social network data and personal data that is commodified and sold to advertising clients.

Figure 4.3 shows the connection of the capital accumulation process of commercial digital media that are based on targeted advertising and the capital accumulation process of advertising clients. They both have their relatively autonomous capital accumulation processes that are based on the exploitation of abstract labour and are interdependent in the form of an exchange process M—C, in which advertising clients exchange their money for the access to user data commodities.

Jhally (1987, 83) argues that "watching is an extension of factory labour" and that the living room is one of the factories today. The factory is the space of wage labour, but it is also in the living room. Outside of wage-labour spaces, the factory is not only in the home—it is everywhere. The Internet is the all-ubiquitous factory and realm of the production of audience commodities. Social media and the mobile Internet make the audience commodity ubiquitous and the factory not limited to your living room and your wage workplace—the

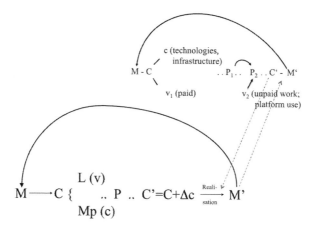

FIGURE 4.3 The dialectic of social media capital accumulation and advertising clients' capital accumulation

factory is also in all in-between spaces, and the entire planet is today a capitalist factory.

The contemporary globalization of capitalism has dispersed the walls of the wage-labour factory all over the globe. Because capital cannot exist without non-wage labour and exploits the commons that are created by all, society has become a factory. Reflecting this development, Mario Tronti has coined the concept of the social factory: "At the highest level of capitalist development social relations become moments of the relations of production, and the whole society becomes an articulation of production. In short, all of society lives as a function of the factory and the factory extends its exclusive domination over all of society" (Mario Tronti, quoted in and translated by Cleaver 1992, 137). "Now we have the factory planet—or the planet factory, a regime that subsumes not just production, consumption, and social reproduction (as in Fordism), but life's genetic and ecological dimensions" (Dyer-Witheford 2010, 485).

The social worker and the social factory are concepts that allow one to go beyond a wage-centric concept of value, labour and exploitation. In fact, especially women, migrant workers, illegal workers, precarious workers, house workers, home workers and the working class in developing countries have long been facing the struggle of surviving in modes of production that feature non-, low- and underpaid work. Especially neo-liberalism has generalized the precarious mode of work so that housewifized work that is insecure, low-paid, temporary, precarious and individualized and lacks social security, unionization, access to health care and other welfare benefits has become the normality of work for many. The concept of the exploitation of the social labourer who works in a global social factory allows connecting Marxist political economy to feminism and studies of race and postcolonialism. There is a global division of labour in the organization of knowledge work. And this division is class-structured, gendered and racist.

There is an inherent connection of class, gender and race in the capitalist mode of production. Dallas Smythe, Marxist feminism and Autonomist Marxism have stressed that exploitation takes place beyond the confines of the traditional wage-labour factory, which opens up connections between these approaches.

Vincent Mosco and Catherine McKercher (2008, 62) stress that Dallas Smythe has "established a groundwork for" the research of voluntary, low-paid and unpaid labour "by describing the extent of audience labor on the home through the sale of people's attention to advertisers. The connection of capitalism, patriarchy and racism has become ever more obvious in recent years, needs to be more analysed and can be a foundation for solidarity between the different exploited groups that we find in capitalism today". Harry Cleaver (2000, 123) argues that capital "tries to shape all 'leisure', or free-time, activities [. . .] in its own interests. Thus, rather than viewing unwaged 'non-labour time' automatically as free time or as time completely antithetical to capital, we are forced to recognize that capital has tried to integrate this time, too, within its process of accumulation. [. . .] Put another way, capital has tried to convert 'individual consumption' into 'produc-tive consumption' by creating the social factory". Capitalist media and culture are shaped by a global mode of production, in which house workers and consumers shop for commodities and actively reproduce labour-power and work as audience for the media; users generate a data commodity on the Internet; slave workers in poor countries extract minerals that are used for the production of hardware; low-paid children, women and other workers in Chinese and other manufactur-ing companies assemble the hardware of computers, phones and printers under extremely hard and dangerous working conditions; highly paid and overworked software engineers work for companies such as Google and Microsoft; relatively low-paid knowledge workers in developing countries create, transform, process or edit cultural content and software for firms that are subcontractors to Western media and communications companies; a feminized low-paid workforce takes care of communications services in call-centres and other service factories; and so on. The contradictory relations between communications workers in an interna-tional division of labour pose the question, "Will knowledge workers of the world unite?" (Mosco and McKercher 2008, 13).

"The urban" is "one of the critical sites for contemporary struggle" (David Harvey, quoted in Harvey, Hardt and Negri 2009). "The metropolis is a factory for the production of the common. [. . .] With the passage to the hegemony of biopolitical production, the space of economic production and the space of the city tend to overlap. There is no longer a factory wall that divides the one from the other, and 'externalities' are no longer external to the site of produc-tion that valorises them. Workers produce throughout the metropolis, in its every crack and crevice. In fact, production of the common is becoming nothing but the life of the city itself" (Hardt and Negri 2009, 250–251). Commercial so-cial media show that the Internet is simultaneously a playground and a factory (Scholz 2011). They lock "networked publics in a 'walled garden' where they can be expropriated, where their relationships are put to work, and where their fascinations and desires are monetized" (ibid., 246). Internet user commodification is part of the tendency of the commodification of everything that has resulted in the generalization of the factory and of exploitation. "Commodification presumes the existence of property rights over processes, things, and social relations, that a price can be put on them, and that they can be traded subject to legal contract. [. . .] In practice, of course, every society sets some bounds on where commodification begins and ends" (Harvey 2007, 165). Neo-liberal capitalism has largely widened the boundaries of what is treated as a commodity. "The commodification of sexuality, culture, history, heritage; of nature as spectacle or as rest cure; [. . .]—these all amount to putting a price on things that were never actually produced as commodities" (ibid., 166).

The outsourcing of work to consumers is a general tendency of contemporary capitalism. Facebook has asked users to translate its site into other languages without payment. Javier Olivan, international manager at Facebook, commented that it would be cool to use the wisdom of the crowds.[4] Pepsi started a competition in which one could win US$10,000 for the best design of a Pepsi can. Ideabounty is a crowdsourcing platform that organizes crowdsourcing projects for corporations, as for example Red Bull, BMW or Unilever. In such projects, most of the employed work is unpaid. Even if single individuals receive symbolic prize money, most of the work time employed by users and consumers is fully unpaid, which allows companies to outsource paid labour time to consumers or fans who work for free.

Value is a complex concept. Göran Bolin (2011) identifies economic value, moral value, news value, public value, cultural value, aesthetic value, social value, educational value, political value and symbolic/sign value as specific interpretations of the term. Marx shared with Adam Smith and David Ricardo an objective concept of value. The value of a commodity is for them the "quantity of the 'value-forming substance', the labour, contained in the article", "the amount of labour socially necessary" for its production (Marx 1867c, 129). Marx argues that goods in capitalism have a dual character. They have a use-value side (they are used for achieving certain aims) and a value side. There are aspects of concrete and abstract labour. Concrete labour generates the commodity's use-value (the good's qualitative character as useful good that satisfies human needs), abstract labour the commodity's value (the good's quantitative side that allows its exchange with other commodities in the form of the relationship x amount of commodity A = y amount of commodity B). Subjective concepts of economic value, as held for example by classical French political economists such as Jean-Baptiste Say and Frederic Bastiat or representatives of the neoclassical Austrian school, assume that the worth of a good is determined by humans' cognitive evaluations and moral judgements; they interpret the notion of value idealistically. They say that the value of a good is the value given to them by the subjective judgements of humans.

One problem of the value concept is that its subjective and objective meaning are often mixed up. As the moral value of capitalism is economic value, one needs a precise concept of value. To focus the meaning of the term "value" on economic value does not automatically mean to speak in favour of capitalism and commodification; it only reflects the important role the capitalist economy has in modern society and stresses commodity logic's tendency to attempt to colonize non-commodified realms. For socialists, an important political goal is a world not dominated by economic value. But achieving this goal does not necessarily need a non-economic definition of the value concept.

Marx made a distinction between the concept of value and the concept of price. When we talk about the value of a good, we talk about the average number of hours needed for its production, whereas the price is expressed in quantities of money. "The expression of the value of a commodity in gold— x commodity A $=$ Y money commodity—is its money-form or price" (Marx 1867c, 189). Marx argued that the value and the price of a commodity do not coincide: "the production price of a commodity is not at all identical with its value. [. . .] It has been shown that the production price of a commodity may stand above or below its value and coincides with it only in exceptional cases" (Marx 1894, 892). He also dealt with the question of how values are transformed into prices. Chapter 9 of *Capital, Volume 3* (ibid., 254–272) is devoted to this question.

Information is a peculiar commodity:

- It is not used up in consumption.
- It can be infinitely shared and copied by one individual without losing the good itself. Several people can own it at the same time.
- It has no physical wear and tear. Its wear and tear is what Marx (1867c, 528) called "moral depreciation": it is caused by competition and the drive of companies to establish new versions of informational commodities, such the newest version of the iPod or iPad or a new song by an artist in order to accumulate ever more capital, and by the creation of symbolic difference postulated by advertising and branding so that the older informational commodities appear for consumers to be "outdated".
- It can be easily and cheaply copied and quickly transmitted.
- It is a social good that reflects the history of social interactions and the history of knowledge.
- The value for producing the initial form of information is relatively high (it includes many hours of development costs), whereas starting with the second copy the value is relatively low (work time mainly is the time of copying and distributing the good).
- Information is, however, normally sold at a price that is higher than its value (measured as the amount of hours needed for its production). The difference between value and price is at the heart of profit-making in the information industries.

An artwork sold at a high price makes use of the value-price differential and the ideological belief of the buyers in the superiority of the artist. Similarly, branding can constitute a value-price differential. It is an ideological mechanism that wants to make consumers believe that a commodity has a symbolic value above its economic value. Consumers' ideological belief in the superiority of a certain commodity allows companies to achieve excess profit, a profit higher than yielded for similar use-values. Related phenomena are financial assets that are sold at prices that do not correspond to the profits the underlying commodities are yielding. Marx (1894) speaks in this respect of fictitious capital and David Harvey (2005) of a temporal fix to over-accumulation that results in the deference of "the re-entry of capital values into circulation into the future" (ibid., 109) so that the difference between profits and asset price can result in financial bubbles. Just like there can be a difference between value and price of a commodity, there can be a difference between profit and financial market worth of a financial asset.

Bolin (2011) argues that in broadcasting, not audiences but statisticians work. The advertisers would buy not audiences but the belief in a certain audience value generated by statisticians who relatively arbitrarily measure audience ratings. "Audiences do not work; It is rather the statisticians and market executives who do" (ibid., 84). From a Marxist perspective (which Smythe employed), audiences' work time is the time they consume commercial media. The exact quantity of labour value can never be determined; therefore Marx said that the "individual commodity counts [...] only as an average sample of its kind" (Marx 1867c, 129–130). Audiences create the value of the commercial media commodity, whereas audience statistics determine the price of the audience commodity by approximating average audience numbers based on a sample of a certain size. Statistical workers are crucial in setting prices and transforming labour values of the media into prices.

On corporate social media, users create content, browse content, establish and maintain relations with others by communication, and update their profiles. All time they spend on these platforms is work time. The Internet prosumer commodity that an advertiser buys on Facebook or Google is based on specific demographic data (age, location, education, gender, workplace, etc.) and interests (e.g. certain keywords typed into Google or certain interests identified on Facebook). Thereby a specific group can be identified as a target group. All time spent by members of this group on the specific social media platform constitutes the value (work time) of a specific Internet prosumer commodity. This work time contains time for social relationship management and cultural activities that generate reputation. One therefore needs to reflect on how economic value production by the media is connected to what Bourdieu termed social, cultural and symbolic capital (Bolin 2011). Users employ social media because they strive for a certain degree to achieve what Bourdieu (1986a, b) terms social capital (the accumulation of social relations), cultural capital (the accumulation of qualification, education, knowledge) and symbolic capital (the accumulation of reputation).

The time that users spend on commercial social media platforms for generating social, cultural and symbolic capital is in the process of prosumer commodification transformed into economic capital. Labour time on commercial social media is the conversion of Bourdieusian social, cultural and symbolic capital into Marxian value and economic capital.

Marx (1894) stressed the difference between a commodity's value and price. The price of production of a commodity may lie above or below its value and in some cases coincides with its value. The value level measures the labour needed for the production of commodities in work hours, the price level measures for which amount of money a commodity is sold. The ratings industry transforms the value of the audience commodity into prices. Advertisements are linked to certain programmes because one expects specific kinds of audiences to watch certain programmes (or to read certain parts of a newspaper). The value of one specific programme that is interrupted by advertisements is the sum of the time all viewers spend viewing the programme (including the advertisements). It is impossible to measure this value exactly. Rather, as Marx (1894) knew, only approximations of the average value of a commodity are possible. If more viewers watch a certain programme because it is popular, then its value increases. This makes it likely that also the audience price will be higher because more advertisements will be watched. However, there is no automatic correspondence between value and price of the audience commodity: if one million young, urban, middle-class youngsters who can be expected to buy a lot of commodities watch one programme and two million elderly rural people watch another programme that has the same length, then the second audience commodity's value is higher. However, because of the expectation that young urban people are more consumption-oriented than elderly rural people, the first commodity audience's price (measured as amount of money that an advertiser needs to pay at a certain point of time in the programme slot for a specific advertisement length in order to reach a defined audience of a particular size) may be higher.

Once value has been created on Facebook by online labour, the resulting data commodities are offered to ad clients with the help of either the pay per click (CPC) or the pay per 1,000 impressions (CPM) methods of payment. At this point of analysis, we leave the value level and the commodity production sphere and enter the price level and the sphere of commodity sales. How is the social media prosumer commodities' price determined and how is value transformed into money profit? Advertising clients are interested in the access to specific groups that can be targeted with individualized advertisements that fit their interests. Access to this group and data about their interests (information about who is member of a specific consumer group that shares certain interests) are sold to advertisers. On Google and Facebook, advertisers set a maximum budget for one campaign and a maximum they are willing to pay for one click on their advertisement or for 1,000 impressions (1 impression = a presentation of an ad on a profile). The exact price for one click or for 1,000 impressions is determined in an automated bidding process, in which all advertisers interested in a specific group (all ads targeted at this specific group) compete. In both models, every user is offered as a commodity and commodified, but only certain user groups are sold as commodity. In the pay-per-click model, value is transformed into money (profit is realized) when a user clicks on an ad. In the pay-per-view model, value is transformed into money (profit is realized) when an ad is presented on a user's profile. The price is mathematically determined by an algorithm and based on bids. The number of hours spent online by a specific group of users determines the value of the social media prosumer commodity. The price of this commodity is algorithmically determined.

All hours spent online by users of Facebook, Google and comparable corporate social media constitute work time, in which data commodities are generated, as well as potential time for profit realization. The maximum time of a single user that is productive (i.e. results in data commodities) is 100% of the time spent online. The maximum time that the same user contributes to profit realization by clicking on ads or viewing ads is the time that s/he spends on a specific platform. In practice, users only click on a small share of presented ads. So in the pay-per-click accumulation model, work time tends to be much larger than profit realization time. Online labour creates a lot of commodities that are offered for sale, but only a certain share of that labour is sold and results in profits. This share is still large enough that companies like Google and Facebook can generate significant profits. Online labour time is at the same time potential profit realization time. Capital tries to increase profit realization time in order to accumulate capital, that is, to make an ever-larger share of productive labour time also profit realization time.

According to Facebook, the price of an ad in a bid is determined by the number of people competing for a specific ad space/target audience, by ad quality and ad performance. On Google AdWords, the price of an ad depends on the maximum bid that one sets/can afford and ad quality. Ad quality is based on an assessment of how relevant and well-targeted the text of an ad is (Google, video "AdWords: Control Your Costs"): the more targeted an ad, the lower the CPC cost. Google's quality score of an ad is based on the number of past clicks for the targeted keyword, the display URL's number of past clicks, the "targetedness" of the ad text and the number of past clicks for the ad (Google AdWords Help: Quality Score). Like Facebook, Google offers both CPC and CPM as payment methods. How exactly Google's and Facebook's pricing algorithms work is not known because they are not open-source.

According to statistics, the most expensive keywords on Google are insurance, loans, mortgage, attorney and credit[5]. The most-viewed ads on Facebook are those from the retail sector (23% of all viewed ads), the food and drink industry (19%), the finance industry (14%), the entertainment industry (11%) and the games industry (11%) (http://allfacebook.com/facebook-advertising-rates-2_b86020). (accessed August 8, 2013).

A study of Facebook advertising conducted by Comscore (2012) argues that:

- Users spend 40% of their Facebook time in the news feed; therefore exposure to ads is larger there than on brand pages.
- According to DoubleClick, click-through-rates are on average 0.1%.
- Many companies would today mistakenly see the number of fans on brand pages as a main success indicator for online advertising.
- People exposed to Facebook ads are more likely to purchase products online or in stores than those who are not. The purchase ratio grows with the length of the advertising campaign. The study therefore suggests the importance of "view-through display ad effectiveness in a medium where click-through rates are known to be lower than average for many campaigns" (ibid., 3).

Time dimensions play a crucial role in determining the price of an ad: the number of times people click on an ad, the number of times an ad or target URL has already been viewed, the number of times a keyword has been entered and the time that a specific user group spends on the platform. Furthermore, the bidding maximums used as well as the number of ad clients competing for ad space influence the ad prices. In the pay-per-view method, Facebook and Google earn more with an ad that is targeted to a group that spends a lot of time on Facebook. The larger the target group, the higher Facebook's and Google's profits tend to be. In the pay-per-click method, Facebook and Google only earn money if users click on an ad. According to studies, the average click-through-rate is 0.1% (Comscore 2012). This means that Facebook and Google tend to gain more profit if ads are presented to more users.

Generally one can say that the higher the total attention time given to ads, the higher Google's and Facebook's profits tend to be. Attention time is determined by the size of a target group and the average time this group spends on the platforms. Online time on corporate social media is both labour time and attention time: All activities are monitored and result in data commodities, so users produce commodities online during their online time. In the pay-per-view mode, specific online time of specifically targeted groups is also attention time that realizes profit for Facebook or Google. In the pay-per-click mode, attention time that realizes profit is only the portion of the online time that users devote to clicking on ads that are presented to them. In both cases, online time is crucial for (a) the production of data commodities and (b) the realization of profit derived from the sales of the data commodities. Both surveillance of online time (in the sphere of production) and attention time (in the sphere of circulation) given to advertisements play an important role in corporate social media's capital accumulation model.

According to Google Trends, Michael Jackson was one of the top trending search keywords on Google on June 27, 2012. Using the Google AdWords traffic estimator (on June 27, 2012) showed that by creating a campaign with a maximum CPC of 10€ and a budget of 1,000€ per day, one can expect to attract

2,867–3,504 impressions and 112–137 clicks for total costs of 900–1100€ per day
if one targets Google users who search for "Michael Jackson". In comparison,
I used the same settings for the keyword "Cat Power" (an American indie rock
singer, much less popular and less sought-after on Google than Michael Jackson).
In a campaign that targets users who google "Cat Power", one can expect to
attract 108–132 impressions and 3.9–4.7 clicks for total costs of 30.96–37.84€
per day. The profit that Google makes with the data commodity associated with
the keyword "Michael Jackson" is much larger than the one it makes with the
keyword "Cat Power" because the first is a more sought-after keyword. And that
a keyword is popular means that users spend more collective usage time per day
entering the keyword and reading result pages than for other keywords. The example shows that popular interests, for whose generation and result consumption
users spend more labour time on the Internet than for not-so-popular keywords,
tend to result in higher profits for Google than interests that are not so popular.

Marx formulated the law of value as saying that "the greater the labour-time
necessary to produce an article, [. . .] the greater its value" (Marx 1867c, 131). The
law of value also applies in the case of commercial social media: The more time
a user spends on commercial social media, the more data about her/his interests
and activities are available and the more advertisements are presented to her/
him. Users spending a lot of time online create more data and more value (work
time) that is potentially transformed into profit. That the law of value applies on
commercial social media can also be observed by the circumstance that there are
high prices for advertisements presented in the context of frequently searched
keywords on Google. A lot of users spend their work time on searching for these
keywords: that is, the value (work time) underlying specific keywords is high. This
makes the corresponding user commodity more precious (it is likely to be a large
group); therefore its price can be set at a high rate.

That surplus-value-generating labour is an emergent property of capitalist production means that production and accumulation will break down if this
labour is withdrawn. It is an essential part of the capitalist production process.
That prosumers conduct surplus-generating labour can also be seen by imagining
what would happen if they would stop using Facebook or Google: The number
of users would drop, advertisers would stop investments because no objects for
their advertising messages and therefore no potential customers for their products
could be found, the profits of the new media corporations would drop and they
would go bankrupt. If such activities were carried out on a large scale, a new
economy crisis would arise. This thought experiment shows that users are essential for generating profit in the new media economy. Furthermore they produce
and co-produce parts of the products and therefore parts of the use-value, value
and surplus value that are objectified in these products.

Not all prosumer work on social media is commodified (just like not
all audience work is commodified). Work that contributes content, attention or comments to non-commercial non-profit projects (such as Wikipedia;

alternative online news media such as Indymedia, Alternet, Democracy Now!, open Democracy, WikiLeaks; or the use of social media by NGOs) is work in the sense that it helps creating use values (alternative news, critical discourse, etc.), but it is non-commodified work, it cannot be exploited, it does not have exchange value and it does not yield profit. Non-commercial non-profit online projects are an expression of the struggle for a society and an Internet that is not ruled by the logic of commodities and exchange value. Although they are frequently precarious, the existence of alternatives shows that social media and media in general are in capitalism shaped by (a) class structures, (b) ideological "incorporation and legitimation" and (c) "gaps and contradictions" that constitute "cracks and fissures" that allow "currents of criticism and movements of contestation" (Golding and Murdock 1978, 353).

Corporate social media have an immanent connection to finance capital. Google's profits were US$9.7 billion in 2011 (SEC Filings Form 10-K 2011), whereas its financial market valuation (stock market capitalization) was US$182 billion on June 26, 2012.[6] Facebook's profits were US$1 billion in 2011 (SEC Filings Form S-1 Registration statement), whereas its stock market capitalization was US$70 billion on June 26, 2012.[7] This shows that the financial market values achieved on the stock market and the profits achieved by Internet prosumer commodification do not coincide. Companies like Facebook and Google are overvalued on the stock market; their profits do not match the high market values. This divergence phenomenon does not lie outside of the logic of Marxist theory, but was rather described by Marx (1894) in the analysis of fictitious capital in *Capital, Volume 3*.

For Marx, financial capital is based on the formula M (money)—M' (more money). "Here we have M—M', money that produces money, self-valorizing value, without the process that mediates the two extremes" (ibid., 515, see also 471). Consumer credits, mortgages, stock, bonds and derivates are all based on this financial type of accumulation. Finance capital does not itself produce profit, it is only an entitlement to payments that are made in the future and derive from profits or wages (the latter for example in the case of consumer credits). Marx therefore characterizes finance capital as fictitious capital (ibid., 596). The "share is nothing but an ownership title, *pro rata,* to the surplus-value which this capital is to realize. A may sell this title to B, and B to C. These transactions have no essential effect on the matter. A or B has then transformed his title into capital, but C has transformed his capital into a mere ownership title to the surplus-value expected from this share capital" (ibid., 597–598). Financial investments in stocks and financial derivates are transformed into operative capital, but they are not capital themselves, only ownership titles to a part of surplus value that is expected to be produced in the future. "All these securities actually represent nothing but accumulated claims, legal titles, to future production" (ibid., 599). The value of shares is therefore speculative and connected not to the actual profits of the company, but only to expectations about future profits that determine buying and selling decisions of stock investors: "The market value of these securities is partly speculative, since it is determined not just by the actual revenue but rather by the anticipated revenue as reckoned in advance" (ibid., 598, see also 608, 641). The result is a high-risk system of speculation that resembles gambling (ibid., 609) and is crisis-prone (ibid., 621). "Monetary crises, independent of real crises or as an intensification of them, are unavoidable" in capitalism (ibid., 649).

Financialization is a crucial aspect of corporate social media platforms like Facebook and Google. Financialization is a mechanism that Marx described as an important element of capitalism. User labour is the source of profit on these platforms. Finance capital invests in platforms like Facebook and Google because it has the expectation of high future profits. The new economy crisis in 2000 has shown that the difference between stock market values and actual profits can result, as Marx knew, in bursting financial bubbles that then result in economic crises. Crises can have multiple sources (e.g. lack of sales = overproduction, underconsumption; class struggle that increases investments and negatively impacts profits (profit-squeeze); over-accumulation; crisis events that trigger large-scale sales of stocks and disappointed investment situations; combinations of some of these sources of crises, etc.). The stock market values of companies like Google and Facebook are based on expectations of how well these corporations will in the future be able to exploit users' and employees' labour and turn it into profit. The actual profit rates influence but do not determine stock market investors' buying and selling decisions. The latter are determined by multiple factors and expectations, especially expectations about potential futures, which is the reason why Marx speaks of fictitious capital.

Capital has the inherent interest to maximize profit. For doing this, it will take all means necessary because the single capitalist risks his/her own bankruptcy if s/he cannot accumulate capital as a result of high investment costs, heavy competition, lack of productivity and other reasons. The wage relation is, as we have argued earlier, a crucial element of class struggle. Capital tries to reduce the wage sum as much as possible in order to maximize profits. If possible, capital will therefore remunerate labour-power below its own value, that is, below the socially necessary costs that are required for survival. The transformation of the value into the price of labour-power and the difference between the two is, as Cleaver (2000) and Bidet (2009) stress, the result of class struggle. Labour legislation and an organized labour movement can struggle for wages that are higher than the value of labour-power. If labour is, however, weak (e.g. because of fascist repression), capital is likely to use any opportunity to reduce wages as much as possible in order to increase profits. Neo-liberalism is a form of governmentality that increases profits by decreasing the wage sum with the help of cutting state expenditures for welfare, care and education; privatizing such services; creating precarious wage-relations that are temporary, insecure and underpaid; weakening the power of labour organizations; decreasing or not increasing wages relatively or absolutely; outsourcing labour to low-paid or unpaid forms of production;

coercing the unemployed to work without payment or for extremely low wages, and so forth. It is a form of politics that aims at helping capital to reduce the price of labour-power as much as possible, if possible even below the minimum value that is needed for human existence. The creation of multiple forms of precarious and unpaid forms of work is an expression of the class struggle of capital to reduce the costs of labour-power. The result is a disjuncture of the value and price of labour-power. Digital labour should be situated in the context of capital's actual struggle to reduce the price of labour-power and potential resistance by the working class. The disjuncture between value and price of labour-power is accompanied by a disjuncture of the value and price of commodities: The financialization of the economy has established stocks and derivatives that have fictitious prices on stock markets that are based on the hope for high future profits and dividends, but these are disjointed from the actual labour values and commodity prices. Contemporary capitalism is a disjuncture economy, in which values, profits and prices tend to be out of joint so that there is a high crisis-proneness.

After analysing the commodity and capital side of corporate social media, I will in the next section discuss changes in the relationship between play and labour and relate them to the digital labour debate.

4.5. Ideology, Play and Digital Labour

Ideology takes on two distinct forms in relationship to contemporary digital media:

(1)   The presentation of social media as a form of participatory culture and new democracy.
(2)   The hidden appearance of exploitation as play.

Ideological claims are not specific for what some term "Web 2.0"; rather earlier claims about the Internet in the 1990s also constituted a "Californian ideology" (Barbrook and Cameron 2001) that stresses individualism, personal responsibility, competition, private property and consumerism, lacks consciousness of inequality and exploitation and is in line with the basic ideas of neo-liberalism (Fisher 2010). Neubauer (2011) stresses in this context the existence of a specific ideology of informational neo-liberalism that combines the belief in the power of ICTs and neo-liberal values.

The turn of the millennium saw a crisis of heavily financialized Internet companies. The "dot-com" crisis destroyed the hopes that the "Internet age" would result in a new age of prosperity and unhampered economic growth. In the years following the crisis, companies such as Facebook (2004), Flickr (2004), LinkedIn (2003), Sina Weibo (2009), Tumblr (2007), Twitter (2006), VK (VKontakte, 2006), Wordpress (2003) and YouTube (2005, sold to Google in 2006) were founded. They provide Internet services that are today among the most accessed web platforms in the world. They represent capitalists' new aspiring hopes to found a new capital accumulation model that is based on targeted advertising.

The rise of these platforms was accompanied by an ideology that celebrated these services as radically new and the rise of an economic democracy and participatory culture. Henry Jenkins (2008, 275) argues that "the Web has become a site of consumer participation" and has supported the rise of a participatory culture. Axel Bruns argues that Flickr, YouTube, MySpace and Facebook are environments of "public participation" (Bruns 2008, 227–228) and give rise to "a produsage-based democratic model" (372). John Hartley (2012) describes the emergence of a "dialogical model of communication" (2), in which "everyone is a producer" (3). His general argument is that with the rise of online platforms that support social networking and user-generated content production and diffusion, journalism, the public sphere, universities, the mass media, citizenship, archives and other institutions have become more democratic because "people have more say in producing as well as consuming" (ibid., 14). Clay Shirky (2008, 297) says that "Web 2.0" means the "democratization of production". Tapscott and Williams see the rise of a new economy they call "wikinomics" that results in the emergence of "a new economic democracy" (Tapscott and Williams 2006, 267).

Especially management gurus and cultural theorists have made the claim that user-generated content platforms have advanced a participatory economy and culture. They have helped to sell "Web 2.0" as the "next big thing" that venture capitalists need to invest in. The hype turned out to be more about capital accumulation than democracy. The discussions about terms such as "social media" and "Web 2.0" started when Tim O'Reilly (2005) introduced the term "Web 2.0" in 2005. Although Tim O'Reilly surely thinks that "Web 2.0" denotes actual changes and says that the crucial fact about it is that users as a collective intelligence co-create the value of platforms like Google, Amazon, Wikipedia or craigslist in a "community of connected users" (O'Reilly and Battelle 2009, 1), he admits that the term was mainly created for identifying the need of new economic strategies of Internet companies after the "dot-com" crisis, in which the bursting of financial bubbles caused the collapse of many Internet companies. So he says in a paper published five years after the creation of the term "Web 2.0" that this category was "a statement about the second coming of the Web after the dotcom bust" at a conference that was "designed to restore confidence in an industry that had lost its way after the dotcom bust" (ibid.). This means that the person who coined the notion of Web 2.0 admits that it is an ideology aimed at attracting investors.

Web 2.0 enthusiasts tend to use the notion of participation in a shallow way, forgetting that it main use stems from participatory democracy theory, in which it signifies the control of ownership, decision-making and value-definition by all (Fuchs 2011a, chapter 7). Statistics such as the ownership structures of Web 2.0 companies, the most viewed videos on YouTube, the most popular Facebook groups, the most popular topics on Google and Twitter and the Twitter users with the highest number of followers show that the corporate Web 2.0 is not a democratic space of equal participants, but a space in which large companies, celebrities and entertainment dominate. They achieve a much higher number of followers, readers, viewers, listeners, re-tweets, likes and so on than the everyday users (ibid.). If a claim about reality is disjointed from actual reality, then one commonly characterizes such a claim as an ideology. "Web 2.0" and "social media", conceived as participatory culture and participatory economy, are ideological categories that serve the interests of the dominant class. They ignore power structures that shape the Internet.

Claims about the power of "social media" are not only trying to attract business investments, but also have a hegemonic side in the life and thought of everyday users. Jodi Dean (2005) speaks in this context of Internet fetishism and argues that it is an ideology to assume that the Internet is inherently political and that "Web 2.0" is a form of politics in itself: "Busy people can think they are active—the technology will act for them, alleviating their guilt while assuring them that nothing will change too much. [. . .] By sending an e-mail, signing a petition, responding to an article on a blog, people can feel political. And that feeling feeds communicative capitalism insofar as it leaves behind the time-consuming, incremental and risky efforts of politics. [. . .] It is a refusal to take a stand, to venture into the dangerous terrain of politicization" (Dean 2005, 70).

But ideology not only takes on the form of overdrawn claims about the democratic implications of "social media". It is also present in the media production process itself, in which exploitation as social relation tends to be hidden in structures of play. The labour side of the capital accumulation strategy of social media corporations is digital playbour. Kücklich (2005) first introduced the term playbour (play+labour). The exploitation of digital playbour is based on the collapse of the distinction between work time and play time. In the Fordist mode of capitalist production, work time was the time of pain and the time of repression and surplus repression of the human drive for pleasure, whereas leisure time was the time of Eros (Marcuse 1955). In contemporary capitalism, play and labour, Eros and Thanatos, the pleasure principle and the death drive, partially converge: workers are expected to have fun during work time and play time becomes productive and work-like. Play time and work time intersect and all human time of existence tends to be exploited for the sake of capital accumulation.

Capitalism connects labour and play in a destructive dialectic. Traditionally, play in the form of enjoyment, sex and entertainment was in capitalism only part of spare time, which was rather unproductive (in the sense of producing commodities for sale) and separate from labour time. Freud (1961) argued that the structure of drives is characterized by a dialectic of Eros (the drive for life, sexuality, lust) and Thanatos (the drive for death, destruction, aggression). Humans according to Freud strive for the permanent realization of Eros (pleasure principle), but culture would only become possible by a temporal negation and suspension of Eros and the transformation of erotic energy into culture and labour. Labour would be a productive form of desexualization—the repression of sexual drives. Freud speaks in this context of the reality principle or sublimation. The reality principle sublates the pleasure principle. Human culture thereby sublates human nature and becomes man's second nature.

Marcuse (1955) connected Freud's theory of drives to Marx's theory of capitalism. He argued that alienated labour, domination and capital accumulation have turned the reality principle into a repressive reality principle—the performance principle: alienated labour constitutes a surplus-repression of Eros. The repression of the pleasure principle takes on a quantity that exceeds the culturally necessary suppression. Marcuse connected Marx's notions of necessary labour and surplus labour/value to the Freudian drive structure of humans and argued that necessary labour on the level of drives corresponds to necessary suppression and surplus labour to surplus-repression. This means that in order to exist, a society needs a certain amount of necessary labour (measured in hours of work) and hence a certain corresponding amount of suppression of the pleasure principle (also measured in hours). The exploitation of surplus value (labour that is performed for free and generates profit) results not only in the circumstance that workers are forced to work for free for capital to a certain extent, but also in the circumstance that the pleasure principle must be additionally suppressed.

"Behind the reality principle lies the fundamental fact of Ananke or scarcity (*Lebensnot*), which means that the struggle for existence takes place in a world too poor for the satisfaction of human needs without constant restraint, renunciation, delay. In other words, whatever satisfaction is possible necessitates work, more or less painful arrangements and undertakings for the procurement of the means for satisfying needs. For the duration of work, which occupies practically the entire existence of the mature individual, pleasure is 'suspended' and pain prevails" (ibid., 35). In societies that are based on the principle of domination, the reality principle takes on the form of the performance principle: Domination "is exercised by a particular group or individual in order to sustain and enhance itself in a privileged situation" (ibid., 36). The performance principle is connected to surplus-repression, a term that describes "the restrictions necessitated by social domination" (ibid., 35). Domination introduces "additional controls over and above those indispensable for civilized human association" (ibid., 37).

Marcuse (1955) argues that the performance principle means that Thanatos governs humans and society and that alienation unleashes aggressive drives within humans (repressive desublimation) that result in an overall violent and aggressive society. Because of the high productivity reached in late-modern society, a historical alternative would be possible: the elimination of the repressive reality principle, the reduction of necessary working time to a minimum and the maximization of free time, an eroticization of society and the body, the shaping of society and humans by Eros and the emergence of libidinous social relations. Such a development would be a historical possibility—but one incompatible with capitalism and patriarchy.

Gilles Deleuze (1995) has pointed out that in contemporary capitalism, disciplinary power is transformed in such a way that humans increasingly discipline themselves without direct external violence. He terms this situation the society of (self-)control. It can for example be observed in the strategies of participatory management. This method promotes the use of incentives and the integration of play into labour. It argues that work should be fun, workers should permanently develop new ideas, realize their creativity, enjoy free time within the factory, and so on. The boundaries between work time and spare time, labour and play, become fuzzy. Work tends to acquire qualities of play, whereas entertainment in spare time tends to become labour-like. Work time and spare time become inseparable. At the same time, work-related stress intensifies and property relations remain unchanged (Boltanski and Chiapello 2007). Corporate social media's exploitation of Internet users is an aspect of this transformation. It signifies that private Internet usage, which is motivated by play, entertainment, fun and joy—aspects of Eros—has become subsumed under capital and has become a sphere of the exploitation of labour. Internet corporations accumulate profit by exploiting the play labour of users.

Luc Boltanski and Ève Chiapello (2007) argue that the rise of participatory management means the emergence of a new spirit of capitalism that subsumes the anti-authoritarian values of the political revolt of 1968 and the subsequently emerging New Left—such as autonomy, spontaneity, mobility, creativity, networking, visions, openness, plurality, informality, authenticity, emancipation, and so on—under capital. The topics of the movement would now be put into the service of those forces that it wanted to destroy. The outcome would have been "the construction of the new, so-called 'network' capitalism" (ibid., 429) so that artistic critique—which calls for authenticity, creativity, freedom and autonomy in contrast to social critique, which calls for equality and overcoming class (37–38)—today "indirectly serves capitalism and is one of the instruments of its ability to endure" (490).

Also paid creative industry work is becoming more like play today. Hesmondhalgh and Baker (2011) show the ambivalence of much creative industry work that is precarious but cherished because of the fun, contacts, reputation, creativity and self-determination that it may involve. The difficulty is that labour feels like play and that exploitation and fun thereby become inseparable. Play and labour are today in certain cases indistinguishable. Eros has become fully subsumed under the repressive reality principle. Play is largely commodified, and spaces and free time that are not exploited by capital hardly exist today. They are difficult to create and to defend. Play is today productive, surplus-value-generating labour that is exploited by capital. All human activities, and therefore also all play, tends under the contemporary conditions to become subsumed under and exploited by capital. Play as an expression of Eros is thereby destroyed, human freedom and human capacities are crippled. On corporate social media, play and labour converge into play labour that is exploited for capital accumulation. The

TABLE 4.1 Pleasures in four modes of society (human essence, society with scarcity, classical capitalism, capitalism in the age of corporate social media)

Essence of human desires	Reality principle in societies with scarcity	Repressive reality principle in classical capitalism	Repressive reality principle in capitalism in the age of corporate social media
immediate satisfaction	delayed satisfaction	delayed satisfaction	immediate online satisfaction
pleasure	restraint of pleasure	leisure time: pleasure; work time: restraint of pleasure, surplus repression of pleasure	collapse of leisure time and work time, leisure time becomes work time and work time leisure time, all time becomes exploited, online leisure time becomes surplus value-generating, wage labour time = surplus repression time of pleasure, play labour time = surplus value-generating pleasure time
joy (play)	toil (work)	leisure time: joy (play); work time: toil (work)	play labour: joy and play as toil and work, toil and work as joy and play
receptiveness	productiveness	leisure time: receptiveness; work time: productiveness	collapse of the distinction between leisure time/work time and receptiveness/productiveness, total commodification of human time
absence of repression of pleasure	repression of pleasure	leisure time: absence of repression of pleasure; work time: repression of pleasure	play labour time: surplus value generation appears to be pleasure-like, but serves the logic of repression (the lack of ownership of capital)

Source: Based on a table from Marcuse (1955, 12).

corporate Internet therefore stands for the total commodification and exploitation of time—all human time tends to become surplus-value-generating time that is exploited by capital. Table 4.1 summarizes the application of Marcuse's theory of play, labour and pleasure to corporate social media.

Some authors have criticized the main arguments advanced in the digital labour debate. In the next section, I present and discuss some of the points of criticism.

4.6. A Critique of the Critique of Digital Labour

David Hesmondhalgh (2010) argues that Internet labour is not exploited because there is much cultural work in society that is unpaid. "Most cultural production in history has been unpaid, and that continues to be the case today. Consider the millions of people across the world, especially young people, who will, on the day you are reading this, be practising musical instruments, or, to use an example from an industry that I would call a leisure industry rather than a cultural industry, imagine how many young people are practising football or basketball. Now it could be argued that all this represents labour (defined here as the expenditure of effort, under some kind of compulsion; it will usually seem preferable to undertake some other more restful activity) which is vital to the realisation of surplus value in the music industry or the football industry. For this work helps to create a reservoir of workers, from whom these industries can draw" (ibid., 277). Hesmondhalgh says that the claim "that contacting friends and uploading photographs on to Facebook represents some kind of exploited labour is, to my mind, more along the lines of arguing that we should demand that all amateur football coaches be paid for their donation of free time: not impossible to argue for, but hardly a priority—and accompanied by the danger that it may commodify forms of activity that we would ultimately prefer to leave outside the market" (278).

Hesmondhalgh mixes up two different types of activity:

(1) hobby or private activities, in which labour-power is reproduced but no commodities are produced (like playing football or sleeping);
(2) hobby activities, in which value is generated that is directly appropriated by capitalist companies (using commercial Internet platforms, watching commercial television, etc.).

Hesmondhalgh conflates different activities—reproductive activity that re-creates labour-power but produces no commodity that is sold, and reproductive activities that recreate labour-power and at the same time create an audience or Internet prosumer commodity. If a wage for either or both of these activities should be demanded (there are pro- and counter-arguments from a left-wing political perspective) is another (political) question, but Hesmondhalgh ignores the direct role of class, commodification and profit in the second type of activity.

The audience and digital labour are definitely exploited on corporate social media because three conditions of exploitation (Wright 1997, 10) are given:

(a) The profit accumulated deprives the audience and users of material benefits (inverse interdependent welfare).
(b) Audience and users are excluded from the ownership of media organizations and the accumulated profit (exclusion).
(c) Capital appropriates the created profit (appropriation).

Pasquinelli (2009, 2010) argues that Google creates and accumulates value by its page rank algorithm. He says that Google's profit is a form of cognitive rent. Caraway (2011, 701) shares this analysis on a more general level and argues, "The economic transaction described by Smythe is *rent*. The media owner rents the use of the medium to the industrial capitalist who is interested in gaining access to an audience. The rental may be either for time (broadcasting) or space (print). It is the job of the media owner to create an environment which is conducive to the formation of a particular audience". Rent theories of the Internet substitute categories like class, surplus value and exploitation with the notion of rent.

Marx (1867c) showed that technology never creates value but is only a tool that is used by living human labour for creating commodities. Therefore it is a technological-deterministic assumption that the page rank algorithm creates value. Marx (1894) argued that rent is exchanged for land and formulated the trinity formula that expresses the three aspects of the value of a commodity (chapter 48): profit (including interest), rent, wages. Profit is attached to capital, rent to land and wages to wage labour. The three kinds of revenue are connected to the selling of commodities, land and labour-power. Rent is obtained by lending land or real estates. Rent is not the direct result of surplus value production and human labour. No new product is created in the renting process. Rent indirectly stems from surplus value because capitalists take part of the surplus in order to rent houses, but it is created in a secondary process, in which surplus value is used for buying real estates. "First we have the use-value land, which has no value, and the exchange-value rent" (ibid., 956). "Value is labour. So surplus-value cannot be earth" (ibid., 954). Therefore, using the category of rent for describing commercial media and Internet practices and their outcomes means to assume that activities on the corporate media and Internet, such as surfing on Google or creating content on YouTube or Facebook, are not exploited and are no form of labour. The category of cognitive rent is not useful for a Critical Political Economy of the Media and the Internet. The notion of the Internet prosumer commodity that is created by exploited knowledge labour is more feasible.

Adam Arvidsson formulated a critique of the digital labour hypothesis and of Smythe's audience commodity approach. "As a consequence, the labor theory of value only holds if labor has a price, if it has been transformed into a commodity that can in some way be bought and sold on a market. It is clear already at this point that it is difficult to apply the labor theory of value to productive practices that do not have a given price, that unfold outside of the wage relation" (Arvidsson 2011, 265). "The circumstance that digital labour has no price and that it becomes impossible to distinguish productive time from unproductive time" would make "it difficult to sustain, as Arvidsson [(2006)], Fuchs [(2009a)], and Cote and Phybus [(2007)] have done, that the Marxist concept of 'exploitation' would apply to processes of customer co-production" (Arvidsson 2011, 266–267). "But since 'free labor' is free, it has no price, and cannot, consequently, be a source of value" (ibid.). Arvidsson's conclusion is that digital labour is not exploited because it has no price (i.e. it is unpaid).

Digital labour is not the only work that has historically been unpaid; one can think also of housework or slave work. Marxist feminists have argued that house workers are an exploited colony of capitalist patriarchy that is a locus of "ongoing primitive accumulation" (Mies, Bennholdt-Thomsen and Werlhof

1988, 6): they are unpaid, unfree and fulfil a function for capitalism. They are therefore a locus of extreme exploitation. The argument of Marxist feminism is that "subsistence production—mainly performed through the non-wage labour of women and other non-wage labourers as slaves, contracted workers and peasants in the colonies—constitutes the perennial basis upon which 'capitalist productive forces' can be built up and exploited" (Mies 1986, 48).

There is a crucial difference between classical slaves, house workers and corporate Internet users because the first are repressed by physical violence (they are likely to be killed if they stop working) and the second are partly coerced by physical violence and feelings of love and affection, whereas the third are ideologically coerced (they are compelled to use the dominant corporate Internet platforms in order to maintain social relations and reputation; if they stop using the platforms, they do not die but are likely to be more isolated). But all three forms of labour produce value that is appropriated by others (the slave master, capitalists and wageworkers, corporations). They are unpaid. Others exploit all of their work time. Arvidsson's false assumption that exploitation is only present if a wage is paid downplays the horrors of exploitation and implies also that classical slaves and house workers are not exploited. His assumption has, therefore, problematic implications in the context of racist modes of production and patriarchy. It is furthermore interesting that Arvidsson criticizes himself for having shared the thesis of the exploitation of free labour in an article published in 2006.

The reality of digital media is that iPhones and Nokia phones, iPads and iMacs are "blood phones", "blood pads" and "blood Macs": Many smartphones, laptops, digital cameras, MP3 players, and the like are made out of minerals (e.g. cassiterite, wolframite, coltan, gold, tungsten, tantalum, tin) that are extracted under slave-like conditions from mines in the Democratic Republic of Congo and other countries. The existence of the Internet in its current dominant capitalist form is based on various forms of labour: the relatively highly paid wage work of software engineers and low-paid proletarianized workers in Internet companies, the unpaid labour of users and the highly exploited bloody Taylorist work and slave work in developing countries producing hardware and extracting "conflict minerals". Arvidsson's approach implies that unpaid Congolese slave workers who extract the material foundations of ICTs are not exploited, which has problematic implications.

Arvidsson's alternative to the labour theory of value is an idealistic and subjectivist concept of value—ethical value understood as "the ability to create the kinds of affectively significant relations" (Arvidsson 2011, 270)—that ignores the reality of material inequality, precarious labour and gaps between the rich and the poor and assumes that everything in the contemporary economy has become affective.

Arvidsson (2011, 273) argues that I have come to the "absurd suggestion that Facebook users are subject to 'infinite levels of exploitation' since the exchange value of their labor is zero". In a comment on one of my digital labour articles (Fuchs 2010b), Arvidsson and Colleoni argue: "If Facebook made a profit of

$355 million in 2010 [. . .], this means that each Facebook user was a 'victim of exploitation of surplus value' to the extent of $0.7 a year, [. . .] hardly [. . .] 'a rate of exploitation that converges towards infinity' as Fuchs claims" (Arvidsson and Colleoni 2012, 138). Fuchs (2012e) provides a more detailed critique of Arvidsson's work. Arvidsson and his colleague mix up value and price. If 500 million people use a corporate platform that is funded by targeted advertising for an average of 90 hours a year (which is on average 15 minutes a day), then the value created is 45 billion hours of digital labour. All of this online time is monitored and creates a traffic commodity that is offered for sale to advertisers; none of the time is paid. Forty-five billion hours of work are therefore exploited. Exploitation is constituted by the unpaid work time that is objectified in a commodity and appropriated by capital. To which extent the data commodity can be sold is a question of the transformation of value into profit. If not enough data commodities are sold, then the profit will be low. Workers are however also exploited if the commodities they create are not sold because value and surplus value of a commodity is created before it is sold. Arvidsson's criticism implies that exploitation is based in the sphere of commodity circulation and not in the sphere of commodity production. This assumption is absurd because it implies that workers who create a commodity that is not sold (e.g. because there is a lack of demand) are not exploited. Arvidsson's criticism is based on a lack of knowledge of Marx.

Marx stressed the difference between a commodity's value and price. The measure of the substance of value of a commodity is the amount of hours needed for its production: "How then is the magnitude of this value [of a commodity] to be measured? By means of the quantity of the 'value-forming substance', the labour, contained in the article. This quantity is measured by its duration, and the labour-time is itself measured on the particular scale of hours, days etc." (Marx 1867c, 129). "Every commodity (product or instrument of production) is = the objectification of a given amount of labour time" (Marx 1857/1858b, 140). Marx formulated the law of value as saying that "the greater the labour-time necessary to produce an article, [. . .] the greater its value. The value of a commodity, therefore, varies directly as the quantity, an inversely as the productivity, of the labour which finds its realisation within the commodity. (Now we know the *substance* of value. It is *labour*. We know the *measure of its magnitude*. It is labour-time" (Marx 1867c, 131).

Price is not the same as value: "The expression of the value of a commodity in gold x commodity A = y money commodity—is its money-form or price" (ibid., 189). "Price is the money-name of the labour objectified in a commodity" (ibid., 195–196). This means that values are determined at the level of working hours and prices at the level of money. Both are quantitative measures, but they use different units of measurement. Value is a measure of the production process, price a measure of the circulation process (selling) of commodities. Labour is extended in time (and space) in the production process, in which commodities are created, and is transformed into profit (measured as a price in money) in the sphere of circulation (i.e. commodity markets, on which commodities are sold for certain prices).

This means that *exploitation of labour takes place before the selling of commodities.* Even if a commodity is not sold, once it is produced, labour has been exploited.

When introducing the concept of brand value in an article that also mentions Smythe, Adam Arvidsson (2005, 238) immediately gives figures of brand values in US dollars, which shows that he thinks of value in terms of money (that signifies only the price of a commodity) and not in working hours (that signify the value of a commodity). The definition of brand value as "the present value of predictable future earnings generated by the brand" (Arvidsson 2005, 238) is not only circular and therefore absurd (definition of value by value), but it also makes clear that Arvidsson defines value only at the price level ("earnings").

4.7. Conclusion

The global capitalist crisis has resulted in cracks, fissures and holes in neo-liberalism and the logic of the commodification of everything. It has, however, brought not an end to neo-liberalism but a phase of uncertainty. There is a renewed interest in Marx's works, critical theory, Critical Political Economy, class and the critique of capitalism. Media and communication studies should see the sign of the times and build a strong focus on Marxism, class and capitalism. The engagement with Dallas Smythe's works today is a contribution to the renewal of Marxist media and communication studies.

Dallas Smythe spoke of the audience commodity and Jhally and Livant of watching as working for analysing media commodification. Internet and media watching/reading/listening/using is value-generating labour, and the audience commodity and the Internet prosumer commodity are commodities created by the work of watching/reading/listening/using. The audience produces itself as commodity; its work creates the audience and users as commodity. Media usage is, in the case of commercial, advertising-funded media, audience labour. Audience time is in value-generating labour time—capital exploits the unremunerated audience. In the case of commercial social media such as Facebook, audience labour time is quite active, social and creative labour time—it is not just audience labour, but prosumer labour. The online character of prosumer labour allows platforms to monitor all activities of the users and to sell targeted advertising space to ad clients that are able to tailor ads according to not just estimations but exact observations of usage behaviour.

We can summarize the main points of this chapter:

- Dallas Smythe reminds us of the importance of engagement with Marx's works for studying the media in capitalism critically.
- Both critical theory and Critical Political Economy of the Media and Communication have been criticized for being one-sided. Such interpretations are mainly based on selective readings. They ignore that in both approaches there has been with different weightings a focus on aspects of media

commodification, audiences, ideology and alternatives. Critical theory and Critical Political Economy are complementary and should be combined in critical media and communication studies today.

- Dallas Smythe's notion of the audience commodity has gained new relevance in the debate about the exploitation of digital labour by corporate Internet providers. The exploitation of digital labour involves processes of coercion, alienation and appropriation.
- Corporate social media use capital accumulation models that are based on the exploitation of the unpaid labour of Internet users and on the commodification of user-generated-data and data about user behaviour that are sold as commodities to advertisers. Targeted advertising and economic surveillance are important aspects of this accumulation model. The category of the audience commodity becomes in the realm of social media transmogrified into the category of the Internet prosumer commodity.
- Corporate "social media" and "Web 2.0" do not imply a democratization of the economy and culture, but are rather ideologies that celebrate new capital accumulation models and thereby help to attract investors.
- The exploitation of the Internet prosumer commodity is a manifestation of a stage of capitalism, in which the boundaries between play and labour have become fuzzy and the exploitation of play labour has become a new principle. Exploitation tends to feel like fun and becomes part of free time.
- Critics of the digital labour debate conflate different work activities, tend to trivialize exploitation and to a certain degree misunderstand concepts like surplus value, value, price and rent.

Capitalism is highly contradictory today. The crisis is a manifestation of capitalism's objective immanent contradictions that it is unable to overcome. The reactions to the crisis are contradictory: they range from hyper-neo-liberalism (politics that want to intensify neo-liberalism by implementing "socialism for the rich and banks" and privatizing and cutting public funding for welfare, education, health, etc.) to uproars, riots, protests, demonstrations and occupations (like the Occupy movement or the protests in Greece, Spain and Portugal) and revolutions (as in Tunisia, Egypt and Libya). These struggles and forms of politics reflect the subjective contradictions of capitalism in crisis times. It is the task of critical intellectuals today to engage in the academic and political struggle for a just world that is based on common goods and services, including the communication commons. Chapters 3 and 4 have contextualized the digital labour debate in the academic landscape of Cultural Studies and Critical Political Economy. A further contextualization that will be undertaken in the next chapter concerns digital labour's embeddedness into the broader societal and economic context that is discussed under headlines such as information society, information economy, creative and cultural industries and knowledge work. In which type of society do we live? Is it an information society? Or is it a capitalist society? The next chapter deals with these questions.

Notes

1 http://www.marxists.org/reference/archive/mao/selected-works/volume-5/mswv5_65.htm. (accessed August 8, 2013).

2 http://www.marxists.org/reference/archive/mao/selected-works/volume-8/mswv8_09.htm (accessed July 9, 2013).

3 http://newsroom.fb.com/content/default.aspx?NewsAreaId=22 (accessed September 17, 2012).

4 http://www.msnbc.msn.com/id/24205912 (accessed August 20, 2011).

5 http://techcrunch.com/2011/07/18/most-expensive-google-adwords-keywords (accessed on July 9, 2013).

6 http://money.cnn.com/data/us_markets/ (accessed July 9, 2013).

7 Ibid. http://money.cnn.com/data/us_markets/. (accessed August 8, 2013).

5

CAPITALISM OR INFORMATION SOCIETY?

This chapter deals with the question, if we live in an information society and/or a capitalist society. The notion of the information society has in recent decades become very popular for describing proclaimed changes societies have been undergoing. In contrast to the term "capitalism" it is a rather neutral or positive-sounding term. A critical theory of society must ask how it positions itself in relation to the information society discourse. This chapter first gives an introduction (5.1) that is followed by the presentation of a classification of information society theories (5.2) as well as of an alternative view of the information society (5.3) and information society indicators (5.4). The notion of knowledge labour is contextualized in a critical interpretation of information society theory.

In 1968, Theodor W. Adorno asked whether people lived in late capitalism or an industrial society. He argued that the fundamental question of society was about the alternatives: late capitalism or industrial society? I argue that the fundamental question of contemporary society is about other alternatives: capitalism or information society?

5.1. Introduction

A search for the phrase "information society" in titles of articles indexed in the Social Sciences Citation Index (SSCI) for various years shows that there has been a continued academic interest in the concept of the information society since the 1980s (figure 5.1). Two significant rises in the amount of published articles took place. The first peak started in the year 1983 (1980: 1 published article, 1981: 2,

1982: 11, 1983: 22, 1984: 21), two years after the introduction of the IBM Personal Computer and around the time when the Apple Macintosh, the first computer with a graphical user interface, was put on the market in 1984. The second significant peak was around 1995, two years after the Mosaic World Wide Web (WWW) graphic browser was introduced that made surfing the WWW very user-friendly (1994: 4 published articles, 1994: 4, 1995: 14, 1996: 24, 1997: 43). The rising popularity of computing in private lives, everyday life and the economy may have resulted at these points in an increased interest in the concept of the information society.

Computerized society, digital society, information society, knowledge society, knowledge-based society, network society, ICT society, Internet society, communication society, cybersociety, media society, post-industrial society, postmodern society, virtual society—one can find many claims about the present structure of Western societies in political discussions, the media, everyday life and academic discourse. Most of these concepts and claims have in common that they stress the importance of knowledge; the production, generation, diffusion and use of information; and the rise of the computer and digital network technologies like the Internet or the mobile phone. Two important questions related to discussions about the information society are how to define the informational dimension of society and how to measure to which degree a certain subsystem or dimension of society is informational. This chapter deals with the first aspect and presents some reflections about the question, If and under which circumstances is it theoretically feasible to speak of an information society?

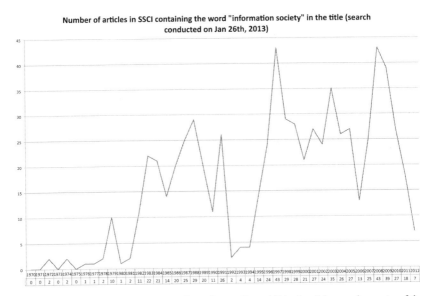

Number of articles in SSCI containing the word "information society" in the title (search conducted on Jan 26th, 2013)

FIGURE 5.1 Development of the number of annually published articles on the topic of the information society

Theodor W. Adorno (1968/2003) asked in 1968, What is the fundamental question of the present structure of society? Do we live in late capitalism or an industrial society? In today's society, where knowledge and creative work, media, the computer and the Internet are said to be important, we can reformulate Adorno's question in the following way: What is the fundamental question of the present structure of society? Do we live in capitalism or an information society? This chapter deals with these questions.

First, I present a classification of information society theories. I discuss radical discontinuous information society theories, sceptic views and continuous information society theories. Second, I introduce an alternative concept that is grounded in Hegelian philosophy and Marxian political economy. Third, I give a methodological note on measuring the information society. Finally, I draw some conclusions.

5.2. A Classification of Information Society Theories

Frank Webster (1995, 2002) has identified five ways of defining an information society: technological innovation, occupational change, economic value, information flows and the expansion of symbols and signs. The theoretical criterion that Webster uses for classifying information society theories is the dimension of society that they primarily focus on. Another classification of theories can be achieved by combining the degree of novelty and the type of sociological theorizing as distinguishing criteria. The information society theory discourse can then be theoretically categorized by making use of two axes: the first axis distinguishes aspects of societal change, the second one the informational qualities of these changes. There are theories that conceive the transformations of the past decades as constituting radical societal change. These are discontinuous theories. Other theories stress more the continuities of modern society. Subjective social theories stress the importance of human individuals and their thinking and actions in society, whereas objective social theories stress structures that transcend single individuals (Giddens 1984, xx). Subjective information society theories put emphasis on the importance of human knowledge (thought, mental activities) in contemporary society, whereas objective information society theories foreground the role of information technologies such as the mass media, the computer, the Internet or the mobile phone. Figure 5.2 shows a typology of information society theories.

Discontinuous subjective concepts are, for example, the knowledge economy (Machlup 1962, Drucker 1969/1992, Porat 1977), the post-industrial society (Bell 1974, Touraine 1974), the postmodern society (Lyotard 1979) or the knowledge-based society (Stehr 1994). Objective discontinuous notions that stress the importance of information technologies are, for example, the network society (Castells 1996, 2000b; van Dijk 2006), the virtual society (Bühl 2000, Woolgar 2002), cybersociety (Jones 1998) or the Internet society (Bakardjieva 2005).

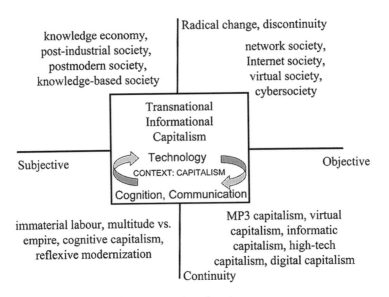

FIGURE 5.2 A typology of information society theories

Discontinuous information society theories prefix certain terms to macro-sociological categories such as society or economy, which implies that they assume that society or the economy has undergone a radical transformation in the past decades and that we now live in a new society or economy. These approaches stress discontinuity, in other words, that we live in a new society that has almost nothing in common with society as it was 100 or 150 years ago. Alain Touraine (1974, 4) for example says that the post-industrial or programmed society is "a new type of society". For Daniel Bell (1974), the "post-industrial society" has brought about "a vast historical change in which old social relations (which were property-bound), existing power structures (centered on narrow elites), and bourgeois culture (based on notions of restraint and delayed gratification) are being rapidly eroded" (37) and "the emergence of a new kind of society [that] brings into question the distributions of wealth, power, and status that are central to any society" (43). Alvin Toffler (1980) argues that a third-wave society, what he also terms the "knowledge age", means a "giant wave of change battering our lives today" (5), a "massive historical shift" (243), "dramatic changes" (243) and a "revolutionary advance" (168) so that the result is a "wholly new society" (261). Peter Drucker argues that the "knowledge society" means "an Age of Discontinuity in world economy and technology" (Drucker 1969/1992, 10) and that "work and workforce, society and polity, are all, in the last decade of this century, qualitatively and quantitatively different both from those of the first years of this century and from anything ever experienced before in human history: different in their configuration, in their processes, in their problems, and in their structures" (Drucker 2001: 227). For Nico Stehr (1994), the emergence of what he terms the knowledge society means that "the age of labor and property is at an end" (viii), that the "emergence of knowledge societies signals first and foremost a radical transformation in the *structure of the economy*" (10) and the "emergence of a new structure and organization of economic activity" (122). For Manuel Castells, the rise of the "network society" means that a "new world is taking shape at this turn of the millennium" and that the "information technology revolution induced the emergence of informationalism, as the material foundation of a new society" (Castells 2000a, 367).

These examples show that many, but certainly not all, information society theorists assume that the effects of information technologies, knowledge, science and communication on society have brought about a new kind of society. It is therefore no surprise that as an answer, approaches have emerged that question the discontinuity hypothesis's claim that society has been radically transformed. "If there is just more information then it is hard to understand why anyone should suggest that we have before us something radically new" (Webster 2002, 26). Nicholas Garnham (1998/2004, 2000b) therefore characterizes information society theory as ideology. Garnham (1998/2004, 165) says that information society theory is "the favoured legitimating ideology for the dominant economic and political powerholders". Garnham's basic argument is that the claim that there is a new information, network, knowledge or post-industrial society denies the continued existence of exploitative class relations between capitalists and workers. "But in terms of the claims for epochal change, we need also to ask whether these characteristics are new or whether on the contrary they are the product of the problems of creating value with information commodities, which drives a constant search for novelty and new cycles of cultural consumption of commodities, which are not destroyed in use" (ibid., 179). The discontinuity hypothesis has ideological character because it says, with the view characteristic for neo-liberal ideology, that we can do nothing about change and have to adapt to existing political realities (Webster 1995, 267). Peter Golding (2000, 170) argues that information society discourse is an ideology that "anticipates and celebrates the privatization of information, and the incorporation of ICT developments into the expansion of the free market". The danger in sociology's fascination of the new is that it would be distracted from the focus on radical potentials and the critique of how these potentials are suppressed (ibid., 171).

Stehr (1994) explicitly discusses such critiques that say that the hypothesis that the knowledge/post-industrial society constitutes a radical change does not take the continuities of contemporary society into account. He says that they ignore the dynamic character of society and cannot explain changes.

> The radical critique of the theory of post-industrial society affirms the con-
> tinuity of the modern world while post-industrial theorists assert that mod-
> ern life is a world of change. But the fixation of the more radical critique of
> the theory of post-industrial society on features of industrial society which
> are more or less persistent, if not permanent, attributes of modern society,
> namely the existence of power elites, social inequality, unemployment, pov-
> erty, a concentration of control in the economy, societal antagonisms and
> contradictions, social control and constraints, can, in my view, only distract
> from gaining insights into the *dynamic* character of modern society. That is,
> the radical critique is long on constant, static and fixed ills and somewhat
> short on dynamic and evolving configurations of socio-economic and po-
> litical realities in modern society. (Stehr 1994, 55)

In a comparable way, Castells (2000a, 367) asks, "After all, if nothing is new under
the sun, why bother to try to investigate, think, write, and read about it?"

The views of Stehr and Castells do not advance the discussion because they
simply posit the notion that there is a radical break against the very critique of
this notion. Stehr is a vehement advocate of the radical break hypothesis. He does
not answer to the criticism that assuming a radical break obscures the continuity
of capital accumulation, inequality, exploitation and stratification in capitalism and
constitutes therefore an affirmative ideology.

Continuous information society theories take the sceptical views to a certain extent into account and stress that we still live in a modern capitalist society, but that certain changes of the forms that express basic capitalist structures
have taken place. Subjective continuous information society concepts are, for
example, reflexive modernization (Beck et al. 1994), cognitive capitalism (Negri
2008, Vercellone 2007), semio-capitalism (Berardi 2009a, b) and general intellect
and immaterial labour (Hardt and Negri 2000, 2005; Virno 2004). They stress the
importance of mental labour for capital accumulation in contemporary capitalism. Objective continuous information society concepts include digital capitalism
(Schiller 2000, Glotz 1999), virtual capitalism (Dawson and Foster 1998), high-
tech capitalism (Haug 2003a), MP3 capitalism (Sennett 2006) and informatic
capitalism (Fitzpatrick 2002). Such approaches stress the continuity of capitalism
but still share the view of continuous information society theories that information technology or knowledge is the central factor in contemporary society.
They hardly account for the continued importance of, for example, very material resources like oil, over which wars are fought, or the importance of finance
capital that has played a crucial role in the emergence of a new global economic
crisis in 2008. In its extreme form, the continuity hypothesis is the claim that
contemporary society does not differ in any significant way from 19th-century
capitalism. For example, Walter Runciman (1993, 65) has argued that "it cannot be claimed that any new sub-type of the capitalist mode of production has
emerged" in Great Britain in the 1970s and 1980s. The United Kingdom would

be a "capitalist-liberal-democratic" society with a "capitalist mode of production", a "liberal mode of persuasion", and a "democratic mode of coercion" (ibid.). "Terms such as 'managerial' capitalism, or 'late' capitalism, or 'finance' capitalism, or 'corporatist' capitalism have all generated more confusion than illumination" (ibid., 54). A similar argument has been forwarded by Jonathan Friedman (2002, 302): "Capitalism has not changed in its general tendencies to the deepening of commodification, the increase in the rate of accumulation of fictitious capital relative to real accumulation, the increasing lumpenization of large portions of the world's population. All these processes are abetted by the new high techno-logy, but they are certainly not its cause, and if anything, they are the symptoms of a capitalism in dire straits, a situation quite predictable from the logic of the system". The only new quality would be the ideological claim that we live in a new society, "the strange air of radical identity or self-identity among those intel-lectuals who are both representatives of the privileged classes and translators of ordinary liberalism into the language of radicalism" (ibid.). There is no doubt that capitalism requires a continuity of the structures of accumulation and exploita-tion to exist. These processes are however not smooth, but rather contradictory and dynamic, which results in the crisis-proneness and reality of capitalist crises. Marx saw the contradictory nature and crisis-riddenness of capitalism as a source of internal capitalist change (and potential transition to socialism). Capitalism re-quires a change of the organization of the structures of accumulation and exploi-tation in order to overcome crises. Crises as "periodic revolutions in value [. . .] confirm what they ostensibly refute: the independence which value acquires as capital, and which is maintained and intensified through its movement" (Marx 1885, 185). "The accumulation of capital, which originally appeared only as its quantitative extension, comes to fruition, as we have seen, through a progressive qualitative change in its composition" (Marx 1867c, 781). The position taken in this chapter is that both the continuity and the discontinuity hypotheses are at the same time to a certain extent right and wrong and that we need a dialectical methodology for understanding the development of society. Such a methodology stresses that development works through preserving changes at a fundamental level by transformations on upper levels of organization of society and that fun-damental changes of society can be grounded in aspects and contradictions taking place on those upper levels. If one applies a dialectical methodology, the rise of transnational informational capitalism is neither only a subjective nor only an objective transformation, but is based on a subject-object dialectic. Objective ap-proaches are techno-deterministic and neglect how forms of labour and agency have changed; subjective approaches neglect that technology is a force that shapes and is shaped by agency. Hence both technology-oriented objective and the sub-jective knowledge-oriented approaches are insufficient. But at the same time they are right in stressing one pole of a dialectic of a larger framework: The notion of transnational informational capitalism sublates both lines of thinking dialectically because information and networks have both an objective and a subjective aspect;

they transform the means of production and the relations of production. The search of capital for new strategies and forms of capital accumulation transforms labour in such a way that cognitive, communicative and cooperative labour forms a significant amount of overall labour time (a development enforced by the rise of the ideology of self-discipline of "participatory management"), but at the same time this labour is heavily mediated by information technologies and produces to a certain extent tangible informational goods (as well as intangible informational services) (Fuchs 2008). The notion of transnational informational capitalism grasps this subject-object dialectic; it conceptualizes contemporary capitalism based on the rise of cognitive, communicative and cooperative labour that is interconnected with the rise of technologies and goods that objectify human cognition, communication and cooperation. Informational capitalism is based on the dialectical interconnection of subjective knowledge and knowledge objectified in information technologies. The reason why I think this approach is better grounded is that dialectics allow conceiving reality as complex and dynamic, which questions one-dimensional and static accounts of reality.

Transnational informational capitalism is the result of the dialectic of continuity and discontinuity that shapes capitalist development. Surplus value, exchange-value, capital, commodities and competition are basic aspects of capitalism; how such forms are exactly produced, objectified, accumulated and circulated is contingent and historical. They manifest themselves differently in different capitalist modes of development. In the informational mode of capitalist development, surplus value production and capital accumulation manifest themselves in symbolic, "immaterial", informational commodities and cognitive, communicative and cooperative labour. Digital media mediates the accumulation of capital, power and definition-capacities on a transnational scale. Roy Bhaskar (1993, 55) has distinguished between "real negation ≥ transformative negation ≥ radical negation" in order to stress the non-deterministic and complex character of sublation. Not all negations of negations are at the fundamental level; there are also partial sublations that are transformative but not radical. The emergence of transnational informational capitalism is a transformational sublation, but not a radical one.

Transnational informational capitalism is a tendency and relative degree in the development of contemporary capitalism, which does not mean that it is the only or the dominant tendency. Capitalism is many things at the same time: it is to a certain degree informational, but at the same time to a certain degree finance capitalism, imperialistic capitalism, hyper-industrial capitalism and so on. We have many capitalisms today existing within one overall capitalist mode of organizing society. Capitalism is at the same time a general mode of production and exploitation and a specific realization, a coexistence and interaction of different types and forms of capitalist production and exploitation. Why do I speak of *transnational* informational capitalism? Hirst and Thompson (1999, 95) have argued that "the extent of the internationalization of business activity is often exaggerated in both popular and academic accounts". Kevin Doogan (2009) therefore speaks of the emergence of "the global ideology of globalization" (65) that "overstates the mobility of capital" (87) and ignores that "processes and mechanisms of globalization have a strong national dimension" (210). In the context of the media economy, some scholars doubt the emergence of global media or argue that their existence is a myth (for example, Hafez 2007, Flew 2007). Foreign direct investment (FDI) stocks have increased from a level of about 5% of world GDP at the beginning of the 1980s to 25%–30% of world GDP at the end of the first decade of the second millennium.[1] This does not prove that capital accumulation is global, but it is an indication that in comparison to the phase of Fordist capitalism, capital exports through the global outsourcing of production in order to reduce labour costs and fixed costs have become more important. The economy has become more global in the past 30 years in comparison to the years 1945–1975 (see also Fuchs 2010a, c). The international share of assets of the world's 100 largest transnational corporations (TNCs) was 62% in 2009, 63% in 2010 and 63% in 2011. Their international share of sales was 66% in 2009, 64% in 2010 and 65% in 2011. Their international share of employment was 57% in 2009, 57% in 2010 and 59% in 2011 (World Investment Report 2012, 25). Table 5.1 shows for the year 2008 the

TABLE 5.1 Transnationality of the world's largest informational TNCs (year 2008)

Company	Industry	Foreign Assets Share	Foreign Sales Share	Foreign Employment Share	Transnationality Index
Vodafone	Telecommunications	92.1%	86.9%	86.9%	88.6%
Siemens	Electronic equipment	77.3%	72.6%	69.1%	73.0%
Telefonica	Telecommunications	68.6%	63.8%	78.3%	70.3%
Deutsche Telekom	Telecommunications	55.4%	53.2%	42.2%	50.3%
France Telecom	Telecommunications	61.4%	46.6%	45.0%	51.0%
Sony	Electronic equipment	46.6%	75.8%	63.0%	61.8%
IBM	Electronic equipment	47.5%	64.6%	71.1%	61.1%
Nokia	Electronic equipment	90.8%	99.3%	80.7%	90.3%
Hewlett-Packard	Electronic equipment	42.6%	68.8%	65.3%	58.9%
Vivendi Universal	Telecommunications	45.5%	37.1%	68.1%	50.2%
Liberty Global	Telecommunications	99.8%	100%	58.9%	86.2%
TeliaSonera	Telecommunications	86.3%	65.4%	66.2%	72.6%
Samsung	Electronic equipment	34.4%	80.6%	47.8%	54.2%
AVERAGE		**65.3%**	**70.4%**	**64.8%**	**66.8%**

Source: UNCTAD Statistics, http://unctad.org/en/Pages/Statistics.aspx/ (accessed July 9, 2013)

international share of assets, sales and employment, as well as the transnationality index (TNI) for those companies in the list of the world's 100 largest TNCs that can be considered informational companies (i.e. companies that create goods or services that are necessary in the context of the production, distribution or consumption of information). Thirteen out of 100 companies are informational companies. Their average international asset share is 65.3%, their average international sales share 70.4%, their average foreign employment share 64.8% and their average TNI 66.8%. UNCTAD's TNI measures the global dimension of a company by a composite index that covers the world's largest companies' shares of assets, sales and employees outside of the home country.

Statistical data suggest that the globalization of media/information corporations is not a myth. There surely is not a purely global media system—as transnational corporations are grounded in their respective national economies. But global production in the form of outsourcing, subcontracting and spatially diffused production seems to be an emergent quality of capitalism and therefore also of information corporations. Indicators such as the TNI, the foreign assets share, the foreign sales share, the foreign employment share and the foreign affiliates share allow one to measure the degree of transnationality of information companies.

5.3. An Alternative View of the Information Society

Marx's distinction between productive forces and relations of production can help one to better understand the discussion about the information society. When scholars such as Alain Touraine (1974), Daniel Bell (1974), Alvin Toffler (1980), Peter Drucker (1969/1992, 2001), Nico Stehr (1994) or Manuel Castells (1996, 2000a, 2000b) speak of the emergence of a post-industrial society/knowledge society/information society/network society, what they actually mean is a change of the productive forces: knowledge and information technology have become important means for producing commodities that serve the purpose of capital accumulation. It is a mistake to characterize this transformation as radical discontinuity or new society because the economy consists not only of the productive forces, but of the interaction of productive forces and relations of production, or what Marx termed the mode of production *(Produktionsweise)*. It is furthermore a mistake to assume that the economy equals society, although it of course forms a central part of society. When scholars such as Nicholas Garnham (1998/2004, 2000a, 2004), Peter Golding (2000) and Frank Webster (1995, 2002) object to the information society hypothesis, they want to warn that a reduction of the contemporary economy to the changes of the productive forces obscures the continued existence of capitalist class relations that are exploitative in character. The argument is that such a reductionism constitutes an ideology which celebrates contemporary society and conceals and denies that changes of the productive forces take place within, advance and are driven by relations of exploitation. When Garnham (1998/2004, 178) says that "the shift from energy to brainpower does not necessarily change the subordination of labour to capital", he does not deny that capitalism is undergoing changes; instead he wants to alert that changes of the productive forces are not revolutionary and do not transform but rather stabilize the capitalist class system. But it is satisfying neither to say that nothing has changed in the contemporary economy nor to say that there are radical changes. It is important to see, like Marx, the dialectical relation of productive forces and relations of production. The information society hypothesis is problematic if interpreted as radical discontinuity in the development of society, but vis-à-vis the continuists, it needs to be stressed that the hypothesis also reminds us that there are significant changes of the productive forces that are needed for the reproduction of capital accumulation and class relations. As Marx knew, capitalism permanently tries to overthrow its productive forces in order to be able to accumulate ever more capital by technically intensifying the exploitation of labour. Even Erik Olin Wright, arguably the most important class analysis scholar and the most important Marxist analyst of class relations and therefore not at all suspect of wanting to conceal the continued existence of capitalism,[2] concedes that the information society thesis has some significance for explaining the inner transformation of capitalism. His empirical analysis of the class structure in the United States showed that the use of knowledge, services and information technology in production brought about a "trajectory of change within developed capitalist societies towards an expansion, rather than a decline, of contradictory locations within class relations" and that as a result it "appears that the class structure of capitalism continues to become increasingly complex" (Wright 2000, 66).

5.4. Information Society Indicators: Measuring the Information Society

It makes sense to empirically analyse to what extent the productive forces are today informational productive forces. This can be done with the help of information society statistics, by calculating the degree of informationalism using certain indicators, as, for example, the share of workers in information industries in the total workforce, the share of information occupations in the total workforce, the share of information industries in total value added, the wage share of workers in information industries in total wages, the share of information companies in total capital assets/total profits/total market value of the world's largest 2,000 corporations, the share of information industries in total foreign direct investment inflows/outflows/instock/outstock, the share of information products in total imports/exports, and so on (for example calculations, see Fuchs 2011a, chapters 3 and 5). It is important to observe the development of these indicators over certain time periods for different countries and for the world economy. Such measurements cannot inform us about the existence of a new society because they only relate to the changes of the productive forces. One therefore should be pragmatic about using these indicators; the task is to show to what degree the productive forces are informational and non-informational. Depending on which indicator is employed, the result will be different. The term "informational productive forces" does not characterize entirely new productive forces, but it does indicate depending on a specific indicator the degree to which a certain aspect of the productive forces is informational and the composite degree to which it is non-informational.

Depending on which indicator one uses for measuring the information-intensity of the capitalist productive forces, one will get different results to the question of to what degree we live in informational capitalism. Informational capitalism is a tendency in the development of the productive forces, not a society. I argue in a pragmatic way that "informational capitalism" should be used as a term that characterizes all those parts of the productive forces that are based on information. To what extent the capitalist economy is information-based can only be determined by empirical research and by a discussion and selection of relevant indicators. Information has traditionally been understood either subjectively (as knowledge stored in the human brain) or objectively (information as a thing, the outcome of mental work that is stored in artefacts). In contrast, I see information as a process of cognition, communication and cooperation, in which human beings form and change their ideas by recognizing the world, symbolically interact with other humans in social relations and communicate in collaborative ways so that they create new qualities of the social world (Fuchs and Hofkirchner 2005). Such a definition of information allows the inclusion of certain industries in the category of the information economy and the exclusion of others. Money is the expression of the price of commodities whose exchange it mediates. The finance industry is a realm that sells money as commodity. Marx (1894) describes the capital accumulation cycle of finance as M—M': money begets more money in a direct way without an active commodity production cycle; money itself is the commodity that is sold. Money's role as the general medium of exchange in the capitalist economy is primarily based not on cognitive or communicative activities, but on the anonymity of exchange that hides actual relations of production in the money form. In contrast, companies like Google or Facebook create software tools that are used by humans for acquiring knowledge about the world and interacting with others. In contrast to banking, these tools are oriented primarily on enabling human cognition and communication. Information economies, especially the Internet industry, are not separate from the finance industry. Google and Facebook are based on venture capital and are listed on the stock market. Although there is the financialization of the information economy, the products of the two realms of finance and the information economy are significantly different in character.

Statistical analysis should not stop at an analysis of the productive forces. It is also important to measure the development of the class structure of capitalist societies. This can, for example, be done with the help of the following indicators: the measurement of the size of the working class, the capitalist class, intermediary classes and the unemployed (Wright 2000); the relation of wage share and profit share; the relation of the poorest and richest groups in society (for example, a 90:10 ratio); the relation of wage growth and living quality growth to GDP growth and the growth of profits; the development of profits of certain companies/company groups/industries; the development of total profits in the world and in certain countries; world gross capital formation; market capitalization of listed companies; the growth of total capital assets; and the growth of capital assets/profits/market values of certain companies/groups of companies/industries/economies. Combining class analysis and analyses of the degrees of informationalism of the productive forces allows one to conclude to what degree capitalism has transformed into informational capitalism. The basic assumption underlying the category of informational capitalism (Fuchs 2008, 2010b, 2010c, 2011a) is that the development of knowledge, services and information technologies in production serves capitalist purposes; that is, it is a conscious class project of the dominant class for advancing new strategies of capital accumulation and surplus value production and for aiming to reduce constant and variable wage costs in order to maximize profits. To what degree these strategies are successful or embedded into crisis-inducing economic antagonisms is another important matter. One should be modest in claiming the existence of informational capitalism. It is unlikely that all aspects of contemporary society or of contemporary capitalist economies are suddenly informational. Therefore the notion of informational capitalism does not make sense as a category of totality. It only makes sense for describing the degree to which the capitalist mode of production is using informational productive forces for accumulating capital within class relations (i.e. by exploiting surplus value). If one analyses the Forbes list of the largest companies in the world according to how capital assets are distributed to industries, then one finds for recent years that finance companies and financial service corporations together account for the vast share of capital assets, that the second largest sector is oil, gas, and utilities and the third largest sector the information sector (comprising the subdomains of telecommunications, technology hardware and equipment, media content, software and semiconductors) (see Fuchs 2011a, 132). So it looks like on the level of productive forces informatization is not the dominant characteristic of the global productive forces, but rather an important, non-dominant trend. Finance capital is the dominant fraction of capital today, which shows that an important characteristic of imperialistic capitalism is present today (Fuchs 2010a, c). Fossil fuels are also still very important in the contemporary economy, which is an indication that industrial society is not over and that we have entered a hyper-industrial era, in which information production, selling and consumption becomes an important factor of the overall economy but does not substitute for the economic importance of finance capital and fossil fuels. Financialization, hyper-industrialization, and informatization characterize contemporary imperialist capitalism. Information companies are important in the global capitalist economy, which reflects a trend towards informatization (that is, the rise of the importance of information in the economy), but they are less important than finance and the oil and gas industry. Such an analysis of the global productive forces can be linked to the relations of production: that is, capital accumulation stands in a relation to the working and living conditions of the mass of the world population. Information corporations are not the dominant corporations. Therefore one can, based on the indicators of assets and profits of the world's largest corporations, *not conclude* that the capitalist mode of production can be characterized as informational capitalism.

In 2007, the profits of the world's largest 2,000 companies amounted to US$2357.06 billion (data source: Forbes 2000 (2008) list). Data about the wage share of African countries is not easily available. But existing data allows calculating an average African unadjusted wage share of 29.5% in the years 2001–2006 (International Labor Organization 2008, appendix A1). There are no reasons to assume that this average number has dramatically increased since 2006, so assuming an African wage share of 30% is feasible. In 2007, the total African GDP was US$1291.7 billion (UNHDR 2009, table M). Assuming an average wage share of 30% gives a total African wage sum of US$387.5 billion. This means that the total profits of the world's largest 2,000 companies were roughly six times as large as the total wages paid to all employees in Africa. This relation shows the huge difference in wealth and income of the capitalist class and the poorest workers in the world. Information companies accounted for 12.4% of the profits of the world's largest 2,000 companies in 2007, which is a sum of US$293.07 billion, roughly US$100 billion less than the total wages of African workers, but it still shows the economic power of global information corporations. These data show that capitalist relations of production are highly stratified: large companies have huge economic money power, whereas workers are, as Marx said, deprived of economic wealth that is directly transformed into capitalist plenitude. The poverty of labour is the wealth of capital.

Table 5.2 shows for selected countries the share of low-paid jobs and the relationship of wages of the 10% that forms the upper income group (usually managers) and the 10% that form the lowest income group. In many countries, the gap between high incomes and low incomes has widened and the share of low-paid jobs in total jobs has climbed to rates that are often above 20%.

"The distance between the lowest paid 10% of workers and the best paid 10% has increased in 17 out of 30 selected countries for which at least one data point is available to compare the periods 1995–2000 and 2007–2009. Although the largest part of this increase in inequality was due to top earners 'flying away' from the majority, another part was due to the so-called 'collapsing bottom', where the distance between median workers and low-paid workers has increased in 12 out of 28 countries" (International Labour Organization 2010, 31).

TABLE 5.2 Share of low-paid jobs and wage inequality in selected countries

Country	Share of low-paid jobs: 1995–2000	2001–2006	2007–2009	Decile ratio D9/D10: 1995–2000	2001–2006	2007–2009
Australia	13.5%	14.5%	16.8%	3.0	3.1	3.3
Canada	22.4%	22.1%	22.0%	3.6	3.7	3.8
Germany	16.6%	19.2%	21.2%	3.1	3.2	3.3
United Kingdom	20.5%	20.6%	20.8%	6.8	7.0	7.2
United States	24.8%	23.8%	24.5%	4.6	4.7	4.9

Source: International Labour Organization (2010)

The wage share is the share of total compensation in total value added. For "the period 1980–2007, 17 out of 24 countries [included in the study] registered a falling wage share" (ibid., 22). This development has especially affected the manufacturing and construction industries, whereas the wage share has generally been rising in finance, real estate, renting and business services (ibid., 25ff).

There are indications that profits have been increasing as a result of the relative decrease of wages and the increase of low-paid precarious employment. The presented data suggest that the capitalist relations of production have in the latter decades of the 20th century and the first decade of the 21st century been shaped by an increase of socio-economic inequality that benefits capital at the expense of labour. Neo-liberalism has been a political class struggle project aimed at the "reconstruction of the power of economic elites" and "a system of justification and legitimation for whatever needed to be done to achieve this goal" (Harvey 2007, 19). The relations of production are shaped by a deep class conflict between the interests of capital and labour.

5.5. Conclusion

In 1968, six years before the publication of Daniel Bell's book *The Coming of Post-Industrial Society,* which was path-breaking for the information society discourse (i.e. in a time before the high rise of the information society hypothesis), Theodor W. Adorno (1968/2003) gave an introductory keynote talk on the topic of "Late Capitalism or Industrial Society?" at the annual meeting of the German Sociological Association. He said that the "fundamental question of the present structure of society" is "about the alternatives: late capitalism or industrial society". It is about "whether the capitalist system still predominates according to its model, however modified, or whether the development of industry has rendered the concept of capitalism obsolete, together with the distinction between capitalist and noncapitalist states and even the critique of capitalism. In other words, the question is whether it is true that Marx is out of date" (ibid., 111). Adorno pointed out that dichotomous answers to this question (either/or) "are themselves predicaments modelled on dilemmas taken from an unfree society" (ibid., 113). He gave an answer to the question that took into account the importance and relation of the productive forces and the relations of production in the capitalist mode of production: "In terms of critical, dialectical theory, I would like to propose as an initial, necessarily abstract answer that contemporary society undoubtedly is an industrial society according to the state of its *forces* of production. Industrial labor has everywhere become the model of society as such, regardless of the frontiers separating differing political systems. It has developed into a totality because methods modeled on those of industry are necessarily extended by the laws of economics to other realms of material production, administration, the sphere of distribution, and those that call themselves culture. In contrast, however, society is capitalist in its *relations* of production. People are still what they were in Marx's analysis in the middle of the nineteenth century. [. . .] Production takes place today, as then, for the sake of profit" (ibid., 117).

Paraphrasing Adorno and transferring his question and answer to a time that is shaped by information society discourse, one can hypothesize that a fundamental question of the present structure of society is about the alternatives capitalism or information society. In terms of critical, dialectical theory, I would like to propose as an initial, necessarily abstract answer that contemporary society is an information society according to the state of its *forces* of production. In contrast, however, contemporary society is capitalist in its *relations* of production. People are still what they were in Marx's analysis in the middle of the nineteenth century. Production takes place today, as then, for the sake of profit, and for achieving this end it to a certain extent makes use of knowledge and information technology in production. Productive forces and relations of production are interlocking phenomena: they contain each other. My argument in this chapter has been that the informational forces of production (knowledge labour, information technology, science, theoretical knowledge) and the capitalist class relations should not be seen as polar opposites and that the discussion about the existence or non-existence of an information society should not be reduced either to the level of the productive forces or to the level of the relations of production. The first reduction will result in the assumption that we live in a new society, the information society, the second reduction in the response that nothing has changed and we still live in a capitalist society. The informational forces of production (just like the non-informational ones) are mediated by class relations, which means that the establishment of information technologies (as part of the instruments of production) and knowledge work (which is characterized by a composition of labour, where mental and communicative features dominate over manual features) as features of economic production are strategies for advancing surplus value exploitation, the reduction of variable and constant capital. Capital thereby hopes to achieve higher profit rates. The idea that the notion of society can today solely be constructed by reference to the informational forces of production is an ideological illusion. The counter-claim that nothing has changed because we still live in a society dominated by capitalist class relations is an understandable reaction and a strategy of ideology critique. But a dialectical analysis cannot leave out that there are certain changes taking place that are intended to support the deepening of the class structure but also contain what Marx termed *Keimformen* (germ forms of an alternative society). That the development of the informational productive forces is itself contradictory and comes in conflict with the capitalist relations of production can be observed by phenomena such as file sharing on the Internet, the discussions about intellectual property rights, the emergence of pirate parties in the political landscape of advanced capitalist countries, or the popularity of free software (Fuchs 2008, 2009). Marx predicted the emergence of informational productive forces as the result of the development of fixed capital, that is, the increasing technical and organic composition of capital that is characterized by an increase of the role of technology in production at the expense of living labour-power. "The development of fixed capital indicates to what degree general social knowledge has become a direct force of production, and to what degree, hence, the conditions of the process of social life itself have come under the control of the general intellect and been transformed in accordance with it. To what degree the powers of social production have been produced, not only in the form of knowledge, but also as immediate organs of social practice, of the real life process" (Marx 1857/1858b, 706).

Marx argued that by technological development "the entire production process" becomes "the technological application of science" (ibid., 699). The "transformation of the production process from the simple labour process into a scientific process [. . .] appears as a quality of fixed capital in contrast to living labour" (ibid., 700). So for Marx, the rise of informational productive forces was immanently connected to capital's need for finding technical ways that allow the accumulation of more profits. That society has to a certain degree become informational is, just like the discourse about this circumstance, a result of the development of capitalism.

Chapters 3, 4 and 5 have set out the academic and societal context of digital labour. In chapters 6–11, we will analyse the reality of labour involved in the production of digital media.

Notes

1 UNCTAD Statistics, http://unctad.org/en/Pages/Statistics.aspx/. (accessed August 8, 2013).
2 The paper "Marxist Class Categories and Income Inequality" (Wright and Perrone 1977) is the most frequently cited paper on issues of economic class analysis in the Social Sciences Citation Index (289 citations, accessed on July 9, 2013).

PART II

Analysing Digital Labour

Case Studies

6

DIGITAL SLAVERY

Slave Work in ICT-Related Mineral Extraction

Look around in the space where you are at the moment and you will probably see different ICTs such as a computer, a printer or a mobile phone. These devices are made out of resources that come from the earth: minerals. By looking at the tools, we do not see under which conditions the minerals they contain have been extracted. This chapter takes a look at the work of miners who extract the resources out of which our daily used digital media tools are made. It documents an unpleasant reality, namely that parts of these minerals are extracted under slave-like conditions. Digital media is connected to digital slavery. Most of the slaves who extract these minerals have never owned a computer or laptop. They work under conditions of high exploitation and violence. If our digital media are based on the blood and death of slave workers, then the question arises of what we should do about it. This chapter wants to point out that there are no easy solutions and that the exploitation of slaves is a phenomenon that stems from the profit orientation of media companies. In order to overcome digital slave labour, we have to start questioning capitalism.

6.1. Introduction

If you look around in the home, office, public space or means of transportation that you currently are at, it is likely that you see at least one computer, laptop or mobile phone that is connected to the Internet. And it is likely that this device has a label on it that says one of the following: Acer, Apple, Asus, BenQ, Compal, Dell, Fujitsu, Hewlett-Packard, HTC, Huawei, Lenovo, LG, Logic Instruments, Motorola, NEC, Nokia, MEDION, Panasonic, Quanta, Samsung, Sony, Sony Ericsson,

Toshiba, Wistron, Wortmann Terra or ZTE. When asked "Where does your computer/phone come from? Who has produced it?", one may therefore be tempted to answer, "Well, it has been produced by the company X". The main information that the ICT user has about his/her device is from which retailer and company s/he bought it. But these companies are only those actors that sell these devices and own the profits made from these sales. The production process itself consists of multiple forms of labour that are invisible to the user. Yet without this labour ICTs would not exist because they are objectifications of complex human labour processes. A computer or mobile phone consists of application programmes, an operating system, cables, a physical case, a display, a battery, a central processing unit, random-access memory (RAM) data storage chips, read-only memory data storage chips, internal storage devices (hard disk, flashcard), a keyboard or other input device and a cooler. All of these components need to be created in complex labour processes and then put together as a computing system that is sold to the end user. Because of the complexity of the production process and the invisibility of the involved complex labour processes in the final ICT product, the question "Who has produced your laptop/computer?" will be answered by many users on second thought with something like "It was produced by company X". But asked if they know where exactly it was manufactured and by whom, they likely will answer: "I do not know. I bought it/ordered it at Y. But the question is interesting and I am interested to find out more about it". Chapters 6–11 deal with the questions "Where does the laptop/computer/mobile phone come from? Who produces it? Which forms of labour are involved?" They analyse and theorize steps in the production processes of ICTs by discussing specific cases of ICT work: the extraction of minerals in African mines (chapter 6), ICT manufacturing and assemblage in China (chapter 7), software engineering in India (chapter 8), call centre service work (chapter 9), software engineering at Google in the context of Silicon Valley (chapter 10) and the digital labour of Internet prosumers/users (chapter 11). The method of analysis that is employed consists of a presentation of existing empirical data and empirical research results that are theoretically interpreted. The theoretical framing is achieved by applying Karl Marx's theory of modes of production to the ICT industry. For this, foundations of this theory are introduced at the beginning of this chapter. The various forms of ICT labour that are needed so that the end user can connect to the Internet on his/her phone, PC or laptop involve a multitude of labour forms, such as mineral extraction, hardware manufacturing and assemblage, software engineering, service work and users' productive consumption. All of these labour forms are objectified in a single ICT device, which shows that ICTs have a complex spatial and temporal history of production that involves an IDDL, in which different forms of labour create the use-values needed for obtaining a computer or mobile phone. These different use-values created at different times in different places by different workers facing certain working conditions all work together and become objectified in single ICT devices. The bigger picture and theoretical results of the IDDL that involves an international division of labour are presented in the concluding chapter.

6.2. Marx on Modes of Production

Michael Porter (1985, 36) introduced the notion of the value chain that he defined as "a collection of activities that are performed to design, produce, market, deliver and support its product". He distinguished between primary activities (inbound and outbound logistics, operations, marketing and sale, service) and support activities (procurement, technology development, human resource management, firm infrastructure). The term "value chain" has since 1985 become a popular category for analysing the organization of capital, which is indicated by the circumstance that 11,682 articles indexed in the academic database Business Source Premier use the term in their abstract (accessed May 21, 2013). The term has also been used in mainstream media economics for analysing the value chains of traditional media and ICTs. Zerdick et al. 2000 (126–135) argue that the stages in the ICT value chain are procurement; the manufacturing of hardware, peripherals, software, operating systems software; the sale of user software; and support services. The problem of the mainstream use of the value chain concept is that it focuses on the stages in commodity production and tends to neglect aspects of working conditions and class relations. An alternative concept that was introduced by critical studies is the notion of the new international division of labour (NIDL): "The development of the world economy has increasingly created conditions (forcing the development of the new international division of labour) in which the survival of more and more companies can only be assured through the relocation of production to new industrial sites, where labour-power is cheap to buy, abundant and well-disciplined; in short, through the transnational reorganization of production" (Fröbel, Heinrichs and Kreye 1981, 15). A further development is that "commodity production is being increasingly subdivided into fragments which can be assigned to whichever part of the world can provide the most profitable combination of capital and labour" (ibid., 14). The notion of the NIDL has been used in contexts such as manufacturing, the underdevelopment of the Third World, women's employment, migration, transformations of the city, the culture industry and the ICT industry (see e.g. Cohen 1981, 1987; Ernst 1980; Feagin and Smith 1987; Folke, Fold and Enevoldsen 1993; Gamsey and Paukert 1987; Henderson 1986; Huws et al. 1983; Huws 2003; Miller et al. 2004). The concept of the NIDL has the advantage that it stresses the class relationship between capital and labour and how in processes of class struggle capital tries to increase profits by decreasing its overall wage costs via the global diffusion of the production process. It is also a concept that encompasses workers' struggles against the negative effects of capitalist restructuring. The approach taken in this chapter stands in the Marxist tradition that stresses class contradictions in the analysis of globalization. It explores how the notion of the mode of production can be connected to the concept of the new international division of labour.

The notion of the mode of production stresses a dialectical interconnection of, on the one hand, class relationships (relations of production) and on the other hand the forms of organization of capital, labour and technology (productive forces). The class relationship is a social relationship that determines who owns private property and has the power to make others produce surplus value that they do not own and that is appropriated by private property owners. Class relationships involve an owning class and a non-owing class: the non-owning class is compelled to produce surplus value that is appropriated by the owning class. The relations of production determine the *property relations*—who owns which share (full, some, none) of labour-power, the means of production, products of labour—the mode of allocation and distribution of goods, the mode of coercion used for defending property relations and the division of labour. Class relationships are forms of organization of the relations of production, in which a dominant class controls the modes of ownership, distribution and coercion for exploiting a subordinated class. In a classless society, humans control ownership and distribution in common. Every economy produces a certain amount of goods per year. Specific resources are invested and there is a specific output. If there is no contraction of the economy due to a crisis, then a surplus product is created, i.e. an excess over the initial resources. The property relations determine who owns the economy's initial resources and surplus. Table 6.3 distinguishes modes of production (patriarchy, slavery, feudalism, capitalism, communism) based on various modes of ownership, i.e. property relations. The *mode of coercion* takes on the form of physical violence (overseers, security forces, military), structural violence (markets, institutionalized wage labour contracts, legal protection of private property, etc.) and cultural violence (ideologies that present the existing order as the best possible or only possible order and try to defer the causes of societal problems by scapegoating). In a free society no mode of coercion is needed. The *mode of allocation and distribution* defines how products are distributed and allocated: In a communist society, each person gets whatever s/he requires to survive and satisfy human needs. In class societies, distribution is organized in the form of exchange: exchange means that one product is exchanged for another. If you have nothing to exchange because you own nothing, then you cannot get hold of other goods and services, except those that are not exchanged but provided for free. There are different forms of how exchange can be organized: general exchange, exchange for exchange-value (x commodity A = y commodity B), exchange for maximum exchange-value, exchange for capital accumulation. The *division of labour* defines who conducts which activities in the household, the economy, politics and culture. Historically there has been a gender division of labour, a division between mental and physical work, a division into many different functions conducted by specialists and an international division of labour that is due to the globalization of production. Marx in contrast imagined a society of generalists that overcomes the divisions of labour so that society is based on well-rounded universally active humans. Marx points out that the central feature of class relationships is the control of surplus-value: "Capital did not invent surplus labour. Wherever a part of society possesses the monopoly of the means of production, the worker, free or unfree, must add to the labour-time necessary for his own maintenance an extra quantity of labour-time in order to produce the means of subsistence for the owner of the means of production, whether this proprietor be an Athenian caloς cagaqoς [aristocrat], an Etruscan theocrat, a *civis romanus,* a Norman baron, an American slave-owner, a Wallachian boyar, a modern landlord or a capitalist" (Marx 1867c, 334–335). Marx (1857/1858b, 238) says that in class society "labour will create alien property and property will command alien labour". The historical alternative is a communist society and mode of production, in which class relationships are dissolved and the surplus product and private property are owned and controlled in common. The relations of production are dialectically connected to the system of the productive forces: I argued in section 2.2.1 of this book (see also figure 2.2 for a visualization) that human subjects have labour-power that in the labour process interacts with the means of production (object). The means of production consist of the object of labour (natural resources, raw materials) and the instruments of labour (technology). In the labour process, humans transform the object of labour (nature, culture) by making use of their labour-power with the help of instruments of labour. The result is a product of labour, which is a Hegelian subject-object, or, as Marx says, a product, in which labour has become bound up in its object: labour is objectified in the product and the object is as a result transformed into a use-value that serves human needs. The productive forces are a system in which subjective productive forces (human labour-power) make use of technical productive forces (part of the objective productive forces) in order to transform parts of the natural productive forces (which are also part of the objective productive forces) so that a labour product emerges. One goal of the development of the system of productive forces is to increase the productivity of labour, that is, the output (amount of products) that labour generates per unit of time. Marx therefore defined the concept of the development of the productive forces (the increase of the productivity of labour) as "an alteration in the labour process of such a kind as to shorten the labour-time socially necessary for the production of a [. . .] [good], and to endow a given quantity of labour with the power of producing a greater quantity of use-value" (Marx 1867c, 431). Another goal of the development of the productive forces can be the enhancement of human self-development by reducing necessary labour time and hard work (toil).

The instruments of work can be the human brain and body, mechanical tools and complex machine systems. They also include specific organizations of space-time, that is, locations of production that are operated at specific time periods. The most important aspect of time is the necessary work time that depends on the level of productivity. It is the work time that is needed per year for guaranteeing the survival of a society. The objects and products of work can be natural, industrial or informational resources or a combination thereof. The human subject possesses labour-power. Reproductive work is work that reproduces, maintains and recreates human existence. It creates humans' means of subsistence that satisfy basic human needs. The organization of the creation of human means of subsistence is organized on three interconnected levels: the individual realm, the social realm and the institutional realm. At all three levels reproduction works on two interconnected levels that affect the human mind and the human body. Humans only exist as interaction of mind and body at individual, social and institutional levels. Table 6.1 summarizes individual, social and institutional structures that organize and create human reproduction.

The arrows in table 6.1 point out that body and mind and corresponding spheres of human existence belong together and cannot be separated. They are dialectically intertwined, which means that they have existences on their own, are interconnected and constitute each other. So for example physical work such as gardening requires bodily movements of the hands as well as creative thinking about how to exactly plant trees, grass and flowers. The way the garden looks and develops over time shapes the gardener's imagination of which improvements to

TABLE 6.1 The human subject's means of subsistence/reproduction

	Mind, information, superstructure, culture and politics	*Body, physical, base, nature, economy*
Institutional needs	Educational institutions, health and medical care, research institutions, media, arts and culture, decision-making institutions, associations	Health and medical care, workplace
Social needs	Social relations, communication, language, love, friendships, cooperation	Procreation, sexual relations, cooperation
Individual needs	Mind, affects, knowledge, skills, creativity, mental health, self-esteem, self-respect, beauty, self-actualization, values, morals, purpose	food, water, air, shelter, sleep, rest, affects, sexuality, housing, bodily health, warmth

make. Conducting these changes brings about a physical differentiation of the garden. Traditionally the body/mind separation has shaped class divisions so that one specific type of activity has been assigned to a specific group and the opposing form of activity to another group (e.g. housework/wage labour, production/management). The second group's control and exploitation exerted in the process

TABLE 6.2 Three modes of organization of the productive forces

Mode	Instruments of work	Objects of work	Products of work
Agricultural productive forces	Body, brain, tools, machines	Nature	Basic products
Industrial productive forces	Body, brain, tools, machines	Basic products, industrial products	Industrial products
Informational productive forces	Body, brain, tools, machines	Experiences, ideas	Informational products

Productive forces ⇔ **Relations of production**

Subject, labour power:
Means of subsistence/reproduction:
individual, social, institutional

Mode of ownership:
Labour power,
means of production,
products of work

Object, means of production
Instruments of work:
body, brain, tools, machines, space-time
Objects of work:
natural, industrial, informational resources

Mode of coercion
None
Physical violence
Structural violence
Ideological violence

Mode of allocation/distribution
To each according to his/her needs,
exchange
exchange for exchange-value,
exchange for maximum exchange-value,
Exchange for capital accumulation

Subject/object, products of work:
Natural products
Industrial products
Informational products

Division of labour:
Household,
physical/mental,
generalists/specialists
politics

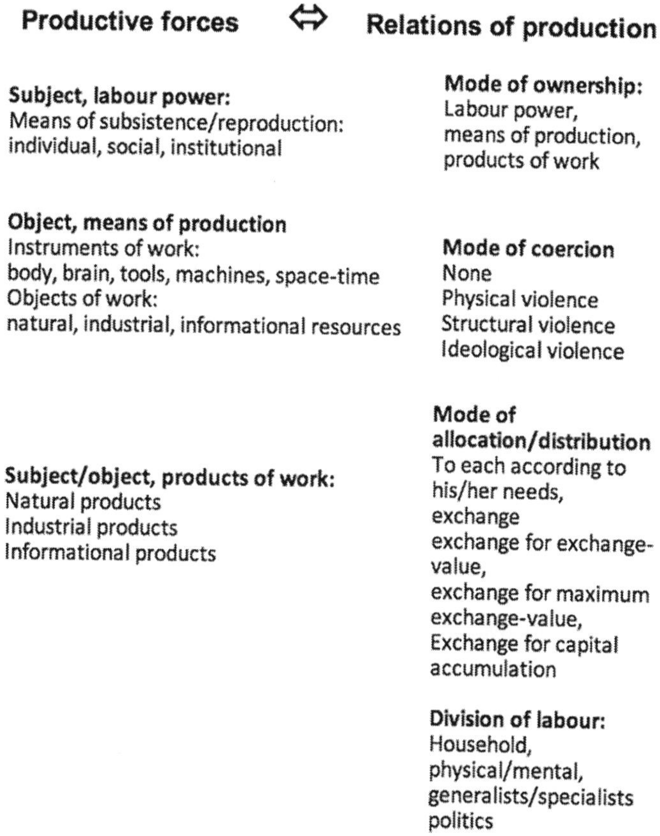

FIGURE 6.1 Dimensions of the productive forces and the relations of production

is ideologically justified by reference to a body/mind dualism that separates the two spheres of the human subject.

The productive forces are a system of production that creates use-values. There are different modes of organization of the productive forces, such as agricultural productive forces, industrial productive forces and informational productive forces. Table 6.2 gives an overview.

Figure 6.1 gives an overview of dimensions of the relations of production and the productive forces.

For Marx, history is a succession and sublation of modes of production. A mode of production is a unity of productive forces and relations of production. If these modes are based on classes as their relations of production, then they have specific contradictions that result in the sublation of one mode of production and the emergence of a new one. History develops in such a way that "an earlier form of intercourse, which has become a fetter, is replaced by a new one corresponding to the more developed productive forces and, hence, to the advanced mode of the self-activity of individuals—a form which in its turn becomes a fetter and is then replaced by another" (Marx and Engels 1845/1846, 91). Class relations and forces of production have historically resulted in a series of contradictions that have brought about the establishment of new modes of production.

In the *Grundrisse*'s section "Forms which precede capitalist production" (Marx 1857/1858b, 471ff), as well as in *The German Ideology*'s section "Feuerbach: Opposition of the materialist and idealist outlooks" (Marx and Engels 1845/1846), Marx discusses the following historical sequence of modes of production:

(1) The tribal community based on the patriarchal family;
(2) Ancient communal property in cities (Rome, Greece);
(3) Feudal production in the countryside;
(4) Capitalism.

So specific historical modes of production that Marx discusses are the family/tribe, ancient slaveholder societies, feudalism and capitalism. In the overview that follows, ancient slaveholder societies and feudalism are discussed in combination because in both the slave is a crucial component of the entire economy. Furthermore, I have added a section that focuses on informational production as a relatively novel development within the capitalist mode of production.

The tribal, ancient and feudal modes of production are according to Marx based on the appropriation of nature: They are forms in which "landed property and agriculture form the basis of the economic order", the earth is "the original instrument of labour as well as its workshop and repository of raw materials" and the "relation to the earth as property is always mediated through the occupation of the land and soil" (Marx 1857/1858b, 485). These are just other expressions for saying that these modes of production are at the level of the productive forces in agricultural societies—nature is the basic object of labour that labour transforms into use-values. The rise of the capitalist mode of production included the creation of large-scale industry and machinery, which means a "separation between these inorganic conditions of human existence [= nature] and this active existence [= labour], a separation which is completely posited only in the relation of wage labour and capital" (ibid., 489). What Marx expresses here is that in large-scale industry, labour does not primarily work in direct contact with earth, but rather takes raw materials and semi-finished goods that stem from nature as objects of labour that are transformed in such a way that a new good or commodity emerges. This means that Marx saw that the rise of capitalism was combined with the rise of industrialism as a mode of the organization of the productive forces. The emergence of capitalism is man's "release from the earth; dissolution of the landed property relations" (ibid., 502). Capitalism therefore also necessarily resulted in the establishment of the factory as a unit of industrial production. This transition entails that the "instruments of labour are converted from tools into machines" (Marx 1867c, 492), a system that consists of a motor mechanism, a transmitting mechanism and a working machine (494) or a combined system of working machines—a machine system (501).

Classical slavery, serfdom and wage labour are three important historical forms of class relations: "With slavery, which attained its fullest development under civilization, came the first great cleavage of society into an exploiting and an exploited class. This cleavage persisted during the whole civilized period. Slavery is the first form of exploitation, the form peculiar to the ancient world; it is succeeded by serfdom in the middle ages, and wage-labor in the more recent period. These are the three great forms of servitude, characteristic of the three great epochs of civilization; open, and in recent times disguised, slavery always accompanies them" (Engels 1884). Table 6.3 provides a classification of modes of production based on the dominant forms of ownership (self-control, partly self-control and partly alien control, full alien control).

TABLE 6.3 The main forms of ownership in various modes of production

	Owner of labour power	Owner of the means of production	Owner of the products of work
Patriarchy	Patriarch	Patriarch	Family
Slavery	Slave master	Slave master	Slave master
Feudalism	Partly self-control, partly lord	Partly self-control, partly lord	Partly self-control, partly lord
Capitalism	Worker	Capitalist	Capitalist
Communism	Self	All	Partly all, partly individual

But how are modes of production related to each other? In a historical way, where they supersede each other, or in a historical-logical way within a specific social formation that sublates older formations but encompasses older modes of production into itself? Jairus Banaji (2011) argues that Stalinism and vulgar Marxism have conceptualized the notion of the mode of production based on the assumption that a specific mode contains only one specific historical form of labour and surplus-value appropriation and eliminates previous modes so that history develops in the form of a linear evolution: slavery => feudalism => capitalism => communism. So for example Althusser and Balibar (1970) argue that the historical development of society is non-dialectical and does not involve sublations, but rather transitions "from one mode of production to another" (ibid., 307) so that one mode succeeds the other. This concept of history is one of the reasons why E.P. Thompson (1978a, 131) has characterized Althusser's approach as "Stalinism at the level of theory". The Stalinist "metaphysical-scholastic formalism" (Banaji 2011, 61) has been reproduced in liberal theory's assumption that there is an evolutionary historical development from the agricultural society to the industrial society to the information society so that each stage eliminates the previous one (as argued, for example, by Bell 1974 and Toffler 1980), which shows that in the realm of theory the liberals of today are contemporary Stalinists. According to Banaji, capitalism often intensified feudal or semi-feudal production relations. In parts of Europe and outside, feudalism would have only developed as a "commodity-producing enterprise" (Banaji 2011, 88). In the Islamic world capitalism would have developed without slavery and feudalism (ibid., 6). Banaji advances, in contrast to formalist interpretations, a complex reading of Marx's theory in which a mode of production is "capable of subsuming often much earlier forms" (ibid., 1), "similar forms of labour-use can be found in very different modes of production" (6), and capitalism is "working through a *multiplicity* of forms of exploitation" (145) and is a combined form of development (358) that integrates "diverse forms of exploitation and ways of organising labour in its drive to produce surplus value" (359). A mode of production is a unity of productive forces and relations of production (Marx and Engels 1845/1846, 91). If these modes are based on classes as their relations of production, then they have specific contradictions that result in the sublation *(Aufhebung)* of one mode of production and the emergence of a new one. The emergence of a new mode of production does not necessarily abolish, but rather sublates *(aufheben)* older modes of production. This means that history is for Marx a dialectical process precisely in Hegel's threefold meaning of the term *Aufhebung* (sublation): (1) uplifting, (2) elimination and (3) preservation, expanded as (1) there are new qualities of the economy, (2) the dominance of an older mode of production vanishes, (3) but this older mode continues to exist in the new mode in a specific form and relation to the new mode. The rise of capitalism, however, did not bring an end to patriarchy, but the latter continued to exist in such a way that a specific household economy emerged that fulfils the role of the reproduction of modern labour-power. A sublation can be more or less fundamental. A transition from capitalism to communism requires a fundamental elimination of capitalism; however, the question is if this is immediately possible. Elimination and preservation can take place to differing degrees. A sublation is also no linear progression. It is always possible that relations that resemble earlier modes of organization are created. Capitalism is at the level of the relations of production organized around relations between capital owners on the one side and paid/unpaid labour and the unemployed on the other side. On the level of the productive forces, it has developed from industrial to informational productive forces. The informational productive forces do not eliminate but sublate *(aufheben)* other productive forces (Adorno 1968/2003, chapter 5 of this book): in order for informational products to exist, a lot of physical production is needed, which in-cludes agricultural production, mining and industrial production. The emergence of informational capitalism has not virtualized production or made it weightless or immaterial; rather it is grounded in physical production (Huws 1999, Maxwell and Miller 2012). Whereas capitalism is a mode of production, the terms "agricul-tural society", "industrial society" and "information society" characterize specific forms of the organization of the productive forces (chapter 5 of this book, Adorno 1968/2003).

The new international division of labour organizes the labour process in space and time in such a way that specific components of the overall commodity are produced in specific spaces in the global economy and are reassembled in order to form a coherent whole that is sold as a commodity. It thereby can command labour on the whole globe and during the whole day. Exploitation has become expanded in time and space. The NIDL is connected to modes of production in two specific ways:

- At the level of the *productive forces,* it globally connects various types of pro-duction, such as agricultural labour, industrial labour, service labour, knowl-edge labour, unpaid consumption and user labour, in the form of a network of production that objectifies itself in products and services, but is not auto-matically visible to the workers and consumers.
- At the level of the *relations of production,* the goal is to maximize profits by decreasing wage costs, which makes use of

  (a) the transferal of specific steps of the production process to countries with precarious working conditions, which makes the working classes in various countries compete and tends to be instrumentalized by neo-liberal politics for downsizing and deregulating workers' protection and the welfare state model of capitalism,
  (b) mobilizing various pre-capitalist class relations (patriarchy, slavery, feu-dalism) in combination with capitalist class relations.

Rosa Luxemburg (1913/2003) argued that capitalism needs non-capitalist milieus and that primitive accumulation is a continuous process that creates new spheres and spaces of accumulation. She wrote that "capitalism needs non-capitalist social organisations" on the one hand and that "capital must go all out to obtain ascendancy over [...] territories and social organizations" on the other hand (ibid., 346).

David Harvey (2005, 2007) has interpreted Luxemburg in such a way that capitalism needs to create new realms of accumulation in order to overcome its own crisis tendencies. The transformation of non-wage labour into wage labour or of public services into capitalist realms of accumulation are specific forms of continuous primitive accumulation. Other forms are the creation of various types of unpaid, pre-capitalist, feudal, patriarchal or slave labour that are connected to capitalist accumulation.

The following sections will use examples to analyse various forms of exploitation in the global production of digital media and how they are related to specific modes of production and organization forms of the productive forces. The discussion that follows will try to show how housework, slavery and the capitalist mode of production's organization models play an interlinked role in the global division of labour that creates digital media. The analysis of continuities, sublations and discontinuities of earlier modes of production and forms of organization of capitalism in the digital media economy helps us to understand that the "information society" is not something completely new, as claimed by neo-liberal and managerialist ideologies, but that exploitation is a crucial aspect of the existence of digital media in contemporary global capitalist society.

6.2.1. Unpaid Work in the Family as Mode of Production

Marx and Engels argue that private property and slavery have their origin in the family: The first form of private property "lies in the family, where wife and children are the slaves of the husband. This latent slavery in the family, though still very crude, is the first form of property, but even at this stage it corresponds perfectly to the definition of modern economists, who call it the power of disposing of the labour-power of others" (Marx and Engels 1845/1846, 52). The family is a mode of production, in which labour-power is no commodity but organized by personal and emotional relationships that result in commitment, which includes family work that is unremunerated and produces affects, social relations and the reproduction of the human mind and body. It can therefore also be called reproductive work. Historically it has mainly been women who have conducted physical and emotional/care work in the family. Coercion of work in the family is mainly emotional and social (the workers feel an emotional commitment that motivates their activities), but also often economical (house workers depend for their and the family's survival on the wage income of other household members) and to a certain share physical (abuse, violence in the family).

But which role does reproductive labour and unpaid labour in general have in capitalism? In a formulation in the *Grundrisse,* Marx sees labour as communal or combined labour (Marx 1857/1858b, 470), as collective worker *(Gesamtar-beiter)*. This idea is also taken up in *Capital, Volume 1,* where he defines the collective worker as "a collective labourer, i.e. a combination of workers" (Marx 1867c, 644), and argues that labour is productive if it is part of the combined labour force: "In order to work productively, it is no longer necessary for the individual himself to put his hand to the object; it is sufficient for him to be an organ of the collective labourer, and to perform any one of its subordinate functions" (ibid.). The collective worker is an "aggregate *worker*" whose "*combined activity* results materially in an *aggregate* product" (ibid., 1040). The "activity of this aggregate labour-power" is "the immediate production of surplus-value, the *immediate conversion of this latter into capital*" (ibid.). This means that in capitalism, the collective worker is a productive worker who creates value, surplus value and capital. The notion of the collective worker allows an interpretation of Marx that is not wage-labour-centric because the collective worker as combined workforce also contains all those activities that are unpaid but directly or indirectly serve capital's needs. Labour-power needs to be reproduced; that is, there are certain activities during a certain time period of the day that help the worker recreate and sustain his/her labour capacity. "The value of labour-power is determined, as in the case of every other commodity, by the labour-time necessary for the production, and consequently also the reproduction, of this specific article" (ibid., 274). This includes means of subsistence for workers and their families, practice, training, education and so on (Marx 1861–1863). This means that there are activities that need to be performed by someone and that reproduce labour-power. One can in this context speak of reproductive labour, which is a form of labour that is mostly unpaid. Non-wage labour "ensures the reproduction of labour power and living conditions" (Mies, Bennholdt-Thomsen and Werlhof 1988, 18). It is labour spent "in the production of life, or subsistence production" (ibid., 70).

6.2.2. Ancient and Feudal Slavery as Modes of Production

Marx and Engels (1845/1846) argue that the form of property common in antiquity (e.g. in ancient Rome) was communal property of citizens. It would have been based on slavery as mode of production. Whereas this form of property was based in the city, feudal property was located in the countryside. Slavery in feudal times took on a specific form: peasants were bondslaves. In the city, artisans emerged as a specific economic group that was based on individual ownership and production. Property "during the feudal epoch primarily consisted on the one hand of landed property with serf labour chained to it, and on the other of the personal labour of the individual who with his small capital commands the labour of journeymen" (ibid., 40).

A wage worker's labour-power has a price, its wage, whereas a slave's labour-power does not have a price—it is not a commodity. However, the slave him/

herself has a price, which means that its entire human body and mind can be sold as a commodity from one slave owner to another, who then commands the entire lifetime of the slave. "As a slave, the worker has exchange value, a value; as a free wage-worker he has no value; it is rather his power of disposing of his labour, effected by exchange with him, which has value" (Marx 1857/1858b, 288–289). So in slavery, money is a means for buying and selling the slave as property (like a means of production), but it is not a means that mediates the relationship between slave owner and slave: "In antiquity, one could buy labour, a slave, directly; but the slave could not buy money with his labour" (ibid., 224). "In Roman law, the servus is therefore correctly defined as one who may not enter into exchange for the purpose of acquiring anything for himself" (ibid., 245).

The slave in both ancient slavery and feudalism is treated like a thing and has the status of a thing: "In the slave relation, he belongs to the individual, particular owner, and is his labouring machine. As a totality of force-expenditure, as labour capacity, he is a thing belonging to another, and hence does not relate as subject to his particular expenditure of force, nor to the act of living labour. In the serf relation he appears as a moment of property in land itself, is an appendage of the soil, exactly like draught-cattle. In the slave relation the worker is nothing but a living labourmachine, which therefore has a value for others, or rather is a value" (ibid., 464–465).

The means of coercion in a slave mode of production is physical violence: "Direct forced labour is the foundation of the ancient world; the community rests on this as its foundation" (ibid., 245). This means that the slave is killed if s/he refuses to work.

6.2.3. The Capitalist Mode of Production

Marx (1867c) points out in *Capital, Volume 1*'s chapter on primitive accumulation ("Part 8: So-called primitive accumulation") that the passage from feudalism to capitalism meant that the worker's body was no longer the private property (of a slave owner or feudal lord), but became property of him/herself so that the worker thereby started to be forced to sell his/her labour-power to capitalists in order to earn a wage for being able to survive. At the same time, artisans and peasants who became wage workers also lost the control of the means of production that became private property. "What does the primitive accumulation of capital, i.e. its historical genesis, resolve itself into? In so far as it is not the direct transformation of slaves and serfs into wage-labourers, and therefore a mere change of form, it only means the expropriation of the immediate producers, i.e. the dissolution of private property based on the labour of its owner" (Marx 1867c, 927). The process of primitive accumulation started, according to Marx, in the 15th and 16th centuries: "The prelude to the revolution that laid the foundation of the capitalist mode of production was played out in the last third of the fifteenth century and the first few decades of the sixteenth. A mass of 'free' and unattached proletarians was hurled onto the labour-market by the dissolution of the bands of feudal retainers. [. . .] Although the royal power, itself a product of bourgeois development, forcibly hastened the dissolution of these bands of retainers in its striving for absolute sovereignty, it was by no means the sole cause of it. It was rather that the great feudal lords, in their defiant opposition to the king and Parliament, created an incomparably larger proletariat by forcibly driving the peasantry from the land, to which the latter had the same feudal title as the lords themselves, and by usurpation of the common lands. The rapid expansion of wool manufacturing in Flanders and the corresponding rise in the price of wool in England provided the direct impulse for these evictions" (ibid., 878–879). Marx sees a double freedom as the specific quality of the worker in capitalism: (1) S/he is free in the sense that no slave owner owns his/her body, but this freedom's positive side immediately resulted in a negative side, namely in the coercion to sell one's labour-power to a capitalist in order to earn a wage. So the resolution of one unfreedom (slavery) resulted in a new freedom that is a new form of unfreedom (wage work/slavery). (2) At the same time, during feudalism artisans and peasants to a certain degree owned the means of production, which in capitalism in a negation of history have become the private property of capitalists so that former owners of means of production were turned into non-owners who are free from ownership. Marx summarizes this double (un)freedom of labour in capitalism in the following passage: "Free workers, in the double sense that they neither form part of the means of production themselves, as would be the case with slaves, serfs, etc., nor do they own the means of production, as would be the case with self-employed peasant proprietors. The free workers are therefore free from, unencumbered by, any means of production of their own. With the polarization of the commodity-market into these two classes, the fundamental conditions of capitalist production are present. The capital-relation presupposes a complete separation between the workers and the ownership of the conditions for the realization of their labour. As soon as capitalist production stands on its own feet, it not only maintains this separation, but reproduces it on a constantly extending scale. The process, therefore, which creates the capital-relation can be nothing other than the process which divorces the worker from the ownership of the conditions of his own labour; it is a process which operates two transformations, whereby the social means of subsistence and production are turned into capital, and the immediate producers are turned into wage-labourers. So-called primitive accumulation, therefore, is nothing else than the historical process of divorcing the producer from the means of production. It appears as 'primitive' because it forms the pre-history of capital, and of the mode of production corresponding to capital" (ibid., 874–875).

6.2.4. Informational Productive Forces

I have pointed out earlier that Marx argues that the rise of capitalism was connected to the transition from an agricultural to an industrial economy. Marx describes how the rise of productivity because of technological innovations results in the sublation of an industrial economy by an informational economy. Marx predicted the emergence of informational productive forces as the result of the development of fixed capital, that is, the increasing technical and organic composition of capital that is characterized by an increase of the role of technology in production at the expense of living labour-power. Marx argued that by technological development, "the entire production process" becomes "the technological application of science" (Marx 1857/1858b, 699). The "transformation of the production process from the simple labour process into a scientific process [...] appears as a quality of fixed capital in contrast to living labour" (ibid., 700). So for Marx, the rise of informational productive forces was immanently connected to capital's need for finding technical ways that allow accumulating more profits. That society has to a certain degree become informational is a result of the development of capitalism.

So Marx predicted the rise of an information economy—"general productive forces of the social brain" (ibid., 694)—that is facing a contradiction between living labour and dead labour that expresses itself in crises and contradictions. He did not, however, assume that the information economy necessarily brings capitalism to an end. This circumstance is evident by the circumstance that today we live in a capitalist information economy, although the social nature of knowledge advances the socialization of work and communist potentials that could result in a communist information economy/society, but will not automatically and with historical necessity do so. The rise of an information economy is a sublation of the industrial economy at the level of the productive forces. It results in new property contradictions (e.g. a contradiction between file sharers and intellectual property rights holders that is based on the nature of culture as common good and its reality as commodity), but has not sublated class relations. The relations of production of contemporary society are capitalist in character, whereas the productive forces are simultaneously informational, industrial and agricultural.

Work in the informational forces of production takes on the form of knowledge work, a work that Marx terms work of the general intellect (ibid., 706), "universal labor of the human spirit" (Marx 1894, 114) or "the power of knowledge, objectified" (Marx 1857/1858b, 706): "The development of fixed capital indicates to what degree general social knowledge has become a direct force of production, and to what degree, hence, the conditions of the process of social life itself have come under the control of the general intellect and been transformed in accordance with it. To what degree the powers of social production have been produced, not only in the form of knowledge, but also as immediate organs of social practice, of the real life process" (ibid.).

Informational productive forces constitute not a new mode of production, but rather a sublation of the mode of the organization of the productive forces. So the information society is rather a change within capitalism. It however contains potentials that advance the socialization of labour and thereby contradict class relations and constitute germ forms of a post-capitalist mode of production.

TABLE 6.4 Major metals in the ICT industry

Type of mineral	Major producing countries	Use in the ICT industry	Largest importers
Beryllium	United States, China, Mozambique	Computers, cellular phones	Russia, Kazakhstan, Japan, Kenya
Cobalt	Democratic Republic of Congo (DRC), Australia, Russia, New Caledonia (France), Zambia, Russia, Canada	Rechargeable batteries in laptops, cellular phones, MP3 players, consoles and digital cameras; coatings for hard disks; headphones	China, Norway, Russia, Canada
Gallium	China, Germany, Japan, Ukraine	Mobile phones	Germany, Canada, United Kingdom, China
Indium	China, Republic of Korea, Japan, Canada, Belgium, Brazil	Laptops, flat screens, cellular phones	China, Canada, Japan, Belgium
Palladium	Russia, South Africa, Canada, United States, Zimbabwe	Mobile phones, computers, capacitors	Russia, South Africa, United Kingdom, Norway
Platinum	South Africa, Russia, Canada, Zimbabwe, United States	Hard disks	Germany, South Africa, United Kingdom, Canada
Rare earths	China, India, Brazil, Malaysia	Cell phones, laptops, computers, digital cameras	China, France, Estonia, Japan
Tantalum/ Coltan	Australia, Brazil, DRC, Rwanda, Mozambique, Canada	Cell phones, computers, digital cameras, capacitors used in various electronics (cell phones, consoles, laptops, MP3 players, etc.)	Brazil, Canada, Germany, Russia
Tin	China, Indonesia, Peru, Bolivia, Brazil, Australia, Vietnam, DRC	Printed circuit boards; solder used in computers, mobile phones, MP3 players and game consoles	Peru, Bolivia, Indonesia, China

Sources: Finnwatch (2007), SOMO (2007), US Geological Survey Statistics (2012)

6.3. Digital Media and Minerals

"Products like laptops, mobile phones, games, MP3 players and webcams contain a substantial amount of metals. Amongst the most important in terms of volume are aluminium, iron, copper, nickel and zinc. However, other metals that are only used in very small amounts, such as beryllium, indium, tantalum and the platinum group of metals, are also essential for today's consumer electronics. It has been estimated that metals constitute 25 percent of a mobile phone's weight, batteries and battery chargers excluded. The biggest variety of metals is found in the circuit board" (SOMO 2007, 10). The statistics in table 6.4 show that African countries (Democratic Republic of Congo, Ethiopia, Mozambique, Rwanda, South Africa, Zambia, Zimbabwe) are among the largest producers of minerals needed for ICTs, whereas they hardly figure among important importing countries. This is an indication that the value chain of ICTs is based on a division of labour, where Africa has the role as an important and relatively cheap source of natural resources (cheap because of highly exploited labour) that are further processed in non-African countries, especially China. In the global ICT value chain, Africa is a highly exploited economic colony. And this colonial status is, as will be shown, based on the highly exploited work and slave work of Africans. Marx has argued that colonies are a form of primitive accumulation. "The discovery of gold and silver in America, the extirpation, enslavement and entombment in mines of the indigenous population of that continent, the beginnings of the conquest and plunder of India, and the conversion of Africa into a preserve for the commercial hunting of blackskins, are all things which characterize the dawn of the era of capitalist production. These idyllic proceedings are the chief moments of primitive accumulation" (Marx 1867c, 916). The contemporary existence of economic colonies shows that primitive accumulation is a continuous process that capitalism uses for getting hold of resources and labour in a way that minimizes investment costs by maximizing exploitation. Whereas the minerals required for ICTs tend to be extracted in Africa and China, the smelting, refinement and enrichment of them often takes place in Asian countries such as Thailand, Malaysia, China and Indonesia, which supply the electronics markets (Finnwatch 2007, 37). "Brand companies of electronics have outsourced much of their production to Asia. As a direct consequence Asian mining companies and traders have turned to the Copperbelt [in the Democratic Republic of Congo and Zambia] to secure metals for manufacturing" (Swedwatch 2007, 8).

Especially cobalt, tantalum (which is extracted from coltan) and cassiterite (a tin oxide metal) are minerals used in ICTs that are mined in the Democratic Republic of Congo (DRC). Thomas Luanda, director of a local NGO in Goma and a native of Walikale, where the Bisie mine is located, says that before "1993, these minerals were not known" (Eichstaedt 2011, 111). The rise of the use of mobile phones, computers and video game consoles since the 1990s has spurred the demand for these minerals and especially for cheap sources that allow the reaping of high profits. It could seem at first glance that the conflict in Eastern DRC has mainly ideological reasons, namely the conflict between the Hutus and the Tutsi. The aspect of ICT-related minerals is a blind spot of the debate of this war, which is also a material and deadly conflict about the control of mines. Nest (2011, 26) estimates that the DRC produced 21% of the world's coltan in 2008. Yager (2012) estimates that in 2010 the DRC accounted for 51% of the world's cobalt extraction, 14% of the world's tantalum extraction and 3% of the world's tin extraction.

A study of the extraction of palladium and platinum in South Africa (SOMO 2007) found evidence of poor working conditions, child labour, the displacement of communities, land degradation, environmental pollution, water pollution, abundant water use, air pollution, respiratory diseases (e.g. silicosis) of workers, low wages, no benefits, poor training, precarious contract work, lack of job security and lack of pay for overtime. In August 2012, miners in the Marikana platinum mine went on strike and demanded higher wages from the mine owner, Lonmin. The police killed 34 striking workers and injured dozens. In a public statement, Lonmin wrote that they feel sorry for the families of the killed workers, that the company engages with unions and that therefore the "illegal strike we've seen is so disappointing and damaging" (Lonmin 2012). This can be interpreted to mean that the fact that the strike was a wildcat strike legitimates the police's killing of workers. The coverage of some of the world's leading news media (BBC, *The Guardian*, *The New York Times*[1]) focused on police violence but neglected to mention that these killings are connected to the ICT industry: platinum is an important material for the production of hard disks. All hard disks contain platinum, and according to estimations platinum makes up on average 35% of a hard drive's alloy.[2] This means that ICTs are based not just on the exploitation of African mine workers, but also on their blood. The deliberate killing of striking workers is not simply an aspect of capitalism, it is (according to theories of fascism) an expression of one specific form of capitalism—fascism. "Fascism is the organization of terrorist vengeance against the working class and the revolutionary section of the peasantry and intelligentsia. In foreign policy, fascism is jingoism in its most brutal form, fomenting bestial hatred of other nations" (Dimitrov 1935). "Fascism is the dictatorship of the Fascist [National Socialist] party, the bureaucracy, the army, and big business, the dictatorship over the whole of the people" (Neumann 1942, 295). The ICT industry is a bloody industry, and its murderous and exploitative character is hidden behind the fetishism of commodities; for instance, a thing like a computer or a hard disk is the outcome of labour relations, but these relations cannot be observed and experienced by looking at the product; they are hidden behind the final product. "Work is ironically the hardest part of the Culture Works to see. In part, this is caused by cultural labor's dispersion and submersion in the contemporary political economy's international division of labor" (Maxwell 2001b, 2). Retailers of ICTs buy products from large ICT producers, who tend to outsource hardware manufacturing and buy the hardware components from other companies that buy metals from processing companies that buy raw materials from middle-men who buy them from primary extractors. This complex global value chain involves many nested social relations so that the underlying social relations are not visible at the upper level. Consumers know which label is on their mobile phone or laptop and from which retailer they bought the device, but the dead thing they possess does not talk; it is rather silent on the living labour relations that created it.

The DRC was a Belgian colony from 1885 until 1960, when it became in-dependent. In 1960, the Mouvement National Congolais won the parliamentary elections and Patrice Lumumba became the first prime minister of the DRC. He was murdered in 1961 by secessionists who were supported by Belgian troops and the United States. From 1971 until 1997, Mobutu Sese Seko ruled the coun-try in a pro-US one-party dictatorship. The Rwandan Civil War (1990–1994) between the Hutus and the Tutsi impacted the DRC because many Hutu sol-diers fled there and formed the FDLR (Forces démocratiques de libération du Rwanda) militia, which resulted in military conflicts in Eastern DRC, which borders Rwanda. The Banyamulenge, who are Tutsi Rwandans living in Eastern DRC and who were attacked by the Hutus and government forces, wanted to force the Hutu Rwandans out of the DRC. Mobutu backed the FDLR and ordered that the Tutsis in Eastern DRC should leave the country, otherwise they would be killed. Mobutu's rule came to an end in the First Congo War (1996–1997), where rebels led by Laurent Kabila and supported by Tutsi-led Rwanda and Uganda took over power. After Kabila allowed Hutu soldiers to again reor-ganize themselves in Eastern DRC, Rwanda and Uganda turned against him, which resulted in the Second Congo War (1998–2003), in which Kabila's troops backed by Angola, Namibia and Zimbabwe fought against rebels supported by Rwanda and Uganda. After Kabila was killed in 2001, his son Joseph took over power. Eastern DRC has remained a region that is plagued by everyday armed conflicts. According to estimations, 5.4 million people were killed in the Congo in the years 1998 to 2007, which makes these wars form "the deadliest human catastrophe since World War II" (Eichstaedt 2011, 8). The poverty and violence the country experienced spurred conditions in which everyone did whatever was necessary in order to survive, which created conditions for the existence of modern forms of slavery.

6.4. The Productive Forces of Mineral Extraction in the International Division of Digital Labour: Labour-Power and the Objects, Tools and Products of Labour

In the DRC, the mining that is relevant for the ICT industry involves tin-ore cassiterite, tantalum-ore coltan (that is by refinement transformed into the metal tantalum), wolframite and gold (Finnwatch and Swedwatch 2010). These minerals are used as raw materials in the production of cell phones, laptops, light bulbs and cars (Free the Slaves 2011). There are high reserves of copper, cobalt, zinc and lead in the Katanga region (ACIDH 2011). Copper in some cases accounts for almost 25% of the material out of which mobile phones are made, especially batteries (ibid.).

In the DRC, mining was privatized in the 1990s when the state-owned mining company Société Minière et Industrielle de Kivu stopped operating (Nest 2011, 36). Artisanal mining methods were introduced in the privatized business in Eastern DRC that was standing in the context of a war economy: The tools used for mining in most cases are not machines: miners instead use their hands, sticks, picks, shovels, pickaxes, crowbars, steel bars, steel rods, buckets and ropes (Eichstaedt 2011, 39, 102, 143; Nest 2011, 34). Artisanal mining is especially prevalent in the extraction of coltan, tin, gold, tungsten and diamonds (Nest 2011, 36).

The take-up of the mining business has resulted in the forced relocation of local communities and pollution of rivers, the air and farmland, as well as a lack of local involvement in decision-making and employment (ACIDH 2011).

6.5. The Relations of Production of Mineral Extraction in the International Division of Digital Labour

Many mines in the DRC are controlled by either armed government forces (FARDC) or rebel armies such as the Hutu militia FDLR, the Tutsi militia CNDP (Congrès national pour la défense du peuple) or the Mai-Mai. Concerning the minerals that are relevant for ICT production, groups that have been involved in the control of coltan mines were the DRC government forces, the FDLR, the CNDP, PARECO (Patriotes résistants congolais), Mai-Mai, the armies of Rwanda and Uganda, RCD-Goma (Rassemblement Congolais pour la démocratie–Goma), RCD-ML (RCD–mouvement de libération) and MLC (Mouvement pour la Liberation du Congo). All of them except MLC have also been involved in the control of the tin mines; the cobalt mines have only been controlled by the government DRC army (Nest 2011, 77, 80).

In 2002, the United Nations (2002) published a report that contains a list of 85 companies said to be trading Congolese conflict minerals. Among them are 18 firms explicitly mentioned for trading or processing coltan: four companies from Belgium; three from the United Kingdom; two each from the United States, Germany, China and Saint Kitts; and one each in Switzerland, Malaysia and Kazakhstan. These firms included Cabot in the United States, H.C. Starck in Germany and Ningxia in China. Some companies say that they have joined the requirements of the Organisation for Economic Co-operation and Development (OECD) Due Diligence Guidance for Supply Chains of Minerals from Conflict-Affected and High-Risk Areas and that they have obtained certifications of responsible supply chain management,[3] whereas others that were listed in the UN report say they were contacted by the UN, but as there were no sanctions they continued the trade (e.g. the Belgian company Traxys—formerly named Umicore—according to an interview conducted by Forestier 2007, 42:30–49:10). This shows that voluntary commitments and public shaming of companies without fines do not necessarily end the problem because money rules more than conscience. After a further UN report published in 2008, Traxys announced it would stop trading conflict minerals from DRC, but allegations that it did not stop this trade still emerged in 2012 (International Business Times 2012). This shows that there is a lack of transparency and enforceable rules in the global mineral business. It is a largely deregulated market, and to trade or not trade conflict minerals is largely a voluntary choice.

Empirical research conducted for the Free the Slaves (2011) report focused on interviewing workers in the Bisie and Omate mines as well as mining workers in Walikale and Masisi (N = 742 interviews). The study found that slavery is widespread in the mining industry, including work in digging, sorting, transporting and the sale of minerals as well as in industries that provide services to miners, such as work as domestic servants, in pubs and in the sex industry. "Several distinctly identifiable forms of modern slavery were found in the mining zones of eastern DRC. These include forced labor enforced by armed groups, debt bondage, peonage, sexual slavery, forced marriage, the use of children by armed groups, and other forms of child slavery" (Free the Slaves 2011, 11). Some 40% of the respondents in the Bisie mine (Free the Slaves 2001)—where 80% of the DRC's tin/cassiterite is mined (Eichstaedt 2011, 121)—worked under conditions of slavery.

The researchers documented *forced labour*, where the government's Forces Armées de la République Démocratique du Congo (FARDC) soldiers forced villagers to work in the Bisie mine without payment and under the threat of being killed if they fled. A citizen of Goma, the capital of North Kivu, says, "They take our resources, they kill people, they steal telephones, they rape our women" (Forestier 2007, 27:46–27:52). The effect is increased inequality, as Joseph, a mineral carrier in the South Kivu capital Bukavu, explains: "They are stealing from the Congolese", they "are getting rich, but not the ordinary Congolese" (ibid., 10:33–10:40). Also a system called *salongo* was documented, in which all mine workers on a particular day of the week have to work for one FARDC official (Free the Slaves 2011, 13). Marx described this system of corvée labour, in which the days worked for the lord create surplus labour and the other days form necessary labour time. Marx argues that as a pure form of production, corvée labour existed "in the Slav countries and the Danubian provinces occupied by the Romans" (Marx 1861–1863). Corvée labour "did not arise on the basis of serfdom; instead serfdom arose, inversely, from *corvée* labour" (ibid.). "The latter is based on a community, and the surplus labour the members of the commune performed over and above that required for their subsistence, which served partly as a (communal) reserve fund, and partly to cover the costs of their communal, political and religious requirements, gradually became transformed into *corvée* labour performed for the families which had usurped the reserve fund and the political and religious offices as their private property" (ibid.). The "days of *corvée*" are " legally at the disposal of the proprietor" and form "the legally established surplus labour" (ibid.). "The *corvée* labourer does the labour necessary for the reproduction of his own labour capacity on the field he himself possesses. He performs surplus labour for the landed proprietor on the seignorial estate". In such a system, the workers have other activities for earning a living and are forced to work for a certain amount of hours per week on the feudal lord's land (or as in the case of the DRC) in his/her mine. "The form of the wage is absent from the whole *corvée* system" (ibid.); it is therefore a premodern form of production, a specific form of slavery.

Another system found in Eastern DRC is that miners have to pay a weekly rent to mine controllers and the government in order to work in a specific mine: "The weekly fee to work in one mine was two dessertspoons (literally) of coltan, the worth about $7.50" (Nest 2011, 43). Between 15,000 and 25,000 people work in the Bisie mine. They extract tin and have to pay fees for mining and for entering and leaving the mine (in order to sell the extracted minerals) to the armed group that controls the mine. The imposed fees are so high that the workers cannot ever get out of the working relation, in which they are trapped— they are slaves (Poulsen 2011, 41:15ff). In the DRC's mining industry, both the classic form of slavery as well as feudal slavery based on rent and corvée slavery exist. Marx described how these two premodern forms of production differ from wage labour: "The wage-form thus extinguishes every trace of the division of the working day into necessary labour and surplus labour, into paid labour and unpaid labour. All labour appears as paid labour. Under the *corvée* system it is different. There the labour of the serf for himself, and his compulsory labour for the lord of the land, are demarcated very clearly both in space and time. In slave labour, even the part of the working day in which the slave is only replacing the value of his own means of subsistence, in which he therefore actually works for himself alone, appears as labour for his master. All his labour appears as unpaid labour. In wage-labour, on the contrary, even surplus labour, or unpaid labour, appears as paid. In the one case, the property-relation conceals the slave's labour for himself; in the other case the money-relation conceals the uncompensated labour of the wage-labourer" (Marx 1867c, 680). In wage labour, the worker is double free and sells his labour-power as a commodity for the whole working week. In classic slavery, the slave is unfree and a property of the slave owner for the entire working week. In the corvée system, the worker is a slave for part of the working week, whereas the other part of the week is free for other activities that are needed for earning a living. "The slave is the property of a particular master; the worker must indeed sell himself to capital, but not to a particular capitalist, and so within certain limitations he may choose to sell himself to whomever he wishes;

and he may also change his master" (ibid., 1032). Both forms of slavery and wage labour have in common that they take place within class relations, which means that there are owners who exploit the unpaid surplus labour of workers for a certain share of the working week: "Capital did not invent surplus labour. Wherever a part of society possesses the monopoly of the means of production, the worker, free or unfree, must add to the labour-time necessary for his own maintenance an extra quantity of labour-time in order to produce the means of subsistence for the owner of the means of production, whether this proprietor be an Athenian caloς cagaqoς [aristocrat], an Etruscan theocrat, a *civis romanus*, a Norman baron, an American slave-owner, a Wallachian boyar, a modern landlord or a capitalist" (ibid., 344–345). In the Free the Slaves (2011) study, a significant share of respondents was facing debt bondage slavery: Money is borrowed at very high interest rates, which forces the debtors to work in a mine. There are fraud schemes that "make it impossible to pay off the debt" (ibid, 14). "Jean, 15-years-old, was sent over 30 kilometers (approximately 18 miles) from his hometown of Mubi to Omate by his mother in order to make money to pay off her US$100 debt. He sells grilled goat meat and is also a digger. His mother and his boss agreed that the boss must 'pay' 8000FC (approximately US$10 at the time he was interviewed) per month for the child's services, of which his mother receives 6000FC to pay off her debt and the boss keeps the balance, ostensibly to provide for the child. Jean says he just wants to go home, enroll in school and run a small business" (ibid.). Also peonage slavery was documented. In this form of slavery, a person is arrested under some charges that are mostly made up and then told that the sentence is that he must work in a mine. Women are generally not allowed to work in mines. They are, however, facing various forms of sexual slavery that are connected to the mining business, as for example unpaid work that is connected to prostitution, where the pub owner takes part or all of the money. Women are also facing rape, forced marriages, genital mutilation conducted by soldiers and the danger of HIV transmission. A third of the interviewed children said that they were recruited by force into an armed group, in which they worked as soldiers or in the mines. This was especially the case in Mai-Mai rebel groups, but also in the FARDC. "'If you can't afford to pay for workers, you'll target children, who are most vulnerable and can be tempted into highly exploitative situations with the simple promise of a meal at the end of the day', was how one NGO worker described the situation" (ibid., 21). Of the interviewed children (N = 31) 89% were living in and working under conditions of slavery. "Children's work includes digging, cleaning, shovelling, picking and transporting minerals, as well as pounding ore with hammer" (ibid., 22). There are no wages or wages that only cover minimal subsistence. The average wage of a Congolese mining worker is US$1–3 per day, and 75% of the miners cannot cover basic needs with their wage (Finnwatch 2007, 29). The slaves are working long hours; there are no or only very weak unions, bad living, unsanitary and unhygienic conditions, a lack of medical supply and services, and as a consequence the workers are constantly facing diseases.

"When unions exist they are, however, often weak and in no position of bringing about real change. In some cases the unions are totally controlled by employers, influencing the election of representatives in order to use them for their own purposes. According to workers at Boss Mining (Camec), membership of the union is compulsory. Every month the employer deducts one dollar from the salary of each worker as a union fee. 'There is only one union. We have elected representatives, but they too have sometimes been threatened by the Managing Director when they have wanted to speak to him about our demands. Finally we went on strike, because the representatives didn't succeed'" (SwedWatch 2007, 36). This example demonstrates the existence of yellow (instead of red) unions in the extractive ICT-related industry. "In addition to the constant threat posed by the lawlessness of the armed groups, inhabitants of the mining zones face numerous threats to their health and personal safety. Miners work without basic equipment and suffer landslides, cave-ins of shafts, and asphyxiation. Malnutrition, exhaustion, physical trauma, poor sanitation, lack of medical treatment, and no clean water supply mean that public health concerns are equally high. Common injuries and ailments include: eye injuries; silicosis; conjunctivitis; bronchitis; tuberculosis; asthma; diarrhoea; skin lesions; deformed muscle and bone in children due to heavy loads; regular dental problems including abscesses, cavities and lesions; tetanus; fractures and contortions; and contusions and severe bruising. Added to these are the impact of extensive drug use and sexually transmitted diseases. The intense crowding—enslaved miners are sometimes forced to sleep jammed together in the mine shafts—means that infectious diseases are rampant. One informant stated that after four to five years working in the mines the body was 'completely deteriorated'; he cited spinal column damage and lung damage, conditions worsened by the extreme pollution of air and water and exposure to toxic chemicals" (Free the Slaves 2011, 7–8).

In the Free the Slaves (2011) study, it became clear that the documented slavery on the one hand works with physical violence: soldiers force children and villagers at gunpoint to work as slaves in the mines. They kill or torture workers if they refuse to work. Also women are violently forced into marrying or having sex with soldiers. But coercion also takes a socio-economic form, in which villagers want to work in the mines or as prostitutes because they live in poverty and have hopes to lift themselves out of poverty. An example: "Janine, age 11, was forced into sexual slavery after arriving in Mubi. She had come to work in a pub in order to support her mother in Walikale. Janine soon discovered that, for a girl, 'bar work' meant that she would not be given a salary for the work she performed. Instead, she was told that she would be 'given an opportunity to be seen by men' who would pay for her sexual services. With nowhere else to go and nothing to eat, Janine was forced to engage in prostitution with bar customers, she said, 'in order to find a bar of soap'. Both CREDDHO [Centre de Recherche sur l'Environnement, la Démocratie et les Droits de l'Homme] and ASSODIP [Association pour le Développement des Initiatives Paysannes] discovered cases in which mothers prostituted their underage daughters in this way. 13-year-old Solange, for example, worked for her mother as a waitress while being trafficked for sex to customers of her pub in Omate" (ibid., 18). Muhanga Kawaya, an enslaved miner in North Kivu, describes his work in the following way: "As you crawl through the tiny hole, using your arms and fingers to scratch, there's not enough space to dig properly and you get badly grazed all over. And then, when you do finally come back out with the cassiterite, the soldiers are waiting to grab it at gunpoint. Which means you have nothing to buy food with. So we're always hungry" (Finnwatch 2007, 20).

6.6. Conclusion

Not every mobile phone, computer, digital camera, hard disk, game console and MP3 player that we use is based, partly or fully, on the blood of East Congolese miners: In 2011, the DRC produced 53% of the world's cobalt, 2.3% of the world's tin (US Geological Survey Statistics 2012) and around 10% of the world's tantalum (Eichstaedt 2011, 140). So the situation varies depending on the type of mineral. The DRC is the world's largest producer of cobalt and a significant producer of tantalum and tin. Independent of these facts is the circumstance that the demand of Western companies for cheap minerals has been an important driver of the violence, slavery and exploitation in Eastern DRC.

The tragedy of the DRC is that a country rich in mineral resources has been the locus of one of the bloodiest conflicts in the world in the 20th and 21st centuries and that this conflict has in the form of conflict minerals a connection to the West and the Western ICT industry. The DRC was in 2011 the least developed country in the world, had a very high inequality rate (Gini) of 44.4%, 59.2% of the population lived in extreme poverty (less than US$1.25 per day for survival) and the life expectancy was 45 years (UNHDR 2011). War and neo-imperialist exploitation of labour and the country's resources, which does not benefit local people but benefits at the end of the value chain primarily Western companies, have created the paradox typical for capitalism that one of the world's countries that is richest in natural resources—45% of the world's cobalt reserves, 25% of the world's diamond reserves (US Geological Survey Statistics 2012) and according to estimates between 7–8% (Nest 2011, 18–20) and 64% (Gootnick 2008) of the world's coltan reserves are located in the DRC—is socially the world's poorest country. In the global ICT industry, African companies are hardly present, but rather companies in the United States, Japan, Taiwan, South Korea, Sweden and Finland dominate the computer hardware industry that requires minerals as its raw materials: the largest computer, communications equipment and periphery producers in the world are Apple (USA), HP (USA), Dell (USA), Fujitsu (Japan) and Quanta Computer (Taiwan); the largest semiconductor producers are Samsung (South Korea), Intel (USA), Taiwan Semiconductor (Taiwan), Texas Instruments (USA) and Applied Materials (USA); the largest communications equipment producers are Cisco (USA), Qualcomm (USA), Ericsson (Sweden), Corning (USA) and Nokia (Finland) (Forbes 2000, 2012). This shows that the profits that are accumulated by the sales of the final products (a mobile phone, a computer, a printer, etc.) go into the pockets of shareholders of Western companies, whereas the immediate extractors of the underlying raw materials are often facing harsh working conditions and are barely able to survive. The major processors of tantalum are the United States' Cabot and Germany's H.C. Starck (Nest 2011, 12). The largest processors of tin were in 2011 Yunnan Tin (China), the Malaysia Smelting Corporation, PT Timah (Indonesia) and Minsur (Peru) (ITRI 2011). In 2010, China was the largest cobalt-processing country and accounted for 43.9% of the worldwide capacity (Shedd 2012). The largest Chinese companies processing cobalt are Jinchuan, Zhejiang Huayou Cobalt Nickel Materials Co. Ltd., Zhejiang Galico Cobalt & Nickel Material Co. Ltd., and Ganzhou Yi Hao Umicore Industries (ibid.). The DRC accounted that year for 8.8% of the processing (ibid.), although it in the same year accounted for 51% of the world's cobalt extraction (Yager 2012). The countries with the largest and most profitable mining and metal-producing companies that are ranked among the world's largest 400 companies are Australia, Brazil, the United Kingdom, Switzerland, China, Canada and Russia (Forbes 2000, 2012), which shows that Africa (with the exception of South Africa) is not a producer of metals in general, but rather only an extractor of minerals that are then sold to other countries, where they are smelted and refined so that the resulting minerals are then further sold for a profit. African countries are at the lowest end of the value chain: they are a locus of highly exploited labour and only get a very small share of the overall profits achieved in the ICT industry and other industries that requires metals (a similar analysis can, for example, be made for the car industry, where there is not a single large automobile manufacturer located in Africa that ranges among the world's largest 2,000 companies).

In order to obtain a functioning ICT tools, the extracted minerals must be used in the manufacturing and assemblage of ICT components. As an illustration, the next chapter will discuss ICT assemblage and manufacturing at Foxconn in China.

Notes

1 A search in the Factiva database for articles in these three media that covered the strike (keyword search: "Lonmin") in the time period from June 23 until December 23, 2012, produced 36 results (conducted on December 23, 2012). None of the results covered aspects of ICTs.

2 http://www.platinum.matthey.com/applications/industrial-applications/hard-disks/ (accessed December 23, 2012).

3 See a statement by H.C. Starck, http://www.hcstarck.com/en/home/hc_starck_group/ the_way_we_move/raw_material_procurement.html (accessed December 26, 2012).

7

EXPLOITATION AT FOXCONN

Primitive Accumulation and the Formal Subsumption of Labour

Do you own an Apple Macintosh, an iPad, an iPod or an iPhone? Have you ever thought about who assembles it and under which working conditions? Think of Apple. Which names do you automatically associate with it? It is unlikely that it is one of the following names: Rong Bo, Ma Xianqian, Li Hongliang, Tian Yu, Li Wei, Liu Zhijun, Rao Shuqin, Ning, Lu Xin, Zhu Chenming, Liang Chao, Nan Chang, Li Hai, He, Chen Lin, Liu, Liu Ming. And it is likely that you think about the following two names: Steve Jobs and Steve Wozniak. The 17 Chinese names are the names of 17 Foxconn workers who attempted to commit suicide between January and August 2010 because they could no longer stand the poor working conditions in the factories, where Apple technologies and other ICTs are assembled. They are largely unknown to the world. In contrast, Steve Jobs and Steve Wozniak are known all over the world as the founders of Apple. Those in power write history, although those who struggle against these powers make history. The task of this chapter is to help remember the stories of those who create the computer technologies that we use every day. It tells the story of working conditions at Foxconn, one of the world's largest ICT manufacturing and assemblage companies. It is a story of exploitation and imperialism that is inscribed into the phones, computers, screens and laptops that we use every day for talking, writing, listening and watching. The story of many ICT tools is the largely unknown story of highly exploited workers.

7.1. Introduction

In 2011, income inequality measured by the Gini coefficient in China was 41.5%, the adult illiteracy rate was 6%, the health-adjusted life expectancy was 66 years, 12.5% of the population lived in multidimensional poverty and 4.5% in severe poverty, and 15.9% of the population had to survive on less than US$1.25 a day (UNHDR 2011). These data show that China has achieved the status of a medium developing country that has been successful in fighting poverty and illiteracy but at the same time has a high level of socio-economic inequality. The global computer hardware market is dominated by US and Taiwanese companies: among the 12 hardware companies listed in the 2012 Forbes 2000 list of the largest corporations in the world are 3 US-based firms (Apple, HP, Dell), which are the largest hardware companies in the world and are also among the 200 largest companies in the world. There are 7 Taiwanese companies, but only 1 Chinese computer hardware producer (Linovo) (Forbes 2000, 2012). Ten of the 15 listed software companies are based in the United States (e.g. Microsoft, Oracle, Symantec); none has its home base in China. There are 29 semiconductor producers in the Forbes 2000 list, of these largest, 14 are American and 4 come from Taiwan, whereas none is from China. In the computer storage market, there is 1 Chinese company (Tencent Holdings) in the Forbes 2000 list in comparison to 4 American ones. In software services, the largest companies are in the United States (IBM, Google). The United States accounts for 8 of the world's 20 largest software service providers, China for 3 (Tencent Holdings, Baidu, Netease), India and France each for 3 also. The largest telecommunications equipment corporations are based in the United States (Cisco, Qualcomm, Corning), Sweden (Ericsson) and Finland (Nokia), whereas there is only one Chinese company (ZTE) in this list. This shows that Chinese companies play a role in the global ICT industry but are embedded into a structure dominated by the United States. The production of consumer electronics is dominated by Japan, which accounts for 8 out of 12 companies in this area in the 2012 Forbes 2000 list (e.g. Panasonic, Fujifilm, Sony, Nintendo). Also 2 Chinese companies are present in this list: TCL Corporation (TVs, video cameras, phones) and Great Wall Technology (memory, power supply, monitors, computers, LCD TVs). The telecommunications market is strongly national in character, with 37 different countries represented in the list of the 62 telecommunications companies that were part of Forbes 2000 in 2012. Among these 62 corporations are 3 Chinese (China Telecom, China Mobile, China Unicom). These data show that China is a significant but not a dominant player in the ICT industry, which is dominated by the United States (hardware, software, semiconductors, software services, telecommunications equipment), Taiwan (hardware) and Japan (consumer electronics).

Tables 7.1 and 7.2 show the development of Chinese computer hardware output over a period of ten years. Some 320 million micro-computers were manufactured in 2011. More than a billion mobile phones were produced in 2011. In

TABLE 7.1 The development of ICT hardware production in China

	2001	*2010*
Integrated circuits	2.2 billion	7.4 billion
Printed circuit boards	382 million square feet	1.1 billion square feet
Light-emitting diodes	1.96 billion	30.3 billion

Source: Statistical Yearbook of the Republic of China (2010)

TABLE 7.2 ICT hardware production in China in 2011

	2011
Integrated circuits	7.2 billion
Micro-computers	320 million
Colour TV sets	122 million
LCD TV sets	103 million
Mobile telephones	1.1 billion

Source: National Bureau of Statistics of China (2012)

the period 2001–2010, the number of manufactured integrated circuits increased from 2.2 billion to 7.4 billion. Yu Hong (2011, 50–51, 55) presents data that show that in 2003 and 2007, computers, electronic components and telecommunications equipment were the primary output (measured in billion CNY, Chinese yuan renminbi) of the Chinese ICT industry, that especially telecommunications equipment and computers attracted large foreign direct investments and that the majority of the output of computers and electronic components was exported. In 2011, the main Chinese exports were data processing components/machines (export value: US$176.3 billion) and clothes (US$153.2 billion) (National Bureau of Statistics of China 2012). Of all Chinese exports 52.4% were foreign-funded (ibid.). Hong (2011, 63–64) presents data that show that ICT exports have been dominated by foreign capital and joint ventures of foreign and Chinese companies. In 2007, 1.3 million people were employed in the manufacturing of computers and 2.1 million in the production of electronic components (ibid., 55). The majority of these workers were assemblers and sales workers (ibid., 53). Foreign companies dominate the Chinese ICT industry: in 2005 these companies accounted for 76.5% of the profits in this industry, but because of special treatment by the government they only accounted for 42.3% of the total taxes paid by the ICT industry (ibid., 38).

These data show that China has an export-oriented economy that is strongly based on the manufacturing of electronics and clothes, cheap labour and land, and the domination of transnational companies (Zhao 2010a). China became the second largest ICT manufacturer in the world in the year 2006 (Hong 2011, 2) and the world's largest producer of laptops, mobile phones, colour and LCD screens and switchers in 2004 (59).

In the publishing industry, there were in 2010 according to official statistics (*Statistical Yearbook of the Republic of China* 2010) 148 software publishers that made up 4.4% of all publishers in China (including publishers of newspapers, periodicals and magazines, books, software, other publishing), which shows that the software industry in comparison to other media industries is comparatively small in China. Jack Qiu (2009, 93–94) argues that foreign capital investments in China focus especially on the electronics industry. Qiu (ibid.) presents statistics that show that since 1978, when Deng Xiaoping started the programme of introducing "market socialism" reforms that introduced "market socialism with Chinese characteristics" (which some prefer to term "neoliberalism with 'Chinese characteristics'", Harvey 2007, chapter 5), there has been a massive decrease of employment in agriculture, fishing and mining and a corresponding increase in manufacturing and low-skill service jobs. Yuezhi Zhao (2007a, 2008) argues convincingly that the digital revolution in China "has been occurring at a time when the Chinese state is progressively liberalizing the Chinese economy and promoting market forces" (Zhao 2007a, 100). The rise of ICTs in China would furthermore have been accomplished by techno-nationalism, military-industrial interests, "convergent interests of domestic bureaucratic and international corporate capital, along with the consuming priorities of China's urban middle class. For this reason, it has been intrinsically connected to the deepening economic inequality and pervasive social injustice facing tens of millions across China. [. . .] As the Chinese economy has grown exponentially and telecommunications market expansion repeatedly surpassed state planners' expectations throughout the 1990s [...], so has inequality" (Zhao 2007a, 101). China would have exactly embraced the consumerism and capitalism that Dallas Smythe (1994) warned about when he visited China in the early 1970s. China's industry and ICT industries have been based on "an FDI-friendly, export-dependent, and market-fundamentalist policy framework" that has "structured China's ICT industries in a way to serve a downstream industrial cluster in the globalized chain of production" and has "established the domination of foreign capital in ICT production" (Hong 2011, 80).

7.2. Foxconn's Productive Forces in the International Division of Digital Labour: Labour-Power and the Objects, Tools and Products of Labour

Hon Hai Precision (also known as Foxconn) is a Taiwanese company that "processes and sells connectors, cable, enclosures, wired/wireless communication products, optics products, power supply modules, and assemblies for use in the information technology, communications, automotive equipment, precision molding, automobile and consumer electronics industries"[1]. (Its headquarters are in Taiwan. With assets of US$47.3 billion, a market value of US$37.8 billion, sales of US$102.7 billion and profits of US$2.6 billion, it was the 156th largest company in the world in 2012 (Forbes 2000, 2012). It had 995,000 employees in 2012 (ibid.). Terry Gou is the company's founder and chairman. He is the world's 184th richest person and his wealth amounted to US$5.5 billion in 2012 (Forbes: The World's Billionaires 2012). According to CNN Global 500 (2012), Foxconn is the fifth largest corporate employer in the world. In 2010, it had 900,000 workers in China, of which 420,000 worked in the Shenzen factory (SACOM 2010, 10). In 2011, Foxconn had enlarged its Chinese workforce to a million, with a majority being young migrant workers who come from the countryside (SACOM 2011a). So a large share of Foxconn's workers is located in Chinese factories, such as in Chengdu, Chongdinq, Guanlan and Longhua (two districts in Shenzhen), Hangzhou, Kunshan, Langfang, Nanhai (in the city Foshan), Tai-yuan, Tianjin and Zhengzhou. Foxconn assembles the iPad, iMac, iPhone, Kindle, and various consoles (by Sony, Nintendo, Microsoft). Its customers are Western companies such as Apple, Dell, HP, Motorola, Nokia, Sony and Sony Ericsson (SACOM 2010, 4).

7.3. Foxconn's Relations of Production in the International Division of Digital Labour

Rong Bo. Ma Xianqian. Li Hongliang. Tian Yu. Li Wei. Liu Zhijun. Rao Shuqin. Ning. Lu Xin. Zhu Chenming. Liang Chao. Nan Chang. Li Hai. He. Chen Lin. Liu. Liu Ming.[2]

These are the names of the 17 Foxconn workers who attempted to commit suicide between January and August 2010: 12 of them were male, 7 female; they were aged between 17 and 25; 16 attempted to commit suicide by jumping from Foxconn buildings, one by slitting his wrists. Four survived. Two suicides took place in the Langfang factory, four in the Guanlan factory, nine in the Longhua factory, one in the Nanhai factory and one in the Kunshan factory (SACOM 2010, 2). Steve Jobs is dead. And he will definitely be remembered by many for having founded Apple. Thirteen of these 17 young workers are dead. How many have ever heard their names? How many will remember their names? Society tends to remember those in power and to forget those on whose labour, sweat and blood this power is built because a class society also has a collective class memory.

Students and Scholars against Corporate Misbehaviour (SACOM 2010) conducted a study in which 100 Foxconn workers in Shenzen and Hangzhou were interviewed and observed. In June 2010, the basic wage of Foxconn Shenzen workers was CNY (Chinese yuan renminbi) 1200 per month, which is around GBP (British pound) 120 and CNY 100 above the local minimum wage (SACOM 2010, 6). The basic wage at the same time was CNY 1250 at Foxconn Hangzhou, CNY 1110 at Foxconn Kunshan, CNY 950 at Foxconn Wuhan and CNY 940 at Foxconn Tianjin (ibid.). SACOM (2010) calculated that the living wage that is needed for surviving in Shenzen should be CNY 2293, CNY 2173 in Hangzhou, CNY 2000 in Kunshan, CNY 1754 in Wuhan and CNY 1685 in Tianjin.

In 2008, Foxconn Guanlan workers on average worked 120 hours overtime per month (SACOM 2010, 7). An engineer at Foxconn Shenzhen says, "We produced the first generation iPad. We were busy throughout a 6-month period and had to work on Sundays. We only had a rest day every 13 days. And there was no overtime premium for weekends. Working for 12 hours a day really made me exhausted" (ibid.). At Foxconn Hangzhou, weekend overtimes were only paid at a rate of 1.5 instead of 2 as required by the law. At Foxconn Taiyuan, overtime beyond 80 hours per month was unremunerated. Unpaid work assemblies that last up to an hour per day before the start of a shift were documented. SACOM (2010) also documented frequent work shift changes, regular working time of over 10 hours per day, a lack of breaks, monotonous work, physical harm caused by chemicals such as benzene or solder paste, lack of protective gear and equipment, forced use of students from vocational schools as interns (in agreement with the school boards) who conduct regular assembly work that does not help their studies, prison-like accommodations with 6–22 workers per dormitory room (SACOM 2011a, 18) who do not know each other, and yellow unions that are managed by company officials and whom the workers do not trust. One worker at Foxconn Longhua says that the union "usually acts in favour of the management. The union workers tend to please the management in order to secure their career paths" (SACOM 2010, 21). Also the food has been reported to be extremely disgusting. One worker in the Chongqing Foxconn factory said, "On the first day, I almost vomited after eating the food in canteen. I've never eaten something which tasted worse than that" (SACOM 2011a, 18).

Tian Yu, a 17-year-old girl who survived an attempted suicide, reports that at Foxconn Longhua she had to work from 7 a.m. to 7 p.m. (Qiu 2010b). "Somebody in the factory scolded me". The overseer argued that she worked too slow. She reports that her salary was not paid on time and that she was told to collect it in another factory campus, where nobody knew about her salary.

SACOM (2011a) conducted interviews with 120 workers in Shenzen, Chengdu and Chongdinq in order to test if, a year after the Foxconn suicides, the working conditions had changed. Interviewees at the Foxconn Chengdu factory that assembles Apple products felt tricked and misled because job ads and government announcements promised CNY 1600–2500 per month, whereas the reality turned out to be CNY 950. The poor working conditions documented in the previous study were confirmed. In addition, the researchers also found miscalculations of wages that never were corrected and left workers with wages lower than guaranteed in their contracts (which were often kept by the employer without issuing a copy to the employees). The basic salary in Chengu was CNY 950 in 2011 and CNY 1300 if the food and housing allowances are included, whereas according to Engel's law it should have been CNY 2600. SACOM (2011b) conducted interviews with workers at the three Foxconn production sites in Zhengzhou, where iPhones are manufactured. The study confirmed all poor working conditions that were previously documented. In 2012, SACOM (2012) conducted a follow-up study comprising 60 interviews with workers in Zhengzhou. The researchers (again) found excessive overtime, a surge in working hours resulting from the release of the iPhone 5, unpaid overtime, monotonous work, lack of breaks, contractual work, health and safety threats, a military management style, the exploitation of forced student interns, arbitrary relocation, workers who have to write confession letters to report misconduct, and a yellow union. A 30-year-old worker reports, "Now, we can only have a day-off every 13 working days. For the machine operators, they do not have a day off throughout a month. It is very difficult to take leave. Apple is everything to Foxconn. [. . .] I do not think I can afford an iPhone with the low wages. [. . .] I feel disappointed about Apple. It only aims to make profit" (ibid., 4–5). A 21-year-old worker explains, "Now, when we have to rush to complete the iPhone 5 orders, the management is inhumane. I do not have a day-off in the past 30 days" (ibid., 5).

World Economy, Ecology and Development (WEED) and SACOM found very similar poor working conditions in the Excelsior Electronics company that assembles motherboards, chips and graphics cards for AMD, Fujitsu Siemens and Intel and in the Compeq Technology company that manufactures printed circuit boards used by such companies as Dell, Lenovo and Nokia (WEED and SACOM 2008). This shows that the Foxconn example is not singular but seems to follow a larger trend in the IDDL. The Fair Labor Association (2012) conducted a survey with N = 35,166 respondents who are employees in Foxconn Chengdu, Guanlan and Longhua. The survey showed that the average working hours were 56.07 per week, the average maximum during the past three months 61.05 hours, and the average longest period during the past three months without rest 11.57 days. Of the respondents, 64.3% think that their salaries do not cover their basic needs. In Chengdu, 72% of the respondents felt the same way, 71.8% disagreed or completely disagreed that the factory canteen's food is good, and 78.6% said that the dorm is a little crowded or crowded. In the survey, 64.9% of the workers in Longhua, 59% in Guanlan and 71% in Chengdu said that they sometimes feel bodily pain after work; 70.2% did not know if the trade union participates in decision-making or not; and 61.4% agreed or completely agreed that their work is often stressful. Workers were asked what three things they would change if they had the chance: salaries were the top priority, followed by benefits/allowances, food quality and working hours. Only 22.1% said that they are union members. A full 72.2% of the respondents were migrant workers, which is relevant because these workers, usually because of discriminatory practices, conduct low-paid routinized jobs and as a result of the hukou registration system are formally seen as rural citizens, who do not belong to the urban centres where they work and are therefore often discriminated against and denied access to public services, which makes them especially vulnerable to the pressures exerted by employers (Qiu 2009, chapters 4 and 6). According to official statistics, there were 252.78 million migrants workers in China in 2011, an increase of 4.4% in comparison to 2010 (National Bureau of Statistics of China 2012). Rural poverty is the basic reason for the Chinese young rural population to migrate to urban areas (Hong 2011, chapter 5). "Being pulled by urban aspirations but pushed by bad urban experiences, frequent job change turns out to be a compromised option and constitutes a typical life trajectory for migrant workers" (ibid., 202).

In the period 2001–2005, 40 million landless peasants were created by government appropriation of rural land, which further spurs migration into cities (ibid., 204). What is happening to Chinese peasants is exactly what Marx (1867c) described as the process of primitive accumulation that started in Europe in the 15th and 16th centuries: primitive accumulation creates an "incomparably larger proletariat by forcibly driving the peasantry from the land [. . .] and by usurpation of the common lands" (ibid., 878). "The newly freed men became sellers of themselves only after they had been robbed of all their own [rural] means of production, and all the guarantees of existence afforded by the old feudal arrangements. And this history, the history of their expropriation, is written in the annals of mankind in letters of blood and fire" (ibid., 875).

Foxconn is a company that is quite characteristic for the Chinese ICT economy, whose employment relations Yu Hong (2011, chapters 3, 5) has analysed in detail based on statistical analysis and 63 interviews with Chinese workers: the high level of foreign direct investment in the ICT industry has created millions of jobs that are, however, mainly "semi-skilled, dead-end, and irregular assembling jobs" (ibid., 103)—informal positions characterized by low wages, low job and social security, low skills, repetitive and laborious work, danger to workers' health and long hours. A large share of these workers in the Chinese ICT industry are young, female and rural migrants. A large share of companies that employ these workers are based in the provinces Guangdong and Fujian (ibid., 112). The "FDI-driven and outward-looking mode of ICT development has created a new working-class stratum who are regionally clustered, largely peasant-based, semi-skilled, low-wage, irregularly employed, and mostly female manual workers" (ibid., 113).

The Fair Labor Association (FLA) has been criticized because the companies it monitors are partly its largest donors. So, for example, Apple became a paying corporate member of the FLA in 2012 at the same time the Fair Labor Association (2012) study of Foxconn was commissioned. The FLA's CEO, Auret van Heerden, after a guided tour of Foxconn, commented that "Foxconn is really not a sweatshop" (Greenhouse 2012). This judgement was made prior to any empirical analysis, and FLA was much criticized for this as being partial and prejudgemental (ibid.). SACOM argues that "the FLA is not independent from Apple and will not criticize the low unit price and short delivery time of its members" (SACOM 2012, 10). Consequently, SACOM criticizes the argument of the FLA (2012) that the cause of overtime is high labour turnover—SACOM's (theoretically correct) perspective is that "high turnover is a symptom of job dissatisfaction instead of a root cause of excessive overtime" (SACOM 2012, 3). The FLA study has the advantage that it is large-scale and has the possibility of access to a large number of workers. At the same time, the FLA's independence is disputed, which may affect the survey and interviews it conducts in a company-friendly way, and workers may feel pressured and may be afraid to answer truthfully if a survey is formally conducted in the company and introduced/supported by the management. They may have fears that anonymity is not guaranteed. In contrast, the SACOM conducts interviews informally and anonymously: students start working in the factories, make contact with workers and then interview them in a private setting. This method guarantees more truthful results but at the same time has resource and time constraints in reaching a large number of respondents. In its Corporate Social & Environmental Responsibility (CSR) Reports, Foxconn (2010, 2011) follows the ideological strategy of avoiding addressing negative reports and research results and instead lists its positive achievements, mainly in the form of claims that are not independently verified. "Foxconn fosters a harmonic work environment that promotes 'health, stability, and development' and strives to improve employee welfare" (Foxconn 2011, 14). Foxconn "creates an atmosphere of health, harmony and advancement" (Foxconn 2010, 15). The chapter "2.2 Employee Welfare" has only five pages, consists mainly of images that show happy employees, has little text and does not address the crucial issues for which Foxconn has been criticized. So for example, it describes as a positive achievement that labour unions "launched a number of fun activities to improve the quality of life at work and all employees were encouraged to attend. These activities included the '2010 Excellent Frontline Worker Award' competition, food and shopping carnival, singing championship—('Who is the Idol'), logo design competition show, stamping worker competition, happy star competition, photographing contest, Care on Women's Day program, and dating activities" (ibid., 17). The question if members feel represented by these unions, if unions represent employees' or rather capitalists' interest (whether they are red or yellow unions), if workers trust union representatives, if unions have decision power and so on are not discussed. The discussed studies show that there are strong doubts that this is the case. Teun van Dijk (1998, 267; 2011, 396–397) explains as part of the ideological square model that one strategy of an ideological discourse in order to distort reality is to express/emphasize information that is positive about "Us", "Us" meaning an in-group, such as Foxconn. Foxconn employs this strategy in its CSR reports.

Apple has introduced Supplier Responsibility Reports. It is questionable whether, if a company itself audits its suppliers, this analysis is conducted fully independently and in a critical manner. Whereas the 2012 report (Apple 2012) claims (based on quite dubious and opaque definitions and empirical methods) that the majority of labour issues are well handled by the suppliers, it says that only 38% of the suppliers respect working hours standards. The 2013 report claims that "we achieved an average of 92 percent compliance with a maximum 60-hour work week" (Apple 2013, 6). Apple's standards of working times say, "Apple's Code sets a maximum of 60 work hours per week and requires at least one day of rest per seven days of work, while allowing exceptions in unusual or emergency circumstances" (Apple 2012, 8). Apple's definition of what are appropriate working hours is arbitrary and does not respect the International Labour Organization's Convention C030—Hours of Work, which says, "Article 3: The hours of work of persons to whom this Convention applies shall not exceed forty-eight hours in the week and eight hours in the day, except as hereinafter otherwise provided. Article 4: The maximum hours of work in the week laid down in Article 3 may be so arranged that hours of work in any day do not exceed ten hours" (ILO 1930). The fact that Apple itself defines what appropriate working conditions are and then itself measures reality against these standards shows the problem of CSR reporting, namely that it is mainly voluntary and not conducted by well-resourced independent agencies that have coercive measures at hand in order to punish corporate offenders and enforce standards. Apple (2013, 18) claims that third-party labour agents and regional labour agencies are responsible for child labour in Apple suppliers' factories. Apple says that it terminates its business with companies that engage in child labour or debt bondage slavery (ibid., 18, 20). Apple does not see any irresponsibility in its own practices, but rather blames "them"—corrupt Chinese companies and labour agencies. Returning children to their parents does not solve the problem of poverty that results in child labour and makes parents willing to send their children to work in factories. If the children are returned, then the family will have less money than before, so its material conditions are likely to worsen. Capitalism necessitates inequality and socio-economic gaps. Apple also does not problematize that its operations in China aim at cost-cutting in order to increase profits. Apple (2013) describes how it audits suppliers: "At each audited facility, the teams conduct physical inspections, interview workers and managers, and observe and grade suppliers based on more than 100 data points corresponding to each category of our Supplier Code of Conduct". The audits are conducted not independently but by Apple itself. Also the worker interviews are conducted on the job and by Apple-recruited interviewers, which makes it likely that the interviewees are afraid to lose their jobs if they say the truth. The general problem of CSR reporting is that it is voluntary and not operated and enforced by an independent institution (Sandoval 2013) that has standard means for evaluation and coercive capacities to seriously fine institutions (e.g. by making companies pay a certain share of the annual revenue to the concerned worker). The audit results are simply presented in reports, but it is not transparent to the public if the study was really conducted this way, if they correspond to reality, if the used methodology is feasible and seen as feasible by established independent scholars. There is no monitoring of Apple's self-selected auditing procedures. CSR reporting has an ideological character in that it wants to create a good public image for company without challenging the capital and power structures underlying corporate irresponsibilities (ibid.).

In its 2011 Supplier Responsibility Report, Apple (2011) claims that it conducted an "independent" analysis of the Foxconn suicides which concluded that it is necessary to hire "a large number of psychological counselors", to establish "a 24-hour care center, and even attaching large nets to the factory buildings to prevent impulsive suicides", and to provide "better training of hotline staff and care center counselors and better monitoring to ensure effectiveness" (ibid., 19). This paragraph reflects a basic attitude, namely that the suicides were due to individual psychological problems, that they have nothing to do with poor working conditions, that as a consequence one only needs a few more psychologists and nets to solve the problem and does not need to change the working conditions. This attitude is not only cynical, superficial and missing an understanding of the roots of the problem, it is also profoundly inhumane. When being questioned about Foxconn in an interview, Steve Jobs celebrated these reports: "We are pretty on top of that. I actually think that Apple does one of the best jobs of any company in our industry and maybe in any industry of understanding the working conditions in our supply chain. [...] Foxconn is not a sweatshop. [...] It is a factory, but my gosh: they have got restaurants and movie theatres and hospitals and swimming pools. I mean for a factory, it is a pretty nice factory" (Jobs 2010, 19:11–20:10). Steve Jobs in fact did a poor ideological job at legitimatizing the exploitation present at Foxconn jobs. For analysing his logic of arguments, Teun van Dijk's (1998, 2011) ideological square model can be used. Jobs stresses positive things about Us (Apple as a company) and negative things about them (the suicide workers). He says that Apple is world-leading in corporate social responsibility reporting and that the workers had psychological problems because they were young and alone away from home for the first time: "They have got a lot of workers who are leaving very poor rural areas, coming to these factories, away from home for the first time, 19 years old, they are probably less prepared to leave home than your typical high school student going to college in this country" (Jobs 2010, 21:07–21:18). So what Jobs rhetorically implies is that Apple and Foxconn have no responsibility because "we" (Apple, Foxconn) have nice factories and corporate social responsibility reporting, whereas "they" (the workers) kill themselves not because of low wages, long hours, maltreatment and inhumane conditions in general, but because they are, according to Jobs, young, stupid peasants. Jobs' logic of arguments not only leaves out everything that has to do with working conditions in Foxconn factories and the fact that the lower these wages, the more profit Apple can make, he furthermore also engages in an age-discriminatory argument and a kind of racism against rural Chinese that communicates that these suicidal persons must be doubly stupid—because they are young and have a rural background. Foxconn workers do not need Jobs' jobs and his understanding of jobs and job problems, but rather different kind of work that are not defined by the corporate ethos of people like Jobs. Foxconn jobs are too much based on the Jobs-ideology, but in order to become humane they need to become not-Jobs, which means that workers as subjects need to realize that they are not just "not-capital, the negation of capital" (Marx 1857/1858b, 274); they need to become conscious of this status in order to politically create the negation of the negative relationship between capital and labour in Foxconn factories, in China, in the West and in global capitalism. One needs to communalize Foxconn and Apple.

The continued high-level exploitation of Foxconn workers has also resulted in resistance: in October 2012, some 4,000 workers went on strike in the Zhengzhou factory because new quality controls for the production of the iPhone 5 put heavy work pressures on employees, who in addition were also required to work during the Chinese national October holiday (China Labor Watch 2012b). In September 2012, a riot involving, according to estimates, between 2,000 and 10,000 workers[3] broke out in Taiyuan, after Foxconn security guards seem to have stabbed a worker who was involved in a brawl with other workers. A worker who was an eyewitness reported, "In Foxconn Taiyuan, the guards have been the common enemy of all workers from early on. Every worker resents them. However, the company turned a blind eye on such issues, disregarding basic respect towards workers. It is just a matter of time until such eruption of emotions occurs. Therefore, the culprit of this 10,000-worker riot at Foxconn Taiyuan is Foxconn itself. No matter how moving the words of Foxconn's spokesperson, none of it can bury the truth of this incident" (China Labor Watch 2012a). Zhao (2007a) points out that neo-liberalism with Chinese characteristics and Chinese digital neo-liberalism do not signify a sealed fate, but are contested in the form of workers' and peasants' struggles that make use of ICTs as well as in the form of the emergence of radical-left online publications and debates. The struggles and riots at Foxconn are an expression that there are struggles "contesting the terms of China's digital revolution"; they show "the unevenness and incommensurability of the digital age" in China and the world (ibid., 113).

At daily assemblies, where attendance is compulsory, workers are urged to work hard to obtain the production target and warned not to talk to journalists and others about the work at Foxconn (SACOM 2010). SACOM (2010) documented harsh management methods, including a lack of breaks, a prohibition that workers move, talk or stretch their bodies, and rules that workers had to stand during production, as well as punishments, beatings and harassments by security guards. Ah Ming, a 19-year-old worker, reports, "I have to stand at least 14 hours a day. [. . .] Basically, we have to stand throughout the day, no matter when we going to work or going back to dorm. When we arrive at the dorm, it's already 9:00 pm. [. . .] The company says overtime work is voluntary, but if I don't stay for overtime work, it will be regarded as work stoppage. [. . .] It's routine. Sleep, work and eat" (SACOM 2011a, 12–13).

"'It is such a cold environment on the shop floor which makes me feel depressed. As a newcomer, I have no one to talk to. If I continue to work at Foxconn, I may commit suicide too,' a young female worker who just resigned from Hangzhou Foxconn" explained (SACOM 2010, 12). Ma Xianqian was, as a punishment, forced by the security guards at Foxconn Shenzen to clean the floors and toilets, after which he killed himself (ibid., 13).

Not just the workplaces but also the accommodations are managed in a military way. "If workers violate the dormitory rules, such as blow-drying their hair inside dormitory rooms and returning to the dormitory after 23:30, their names will be documented and they will be made to clean the dormitory as 'volunteers'. Furthermore, workers have to confess every breach of dormitory rules. On the confession letter, the name, worker I.D. number, worker card with photo will be shown. It states: 'It is my fault. I will never blow my hair inside my room. I have done something wrong. I will never do it again'" (SACOM 2010, 19).

7.4. Conclusion

Studies of working conditions at Foxconn documented low wages, unpaid parts of the workday, no breaks, long working hours, working environments that are hazardous to physical and psychological health, forced overtime, forced student labour, military management including punishments and beatings, and employer-friendly pseudo-unions. "In order to maximize productivity, workers at Foxconn are made to work like machines" (ibid., 10). The ICT workers encountered at Foxconn are dialectical sublations *(Aufhebung)* of the ICT workers we encounter in Congolese mines: The slave-character of the latter is preserved in the first. There are students from vocational schools working at Foxconn, who according to SACOM are forced by their teachers in cooperation with Foxconn to work in the factories at hard conditions that are illegal under Chinese law (overtime, work that is irrelevant for students' studies). Like the mineworker slaves in Congo, these youngsters do not have the possibility to leave the employment relationship. In contrast to the slave miners in the DRC, there are also double-free wageworkers in the Foxconn factories. They can choose to which capitalist they want to sell their labour and can also leave an employment relationship (which slaves and the Foxconn intern students cannot), but this freedom is at the same time the unfreedom of having to sell labour-power as a commodity and to produce goods that do not belong to oneself. There is a large share of young rural migrants among the informal and precarious Chinese ICT workers. They have partly been driven off the land in processes of primitive accumulation that expropriated rural land and made them property-less. Women constitute a significant share of the young migrant workforce and are highly exploited. There is a kind of feminization of work in a double sense: there is a high level of low-paid female workers among Chinese ICT workers and insecure, precarious, low-paid employment is a general pattern in the Chinese ICT assemblage industry.

The conditions found in Foxconn factories are quite similar to those that Marx described in 19th-century Britain: highly exploited young people are put to work. Marx describes the working conditions in a Scottish factory that produces matches: "Half the workers are children under 13 and young persons under 18. [. . .] Of the witnesses examined by Commissioner White (1863), 270 were under 18, fifty under 10, ten only 8, and five only 6 years old. With a working day ranging from 12 to 14 or 15 hours, night-labour, irregular meal-times, and meals mostly taken in the workrooms themselves, pestilent with phosphorus" (Marx 1867c, 356). Similarly, Marx describes fabric inspectors' reports on the working conditions in a wallpaper factory: "I have seen when the children could none of them keep their eyes open for the work; indeed, none of us could. [. . .] J. Lightbourne: 'Am 13 [. . .] We worked last winter till 9 (evening), and the winter before till 10. I used to cry with sore feet every night last winter'. [. . .] Smith, the managing partner of a Manchester factory: 'We [. . .] work on, with no stoppage for meals, so that the day's work of lot hours is finished by 4.30 p.m., and all after that is overtime'. [. . .] 'We [. . .] seldom leave off working before 6 p.m.' (he means leave off from consuming 'our' labour-power machines), 'so that we' (the same man again) 'are really working overtime the whole year round . . . For all these, children and adults alike (152 children and young persons and 140 adults), the average work for the last 18 months has been at the very least 7 days, 5 hours, or 78!-hours a week" (ibid., 357).

If one would put these descriptions into one of the SACOM reports, then most readers would probably not recognize that there are different historical and geographical contexts because the description of the working conditions that Marx described in the second half of the 19th century sounds so similar to those described by SACOM, which is an indication that Foxconn resembles working conditions that represent a stage of capitalist production in which absolute surplus-value production is enforced with a high level of physical violence and the disciplining of human bodies.

There is another parallel between the example cases presented by Marx and Engels and watchdog organizations' studies of Foxconn and related companies. Marx and Engels relied on the reports of factory inspectors for obtaining empirical material that they used for illustrating and verifying theory. SACOM and other corporate watchdog organizations are contemporary factory inspectors: they aim to systematically inspect what is going on in factories that are part of international divisions of labour. A difference is, however, that the 19th-century factory inspectors were backed by the law and state resources, which also enabled certain possibilities for sanctions against companies, whereas organizations like SACOM are civil society organizations, which means more independence but precarious work and often little resources, and therefore with problems attempting to hold corporations accountable and make their behaviour transparent to the public. The working day has two parts: one that is paid and one that is unpaid. The worker receives a wage only for the first. This circumstance can easily be imagined, as commodities are sold at prices that are higher than the investment costs (wages, resource costs, infrastructure costs) in order to achieve a profit. But the part of the working day (at the level of working time or what Marx terms value) that corresponds to the production of profit (at the level of prices) forms a part of the sales price that is artificially separated from the wages by companies' legal ownership rights that allow them to possess the commodities produced by the workers and the profit that can be achieved from it. So wages correspond to one part of the working day and profits to another. Marx calls the first necessary labour time and the second surplus labour time. The first is paid, the second unpaid. Marx describes two methods of how capitalists can try to organize the working day in order to accumulate ever more profit: "The prolongation of the working day beyond the point at which the worker would have produced an exact equivalent for the value of his labour-power, and the appropriation of that surplus labour by capital—this is the process which constitutes the production of absolute surplus-value. It forms the general foundation of the capitalist system, and the starting-point for the production of relative surplus-value. The latter presupposes that the working day is already divided into two parts, necessary labour and surplus labour. In order to prolong the surplus labour, the necessary labour is shortened by methods for producing the equivalent of the wage of labour in a shorter time. The production of absolute surplus-value turns exclusively on the length of the working day, whereas the production of relative surplus-value completely revolutionizes the technical processes of labour and the groupings into which society is divided" (Marx 1867c, 645). The first method changes (increases) the quantity of labour, the second the quality of labour. Absolute surplus-value production means that workers work more hours unpaid because the working day is prolonged, whereas in relative surplus-value production, working time remains the same but work becomes more productive and undergoes a speed-up so that more surplus value is produced in the same amount of time as before.

The analysed reports make clear that in Foxconn factories mainly absolute methods of surplus-value production are used in order to increase profits: one finds in these factories unpaid overtime, hardly any breaks, long working days of up to 12 hours, working weeks with six working days, work without a day off for up to two weeks' time, and so on. A certain wage is paid, but the management strategy is in exchange to try to press as many hours of work out of the workers as possible. The working day is clearly separated from free time that is scarce and during which workers tend to be very exhausted because they have to work and stand for long hours. Therefore a common Foxconn day is described by the employees as "work, eat and sleep" and they say that they "haven't got time for fun" (SACOM 2011a, 12). Being asked "what they would like do on holiday, most of them respond, 'sleep'" (ibid.). This circumstance shows that although free time and working time are separate, they are also strongly connected and form a dialectic: working time in the method of absolute surplus-value production is extended so that it encroaches on and impoverishes free time; it soaks up the living time of workers and transforms it into working time, during which they are exploited.

Marx argues that absolute surplus-value production has material limits: The "working day does have a maximum limit. It cannot be prolonged beyond a certain point. This maximum limit is conditioned by two things. First by the physical limits to labour-power. Within the 24 hours of the natural day a man can only expend a certain quantity of his vital force. Similarly, a horse can work regularly for only 8 hours a day. During part of the day the vital force must rest, sleep; during another part the man has to satisfy other physical needs, to feed, wash and clothe himself. Besides these purely physical limitations, the extension of the working day encounters moral obstacles. The worker needs time in which to satisfy his intellectual and social requirements, and the extent and the number of these requirements is conditioned by the general level of civilization. The length of the working day therefore fluctuates within boundaries both physical and social. But these limiting conditions are of a very elastic nature, and allow a tremendous amount of latitude" (Marx 1867c, 341). In the case of the Foxconn workers, reports show that working time is stretched to high levels, which affects workers' reproduction requirements in terms of sleep and social relations so that their sleeping time and social time becomes impoverished. Also the wages are so low that they hardly guarantee survival, which means that this lack of income has to be compensated, either by abstinence (e.g. from an adequate amount of food, which can negatively impact health) or by trying to get hold of resources that are needed for survival by other means (e.g. crime). The reports also show that absolute surplus-value production is to a certain, although lesser, degree combined with relative surplus-value production: the military system of worker surveillance and coercion that uses drill, control and punishment aims at disciplining them in such a way that they not only work long hours without breaks, but also work in an intense manner, that is, produce as many items per hour as possible. There is a tendency for production targets to be increased by management: "Workers are not allowed to talk on [the] production line and can only repeat the same motion for hundreds or even thousands times a day. The production target keeps rising. And they have to work faster and faster" (SACOM 2011a, 15). Overseers put pressure on workers that they work harder: "Basically, we can accomplish the production target. However, the frontline supervisor usually pressures us to work faster at around 7:00pm, an hour before the work shift ends. We have to stand for the whole day during work. The company promises that we can have a 10-minute break every 2 hours. It's a lie. When I go back to the dormitory, my legs shiver due to exhaustion. The turnover rate is quite high. There are many people who resign within the first month" (SACOM 2011b, 9). "The production target is usually set at 5000 pieces per day. If there is an influx of orders, the target will be raised to 1000 pieces per hour. Production targets keeps [*sic*] soaring. Management always test the capacity of the workers. If workers can finish the quota, the target will be increased day by day until the capacity of the workers maximize" (SACOM 2010, 12). Marx (1867c, 1019–1023, 1025–1034) argues that the formal subsumption of labour under capital entails on the one hand the creation of relations of production, in which labour is organized as wage-labour, and as the method of absolute surplus-value production, where capital tries to extend the working day as much as possible. The real subsumption of labour under capital (ibid., 1023–1025, 1034–1038) is based on relative surplus-value production, for example, with the help of cooperative work, the division of labour, the use of machinery or scientific planning of the production process (1024). Marx argues that the formal and the real subsumption of labour are "two distinct forms of capitalist production" (ibid., 1025). The formal subsumption of labour under capital entails quantitative changes of the mode of production/the productive forces, whereas the real subsumption changes the productive forces qualitatively. Marx argues that in early stages, where capitalism is introduced, the method of formal subsumption necessarily prevails, whereas the real subsumption can coincide with formal subsumption. Foxconn is a company for which both forms of capitalist production coincide in such way that there is a predominance of absolute surplus-value production. China has effectively introduced a relatively pure capitalist system since 1978. In 2011, 58.0% of the profits achieved in China were owned by share-holding enterprises, 25.7% by foreign investors and only 1.6% by collective enterprises (National Bureau of Statistics of China 2012). In contrast, there were no foreign investors and almost 100% collective and state ownership in 1978 (Qiu 2009, 89). So it is no surprise that the formal subsumption of labour under capital features very prominently because it "is the general form of every capitalist process of production" (Marx 1867c, 1019) and "production as an end in itself—does indeed come on the scene with the formal subsumption of labour under capital" (1037).

Jack Qiu (2009, x) argues that China has "the largest exploited working class of the global information age". He therefore characterizes China as undergoing a change which has resulted in the emergence of a working-class network society (Qiu 2009, 2010c) that is especially characterized by what he terms the "information have-less: low-end ICT users, service providers, and laborers who are manufacturing these electronics" (Qiu 2009, 3–4). This class would consist of migrant workers (who have migrated from rural to urban areas), unemployed and underemployed workers, micro-entrepreneurs, youth, students and retirees struggling to make a living, those who to a certain degree are "grey-collar" workers who have highly repetitive jobs in industries such as software engineering, design, marketing, advertising, telecommunications and customer services (ibid., 104–105, 93, 113). Qiu (2009, 83) says they are called "grey-collar" because they "often wear grey uniforms". There is however another dimension: Grey is the colour that results from mixing white and blue, so the term may express an in-between status (between white- and blue-collar). Not only that, but also, although these are tertiary jobs, they are heavily standardized like Taylorist industrial work, so they represent a specific kind of industrialization of service work, a negative dialectic of industrial and service work that results in standardization, precarization and proletarianization.

In order for a computer to be used, software (operating system, application software) as well as hardware is needed. Software is produced under certain working conditions in different parts of the world. In the next chapter, we will have a look at work in the Indian software industry.

Notes

1 Company profile: http://www.forbes.com/companies/hon-hai-precision (accessed December 27, 2012).
2 SACOM 2010, 2.
3 http://www.chinalaborwatch.org/news/new-427.html, http://www.nytimes.com/2012/09/25/business/global/foxconn-riot-underscores-labor-rift-in-china.html?_r=0 (accessed on July 9, 2013).

8

THE NEW IMPERIALISM'S DIVISION OF LABOUR

Work in the Indian Software Industry

In 2000, the conservative German politician Jürgen Rüttgers popularized the slogan "Kinder statt Inder" (Children instead of Indians). He wanted to express that Germans should beget more children because the software industry needs workers. He argued that software engineers are increasingly recruited from India, whereas German children instead of Indians should be professional computer users. Many observers expressed that this slogan was overtly racist and xenophobic.

Why is it that Indian work tends in the West to be associated with either restaurants or software? This chapter aims to shed light on the role of software engineering in the Indian economy. It shows that we cannot discuss the Indian software industry without discussing the global division of labour in the ICT industry. A closer analysis reveals structures of a new form of imperialism, where Western capitalism benefits from the exploitation of Indian labour.

8.1. Introduction

Table 8.1 shows the employment structure of the Indian economy in 2010. Based on this indicator, one can say that the Indian economy is predominantly an agricultural economy. In the service sector, the largest employment sector is the one that comprises wholesale and retail trade and repairs: it accounts for 9.5% of total employment. The Indian construction industry (which is part of the secondary sector) also comprises a relatively large share of the Indian non-agricultural workers, namely 9.5% of all Indian employees. Table 8.1, however, also shows that the structure of value added in the Indian economy follows a quite different pattern: the largest share of value added is located in services, whereas agriculture makes up the lowest share. This shows that the Indian economy has a quite uneven structure: it is a service economy in relation to capital and an agricultural economy in relation to labour. A large share of Indian employment is made up by self-employees, especially in agriculture (ICSSR 2012, 38–39). In 2010, 50.6% of all Indian workers were self-employed, 32.8% had informal and casual jobs and only 16.7% a regular waged employment (ibid., 19). A major problem of the Indian economy is the existence of working poor who account for more than 20% of all employees (ibid., 46). Only about 8% of all workers have social security (ibid., 55).

The ICSSR (2012) report shows that the secondary sector—especially the manufacturing of rubber, plastic and coal products, textile and leather products, machinery, transport equipment, chemical and paper products—had high employment growth rates in the period 1983–2005 that were due to the export orientation of these sectors and foreign direct investments. HCL Technologies is the largest Indian software corporation. It was in 2012 ranked the 1868th largest company and the 16th largest software company in the world (Forbes 2000, 2012). In 2011, its capital assets were US$3.3 billion, its market value US$6.9 billion and its profits US$0.4 billion (ibid.). In the realm of computer services, Tata Consultancy Services (#667), Infosys Technologies (#784) and Wipro (#788) are leading global companies from India. The 2011 profits of these companies were US$2 billion, US$1.5 billion and US$1.2 billion (ibid.). All three companies are based in Hyderabad, the capital of the Indian state of Andhra Pradesh. In telecommunication services, Bharti Airtel (#377) and Reliance Communications (#1520) are among the largest companies in the world. In other media and ICT sectors, namely broadcasting, computer hardware, telecommunications equipment, computer storage devices, consumer electronics, printing and publishing, and semiconductors, there were no Indian companies among the world's largest corporations in 2012. The data indicate that the software industry is India's strongest media industry. Labour in this industry therefore deserves particular attention when one discusses the role of India in the global division of labour of the ICT industry.

TABLE 8.1 Share of employment in three sectors of the Indian economy in 2010

Sector	Employment share	GDP share
Primary economic sector (agriculture and mining)	53.7%	17.0%
Secondary economic sector (manufacturing)	20.9%	24.2%
Tertiary economic sector (services)	25.4%	58.9%

Source: NSSO (2012, table S36), ICSSR (2012, 36)[1]

8.2. The Indian Software Industry's Productive Forces in the International Division of Digital Labour: Labour-Power and the Objects, Tools and Products of Labour

In the mid-1980s, the Indian government started to progressively liberalize regulations in order to attract investments by international capital to the software industry (Lakha 1994). After the assassination of Indira Gandhi in 1984, Rajiv Gandhi became the new Indian prime minister and substituted the old politics of techno-nationalism by politics that modernized and liberalized communications, which resulted in a deregulation of the computer industry and the focus on the attraction of foreign capital and export orientation of the Indian ICT economy (Chakravartty 2004, Upadhya and Vasavi 2008). Software technology parks emerged in Bangalore, Bhubaneswar, Pune, Madras and Hyderabad. International software companies feel attracted by India's high amount of university-educated engineers, relatively good English skills and low-level wages (Lakha 1994). Citigroup (USA) and Texas Instruments (USA) are two of the TNCs that entered the Indian software market relatively early in the mid-1980s; later others such as Alcatel, British Telecom, Cadence, HP, IBM, LG Electronics, Microsoft, Motorola, Oracle and Philips followed (Arora, Gambardella and Torrisi 2001; D'Costa 2002).

In 2012, India attracted 58% of all outsourced IT and business processes (call centres, customer services, HR, finance, accounting) (NASSCOM 2012), which shows the importance of the Indian software sector in the IDDL. Table 8.2 shows that the export orientation of parts of the Indian manufacturing industry has also characterized the Indian software industry: in the decade 2000–2009, it had annual growth rates between 11% and 51%. At the same time, the export orientation of the industry has increased from roughly 50% to more than 75%. In 2010, software services accounted for 54.4% of all exported services in India (Ministry of Finance 2011, 166). In 2011, this value increased to around 58% (NASSCOM 2012). In 1997–1998, the United States accounted for 58% of all Indian software exports (Arora, Gambardella and Torrisi 2001). In 2009, exported software accounted for 58.7% of the value of the Indian electronics and IT (hardware and software) production, domestic software only for 15.5% (Ministry of Finance 2011, 221). In 2010, total FDI inflows into the hardware and software industry accounted for 3.0% of all FDI inflows, whereas in 2009 they accounted for 7.8%, which shows that the global capitalist crisis has negatively affected capital export in the software industry (ibid., 225). The total volume of FDI inflows in the Indian software industry decreased by 58.6% in 2010 in comparison to 2009 (ibid.). Although the Indian software industry has had a huge growth rate and a large share of exports in services, in 2009 it accounted for only 0.5% of the total Indian labour force and in 2012 for 0.6%. This circumstance shows that given the fact that India is the second largest country in the world (following China), its mere size poses an attractive location for the outsourcing of ICT services for Western companies in order to increase profit rates by decreasing overall wage costs. The

TABLE 8.2 Employment in the Indian software industry

Year	Employment in software and software services	Export share of employment	Annual employment growth rate	Share of total workforce[2]
2000	284,000	53.5%		
2001	430,100	53.9%	51.4%	
2002	522,200	52.9%	21.4%	
2003	670,000	56.9%	28.3%	
2004	833,000	61.5%	24.3%	
2005	1,058,000	66.7%	27.0%	
2006	1,293,000	71.8%	22.2%	
2007	1,621,000	76.7%	25.4%	
2008	2,010,000	77.6%	24.0%	
2009	2,236,614	77.6%	11.3%	0.5%
2012	2.8 million			0.6%

Source: ICSSR (2012, 22), NASSCOM (2012, 5)[2]

overall employment impact was nonetheless modest within the Indian economy. But the Indian software sector accounted for 7.5% of the Indian GDP in 2012, according to estimations (NASSCOM 2012).

The presented data show that the growth of the Indian software industry has been based on an export-orientation model and an attraction of foreign capital investments. Software is particularly important in Indian service export and has attracted relatively high levels of FDI, which is an indication that the Indian software industry plays an important role in the IDDL. Therefore we want to further analyse this industry.

8.3. The Indian Software Industry's Relations of Production in the International Division of Digital Labour

In India, there are large gaps between the rich and the poor, the educated and the illiterate, urban entrepreneurs in the tech business and rural landless workers and peasants, as well as between large cities and small towns and between the South and the East (D'Costa 2002). D'Costa (2002) argues that Indian software development is embedded into an uneven and combined development of Indian capitalism that produces winners and losers and develops some regions, cities and groups at the expense of others. In 2011, income inequality measured by the Gini coefficient was 36.8% in India, the adult illiteracy rate 37.2% and the health-adjusted life expectancy 56 years; 53.7% of the population lived in multidimensional poverty, 28.6% in severe poverty; and 41.6% of the population had to survive on less than US$1.25 a day (UNHDR 2011). Ilavarasan (2007) concludes, based on empirical research, that the Indian ICT workforce has large urban-rural and gender differences and that these differences contribute to uneven development in India. Indian software workers would mainly come from the middle and upper class and be highly educated. Lower-class people from poorer families that tend to have less formal education would hardly become software engineers (Ilavarasan 2008).

Indian software engineers are almost all college-educated and highly qualified, and often they are overqualified for the tasks they perform (Upadhya and Vasavi 2008). Indian software firms mainly provide low-level coding, designing and testing of software for the export market, whereas the domestic software market focuses on more complex software engineering projects that entail the entire software lifecycle in the production process (Arora et al. 1999, 2001). "Managers at most of the US firms we interviewed [. . .] agreed that the type of work outsourced was neither technologically very sophisticated nor critical to their business" (Arora et al. 2001, 1274). "Not only is the work outsourced technologically undemanding, the projects are typically small" (Arora et al. 2001, 1287). Ilavarasan (2008) conducted a labour process analysis in two Indian software companies. He identified four different positions (developer, module leader, project leader, project manager) that all involved conception and execution. There would be no division between those who perform conception and execution. Tasks would not be separated in a Taylorist manner into high-skill activities and routinized low-skill activities. The study shows that activities in Indian software companies seem to be distributed in such a way that everyone participates in various work tasks. Depending on how demanding the incoming projects are (if they require only coding, testing, delivery and installation or also requirement specification and design), Indian ICT workers will perform more or less conception and/or execution tasks.

Arora et al. (2001) conducted 75 interviews with senior managers and software professionals in 40 software firms and in addition brief interviews with 60 software engineers in India. They identified three forms of software outsourcing to India: (1) onsite consultancy or engineering in overseas companies, (2) a combination of onsite and offshore work of Indian software engineers, and (3) creation of Offshore Development Centers in order to cut costs. In the conducted study, 42.7% of the total work was conducted offshore.

Xiang Biao (2007) conducted more than 90 interviews in his study of "global body shopping" in the IT industry. Body shopping means the "physical practice of securing work visas for Indian programmers and bringing them to the United States [or other countries] to work on site" (Aneesh 2006, 3). "Body shopping is arguably a uniquely Indian practice whereby an Indian-run consultancy (body shop) anywhere in the world recruits IT workers, in most cases from India, to be placed out as project-based labor with different clients. Unlike conventional recruitment agents who *introduce* employees to employers, body shops *manage* workers on behalf of employers—from sponsoring their temporary work visas to paying their salaries, arranging for accommodation and the like. Thus, workers do not enter into any direct relationships with their contract employers and can be retrenched at any time, whereupon the body-shop sponsor either is able to place them out to a different client or puts them on the bench to await a placement. Acting in association, body-shop operators link up with each other in the same region or in different countries, sending IT workers to where they are required" (Biao 2007, 4). Biao found that "bodyshopped" Indian programmers tend to conduct monotonous, relatively low-paid programming that they consider as "donkey work" (ibid., 5), often have to pay part of their salaries as fees to Indian "body shops" for being sent to the United States or another country, tend to have temporal contracts that often contain clauses that prohibit them from finding other work and often have contracts that are highly individualized, unclear and uncertain. As a result of ICT body shopping in India, "little wealth is passed downward from the global to the local, though conversely, value is pumped both upward and outward (to the West) from the local" (ibid., 112). A. Aneesh (2006, 43) describes the effects of body shopping: a Western company can "trim its workforce, take these temporary workers into service only in times of need, and economize on long-term benefits—social security, retirement contributions, health insurance, and unemployment insurance—that must be provided to permanent employees".The Indian body shops would often get one-third or two-thirds of the employee's salary. Aneesh also analysed a second common strategy that he terms virtual migration: "The concept of virtual migration underscores that a programmer sitting in India and working for a local firm can directly provide services in the United States" (ibid., 2). "It may range from the real-time work performed on mainframe computers and servers in the United States by a worker based in India to a distributed work design, allowing a firm to be geographically dispersed, without a central work station, among several sites throughout the world" (ibid., 69). Different time zones would become integrated in such a way that ICT companies become globally dispersed entities, in which labour operates 24 hours a day. One Indian programmer explains, "Basically [when] it's night in the U.S., it's early morning here. [. . .] At the end of their day [the Americans] just have to [compile] their problems and the changes they want us to do, and we can fix them in our normal working hours, fix them just in time, and it will be there next morning when they come to their office" (ibid., 84). Body shopping and virtual migration are strategies for organizing labour in such a way that it is highly exploited, individualized, dispersed, isolated, precarious, non-unionized and for cheapening labour-power so that the wage costs are low and profits can be maximized. Both strategies organize space in a racist manner for exploiting Indian workers:

- In body shopping, Indian workers are exported as commodities wherever ICT capital wants to have them. Workers enter contracts that limit their freedom of movement. They have to go wherever capital commands them to go for whatever time desired by the ICT corporations. The result may be that they are permanently on the move, serving the interests of capitals in such a way that they are always available whenever ICT capital wants them to be available and moving on as soon as their competence is no longer needed.

- In virtual migration, spatial flexibility means that the company extends its operations into India. The Indian workers do not physically migrate to a host country, but remain in India and perform tasks for Western ICT capitalists from there. Space is organized in such a way that ICT-mediated communication and data transmission enables a specific form of work collaboration so that Indian software engineers provide parts of the code that is needed for software projects.

Both strategies reduce wage costs by paying lower wages to Indian workers than to workers under regular conditions. Being an Indian worker then means being highly exploited. Origin is transformed into a higher level of exploitation and a more insecure employment strategy. Body shopping and virtual migration are highly racist forms of knowledge production that flexibilize space in order to increase exploitation, which results in rising profits.

Indian IT salaries range between 7% and 40% of US standards (D'Costa 2002). Another estimation is that software engineering outsourced to India costs around one-third to one-fifth of the price a company has to pay for the same work in the United States (Arora et al. 2001, 1278). "The single greatest motivation for considering India for offshoring from a developed country is lower labor costs" (Dossani and Kenney 2007, 777). Software developers' wages are among the highest in India (Ilavarasan 2007), which shows that there is generally a large wealth and wage gap between developing and developed countries and within India. Commander et al. (2008) conducted a survey among 225 Indian and 60 US software firms. They found that wages in the Indian software industry are relatively high, but there are large differences within companies: conceptualizers earned on average 29.8% less than managers, software developers 53.2% less than managers, modifiers 62.0% less and support staff 67.0% less. Average wages for managers in the Indian companies were 12% of their US equivalents; this rate was 10% for conceptualizers and modifiers, 9% for developers and 7% for supporters. This means that the average wages in Indian software companies were in this study 9.6% of the wages in US software firms. Commander et al. (2008) report that this wage differential is the cause of a large "brain drain" of educated Indian professionals to the United States. Paula Chakravartty (2006) argues that in the United States right-wing xenophobic discourses in media and politics have put forward the ideology that Indian software engineers who immigrate to the United States or take up jobs outsourced from the United States to India are responsible for wage dumping of white-collar jobs because they work for low wages. But the reality of Indian immigrants who have a H1-B temporary visa that allows them to work in the US software industry is that they are highly exploited and work long hours and overtime without extra payment. In India, the middle class would celebrate software engineers who have immigrated to the United States as heroes of India's national economic development. Both discourses are for Chakravartty forms of "white-collar nationalism" that focus on individual blame or celebration and thereby overlook the reality of global capitalism that shapes the ICT industry, which tries to maximize profits by reducing wage costs.

Based on 50 interviews in a Mumbai-based software company (IN-Sync, export- and domestic-oriented), D'Mello and Sahay (2007) identified three forms of mobility Indian software engineers are confronted with: geographical mobility (long commuting times, work at home, frequent overseas work, relocation due to job change), social mobility (strong social networks inside the company due to long working hours, upward social mobility with relative affluence, changing caste relations), and existential mobility (lack of time for family life, free time is transformed into working time; health risks and suicides due to overwork, work pressure, constant deadlines, etc.; insecure employment contracts that allow firing workers any time; career trajectories result in more responsibilities, tensions and stress, growing frustration and resignation). Indian ICT workers are "'high tech' nomadic" workers (Upadhya and Vasavi 2008, 20). Mohan, a project manager in his mid-30s, explained, "Work takes a priority. [. . .] The area occupied by family and others keeps reducing" (D'Mello and Sahay 2007, 179). Another interviewee said "Sometimes you start at 8 am and then finish at 10–11 pm, five days a week. And anytime you can be called [. . .] Also you don't develop any hobbies" (ibid.). And a third one argued, "Because of inevitable long hours at work, IT people build up strong social networks within the company. Outside the office, apart from family members, there is little time and energy to socialize. This phenomenon, along with overseas travel impacts family relationships. [. . .] On the one hand, my family can be with me overseas for short vacations which are great. However, my family seems to have found other support systems in my absence and sometimes I wonder about my place in the home!" (ibid., 177).

Housewifization means that jobs take on insecure and precarious traits that have traditionally characterized housework (Mies, Bennholdt-Thomsen and Werlhof 1988; Mies 1986; Werlhof 1991). Indian software engineers are different from house workers in the respect that they are waged workers, but the kind of flexibilities they have to deal with are an aspect of housewifization: like house workers they have to be constantly available, be ready to switch between different tasks and invest long hours of work without having enough time for themselves.

Ilavarasan (2007) conducted a survey (N = 114) as well as 62 interviews in two large Indian software companies that confirm the results of D'Mello and Sahay (2007). He found that most employees have flexible working times and often work during the night. Some 56% said they also work on holidays, 86% said they are not paid for overtime. Actual working hours per week would be far more than the 40 hours that are formally required.

Valk and Srinivasan (2011) show based on 13 semi-structured interviews that female Indian IT professionals value their identity as IT workers, but also feel strong responsibility for their joint families, where care of the elderly, sick and children is part of family life. Work pressure, travelling and hard deadlines poses problems for work-family balance. These results show that the high levels of stress in the Indian software industry pose special problems for women. Infosys has adopted the Google model of workplace design by creating playful workplaces that have gyms, basketball and badminton courts, a range of restaurants, various games, and so on (Mathew, Ogbonna and Harris 2012). This workplace organization model is characteristic of a broader trend in the Indian software industry and more generally, where soft management techniques are used that stress teamwork, participation, an open and transparent culture, internalization of management goals by employees, self-discipline, social events, peer group pressure and control, corporate culture/philosophy and cultural training programmes (Upadhya and Vasavi 2008). The result is competition among employees and a strong individualization. At the same time, soft management techniques are often combined with panoptic work surveillance: "This combination of direct and indirect techniques of organisational control allows companies to extract the maximum work out of their employees and hence to maximise productivity. But it also contains a contradiction: workers are expected to transform themselves into individualised, self-managed and self-directed 'entrepreneurial' employees while at the same time they must perform within a tightly controlled and impersonal management system that traces their every move and moment" (ibid., 29).

Trade union organization has been difficult in the IT industry because many workers and managers have viewed unions as harming Indian capitalism and because Indian ICT employees do not tend to see themselves as workers but as knowledge professionals (Mukherjee 2008). The state of West Bengal has even banned strikes in the IT sector (Stevens and Mosco 2010). Another problem for unionization in India is that the population tends to see unions as too much bound up with political parties (James and Vira 2010). Also the use of soft management techniques in the Indian ICT industry that has advanced individualization and undercut collective bargaining has had negative effects on unionization (Upadhya and Vasavi 2008). Stevens and Mosco (2010) describe attempts at unionizing the Indian ICT sector. An example is the Union for IT-Enabled Service Professionals (UNITES) that has established itself but is struggling to attract a broad membership base.

8.4. Conclusion

Edward Said (1978, 153) argues that Karl Marx wrote about India that "in destroying Asia, Britain was making possible there a real social revolution" and that he thereby accepted "the sufferings of Orientals while their society is being violently transformed" as "historical necessity". Kevin Anderson (2010, 20) acknowledges that there are problems with Marx's view that all societies are likely to have the same development path as the West and that he viewed the latter's pathway as a ultimate model of development, but this "in no way implies a lack of sympathy for the human beings suffering". Marx in his articles on India indeed wrote that "the English interference" destroyed Indian communities and their economy and thereby brought about "the only social revolution ever heard of in Asia" (Marx 1853a). Marx also wrote that "England has to fulfill a double mission in India: one destructive, the other regenerating the annihilation of old Asiatic society, and the laying the material foundations of Western society in Asia" (Marx 1853b). But this is not the whole reality of Marx's 1853 articles on India. He says that the bourgeoisie is, in India and wherever it is active, "dragging individuals and people through blood and dirt, through misery and degradation" (ibid.). And he concludes, "The Indians will not reap the fruits of the new elements of society scattered among them by the British bourgeoisie, till in Great Britain itself the now ruling classes shall have been supplanted by the industrial proletariat, or till the Hindoos themselves shall have grown strong enough to throw off the English yoke altogether" (ibid.). This passage shows that Marx anticipated and was in favour of the "rise of an Indian liberation movement" (Anderson 2010, 24) and that he felt sympathy with such a perspective. He did not conceive the Indian people as passive and incapable of revolution, but rather thought that all rule of the bourgeoisie results in misery, blood, dirt and degradation and that this is shown by the Indian case. He furthermore said that Indians would not benefit from this capitalist and colonial rule. Given capitalism's exploitative and imperialistic character, social revolutions would be needed in India, Britain and the world in order to attain a human society. This is the ultimate conclusion of Marx's writings on India. A Marxist analysis of India is also important today.

A neo-liberal programme of liberalization, deregulation and privatization has characterized India in the past decades. Arundhati Roy (2003) says in this context that India "is currently at the forefront of the corporate globalization project. [...] Corporatization and Privatization are being welcomed by the Government and the Indian elite". She argues that India is run by a handful of companies such as Reliance Industries Limited (RIL), Tatas, Jindals, Vedanta, Mittals, Infosys, Essar and ADAG Reliance (Roy 2012). "The era of the Privatisation of Everything has made the Indian economy one of the fastest growing in the world" (ibid.). At the same time this wealth would be based on the dispossession of peasants and the rural population as well as the exploitation of workers so that an extremely uneven development would have emerged in India: "In India, the 300 million of us who belong to the new, post-IMF 'reforms' middle class—the market— live side by side with spirits of the nether world, the poltergeists of dead rivers, dry wells, bald mountains and denuded forests; the ghosts of 2,50,000 [sic] debt-ridden farmers who have killed themselves, and of the 800 million who have been impoverished and dispossessed to make way for us. And who survive on less than twenty rupees a day" (ibid.).

The software industry has in the neo-liberal policy framework become a strategic focus of economic policy-making in India, and its deregulation, export orientation and attraction of foreign capital investments have created a specific case of capital accumulation in India. Software is India's most important service export sector and the most important sector of its ICT industry. The Indian software industry creates a lot of value but has only a limited employment share. The vast majority of this value (75%) is exported to foreign countries, predominantly the United States, where capital investors have their home bases.

Foreign capitalists mainly outsource software engineering to India because they hope to cut costs and increase profits. A general tendency is that labour costs in the Indian software industry are only a fraction of Western standards (between 7% and 40%) so that profits of Western companies can be maximized. Casualization of work means the "process in which work increasingly takes place in an unregulated setting and a growing number of jobs differs from the typical situation of full-time work, protection by labor legislation, permanent employment contracts and guaranteed job security" (Riethof 2005, 64; see also Huws 2011). Casualization involves the informalization of work (lack of legal protection, collective bargaining) and flexibilization (flexibilization of work: outsourcing, variable working hours and wages; flexibilization of labour markets: mobility of workers). Neo-liberalism has advanced the casualization of work (Saad-Filho and Johnston 2005). In the Indian software industry, casualization means especially the flexibilization of working hours and the required spatial mobility of workers. Employees must work whenever capital wishes to, they must be prepared to take on various tasks any time and to shift between them and to work very long hours. Western capital investments have monetarily improved many Indian software engineers' lives, but these monetary benefits come at the expense of overwork, increased stress, compulsory flexibility and mobility, lack of work-life and work-family balance, resulting dangers to health and insecure employment. The flexibilities and mobilities they have to afford are an aspect of the housewifization of work. Despite these difficult circumstances, it has been rather difficult to unionize the sector. The neo-liberal focus on the software sector is embedded into an uneven development between the rich and the poor, urban and rural areas, the educated and the illiterate. Indian software engineers are not Taylorist workers that conduct unqualified and repetitive jobs: they need to be university-educated for conducting work that requires a high level of logical comprehension and reasoning. So there is a clear difference between these jobs and the ones conducted by hardware assemblers that much more often undergo Taylorist standardization. Indian software engineers are highly qualified and highly exploited workers. Lenin (1917, 215) has characterized capital export as an important feature of imperialism: "Under modern capitalism, when monopolies prevail, the export of capital has become the typical feature". The goal would be to achieve high profits by exporting capital to countries in which "capital is scarce, the price of land is relatively low, wages are low, raw materials are cheap" (ibid., 216). Exploiting labour in colonies with high exploitation rates can be achieved by military means (annexation of a country) and/or by economic means. David Harvey (2005) characterizes the contemporary new imperialism as a form of accumulation by dispossession. In the Indian software industry, the new imperialism takes on a specific economic form, in which foreign capital controls the industry, pays internationally comparatively low wages (which is supported by the deregulation of the sector) and thereby achieves high returns. The value created by Indian software engineers to a large degree does not stay in the country and does not benefit all, but rather is appropriated and owned by Western capital, which accumulates capital by selling software based on the dispossession of the value created by Indian software engineers in such a way that high exploitation rates are given. The Indian software industry is part of a global division of labour that is shaped by the new imperialism in such a form that there is a very high rate of exploitation as value from India is exported to Western countries. As a result, there is an uneven global development in the ICT industry and the creation and amplification of uneven development within India. Marx wrote about India that the "aristocracy wanted to conquer it, the moneyocracy to plunder it, and the millocracy to undersell it" (Marx 1853b). Contemporary forms of neo-imperialism are still based on the exploitation of colonies: Western capital acts as "moneyocracy" that plunders India and other countries in the global south. This plunder takes on a specific form. The Indian software industry is a strategic industry in the new imperialistic division of labour of the global ICT industry. Just like Marx wrote in 1853, also today the large share of Indians do "not reap the fruits of the new elements of [the information] society" (ibid.) that exist in India in the software sector.

Hubs of software engineering can be found in various countries under specific working conditions. One of these contexts is the Silicon Valley. And one important ICT company that has its headquarters in this region is Google. The next chapter focuses on software engineering at Google and work in Silicon Valley.

Notes

1 The three-sector model of the Indian economy has been based on a mapping of statistical categories to economic sectors that has been undertaken in the following way: (1) Primary sector (agriculture, mining): Section A: Agriculture, hunting and forestry; Section B: Fishing Section; Section C: Mining and quarrying; (2) Secondary sector (industry): Section D: Manufacturing; Section E: Electricity, gas and water supply; Section F: Construction; (3) Tertiary sector (services): Section G: Wholesale and retail trade, repair of motor vehicles, motorcycles and personal and household goods; Section H: Hotels and restaurants; Section I: Transport, storage and communications; Section J: Financial intermediation; Section K: Real estate, renting and business activities; Section L: Public administration and defence, compulsory social security;

Section M: Education; Section N: Health and social work; Section O: Other community, social and personal service activities; Section P: Activities of private households as employers and undifferentiated production activities of private households; Section Q: Extraterritorial organizations and bodies.

2 According to statistics, the total Indian workforce was 467 million in 2009 (http://www.indexmundi.com/g/g.aspx?c=in&v=72, accessed January 2, 2013, based on CIA World Factbook) and 487.6 million in 2011 (https://www.cia.gov/library/publications/the-world-factbook/geos/in.html, accessed January 3, 2013).

9

THE SILICON VALLEY OF DREAMS AND NIGHTMARES OF EXPLOITATION

The Google Labour Aristocracy and Its Context

Think for a moment about the term "Silicon Valley" before you continue reading. What are your associations? Pause half a minute and reflect: SILICON VALLEY . . . It is likely that your associations include California, computers, software, microprocessors, Intel, Google, Apple, HP, Adobe, Oracle, Facebook. Silicon Valley is an area south of San Francisco where historically the ICT industry has played a crucial role. We tend to associate specific computer technologies and ICT companies with the term. Many think that Silicon Valley is the home of the American dream. It has played an important role in the history of computing. But the history of computing is not just a history of technologies and companies. It is also a history of digital labour engaged in producing ICTs. This chapter wants to illuminate the working conditions in Silicon Valley's ICT industry by focusing on the examples of hardware assemblage and software engineering at Google. It shows that the story of Silicon Valley is not just the story of how the computer makes dreams come true of getting rich, speeding up society and increasing the efficiency of the economy, but is also a story of nightmares: exploitation, racism, toxic workplaces, toxic soil, toxic air, toxic water, the contamination and resulting death of workers, high levels of stress and overtime. Silicon Valley is not the valley where the American dream comes true, but the valley of exploitation and environmental injustice.

9.1. Introduction

Silicon Valley is the name for the area located in the Santa Clara Valley, south of San Francisco. It includes cities such as Cupertino, Los Altos, Mountain View, Palo Alto, San Jose, Santa Clara and Sunnyvale. The term indicates the large presence of ICT companies in this part of California. In 1971, the Intel

4004, one of the world's first commercially available microprocessors, was released by Intel Corporation, which has its headquarters in Santa Clara. Some of the first microcomputers were developed in Silicon Valley, such as HP's 9100 (1968). HP has its headquarters in Palo Alto. The rise of Silicon Valley was based on investments by the US Department of Defense that enabled research and development around microprocessors and transistors for warfare purposes and the interests of the US defence industry in the Cold War (Pellow and Park 2002, chapter 4). In 2012, there were 21 Silicon Valley–based companies among the world's largest 2,000 companies (Forbes 2000, 2012) in various ICT industries:

- Hardware: Apple (#22, Cupertino), HP (#67, Palo Alto);
- Computer services: Google (#103, Mountain View), Yahoo! (#756, Sunnyvale);
- Computer storage devices: SanDisk (#888, Milpitas), NetApp (#970, Sunnyvale);
- Internet retail: eBay (#322, San Jose);
- Semiconductors: Intel (#85, Santa Clara), Applied Materials (#583, Santa Clara), Altera (#1260, San Jose), KLA-Tencor (#1384, Milpitas), Nvidia (#1411, Santa Clara), Advanced Micro Devices (#1416, Sunnyvale), Xilinx (#1432, San Jose), Maxim Integrated Products (#1553, San Jose), Linear Technology (#1586, Milpitas);
- Software: Oracle (#109, Santa Clara), Symantec (#815, Sunnyvale), VMWare (#984, Palo Alto), Adobe Systems (#1010, San Jose), Intuit (#1154, Mountain View).

These Silicon Valley companies accounted in 2012 for 84.9% of the profits of the world's largest hardware companies, 26.2% in the area of computer services, 26.2% in the field of computer storage devices, 68.1% in the Internet retail business, 39.4% in the semiconductor industry and 27.1% in the software industry. These data show that Silicon Valley is a major geographical hub in the world's ICT industry, where a lot of ICT-oriented capital is located. This circumstance gives us reason to have a look at what working conditions look like in Silicon Valley in order to see if it is the "valley of dreams".

Tables 9.1 and 9.2 show that after the world economic crisis had started in 2008, employment in almost all software- and Internet-oriented industries in Silicon Valley continued to grow. Table 9.2 shows that the average wages of employees in these industries were in 2011 between 2 and 5.6 times as high as the general US wage average (the latter for Internet publishing and web search portals, the former for other computer-related services). Practically this means that if one works for Google in Silicon Valley, one can expect to have a pretty high salary. The software industry in Silicon Valley seems to be a winner of the crisis. Other industries have however been hit hard by the crisis: In the newspaper industry in Santa Clara County, the average annual pay decreased from US$62,381 in 2008 to US$59,684 in 2011 and the number of employees from 1,506 in 2007 to 932 in 2011 (US Bureau of Labor Statistics, Quarterly Census of Employment and Wages). In 2008 and 2009, 30,278 newspaper employees were fired in the United States, while at the same time US newspapers' revenues decreased in 2008 by 17% and in 2009 by 27%.[1] In the entire state of California, in the period 2008–2011, a total of 8,155 employees were laid off in the publishing industries (except Internet), 200,749 in the motion picture and sound recording industries, 7,448 in broadcasting (except Internet) and 10,645 in telecommunications (Western Information Office: Mass layoffs in California—2011 annual totals[2]). These data show that the information industry in California and Silicon Valley was overall hit hard by the crisis. The software and Internet industry seems to have been an exception from this crisis. But although the software and Internet industry in Silicon Valley overall generated job growth, there were also larger layoffs by ICT firms: Yahoo! fired 236 employees in 2008 and 295 in 2009, Intel more than 650 in 2008, Sun Microsystems 246 in 2010, Cisco 233 in 2009, Adobe 196 in 2010.[3] The job gain seems to have been unequal. In the semiconductor industry, the other big ICT industry besides software in Silicon Valley, the number of jobs in Silicon Valley decreased from 47,633 in 2007 to 42,328 in 2011 (US Bureau of Labor Statistics, Quarterly Census of Employment and Wages). But also within the Internet and software industry, the development was uneven: For example, if you were after the start of the crisis working not for Google but for its competitor Yahoo!, then you were much more likely to lose your job. In April 2012, Yahoo! announced the layoff of 2,000 employees.[4] In 2008, Yahoo!'s profits shrank from US$640 million to US$419 million, which may be a partial explanation for the job cuts. In the subsequent years, Yahoo!'s profits were US$598 million in 2009, US$1.2 billion in 2010 and US$1 billion in 2011 (Yahoo! Inc., SEC Filings, Form 10-K for 2011). In parallel, the profits for Google—Yahoo!'s strongest

TABLE 9.1 Employment numbers in selected industries in Santa Clara County

	Software publishing	Data processing and hosting	Internet publishing and web search portals	Custom computer programming service	Computer systems design services	Other computer-related services
2007	10,549	4,653	12,872	28,403	20,166	996
2008	10,482	4,666	15,007	27,698	21,802	1,035
2009	10,340	4,628	15,006	24,788	19,047	1,076
2010	11,421	4,693	16,758	25,944	19,324	1,213
2011	13,505	4,921	19,587	28,009	21,104	1,200

Source: US Bureau of Labor Statistics, Quarterly Census of Employment and Wages

TABLE 9.2 Average annual wages in selected industries in Santa Clara County, in US$

	Software publishing	Data processing and hosting	Internet publishing and web search portals	Custom computer programming service	Computer systems design services	Other computer-related services	Average annual pay (US-wide, all employment)
2007	191,267	170,562	258,151	137,687	136,167	88,892	44,458
2008	201,640	151,876	216,316	148,116	124,562	95,395	45,563
2009	175,085	155,119	217,643	133,793	128,988	96,168	45,559
2010	235,226	233,153	236,885	146,329	148,575	100,899	46,751
2011	239,930	197,842	269,258	154,342	163,093	100,491	48,043

Source: US Bureau of Labor Statistics, Quarterly Census of Employment and Wages

opponent in the search and online service and advertising industry—profits increased from US$4.5 billion in 2007 and 2008 to US$6.5 billion in 2009, US$8.5 billion in 2010 and US$9.7 billion in 2011 (Google Inc., SEC Filings, Form 10-K for 2011 and 2009).Yahoo! reacted with layoffs to the heavy competition, which first increased its profits, but then resulted in a backlash in 2011, to which it again reacted with layoffs in 2012. Notwithstanding the 2,000 layoffs conducted in 2012,Yahoo! reduced its employees from 14,300 in 2007 to 14,100 in 2011 (Yahoo! SEC Filings, Form 10-K for 2011 and 2007), whereas Google increased its employees from 16,805 in 2007 to 32,467 employees in 2011 (Google SEC Filing, Form 10-K for 2011 and 2007).

9.2. Silicon Valley's Productive Forces in the International Division of Digital Labour: Labour-Power and the Objects, Tools and Products of Labour

The following table displays the average employment in selected industries in Santa Clara County in 2011 and 2000. It shows that the manufacturing of computer and electronic products constitutes a significant share of the employment in Silicon Valley.The employment share has decreased from 18.4% in 2000 to 13.8% in 2011, which is an indication of overseas outsourcing of ICT manufacturing. But nonetheless, this area constitutes the largest employment sector in Silicon Valley. If we consider the software sector as consisting of software publishing (5,112), Internet publishing and broadcasting (516), ISPs, search portals and data processing (518), and computer systems design and related services (5,415), then this sector constituted 9.1% of SiliconValley's employment in 2000 and more than 8.7% in 2011. Other large employment sectors in Silicon Valley are retail trade (10.0% in 2011), health care and social assistance (9.9% in 2011) and accommodation and food services (8.2% in 2011).

TABLE 9.3 Employment shares (in %) of selected industries in total employment in Santa Clara County

NAICS Code	Industry	2011	2000
	Total	783,785	943,574
11	Agriculture, Forestry, Fishing and Hunting	0.4	0.5
21	Mining	0.0	0.0
22	Utilities	0.2	0.2
23	Construction	3.9	5.1
31–33	Manufacturing	19.8	26.9
334	Computer and Electronic Product Manufacturing	13.8	18.4
3341	Computers and Peripheral Equipment	4.8	5.0
334111	Electronic Computer Manufacturing	4.5	4.1
334112	Computer Storage Device Manufacturing	0.1	0.4
334118	Computer Terminal and Peripheral Equip. Mfg.	0.2	0.5
3342	Communications Equipment Manufacturing	1.3	1.6
33422	Broadcast and Wireless Communication Equip.	0.6	0.5
3344	Semiconductor and Electronic Components	5.4	8.0
42	Wholesale Trade	4.5	4.4
44–45	Retail Trade	10.0	9.7
48–49	Transportation and Warehousing	1.3	1.6
51	Information	6.2	4.5
511	Publishing Industries	1.9	1.5
5111	Newspaper, Book and Directory Publishers	0.2	0.4
5112	Software Publishers	1.7	1.1
512	Motion Picture and Sound Recording Industry	0.2	0.2
515	Broadcasting (except Internet)	0.2	0.1
516	Internet Publishing and Broadcasting	N/A	0.2
517	Telecommunications	0.7	0.8
518	ISPs, Search Portals and Data Processing	0.6	1.7
519	Other Information Services	2.5	0.0
52	Finance and Insurance	2.4	2.0
53	Real Estate and Rental and Leasing	1.6	1.6
54	Professional and Technical Services	14.1	13.5
5411	Legal Services	0.9	1.0
5412	Accounting and Bookkeeping Services	1.0	0.7
5413	Architectural and Engineering Services	1.5	2.1
5414	Specialized Design Services	0.1	0.2
5415	Computer Systems Design and Related Services	6.4	6.1
5416	Management and Technical Consulting Svc.	1.1	0.8
5417	Scientific Research and Development Svc.	2.4	2.0
5418	Advertising and Related Services	0.2	0.4
5419	Other Professional and Technical Services	0.4	0.3
55	Management of Companies and Enterprises	1.2	2.3
56	Administrative and Waste Services	6.2	8.3
61	Educational Services	4.0	2.4

(Continued)

TABLE 9.3—(*Continued*)

NAICS Code	Industry	2011	2000
62	Health Care and Social Assistance	9.9	6.5
71	Arts, Entertainment and Recreation	1.4	1.1
72	Accommodation and Food Services	8.2	6.5
81	Other Services, Ex. Public Admin.	3.9	2.7

Source: State of California Employment Department, data for private industry

Table 9.4 shows that the manufacturing of electronic products and computers as well as the information industries are among the economic sectors in Silicon Valley that produce the largest relative shares of value. This shows the importance of these industries in this geographical area. The manufacturing of computers and electronic products accounted for 19.0% of the region's GDP in 2001 and 18.8% in 2009, the information industry for 6.4% in 2001 and 12.0% in 2009. Also wholesale and retail trade (11.0% of the local GDP in 2009) and real estate (12.4%) are important loci of value generation in Silicon Valley. That the employment share in ICT manufacturing decreased while the created value share remained constant is an indication that the industry reduced its labour costs (by productivity increases, the outsourcing of labour and the precarization of labour). The San Jose–Sunnyvale–Santa Clara metropolitan area accounts for only about 1% of the total value produced in the United States, but nonetheless it accounted for 16.5% of the total value of ICT manufacturing in 2001 and 12.5% in 2009 as well as for 8.8% of the total value in the entire ICT sector in 2001 and 8.0% in 2006. These data show the relevance of Silicon Valley's software industry and ICT manufacturing industry for the United States' total information economy. Given the important role of Silicon Valley's software engineering, software and Internet services as well as ICT manufacturing in ICT value creation, the question that arises next is how the working conditions look in these industries.

9.3. The Relations of Production of Google and the Silicon Valley in the International Division of Digital Labour

Chris Benner (2002) shows that labour in Silicon Valley has been characterized by an increase of nonstandard employment (temporary work, part-time work, outsourced work, contracted work, single-employee businesses), a high turnover rate of labour and high skills obsolescence. There is high wage inequality between professionals, especially managers on the one hand and manufacturing workers on the other hand (see also Carnoy, Castells and Benner 1997). "Between 1991 and 2000 the average compensation of the top 100 executives in Silicon Valley's largest companies grew by over 2,000 percent in real terms, while the average

TABLE 9.4 Share of selected industries in the GDP of private industry in the San Jose–Sunnyvale–Santa Clara metropolitan area/the total private US economy

	2009 (local share)	2006 (local share)	2001 (local share)	2009 USA (total share)	2006 USA (total share)	2001 USA (total share)
Computer and electronic product manufacturing	18.8%		19.0%	12.5%		16.5%
Information (publishing industries, software, motion pictures and sound recording, broadcasting, telecommunications, information and data processing services)	12.0%		6.4%	2.7%		1.6%
Wholesale and retail trade	11.0%		12.5%	1.0%		1.1%
Real estate	12.4%		11.5%	1.0%		1.1%
ICT sector: manufacturing of computer and electronic products, information (publishing including software, information and data processing services), professional and business services (computer systems design and related services)	N/A	34.1%	30.1%	N/A	8.0%	8.8%
Total private industry GDP				1.2%	1.1%	1.2%

Source: Bureau of Economic Analysis

annual income for production workers in the electronics industry declined by 7 percent" (Benner 2002, 213). Whereas white people constitute a large share of officials, managers and professionals, especially Hispanic and Asian employees make up the large share of semi- and unskilled production and service workers in Silicon Valley (Benner 2002, Pellow and Park 2002). "Thus race, class, and gender operated in ways that generally disadvantaged people of color and women in Silicon Valley" (Pellow and Park 2002, 68). Since Benner and Pellow and Park published their analyses in 2002, wage inequality in the ICT industry continued to rise in California (see table 9.5): In 2004, a computer and information system manager's annual salary was on average 4.1 times as high as the one of an electronic equipment assembler and 3.1 times as high as the one of a semiconductor processor. In 2012, these ratios had risen to 4.4 and 4.0. In 2002, a Californian systems software developer earned on average 3.3 times the salary of an electronic equipment assembler and 3.1 times the salary of a semiconductor processor. In 2012, the ratios were 3.5 and 3.2.

Benner (2002) found that Internet and software have been the largest growth sectors in Silicon Valley since the 1990s. Especially the semiconductor and computer manufacturing industry has experienced a lot of overseas outsourcing of labour. At the same time, the software industry has a high turnover rate of employees because of its project-based character. Software engineers are twice as likely to change their career in comparison to other occupations (Benner 2002, 65).

Pellow and Park (2002) have analysed the working conditions in Silicon Valley's ICT manufacturing industry. They show that the wealth of this industry and its beneficiaries is linked to the "hyperexploitation of undocumented and documented persons by employers" (ibid., 6) and to toxic workplaces that are highly gendered and racially structured; that is, immigrant women especially have low-wage jobs where they are exposed to toxic substances in Silicon Valley's ICT manufacturing. Toxic substances that have frequently been released into the workplace and breathed in by workers include arsenic, asbestos, chlorine gas, cyanide, Freon, glycol ether, hydrochloric acid, isopropyl alcohol, lead, nitric acid, silica, solder, sulphate, sulphur, toluene, trichloroethylene (TCE), ultraviolet ink and xylene. They have especially caused health impacts on female workers' reproductive systems. Resulting effects include "[m]iscarriages, birth defects, sterility, distorted menstrual cycles, toxic breast milk, and breast cancer" (ibid., 12), an increase of the rate of babies that have defects of the heart and neural tubes, allergies, asthma, bronchitis and cancer of the respiratory system and the larynx. The racist and patriarchal division of labour in Silicon Valley has also resulted in segregated residential areas and schools. Toxic heavy metals created by ICT manufacturing such as cadmium, cyanide, lead and nickel have also contaminated water, air and the soil, predominantly in immigrants' residential areas, which means that many of them have been doubly exposed and contaminated—at the workplace and in their homes. Unions have traditionally been weak in Silicon Valley, and it has been difficult to unionize the workforce in the ICT industry (Pellow

TABLE 9.5 Development of average annual wages (in US$) in specific occupations in California

	2012	2010	2008	2006	2004	2002
Manager	123,364	117,810	109,503	100,772	98,074	N/A
Computer and Information System Manager	145,873	138,826	128,937	119,418	111,416	N/A
Computer and Information Research Scientist	117,972	123,743	120,606	116,277	100,959	90,646
Computer Systems Analyst	90,252	84,962	81,166	75,527	71,124	68,341
Computer Programmers	86,626	84,683	81,320	76,691	75,896	70,858
Software Developers, Applications	105,806	102,995	98,261	90,605	89,136	82,643
Software Developers, Systems Software	115,424	110,220	102,752	94,397	90,320	84,297
Electrical and Electronic Equipment Assemblers	33,179	31,845	29,937	29,000	26,680	25,204
Semiconductor Processor	36,584	34,158	40,008	38,917	30,094	27,423

Source: State of California Employment Development Department

and Park 2002). A lot of the manufacturing employees work under temporary and precarious conditions, are highly vulnerable to losing their jobs and are therefore afraid. A Cambodian worker exposed to toxic substances reports, "I talked to my co-workers who felt the same way [that I did] but they never brought it up, out of fear of losing their job" (ibid., 139). In 2011, only 17.1% of workers employed in California were members of a union (Bureau of Labor Statistics). As a consequence, workers' negotiation power is low, wages in low-skills jobs tend to be quite low and the number of layoffs is high. In the years 2000–2011 there was a total of 60,600 layoff events in California (Bureau of Labor Statistics) with high peaks during phases of economic crisis such as in 2000–2002 and in 2008 and 2009. Civil society groups such as the Occupation Health Clinic, the Santa Clara Center for Occupational Health or the Silicon Valley Toxics Coalition have continuously worked on documenting and struggling against the contamination of workers and the environment. Pellow and Park (2002) also show that home-based piecework occurred, where whole immigrant families work in their homes on the cleaning of ICT components with toxic substances. This piecework is especially used for the assembly of printed circuit boards or cables. Many of these workers are paid per assembled piece, sometimes "as little as a penny for each component produced" (ibid., 158). The piece wage puts working pressure on assemblers. They have no fixed hourly wage, so if they do not work fast enough and do not assemble enough components, they are not able to earn a living. Marx characterized piece wages as "the most fruitful source of reductions in wages, and of frauds committed by the capitalists" (Marx 1867c, 694). He describes how the "subletting of labour" is typical for piecework. And indeed, in the home work in Silicon Valley that Pellow and Park (2002) describe, whole families, including children, are engaged in this form of ICT manufacturing. "The piece-wage is a form of the intensification of labour and the extension of the work day: Given the system of piece wages, it is naturally in the personal interest of the worker that he should strain his labour-power as intensely as possible; this in turn enables the capitalist to raise the normal degree of intensity of labour more easily. Moreover, the lengthening of the working day is now in the personal interest of the worker, since with it his daily or weekly wages rise" (Marx 1867c, 695).

So there are highly exploitative, low-paid and dangerous jobs in Silicon Valley's ICT manufacturing and assemblage industry. But what do working conditions look like in knowledge-intense jobs, such as software engineering? To test this, we want to have a look at labour in one of Silicon Valley's most well-known companies—Google. Google, which was founded in 1998 by Larry Page and Sergey Brin, was transformed into a public company on August 19, 2004 (Vise 2005, 4). Google acquired the video sharing platform YouTube for US$1.65 billion in 2006 and the online advertising service company DoubleClick for US$3.1 billion in 2008 (Stross 2008, 2). In 2012, Google was, after IBM, the second largest computer service company in the world (Forbes Global 2000, 2012 list). In the list of the world's largest companies, Google has rapidly increased its ranking (table 9.6). The year 2012 has been a record profitable year for Google: its profits were US$10.79 billion (Google SEC Filings, Annual Report 2011), the largest amount since the company's creation in 1998. Since 2004, Google's annual profits have rapidly increased (see figure 9.1).

Glassdoor is "a free jobs and career community that offers the world an inside look at jobs and companies" (www.glassdoor.com/about/index_input.htm). It has collected millions of reviews of work, interviewing and salaries in specific companies. I analysed job reviews for Google that contained a job title related to the keyword "software". In addition, I analysed a thread on reddit that asked people to report anonymously on working conditions at Google.[5] I searched for and analysed postings in which workers talked about working time issues. The 307 postings on Glassdoor that fit into my search criteria were written between

TABLE 9.6 Google's ranking in the list of the largest public companies in the world

2004	2005	2006	2007	2008	2009	2010	2011
904	439	289	213	155	120	120	103

Source: Forbes Global 2000, various years; the ranking is based on a composite index of profits, sales, assets and market value

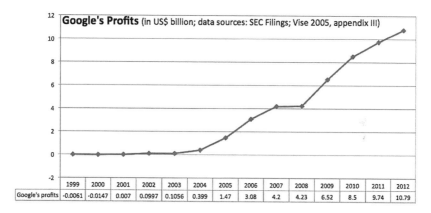

	1999	2000	2001	2002	2003	2004	2005	2006	2007	2008	2009	2010	2011	2012
Google's profits	-0.0061	-0.0147	0.007	0.0997	0.1056	0.399	1.47	3.08	4.2	4.23	6.52	8.5	9.74	10.79

FIGURE 9.1 The development of Google's profits

February 5, 2008, and December 15, 2012. This resulted in a sample of 75 postings, 10 from the reddit thread and 65 from Glassdoor. Glassdoor calculates salary averages for certain job positions. On January 17, 2013, the average salary for a Google software engineer in the United States was US$112,915 (N = 2744) and for a senior software engineer US$144,692 (N = 187). Given that the average salary of an application software developer was US$105,806 in California in 2012 (State of California Employment Development Department, see table 9.5), it seems that Google pays salaries that are somewhat above the average. Most postings say nothing about working time, but rather focus on aspects such as free food. They therefore had to be excluded from the working time analysis. In the conducted analysis, 18 postings mentioned positive aspects of working time at Google: 14 (78%) of them said that they value that there are flexible working times. A minority said that there is a good work-life balance (3, 17%) or that they work a regular eight-hour day (1, 5%). Fifty-eight postings mentioned negative aspects of working times at Google. The issue that all of these 58 postings exclusively focused on in relation to working time were long working hours and a resulting poor work-life balance. I have summarized typical comments in table 9.7. The picture that emerges from this analysis is that people tend to work long hours at Google; they feel that the nice working environment which features free food, sports facilities, restaurants, cafés, events, tech-talks and other perks encourages employees to stay and work longer, that working long hours is not

TABLE 9.7 A selection of typical comments of Google employees about working hours

ID	Comment
5	I dont have much of a social life yet (workin on it) so I tend to be at the office at retarded hours. [. . .] People dont look twice when I show up at noon. :3
6	The downside to google, youre asking? Thats easy. Everything they do for you is in the interest of keeping you in the office as much as possible. Theyll give you breakfast, lunch, dinner (all delicious, no crap). Theres gyms, theyll do your laundry, theyll get you a massage, you can play sports, you can bring a pet. So for some people this is AWESOME. All I see is a bunch of people who are at the office 5070 hours a week of their own volition, and dont separate their work from their everyday life.
7	Its not uncommon for people to be there late, work late @home, and work a few hours over the weekend.
8	By the end my typical day was 14 hours long and I was starting to underperform on my primary responsibilities. [. . .] The fast pace and competitive environment simply make it an easy trap for Googlers to fall into.
9	Google is specifically catering to people who work very long hours. The breakfast is at 8:30, and the dinner is at 6:30 (and its considered tacky to eat dinner and leave right away).
14	The food was great, and while I stayed in the office for long hours every day, my work schedule didnt feel oppressive to me, simply because it was such a nice work environment.
17	In my group, people usually work from 9:00am to 7:00pm everyday.
24	Everybody is very very career focused, they mostly dont have any other aspiration in life. So they spent a lot of hour in office. And it creates tremendous peer pressure. [. . .] If you want a stable work pressure, with stable work life balance, and other interest than the job, this is not your place for sure.
26	All the benefits are designed to get you to work more.
27	Cons—Too much time spent at work (50–60hrs/week)
29	Cons—over-time work. seems everyone works late on weekends.
32	Cons—too much time spent on work, sometimes too much time thinking of work even when you're out.
33	The opportunities for 20% time are real, but you may not have enough time and energy to make use of them.
35	Also, the availability of free food, gym, etc. on campus and the plenty of fun distractions on its corp network make it easy to spend more time there.
37	Cons—Company policy, not that fun when you working, pressure, dead line, pushing, sometime you have to give up some life for the work.
38	ProsThe free food is good. Cons—The working hours are long. The pay is not worth all the time spent at work. Management is not great.
43	Cons—too much work and very weird hours! Advice to Senior Managementhave a good work life balance
45	"Death march" schedules and random priority changes becoming more common.
47	Bad balance between work and personal life.
49	Cons—Growth within the company is difficult unless youre prepared to sacrifice personal life and sleep.
50	There may not be a lot of external pressure from management to pull long hours, but folks tend to do it anyway because they want to accomplish something great. Its an easy place to feel youre below average, even when youve been tops everywhere else.

(*Continued*)

ID	Comment
51	[B]ad work/life balance.
54	Cons—Very long hours. At least where I was, people would seriously work 1214 hours a day (out of which 90% would be effective hours, churning away tons of code). [. . .] Google is not that magic place to work for anymore: pay better, think of the work-life balance (I mean, actually think of it, not just pretend you are).
56	Cons—Long work hours10+ hours/day is typical for many engineers.
58	Cons—Many people work very long hours, so it feels that you must do likewise in order to be considered a good employee.
61	Because the peer group is so good, expectations run high, as a result many people have to put in long hours.
62	Work-life balance doesnt really exist, as working 10+ hours a day seemed to be expected with people working 89 hours at work and then 2+ hours at home at night. [. . .] Advice to Senior Management—Dont stress working so much and be more open in general.
63	Cons—Can have long hours because you dont want to disappoint high-achieving coworkers.
65	Cons—There is a culture of working long hours there, and 20% time is pretty much a myth now. If anything, its 120% time.
67	Theres a culture of working long hours.
70	Culture encourages one to give up the rest of his/her life for their job.
73	Cons—Long hours! Not the place for people who want to have a life outside of work, but then they arent the type who wind up getting hired anyway.
74	Cons—Because of the large amounts of benefits (such as free foods) there seems to be an unsaid rule that employees are expected to work longer hours. Many people work more than 8 hours a day and then will be on email or work for a couple hours at home, at night as well (or on the weekends). It may be hard to perform extremely well with a good work/life balance. Advice to Senior ManagementGive engineers more freedom to use 20% time to work on cool projects without the stress of having to do 120% work.

formally dictated by the management but rather built into the company culture so that there is a lot of competitive peer pressure to work long hours, and that one tends not to have enough time to make use of the 20% work for one's own projects or has to add these hours to more than 100% of their working time.

For a study of the working conditions of IT professionals in Europe (Valenduc 2007) that was conducted as part of the EU FP6 project WORKS—Work Organisation and Restructuring in the Knowledge Society, scholars interviewed 57 software engineers in seven countries. It was found that "[w]ages are individualised, [. . .] individual wage negotiation often escape any regulatory framework" (ibid., 96). The typical work schedule would have a core working time and flexible working times that are based on project workloads (ibid., 90). In five of the seven countries, overtime was found to be very frequent, in four of them it was unpaid (ibid.). At the same time, the interviewed employees said that they value that work time management allows them quite some flexibility and that a high workload is unavoidable in project work (ibid.). "Flexibility in working time arrangements is positively appraised and compensates the high workload" (ibid., 92). The WORKS project's empirical results can be confirmed for the case of Google: Employees on the one hand tend to have long working hours and a lot of overtime, whereas on the other hand office hours are completely flexibilized and management does not see it as a negative feature if somebody does not work from 9 to 5. Rosalind Gill (2002) conducted a study with 125 freelance digital media workers (digital content creators) in six European countries. In another study, she interviewed 34 Dutch digital media workers who were programmers, designers, artists, project managers and content creators (Gill 2006). The studies deconstruct the myth that work in the digital media industry is cool, relaxed, non-hierarchical, diverse, creative and egalitarian. The analyses show that in their everyday reality digital media workers are often confronted with stress resulting from project-based work, low incomes (in the first study the average annual income of men was €16,000 and of women €10,000; in the second study only one-third of the interviewees earned more than the average national income and around 85% of the interviewed freelancers earned less than the average wage), long working hours, high insecurity, an individualization of risk, "intense round-the-clock working for a short period [. . .] followed by several weeks with no (new media) work at all" (Gill 2002, 83–84)—Pratt (2000) and Gill and Pratt (2008) call this phenomenon bulimic work—as well as the difficulty of combining career, family and children, which resulted in the circumstance that most respondents had no kids. The freelancers in the studies tended not to take holidays, and most had no pensions and unemployment insurance. They were largely precarious workers and precarity is gendered (i.e. affects women in particular ways). At the same time Gill (2002, 2006) found that digital media workers are mostly university educated and passionate for and enthusiastic about their jobs, which they tend to see as creative and a source of autonomy. Hesmondhalgh and Baker (2011) confirmed the results of Rosalind Gill's work in interviews with 63 creative workers in TV, music recording and magazine publishing, which show the ambivalence of much creative industry work as precarious but cherished because of the fun, contacts, reputation, creativity and self-determination that it may involve. Juliet Webster (2011) summarizes results of feminist studies of labour in digital media industries: "In ICT development projects, women are particularly absent and even where present, invisible. They are badly represented among ICT professionals [. . .] and, as ICT users, tend to be clustered in low status jobs with little influence over change processes" (ibid., 6). The gendering of digital media labour means that women tend to be facing precarious work and exclusion. Andrew Ross (2003) conducted a study of digital media workers in New York City. He found that one crucial aspect of this work is that "it can enlist employees' freest thoughts and impulses in the service of salaried time. In knowledge companies that trade in creative ideas, services, and solutions, everything that employees do, think, or say in their waking moments is potential grist for the industrial mill [. . .] there are no longer any boundaries between work and leisure. Their occupation becomes a support system for everything else. No one who held a New Economy job was immune to this biohazard" (ibid., 19). Ross' study confirms the phenomenon that we found as typical for Google, namely that in digital media jobs work time tends to absorb free time and that corporate ideology presents this development in terms of freedom, flexibility and the social workplace where work is play and fun. The result would be an ideology that he terms "no-collar": a work culture that embraces "openness, cooperation and self-management", an "anti-authoritarian work mentality", "open communication and self-direction, adopting new modes and myths of independence along the way" (Ross 2003, 9–10). No-collar workers would be "a *self-justifying*" knowledge workforce that does not question capital interests. "Deeply caffeinated 85-hour work-weeks without overtime pay are a way of life for Webshop workers on flexible contracts, who invest a massive share of sweat equity in the mostly futile hope that their stock options will pay off. Even the lowliest employee feels like an entrepreneurial investor as a result. In most cases, the stock options turn into pink slips when the company goes belly-up, or, in some cases, employees are fired before their stock options are due to mature" (Ross 2001, 82). The political task would be that knowledge labour organizes and emancipates itself: "while the chief blight of these centuries had been chattel slavery, serfdom, and indentured labour (and we are not done with these), we must now respond to that moment in the soulful lullaby of 'Redemption Song' where Bob Marley soberly advises us: 'Emancipate yourself from mental slavery'" (ibid, 86). Precarious labour has become a large-scale trend in capitalist economies. Neo-liberalism has resulted in a housewifization (Mies 1986; Mies, Bennholdt-Thomsen and Werlhof 1988) of labour. Many workers today are facing conditions of a *"precariat"* that is "somehow linked by shared concerns about the insecurity of all aspects of their lives" (Ross 2008, 34–35). Knowledge and other workers are depending on their concrete situation affected to different degrees by precarity: some have a permanent contract, whereas others work on temporary contracts or are self-employed; some have higher wages, other lower (the wage differential seems to be gendered and depending on the level of individualization of the work situation); some have pensions and unemployment insurance, others do not; most work long hours, have irregular working days and spaces, where work and play blur. Many workers today experience some aspect of precarity. Precarity means that workers invest a lot of time in their work and have insecure living conditions. Precarity is a form of absolute surplus-value production: one works long hours that under conditions of highly unionized and organized labour could look differently and the social costs are outsourced to the individuals. The total wage and investment costs (including the costs for contract labour) of those who make high profits are thereby minimized, which increases the rate of exploitation and profits. Software engineers at Google tend to share some of the characteristics of the precariat: they have long working hours and face the problem of combining working life with family, friends and social life outside the job. They tend to be relatively high paid. They are at the same time precarious workers who have precarious working times and aristocratic workers who earn surplus wages. Yet not all Google workers seem to have relatively high wages: in 2011 Andrew Normal Wilson was fired because he filmed and talked to data entry workers who scan books for Google Books.[6] They are, according to observations, mostly people of colour who do not have the privileges that other Google workers enjoy.[7] Where can long working hours lead? Employees sleep under their desks in order to maximize performance. Former Google vice president Marissa Mayer reports about her time at Google: "Part of Google was it was the right time and we had a great technology, but the other part was we worked really, really hard. [. . .] It was 130 hour weeks. People say, 'there's only 168 hours in a week, how can you do it?' Well, if you're strategic about when you shower and sleeping under your desk, it can be done".[8] The ultimate consequence of such behaviour is that there is no life outside Google—life becomes Google and thereby one-dimensional. What is very striking about Google is a management strategy that uses soft and social forms of coercion: there is no formal contractual requirement to work overtime, but the company culture is based on project-based work, social pressure between colleagues, competition, positive identification with the job, a fun and play culture, performance-based promotion, incentives to spend a lot of time at the workplace (sports, restaurants, cafés, massages, social events, lectures, etc.) and a blurring of the boundaries between work and play. As a result, employees tend to work long hours, work-life balance is damaged and Google tends to become synonymous with life itself: life time becomes work time and time spent creating value for Google. Google is a prototypical company for the realization of what Luc Boltanski and Éve Chiapello (2007) call the new spirit of capitalism: the anti-authoritarian values of the political revolt of 1968 and the subsequently emerging New Left, such as autonomy, play, freedom, spontaneity, mobility, creativity, networking, visions, openness, plurality, informality, authenticity and emancipation, are subsumed under the logic of capital. In the early times of capitalism that Marx describes in *Capital, Volume 1,* the lengthening of the working day was achieved by control, surveillance, disciplinary measures and legitimation by state laws. The price was an increase of class struggles that pressed for reducing working hours. Google's main way of increasing surplus-value production is also absolute surplus-value production (i.e. the lengthening of the working day), but it takes a different approach: the coercion is ideological and social, built into the company's culture of fun, play-bour (play labour), employee services and peer pressure. The result is that the total average working time and unpaid working hours per employee tend to increase. Marx described this case as a specific method of absolute and relative surplus-value production, in which the productivity and intensity of labour remain constant, whereas the length of the working day is variable: If the working day is lengthened and the price of labour (wages) remain the same, "the surplus-value increases both absolutely and relatively. Although there is no absolute change in the value of labour-power, it suffers a relative fall. [. . .] Here, [. . .] the change of relative magnitude in the value of labour-power is the result of the change of absolute magnitude in surplus-value" (Marx 1867c, 663). What Marx explains in this passage is that the wages tend to relatively decrease the more hours employees work unpaid overtime because they then create additional surplus value and profit. This can be illustrated for the case of Google: 12 of the analysed postings indicated average working hours per week, which allows calculation of an average weekly working time of 62 hours.[9] This evidence is certainly only anecdotal, but given the large number of comments that stated working long hours is common at Google, this result seems to be indicative. The Fair US Labor Standards Act (Section 13 (a) 17) provides an exemption from overtime pay for computer systems analysts, software engineers or similar workers if they earn at least US$27.63 an hour. This means that if it is assumed that software engineers at Google on average work 22 hours of overtime per week, their salary average of US$112,915 stands for a 155% time employment, which means 55% of the working time is unpaid extra work time. During these 22 hours a week, the employee creates surplus value and profit for Google. If we assume 47 weeks of work per year, then the unpaid overtime lengthens work on average by 1,034 hours a year. In comparison to Californian semiconductor processors, who in 2012 earned on average earned US$36,584 in 2012, and Californian electronic equipment assemblers, whose average wage was US$33,179 in 2012 (State of California Employment Development Department), the average 2012 wage of a Google software engineer (US$112,915) was 3.1 times and 3.4 times higher respectively. This shows that there is a significant wage gap in the ICT industry between assemblers and software engineers. Both types of labour are exploited and necessary for capital accumulation in the ICT industry. Software engineers at Google (and other companies) form what Engels termed the "labour aristocracy": Engels describes that in 1885 in the United Kingdom, there were workers whose "state of misery and insecurity in which they live now is as low as ever", but there was also "an aristocracy among the working-class" (engineers, carpenters, joiners, bricklayers) that has "succeeded in enforcing for themselves a relatively comfortable position" (Engels 1892). Also Lenin (1920), based on Engels, spoke of a labour aristocracy that consists of "workers-turned-bourgeois", "who are quite philistine in their mode of life, in the size of their earnings and in their entire outlook" and are "the real *agents of the bourgeoisie in the working-class* movement, the labour lieutenants of the capitalist class". Google workers in comparison to ICT manufacturers have much higher wages and privileges, which also means that they are more unlikely to resist, which is, as Engels describes, typical for the labour aristocracy: "they are very nice people indeed nowadays to deal with, for any sensible capitalist in particular and for the whole capitalist class in general" (Engels 1892).

Slavoj Žižek (2012, 12) has inappropriately described the Occupy movement as a salaried bourgeoisie that consists of "privileged workers who have guaranteed jobs" and are "driven by fear of losing their surplus wage". But what he really described in this passage, without knowing it, are Google professionals, who as a labour aristocracy have in comparison to ICT manufacturers relatively high wages. If the ICT industry is seen as a combined industry and its profits as combined profits, then Google software engineers have a wage that is higher by a certain surplus in contrast to poorly paid ICT assemblers. This relative surplus wage comes, however, at a price: long working hours, high stress, a relative high turnover of labour in the software industry, poor work-life balance, and the tendency to have no social life outside the company. The term "labour aristocracy" is meant in an objective and not necessarily subjective sense: Google's software engineers have surplus wages relative to ICT manufacturing workers. Whether this status results in bourgeois consciousness that is quite homologous to the one of Google's managers and owners can only be determined empirically. Google totalizes labour time to lifetime. It pays relatively high wages as incentives to exploit high volumes of unpaid labour time.

Social media tend to enhance the stress of workers who typically work in companies like Google and other companies in the knowledge industries. Melissa Gregg (2011) shows how neo-liberalism forces knowledge professionals to put work above concerns for intimacy and how ICTs and especially mobile phones and social media like Facebook exacerbate this trend. There would be a neo-liberal demand to be always present, which she terms the "presence bleed" (ibid., 2). Communication technologies such as Facebook would add another layer of work on top of what is already expected" (ibid., 17). "Facebook's rise to prominence reflects the significance of work in the lives of white-collar professionals" (ibid., 88) and it is "synonymous with a new kind of presence" (101). Employees are today increasingly facing the demand, in addition of their regular work, to manage Twitter feeds, Facebook profiles, YouTube videos and so on and to use their private profiles for promoting their employer's company.

Convergence has been described in relation to dimensions such as media technologies, companies, institutions, industries, spaces, production and consumption, culture and politics (Jenkins 2008, Meikle and Young 2012; Mosco and McKercher 2008). Mosco and McKercher (2008) point out that convergence affects not just these realms, but also the world of labour, where the globalization of capitalism and convergence of capitalist industries and corporations would create a demand for labour union convergence in order to better organize class struggles. Deuze (2007) points out that the boundaries between life, work and play tend to become liquid and that the media support this development. Gregg's (2011) study can be interpreted as showing that contemporary capitalism, mobile and social media advance the convergence of labour: work that was traditionally handled by managers, secretaries, advertising public relations departments and call centres is outsourced to knowledge workers who are always available via mobile phones, laptops, Internet connections, voice over IP and social media, which requires them to manage a multitude of different activities in limited available time. Knowledge labour convergence seems to result in more tasks and different knowledge jobs converging in one job, which can easily put high demands and pressure on knowledge workers. Labour convergence interacts with the convergence of technologies and industries. Labour union convergence is an appropriate political response (Mosco and McKercher 2008).

9.4. Conclusion

Silicon Valley is not simply a space of ICT production but also a space of capital accumulation in ICT production that is based on a geography and social reality of inequality. Especially women and immigrants work in low-paid ICT manufacturing jobs that is partly based on piecework and because of the contamination of workplaces, air, soil and drinking water tend to result in health threats such as cancer, respiratory diseases, miscarriages and birth defects of babies. ICT manufacturing in Silicon Valley is based on a gendered and racist political economy that highly exploits and physically cripples workers and their families and destroys nature. The ICT industry increases its profits by decreasing wage costs and investment costs. Costs for workplace health, safety and environmental protection are reduced by physically harming workers and nature. Silicon Valley is a very good example of the circumstance observed by Marx that "[c]apitalist production [. . .] only develops the techniques and the degree of combination of the social process of production by simultaneously undermining the original sources of all wealth— the soil and the worker" (Marx 1867c, 638). James O'Connor (1998) argues that besides a contradiction between productive forces and production relations that takes on the form of a contradiction between production and realization of value there is a "second contradiction of capitalism" (ibid., 158–177): "the contradiction between capitalist production relations (and productive forces) and the conditions of capitalist production, or 'capitalist relations and forces of social reproduction'" (ibid., 160). In the case of ICT manufacturing, one can observe how the class contradiction between capital and labour is in the form of a negative dialectic connected to the antagonism between the capitalist mode of production and the natural forces so that the destructive forces of capital destroy both humans and nature, destroy humans by destroying nature (contaminated air, water and soil), and destroy humans' nature by destroying humans and nature (babies with birth defects). In Silicon Valley, the ecological antagonism and the social antagonism of capitalism are directly coupled.

In the *Grundrisse,* Marx describes conditions of production, such as a high demand of labour in one specific industry, in which certain workers gain "surplus wages" that represent a "small share of [. . .] surplus labour" (Marx 1857/1858b, 438). Martin Nicolaus therefore writes in the foreword that Marx shows that it is "theoretically possible, quite apart from the question of the economic cycle, for one fraction of the working class (but not the whole) to receive, via the mechanisms of the distribution of profit among the different capitalists, 'an extremely small share of' the surplus value produced by themselves in the form of 'surplus wages' (p. 438)" (ibid., 48). Google workers have, in contrast to ICT manufacturers, relatively high wages: they are highly paid and highly stressed. The antagonism between nature and class, on which the exploitation of ICT manufacturing workers is based in Silicon Valley, is complemented by an antagonism that fractionizes the ICT working class into a low-paid manufacturing proletariat and a highly paid and highly stressed labour aristocracy that enjoys relative surplus wages at the expense of transforming its life time into work time for Google.

Silicon Valley is only the valley of dreams for some: it is the valley of dreams for the class made up of those who reap high profits in the ICT industry precisely because it is the valley of death for ICT manufacturing workers and the valley of stress for the labour aristocracy in software engineering. Silicon Valley is shaped by a geography of inequality, death, stress and the destruction of nature and human livelihood that is the foundation of the capitalist ICT industry and its profits. Selling a commodity in an information society requires propaganda for this good and the monitoring and analysis of customer interests as well as responses to inquiries and problems of customers. Call centres are spaces of a specific type of service work that takes care of all such tasks. This type of work of not specific for managing the sales of ICTs; it can be found in all commercial industries. Call centre work is affective and communicative. It always makes use of phones and often of networked computers for managing customer databases, entering data and so on. Therefore, call centre work is a case that is particularly interesting for studying labour in the IDDL.

Notes

1 http://newsosaur.blogspot.se/2011/12/newspaper-job-cuts-surged-30-in-2011.html (accessed on July 9, 2013)
2 http://www.bls.gov/ro9/mlsca.htm (accessed on July 9, 2013).
3 California Layoffs Database, http://www.mercurynews.com/business/ci_12277251 (accessed on July 9, 2013).
4 http://content.usatoday.com/communities/technologylive/post/2012/04/yahoo-layoffs-read-the-email-to-employees/1#.UOzIGhhR97w (accessed on July 9, 2013).
5 www.reddit.com/r/AskReddit/comments/clz1m/google_employees_on_reddit_fire_up_your_throwaway/ (accessed on July 9, 2013).
6 http://www.youtube.com/watch?v=w0RTgOuoi2k&feature=share (accessed March 27, 2013).
7 Ibid.
8 http://it-jobs.fins.com/Articles/SBB0001424052702303404704577309493661513690/How-Google-s-Marissa-Mayer-Manages-Burnout (accessed March 16, 2013).
9 If an employee wrote, e.g., that s/he works 55–70 hours per week, then this circumstance was coded as an average of 62.5 hours.

10

TAYLORISTIC, HOUSEWIFIZED SERVICE LABOUR

The Example of Call Centre Work

"Good afternoon. Thank you for calling X. My name is Y. How can I help you, sir/madam?" These sentences are typical for the start of a phone conversation between you and a call centre agent. We call such centres for organizing our bank accounts, for setting up and managing customer accounts, for accessing technical expertise if a tool that we possess does not work, for resetting passwords that we have forgot, for filing complaints, and more. There are also call centre agents who call us to ask us to participate in surveys, to try to sell things to us, to update customer accounts, to try to convince us that we should prolong the subscription to X, not just possess Y but in addition also buy Z, and so on. Call centre work involves not only phones but also computer databases. It is a specific form of digital service labour. But how is it to work in a cell centre? This chapter engages with this question.

The German investigative journalist and undercover reporter Günter Wallraff worked undercover in call centres in order to document the working conditions there. He writes, "60 computer work stations are installed in a confined space. The setting: a flat screen, a headset and software that calls stored numbers after a mouse click. As soon as a connection is established the address of the participant and the origin of the addresses are displayed. [. . .] I ask myself: Why do these workers stoop to do this? Who forces them? The woman at CallOn who left ZIU had defended her former colleagues: They are often desperate people who were unemployed for a long time and clutch at the last straw. They now must convey energy and good spirits on the phone although they have a hard time. But what consequences does such labour have for the employees? [. . .] Already the

(Continued)

furnishing of the office gives an answer: A board hangs on the wall, on which sales are recorded by name. If somebody has brought about a new deal, s/he goes to the front and notes it. This automatically creates a pressure to succeed and compete"[1]. Let's have a look at a closer analysis of call centre work as a specific type of digital labour.

10.1. Introduction

In 2010, there were 8,240 companies in the EU27 countries that specialized in call centre activities. They generated a value added at factor costs of €10.6 billion, made a gross operating surplus of €861.54 million and employed 4.3 million people (Eurostat[2]). These economic activities make up 0.18% of the value added, 0.04% of operating surplus and 3.2% of all employees in the industry and service sector (excluding finance and insurance) of the EU27 countries (Eurostat). These data show that the call centre sector is economically quite relevant in terms of employment, value and profits and therefore deserves further attention.

In the EU project STILE, coders from national statistic offices were asked to code various job descriptions according to the International Standard Classification of Occupations (ISCO). Thirty-four cases involved call centre work. There was only agreement on how to code two of them. "It seems that call centres provide a paradigmatic example of the difficulty of classifying activities in the new economy, sitting as they do at the interfaces between businesses and their customers, between products and services and between internal and external processes" (Bertin et al. 2004, 76).

STILE showed the difficulty of understanding call centre activities. So how can call centre work be defined? The 2008 version of the International Standard Classification of Occupations (ISCO-08) contains two categories that describe call centre workers:

- 4222 Contact centre information clerks:

  "Contact centre information clerks provide advice and information to clients, respond to queries regarding a company's or an organization's goods, services or policies, and process financial transactions using the telephone or electronic communications media, such as email. They are located in premises that may be remote from clients or other operations of the organizations or companies about whom information is provided" (ISCO-08).

- 5244 Contact centre sales person:

  "Contact centre salespersons contact existing and prospective customers, using the telephone or other electronic communications media, to promote goods and services, obtain sales and arrange sales visits. They may work from a customer contact centre or from non-centralised premises" (ibid.).

The International Standard Industrial Classification of All Economic Activities (ISIC Rev. 4) contains a category for the call centre sector—8220 Activities of call centres:

> "This class includes:
>
> —activities of inbound call centres, answering calls from clients by using human operators, automatic call distribution, computer telephone integration, interactive voice response systems or similar methods to receive orders, provide product information, deal with customer requests for assistance or address customer complaints
> —activities of outbound call centres using similar methods to sell or market goods or services to potential customers, undertake market research or public opinion polling and similar activities for clients" (ISIC Rev. 4, 242).

The EU project TOSCA provides a synthetical definition of a call centre as "an office employing people in specialist posts involving the use of a computer and a telecommunications link to process communications in voice or electronic form" (Paul and Huws 2002, 10). Call centre work involves the use of ICTs (phones, computers, Internet); it is white-collar work that has some features of the standardization characteristic of some manufacturing; and it involves spatially and temporally disembedded activities (outsourcing, flexible working times).

10.2. The Call Centre's Productive Forces in the International Division of Digital Labour: Labour-Power and the Objects, Tools and Products of Labour

Paul and Huws (2002) argue that telephone services have existed for a long time but that advances in telecommunications, the growth of consumer culture and increasing media skills have created the context for the emergence of call centres.

Call centres typically focus on customer relations. Customer relations can be business-to-business or business-to-consumer. They can be inbound (customers call) or outbound (company calls actual or potential customers, e.g. marketing research) or both. Around 75% of call centres are oriented on the mass customer services market, and about 25% are business-to-business centres (Holman, Batt and Holtgrewe 2007). The first have around 80% of the total workforce (ibid.). The largest share of call centres exists in telecommunications and financial services (ibid.). Of the total number, 79% are inbound and 21% outbound call centres (ibid.). Subcontractors that have clients who outsource their services to these call centres make up 33% of all call centres but account for 56% of the employees, which shows that they tend to be fairly large in size.

The technologies that are needed for operating a call centres involve a phone line for speaking to the customers and networked computers that give employees access to a database that stores information on customers and into which they enter the data obtained in the phone calls. Frequently, employee monitoring software is also used.

10.3. The Call Centre's Relations of Production in the International Division of Digital Labour

The EU project TOSCA carried out research on call centres in Europe. It found that call centre work tends to be very repetitive, highly monitored and stressful. One could therefore speak of "modern-day sweat-shops" (Paul and Huws 2002, 14). The resulting stress and negative health impacts lead to high levels of absence of up to 25% of the employees. The employees are typically female and have a low level of education and flexible working hours so that call centres can operate 24 hours. These conditions result in a high worker turnover of up to 40%. Also a low level of union presence was found in call centres.

The Global Call Center Project (www.ilr.cornell.edu/globalcallcenter) is a research network that has studied call centre work in 20 countries. The project conducted a survey (Holman, Batt and Holtgrewe 2007) that covered 2,500 call centres in 17 countries: Austria, Brazil, Canada, Denmark, France, Germany, India, Ireland, Israel, the Netherlands, Poland, South Africa, South Korea, Spain, Sweden, the United Kingdom and the United States of America. At the time of the survey (2007), the typical call centre was eight years old, which shows that call centres are a relatively new development in the knowledge industry. Of the call centres involved in the study, 14% serve international clients. But in India, 73% of the call centre clients are international. Besides India, Canada and Ireland also have a relatively large focus on an international client base (Holtgrewe et al. 2009). Of the studied call centres, 67% are part of larger companies and 33% are subcontractors that work for companies that outsource the call centre work.

In all countries, there was a high level of women in the workforce. Women accounted in total for 69% of the employees. Seventy-one per cent of the employees were full-time, 17% part-time and 12% temporary workers. In some countries, however, the share of part-time workers was larger: 48% in Israel, 46% in the Netherlands and 44% in Spain. In South Korea, 60% of the call centre employees were temporary workers. Forty per cent of the call centres had collective bargaining agreements, 50% a form of collective representation. Whereas collective bargaining and representation mechanisms were found to be high in a number of countries such as France, the Netherlands and Brazil, there was a significant number of countries where such mechanisms were hardly existent (Israel, Canada, United States, India, Poland, South Korea). Of the call centres, 15.3% had performance-based payment; however, in the Netherlands this value was 41%. The study also showed that wages were higher in companies with collective bargaining. In coordinated economies, the median annual pay of a call centre agent was US$23,599, in liberal economies US$32,925 and in industrializing countries US$19,105. Managers' median wages were 111.0%/58.0%/59.1% higher respectively. Labour costs on average made up 65% of the total costs. The median turnover rate of personnel was 20% (that includes people who quit the job, are dismissed, are promoted or retire), which means that 1 out of 5 employees leaves every year. Call centres that serve international customers (meaning subcontractors) who outsource their services can especially be found in Canada, India and Ireland. Workers typically handle 80 calls per day in subcontracting call centres and 65 in in-house call centres. Employees working for subcontractors typically have lower complexity tasks, less training and more insecure employment contracts (temporary, part-time) than workers in in-house call centres. There is also more surveillance and lower job discretion in such companies. There is less collective bargaining, and employees get wages that are on average 18% lower.

Call centres extensively use call monitoring and software for call performance metrics (Holman, Batt and Holtgrewe 2007, 9–10). "The call handling time of the typical call centre provides one indicator of the relative standardization of work across call centres in different countries. The typical worksite in this report has an average call handling time of 190 seconds, or 3 minutes and 10 seconds" (ibid., 10). Call centres in three countries—France, India and Canada—primarily (more than 50%) hire college graduates. In nine countries, this rate is below 20% and in five it is between 20% and 40%. This shows that call centre workers tend to have lower education with the exception of a few specific countries. Performance monitoring (call handling times, task times, call waiting times) typically occurs more than once a week in recently industrialized countries, every two weeks in countries with liberal economies and once a month in countries with coordinated economies.

Job discretion (the influence employees can have on the pace of work, work methods, the timing of breaks, task completion and the way customer responses are handled) was found to be rather low: 2.6 on a scale that ranges from 1 to 5 (maximum). The study found that 39% of the analysed call centres have low- to very-low-quality jobs that feature relatively low job discretion and relatively high performance monitoring. Another result was that 36% of the employees have very-low-quality jobs, 67% low- to very-low-quality jobs and only 14% high- or very-high-quality jobs. "Our findings indicate that performance monitoring in call centres works by ensuring that employees sustain a high level of task effort. [. . .] [H]igh levels of monitoring hasten the depletion of physical and mental resources, which leads to lower levels of well-being" (Holman, Batt and Holtgrewe 2007, 42–43). Low-quality jobs can also result in increased stress and in turn increased levels of sickness and leave, which is indicated by the circumstance that the median number of sick days per employee was six per year.

The Global Call Center Project in general found a high level of standardization of call centre jobs, high performance monitoring, low level of employees' influence on decisions about the work process, low job quality and a high rate of female employment. The study found some variation that is explained by higher union power and influence in those countries where call centre job have higher quality and lower turnover and where wages are less dispersed. "There is ample evidence to show that heavy reliance on a cost-focused model not only creates low quality jobs but also breeds customer dissatisfaction and employee turnover" (Holman, Batt and Holtgrewe 2007, 45).

English-speaking countries' preferred location for outsourced jobs (banking, energy, entertainment, insurance, media, retail, technology, telecommunications, travel, utilities) is India (James and Vira 2010). Four hundred of the Fortune 500 companies have call centres in India (ibid.), especially in Bangalore, Delhi and Mumbai. Overall, 25–50% of the costs can be saved by call centre offshoring. India attracts the majority of internationally outsourced call centre work. Studies found that call centre work in India is repetitive, features rigid discipline and large-scale surveillance of employees, has negative health impacts for employees (muscle tension, headaches, eyestrains, repetitive strain injury [RSI], voice loss, hearing problems, stress, nausea, dizziness and panic attacks), and has a hierarchical character with a lack of participation in decision-making (ibid.). James and Vira (2010) present the results of interviews with 42 Indian call centre workers and of a survey among such workers (N = 511). Entry salaries were found to be on average INR 9272 (Indian rupee) per month, which is three times the per capita income in India. Indian call centre agents see themselves as highly qualified white-collar professionals, 79% of the respondents were university graduates and 75% of agents think that unions damage the industry. Indian call centre workers are often college-educated, so many times they are overqualified for the tasks they perform (Upadhya and Vasavi 2008). Ramesh (2008) conducted a survey among Indian call centre workers (N = 277). Ninety-seven per cent of them were university educated. Only 13% had their job for more than two years, which is an indication that because of their overqualification, employees do not see the call centre as a long-term opportunity, but "rather as a stop-gap arrangement to earn money before moving on to another career or further education" (Upadhya and Vasavi 2008, 19). Some 53% of the respondents earned more than INR 10,000, 19% between INR 8,000 and 10,000. Indian call centre work typically involves night shifts in order to comply with the needs of Western clients. There is a high level of control and surveillance in the form of recorded calls, computer-assisted performance monitoring and card-based registration systems. A certain number of calls are set as an individual target for each worker, and these targets would be constantly pushed up in performance reviews. Peer pressure would be generated by the public display of the performance of all employees. D'Cruz and Noronha (2009) show that Indian call centre workers are often bullied by managers.

10.4. Conclusion

Call centre work tends to be repetitive, standardized, stressful and highly monitored and often features shift and flexible work that poses problems for work-life and work-family balance. Influence on on-the-job decision-making and job quality tend to be low. Call centre workers are to a large degree female.

Many call centre workers do not define themselves as such, but rather consider their identity as something quite different (Huws 2009, Paul and Huws 2002): they tend to see themselves as being only transiently in the call centre business, which shows that call centre agent is, as a result of its features, a job that does not and probably cannot have a high status among the workforce and in society. Ursula Huws (2009) argues that there is a "callcenterisation" of work that "destabilises many features of work that were formerly taken for granted" (Huws 2009, 7): many call centre employees and workers in general have to manage the difficult interfaces between company and customers, which requires significant affective labour endeavours, between local work and the global nature of capital, and between working life and family life. Rosa Luxemburg (1913/2003) argued that capital accumulation feeds on the exploitation of milieus that are drawn into the capitalist system: "capital feeds on the ruins of such organisations, and, although this non-capitalist milieu is indispensable for accumulation, the latter proceeds, at the cost of this medium nevertheless, by eating it up" (ibid., 363). This idea was used to explain the existence of colonies of imperialism by Luxemburg and was applied by Marxist feminism in order to argue that unpaid reproductive labour can be considered as an inner colony and milieu of primitive accumulation of capitalism (Mies, Bennholdt-Thomsen and Werlhof 1988; Mies 1986; Werlhof 1991). Non-wage labour "ensures the reproduction of labour-power and living conditions" (Mies, Bennholdt-Thomsen and Werlhof 1988, 18). It is labour spent "in the production of life, or subsistence production" (ibid., 70). Primitive accumulation "is overt violence, with the aim of robbery wherever, whenever, and against whomever this is 'economically' necessary, politically possible and technically feasible" (ibid., 102). In post-Fordist capitalism, the inner colonies of capitalism are expanded so that profits rise by generating milieus of low-paid and unpaid labour. The formation of these colonies is a form of ongoing primitive accumulation that uses violence for expropriating labour. "Women, colonies and nature" are "the main targets of this process of ongoing primitive accumulation" (ibid., 6). This phenomenon has been termed "housewifisation" (Mies, Bennholdt-Thomsen and Werlhof 1988; Mies 1986): more and more people live and work under precarious conditions that have traditionally been characteristic of patriarchal relations. People working under such conditions are, like housewives, a source of uncontrolled and unlimited exploitation. Housewifization transforms labour so that it "bears the characteristics of housework, namely, labour not protected by trade unions or labour laws, that is available at any time, for any price, that is not recognized as 'labour' but as an 'activity', as in the 'income generating activities', meaning isolated and unorganized and so on" (Mies, Bennholdt-Thomsen and Werlhof 1988, 10). Housewifized labour is characterized by "no job permanency, the lowest wages, longest working hours, most monotonous work, no trade unions, no opportunity to obtain higher qualifications, no promotion, no rights and no social security" (ibid., 169). Such informal work is "a source of unchecked, unlimited exploitation" (Mies 1986, 16). Housewifized labour is "superexploitation of non-wage labourers [. . .] upon which wage labour exploitation then is possible" (ibid., 48) because it involves the "externalization, or ex-territorialization of costs which otherwise would have to be covered by the capitalists" (110).

Zillah Eisenstein (1979, 33) argues that the gender division of labour that shapes capitalist patriarchy assigns five types of labour to women: reproduction, child-rearing, maintenance of home, sexuality and organization of consumption. Call centre labour shows that the gender division of labour extends from the home into the capitalist workplace: in the home, women are compelled to take care of biological reproduction and child-rearing; in call centre work this role is reproduced because a patriarchal ideology is at play that sees women as being affective, social, friendly and caring not just for children and the family in the home, but also for customers on the phone. The activity of keeping constant order in the home gets reproduced in the call centre as assigning employees the task of keeping order in the customer database so that the clients continue buying the offered commodities. In the household, patriarchy assigns women the role of organizing consumption of the family—buying and preparing food, informing herself about new consumer goods that could improve family life, and so on. In the call centre, workers are also in charge of organizing consumption—they respond to the consumer needs of customers and have to try to help them fix problems that relate to consumption and improving the consumption experience. Last, but not least, also sexual work and desire gets reproduced from patriarchal relations to the call centre: talking to a woman at customer service may easier please male customers because it may invoke sexual desires. Just like the tele-communicated form of prostitution—paid phone sex—provides a sexual service to men, the female call centre agent provides services that may easier please male customers if they are reminded of the submissive and sexual connotations of women that the phone carries in the culture of capitalist patriarchy. All five types of housework that Eisenstein distinguishes—reproduction, child-rearing, maintenance of home, sexuality, organization of consumption—get reproduced in the call centre. It is therefore no surprise that the majority of call centre agents are female—capitalism uses patriarchal ideologies, such as the identification of women with being social, caring, affective, sexual, relational and communicative, to create housewifized employment relations. In call centres, like in the home, "the biological distinction male/female" is ideologically used "to distinguish so-cial functions and individual power" (ibid., 17) and the position of employees "as paid workers is defined in terms of being a woman" (30). Like housework, call centre work relies on workers' temporal availability and alienated flexibility: house workers often have to be available around the clock for children and the whole family, call centres tend to be open 24 hours, which requires around-the-clock availability of the collective call centre worker. This can bring problems for health and family life.

And yet there is of course an important difference between house workers and call centre workers: the latter are often paid poorly, the first are not paid at all.

Domestic "slaves are not exploited in the same way as wage slaves. They would have to be paid a wage for this to be true" (ibid., 23). The "callcenterisation" and housewifization of work creates and extends the "free labor pool" and the "cheap labor pool" (ibid., 31) in order to maximize profits.

The call centre agent's work—insecure, precarious, stressful, standardized work that entails spatio-temporal flexibility requirements defined by capital's needs—has become the model for the creation of an entire economy of insecure and precarious jobs that especially affects and negatively influences young people's lives. What Ursula Huws (2009) calls the "callcenterisation" of work is at the same time a housewifization of work—the creation of forms of labour that re-semble the difficulties with which women had to struggle for a long time because of the gender division of labour. The "callcenterisation" and housewifization of work follow one purpose—to cut labour costs in order to maximize profits (i.e. to make workers labour for less than what could be expected as a wage under non-housewifized conditions). Cutting labour costs by housewifization is a form of absolute surplus-value production—the part of the day that produces surplus value and profit is lengthened. Ideology defines women as working mothers in order to pay them less than men. Call centre work is highly monitored and standardized—it is a kind of Taylorist white-collar work that blurs the boundaries between blue- and white-collar work. It could be called grey-collar work because grey is the colour that results from mixing blue and white. The standardization and surveillance of work, accompanied by precarization that puts workers under survival pressures, is a method of relative surplus-value production—constant control and pressure is aimed at making workers discipline their brains and bodies in such a form that they work more intensively (i.e. take care of more customers in less time and so increase productivity). Call centre work is characterized both by the formal and the real subsumption of labour under capital: methods of both absolute surplus-value production (cutting wage costs) and relative surplus-value production (standardization, surveillance, grey-collar Taylorism) are used for advancing capital accumulation.

There is another type of work in the IDDL that needs to be considered: the unpaid digital labour of the users, especially social media users. We will analyse this form of labour in the next chapter.

Notes

1 My translation from German. Original text: "Auf engstem Raum sind hier 60 Computerarbeitsplätze installiert. Die Ausstattung: Flachbildschirm, Headset und Software, die gespeicherte Nummern nach Mausklick anwählt. Sobald eine Verbindung zustande kommt, erscheinen auf dem Bildschirm die Anschrift des Teilnehmers und die Herkunft der Adresse. [. . .] Ich frage mich: Warum geben sie sich dafür her? Wer zwingt sie dazu? Die Frau bei CallOn, die bei ZIU ausgestiegen war, hatte ihre früheren Kollegen in Schutz genommen: Es seien oft Verzweifelte, die über lange Zeit arbeitslos gewesen seien und sich an den letzten Strohhalm klammerten. Die nun am Telefon Energie und gute

Laune versprühen müssten, obwohl es ihnen dreckig gehe. Aber welche Auswirkungen hat eine solche Arbeit auf die Beschäftigten? Einmal unterstellt, dass hier keine Betrüger am Werke sind, die lustvoll andere ausnehmen. Schon die Einrichtung des Büros gibt eine Antwort: An der Wand hängt eine Tafel, auf der die Verkaufsabschlüsse namentlich erfasst werden. Wer einen neuen Abschluss zustande gebracht hat, geht nach vorn und notiert das. So entsteht automatisch Erfolgs- und Konkurrenzdruck" (Wallraff 2009).

2 http://epp.eurostat.ec.europa.eu (accessed August 8, 2013).

11

THEORIZING DIGITAL LABOUR ON SOCIAL MEDIA[1]

- "Connect with friends and the world around you on Facebook". "Facebook's mission is to give people the power to share and make the world more open and connected".
- "YouTube allows billions of people to discover, watch and share originally-created videos. YouTube provides a forum for people to connect, inform, and inspire others across the globe and acts as a distribution platform for original content creators and advertisers large and small".
- "Welcome to Twitter. Find out what's happening, right now, with the people and organizations you care about". "Twitter is a real-time information network that connects you to the latest stories, ideas, opinions and news about what you find interesting. Simply find the accounts you find most compelling and follow the conversations".
- "Blogger: Create a blog. It's free".
- "Over 200 million professionals use LinkedIn to exchange information, ideas and opportunities. Stay informed about your contacts and industry. Find the people & knowledge you need to achieve your goals. Control your professional identity online".
- "What can you do on VK? Find people with whom you've studied, worked or met on vacation. Learn more about people around you and make new friends. Stay in touch with loved ones".
- "tumblr. Follow the world's creators. Tumblr lets you effortlessly share anything". "Post text, photos, quotes, links, music, and videos from

(Continued)

your browser, phone, desktop, email or wherever you happen to be. You can customize everything, from colors to your theme's HTML".

- "Pinterest. Collect and organize the things you love".
- "Meet Instagram. It's a fast, beautiful and fun way to share your photos with friends and family. Snap a picture, choose a filter to transform its look and feel, then post to Instagram. Share to Facebook, Twitter, and Tumblr too—it's as easy as pie. It's photo sharing, reinvented. Oh yeah, did we mention it's free?"
- "Discover and share great places with friends. Over 30 million people use Foursquare to make the most of where they are. Discover and learn about great places nearby, search for what you're craving, and get deals and tips along the way. Best of all, Foursquare is personalized. With every check-in, we get even better at recommending places for you to try".
- Weibo: "Sina microblogging account? Join now". "Hi! I am the audience".

These are invitations for users to join on some of the world's most popular social media platforms: Facebook, YouTube, Twitter, Blogger, LinkedIn, VK, tumblr, Pinterest, Instagram, Foursquare, Weibo. They promise users possibilities to connect, share, open the world, discover, watch, create, inform, inspire, find out, care, exchange, contact, learn, follow, post, collect, organize, fun, recommend, and enjoy beauty, freedom and opportunities.

Corporate social media publish a flood of positive promises and associations. But how does this all work? And who works to make it work? And who owns the results of this work? Understanding corporate social media requires a critical discussion of digital labour and digital work and an engagement with these questions: What are digital work and digital labour on social media?

11.1. Introduction

Users act as buyers and consumers of ICTs in many different ways: for example, they buy and use desktop computers, monitors, laptops, mobile phones, tablets, printers, keyboards, mice, game consoles, operating systems, application software or online access to music, texts, videos and images. In all of these roles, they act as consumers, who exchange money with commodities, whereby capital is transformed from the commodity form into the money form, or, as Marx (1867c, 1885) says, profit is realized from the potential form that it has in the commodity in the form of crystallized surplus labour into the actual form it has as money that the consumer pays for obtaining ownership of or access to ICTs. In the examples just described, users are not ICT workers but rather consumers; the capital accumulation process M (money)—C (commodities: means of production, labour-power) .. P (production) .. C' (new commodity)—M' (more money) comes to an end in the consumers' buying process just in order to start anew when part of the achieved profit is reinvested into new production so that a new cycle of accumulation can start. So the users' role is precisely in the stage C'—M', in which s/he exchanges money with commodities and obtains a use-value for consumption. In the consumption process itself, users engage in the cultural process of meaning-making; they create various meanings of commodities in the usage of these goods in everyday life. They may for example find a new computer game entertaining, boring, funny, too violent, individualizing, a good form for socializing with other players, and so on. What they produce is meaning in the usage and consumption process of cultural goods. These roles of ICT users as consumers as partly changing towards what some have called Internet prosumption (Fuchs 2010b, Ritzer and Jurgenson 2010) or consumption work (Huws 2003, 37–38, 44; Huws 2012) of ICT users. So what are these changes all about?

11.2. Users and the Productive Forces in the International Division of Digital Labour: Labour-Power and the Objects, Tools and Products of Labour

In early 2013, 46% of all Internet users searched online for information with the help of Google and 13% with the help of Baidu, 43% were users of Facebook, 32% watched videos on YouTube, 7% tweeted, 6% were reading or writing blogs on Blogspot and 5% used LinkedIn (alexa.com, three-month average usage statistics, accessed January 18, 2013). These platforms are different in that they enable different forms of usage—searching, social networking, sharing and watching user-generated content, blogging and short message blogging (microblogging). What they all have in common is not necessarily that they are "social" and that other forms of Internet usage (such as reading an online newspaper or sending an email) are "non-social". They rather imply a form of sociality focused on sharing, community and collaboration that is combined with information and communication, which are two other forms of socialization. What all of these platforms have in common is that they use a business model that is based on targeted advertising and that turn users' data (content, profiles, social networks, online behaviour) into a commodity. The use, monitoring and commodification of user data is typically legally defined in terms of use and privacy policies. Internet prosumer commodification is enabled by privacy policies and terms of use. Here are three examples of such provisions:

- "We use the information we receive to deliver ads and to make them more relevant to you. This includes all of the things you share and do on Facebook, such as the Pages you like or key words from your stories, and the things we infer from your use of Facebook" (Facebook Data Use Policy, June 8, 2012).

- "We also use this information to offer you tailored content—such as giving you more relevant search results and ads" (Google Privacy Policy, July 27, 2012).
- "The Services may include advertisements, which may be targeted to the Content or information on the Services, queries made through the Services, or other information" (Twitter Terms of Use, June 25, 2012).

Commodities have producers who create them; otherwise they cannot exist. So if the commodity of the mentioned Internet platforms is user data, then the process of creating these data must be considered to be value-generating labour. This means that this type of Internet usage is productive consumption or pro-sumption in the sense that it creates value and a commodity that is sold. In this context, the notion of digital labour has gained prominence (Burston, Dyer-Witheford and Hearn 2010; Scholz 2013), and Dallas Smythe's concept of the audience commodity has been revived and transformed into the concept of the Internet prosumer commodity. Digital labour creates on social media the Internet prosumer commodity that is sold by Internet platforms to advertising clients, which in return present targeted ads to users.

Management thinkers have recommended to companies the outsourcing of labour to users and consumers in order to increase profits by decreasing labour costs. Jeff Howe has in this context introduced the concept of crowdsourcing: "Simply defined, crowdsourcing represents the act of a company or institution taking a function once performed by employees and outsourcing it to an undefined (and generally large) network of people in the form of an open call. This can take the form of peer-production (when the job is performed collaboratively), but is also often undertaken by sole individuals. The crucial prerequisite is the use of the open call format and the large network of potential laborers" (Howe 2006). Howe (2008) has argued that crowdsourcing results in a democratization of capitalism: "Crowdsourcing engenders another form of collaboration as well, between companies and customers. Toffler was right: people don't want to consume passively; they'd rather participate in the development and creation of products meaningful to them. Crowdsourcing is just one manifestation of a larger trend toward greater democratization in commerce" (ibid., 14). That management gurus make such recommendations and present them in an ideological form as economic democracy is an indication that a new capital accumulation model has emerged.

11.3. Users and the Relations of Production in the International Division of Digital Labour

In this section, we will discuss how to apply Marx's theory of work and labour to the realm of online media. We on the one hand develop general arguments and on the other hand use Facebook as an example to make the abstract discussion more concrete. Facebook is particularly suited as a case study because it is the most popular "social medium" and uses a capital accumulation model that cannot work without the commodification of users' online activities. The discussion can also be applied to other forms of social media. We will use the distinction between work and labour that was introduced in chapter 3 to analyse general and capitalism-specific characteristics of online work. The section is divided into three parts: the first one discusses digital work on social media (11.3.1), the second one digital labour on social media (11.3.2), the third one on the law of value on social media (11.3.3).

11.3.1. Digital Work on Social Media

Raymond Williams focuses in his essay "Means of Communication as Means of Production" on the structures of communication, that is, media (including language and mass media), and argues that they are means of production and therefore "indispensable elements both of the productive forces and of the relations of production" (Williams 1980, 50). His focus on structures, however, leaves out the focus on the subjects' practices and the question whether communication is a form of work. The most concrete way he addresses this issue is by saying that languages and communication are "forms of social production" (ibid., 55). A question related to the relationship of work and communication is the role of nature in production and the issue of whether the object of work is necessarily taken from nature. "It is possible that the material of labour, the object to be appropriated by means of labour for a specific need, is available in nature without the assistance of human labour: the fish caught in water for example, or the wood felled in the primeval forest, or the ore brought up out of the pit. In such a case only the means of labour itself is a product of previous human labour. This characterises everything that can be called extractive industry; it only applies to agriculture to the extent that, say, virgin soil is being cultivated" (Marx 1861–1863). This quotation shows that Marx considered nature just one possible object of work that occurs in agricultural work and mining. This implies that also fabricated nature and ideas can be the object of work. Agricultural and extractive work takes nature as the object, industrial work takes fabricated nature as the object, information work takes ideas and human subjectivity as the object. Marx described the latter possibility in the *Grundrisse*'s "Fragment on Machines" as a consequence of capitalism's technological progress, in which fixed constant capital in the form of machines becomes historically ever more important in production in order to increase productivity, which is a development that is accompanied by the rising relevance of information work. He coined the notion of the general intellect in this context: "The development of fixed capital indicates to what degree general social knowledge has become a direct force of production, and to what degree, hence, the conditions of the process of social life itself have come under the control of the general intellect and been transformed in accordance with it. To what degree the powers of social production have been produced, not only in the form of knowledge, but also as immediate organs of social practice, of the real life process"

(Marx 1857/1858b, 706). Most Marxist approaches that have given attention to the communication process at a theoretical level have focused on the communicative character of work but have neglected the question if communication is work. They stress that work requires communication and is organized with the help of communication and human communication emerged and is reproduced in interaction with human work. Conventional communication theory sees the material and the ideal as two separate realms of society, labour and interaction are seen as being alien to and independent from each other (Hund 1976, 272–273).

Language is the result of human activities over many generations. Words are not natural objects but produced by humans together in their culture. As being produced by humans, information is the product of human work. Hands, head, ears, mouth—body and brain—work together in order to enable speech. Work has a dual character: it has physical and social dimensions. Thinking and speaking that result in the production of information and symbols form the physical aspect, human relations the social dimension of communication (Hund and Kirchhoff-Hund 1980).

Information can be conceived as a threefold process of cognition, communication and cooperation (Fuchs and Hofkirchner 2005, Fuchs et al. 2010, Hofkirchner 2002). The following table gives an overview of the dimensions of cognitive, communicative and cooperative work.

Figure 11.1 shows that these three processes are connected dialectically and form together the process of information work. Each of the three behaviours—cognition, communication and cooperation—is a work process: cognition is work of the human brain, communication work of human groups and cooperation collaborative work of human groups. Communication is based on cognition and uses the products of cognition—ideas—as its object of work. Cooperation is based on communication and uses the products of communication—meanings—as object

TABLE 11.1 The subject, object and subject-object of cognitive, communicative and cooperative work

	Subject	*Object of work*	*Instruments of work*	*Product of work*
Cognition = human brain work	Human being	Experiences	Brain	Thoughts, cognitive patterns, ideas
Communication = human group work	Group of humans	Thoughts	Brain, mouth, ears	Meaning
Cooperation = collaborative human group work	Group of humans	Meaning	Brain, mouth, ears, body	Information product with shared and co-created meaning

of work. Information is a work process, in which cognitive work creates ideas, communicative work creates meanings and cooperative work co-creates information products that have shared and co-created meaning. Information is a dialectical process of human work, in which cognition, communication and cooperation are dialectically connected. Each of these three processes forms a work process that has its own subject-object dialectic in itself.

Using the Hegel-Marxist triangle model of the work process (see the "Dialectical triangle of the work process" in chapter 2, figure 2.2), one can argue that the development that Marx points out on behalf of the notion of the general intellect can be formalized as follows: S-O > SO ... S-SO > SSO ... S-SSO > SSSO and so forth. The object position of a dialectical work triangle starts with the result, the subject-object of a previous triangle, and so on.

An example: A person likes reading books about gardening and builds up a sophisticated knowledge of how to create and maintain a good-looking garden by reading more and more books and applying this knowledge in his/her garden. The created knowledge is a use-value in the sense that it helps him/her organize his/her own garden in a nice-looking manner. S/he meets another person who has comparable knowledge. They start exchanging ideas on gardening. In this communication process, the shared knowledge of one person forms an object that is interpreted by the other person so that meaning (i.e. an interpretation of parts of the world) is formed. The process also works vice versa. As a result, meanings are created as use-values on both sides, and each person understands something about the other. After continuous conversations and mutual learning, the two hobby gardeners decide to write a book about gardening. They develop new ideas by discussing and bring their experiences together, whereby synergies,

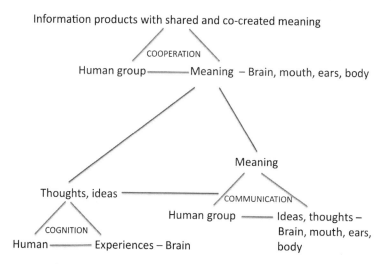

FIGURE 11.1 The information process as work process

new experiences and new gardening methods emerge. In the book, they describe these new methods that they have tried in practice in a jointly run garden. The representations of the joint experiences and of the co-created methods in the form of a book are a use-value not just for the two, but for others too.

Work requires information processes, and information creation is itself a work process. This model allows (in contrast to Habermas' approach) a non-dualistic solution to the question of how work and information/interaction are connected. It avoids separations between nature/culture, work/interaction, base/superstructure, but rather it argues that information has its own economy—it is work that creates specific use-values. These use-values are individual in character only at the level of cognition—the human thinks and develops new ideas—whereas they have a direct social character at the level of communication and cooperation. But humans do not exist as monads: the objects of cognitive work stem to a large degree from society itself and from human experiences. To interpret the information creation process as work is not philosophical idealism because idealism sees spirit as an independently existing entity that is not connected to human labour. Ideas, meanings and co-created information products are objects of labour that reflect society in complex ways. Every work process requires cognition, communication and cooperation as tools of production. Therefore, the physical production of goods in manufacturing as well as agricultural work and mining are never separate from information processes. This aspect has been stressed in many Marxist analyses of the connection of communication and work. In these production forms, information is not a product but a means of production. Work requires information. The other way round, information is also work: there is an informational organization of the capitalist mode of production that has grown in size in the 20th century (in terms of the population active in it and share of the overall created value in the economy): it focuses on the production of informational goods and services. It is this kind of production that is the main focus in this chapter. Work requires information and communication. But at the same time, it is important to give attention to information and communication as forms of work.

In concrete work, human subjects equipped with labour-power apply instruments to objects in order to create products that satisfy human needs. On Facebook, labour-power is predominantly informational work. Information is a threefold process of cognition, communication and cooperation. On Facebook, users publish information about their life, which means they objectify their subjective knowledge that is grounded in their experiences in society in such a way that they create and update their user profiles. This is the stage of cognitive work on Facebook. Users also communicate with others by using the messaging function or writing comments on walls or community pages. In this process, users externalize parts of their cognitive knowledge in the symbolic exchange of messages with other users. If the interaction is reciprocal, then subjective knowledge of one user becomes objectified in the brains of at least one other user and the other way round. This objectification of subjective knowledge means that users interpret the messages of others and thereby change their thought patterns to a certain degree. Communicative work on Facebook means the mutual symbolic interchange of subjective knowledge, which results in meaning-making that is internalized. Facebook is also a community, which means that repeated communication between users results in or maintains friendships and personal relations that involve feelings of belonging together. Furthermore, it is also a space of collaboration, where users together try to strategically achieve goals such as saving money by organizing online ridesharing, exchanging or giving away furniture or clothes, or setting up community pages that enable the joint activities of guerrilla gardeners, guerrilla knitters and others. Online community and online collaboration are both expressions of cooperation: humans come together online to create something new, either social relations that involve feelings of togetherness or social relations that enable the collaborative creation of novel objects in the world. These cooperation processes are enabled by Facebook, and they are grounded in human cognition and communication, from which a new quality of a social system emerges by repeated and routinized interactions that create results on a higher level of social organization. Facebook is a realm of cognitive, communicative and cooperative activities. But why are these activities work? According to Marx, in order to speak of work, there must be an interaction of labour-power with objects and instruments of work so that use-values are created as products. The following table summarizes these elements in relation to the three forms of digital work and in the context of Internet usage. In cognitive digital work, humans make use of their brains, mouths, speech, ears, hands, the Internet and platforms (such as Facebook) as instruments to organize parts of their experiences that form an object so that a transmogrified representation of these experiences is created in the online realm (e.g. in the form of a blog post, a user profile or an online video). In communicative digital work, experiences of at least two human subjects (either objectified in an online form or in human brains) form an object which is transformed with the help of symbolic interaction that is enabled by online media, human brains, mouths, speech and ears so that new meanings about the world and new experiences are created on the side of the involved individuals and social relationships are established. New meanings and (the creation or maintenance of) social relations are the use-values of communicative work. Cooperative digital work organizes human experiences that are given in the form of human thought, online information or joint meanings and existing social relations with the help of online media, human brains, mouths, speech, ears and hands in such a way that new artefacts, communities or social systems are created. A social system is a routinized social relationship involving behaviour that follows certain rules and exists over a longer time period. All three forms of digital work have a common ground: Digital work is the organization of human experiences with the help of the human brain, digital media and speech in such a way that new products are created. These products can be online information,

TABLE 11.2 Three forms of digital work on social media

	Object of work	Instruments of work	Product, use-value
Cognitive digital work	Human experiences	Human brains, hands, mouths, ears, speech, Internet, platforms	Online information, profiles
Communicative digital work	Human experiences, online information	Human brains, hands, mouths, ears, speech, Internet, platforms	New meanings established in social relationships
Cooperative digital work	Human experiences, online information, online social relations	Human brains, hands, mouths, ears, speech, Internet, platforms	Artefacts, communities, social systems

meanings, social relations, artefacts or social systems. Digital work is grounded in what Marx termed the species-being and the sensuous being of humans, which means that they are creative and productive as well as social beings with language competence. Man is "a social (i.e. human) being" (Marx 1844, 102), and his/her "existence is social activity. Therefore what I create from myself I create for society" (ibid.).[2]

That "general social knowledge has become a direct force of production" means that at a certain stage of development, knowledge not only plays an indirect role for the economy in the form of educational skills provided by schools, universities, libraries and other cultural institutions, but it has also a role in the economy in the form of information work that creates informational products. Based on a reading of Marx's "Fragment on Machines", Italian Autonomist Marxists have formulated the concept of immaterial labour. Maurizio Lazzarato introduced this term, by which he means "labour that produces the informational and cultural content of the commodity" (Lazzarato 1996, 133). Michael Hardt and Antonio Negri have popularized this notion and define immaterial labour as labour "that creates immaterial products, such as knowledge, information, communication, a relationship, or an emotional response" (Hardt and Negri 2005, 108). The term "immaterial" creates the impression that information work is detached from nature and matter and that there are two substances in the world—matter and spirit—that result in two different types of work. Information work is however not detached from nature and matter, but is material itself. It is based on the activity of the human brain, which is a material system that is part of the human's materiality. If one presents the spirit as being detached from nature and matter, as post-Operaist accounts often do, then one leaves the realm of a materialistic analysis of society and enters the realm of spiritualism, esoterics and religion, in which spirit is an immortal substance.

Are human cognition, communication and cooperation really work? Jürgen Habermas has contested this view. He argues that Marx, Lukács, Horkheimer and Adorno expanded "the teleological concept of action" and thereby relativized "purposive rationality against a model of reaching understanding" (Habermas 1984, 343). The strong focus on instrumental reason would not provide enough consideration of communicative rationality. Marx would therefore dialectically clamp together "system and life-world" so that the "intersubjectivity of workers associated in large industries is crippled under the self-movement of capital" (Habermas 1987, 340). As a consequence, Habermas makes a sharp distinction between on the one hand purposive (instrumental, strategic) action that is oriented to success and on the other hand communicative action that is oriented on reaching understanding (Habermas 1984, 285–286). Work is for Habermas always an instrumental, strategic and purposive form of action.

Habermas misinterprets Marx by not seeing that the latter gives attention to both the anthropological and historical side of human activity. In the concepts of the species-being and the sensuous being, Marx conceives the human as a producing and communicating being. He uses in this context the notion of the species-being and the sensuous being. The species-being is an economically producing (i.e. working) being: "It is just in the working-up of the objective world, therefore, that man first really proves himself to be a species being. This production is his active species life. Through and because of this production, nature appears as his work and his reality" (Marx 1844, 77). The sensuous being is among other things a speaking and communicating being: "The element of thought itself—the element of thought's living expression—language—is of a sensuous nature. The social reality of nature, and human natural science, or the natural science about man, are identical terms" (Marx 1844, 111). Communication is enabled by the interaction of the two human senses of speaking and hearing. But these senses can, as Marx points out, never exist in isolation, only in social relations: "For his [the human's] own sensuousness first exists as human sensuousness for himself through the other man" (ibid.). "Language itself is the product of a community, just as it is in another respect itself the presence of the community" (Marx 1857/1858b, 490). Language "is practical, real consciousness that exists also for other men as well, and only therefore does it also exist for me; language, like consciousness, only arises from the need, the necessity of intercourse with other men" (Marx and Engels 1845/1846, 49). For Marx, the human being is not necessarily an instrumental being, because he stresses on the one hand the dimensions of sensuousness, speech and communication and on the other hand points out that work is not always and not necessarily a necessity and an instrument to achieve goals, but under communism it becomes a free activity beyond necessity and instrumentality.

Habermas mistakenly claims that Marx did not take into account communication when describing humans in society but focused on work and instrumentality instead. As we have tried to show, Marx in his analysis of the human as species-being and sensuous being saw both the aspects of work and information as constitutive of human existence. The Italian post-operaists have foregrounded based on Marx that information has become a productive force in many contemporary economies. The analytical consequence we can draw from this discussion is that it does not make sense to separate information and work as two realms of human existence, as Habermas does in his theory. One should rather see work as a broad category constitutive of the human that includes different types of work, such as agricultural work, industrial work and informational work. Work on Facebook is informational work that is organized with the help of digital media based on the Internet. Digital work on social media is a specific form of informational work that makes use of digital media as an instrument of work which is employed together with the human brain to organize human experiences in such a way that symbolic representations, social relations, artefacts, social systems and communities emerge as new qualities.

11.3.2. Digital Labour on Social Media

I have argued that a conceptual distinction between work and labour should be made and that labour is based on a fourfold alienation of the human being: the alienation from oneself, the alienation from the objects of labour (alienation from the instruments of labour, alienation from the objects of labour) and the alienation from the created products. This fourfold alienation constitutes an alienation from the whole production process that is due to the existence of class relations and results in exploitation. We will now apply this discussion to the realm of the digital and the case of Facebook.

Alienation of labour-power means for Marx that humans have to let capital control their productive activities for a certain share of the day in order to be able to survive. One argument that one can sometimes hear about digital labour is that Facebook users are not exploited because nobody forces them to use the platform; they rather do so voluntarily and have fun in doing so. In order to exist humans not only have to eat, but also must enter social relations, communicate and form friendships. Isolation of an individual from communication and social networking will ultimately result in either death or an animal-like existence. Speech and the brain are at the heart of human communication power. They can only be put to use in social relations, in the connection with other humans. In an information society, digital media have for many become important means of interaction that humans employ for putting to use their communication power. Labour-power is therefore partly communication power. If one wants to use a social networking site (SNS) for communicating with others, then Facebook is the most likely option because it controls a very large number of users and their profiles, which makes it very likely that individuals engage in a significant number of meaningful communications if they access Facebook. If they do not use Facebook, their lives may involve a smaller number of meaningful interactions. This is especially true for young people, who are the most active users of Facebook and who tend to organize everyday activities (such as parties, going out, small talk, entertainment, etc.) with the help of social media. The coercion exercised by Facebook on users is not one that makes them die physically as in the case of the worker, who does not find paid employment and gets no benefits; it is rather a social form of co-ercion that threatens the user with isolation and social disadvantages. Facebook users are not paid for their labour, they are unpaid workers. For Marx, exploitation does not necessarily presuppose a wage. Slaves or house workers are examples of unpaid workers who are exploited by slave masters and family heads. Both slaves and house workers existed in pre-capitalist modes of production that have been transformed but not abolished in capitalism. They are part of a collective worker that creates value and is in this process exploited by capital.

The main *instruments of labour* on Facebook are the platform itself and the brains of its human users. Alienation of users' brains means that there are attempts to dif-fuse ideologies that present Facebook and other corporate platforms as purely positive and as not having negative impacts. These ideologies can be summarized with statements such as these: "Web 2.0 is a form of democratic communication and participatory culture", "Facebook is free and always will be", "The world will be better if you share more", "Facebook makes the world more open and con-nected", "Facebook helps promoting understanding between people", "Facebook creates an open society", "Facebook revolutionizes how people spread and con-sume information", "Facebook gives people a voice", "The Arab spring was a Facebook revolution", "Facebook is a network built from the bottom-up rather than one of the monolithic top-down structures that have existed to date", and so on. What the role of Facebook is in culture, everyday life and politics is a separate question, but it is a fact that such statements typically used in marketing, public relations and advertising leave out talking about negative impacts, commodifica-tion and who controls ownership and profits. That these are ideologies does not mean that users are necessarily duped by them, but there are attempts to paint one-sided pictures of Facebook and other media that leave out a problematization of parts of the reality of Facebook. The overall aim is to achieve more users and make users spend ever more time on Facebook. Similar ideologies can be found also in the context of other corporate online media. Facebook's capital accumula-tion model is based on targeted advertisements. The content of these ads is mainly focused on promoting certain commodities. Facebook ads aim at hailing the users to buy specific commodities. Ads are ideological in the sense that they often make overdrawn claims about commodities and present the latter as the best thing that exists in the world and as something that one must possess in order to lead a good life. The goal is to make consumers buy these commodities and to shape their needs and desires in such a way that they feel that they have to possess these goods. The instrumentalization of users' brains, hands, mouths, ears and speech, the Inter-net and platforms for advertising constitutes a crucial part of the alienation of the instruments of labour from the users on Facebook and other corporate social media. Alienation of the instruments of labour also means in the context of Facebook that the users do not own and control the platform. After Facebook's initial public offering, its 12 executive officers and directors controlled together 61.1% of the class B stock (Facebook Registration Statement, Form S-1). For a class B stock, there are ten votes per share in contrast to the Facebook class A stock, where every share means one vote (ibid.). Other Facebook shareholders include the companies Accel Partners, DST Global Ltd., Elevation Partners, Goldman Sachs, Greylock Partners, Mail.ru Group Ltd, Meritech Capital Partners, Microsoft, Reid Hoffman, T. Rowe Price Associations Inc., Tiger Global Management and Valiant Capital Opportunities LLC (ibid.). These data shows that Facebook is owned not by its users, but rather by its directors and some companies. There is a class relationship between stock-owners and users = non-owners at the heart of Facebook. The first are Facebook's economic poor who do not control ownership and create the wealth that is controlled and owned by the stockholders. The class of Facebook users is also politically poor because they do not have the decision power to influence Facebook's rules and design, such as the content of the terms of use and the privacy policy, the privacy settings, the use of advertisements, which user data is sold for advertising purposes, the standard settings (e.g. opt-in or opt-out of targeted ads), required registration data, the placement of commercial and non-commercial content on the screen, and so on. In 2009, Facebook introduced a governance page, on which users can discuss changes. It also provides votes about these changes. Facebook says that "if more than 30% of all active registered users vote, the results will be binding".[3] These votes only concern acceptance or rejection of certain policy changes, but do not cover more fundamental questions such as if advertising should be used or not or who owns Facebook. The 30% restriction clause seems to have been taken in order to minimize influence of users. Facebook also owns and controls paid employees and technologies (especially servers) that are necessary for providing, developing and maintaining the platform as a means of production. Facebook's *object of labour* is human experiences. These experiences are first isolated, private and not connected to each other. On Facebook they can be made public and socially connected with each other. They therefore can be considered basic resources and building blocks of the labour conducted by users. By signing up to Facebook, a user agrees to the privacy policy and the terms of use. These documents state that the user agrees that all his/her shared experiences can be used by Facebook for economic purposes. Thereby users give Facebook the right to use data that represent these experiences for accumulating capital. The experiences are still stored in the users' brains and not detachable from them because knowledge is a good that is not used up in consumption or when shared. But in economic terms, Facebook gains the right to use representations of these experiences that are stored on the platform for capital accumulation. This means that the users lose control of how and for what their social media activities are economically utilized. Losing this control also means that Facebook gains the right to monitor all activities of its users and to use the resulting data for economic ends.

The legal statements that enable Facebook to control users' data alienate the users from the control of the experiences that they share online. They are alienated through a legally binding agreement. These statements are the privacy terms and the terms of use that, for example, grant Facebook the following rights: "We use the information we receive to deliver ads and to make them more relevant to you. This includes all of the things you share and do on Facebook, such as the Pages you like or key words from your stories, and the things we infer from your use of Facebook" (Facebook Data Use Policy[4]). "For content that is covered by intellectual property rights, like photos and videos (IP content), you specifically give us the following permission, subject to your privacy and application settings: you grant us a non-exclusive, transferable, sub-licensable, royalty-free, worldwide license to use any IP content that you post on or in connection with Facebook (IP License)" (Facebook Statement of Rights and Responsibilities[5]). Facebook's *product of labour* is the result of a process in which the Facebook platform and human brains as instruments are used for organizing human experiences in such a way that data representing individual and social experiences and available publicly or to a defined social group is created as use-value that satisfies the users' needs of making parts of their lives visible to others, communication and cooperation. Examples are that a user has certain ideas that form the object of labour and then publishes them on his/her Facebook profile or another user's wall, whereby they become a product of her/his online work (i.e. a use-value that satisfies the social needs of a community). Another example is that a user has created an image or video that s/he stores on his/her hard disk. This object becomes a use-value if the user uploads it to Facebook. Another user has certain ideas in his/her head. They represent his/her experiences. If s/he shares them on Facebook by sending a message to friends, the ideas become a use-value for others. Processes such as updating profiles, uploading content and communicating with others are concrete work process that create products that satisfy the informational, communicative and social needs of human groups. Marx argued that in capitalism labour has at the same time an abstract and a concrete dimension: it creates value and use-values. This means that the products that are created by Facebook users do not just satisfy the users' human needs but also serve Facebook's profit interests. Facebook turns personal profile data, usage behaviour data on the Facebook platform, usage behaviour data on other platforms, social network data and content data (images, videos, messages, postings) into data commodities. This means that the use-values that Facebook users create are at the same time commodities that Facebook offers for sale on a market. Facebook usage is work (concrete labour) and labour (abstract labour) at the same time: it generates use-values and economic value. Facebook usage is the connection of a work and a valorization process. Human subjectivity and human sociality is put to use for capital accumulation. All online time of a user is productive work time: it is permanently monitored and stored and packaged together with similar users' data into a data commodity that is offered for sale to advertising clients. The creation of this data commodity is based on not only all time the involved users spend on Facebook, but also the work time of those who are employed in Facebook's advertising department. Data commodities are packaged in such a form that they represent specific user groups with certain demographic characteristics and interests. They are offered to advertising clients, who by purchasing the commodity obtain as a use-value the possibility to present targeted advertising messages to the defined user group. Facebook first controls the data commodity as a use-value but is only interested in its exchange value, that is, the money sum it can obtain by selling it. In the sales process, Facebook exchanges use-value for money and the advertising clients obtain use-value by paying money.

It is important to note that Facebook users create two differing use-values by the same digital work: communication and public visibility as their own needs and the possibility that they are confronted with targeted ads. We can therefore speak of the double character of Facebook's use-value: on the one hand, users produce use-values for themselves and others; they create a social relation between users and public visibility. On the other hand, users produce use-values for capital, that is, targeted advertising space for the advertising industry. For Facebook, both use-values are instrumental for achieving exchange value—selling to the advertising industry what it wants (ad space) and what is produced by the users. The dual character of use-value stems from the circumstance that the Facebook product/use-value is informational: it can be exchanged with money and at the same time stay under the control of the users. This double character of the use-value makes the Facebook product a peculiar product: it serves users' own social needs and the commercial needs of advertisers. At the same time, the commercial use-value is first controlled by Facebook and enables the exchange-value character and commodification of user data. Information has a peculiar character: "The problem with cultural and informational goods is that, because their use value is almost limitless (they cannot be destroyed or consumed by use) it is extremely difficult to attach an exchange value to them" (Garnham 1990, 38).

Value on Facebook means the average time that users spend on the platform. The law of value on Facebook means that the more time a certain group spends on the platform, the more valuable the corresponding data commodity gets. A group that on average spends a lot of minutes per day on Facebook (e.g. the group of those aged 15–25) compared to another group (e.g. the group of those aged 75–85) constitutes a more valuable data commodity because (a) it has a higher average labour/online time per day that generates more data that can be sold and (b) it spends more time online, during which targeted ads are presented to this group.

Mark Andrejevic (2012, 85) argues "users have little choice over whether" transaction data on commercial social media "is generated and little say in how it is used: in this sense we might describe the generation and use of this data as the alienated or estranged dimension of their activity". Andrejevic (2013, 154) argues that in this form of estranged free labour, users do not have "control over productive activity" and "its product". Users "sacrifice a degree of control over how our activity is used when we agree to the terms of service for a particular website or online service" (ibid., 156). Eran Fisher (2012, 173) argues that on Facebook, less alienation—understood as "a greater possibility to express oneself, to control one's production process, to objectify one's essence and connect and communicate with others"—results in more exploitation in comparison with traditional mass media. Facebook would result in de-alienation because the "audience is actively engaged in the production of media content. Audiencing entails deep engagement with the media, opening up the opportunity for authentic self-expression, and for communication and collaboration with others. [. . .] a high level of exploitation of audience work enabled by social media is dialectically linked with a low level of alienation" (ibid., 182). For PJ Rey (2012), usage of corporate social media is non-alienated because the "immaterial" labour conducted there does not separate intellectual and physical activities and usage would be voluntary, self-motivated and spontaneous. All three approaches agree that digital labour is exploited by capital. They differ however in the understanding of the concept of alienation. Whereas for Andrejevic alienation is a more structural process that has to do with the users' non-control of online surveillance processes and non-ownership of the products (profits) of surveillance, Fisher and Rey have a more subjective concept of alienation that has to do with isolation, (in)voluntary action and intellectual activity. This difference can be overcome by distinguishing between objective conditions of alienation and subjective feelings of alienation. In a passage in the *Grundrisse,* Marx makes clear which elements of alienation there are in capitalism: the worker is alienated from (a) herself/himself because labour is controlled by capital, (b) the material of labour, (c) the object of labour and (d) the product of labour. "The material on which it [labour] works is alien material; the instrument is likewise an alien instrument; its labour appears as a mere accessory to their substance and hence objectifies itself in things not belonging to it. Indeed, living labour itself appears as alien vis-à-vis living labour capacity, whose labour it is, whose own life's expression it is, for it has been surrendered to capital in exchange for objectified labour, for the product of labour itself. [. . .] [L]abour capacity's own labour is as alien to it—and it really is, as regards its direction etc.—as are material and instrument. Which is why the product then appears to it as a combination of alien material, alien instrument and alien labour—as alien property" (Marx 1857/1858b, 462). These four elements of alienation can be related to the labour process that consists in a Hegelian sense of a subject, an object and a subject-object. Alienation is alienation of the subject from itself (labour-power is put to use for and is controlled by capital), alienation from the object (the objects of labour and the instruments of labour) and alienation from the subject-object (the products of labour). On social media, users are objectively alienated because in relation to subjectivity they (a) are coerced by isolation and social disadvantage if they leave monopoly capital platforms (such as Facebook), in relation to the objects of labour; (b) their human experiences come under the control of capital, in relation to the instruments of labour; (c) the platforms are owned not by users but by private companies that also commodify user data, and in relation to the product of labour; (d) monetary profit is individually controlled by the platform's owners. These four forms of alienation constitute together capital's exploitation of digital labour on social media. Alienation of digital labour concerns labour-power, the object and instruments of labour and the created products. Figure 11.2 summarizes this manifold alienation process in the case of Facebook.

Congolese miners, Foxconn workers, Indian and Californian software engineers, call centre workers and social media prosumers are all alienated in the sense that they do not own the profits and products they produce. In the case of social media users, the situation is, however, somehow different. They create two different use-values by the same digital work: communication and public visibility, and the possibility that they are confronted with targeted ads. We can therefore speak of the double character of use-values on corporate social media: on the one hand, users produce use-values for themselves and others—they create a social relation between users and public visibility. On the other hand, users produce use-values for capital, that is, targeted advertising space for the advertising industry. The dual character of the use-value makes the Facebook product peculiar: it serves users' own social needs and the commercial needs of advertisers. At the same time, the commercial use-value is first controlled by corporate platforms and enables the exchange-value character and commodification of user data. There is also a specific form of coercion that takes on a social form: leaving a corporate platform is

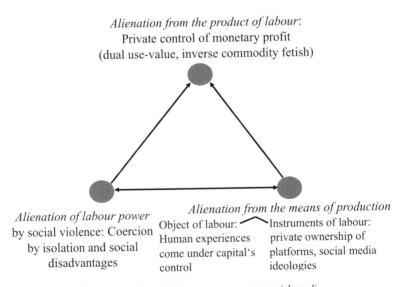

Alienation from the product of labour:
Private control of monetary profit
(dual use-value, inverse commodity fetish)

Alienation of labour power
by social violence: Coercion
by isolation and social
disadvantages

Alienation from the means of production
Object of labour: Instruments of labour:
Human experiences private ownership of
come under capital's platforms, social media
control ideologies

FIGURE 11.2 The alienation of digital labour on corporate social media

not so easy if one has many contacts there because one is facing the threat of fewer contacts and communicative impoverishment.

Marx argued that commodities have an ideological character that he termed the fetish character of the commodity: "The mysterious character of the commodity-form consists therefore simply in the fact that the commodity reflects the societal characteristics of men's own labour as objective characteristics of the products of labour themselves, as the socio-natural properties of these things. Hence it also reflects the social relation of the producers to the sum total of labour as a social relation between objects, a relation which exists apart from and outside the producers" (Marx 1867c, 164–165). This means that the social relations that form a commodity are not visible in the commodity itself as it presents itself to the consumer. In the world of digital labour on social media, the fetish character of the commodity takes on an inverted form. We can speak of an inverse fetish character of the social media commodity. The commodity character of Facebook data is hidden behind the social use-value of Facebook (i.e. the social relations and functions enabled by platform use). The inverse fetish of Facebook is typically expressed in statements like "Facebook does not exploit me because I benefit from it by connecting to other users". The object status of users—that is, the fact that they serve the profit interests of Facebook—is hidden behind the social net-working enabled by Facebook. The impression that Facebook only benefits users socially is one-sided because it forgets that this social benefit, the social relations and the obtained visibility, are at the heart of the commercial and corporate side of Facebook, its exchange-value and commodity dimension. Exchange-value gets hidden in use-value; the object side of Facebook hides itself in social relations. The object side of Facebook is grounded in social relations between Facebook, ad clients and users: the exchange relation between Facebook and advertisers on the one hand and coupled to it the advertising relation between advertisers and users. Both relations are necessary for creating profit for both Facebook and the adver-tisers. These commercial relations do not immediately present themselves to the users, who mainly see the relationships between themselves and other users. The commercial relations that constitute the commodity side of Facebook are hidden behind the social relations between users. Facebook takes advantage of its inverse fetish character by presenting itself as organization that is about sharing and social relations and not about profit. The discussion shows that there is a class relation between Facebook and its users that constitutes a process of economic exploita-tion. Facebook is rich in data about its users; it is one of the largest data controllers in the world. It is also rich in the sense that it generates profit from selling these data as commodities. The users appear to primarily benefit from Facebook usage, to become richer in social relations by this use. But their poverty is hidden behind the appearance of social wealth. They are the online poor because they lack the freedom to enter online relations that are not controlled by capital (the poverty of digital labour-power: almost the entire Internet is controlled by companies), they lack the ownership and control of corporate online platforms (poverty in relation to the instruments of labour), they lack control over expressing their experiences online independently from capital (poverty in relation to the objects of labour) and finally they lack the ownership of the data commodities they create and the monetary profit that is thereby generated (poverty in relation to the products of labour). This manifold poverty of the digital working class is at the same time the source of wealth: they are the producers of online wealth that is appropriated by capital: the online time they spend on platforms is productive work and labour time that is valorized and produces money capital that is created but not owned by the users. The class of the few (the owners of Facebook) benefits at the expense of the class of the many (the users of Facebook). The fact that users are the source of online wealth enables them in principle to overcome their own poverty by becoming the collective master of their collective wealth.

But there is also a subjective dimension of alienation on Facebook. In his book *The Long Revolution,* Raymond Williams (1961, 64) defined the notion of the structure of feeling as "a particular sense of life", "a particular community of experience", through which a way of life obtains "a particular and characteristic colour". It is the "culture of a period" (ibid.) and communication depends on it (65). It is the way a generation "responds in its own ways to the unique world it is inheriting" (ibid.). It gets expressed, for example, in the "documentary culture", such as poems, buildings and dress-fashions. The structure of feeling is an expression of the experience of how it is to live in a certain time under certain societal conditions. Given that each modern time has its own class structures and social conflicts, each period must have its own conflicting structures of feelings. It may therefore be better to speak not of a structure of feeling in the singular but of antagonistic structures of feeling in the plural. Williams (1961, 307) also says that the "experience of isolation, of alienation, and of self-exile is an important part of the contemporary structure of feeling". He here hints at the circumstance that feelings of alienation can be part of the structure of feelings of a particular class. What structure of feelings do users of Facebook display? The structure of feeling of a social media platform is formed by the users' typical pattern of values, sense of usage and affects. Their dominant structure of feeling is likely to be different from the ones of platform owners because they experience the platform in a different social role. Structures of feeling of the users can also be internally contradictory and contested, and the dominant user structure of feeling can change over time. So Facebook and other corporate social media are likely to have conflicting structures of feeling. The empirical question if corporate social media use is experienced as unalienated, although it is objectively alienated in the fourfold sense pointed out earlier, is a question about corporate social media users' structure of feelings. We can distinguish between the objective conditions of alienation and users' structures of feelings on social media. They are dialectically mediated with each other: the objective conditions of social media (such as the market conditions, e.g. monopoly, ownership structures, data processing, the terms of use and privacy policy, the form of the use of advertising, etc.) condition certain user experiences and structures of feelings. The dominant structure of feelings of the users in return can influence the objective conditions of platforms. If users massively protest against perceived privacy violations, leave a platform and join another one, then their objective conditions of usage change from one context (e.g. Facebook) to another one (e.g. Diaspora*). This distinction allows one to grasp both subjective and objective dimensions of social media alienation and their interconnection.

Facebook labour creates commodities and profits. It is therefore productive work. It is, however, unpaid work and in this respect shares characteristics of other irregular workforces, especially house workers and slaves, who are also unpaid. At the same time, Facebook users are facing quite different working conditions in the respect that house workers' activities are predominantly involving care work, sexual work and exhausting physical work and that slaves are the private property of slave masters, by whom they can be killed if they refuse work. What these work types share is the characteristic that the workers are all unpaid and as unpaid workers create more surplus value and profit than in a situation in which their labour would be conducted by regular labour that is paid. One hundred per cent of their labour time is surplus labour time, which allows capitalists to generate extra surplus value and extra profits.

Antonio Negri uses the term "social worker" for arguing that there is a broadening of the proletariat—"a new working class" that is "now extended throughout the entire span of production and reproduction" (Negri 1982/1988, 209). He here takes up Marx's idea of the collective worker that forms an aggregated and combined workforce, is heterogeneous and forms a whole of singularities that is necessary for creating profit. Negri (1971/1988) first developed this concept in a reading of Marx's "Fragment on Machines" in the *Grundrisse*. He argued that the main contradiction of capitalism is that money is the specific measure of value, while labour with the development of the productive forces acquires an increasingly social character and so questions value. The socialization of labour would have resulted in the "emergence of a massified and socialised working class" (ibid., 104). The notion of the socialized working class was later developed into the concept of the social worker (Negri 1982/1988), which emerged by a reorganization of capitalism that dissolved the mass worker that had been characterized by Taylorism, Fordism, Keynesianism and the planner-state (ibid., 205). The social worker signifies "a growing awareness of the interconnection between productive labour and the labour of reproduction" (ibid., 209), the emergence of "diffuse labour" (= outsourced labour, 214) and mobile labour (= labour flexibility, 218). The advantage of the concept of the social worker, which is a reformulation of Marx's notion of the collective worker in the context of informational and post-Fordist capitalism, is that it allows us to consider also irregular and unpaid workers (house workers, slaves, precarious workers, migrant workers, education workers, public service workers, the unemployed, etc.) as productive labourers (Fuchs 2010b). Negri, however, goes so far as to say that "labour time" as a consequence of this tendency "becomes increasingly irrelevant in the context of a full sociali-sation of the productive machine" (Negri 1971/1988, 100). This is just another formulation for saying that the law of value ceases to exist—it is "in the process of extinction" (ibid., 148). As a consequence, Negri assumes that communism is near: "communism is the present-day tendency, an active force operating in the here and now" (ibid., 112). The law of value operates as long as capitalism ex-ists: it does not stop operating because of the emergence of social or knowledge work and has in fact not stopped operating in all the years that have passed since Negri first formulated this idea. The labour time of a specific part of the social worker can perfectly be measured: it is the average number of hours of unpaid work performed by a specific group or overall in a society. That the socialization of work increases because of the rise of productivity means that the time needed for producing certain goods has historically decreased. High productivity is a precondition of communism, but it is not communism itself and does not auto-matically lead to communism. There are communist potentials within capitalism; however, communism can only be established by struggles. Notwithstanding these limits of Negri's approach, the logical consequence of the concept of the social or collective worker is that one is exploited and productive if one is part of the collective worker that produces commodities. Digital labour on Facebook and other corporate digital media is enabled by and connected to an entire value chain and global sphere of exploitation that constitutes the ICT industry. The reality of ICTs today is enabled by the existence of a plenitude of exploited labour: the slave labour of people of colour in Africa who extract minerals, out of which ICT hardware is produced, the highly exploited labour of industrial workers in China and other countries who assemble hardware tools, the labour of low-paid software engineers and knowledge workers in developing countries, the activities of a labour aristocracy of highly paid and highly stressed engineers in Western software companies, the labour of precarious service workers in the knowledge industry that process data (e.g. call-centre workers) and the digital labour of unpaid users. All of these varied forms of exploited labour depend on each other and are needed for creating profits in the ICT industry. Knowledge workers of the world are therefore connected by the circumstance that they are all exploited by capital. They form a combined labour force, the social ICT and knowledge worker that forms a knowledge proletariat. The question that there-fore arises is if the social knowledge proletariat of the world will organize itself politically and become a class-for-itself that struggles against capitalism.

In the digital labour debate, on the one hand some scholars have stressed that "social media" enable participatory culture (Jenkins 2008) or enable a "'making and doing' culture" (Gauntlett 2011, 11) and everyday creativity (ibid., 221). The stress is on participatory culture and new forms of sharing, connecting, making and creativity (Bruns 2008; Gauntlett 2011; Jenkins 2008; Shirky 2008, 2011). On the other hand, there are authors who stress that Facebook and other commercial online media whose profits are based on targeted advertising are grounded in the exploitation of users' labour and the commodification of personal data (e.g. Andrejevic 2011, 2012; Fuchs 2010b). In this context, Marxist labour theories of value that were applied to commercial mass media have been employed and updated, namely Dallas Smythe's (1977a, 1981) concept of audience work/audience commodity (Fuchs 2010b) and Sut Jhally and Bill Livant's (1986/2006) notion of the work of watching (Andrejevic 2009). There are scholars who have pointed out that claims about social media and participatory culture are ideological and overdrawn and celebrate capitalism and that the reality of "social media" is a new form of exploitation and alienation (Andrejevic 2012; Curran, Fenton and Freedman 2012; Fuchs 2010b, 2013; van Dijck 2013). This debate can be interpreted with the help of Marx's analysis of the dual character of labour as concrete work that produces use-values and abstract labour that generates value.

Marx (1867c, 131) has argued that a commodity is "an object with a dual character, possessing both use-value and exchange-value". It satisfies human needs and is exchanged against money. The satisfaction of human needs has thereby become dependent on the commodity and money form. Given that the commodity has a dual character, the work that creates the commodity also has a dual character: it generates both use-values (work) and value (labour). Use-value generation is an anthropological feature of economic production, whereas value and exchange-value are historical features. Marx theorized both the essential and the historical features of society by pointing out the dialectical character of capitalism, labour and commodities. Given that "social media" result in the accumulation of capital, they are connected to the commodity form and therefore the dual character of the commodity and the work process also must apply to these type of media. The dual character of commodities and work is often overlooked if claims are made that social media are either new forms of creativity, sociality and participation or new forms of exploitation. The first claim focuses on the use-value form, the second on the exchange-value form of social media. But commodities have both a use-value and exchange-value form and are crystallizations of concrete labour (work) and abstract labour. So the two claims about social media are inherently intertwined, and dialectical thinking allows us to understand this connection: for Facebook, Twitter, YouTube and corporate blog platforms to exist, users need to be quite active, social, creative and networked. The online work they perform on social media is informational work, affective work, cognitive work, communicative work, community work and collaborative work. This work creates profiles, content, transaction data and social relations. The use-value of social media is that they allow users to inform themselves, share, communicate and collaborate as well as build and maintain communities. Social media's use-value are its informational features: they are tools for cognition, communication and cooperation. But this use-value is subsumed under the exchange-value of social media that requires and is grounded in concrete work processes: the activities, social relations and creative expressions that create the use-value of social media also form economic value and thereby create data commodities that are sold to targeted advertisers, achieve a market price and help social media corporations to achieve profits. Users' creativity, sharing and activity connecting is generating use-value and exchange-value—it is concrete work and abstract labour. The use-value of social media is subsumed under exchange-value but at the same time represents a socialization of labour that points to and has the potential to go beyond the commodity form. It is one of the germs of a use-value economy.

Capitalism connects labour and play in a destructive dialectic. Traditionally, play in the form of enjoyment, sex and entertainment was in capitalism only part of spare time, which was unproductive and separate from labour. Sigmund Freud (1961) argued that the structure of drives is characterized by a dialectic of Eros (drive for life, sexuality, lust) and Thanatos (drive for death, destruction, aggression). Humans would strive for the permanent realization of Eros (pleasure principle), but culture would only become possible by a temporal negation and suspension of Eros and the transformation of erotic energy into culture and labour. Labour would be a productive form of desexualization—the repression of sexual drives. Freud speaks in this context of the reality principle or sublimation. The reality principle sublates the pleasure principle; human culture sublates human nature and becomes man's second nature. Marcuse (1955) connected Freud's theory of drives to Marx's theory of capitalism. He argued that alienated labour, domination, and capital accumulation have turned the reality principle into a repressive reality principle—the performance principle: alienated labour constitutes a surplus-repression of Eros. The repression of the pleasure principle takes on a quantity that exceeds the culturally necessary suppression. Marcuse connected Marx's notions of necessary labour and surplus labour/value to the Freudian drive structure of humans and argued that necessary labour on the level of drives corresponds to necessary suppression and surplus labour to surplus-repression. This means that in order to exist, a society needs a certain amount of necessary labour (measured in hours of work) and hence a certain corresponding amount of suppression of the pleasure principle (also measured in hours). The exploitation of surplus value (labour that is performed for free and generates profit) would mean not only that workers are forced to work for free for capital to a certain extent, but also that the pleasure principle must be additionally suppressed.

"Behind the reality principle lies the fundamental fact of Ananke or scarcity (*Lebensnot*), which means that the struggle for existence takes place in a world too poor for the satisfaction of human needs without constant restraint, renunciation, delay. In other words, whatever satisfaction is possible necessitates work, more or less painful arrangements and undertakings for the procurement of the means for satisfying needs. For the duration of work, which occupies practically the entire existence of the mature individual, pleasure is 'suspended' and pain prevails" (Marcuse 1955, 35). In societies that are based on the principle of domination, the reality principle takes on the form of the performance principle. Domination "is exercised by a particular group or individual in order to sustain and enhance itself in a privileged situation" (ibid., 36). The performance principle is connected to surplus-repression, a term that describes "the restrictions necessitated by so-cial domination" (ibid., 35). Domination introduces "additional controls over and above those indispensable for civilized human association" (ibid., 37).

Marcuse (1955) argues that the performance principle means Thanatos gov-erns humans and society and alienation unleashes aggressive drives within humans (repressive desublimation) that result in an overall violent and aggressive society. As a result of the high productivity reached in late-modern society, a historical alternative would be possible: the elimination of the repressive reality principle, the reduction of necessary working time to a minimum and the maximization of free time, an eroticization of society and the body, the shaping of society and humans by Eros, and the emergence of libidinous social relations. Such a devel-opment would be a historical possibility—but one incompatible with capitalism and patriarchy.

Luc Boltanski and Ève Chiapello (2007) argue that the rise of participatory management means the emergence of a new spirit of capitalism that subsumes the anti-authoritarian values of the political revolt of 1968 and the subsequently emerging New Left—such as autonomy, spontaneity, mobility, creativity, net-working, visions, openness, plurality, informality, authenticity, emancipation, and so on—under capital. The topics of the movement would now be put into the service of those forces that it wanted to destroy. The outcome would have been "the construction of the new, so-called 'network' capitalism" (ibid., 429) so that artistic critique—which calls for authenticity, creativity, freedom and autonomy in contrast to social critique, which calls for equality and overcoming class (37–38)—today "indirectly serves capitalism and is one of the instruments of its ability to endure" (490). Play labour is a new ideology of capitalism: objectively alienated labour is presented as creativity, freedom and autonomy that is fun for workers. That workers should have fun and love their objective alienation has become a new ideological strategy of capital and management theory. Facebook labour is an expression of play labour ideology as an element of the new spirit of capitalism.

Gilles Deleuze (1995) has pointed out that in contemporary capitalism, disci-plines are transformed in such a way that humans increasingly discipline them-selves without direct external violence. He terms this situation the society of (self-)control. It can for example be observed in the strategies of participatory management. This method promotes the use of incentives and the integration of play into labour. It argues that work should be fun and workers should perma-nently develop new ideas, realize their creativity, enjoy free time within the factory and so on. The boundaries between work time and spare time, labour and play, become fuzzy. Work tends to acquire qualities of play, and entertainment in spare time tends to become labour-like. Working time and spare time become insepa-rable. The factory extends its boundaries into society and becomes what Mario Tronti (1962) has termed a social factory: "The more capitalist development pro-ceeds, i.e. the more the production of relative surplus value asserts and extends itself, the more the cycle production—distribution—exchange—consumption closes itself inevitably, the societal relation between capitalist production and bourgeois society, between factory and society, between society and the state become more and more organic. At the highest level of capitalist development the societal relation becomes a moment of the relations of production, and the whole of society becomes cause and expression of production, i.e. the whole society lives as a function of the factory and the factory extends its exclusive domination to the whole of society. [. . .] When the factory raises itself to the master of the whole of society—the entire societal production becomes industrial production—, then the specific characteristics of the factory get lost inside of the general characteristics of society" (ibid., 30–31, translation from German). At the same time as work time and spare time get blurred in the social factory, work-related stress intensifies and property relations remain unchanged. The exploitation of Internet users by Facebook (and other Internet companies) is an aspect of this transformation. It signifies that private Internet usage, which is motivated by play, entertainment, fun and joy—aspects of Eros—has become subsumed under capital and has become a sphere of the exploitation of labour. It produces surplus value for capital and is exploited by the latter so that Internet corporations accumulate profit. Play and labour are today indistinguishable. Eros has become fully subsumed under the repressive reality principle. Play is largely commodified; there is no longer free time or spaces that are not exploited by capital. Play is today productive, surplus-value-generating labour that is exploited by capital. All human activities, and therefore also all play, tends under the contemporary conditions to become subsumed under and exploited by capital. Play as an expression of Eros is thereby destroyed, human freedom and human capacities crippled. On Facebook, play and labour converge into play labour that is exploited for capital accumulation. Facebook therefore stands for the total commodification and exploitation of time—all human time tends to become surplus-value-generating time that is exploited by capital. Table 11.3 summarizes the application of Marcuse's theory of play, labour and pleasure to Facebook and social media.

Work stands in a dialectical relation with play: In play, humans have the freedom to do with the objects of play whatever one wants to do: "In a single toss of a ball, the player achieves an infinitely greater triumph of human freedom over the objective world than in the most massive accomplishment of technical labor" (Marcuse 1933, 128). Play has "no duration or permanence. It happens essentially in 'intervals', 'between' the times of other doings that continually dominate human Dasein" (ibid.). In societies where work is toil, play would be dialectically related to work in such a way that it is an escape from it: "Play is self-distraction, self-relaxation, self-recuperation *for the purpose* of a new concentration, tension, etc. Thus play is in its totality necessarily related to an other from which it comes and at which it is aimed, and this other is already preconceived as *labor* through the characteristics of regimentation, tension, toil, etc." (ibid.). Work is a durable and permanent process that produces objects in the world that satisfy human needs.

TABLE 11.3 Pleasures in four modes of society (human essence, society with scarcity, classical capitalism, capitalism in the age of Facebook)

Essence of human desires	Reality principle in societies with scarcity	Repressive reality principle in classical capitalism	Repressive reality principle in capitalism in the age of Facebook
immediate satisfaction	delayed satisfaction	delayed satisfaction	Immediate online satisfaction
pleasure	restraint of pleasure	leisure time: pleasure; work time: restraint of pleasure, surplus repression of pleasure	Collapse of leisure time and work time, leisure time becomes work time and work time leisure time, all time becomes exploited, online leisure time becomes surplus value-generating, wage labour time = surplus repression of pleasure, play labour time = surplus value-generating pleasure time
joy (play)	toil (work)	leisure time: joy (play); work time: toil (work)	play labour: joy and play as toil and work, toil and work as joy and play
receptiveness	productiveness	leisure time: receptiveness; work time: productiveness	Collapse of the distinction between leisure time/work time and receptiveness/ productiveness, total commodification of human time
absence of repression of pleasure	repression of pleasure	leisure time: absence of repression of pleasure; work time: repression of pleasure	play labour time: surplus value generation appea rs to be pleasure-like but serves the logic of repression (the lack of ownership of capital)

Source: Based on a table from Marcuse (1955, 12)

Play in contrast takes place unregularly and does not involve the necessity to create use-values that satisfy human needs: play has the freedom to do with objects whatever one likes to. This can involve creating new objects, but also destroying existing objects or engaging in unproductive activity that is pure individual joy and does not create anything new. This means that in playing with a ball one can develop a new form of game, destroy the ball or just toss it around for fun. In play labour (playbour), the relationship between play and labour has changed: Whereas labour is permanent and play irregular, Facebook playbour does not take place at specific times either during "free time" or "work time"; rather it can take place any time during wage labour time, at home or on the move (via mobile devices). Play labour is irregular in the sense that it takes place at irregular times and intervals, but it is permanent because users tend to return and update their profiles and repeat their activities. Whereas labour creates new objects that have a permanency in the world and satisfy human needs and play has the freedom to do with an object whatever one pleases, the Facebook user has the freedom to design his/her profile however s/he wants to (but given strict limits by Facebook such as the available input fields, what kind of images, videos and comments are allowed to be uploaded), but every browsing behaviour and activity on Facebook is made permanent by being in the form of data that are stored, processed, analysed and commodified for the purpose of targeted advertising. Whereas play is relaxation and distraction from the unfreedom and hardships of labour and at the same time recreation of labour-power, playbour explodes the relative temporal and spatial separateness of play and labour: Facebook usage is relaxation, joy and fun, and at the same time, like labour, it creates economic value that results or can result in monetary profits. It is recreation that generates value, consumption that is productive, play that is labour. Play is a free activity without duration and permanence; labour is an unfree activity with duration and permanence. Play labour has the semblance of freedom but is unfree in that it creates wealth and profits that are controlled by others; it is regular in its irregularity, creating permanence of data storage and usage in its impermanence of usage (irregular times, no need to create something new or useful, etc.). It is fun and joy that is not like play mainly an end-in-itself or like labouring an end-for-others. It is rather as fun an end-in-itself, as social activity an end-for-others and as value-creating activity an end-for-capital, that is, a particularistic end-for-others that monetarily benefits private property owners at the expense of play workers. The question if users see digital labour on social media as a form of exploitation or a fair exchange of access to platforms for real-time monitoring and commodification of user data is mainly an empirical question that needs to be studied with the help of social science methods. We need not only digital labour theory, digital labour ethics and digital labour politics, but also critical empirical digital labour research. There are examples that indicate that users politically question the commodification of social media and the exploitation of digital labour. Couchsurfing.org is a community of travellers who use this platform for finding places to stay overnight and to offer a couch or a room to travellers who come to their home cities. It is a community that is based on the ideas of mutual aid in travelling and making travelling affordable. Founded in 2003 as a non-profit organization, Couchsurfing "connects travelers and locals who meet offline to share cultures, hospitality and adventures—whether on the road or in their hometowns. Our Mission is simple: Create inspiring experiences. We envision a world where everyone can explore and create meaningful connections with the people and places they encounter. Building meaningful connections across cultures enables us to respond to differences with curiosity, appreciation and respect. The appreciation of diversity spreads tolerance and creates a global community".[6] Couchsurfing's character as non-profit organization fitted the overall spirit of the Couchsurfing community as mutual aid community quite well. In 2011, Couchsurfing was incorporated. Founder Casey Fenton explained that the economic crisis made survival difficult and that being non-profit is not Couchsurfing's core value: "The non-profit structure [...] can really limit our ability to innovate". Being a non-profit "isn't Couchsurfing's core identity. Our identity is our vision and mission: We get people together".[7] In 2011, Couchsurfing raised US$7.6 million in venture capital investments that was provided by Omidyar Ventures and VC Benchmark Capital.[8] Couchsurfing became a so-called B-corporation, which is a corporation that is for-profit and has its "social responsibility" certified: the company's accountability, environmental and consumer friendliness, employees' working conditions and community character are assessed in order to calculate an overall B score that is regularly published.[9] This score ignores the overall question if capital accumulation can ever be responsible or rather necessarily results in inequalities. The Couchsurfing community has been rather critical of the commodification of its platform. It started, for example, an Avaaz petition that called for returning the platform's control and ownership to the users: "We, the community of CouchSurfing, are the ones who built everything from scratch in voluntary work. [...] As this community was giving such a high social reward to all it's users, and as we won't just watch how this all is destroyed by the profit-seeking share holders, we decided to fight for the future of our community and will do our best to put it back to the track of the user based community it has been for a long time!"[10] The petition expresses users' concerns that their voluntary digital work is turned into digital labour which is exploited and generates profit owned by private stockholders. They feel betrayed and exploited. Their use-value-generating work was turned into exchange-value-generating labour without their consent, and there is the implication that profits are generated that are owned by private investors but generated by the users' labour. Another example of the commodification of a social media platform is the Huffington Post. Arianna Huffington founded it in 2005 as a political blog that developed into the most successful Internet newspaper/news blog. On January 18, 2013, it was the world's 83rd most accessed website (alexa.com). In February 2011, AOL bought the Huffington Post for US$315 million and it became an advertising-financed platform. A number of writers had contributed texts voluntarily and without payment. Given the commodification and incorporation of the Huffington Post, many of them felt not only betrayed but also exploited. The writer Jonathan Tasini as a consequence filed a $105 million class action suit against the Huffington Post that argued that the platform engaged in unjust enrichment. He said, "In my view, the Huffington Post's bloggers have essentially been turned into modern-day slaves on Arianna Huffington's plantation. [...] She wants to pocket the tens of millions of dollars she reaped from the hard work of those bloggers. [. . .] This all could have been avoided had Arianna Huffington not acted like the Wal-Marts, the Waltons, Lloyd Blankfein, which is basically to say, 'Go screw yourselves, this is my money'" (Forbes 2011).

Arianna Huffington responded that bloggers contribute for fun and creativity, not for the purpose of money, and that they obtain other indirect forms of payment: "People blog on HuffPost for free for the same reason they go on cable TV shows every night for free: either because they are passionate about their ideas or because they have something to promote and want exposure to large and multiple audiences. [. . .] Our bloggers are repeatedly invited on TV to discuss their posts and have received everything from paid speech opportunities and book deals to a TV show" (Los Angeles Times 2011). These two arguments are often voiced in the context of discussions on digital labour. The first one basically says that users are only interested in the use-value they get out of social media. It ignores the exchange-value side and that the same activities that create use-value on social media for users also create value and exchange-value from which private company owners rather than the users benefit in a monetary way. The second argument says that there are indirect or non-monetary payments for the users of corporate social media. One common argument in this context is that they are paid in-kind with platform access. This argument misperceives the central role of money and monetary profits in capitalism: money is the only commodity that can be exchanged for all other forms of commodities. In capitalism, one cannot buy food with platform access, only with money. Arianna Huffington's form of the argument is that bloggers get publicity in return for their activities. This logic decentres attention from the ownership structures of the Huffington Post and the circumstance that the bloggers' content has become part of a for-profit company, accumulating capital in connection with these contents and leaving bloggers unremunerated. Couchsurfing and the Huffington Post are two examples of how the voluntary work of social network users and bloggers is turned from digital work into digital labour that creates value and profit for corporations. In the case of Google, Facebook and YouTube, the for-profit purpose was there from the beginning, which means that the exploitation of digital labour was on the agenda right from the beginning. In the case of Twitter, there was from the beginning a for-profit purpose, but it took several years until advertising and with it the exploitation of digital labour was introduced. Digital labour is a housewifized form of labour. "Housewifization" (Mies, Bennholdt-Thomsen and Werlhof 1988; Mies 1986) means that work or labour is transformed in a way that resembles the working conditions housewives traditionally have had to face. Housewifized labour "bears the characteristics of housework, namely, labour not protected by trade unions or labour laws, that is available at any time, for any price, that is not recognized as 'labour' but as an 'activity', as in the 'income generating activities', meaning isolated and unorganized and so on" (Mies, Bennholdt-Thomsen and Werlhof 1988, 10). Housewifized labour is characterized by "no job permanency, the lowest wages, longest working hours, most monotonous work, no trade unions, no opportunity to obtain higher qualifications, no promotion, no rights and no social security" (ibid., 169). Digital labour on "social media" resembles housework because it has no wages, is mainly conducted during spare time, has no trade union representation and is difficult to perceive as being labour. Like housework, it involves the "externalization, or ex-territorialization of costs which otherwise would have to be covered by the capitalists" (Mies 1986, 110). The term "crowdsourcing" expresses exactly this outsourcing process that helps capital to save labour costs. Like housework, digital labour is "a source of unchecked, unlimited exploitation" (ibid., 16).

In slave work, there are no wages and the exploitation is unlimited in the sense that the entire working day is unpaid. Necessary labour time is minimized, surplus-value-generating labour time is maximized. Digital labour has in common with classical slavery that the work is unpaid and highly exploited. There are however important differences concerning the mode of coercion. Neither the digital worker's nor the classical slave's labour is a commodity: they both do not sell their labour-power as a commodity on the labour market. A crucial difference is the mode of coercion: the slave is the slave owner's private property, whereas the digital worker is not a private property. Therefore, more like a housewife, the digital worker is creating value in conditions that are detached from property relations, whereas the slave is a form of private property himself/herself. In both the slave's and the digital worker's labour, play and labour converge—for both all play time is work time. The difference is that slave work tends to be hard manual work that is physically exhausting and does not feel like play, whereas digital labour is information work that feels almost exclusively or to a large degree like play. Slaves are violently coerced with hands, whips, bullets—they are tortured, beaten or killed if they refuse to work. The violence exercised against them is primarily physical in nature. House workers are also partly physically coerced in cases of domestic violence. In addition, they are coerced by feelings of love, commitment and responsibility that make them work for the family. The main coercion in patriarchal housework is conducted by affective feelings. In the case of the digital worker, coercion is mainly social in nature: large platforms like Facebook have successfully monopolized the supply of certain services, such as online social networking, and have more than a billion users, which allows them to exercise a soft and almost invisible form of coercion, in which users are chained to commercial platforms because all of their friends and important contacts are there and they do not want to lose these contacts and therefore cannot simply leave these platforms. Non-commercial alternatives exist but have problems attracting users because of the monopoly status of commercial players and the lack of budget for public relations.

Capitalism is connected to a patriarchal ideology, in which, as Leopoldina Fortunati (1995) argues, "production both *is* and *appears* as the creation of value, [while] reproduction *is* the creation of value but *appears otherwise*". The dual character of labour contains not only a division between use-value and exchange-value, but also one between production and reproduction as well as productive and unproductive labour: patriarchal ideologies present wage labour as productive, housework as unproductive. *"It is the positioning of reproduction as non-value that enables both production and reproduction to function as the production of value"* (ibid., 9). The "subjective conditions of reproduction work are posited as separate from those of production work" (ibid., 12). There are certain parallels between housework and user labour on corporate social media: both are unpaid forms of value-generating labour. And both are the subject of ideologies that present these forms of labour as unproductive to hide the exploitation of house workers and users, which allows maximizing capitalists' profits. The patriarchal-ideological denial of the productivity of housework that Fortunati analyses finds a parallel in the ideological denial of the productivity of user labour on corporate Internet platforms that live by user-generated content and its commodification. What makes user labour difficult to perceive as labour that is exploited is the circumstance that it often feels like fun and is conducted in one's spare time. Just like in housework, the boundary between working time and spare time is blurred in user labour; play time and spare time are working time. An example of the ideological separation of user labour and exploitation is the verdict in the class action lawsuit *Jonathan Tasini v. AOL/ The Huffington Post*. Tasini, a blogger, sued the Huffington Post after AOL had bought it for US$315 million and had transformed it into a commercial platform, arguing that the commodification of Huffington Post resulted in the exploitation of the unpaid labour of bloggers who contributed to the Post and in unfair enrichment. In the verdict, the judge dismissed the claim, arguing that "under New York law, a plaintiff must plead some expectation of compensation that was denied in order to recover under a theory of unjust enrichment. The Complaint fails to do so and the claim for unjust enrichment must therefore be dismissed. [. . .] No one forced the plaintiffs to give their work to The Huffington Post for publication and the plaintiffs candidly admit that they did not expect compensation" (United States District Court Southern District of New York 2012, 12–13). The argument of the judge is that if a worker does not expect payment (e.g. because the work is part of family or friendship relations or is conducted because the worker believes in the public usefulness of the project), there can be no exploitation. The verdict subjectivizes exploitation and does not see that in both (a) housework and (b) unpaid user work for corporate social media, companies benefit materially by accumulating capital that is enabled by (a) housework that reproduces labour-power and (b) user work that creates a data commodity. The judge furthermore argues that if somebody submits voluntarily to exploitation, it is not exploitation. Assume a slave has to choose if he goes free or stays enslaved and s/he for some reasons chooses slavery. Although his/her choice may be hard to understand, s/he would still continue to be exploited. It does not matter for the givenness of exploitation for which reasons house workers and users choose to be in these roles, if it is voluntary labour or not and if they expect compensation for it or not. The circumstance that capital benefits from these forms of labour is an indication for the existence of the exploitation. There are objective criteria of exploitation; patriarchal and capitalist ideologies try to subjectivize exploitation in order to deny that it takes place.

11.3.3. Digital Labour and the Law of Value on Social Media

Certain scholars argue that the rise of a "knowledge society" or "cognitive capitalism" as well as of "social media" has resulted in an outdatedness and non-applicability of the labour theory of value to contemporary capitalism. Virno (2004, 100) says that the law of value is "shattered and refuted by capitalist development itself". Hardt and Negri (2005, 145) argue that the "temporal unity of labor as the basic measure of value today makes no sense". Vercellone (2010, 90) writes that "cognitive capitalism" has resulted in the "crisis of the law of value" and "a crisis of measurement that destabilizes the very sense of the fundamental categories of the political economy; labor, capital and obviously, value". The rise of knowledge in production, what Marx (1857/1858b) termed the general intellect, would result in the circumstance that labour, particularly knowledge labour, "can no longer be measured on the basis of labour time directly dedicated to production" (Vercellone 2007, 30). Abstract labour, "measured in a unit of time", would no longer be "the tool allowing for the control over the labor and simultaneously favouring the growth of social productivity" (Vercellone 2010, 90). Creativity and knowledge would today form "the main source of value" (ibid., 105).

The assumption of many Autonomist Marxists that the law of value no longer applies today is not feasible because this law is a foundation of the existence of capitalism and because the assumption is based on a false interpretation of a passage from Marx's *Grundrisse* (see e.g. Vercellone 2007, 29–30), in which Marx says that "labour time ceases and must cease to be" the measure of wealth (Marx 1857/1858b, 705). The misinterpretation is precisely that Marx here describes a transformation within capitalism. Instead Marx in the same passage makes clear that he talks about a situation in which the "mass of workers" has appropriated "their own surplus labour" (ibid., 708). As long as capitalism exists, value is set as the standard of production, although the value of commodities tends to historically diminish, which advances capitalism's crisis-proneness. Harry Cleaver has pointed out that the Marx passage is based on a framework that results from the circumstance that class struggle "explodes the system and founds a new one" (Cleaver 2000, 92).

In the specific passage in the *Grundrisse,* Marx says, "Once they have done so— and *disposable time* thereby ceases to have an *antithetical* existence—then, on one side, necessary labour time will be measured by the needs of the social individual, and, on the other, the development of the power of social production will grow so rapidly that, even though production is now calculated for the wealth of all, *disposable time* will grow for all" (Marx 1857/1858, 708). Marx talks about a society in which "production based on exchange value breaks down" (ibid., 705)—a communist society.

Adam Arvidsson (2011) shares with circulation-fetishistic approaches like the one of Heinrich the assumption that "the labor theory of value only holds if labor has a price" (ibid., 265). He wants to point out with this assumption that users of Facebook and other corporate "social media" are not exploited because they do not receive a wage (for a detailed criticism of Arvidsson's approach see Fuchs 2012e). The question that arises in this context is whether slaves, who do not receive wages, are not exploited. As this assumption is difficult to make, it becomes clear that Arvidsson's approach has quite problematic implications.

On corporate "social media", the "time spent online viewing or interacting with a particular site is not the critical parameter for defining or measuring value in the online advertising environment"; rather "affective engagements" and "user affect" (e.g. measured by social buttons, sentiment analysis, network analysis) would be the "source of value" (Arvidsson and Colleoni 2012, 144). This means that Facebook constantly monitors interests, usage behaviour, browsing behaviour, demographic data, user-generated content, social relations and so forth. These are individual, affective, social, economic, political, cultural data about users. The more time a user spends on Facebook, the more data is generated about him/her that is offered as a commodity to advertising clients. Exploitation happens in this commodification and production process, whereas the data commodities are offered for sale to advertising clients after the production/exploitation process. The more time a user spends online, the more data is available about him/her that can potentially be sold and the more advertisements can be presented to him/her. Time therefore plays a crucial role on corporate social media. Users employ social media because they strive to a certain degree for achieving what Bourdieu (1986a, b) terms social capital (the accumulation of social relations), cultural capital (the accumulation of qualification, education, knowledge) and symbolic capital (the accumulation of reputation). The time that users spend on commercial social media platforms for generating social, cultural and symbolic capital is in the process of prosumer commodification transformed into economic capital. Labour time on commercial social media is the conversion of Bourdieusian social, cultural and symbolic capital into Marxian value and economic capital.

Arvidsson and Colleoni (2012) ignore that the labour that generates content, affects, likes, social relations and networks is organized in time and space and that Facebook usage time is productive labour time. All hours spent online by users of Facebook, Google and comparable corporate social media constitute work time, in which data commodities are generated, and potential time for profit realization.

Arvidsson ignores the material realities and power of actual capital accumulation by substituting a materialistic concept of value and labour by a subjectivistic, idealistic concept of value. He substitutes the economic concept of value with a moral concept of value. This move is not a generalization of the value concept, as in Grossberg's approach, but a subjectification of value that corresponds to neo-classical economic theories which question Marx's concept of value as substance constituted as societal phenomenon in the production process.

The discussion of contemporary Cultural Studies in chapter 3 and this section have shown that the labour theory of value is an ideological object that is frequently used to argue that Marx's theory is out of date. Resulting claims are that value has been generalized and pluralized (Grossberg) and stems from affects (Arvidsson) or social networks (Hartley), but is not constituted by labour and measured by labour time. The implications of these approaches are diverse, but they all share the consequence that the immediateness of the radical critique of capitalism and capitalist media is either reduced in importance or altogether rejected.

Not all Autonomist Marxists share the assumption that there is an end of the law of value today. Karl Heinz Roth (2005, 60) stresses the large number of unpaid and underpaid workers in the world today. Examples that he mentions are reproductive work in the family, precarious and informal labour, slave workers, prison labour (Roth 2005), temporal work, seasonal workers, migrant workers and precarious self-employment (Roth and van der Linden 2009). Karl Heinz Roth and Marcel van der Linden (2009, 560) say that these workers constitute the global worker *(Weltarbeiterklasse)* that is "a multiversum of strata and social groups". Nick Dyer-Witheford (2010, 490) argues that the global worker (a) is based on the globalization of capital, (b) is based on a complex division of labour, (c) is based on underpaid and unpaid labour (migrants, house workers, etc.), (d) is embedded into global communication networks, (e) is facing precarious conditions, and (f) has worldwide effects. Slave workers who are unpaid would also produce value, although their labour-power does not have a price for which it is rented to an owner, but rather it is the private property of a slave master (Roth and van der Linden 2009, 581–587). Roth and van der Linden use the example of the slave worker in order to argue that exploitation and value production do not presuppose a wage relationship. They argue for a dynamic labour theory of value (ibid., 590–600) that assumes that all humans who contribute to the production of money profit by entering a relationship with capital—in which the latter controls and owns their personality (slaves), labour-power (wage workers), the means of production and subsistence (outsourced contractual labour), the products of labour (unpaid and underpaid labour) or the sphere of reproduction (reproductive labour)—are part of the exploited class. Capital has the inherent interest to maximize profit. To do this, it will take all means necessary because the single capitalist risks his/her own bankruptcy if s/he cannot accumulate capital as a result of high investment costs, heavy competition, lack of productivity and so on. The wage relation is, as argued earlier, a crucial element of class struggle. Capital tries to reduce the wage sum as much as possible in order to maximize profits. If possible, capital will therefore remunerate labour-power below its own value, that is, below the socially necessary costs that are required for survival. The transformation of the value into the price of labour-power and the difference between the two is, as Cleaver (2000) and Bidet (2009) stress, the result of class struggle. Labour legislation and an organized labour movement can struggle for wages that are higher than the value of labour-power. If labour is, however, weak (e.g. because of fascist repression), capital is likely to use any opportunity to reduce wages as much as possible in order to increase profits. Neo-liberalism is a form of governmentality that increases profits by decreasing the wage sum with the help of cutting state expenditures for welfare, care and education; privatizing such services; creating precarious wage-relations that are temporary, insecure and underpaid; weakening the power of labour organizations; decreasing or not increasing wages relatively or absolutely; outsourcing labour to low-paid or unpaid forms of production; coercing the unemployed to work without payment or for extremely low wages, and so on. It is a form of politics that aims at helping capital to reduce the price of labour-power as much as possible, if possible even below the minimum value that is needed for human existence. The creation of multiple forms of precarious and unpaid forms of work is an expression of the class struggle of capital to reduce the costs of labour-power. The result is a disjuncture of the value and price of labour-power. The disjuncture between value and price of labour-power is accompanied by a disjuncture of the value and price of commodities: The financialization of the economy has established stocks and derivatives that have fictitious prices on stock markets that are based on the hope for high future profits and dividends, but are disjointed from the actual labour values and commodity prices. Contemporary capitalism is a disjuncture economy, in which values, profits and prices tend to be out of joint so that there is a high crisis-proneness. Digital media scholars, entrepreneurs, managers, consultants and politicians often celebrate the rise of "social media" like Facebook, Twitter and YouTube as the rise of a democratic and participatory economy, in which users control the means of communication and intellectual production and consumers can actively and creatively shape the economy. Seen from the view of a dynamical labour theory of value, corporate social media are in contrast forms of the exploitation of unpaid labour: all time users spend on such platforms is recorded and analysed and creates data commodities containing personal and usage data and are sold to advertising clients that provide targeted ads to the users. The price of the users' labour-power is zero: they are unpaid, which allows capital to maximize profits by reducing the price of labour-power as much below its value as possible. The multiverse of the global worker does not consist of separate types of work and relations of production, but rather of interdependent production relations that form a whole. Nick Dyer-Witheford (2002, 2010) therefore speaks of the emergence of a global value subject that forms a value chain organized by multinational corporations in the form of a global factory. He stresses that the emergence of knowledge work and the global worker does not mean an end of the law of value, but rather an expansion of exploitation and the law of value from the workplace as the "traditional locus of exploitation" (2002, 8) to the "factory planet" (2010, 485). The exploitation of user labour on commercial Internet platforms like Facebook and Google is indicative of a phase of capitalism in which we find an all-ubiquitous factory that is a space of the exploitation of labour. Social media and the mobile Internet make the audience commodity ubiquitous and the factory not limited to your living room and your wage work place—the factory and workplace surveillance are also in all in-between spaces. The entire planet is today a capitalist factory. The exploitation of Internet users/prosumers is not isolated; it is part of a larger value chain of computing, in which African slave workers extract raw materials, underpaid workers in developing countries (and Western countries) assemble hardware, underpaid workers in developing countries and highly paid workers in the West engineer software and precariously working service workers (e.g. in call centres) provide support. So the global value subjects are "subject to the law of value constituted and constrained by the logics of the world-market" (Dyer-Witheford 2002, 9). But they also have the potential power to subvert the law of value by refusals to work (protests, strikes, occupations and, in the most extreme form, as in the case of Foxconn, suicide), refusals to consume (stopping the use of certain products and favouring the use of non-commercial products) and the creation of alternative forms of valuation/production that transcend monetary values and are non-profit and non-commercial in character (e.g. non-proprietary software/operating systems, non-commercial social networking sites, self-managed alternative IT companies, etc.). Göran Bolin (2011) stresses in this context that economic value is not the only moral value that can shape the media. Nick Couldry (2010) points out that neo-liberalism reduces the possibilities for the expression of voices that constitute an alternative moral value to economic logic. Expressed in another way, the value of capitalism is value, which reduces the status of the human to a voiceless and exploited cog in the machine, and although perceiving itself as permanently talking, it mostly has a voice and power without real effects. What we need to achieve is the sublation of economic value so that (economic) value is no longer the primary (moral) value.

The law of value has not lost its force. It is in full effect everywhere in the world where exploitation takes place. It has been extended to underpaid and unpaid forms of labour, corporate media prosumption being just one of them. As a result of technical increases in productivity, the value of commodities tends to historically decrease. At the same time, value is the only source of capital, commodities and profit in capitalism. The contradictions of value have resulted in a disjuncture of values, profits and prices that contributes to actual or potential crises, which shows that crises are inherent to capitalism. This it turn makes it feasible to replace capitalism with a commons-based system of existence, in which not value but creativity, social relations, free time and play are the source of value. Such a society is called communism and is the negation of the negativity of capitalism.

11.4. Conclusion

On corporate social media platforms such as Facebook, Twitter, YouTube and Google, users are not just consumers of information, but also prosumers—productive consumers, who produce profiles, content, connections, social relations, networks and communities as use-values. They are creative, active, networked digital workers. Furthermore, data about all of these activities is produced and sold to targeted advertisers, who obtain access to the users' preferences and data in exchange for money and present customized ads to the users. The use-value of social media becomes in this way alienated from the users themselves, which results in an alienation from the control of activities, data, experiences, platforms and the generated monetary profits. The effect is that they are exploited digital workers who create surplus value and monetary profits. Digital labour on "social media" resembles housework because it has no wages, is mainly conducted during spare time, has no trade union representation and is difficult to perceive as being labour. House workers, slaves and digital workers on social media have in common that they have no wages and are highly exploited, which means that all or large parts of their work days create surplus value. They experience different modes of coercion that are emotional, physical and social in character. Slave workers in the Democratic Republic of Congo who extract conflict minerals that are the physical foundation of ICTs are likely to be killed if they refuse the physically hard extraction work. Facebook users are likely to be more socially isolated if they refuse the fun work of mailing, connecting, browsing, commenting, reading, watching and so on. The first type of labour is no fun at all, deadly serious and bloody, the second type of labour is playful and does hardly feel like labour. Besides these differences that make a difference, what both share is that they are performed in the IDDL, are activities necessary for capital accumulation and are hardly monetarily remunerated. The first is physical labour, the second is a special form of information work—play information labour. Digital play workers on social media are objectively alienated from the control of sociality, the control of platforms, the control of what happens with the data of their online experiences and the control of the derived monetary profits. They furthermore have individual structures of usage feeling that translate into one or several collective structures of usage feeling which are more or less subjectively alienated.

This chapter has dealt with the question: What are digital work and digital labour on social media? For providing possible answers, theoretical notions of work and labour are needed. We have explored the use of Marx's theory in this context. Marx distinguishes between an anthropological and a historical quality of collective activities that satisfy human needs: work and labour. This distinction is reflected in capitalism in the dual character of the commodity that is both use-value and (exchange-)value at the same time. We have set out a Hegelian-Marxist framework for understanding the work process as dialectical interconnection of human subjects (labour-power) that use instruments on objects so that products emerge that satisfy human needs. Alienation in capitalist societies is alienation of workers from all poles of this dialectic and from the whole process itself that constitutes class relations and exploitation. An answer to the question posed earlier and that sometimes divides representatives of the approaches of (a) the Political Economy and (b) Cultural Studies of social media—namely if the usage of commercial social media results is exploitation of digital labour or a creative and participatory culture—can be given by approaching this issue with the help of Marx's characterization of work in capitalism as a process of concrete labour that creates use-values and abstract labour that creates the value of commodities. Users of social media are creative, social, and active prosumers who engage in a culture of sharing, doing, connecting and making and in these work activities create social use-values (content, social relations, cooperation). On corporate social media that use targeted advertising, this creativity is a form of labour that is the source of the value of a data commodity sold to advertisers and resulting in profits. Facebook achieved revenues of US$3.7 billion in 2011 (Facebook Registration Statement Form S-1). Its founder Mark Zuckerberg was in 2012 the 35th richest person in the world, controlling a wealth of US$17.5 billion (Forbes 2012 List of the World's Billionaires[11]). The forecast for Facebook's 2012 earnings are US$4.991 billion.[12] At the same time, the Facebook stock lost value during 2012 after the initial public offering in May, where the price per share was set at US$38. It was down to less than US$20 in early September 2012 and then rose to a little above US$30 at the end of January 2013 (money.cnn.com, accessed January 27, 2013). This means that there is a difference between Facebook's share value and capital accumulation. Facebook tries to attract investors and to thereby increase its capital base and operations. The question is if profits and share values will be stable overall or if the gap between them will persist.

The argument put forward by this chapter is that the wealth of Facebook's owners and the profits of the company are grounded in the exploitation of users' labour that is unpaid and part of a collective global ICT worker. Digital labour is alienated digital work: it is alienated from itself, from the instruments and objects of labour and from the products of labour. It is exploited, although this exploitation does on social media tend not to feel like exploitation because digital labour is play labour that hides the reality of exploitation behind the fun of connecting with and meeting other users. That Facebook has gone public poses the question if it will attract large capital investments and if the expectations these investments raise for profit growth can be matched by actual capital accumulation. Its public listing as a stock market company has made Facebook definitely more prone to crisis and therefore more inclined to extend and intensify the exploitation of users. The capitalist Internet has faced a financial bubble before. Capitalism has slid into a big crisis since the bursting of the housing bubble in 2008. The social media economy's financialization may result in the next big bubble. The only alternative to exit the Internet crisis and exploitation economy is to exit from digital labour, to overcome alienation, to substitute the logic of capital with the logic of the commons and to transform digital labour into digital work.

Notes

1 Sebastian Sevignani co-authored sections 11.3.1 and 11.3.2 of this chapter.
2 http://www.marxists.org/archive/marx/works/1844/epm/3rd.htm (accessed July 9, 013).
3 https://www.facebook.com/fbsitegovernance/app_4949752878 (accessed November 17, 2009).
4 https://www.facebook.com/full_data_use_policy, version from June 8, 2012 (accessed November 18, 2012).
5 https://www.facebook.com/legal/terms, version from June 8, 2012 (accessed November 18, 2012).
6 https://www.couchsurfing.org/n/about (accessed January 18, 2013).
7 http://www.couchsurfing.org/bcorp (accessed January 18, 2013).
8 http://techcrunch.com/2011/08/24/couchsurfing-raises-7-6-m-will-users-cry-sell-out/ (accessed January 18, 2013).
9 http://www.bcorporation.net/community/directory/couchsurfing (accessed January 18, 2013).
10 http://www.avaaz.org/en/petition/For_a_strong_Community_behind_CouchSurfing (accessed January 18, 2013).
11 http://www.forbes.com/billionaires/#p_1_s_a0_Technology%20%20%20%20%20 %20%20%20%20%20%20%20%20%20%20%20%20%20%20%20_All%20countries_ All%20states_ (accessed November 18, 2012).
12 http://www.4-traders.com/FACEBOOK-INC-10547141/calendar/ (accessed November 18, 2012).

PART III
Conclusions

12

DIGITAL LABOUR AND STRUGGLES FOR DIGITAL WORK

The Occupy Movement as a New Working-Class Movement? Social Media as Working-Class Social Media?

- "Occupy Wall Street is a people-powered movement that began on September 17, 2011 in Liberty Square in Manhattan's Financial District, and has spread to over 100 cities in the United States and actions in over 1,500 cities globally. #ows is fighting back against the corrosive power of major banks and multinational corporations over the democratic process, and the role of Wall Street in creating an economic collapse that has caused the greatest recession in generations. The movement is inspired by popular uprisings in Egypt and Tunisia, and aims to fight back against the richest 1% of people that are writing the rules of an unfair global economy that is foreclosing on our future".
- "Occupy London is part of the global social movement that has brought together concerned citizens from across the world against this injustice and to fight for a sustainable economy that puts people and the environment we live in before corporate profits".

The year 2011 was one of revolutions and the emergence of new protest movements in many countries. The Occupy movement is one of these movements. The self-descriptions show that it is a movement that focuses on socio-economic issues such as labour, injustice, economic crisis, exploitation, the gap between the rich and the poor, and class relations. This circumstance is summarized in the slogan "We are the 99%", which sees the people opposed to the 1% of the wealthy and owning elite.

(Continued)

> In this chapter, I give an overall summary of the book. Corporate digital media are based on a class system in which multiple forms of digital labour are exploited. This chapter asks the question of how these forms of exploitation can be resisted. Is the Occupy movement a new working-class movement? Does its use of digital media constitute working-class ICTs? How can alternative social media and digital work that is performed on it look?

12.1. Conclusion of Chapters 2–11

When you use a mobile phone, iPad or laptop for conducting a Google search or posting a status message or comment on Facebook, then the whole process feels immediate and simple and it happens at high speed. This immediacy, simplicity and high speed of the usage of networked ICTs hides the circumstance that in order for this process to happen, a complex chain of globally dispersed but necessarily interconnected labour processes has to be conducted—the international division of digital labour (IDDL). ICTs in contemporary capitalist society do not only advance an ideological technological fetishism—what Jodi Dean (2005) terms Internet fetishism—that stems from management theory and the capitalist class and advances the idea that the Internet and social media automatically make a better and radically new world. There is also a form of Internet fetishism that is immanent to the relations of production: the global value chain of ICT production is so complex and globally dispersed that it becomes very difficult to trace which forms of labour and exploitation are exactly objectified in the device and service one is using at a certain point of time.

The producers of various aspects of computers, content disseminated by computers, products created by computers, and the owners of the companies in which these components are organized are independent and separate and at the same time anonymously connected by the IDDL. They are formally independent but materially related by a division of labour. In "the commodity-capitalist economy, production-work relations among people necessarily acquire the form of the value of things, and can appear only in this material form" (Rubin 2008, 62). The user of ICTs is confronted with a thing that represent, as Marx says, "the definite social relation between men themselves" that appears as "the fantastic form of a relation between things" (Marx 1867c, 165). This is precisely what Marx terms the fetishism of commodities. Value "does not have its description branded on its forehead": the relations of slavery, exploitation, imperialism, housewifized work and primitive accumulation that are at the heart of labour relations of the ICT industry do not speak out of the digital media artefact. They are rather objectified in it and therefore invisible and undecipherable to the users: value "transforms every product of labour into a social hieroglyphic. Later on, men try to decipher the hyroglyphic, to get behind the secret of their own social product" (ibid., 167). The societal (i.e. exploitative) character of the digital commodity is hidden in its immediate form of appearance as thing.

Maxwell and Miller (2012) argue that media technologies are contemporary opiates of the people: "Adorned with human characteristics of beauty, taste, serenity, and the like, media technologies compensate for the absence of these qualities in everyday capitalism, via a 'permanent opium war' of symbolic intoxication" (ibid., 21). The "dirty work is concealed within the toys of machines that others use to relax" (ibid., 89).

Wolfgang Fritz Haug has, in this context based on Marx's theory of commodity fetishism, coined the notion of commodity aesthetics: commodities are designed in appealing ways in order to sell them. They make what Haug calls a use-value promise: "The basic law of commodity aesthetics is the condition that not use-value but rather use-value promise triggers the act of exchange of purchase" (Haug 1987, 147).

The Apple MacBook, iPhone or iPad not only look nice, they are also symbols of a flexible and mobile lifestyle, success, being part of the group of knowledge professionals, modernity and progress. It is "cool" to possess an Apple device. And this coolness hides the labour conditions that underlie the production of ICTs. ICTs often have a commodity aesthetic ideology that deceives, hides and recodes the actuality of blood and sweat into play, desire, good looks, appealing design and lifestyle ideologies. ICT's commodity aesthetic ideology is characteristic for what Jim McGuigan (2009) calls the ideology of cool capitalism and Vincent Mosco (2004) the digital sublime.

I have tried to show, with the help of a discussion of a variety of empirical research results and the theoretical interpretation of these results, that the IDDL involves various forms of labour, exploitation and mode of production that are anonymously networked with each other and all form necessary elements for the production, usage and application of digital media. Table 12.1 summarizes the various forms of labour involved in the IDDL that were discussed in chapters 6-11. Note that the concepts mentioned are not necessarily specific for just one of the specific forms of IDDL. Rather these chapters are example case studies that show how to apply specific Marxist concepts that form a digital labour theory-toolbox. The dynamic character of capitalism results in the circumstance that one category of this toolbox can often be applied to several activities within the IDDL.

The most direct, although not necessarily most visible and conscious, form of labour that users are confronted with when connecting, writing, reading and watching on corporate social media is Internet prosumption labour. This means users consume existing information and create information, profiles, social relations and affects and in this process create transaction data that is commodified by advertising companies like Facebook, Google and Twitter, which sell this data as commodity to ad clients that provide targeted ads to users. This type of labour was discussed in chapter 11.

TABLE 12.1 Aspects of the productive forces and relationships of production in the digital media industry's division of labour

Dimension of the IDDL	Relations of production	Productive forces	Labour power (subject)	Object of work	Tools of work
Slave mineral workers	Slave—slave owner	Agricultural production	Private property of the slave owner	Nature	Mining equipment
Taylorist hardware assemblers	Worker—capital	Industrial production	Commodity	Minerals, semiconductors, ICT parts	Machine system
Imperialistically exploited knowledge workers in developing countries	Workers—capital	Information production	Commodity	Data	Computers, brains

Product of work	Relationship between work time and play time	Typical working conditions	Form of coercion	Typical examples
Minerals: cassiterite (the foundation of tin), wolframite, coltan (the foundation of tantalum), gold, tungsten	Life tends to be no play and fun at all, but rather extreme toil with death threats and without play	There are slave workers who are the property or part-time property (in the system of corvée labour) of slave masters who can kill them if they do not obey the set rules of work. This slave work is embedded into a new imperialistic system, in which slave work in developing countries produces profits for Western digital media companies by extracting minerals	Physical violence, military control of the workforce: threat of being killed if work is refused	African slave mineral workers
Semiconductors, computers, periphery	Separation of work time and play time	Taylorist industrial work that can feature high standardization, military drill, a deadly formal subsumption of labour under capital to the degree that workers are at a high risk of dying, being seriously injured or poisoned or to commit suicide, primitive accumulation where peasants are driven from the land into urban regions to become wage-workers, contamination of workers, soil, earth, air, water, families (destruction of nature and workers), piecework. Such work is frequently predominantly or to a significant degree conducted by women	Double-free wage labour, surveillance, military drill, surveillance, punishments	ICT assemblage and manu-facturing industry in China and the Silicon Valley
Software, objectified knowledge	Free time tends to be absorbed by work time, manage-ment tries to present work as fun and play	Knowledge workers that are exploited in the form of a new imperialism that outsources knowledge work to developing countries in order to save costs and maximize profits and that tends to implement absolute and compulsory temporal and spatial mobility (high-tech nomads, global body shopping, virtual migration)	Management language of freedom and participation, silent coercion, self-discipline out of fear of losing ones job, low degree of unionization makes resistance difficult	Indian software engineers

(Continued)

TABLE 12.1—*(Continued)*

Dimension of the IDDL	Relations of production	Productive forces	Labour power (subject)	Object of work	Tools of work
Precarious service workers	Workers—capital	Industrialized information production, information production	Commodity	Culture	Computers, phones, brains
Highly paid knowledge workers	Precarious workers— highly paid knowledge workers— capital	Information production	Commodity	Culture	Computers, brains

Product of work	Relationship between work time and play time	Typical working conditions	Form of coercion	Typical examples
Customer relations, public relations, content, software	Separation between work time and play time	Taylorist service work (grey-collar) that tends to be highly standardized, repetitive and highly monitored (control as method of relative surplus value production), relatively lowly remunerated in comparison to the professional work of the knowledge labour aristocracy, and that tends to feature a high level of female workers. Precarious service work is especially gendered and comparable to the labour of houseworkers and in a manifold way because these workers are often women, hardly or not at all represented by unions, receive the lowest remuneration while having the longest working hours, engage in highly monotonous work, in affectual activities (selling and service as customer care work), and conduct work that organizes consumption and has sexual connotations. Also other forms of digital labour are often housewifized and strongly gendered, but precarious service work tends to be a form of highly and multidimensional housewifized labour	Double-free wage work, performance surveillance, Taylorist work standardization	Call centre workers
Content, software	Play labour: blurred boundary between work and play time – free time turns into labour time, labour time is presented and partly experienced as play	Digital labour aristocracy with high wages that are surplus wages in comparison to low paid work in the international division of digital labour, but comes at the price of working very long hours (absolute surplus-value production). Highly paid and highly stressed workers	Self-discipline, new spirit of capitalism, social and peer pressure, incentives to spend a lot of time in the work context (restaurant, sports facilities, social events, etc.)	Google software engineers

(Continued)

TABLE 12.1—(*Continued*)

Dimension of the IDDL	Relations of production	Productive forces	Labour power (subject)	Object of work	Tools of work
Internet prosumer labour	Prosumers — capital	Information production	No commodity	Cultures	Computers, brains

Internet prosumer labour is play labour that is mainly fun and conducted as non-paid spare time activity in the social factory. It is feminized and house-wifized labour because it resembles housework in that it is unpaid, non-unionized and highly exploited. At the same time, it differs from slavery and housework because the type of coercion is primarily based on neither physical violence nor love, but on a specific form of social coercion that threatens users with isolation and the loss of social contacts. For using the Internet, various types of application and operating system software are needed that are created by software engineers under various working conditions. There are on the one hand highly paid and highly stressed software engineers like the Google engineer who is part of the digital labour aristocracy (chapter 9). They are confronted with workplayplaces—places, where work and play converge, where the boundaries between work time and play time are highly blurred, so that absolute surplus-value production (working long hours), peer pressure and self-disciplining are an everyday reality that benefits the capital owners of Internet and software companies. They form on the level of objective class relations a labour aristocracy that enjoys surplus wages in contrast to other ICT workers. On the other hand there is software engineering that has been outsourced to developing countries or emerging economies, especially India, where the wage levels are lower than in Western countries, which allows a new imperialistic transfer of value from developing countries to Western corporations that reap high profits from the exploitation of workers in Asia and other poorer parts of the world (chapter 8). Software engineers in these countries are relatively privileged within their countries, which hides the circumstance that their exploitation produces high profits for Western companies that save labour costs by outsourcing work.

Another type of labour involved in the IDDL is low-paid, highly precarious service work, ideally represented by call centre agents (chapter 10). The work in

Product of work	Relationship between work time and play time	Typical working conditions	Form of coercion	Typical examples
Content, software, social networks, user-generated content; behavioural data, profile data, social network data	Play labour: play time is unremunerated labour time	This form of digital labour shares some of the characteristics of housework: it is unpaid, completely non-unionized and infinitely highly exploited. It creates a dual use-value (sociality and data commodity) and is confronted by an inverted commodity fetishism (the commodity character is hidden behind social benefits)	Self-discipline, social coercion	Users of corporate social networking sites and corporate social media (Facebook, YouTube, Google, Twitter, etc.)

call centres is highly Tayloristic and Fordistic in that it is standardized and repetitive, does not allow a lot of creativity and is highly monitored and subject to workplace surveillance. The Tayloristic aspect of call centre work is a multidimensional form of relative surplus-value production. Call centre work is a multidimensional form of housewifized and feminized labour because it involves affective care for the customer, the task of organizing consumption and the projection of clients' sexual desires by talking to female call centre agents, which evokes the association of phone sex. The housewifization of call centre work makes this work poorly paid, which means that this process is a form of absolute surplus-value production because the exercise of high pressure, the low degree of unionization and high coercion create fears of job loss that make call centre agents accept poor wages in comparison to highly paid ICT workers (such as Google employees).

In order for a computer, mobile phone, laptop or printer to be used, its parts need to be physically produced and assembled. This labour is conducted by Taylorist hardware assemblers in various places (such as Silicon Valley or China, chapters 9 and 7 respectively). In China, peasants are in processes of primitive accumulation made landless and transformed into migrant workers who work under highly exploitative and health-threatening conditions in the ICT manufacturing industry, which is located in large urban centres. This work is highly feminized in the sense that (a) there is a large degree of female workers and (b) the work is insecure, precarious and low-paid and in this respect resembles housework. In chapter 7, the example of hardware assemblage at Foxconn was discussed. Similar working conditions can be encountered in the ICT manufacturing industry in Silicon Valley (chapter 9), where work is based on a highly gendered and racist political economy that creates toxic working and living conditions in the sense that workers, workplaces, the air, the soil, drinking water, homes and entire families are contaminated by toxic substances that are by-products of ICT manufacturing and assemblage.

Finally, at the very foundation of the IDDL are working conditions representative of agricultural society and the slave mode of production, where physically coerced workers who are the de facto property of slave owners are compelled to extract "conflict minerals" (such as cassiterite, wolframite, coltan, gold, tungsten) in African (and other) mines, where they are threatened with being killed, tortured and punished. The bloody history of slavery is not over but rather persists in the IDDL and other forms of labour. This type of labour was discussed in chapter 6.

The IDDL shows that various forms of labour characteristic of various stages of capitalism and various modes of capitalist and pre-capitalist modes of production interact so that different forms of separated and highly exploited double-free wage labour, unpaid "free" labour, casualized and housewifized labour and slave labour compose a global network of exploited labour that creates value and forms profits of the variety of companies involved in the capitalist ICT industry. The global division of digital labour shows that stages of capitalist development and historical modes of production (such as patriarchal housework, classical slavery, feudalism, capitalism in general) and modes of organization of the productive forces (such as agriculture, industrialism, informationalism) are not simply successive stages of economic development, where one form substitutes an older one, but that they are all dialectically mediated. Dialectical mediation here means Hegel's notion of *Aufhebung* (sublation): a new stage or mode of production sublates a previous one, which means that a new model emerges, but the old model can be preserved in the new model, can continue to exist in a new form, although its dominance is eliminated. Capitalism has not destroyed the possibility of slavery: on the one hand slavery exists in a new form as wage slavery, and on the other hand possibilities for the existence of classical and feudal forms of slavery remain and, as the example of slavery in mining shows, exists today in a way that benefits Western ICT companies.

The earliest form of private property was constituted in the patriarchal family. The patriarchal mode of production and housework continue to exist in the ICT value chain in the form of casualized and housewifized work of the "free" online workers of Google, Facebook, YouTube, Twitter and others and of the highly controlled and exploited work of call centre agents and ICT manufacturers. Classical and feudal forms of slavery, in which workers are not double free but rather the property of slave owners who physically coerce and almost limitlessly exploit them, persist in the extraction of conflict minerals that form the physical foundation of ICTs. Capitalism is based not only on capital accumulation, but also on double-free wage labour, which means that workers are by the threat of dying of hunger compelled to sell their labour-power as commodity to capitalists, which alienates them from the process and the products of capitalist production and installs wage labour as a specific form of exploitation of labour. Double-free wage labour takes on several specific forms in the ICT value chain. First, there are wage workers who work under conditions that resemble the early stage of industrial capitalism. These are manufacturing and assemblage workers, who risks their health and lives at work. Their work is no fun at all. They are subject to high levels of control, workplace surveillance and standardized work, which shows that Taylorist and Fordist factory work continues to exist under new conditions in the information society. Also call centre agents are facing a kind of Taylorist work situation, with the difference that their labour is, in contrast to ICT manufacturing and assemblage, not primarily physical but informational in nature in that their main activities are talking, convincing with affects, typing, using phone systems and accessing databases. The IDDL also involves relatively new forms of wage labour that are types of highly paid and highly stressful play work, as represented by the Google worker.

This book does not focus on the disposal of ICTs because the topic of the negative impacts of e-waste on humans and society and e-waste labour can fill entire books themselves. So the exclusion of the topic of e-waste in this book does not mean that it is not important, but rather that it is so important that entire books instead of just single chapters need to be devoted to it. An excellent study of e-waste and environmental aspects of media technologies is Richard Maxwell and Toby Miller's (2012) *Greening the Media*. "Beyond production lies the problem of e-waste, which is growing as part of a profitable salvage industry that continues to flourish in the absence of global enforcement" (ibid., 159). The disposal of ICTs succeeds their usage; it is the terminal phase of a single ICT device. Yet it also involves aspects of labour and production: transport workers bring the devices to the sites of disposal and salvage workers disassemble and partly reassemble them. Maxwell and Miller (2012) show that e-waste is mainly produced in rich countries and dumped in poor countries, where it negatively affects the living conditions of residents by contaminating the soil, water and air. ICTs are often disassembled in order to "collect remaining parts and valuable metals, such as gold, silver, copper, and rare-earth elements. This process causes serious health risks to bones, brains, stomachs, lungs, and other vital organs, in addition to birth defects and disrupted biological development in children" (ibid., 3). E-waste labour is an aspect of the IDDL that organizes the disposal of devices. It is a profit-generating business that harms humans and nature.

Jairus Banaji stresses that Marx's theory of the mode of production shows that "capitalist relations of production are compatible with a wide variety of forms of labour, from chattel-slavery, sharecropping, or the domination of casual labour-markets, to the coerced wage-labour peculiar to colonial regimes and, of course, 'free' wage-labour" (Banaji 2011, 359). This book has shown that Banaji's concept of the mode of production matters for understanding the digital media economy because in this economy a variety of modes of production and organizations of the productive forces (= variations within a specific mode of production) are articulated, including slavery in mineral extraction, military forms of Taylorist industrialism in hardware assemblage, an informational organization of the productive forces of capitalism that articulates a highly paid knowledge labour aristocracy, precarious service workers, imperialistically exploited knowledge workers in developing countries and industrial recycling and management of e-waste as well as highly hazardous informal physical e-waste labour.

The "information economy" is not new, postmodern or radically discontinuous. It is rather a highly complex formation in which various contemporary and historical forms of labour, exploitation, different forms of organization of the productive forces, and different modes of production are articulated with each other and form a dialectic of exploitation. When using a single ICT device, such as a computer, a laptop, a printer or a mobile phone, this complexity is reduced to simple, immediate and high-speed usage—exploitation is hidden behind immediate satisfaction of informational needs. ICT usage helps in many situations to achieve goals and to attain pleasures (except in those not so infrequent situations where these technologies fail, which often results in a release of aggression that is characteristic for our high dependence on ICTs for organizing our lives). This positive use-value hides the relations of exploitation that are invisible to the single user and are difficult to trace. The IDDL represents the history and articulation of forms of exploitation. The history of class societies is a history of exploitation. This history forms the heart of and is objectified in the capitalist organization of production, diffusion and consumption of ICTs.

The discussion results show that the global collective ICT worker consists of many different workers: unpaid digital labourers, a highly paid and highly stressed knowledge worker aristocracy, knowledge workers in developing countries, Taylorist call centre wage workers, Taylorist hardware assemblers and manufacturers, slave mine workers and others. This shows that " double-free" wage labour in the ICT industry, as Marcel van der Linden and Karl Heinz Roth (2009) argue, in general is "no longer the strategic and privileged part of the global working class and that slaves, contract workers, (pseudo-) self-employment and others are equally important for theorising capitalism" (ibid., 24; translation from German).

Digital labour has thus far mainly been used as a term characterizing unpaid labour conducted by social media users (see the contributions in Scholz 2013). We can conclude from the discussion in this book that social media prosumption is just one form of digital labour which is networked with and connected to other forms of digital labour that together constitute a global ecology of exploitation enabling the existence of digital media. It is time to broaden the meaning of the term "digital labour" to include all forms of paid and unpaid labour that are needed for existence, production, diffusion and use of digital media. Digital labour is relational in a twofold sense: it is a relation between labour and capital and relational at the level of the IDDL that is shaped by articulated modes of production, forms of the organization of productive forces and variations of the dominant capitalist mode of production.

The question that arises next and to which the rest of this book is devoted is if alternatives to the exploitation of the various forms of work engaged in the ICT value chain are possible and how they can be achieved. Section 12.2 discusses the relationship of digital work and the commons. Sections 12.3 and 12.4 analyse one specific social movement, namely Occupy, and its social media use.

12.2. Digital Work and the Commons

The Internet is controlled by capitalist companies. If one takes a look at the list of the 100 most frequently accessed web platforms in the world (www.alexa.com/topsites), then only few exceptions can be found: Wikipedia and BBC Online. Wikipedia is operated by a non-commercial, non-profit organization, the Wikimedia Foundation (see Firer-Blaess and Fuchs 2012). It funds its activities by donations, does not have advertisements and does not sell commodities. The BBC is a British public service media provider that is predominantly funded by the licence fee but on its international broadcasting and web outlets also sells advertisements for co-funding its domestic UK operations.[1] This means most web usage is digital labour which creates commodities and profit that is owned by private companies. The Internet is largely dominated by the exploitation of digital labour. The question that now arises is how the Internet can be de-commodified. We have ideas about what public service media look like in the realm of broadcasting, whereas the idea of the public good is much more uncommon in the online world because the latter is so much grounded in commercial and corporate values and control.

An important analytical and political question is if users are satisfied with the labour they perform for Facebook and other commercial social media and happily accept a trade-off between personal data commodification and access to corporate platforms without payment. This question cannot be theoretically decided; rather it can only be answered by social research. Research results suggest that users are rather critical of targeted advertising. In a survey conducted in the research project "Social networking sites in the surveillance society" (see sns3.uti.at) that I coordinated, 82.1% of the respondents said they do not want to have targeted advertising on the websites they visit (N = 3558) (see figure 12.1).

A counter-argument one sometimes hears is that targeted ads are not privacy-invasive because they only aggregate data and do not give advertisers direct access to personal data. Our study also showed that 59% say that they do not wish to have targeted ads on Facebook even if the data are not shared with

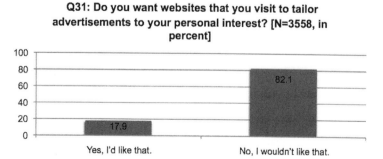

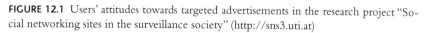

FIGURE 12.1 Users' attitudes towards targeted advertisements in the research project "Social networking sites in the surveillance society" (http://sns3.uti.at)

TABLE 12.2 Users' attitudes towards targeted advertisements in the research project "Social networking sites in the surveillance society" (http://sns3.uti.at)

Is it ok for you that based on your Facebook profile data ... (N=3948)

	Yes	No	I do not know
ads on Facebook are targeted to your personal interests without Facebook providing these data to external advertising clients	1,235 (31.3%)	2,331 (59.0%)	382 (9.7%)
ads on other websites are targeted to your personal interests by Facebook providing these data to external advertising clients	73 (1.8%)	3,738 (94.7%)	137 (3.5%)

advertisers (N = 3558) (see table 12.2). A full 94.7% say they oppose targeted ads on other platforms for which Facebook provides personal data to advertisers (N = 3948).

In a European-wide survey, 54% of the respondents said that they feel uncomfortable about targeted advertising (Special Eurobarometer 359: Attitudes on Data Protection and Electronic Identity in the European Union).

Such data show that one cannot assume that users are happy about a trade-off between data commodification and "free" access, that they are rather critical of such a trade-off model and that there is a need for discussing alternatives to targeted advertising and corporate Internet platforms.

A humanization of the Internet requires a commons-based Internet in a society of the commons. It requires an Internet that is not controlled by the logic of capital and by private profit-making; an Internet that is controlled by all users and benefits all users; an Internet that is grounded in the logic of the information gift that is inexhaustible by consumption; an Internet that is accessible to all without payments; an Internet that is based on the logic of common access to technology and knowledge; an Internet of common production, common ownership, common control, common interests beyond class, common benefits. The logic of the commons then becomes the reality of the society of the commons. Michael Hardt (2010, 136) argues that there are two types of the common: the natural common (earth, land, forests, water, air, minerals, etc.) and the artificial common (ideas, language, affects, information, images, knowledges, codes, social relationships, affects). Slavoj Žižek (2010a, 212–213) draws a distinction between the cultural commons (language, means of communication, education, infrastructures), the commons of external nature (the natural environment) and the commons of internal nature (the human being). For Hardt, the commons are the "escape [of] the boundaries of property" (Hardt 2010, 136).

Hardt's and Žižek's definitions of the commons create the impression that the commons are based on specific inherent qualities of goods, namely that they are not created by single individuals and to a certain extent resist commodification. But the problem of these definitions and the argument that they base on it—that a society of the commons is grounded in the commons—is that they imply politically that only certain goods should be owned and controlled collectively in a society of the commons, namely nature, culture, knowledge and general infrastructures. So the private property status of other goods is not automatically questioned.

Let us take the example of the production of bicycles. A bicycle is different from fresh air and knowledge in the respect that only a limited number of people can consume it at one point of time. It is a good whose consumption is exclusive. Nonetheless, one can argue that bicycles should become a common good in a society of the commons: their production process should be controlled by the producers, who should also own the instruments and objects of labour, and the results of production—bicycles—would either be made available publicly to all so that one can use a bike whenever one needs one or everyone would get his/her own bicycle for free so that everybody has one. The difference that knowledge has in contrast to bicycles is that it is more difficult to exclude others from consumption: knowledge has no wear and tear, it can in principle be used at the same point of time by an endless number of consumers and it can easily and quickly be copied. To turn it into a commodity, legal rules that are carried out by state apparatuses and enforce the commodity status and outlaw copying are needed. Nonetheless, many goods—not just culture, information, nature and infrastructures—can be turned into common goods (and vice versa into commodities).

On Facebook and other social media, the created content is commodified, but this commodification does not result in the full separation of the content from the producers, but rather it results in the users' separation from the economic usage rights and the monetary profits gained with these rights. The specific characteristics of knowledge as peculiar good that it is not used up by consumption, can be simultaneously used by many and can be easily and endlessly copied make it a good that can be more easily turned into a common property than bicycles, but at the same time it can create the (inverse) ideological fetishism that commodification of knowledge on platforms such as Facebook is not problematic because one can still access one's own knowledge and does not lose access to it by commodification. Knowledge concurrently displays germs of a society of the commons and ideologies directed against such a society. Commons are not specific goods, but rather any good can be turned into a private property, just like it can become a common good:

(1) Subject: Labour-power is not a commodity; instead productivity is so high that there are well-rounded individuals who are not facing scarcity and necessity and who freely choose their activities.
(2) Means of production: The objects of labour are owned and controlled in common.
(3) Means of production: The instruments of labour are owned and controlled in common.
(4) Subject-object: The work products are commonly controlled and accessible to all people in society without payment.

In a society of the commons, the entire work process is jointly controlled. Figure 12.2 visualizes the dimensions of a common good in a society of the commons.

A commons-based social networking platform therefore has the following dimensions:

(1) Subject: Usage does not have an instrumental character, and no commodity is created by it, only use-values that satisfy social needs.
(2) Means of production: Experiences are seen as something that is worth sharing with others. People feel no necessity to keep their experiences apart

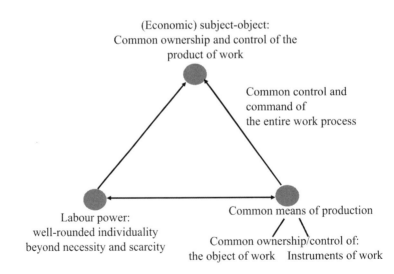

FIGURE 12.2 Dimensions of the commons

from others and as a private secret. The idea of keeping knowledge hidden from others and private is less important. The concept and reality of privacy do not vanish but take on a different role. The idea of public communication becomes a crucial element of society.

(3)   Means of production: A commons-based social medium is a non-commercial, non-profit organization that is controlled and owned by all its users.

(4)   Subject-object: The products of online work have no commodity character; they serve purely social needs: that people inform themselves, communicate and collaborate with each other.

In a commons-oriented society (a society of the commons), digital labour becomes digital work. The use-value created is informational: digital work creates shared cognition, communication (social relations) and cooperation (communities, collaborative work). Information's commodity character is abolished and it becomes a truly common good. Figure 12.3 visualizes the dimensions of a commons-based Internet platform in a society of a commons. Only a commons-based Internet is a truly and fully "social medium" in the sense that the subject, objects and subject-objects of work become controlled by society as a whole and stop being owned by private individuals who accumulate capital. Social media can then become common media, a "commonsnet" operated and controlled in common by the people.

Attempts at establishing non-commercial alternatives to Facebook exist. Examples are the social networking sites Diaspora* (Sevignani 2012), Occupii and N-1.

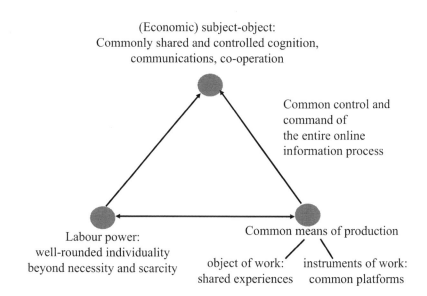

(Economic) subject-object:
Commonly shared and controlled cognition,
communications, co-operation

Common control and
command of
the entire online
information process

Labour power:
well-rounded individuality
beyond necessity and scarcity

Common means of production

object of work: instruments of work:
shared experiences   common platforms

FIGURE 12.3 Dimensions of a commons-based Internet (commonsnet)

Diaspora★ describes itself as "the community-run, distributed social-network".[2] Occupii is a non-commercial SNS created by the Occupy movement that serves the purpose of networking activists. N-1 is a non-commercial SNS that describes itself as "social networks by the people for the people" and explains its existence by saying that "the master's tools will never dismantle the master's house".[3] Usage of these platforms is not digital labour but digital work: online activity creates use-value (communication, social relations, publicity) but no commodities. These platforms are shaped by the logic of the commons and not by the logic of capital and commodities. They are foundations of a commons-based Internet. A commons-based Internet is characterized by common access for all and common ownership, is a common space of communication, provides the common capacity to produce and share knowledge, is a common space for the co-creation of shared meanings (cooperation), and is a common space for political debate, a common space for co-forming collective values and identities and a common space for struggles against the colonization of the commons (Fuchs 2011a, chapter 9).

However, alternative social media currently exist within capitalism, which means that certain goods necessary for the operation (especially servers, domain names and bandwidth) have to be purchased as commodities. The employed software is free software developed in common. But within capitalism, free software development requires time and time is a scarce resource. So many free software developers have a day job for earning a living and contribute to software development voluntarily and unpaid during their spare time. Facebook and other commercial platforms in contrast have a revenue stream that stems from Internet prosumer commodification, which allows them to employ software engineers and other operational personnel, to buy servers and other goods that are necessary for operating and to engage in public relations by running ads and campaigns that promote Facebook usage. Platforms like Facebook and Google also have reputational power and political influence because they are huge organizations that control access to a large global user community.

Alternative platforms in contrast depend on donations and voluntary work. Money is the dominant medium of capitalism; as the general equivalent of exchange—the general commodity—it can be used for obtaining most other goods. It is the outcome of capitalist production. Those who control and accumulate money power are therefore equipped with a resource that puts them at a strategic advantage. This means that alternative online platforms in capitalism are facing power inequalities that stem from the asymmetric distributions of money and other resources that are inherent in capitalism. Practically this means that alternative platforms have less money and fewer users than Facebook. Facebook had around 1.0 billion users in November 2012.[4] In contrast, Diaspora★[5] had at the same time around 90,000 users, Occupii 5,303 members and N-1 44,414 members. This circumstance shows that Facebook controls monetary, reputational and usage power that puts alternative players at a disadvantage and makes it difficult for them to challenge the de facto monopoly of Facebook in the realm of social networking sites. Using social networking sites is predominantly and to a large degree social labour that is alienated and not social work that focuses on a pure social logic and transcends the private logic of capital accumulation. Using platforms such as Diaspora*, Occupii and N-1 is digital work, but this work is embedded into the unequal political economy of the Internet that is shaped by capitalism.

How can alternatives be strengthened? How can common media be built? One argument is that Facebook usage should be remunerated, that social media unions should be founded and that the struggle for an online wage is needed. Digital labour creates value, but to a large degree digital labour-power is not a commodity. It is unpaid and not sold as a commodity. The failure of social democracy has been that it has for a long time not struggled against the commodity form and for the abolishment of labour, but only for the increase of wages, which does not question the commodification of labour-power as such. Labour-power can be de-commodified by creating self-managed or public companies that do not follow profit logic. As long as the logic of money exists, such work can be remunerated, but it does not create profit in such companies because these are organizations that follow the logic of the public or common good. Once a wage relationship is installed, it is easier to struggle for wage increases than for the establishment of alternative forms of organizing work.

I oppose the idea of paying a wage to users of Facebook, Google and other corporate platforms that exploit unpaid digital labour, and, rather, argue for establishing and nourishing the existing alternative Internet platforms by user support, donations and public funding. Occupii and N-1 are more political activist platforms, whereas Diaspora* has set out to become an alternative to Facebook. We think that a combined political strategy of class struggle of the digital working class is needed that seeks both breadth and depth: on the one hand, it should aim at providing a non-commercial, commons-based alternative to Facebook that attracts a lot of users and in the end results in a collective exodus from Facebook that at once and as a combined act transfers all users to alternative platforms; on the other hand, the strategy requires the networking of activists as a social movement that challenges class relations. The Occupy movement is a class struggle movement that questions the power of capital. It also makes use of social media and has created its own social media (such as Occupii and the Global Square). Facebook and other corporate social media are part of the 1% but are nourished by the digital labour of the 99%. Occupying the Internet requires a movement for the commons that politicizes the Internet and makes use of its own platforms for networking activists and of existing commercial platforms for reaching out to users and preparing the exodus from corporate platforms as a class struggle strategy. The overall goal is the sublation of online alienation, that is, the self-determination of digital labour-power and the common control of online platforms, online experiences and online interactions. We require the transformation of digital labour into digital work. We require a true social media revolution.

Jack Qiu argues that the Chinese working class uses and adopts cheap ICTs that he calls "working-class ICTs" (Qiu 2009, 2010c): they include the sale of second-hand phones, refurbished computers, pirated DVDs, pirated software and refilled printer cartridges and the use of prepaid mobile phones, Internet cafés, Little Smart wireless phones, blogs, computer games, peer-to-peer networks and QQ Internet messaging (one today can probably add the social networking site RenRen and the microblog Weibo). They use these ICTs for networking for the purposes of survival, entertainment, social relations, education, mutual support and politics. Qiu's (2009) book is an interesting, empirically sound study that makes clear the role of highly exploited labour in the ICT industry in China. His analysis is enlightening and a critique of the conditions that disenfranchised workers in China have to face. What makes it sympathetic is the class solidarity of the author that one feels when reading the book. One theoretical question that arises is how the term "working-class ICTs" should be used. For Qiu, this term signifies an informal economy of ICT production as well as the new working class's use of relatively cheap ICTs and online working-class culture. What characterizes the working class is that it is not-capital: it does not own and control capital—it is therefore economically poor. Labour is "not-value", "not-capital", "not-raw-material", "not-instrument of labour", "not-raw-product" (Marx 1857/1858b, 295): it is "absolute poverty", which means an "exclusion from objective wealth" (ibid., 296) and at the same time the constitution of labour as the "living source of value", the "general possibility" of wealth (ibid.). Given that labour is not-capital and stands in a class antagonism with capital, working-class ICTs can be conceived as ICTs whose production and output is controlled and owned by workers (i.e. self-managed ICT companies). To the extent that Chinese workers create an informal economy in which they create ICTs (e.g. pirated DVDs), one can speak of the attempt of the "information have-less" to find ways to control ICT production. The category of working-class ICTs is theoretically interesting and can be quite fruitful. The question is if this notion should encompass the use of cheap ICTs that are sold by capitalist companies to workers. The basic logic for capital is that although these workers are poor, the fact that there are a hundred millions of them creates a profitable market segment. These companies are, however, not worker-controlled and in fact exist by the exploitation of workers as well as the exploitation of users (the latter is the case if targeted advertising is used as a capital accumulation model). The working class is universal in that its emancipation puts an end not only to capital, but to all classes. So working-class ICTs can conceptually best be defined as ICTs that try to explode the class character, that is, ICTs that are collectively owned, controlled, operated and used by the immediate producers and prosumers. Such a definition is similar to saying that these ICTs are part of the commons or digital media commons. ICTs that are controlled by capitalist companies such as Tencent (QQ), Renren Inc., Sina Inc., Youku Inc., NetEase Inc. (163.com), which make profit by exploiting producers and prosumers, can then by definition not be working-class ICTs. A Marxist definition of the term "working-class ICTs" also implies a struggle between commons-based ICTs and capitalist ICTs for the method of how surplus is controlled.

A concept of ICT use by the working class needs to reflect the difference between a class-in-itself and a class-for-itself: the difference between the working class in its position in the relations of production with any form of subjectivity and a politically conscious working class engaged in political struggles. One can use the two terms "proletariat" and "working class" to draw a distinction between the subjective and the objective class dimension, meaning that based on such a distinction, the working class is the politically conscious and politically (self-) organized struggling proletariat, the class-in-and-for-itself, a self-constituting collective political power. The becoming working class of the proletariat is then a political process taking place in social struggles. The *Communist Manifesto* ends with the words "Proletarier aller Länder, vereinigt Euch!" (Proletarians of all countries, unite!) (Marx and Engels 1848, 493). This is an indication that Marx and Engels saw the working-class-in-itself as the proletariat. The proletariat is the not-yet politically organized, not-yet united and not-yet conscious class that organizes itself to become the working class that struggles for its own abolition and thereby the abolition of all classes and class society. Karl Heinz Roth and Marcel van der Linden (2009, 592; translation from German) define the global proletariat as the "multiverse of the exploited", those who are in the situation of the "expropriation, disciplining and the externalisation as well as alienation and valorisation of their labour power", and the global working class *(Weltarbeiterklasse)* as those resisting the exploitation and valorization of their labour. If one makes a theoretical distinction between the proletariat and the working class, then a differentiation between "proletarian ICTs" and "working-class ICTs" can be made. For both, we find different aspects of (a) production, (b) distribution and (c) use of ICTs for economic, political and cultural purposes. The proletariat uses ICTs for all sorts of purposes and in a context where the proletariat is large enough, this becomes a profitable industry, a kind of industry of selling cheap ICTs to proletarians. At the same time, if proletarian ICTs are organized by capital and in the form of commodities, then exploitation and the deepening of the class antagonism is a structural feature of proletarian ICTs. As a working class, proletarians have the interest not to be exploited because exploitation limits their opportunities and is the structural cause of inequality. So the becoming working class of proletarians then entails specific features, namely that ICTs are used in working-class struggles. In addition, if the working class is the universal class that wants to overcome its exploitation and thereby that of all classes, then in the realm of ICTs it also stands for qualitatively different ownership and organization structures of ICTs, namely ICTs that are no longer commodities but are worker-controlled and worker-owned (i.e. self-managed ICTs or commons-based ICTs). The notion of working-class ICTs then also entails the becoming-common (goods) of ICTs. Commons are structures that are produced and created by all people. Therefore communication is also a commons. Communication is a social means of survival of humanity. Commodification therefore contradicts the essence of communication. Commodification is in conflict with communicative work or the communications that we all produce in order to exist. A large part of the Internet is today based on commodity logic and capital accumulation. A political task today is to struggle for a commons-based Internet or working-class Internet.

The difference between a Weberian and a Marxian concept of class is that in the first a class consists of individuals who have similar living conditions and opportunities, whereas in a Marxian definition of class there is an inverse interdependent welfare between two classes, exclusion of one class from the ownership of wealth and appropriation of the fruits of labour by the ruling class (Wright 1997, 10; Wright 2005, 23). This means that for Marx, class is a relationship of exploitation between a ruling and a dominated class, and those who control and own capital have the power to appropriate (i.e. make their property, which implies a sales right) the surplus time and product that workers create because they are forced to work under the control of capital in order to survive. The Marxist approach to class is strongly relational (Gubbay 1997)—class is a dialectical relation between opposing positions in the structure of production: each class requires the other to exist in capitalism and they have contradictory interests that relate to the question how the surplus should be distributed (ownership of all or a part of surplus value by capital implies non-ownership by labour).

In a Weberian approach, the "information have-less" are a separate class (like the "middle class" or "upper class") because they have similar living conditions that are characterized by precarity and struggle for survival. In a Marxist approach, the information have-less are a group that belong to one overall class—the working class: they have something in common with Congolese slave workers, American automobile workers, Indian software workers and so on—namely that they are exploited by capital and in this exploitation lies a joint and universal interest to emancipate themselves from exploitation. So the information have-less in a Marxist approach do not form a separate class, but make up a faction or subgroup within the working class. A Marxist concept of class is relational, focusing on exploitation and struggle.

A Marxist concept of the knowledge working class has the advantage that it is relational and can thereby stress that the situation workers are facing is due to the exploitative relations with companies, the global division of labour in the ICT value chain. The solution to these antagonisms lies in class struggle and the establishment of a qualitatively different ICT economy. A Weberian concept is much more focused on internal similarities and characteristics of groups, not so much on relations between groups.

The postmodern turn in the social sciences has been a turn away from class. Class was deliberately not discussed or analysed. Therefore, any return to class as an analytical category is important today. But a pluralistic concept of class is not necessarily more complex; it can simply be a postulation of dimensions that do not easily fit together. Both the Marxian and the Weberian approach are concerned with socio-economic inequality. The difference is theoretical and political: Marx's approach allows one to analyse antagonistic relations of exploitation and calls for the abolishment of the root causes of exploitation. Weberian approaches have a stress on class positions and situations. They do not necessarily see a class antagonism because they politically tend to advocate class compromise. Class positions and situations are defined as arising from the distribution of life chances in the economy. Individuals are seen as being part of one class because they have a comparable amount of income, wealth, and household consumption patterns, a comparable lifestyle, occupation, social status, social security, social mobility, skills and the like. Two well-known contemporary Weberian class approaches have been advanced by John Goldthorpe (2000) and Anthony Giddens (1980). How one defines class has quite important theoretical and political implications. Given a world of exploding inequalities that are grounded in multiple relationships of exploitation, a Marxian analysis of global society is the most adequate approach.

The distinction between a Weberian and a Marxist concept of class has implications for the theoretical concept of working-class ICTs. In a Weberian notion of working-class ICTs, these media are defined via similar life chances of users, as for example the degree of ICT use. One then speaks of working-class ICTs if wage earners have significant access to certain ICTs and make use of them. The resulting central political problem then is that workers do not have usage access to certain ICTs and the problem is solved once they have. In a Marxian concept of working-class ICTs, ownership plays a crucial role—the production process of ICTs, the means and the results of production are collectively owned by workers. If in contrast certain ICTs are produced in a capitalist manner, then this production implies the exploitation of workers, so these ICTs contradict workers' objective interests and can therefore not be defined as working-class ICTs. The corresponding political problem is one of class struggle against the capitalist character of ICTs and society. The Weberian approach is focused on access and use, the Marxian approach on ownership and control of the surplus product.

There is a difference between proletarian digital media and working-class digital media. Proletarian digital media often feature capitalist ownership structures, although they can also be non-profit and non-commercial. Working-class digital media are media of struggle controlled by workers in processes of self-management. What a struggling true working class struggles for is the abolishment of classes by the establishment of an economic democracy. Working-class media strive towards media of the commons just like working-class struggles strive towards a society of the commons. Worker self-management is not limited to knowledge work and the Internet. It can be applied to any form of production, as the example of mining cooperatives shows: Policy discussions have involved suggestions to ban conflict mineral imports from the DRC (the Dodd-Frank Act in the United States). But given that many workers' only income opportunity is mining, such measures ultimately negatively impact the socio-economic situation in the country and can thereby further advance violence and poverty, the conditions that form the root of slavery (Finnwatch and Swedwatch 2010). A viable alternative is the support of the creation of mining cooperatives that are worker-controlled and worker-owned. So, for example, in Walikale, where the Bisie mine is located, there is a mineral-buying cooperative, the Vin de Minier M'Pama du Bisie (Eichstaedt 2011, 114). Gilber Kalinda, member of the local parliament in Walikale, says that cooperatives are the viable alternative to the armed militia's control of the mines and "can reduce the possibilities that militias will use the minerals for war" (ibid., 133). Jotham Vwemeye, director of the mining cooperative Co-operama in Masisi, says that the "cooperative is a means of improving the lives of people at a local level" (ibid., 147).

The question is how working-class struggles look today, what relevance and problems they have and what role media and communication play in them. This book cannot give a thorough discussion of contemporary working-class struggles; rather it has to restrict itself to one example, namely the Occupy movement in Europe and the United States. The focus on this movement does not at all imply that other struggles, such as the ones by Chinese workers (see Qiu 2009, Zhao 2008), are less important or that the important changes have to take place in the West. Capitalism is global and struggles take place in many parts of the world. Significant transformations can, as the Arab Spring has shown, take place anywhere. The choice of Occupy is rather motivated by the circumstance that the author possesses the linguistic skills to analyse this movement but cannot analyse many other movements. Analysis of movements such as the Arab Spring, the Chinese working-class movement, popular movements in Latin America and so forth is of crucial importance and should be advanced and supported.

Section 12.3 will discuss what kind of movement Occupy is. Based on this analysis, section 12.4 analyses Occupy's social media use and connects this discussion to the notion of working-class media.

12.3. The Occupy Movement: A New Working-Class Movement?

In 2008, a phase of global economic crisis started. David Graeber (2011) argues that neo-liberalism broke the link between productivity and wages so that rising productivity did not increase wages. The latter rather stagnated or decreased. Capitalism "became the organizing principle of almost everything" (ibid., 376). Citizens were turned into debtors who were forced to live off credit cards and were encouraged to mortgage or remortgage their houses. The big crisis would have occurred because it "proved no more possible to really turn everyone in the world into micro-corporations, or to 'democratize credit'" (ibid., 381). As an answer to the crisis, governments were "forced to decide who really gets to make money out of nothing: the financiers, or ordinary citizens. [. . .] Financiers were 'bailed out with taxpayer money'" (ibid.).

The Occupy movements in the United States and Europe, just like the Arab Spring, are social movements that are situated in the context of this crisis. This section asks the question, what kind of movement is the Occupy movement? To offer an answer to this question, first a brief overview of how social movements have been theoretically conceptualized is given in section 12.3.1. In section 12.3.2, I discuss how some major political theorists have theorized the Occupy movement in recent writings and compare their insights to new social movement theory. In section 12.3.3, I move from the level of theoretical conceptualization to the level of subjectivity. By analysing key documents of the Occupy movement, I want to show how the movement conceptualizes itself. Finally, some conclusions are drawn in section 12.3.4.

12.3.1. Social Movement Theory

Social movements are in this type of literature characterized as informal, conflict-oriented collectives (Diani 2003, della Porta and Diani 2006) that want to establish collectively binding goals (Offe 1985, Touraine 1985); are oriented on social change (McCarthy 1996, 145; McCarthy and Zald 1977); are political (Kriesi 1996); involve direct participation; protest politics; are loose, decentralized, grassroots and an expression of participatory democracy (della Porta and Diani 2006, 145–150; Rucht 1996); and engage in multi-issue direct activism with permanent campaigns (Bennett 2005). *Non-governmental organizations (NGOs)* are, just like social movements, considered as being political (Kriesi 1996) and as wanting to establish collectively binding goals (Offe 1985, Touraine 1985). They are however seen as being more formal (Rucht 1996); having more focus on lobbying than on social change and protest (Roth and Rucht 2008, 18); involving hierarchies, leadership and representation (della Porta and Diani 2006, 145–150); and being more centralized and focused on single issues and policy reforms (Bennett 2005). Both social movements and NGOs are seen as part of civil society's political public sphere. Della Porta and Diani (2006, 20ff) see (political or cultural) conflicts, opponents, informal networks and collective identity as characteristic of social movements.

Protest movements are a reaction to social problems, an expression of fear and dissatisfaction with society as it is and a call for changes and the solution to problems (Fuchs 2006). Protest movements are political answers of civil society to modern society's ecological, economic, political, social and cultural problems. The problems produced by the antagonistic structures of society are a condition for the emergence of protest that organizes itself within the civil society subsystem of the political system. Each protest movement is reactive in the sense that it reacts to strains and protests against the existence of certain social structures, but each is also proactive in the sense that it wants to transform society and holds certain values and goals that shall guide these transformation processes. The emergence of a protest movement presupposes societal problems as a material base (ibid.). Protest is a negation of existing structures that result in frictions and problems and is a political struggle that aims at the transformation of certain aspects of society or of society as a whole. Neither the aggravation of problems, the structural opening of new political opportunities nor the increase of resources for protest movements results automatically in protest (ibid.). Only if social problems are perceived as problems and if this perception guides practices does protest emerge. The difference between objective structures and subjective values and practices is an important aspect of protest. Protest presupposes societal problems, the perception of these problems as problems by human actors, the assessment that these problems are unbearable and a moral indignation that activates and mobilizes practices. That a problem is perceived as a problem that should be solved does not automatically result in the emergence of protest, but maybe results in attempts to organize protest. Such attempts are only successful if possibilities and resources for protest can be found and mobilized. Protest is a collective search for and a production of alternative meanings and values. Each protest group has a certain identity, an adversary and goals.

Alain Touraine argues that each type of modern society (commercial, industrial, post-industrial) is based on a central conflict and a single social movement that animates these struggles. Whereas industrial societies would have been based on class struggle, post-industrial society would be based on struggles over the production of symbolic goods (information, images, culture, Touraine 1985, 774). In post-industrial society, struggles would be more based on biological and natural entities such as the environment, gender, youth and age and they would be struggles for happiness (Touraine 1988, 111). Jürgen Habermas argues that new social movements do not focus on conflicts over distribution, but that rather "these new conflicts arise in domains of cultural reproduction, social integration, and socialisation. [. . .] In short, the new conflicts are not ignited by distribution problems but by questions having to do with the grammar of forms of life" (Habermas 1987, 392). Laclau and Mouffe (1985) argue that the novelty of social movements is due to their feature that they question new forms of subordination that are defined not by class but by, for example, sexuality, gender, ethnicity and nature. Society would today be based on a plurality of antagonisms that manifests itself in separate struggles, the autonomization of spheres of struggles and a plurality of subjects that opens up the possibility for a radical, pluralistic democracy. For Offe (1985), new aspects are that new social movements (NSMs) are not socio-economic groups acting as groups, but act on behalf of ascriptive collectivities, that they are concerned with not purely economic issues, that autonomy and identity are their central values, and that they have a high degree of informality and spontaneity and a low degree of horizontal and vertical differentiation. Eder (1993) suggests that nature is a new field of class struggle. New social movements would be struggles for the control of the means of producing identities and the means of cultural expression; they would protest against the exclusion from identity-construction and fight for the control of identity as a symbolic and invisible good as well as for alternative values (good life, community).

These approaches share the assumption that new social movements are not primarily oriented on class struggle, questions of distributive justice and socio-economic issues, but rather focus on identity politics and struggles that relate to culture and human beings' internal and external nature. The emergence of the Global Justice Movement challenged these assumptions. It is a global social movement that opposes neo-liberal globalization and calls for social justice and participatory democracy (della Porta 2007a).

The Global Justice Movement reacted "to the effects of the liberalization of markets, framing them as consequences of political decisions dominated by the neoliberal agenda" (ibid., 22) and to the "retrenchment of the welfare state and the increasing inequalities" (della Porta 2007b, 236). It was not a single-issue new social movement, but is characterized by the "resurgence of social issues, although blended with 'new social movement' issues" (ibid.). The movement gave special attention to economic globalization, and the "re-emergence of social issues" (ibid., 242) in the Global Justice Movement challenged "some previous hypotheses [of e.g. postmodernism and new social movement theory], such as the steady decline of class cleavages" (ibid., 250). Nick Crossley (2003) analyses the *altermondialiste* movement based on Habermas. It would be a reaction to the colonization of the "lifeworld" by the market and capital. Whereas Habermas has stressed colonization by the economy and bureaucracy, contemporary colonization would primarily be based on the market.

Whereas in the 1970s and 1980s political struggles were strongly oriented on the recognition of marginalized identities (women, gays and lesbians, transsexuals, etc.) and the recognition of nature as a value (ecological movement), these specific struggles have to a certain extent become unified by the re-emergence of class issues because of the rise of strong socio-economic inequality. The Global Justice Movement constituted a movement of movements that aims at reclaiming the commons that have increasingly been privatized and commodified by capitalism (Klein 2004). This movement unified particular struggles and refocuses on class issues by questioning corporate domination.

12.3.2. The Occupy Movement in Contemporary Political Theory

Hardt and Negri (2012, "Opening") argue that whereas the movement for democratic globalization was nomadic (following global institutions to their meetings), the Occupy movements are sedentary: they "refuse to move" from occupied spaces. They are "struggles for the common, then, in the sense that they contest the injustices of neoliberalism and, ultimately, the rule of private property" (ibid.). For Hardt and Negri, there are four causes of contemporary uprisings: finance capitalism's creation of the indebted, IT's creation of the mediatized, the security regime's creation of the securitized, and the corrupt state's creation of the represented (ibid., chapter 1). So Hardt and Negri see three causes and dimensions of Occupy: class, the media and politics (surveillance and securitization, corruption and lack of democracy).

This is a rather dualistic analysis that postulates multiple causes and goals but does not discuss if and how these dimensions are related and if certain elements weigh stronger than others. The dimensions of the media and politics are not independent from capitalism: social media such as Twitter, Google and Facebook are operated by capitalist companies that use targeted advertising as their business models. They became especially popular after the 2000 dot.com crisis when the Internet industry was looking for new ways to attract financial investments. The intensification and extension of surveillance in society has taken place in the context of 9/11 and the subsequent phase of global war (Bigo 2010, Gandy 2009, Lyon 2003, Mattelart 2010). There has been both an inner and outer militarization of society. After 9/11, the United States tried to secure its global hegemony by military means and symbolic wars in Afghanistan and Iraq that also secured Western access to oil as a strategic economic resource. New imperialism has aspects of both global capital accumulation and global hegemony (Fuchs 2010a, Hardt and Negri 2000, Harvey 2005, Panitch and Gindin 2004, Wood 2003). Occupy is not, as conceived by Hardt and Negri, a movement that stands in the context of independent changes of the economy (the rise of the indebted), the media (the emergence of the mediated) and politics (the rise of the securitized and the represented); it is rather situated in the interdependent changes of global capitalism (financialization, neo-liberalism, the new imperialism and militarized capitalism, crisis, new spheres and models of capital accumulation).

Slavoj Žižek (2012, 10) argues that managers are salaried workers and that they "are paid rather more than the proletarian 'minimum wage' [. . .] and it is this distinction from common proletarians which determines their status". He speaks in this context of a surplus wage. The Occupy movement and contemporary student protests are not proletarian protests but protests of "privileged workers who have guaranteed jobs (mostly in the civil service: police and other law enforcers, teachers, public transport workers, etcetera") (ibid., 12)—protests of "a 'salaried bourgeoisie' driven by fear of losing their surplus wage". Student protests are a sign of students' "fear that higher education will no longer guarantee them a surplus wage in later life" (ibid.).

The problem of Žižek's analysis is that he compares people who partly are facing precarious jobs and unemployment with managers, who often have high salaries and bonuses. Students, public service workers and many knowledge workers in general do not have high salaries but are facing precariousness. Just think of low-paid call centre agents and the fact that many young people in countries like Greece and Spain are unemployed, although they have completed higher education. Žižek overestimates the category of the bourgeoisie and underestimates the degree of proletarianization of knowledge work.

In chapter 7 of the same book, in which he classifies the Occupy movement as revolt of the salaried bourgeoisie, Žižek (2012) contradicts his own analysis given in the introduction and the solidarity he expressed in a speech he gave at Occupy Wall Street (Žižek 2011), where he warned that the movement should not fall in love with itself, not listen to those who want to turn it into or interpret it as a harmless moral protest—a "decaffeinated protest", but to remember that the "problem is the system" and that the question to ask is, "What social organization can replace capitalism"? (ibid., 68). Žižek (2012) argues that new social movements had abolished "class-struggle essentialism" by stressing the "plurality of anti-racist, feminist and other struggles", whereas the Occupy movement sees "capitalism" as "the name of the problem" (ibid., 77). The activists would "care about the commons—the commons of nature, of knowledge—which are threatened by the system" (ibid., 83). The Occupy movement would be discontent with "capitalism as a system" and with the reduction of democracy to representation (ibid., 87).

So Žižek's position is ambivalent. Whereas on the one hand he describes Occupy as a movement of the salaried bourgeoisie, on the other hand he stresses its anti-capitalist potential. In contrast, Alain Badiou (2012) argues that the Occupy movement and other contemporary movements (such as the revolutionary Arab Spring movements in Egypt and Spain) are communist movements because they call for the realization of the common interests of all people (the Communist Idea) and transcend class structures in their internal organization—Occupy constitutes a "movement communism" and stands for the "creation in common of the collective destiny" (ibid., 111).

Jodi Dean (2012, 85) argues that class conflict today is between "the rich and the rest of us". The Occupy movement would advance "a new assertion of the common and commons" (ibid., 178) and would be "a political form for the incompatibility between capitalism and the people" (214) and "the organized collective opposition to the capitalist expropriation of our lives and futures" (223). Its slogan "We are the 99%" would voice the class relation between the rich and the rest of us—"those who have and control the common wealth and those who do not" (ibid., 201). Although the Occupy movement would stress consensus and grassroots decisions, it would be a new form of communist party because it would not be but rather represent the 99% (ibid., 229)—it is, so to speak, the party of the 99%.

For Noam Chomsky (2012), Occupy is a reaction to the "tremendous concentration of wealth" that also yields "concentration of political power. And concentration of political power gives rise to legislation that increases and accelerates the cycle" (ibid., 28–29). The problem is a contradiction between a precariat and a plutonomy (ibid., 34).

David Harvey argues that the financialization of the housing market and the growth of inequality have been reflected in urban spaces as an "urban crisis" (Harvey 2012, 51). The emergence of a precariat facing "insecure, often part-time and disorganized low-paid labor" (ibid., xiv) and the privatization and financialization of urban space would have resulted in the emergence of urban social movements that reclaim "their right to the city—their right to change the world, to change life, and to reinvent the city more after their hearts' desire" (25) and the right to urban commons that were created by collective labour (78). Harvey conceives the Occupy movement (and other movements such as the Arab Spring revolutions) as an urban movement that confronts "the Party of Wall Street and its unalloyed money power" (ibid., 161).

Hardt and Negri see three independent dimensions and causes of the emergence of the Occupy movement (capitalism, the media, politics). In contrast, Žižek, Badiou, Dean, Chomsky and Harvey stress the importance of the socio-economic dimension and capitalism in their analyses of Occupy. Whereas Žižek gives a somewhat ambivalent and immanently contradictory analysis (is Occupy a reformist movement of the salaried bourgeoisie that wants to defend its privileges against the "real" working class or is it an anti-capitalist new working-class movement?), Badiou, Dean, Chomsky and Harvey give overall consistent analyses that focus on aspects of a class struggle that challenges capitalism. Alain Badiou points out that Occupy is a movement that struggles for the defence of common interests, for common control of society and common property. It would create a common project for the commons and try to realize the communist idea. In line with Badiou's analysis, Jodi Dean points out that Occupy is a new communist movement. Noam Chomsky foregrounds the class-struggle dimension of this movement, whereas David Harvey adds to the analysis that this class struggle takes place in an urban context and that Occupy is an urban movement that wants to reclaim the urban commons.

There is a clear difference between these analyses and the analysis of new social movements in the 1980s that seems to indicate changes in the politics of social movements. Žižek, Touraine, Habermas, Offe and Laclau and Mouffe, as well as others, argued that new social movements are new because they focus on non-class issues: culture, nature, gender, youth, age, happiness, information, ethnicity, identity. In contrast, Žižek, Badiou, Dean, Chomsky and Harvey foreground that the Occupy movement's central issues are class and capitalism. The focus on class politics instead of identity politics signifies a shift of politics from a focus on freedom and pluralistic democracy to one of justice and participatory democracy that foregrounds the need for economic democracy and stresses the crucial role the economy has in modern society. The Global Justice Movement that emerged with the "battle of Seattle" in 1999 was an early indication of the return of class politics. What mainly differed in comparison to Occupy was the societal context: there was no global economic crisis. The crisis that started in 2008 marks a big rupture: it suddenly became evident through economic reality that capitalism is a crisis-ridden system and that neo-liberalism fosters massive socio-economic inequality. The Global Justice Movement constantly warned about the consequences of financialization and neo-liberalism, but these warnings could be more easily ignored or downplayed by those in power. In 2008, the contradictions of contemporary capitalism exploded in a global crisis. The warnings can now no longer be ignored or downplayed ideologically, but rather have become economic reality that manifests itself in bankruptcy, debt, unemployment, evictions, food crisis, misery, austerity—and protests.

Not only context but also strategy distinguish Occupy from the Global Justice Movement. Whereas the latter followed mainly the strategy of trying to block events where the global political-economic elite meets and takes decisions that affect the lives of people globally, in combination with organizing counter-summits such as the World Social Forum or the European Social Forum, Occupy does not move flexibly in space but occupies and encamps places. The Global Justice Movement's occupations were temporary (there was a planned beginning and end) and took the form of demonstrations in certain places where the powerful met, so space was appropriated in a temporally limited manner and in a spatially flexible way, depending on where the powerful were meeting. In contrast, a strategy of the Occupy movements—not only in the United States and Europe, but also in the Arab Spring—was to claim strategic urban places (such as Tahrir Square in Cairo, Syntagma Square in Athens, Puerta del Sol in Madrid, Plaça Catalunya in Barcelona or Zuccotti Park in New York) as common property of the movement, where protest practices happen for an undefined period of time. Whereas the Global Justice Movement was placeless and dynamically located in global space, Occupy is a place-based movement. David Harvey (2012) points out this circumstance by characterizing Occupy as urban movement. The assembly of a large number of people in squares and the organization of these squares as political places controlled by activists is a threat to those in power. It makes visible the discontents of people in a central spatial environment. The claim to urban space as a common also reflects the dissatisfaction with capitalism's exploitation and destructions of commons such as housing, social security, communication, culture, nature, education, health care and human survival. Reclaiming space is at the same time the symbol for the political demand to reclaim all of society from the control exerted by capital. But not only the control of spaces and the reclaiming of certain urban spaces as common property of the people is a strategy of resistance; the control of time is also a threat to those in power: whereas a demonstration or campaign is planned for a limited time, the encampments and occupations do not plan a temporal limit but make the political claim that spaces are liberated and that this liberation has started and will never stop. Of course there are different temporal outcomes of such urban rebellions: whereas Occupy Wall Street was dissolved by police violence, which put an artificial temporal end point to the occupation, the struggles in Egypt and Tunisia turned into successful revolutions that occupied time in another sense: they put an end to old regimes and opened up space and time for new political opportunities. Whereas Manuel Castells (1996) described contemporary society as moving from the logic of the space of places to the logic of the space of flows that is characterized by timeless time and placeless space so that contemporary movements are timeless and placeless movements (Castells

1997), the Occupy movement makes clear that the space of flows was primarily the space of capital and that the logic of common places can be a global and networked logic of resistance. It grounds resistances in places, so it is not placeless, but it uses places as a form of power. It understands timelessness not primarily as the overcoming of temporal distance in globalization processes, but as the claim that the revolution/rebellion has started and will not stop until those in power are gone and new economic and political times can begin. Occupy is the attempt to open up time, to make time historical in the process of revolution. In contrast to the reformist characteristics of new social movements, Occupy is a revolutionary movement, which means that it wants to create new spaces and new times for a new society.

12.3.3. The Occupy Movement's Self-Understanding

What kind of movement is Occupy? The Occupy Wall Street movement started on September 17, 2011, when activists occupied Zuccotti Park in New York. The police made them leave the park on November 15. The two makers of *Adbusters Magazine* (Kalle Lasn and Micah White) had the idea for the occupation, set up the website occupywallstreet.org and spread the occupation idea to its subscribers via the magazine, a mailing list and a blog. The call text read: "On September 17, we want to see 20,000 people flood into lower Manhattan, set up tents, kitchens, peaceful barricades and occupy Wall Street for a few months. Once there, we shall incessantly repeat one simple demand in a plurality of voices. [. . .] [W]e demand that Barack Obama ordain a Presidential Commission tasked with ending the influence money has over our representatives in Washington. It's time for DEMOCRACY NOT CORPORATOCRACY, we're doomed without it. [. . .] Beginning from one simple demand—a presidential commission to separate money from politics—we start setting the agenda for a new America" (Adbusters 2012).

The basic demand in the initial call was that the government should limit the influence of capital on politics. The focus was not so much on inequality and class, but more on the relationship between corporate power and the state that, according to the demand, should be separated. This focus was, however, broadened in the actual politics of the movement.

In a self-understanding published on the website occupywallst.org, the Occupy movement describes itself as being the "99% that will no longer tolerate the greed and corruption of the 1%" (occupywallst.org). In the United States, the top 20% of households controlled 50.0% of the (equivalized) income in 2011, whereas the poorest 20% only had a share of 3.4% (source for all US data that follow in this paragraph: US Bureau of the Census 2012, table A-3). The top 5% controlled 22.1% of the total income. The share of the upper 20% in total household income has historically constantly increased: it was 48.6% in 2000, 45.1% in 1990, 41.9% in 1980, 41.5% in 1970. In contrast, the total household income share of the lower 20% has decreased: 3.4% in 2011, 4.1% in 2000, 4.4% in 1990,

5.2% in 1980, 5.7% in 1970. The United States' Gini coefficient, which measures income inequality, was 0.463 in 2011, 0.442 in 2000, 0.406 in 1990, 0.367 in 1980 and 0.357 in 1970. These data are an indication that class inequality has been rising during the past decades and that the poor's income share has been decreasing precisely because the income of the wealthiest has been sharply rising. In the EU15 countries (those 15 countries that were members of the EU prior to May 1, 2004), the top 20% of households controlled 38.2% of the total income in 2011 and 37% in 2000 (source for all EU data that follow in this paragraph: Eurostat). In contrast, the lower 20% had an income share of just 7.1% in 2011 and 9% in 2000. The Gini coefficient increased from 0.3 in 2003 to 0.305 in 2010. These data show that class disparities are less deep in Europe than in the United States but that they nonetheless exist and are significant. The Occupy movement is reacting to the existence of the socio-economic inequality indicated by these data.

David Harvey identifies four specific mechanisms that characterize neo-liberal capitalism: financialization, the deliberate creation of crises, privatization and commodification, and state redistributions which favour capital at the expense of labour (Harvey 2007, 160–165; Harvey 2006, 44–50). The first and the second mechanism create individuals and states as debtors, the third and the fourth directly decrease the income of working people. All together these mechanisms redistribute money from the pockets of the working class to corporations and the rich. Occupy is situated in the context of neo-liberal capitalism, which forms its objective foundation.

Occupy Wall Street positions itself as class struggle against the 1%: "#ows is fighting back against the corrosive power of major banks and multinational corporations over the democratic process, and the role of Wall Street in creating an economic collapse that has caused the greatest recession in generations. The movement is inspired by popular uprisings in Egypt and Tunisia, and aims to fight back against the richest 1% of people that are writing the rules of an unfair global economy that is foreclosing on our future" (occupywallst.org/about/).

The *Declaration of the Occupation of New York City* (www.nycga.net/resources/documents/declaration) speaks out against "corporations, which place profit over people, self-interest over justice, and oppression over equality". In this declaration, the movement says that it is critical of the negative impacts of corporations on housing, bailouts, workplace inequality and discrimination, food supply, animal rights, unionization, higher education, workers' healthcare and wages, privacy protection, freedom of the press, nature, energy supply, medicine, the media and international relations. This shows that the Occupy movement stresses how capitalist interests interact with the social, cultural, political, ecological and technological realms of society and create negative effects on these realms.

Occupy London describes itself as a movement "against this injustice and to fight for a sustainable economy that puts people and the environment we live in before corporate profits" (occupylondon.org.uk/about). In its Initial Statement passed on October 26, 2011, Occupy London stresses that the current system is unsustainable, undemocratic and unjust and has negative impacts on citizens, democracy, health services, welfare, education, employment, peace and the planet (ibid.).

The analyses and demands presented on the websites of Occupy Wall Street and Occupy London go further than the original Adbusters text. They stress more issues of class and inequality and that capitalism has negative impacts on multiple realms. Just like the Global Justice Movement, the Occupy movement brings together demands and topics addressed traditionally by various new social movements, such as the student movement, the ecological movement, the anti-racist movement, the peace movement, the third world solidarity movement and others. It is a movement of movement and networked movement. What is specific about it is the emphasis on capitalism and class as a unifying topic and dimension. The Occupy movement stresses that contemporary societal problems take place in the context of capitalism and that corporate interests have negative impacts on multiple realms of society and need to be challenged. So the multitude of topics and demands is not seen in an isolated manner, but is rather unified and connected by the economic dimension of capitalism and class. Occupy is not a fragmented movement of movements but a topically unified movement of movements. Angela Davis (2011) points out in this contexts that many new social movements "have appealed to specific communities", that coalition-building was difficult and that the Occupy movement is "strikingly different" because it "imagines itself from the beginning as the broadest possible community of resistance—the 99%, as against the 1%". Class would be the unifying topic of this movement that transcends diversity. Paolo Gerbaudo (2012, 120) argues that Occupy's "intention to represent the majority"—as expressed in the slogan "We are the 99%", created by David Graeber—that is, its "majoritarian ambition", "constitutes precisely the difference between Occupy and the anti-globalisation movement".

Castells (2012, 194) argues with some caution that Occupy is a class struggle movement: "what is relatively new and meaningful is that there are indications that Occupy Wall Street has shaped the awareness of Americans on the reality of what I would dare to call class struggle". But he immediately limits the implications of this thought by saying that the movement is not anti-capitalist, it wants to reform capitalism: "The criticism is focused on financial capitalism and on its influence on government, not on capitalism as such. The movement does not embrace ideologies of the past. Its quest aims at eradicating evil in the present, while reinventing community for the future. Its fundamental achievement has been to rekindle hope that another life is possible" (ibid., 197). He seems to base this argument on a Fox News Poll survey from October 2011, in which a relative majority of 46% of the respondents said that it does not think that the Occupy Wall Street movement is anti-capitalist (ibid., 290). There is, however, a flaw in the applied logic: that the majority of a sample consisting of a selection of respondents from the general population answered this way does not mean that Occupy activists do not consider themselves anti-capitalist. Only surveys conducted among activists can give a clearer picture. Castells is drawing premature conclusions that more reflect his own political ideology than reality. Consequently, although he once mentions class struggle as an aspect of the Occupy movement, he overall rather neglects the economic dimension of contemporary movements, reduces them to political struggles for the reform of democracy and neglects the dimension of struggles against capitalism. As a conclusion in his books, Castells therefore desires a "love between social activism and political reformism" (ibid., 237). For Castells, these movements fit well into the Western liberal framework of democracy that only talks about democracy in politics, but never questions the actual existing dictatorship in the capitalist economy. He says that they want to "transform the state" (ibid., 227), are cultural movements with new values (231–232) and are movements for real democracy (124). By "real democracy" Castells means political-institutional reforms and not transformations of the economy. He does not see the entanglement of politics and the economy and consequently would not agree with Marx and Engels (1848) that communism is the "struggle for democracy".

A social movement can be working class according to (a) its social structure and (b) its goals. Some data about the social structure of the Occupy movement is available from the Occupy Research General Survey (http://occupyresearch. wikispaces.com/ N = 5074), which was mainly conducted in the United States. Of the respondents, 39% described themselves as working class or lower middle class, 29.3% as middle class, 10.9% as upper middle or upper class. This means that the relative majority considers itself to have a relatively lower social status. Also, 17.6% of the respondents were students, 31.6% full-time employees, 14.4% part-time employees, 14.8% self-employed, 3.4% full-time house workers, 1.2% seasonal workers, 7.6% underemployed, 8.6% unemployed and 5.3% disabled. The share of irregularly employed people (part-time workers, house workers, seasonal workers, underemployed, unemployed and disabled: 40.5%) in the survey is larger than the one of full-time employees (31.6%). They form the relative majority of the movement. Žižek's (2012) assumption that the Occupy movement is made up of a salaried bourgeoisie therefore does not have empirical grounds. Statistically, the middle class is defined as people who have a median income. In 2011, the median household income in the United States was US$50,054 (US Bureau of the Census 2012). The income in the lowest quintile was US$20,263 or less, the income in the second lowest quintile between US$20,263 and $38,520 (ibid.). In the Occupy survey, 25.7% had an income below US$20,000, 23.9% an income between US$20,000 and $39,999 and 9.7% an income between US$40,000 and $49,999. This means that 59.3% of the respondents (N = 3341) had a household income below the median income; that is, the survey indicates that almost two-thirds of the US Occupy movement are not middle class but belong to the lower income group. The self-perception of being middle class is often larger than the actual income distribution because the latter is not visible to many citizens. This circumstance seems to hold also for the Occupy movement. A full 70.9% of the respondents have a university degree. The data indicate that the US Occupy activists are highly educated and predominantly precarious workers with relatively low household incomes. They can therefore be described as precarious and proletarianized knowledge workers.

When participants were asked what the highest concern that motivates participation in the Occupy movement is, issues relating to capitalism were most prominent: (income) inequality (#1, #2; ranked in terms of the frequency of mentionings), corporations (#7), corporate personhood (#8), injustice (#9), social justice (#10), corporate greed (#11), anti-capitalism (#12), unemployment (#14), equality (#16), poverty (#19). This means that the answers given most frequently to the question of the main motivation for participating in the Occupy movement related to the criticism of socio-economic class relations, whereas classical left-liberal topics such as (government) corruption (#4, #18), democracy (#21) and freedom (#23) were much less prominent. This shows that the Occupy movement is much more a movement motivated by socialist interests that relate to class structures than a liberal movement motivated by concerns about individual liberties.

The data indicate that Occupy is a working-class movement in terms of both its social structure and its goals. This status of Occupy as new working-class movement can also be put into theoretical terms.

In a passage in the *Grundrisse,* Marx sees labour as communal or combined labour (Marx 1857/1858b, 470), as collective worker *(Gesamtarbeiter).* This idea was also taken up in *Capital, Volume 1,* where he defines the collective worker as "a collective labourer, i.e. a combination of workers" (Marx 1867c, 644), and argues that labour is productive if it is part of the combined labour force: "In order to work productively, it is no longer necessary for the individual himself to put his hand to the object; it is sufficient for him to be an organ of the collective labourer, and to perform any one of its subordinate functions" (ibid.). The collective worker is an "aggregate *worker*" whose "*combined activity* results materially in an *aggregate* product" (ibid., 1040). The "activity of this aggregate labour-power" is "the immediate production of surplus-value, the *immediate conversion of this latter into capital*" (ibid.). This means that in capitalism, the collective worker is a productive worker that creates value, surplus value and capital. The notion of the collective worker allows an interpretation of Marx that is not wage-labour-centric because the collective worker as combined workforce also contains all those activities that are unpaid but directly or indirectly serve capital's needs.

Inspired by Marx, Antonio Negri uses the term "social worker" for arguing that there is a broadening of the proletariat—"a new working class" that is "now extended throughout the entire span of production and reproduction" (Negri 1982/1988, 209). He here takes up Marx's idea of the collective worker that forms an aggregated and combined workforce, is heterogeneous and forms a whole of singularities that are necessary for creating profit. Negri (1971/1988) first developed this concept in a reading of Marx's "Fragment on Machines" in the *Grundrisse*. He argued that the main contradiction of capitalism is that money is the specific measure of value, while labour with the development of the productive forces acquires an increasingly social character and so questions value. The socialization of labour would have resulted in the "emergence of a massified and socialised working class" (ibid., 104). The notion of the socialized working class was later developed into the concept of the social worker (Negri 1982/1988), which emerged by a reorganization of capitalism that dissolved the mass worker characterized by Taylorism, Fordism, Keynesianism and the planner-state (ibid., 205). The social worker signifies "a growing awareness of the interconnection between productive labour and the labour of reproduction" (ibid., 209) and the emergence of "diffuse labour" (=outsourced labour, 214) and mobile labour (=labour flexibility, 218).

Hardt and Negri (2005) have turned the notion of the social worker into the concept of the multitude that produces the commons of nature and culture exploited by capital. Hence, exploitation today is "the expropriation of the common" (ibid., 150). The multitude or proletariat today are "all those who labour and produce under the rule of capital" (ibid., 106), "all those whose labour is directly or indirectly exploited by and subjected to capitalist norms of production and reproduction" (Hardt and Negri 2000, 52).

The whole of society, except capital, forms a body which produces the commons that are needed for survival. Some commons are given by nature (the environment, the human body), others are created by cooperative human activities (knowledge, communication, social relations, education, health care, e-culture). What has happened in neo-liberal capitalism is that the commons have been commodified, privatized and turned into monetary profit. The work of the collective worker of society has increasingly been economically exploited. The result was large-scale socio-economic inequality. Occupy is a movement that questions this reality. It is a movement of the collective worker, a collective working-class movement that questions the commodification of the commons it produces and demands reclaiming the commons. It is a new working-class movement because it claims collective control of the fruits of the collective work of society. The attempt to make use-values common property is precisely the purpose of a society of the commons.

12.3.4. What Is the Occupy Movement?

Post-Marxism sees universality as a totalitarian project (Laclau and Mouffe 1985, 188) and argues for the primacy of a plurality of political subjects that are at best loosely connected. Laclau and Mouffe (1985) speak in this context of "the plurality of diverse and frequently contradictory positions" (84), "decentred subject positions" (87), the "plurality of political spaces" (137), the "rejection of privileged points of rupture and the confluence of struggles into a unified political space" (152), or the "polysemic character of every antagonism" (170). Laclau and Mouffe have celebrated the rise of plural new social movements which overcome the unity of class politics that characterized the working class.

In this section, I have argued that the Occupy movement signifies a new stage in the development of social movements that is a kind of Hegelian sublation of social movements. In one sense, it is a return to politics that focus on class, capitalism and class struggle. Class is perceived as a unifying motive that puts 99% of the population against the dominant 1%. In terms of its political topics, Occupy is a new working-class movement. In terms of its structure, the relative majority of activists are precarious and proletarianized knowledge workers. Work is also an issue in the context of the commons: all humans create as collective worker the commons of nature, welfare, reproduction and culture. Neo-liberal capitalism has been a project for the commodification and dispossession of the commons, a project of the exploitation of the collective worker of society. Occupy reacts to this situation by demanding to reclaim the commons. It is therefore a collective working-class movement. But topics that have been characteristic of new social movements, such as racism, gender, war, nature, identity and the human body, have not been eliminated by Occupy, but rather unified and lifted to a new level. They continue to exist in this movement, not separated in different movements, as typical for the plural and therefore fragmented politics of new social movements, but in one movement that sees how different dimensions of stratification and struggle are interdependent and unified by the articulation with class and capitalism. A major difference between new social movements and Occupy is that the latter is a revolutionary movement aimed at creating a new society that opens up new spaces and new times. The occupation of urban spaces in the form of encampments signifies the political demand to reclaim the commons.

Slavoj Žižek has in my opinion correctly noted that postmodernism and post-Marxism have, by assuming an "irreducible plurality of struggles", accepted "capitalism as 'the only game in town'" and have renounced "any real attempt to overcome the existing capitalist liberal regime" (Butler, Laclau and Žižek 2000, 95). Subordinating or equalizing the category of class to other antagonistic categories (gender, ethnicity, age, capabilities, etc.) poses the danger of burying the project and the demand to establish participatory alternatives to the capitalist totality. The Occupy movement shows that all non-class antagonisms are articulated with class, whereas not all non-class antagonisms are articulated with each other, which means that all antagonisms of contemporary society have class aspects and are conditioned by class. Class is the antagonism that binds all other antagonisms together; it prefigures, conditions, enables and constrains, and exerts pressure on possibilities for other antagonisms. At the same time, non-class antagonisms influence the class antagonism so that complex dynamic relationships are present. If class is the super-antagonism of capitalism that does not determine or overdetermine but conditions other antagonisms, then it is important to give specific attention to this category.

Within a global system of capitalism that Hardt and Negri (2000) have termed the empire, capital exploits the common that is created by the multitude. Although Hardt and Negri see Hegelian dialectics as deterministic and teleological (ibid., 51) and therefore base their approach explicitly on Spinoza's immanence rather than on Hegel's dialectics, Hegelian dialectics has shaped Hardt's and Negri's own work behind their backs. Žižek has in another context also observed the "'wild' [. . .] use of Hegelian categories" by Negri, "which so blatantly contradicts his professed anti-Hegelianism" (Žižek 2008, 353). Hardt's and Negri's concepts/books of the multitude (Hardt and Negri 2005), the empire (Hardt and Negri 2000) and the commonwealth (Hardt and Negri 2009) can be logically organized in a dialectical triad: (1) The multitude produces the commons by immaterial labour. The commons are exploited by capital that is organized as a (2) global empire. The multitude and capital form a contradiction: capital dominates and exploits the multitude. They stand in a negative relation. Capital requires the multitude because it produces the commons and at the same time excludes it. The multitude does not similarly relate to capital. Unfortunately Hardt and Negri create the impression that the multitude always and automatically struggles against capital, so for them the effect from multitude on empire is not a mere potential but a deterministic necessity. And (3),Commonwealth, a new self-managed form of society that is based on the common wealth created by immaterial labour, is the vision of the negation of the negative relation of capital and empire.

The Occupy movement is situated in the dialectical triangle of capitalism, collective worker and the commonwealth: Humans create the commons of society as collective worker. They form a contemporary working class that includes all those who create and recreate the commons (i.e. all humans). The commons have become increasingly commodified and the collective worker exploited by capital. There is a contradiction of capitalism and the collective worker. Occupy signifies the subjectification of this objective contradiction: It is a collective insight and response of the working class to its exploitation, the form of political organization that questions the underlying class relation and struggles for a society in which humans control the economy and society in common. They struggle as and for a project for the commons.

The importance of the Occupy movement is that it shows the topicality of capitalism, exploitation and class and that it has put the need for a discussion about a commons-based society as an alternative to capitalism on the agenda.

12.4. Occupy, Digital Work and Working-Class Social Media

This sections deals with the research question, Which online social media does the Occupy movement use? This requires an understanding of the role of media in social movements and what is social about social media. First, section 12.4.1 presents a brief introduction to the analysis and conceptualization of the role of the Internet and social media in social movements. Then, a literature review shows how theorists have conceptualized the role of social media in the Occupy movement (section 12.4.2). Section 12.4.3 outlines a theoretical classification of Occupy's social media use.

12.4.1. Social Movements, the Internet and Social Media

The media are a source of political information and a tool for political communication. They are one mechanism that civil society needs for becoming and acting politically, that is, for making political demands. Politics are today heavily mediated (Bennett and Entman 2001). Although the degree of influence of the Internet on social movements is contested, a general observation is that it has potentials that can help coordinating protests (Della Porta and Diani 2006, 132–133, 155–156). For analysing social movements' use of the Internet for information, communication and coordination purposes in political mobilizations and protests, terms like "cyberprotest" (Donk et al. 2004) and "cyberactivism" (McCaughey and Ayers 2003) have been coined. Bennett (2003, 2005) argues that the Internet is a social technology that enables the combination of online and offline relationship building, the globalization of social movements and the formation of non-hierarchical, distributed, flexible protest networks. Rucht (2004) stresses that the Internet has a potential to support counter-public spheres, but it cannot replace personal contacts of activists.

Studies of social movements and social media have, for example, focused on the use of social media in the environmental movement (Castells 2009), the Global Justice Movement (ibid., Kavada 2012), anti-war activism and war propaganda (Christensen 2008; Gillan, Pickerill and Webster 2008), feminism (Hartcourt 2011), blog politics (Dean 2010, Kahn and Kellner 2004), YouTube activism (Thorson et al. 2010; Zoonen, Vis and Mihelj 2010), the role of Twitter and Facebook in the Arab Spring (Aouragh 2012, Aouragh and Alexander 2011, Bratich 2011, Lotan et al. 2011, Mansour 2012, Nanabhay and Farmanfarmaian 2011, Sayed 2011, Khamis and Vaughn 2011), the Occupy movement (Juris 2012), and the emergence of a private sphere and virtual sphere 2.0 for politics (Papacharissi 2009, 2010).

Some empirical studies of the role of social media in the Occupy movement have been published. A few examples can be mentioned. The discussion is necessarily incomplete because of spatial constraints. Sasha Costanza-Chock (2012, 379) reports some results from the Occupy Research General Survey, in which 77.3% of the activists reported that they had posted about Occupy on social media (Facebook, Twitter or other), 75.7% said they had had a face-to-face discussion about Occupy, 19.1% said they had written a blog post about Occupy and 8.2% answered that they had made a video about Occupy (N = 4877). Gaby and Caren (2012, 372) analysed 100 posts that attracted many new users to Facebook Occupy groups. Many of these postings featured personal narratives and in roughly 60% "pictures and videos were the medium for these messages". Based on participant observation at Occupy Philadelphia, Alice Mattoni (2012) argues that social media form part of a rich repertoire of protest communication in the Occupy movement.

Paolo Gerbaudo (2012) interviewed 80 activists in the United States, Egypt, Spain, the United Kingdom, Tunisia and Greece about their use of social media in protests. He found that although contemporary social movements as well as analysts (such as Manuel Castells, Jeffrey Juris, Michael Hardt and Antonio Negri) claim that they are leaderless networks, there are soft leaders who make use of social media for choreographing protests and "constructing a *choreography of assembly*" (ibid., 139): "a handful of people control most of the communication flow" (135). The choreography of assembly means "the use of social media in directing people towards specific protest events, in providing participants with suggestions and instructions about how to act, and in the construction of an emotional narration to sustain their coming together in public space" (ibid., 12).

The movements' spontaneity would be organized "precisely because it is a highly mediated one [movement]" (ibid., 164). The ethical problem would not be this movement choreography, but would be the denial that there are leaders because this would result in unaccountability. Facebook "has been employed as something akin to a recruitment and training ground, to facilitate the emotional condensation and common identification of a largely un-politicised middle-class youth. Twitter, in contrast, has been mainly used as a vehicle for 'live' internal co-ordination within the activist elite, besides its many largely 'external' uses, including as a means for citizen journalists to document police brutality" (ibid., 135). "Facebook was used by movement leaders, or to use a more neutral term 'organisers' or 'activists' to mobilise people from the outside of the space of participation, while Twitter was important for purposes of internal organisation" (ibid., 145). In the Global Justice Movement, Indymedia would have had the role that Facebook now has in the Occupy movement (external mobilization), and mailing lists the role that Twitter has today (internal organization and coordination) (ibid., 150). Based on his interviews, Gerbaudo argues that in the Occupy Wall Street movement, Twitter was a tactical tool and "the key Twitter tactical accounts were managed by a core group of movement organisers, composed of around 20 people. These people also tended to be highly involved in ground operations, in the General Assembly, and in the different commissions. During the occupation in Zuccotti Park this core group used an office space made available by the New York Teachers Union" as a kind of headquarter (ibid., 129). Gerbaudo challenges assumptions such as the one by Hardt and Negri (2012, chapter 2) that social media would be good for the "decentralized multitude of singularities [. . .] because they correspond to their organizational form". Hardt and Negri (2012, "Next: Event of the Commoner") argue that the contemporary movements "are powerful not despite their lack of leaders but because of it. They are organised horizontally as multitudes, and their insistence on democracy at all levels is more than a virtue but a key to their power". Their power would be that they burn down the "churches of the Left".

The occupations, protests and revolutions of 2011 have received a lot of public attention. Therefore also political theorists have tried to understand the causes of these collective political actions and have published on this issue. One question that arises is what theoretical positions we can discern concerning the question what role social media have in the Occupy movement.

12.4.2. The Occupy Movement and Social Media

Four common positions on the role of social media in the Occupy movement can be identified. These four positions represent four logical possibilities of connecting technology and society (technology as the determining factor, society as the determining factor, two independent factors and a mutual and contradictory relationship).

12.4.2.1. Position 1—Technological Determinism: The Occupy Movement (and Other Rebellions) Are Internet Rebellions

Manuel Castells (2012, 2) argues that we live in a network society and that therefore "movements spread by contagion in a world networked by the wireless Internet". Revolutions would be connected to economic, political, military, ideological and cultural contradictions of power (ibid., 79; see also p. 12), but they could only form if there are the emotions of hope and outrage and these emotions are communicated to others on a large scale (ibid., 14). A "condition for individual experiences to link up and form a movement is the existence of a communication process that propagates the events and the emotions attached to it. [. . .] In our time, multimodal digital networks of horizontal communication are the fastest and most autonomous, interactive, reprogrammable and self-expanding means of communication in history. [. . .] [T]he networked social movements of the digital age represent a new species of social movement" (ibid., 15). Castells is certainly correct in stressing that for a protest movement or revolution to emerge there need to be objective conditions (problems in society) and subjective insight into these conditions—the perception of a mass of people that the objective conditions are unbearable, that society therefore needs to be changed by them and that this requires their collective political action (Fuchs 2006). This is precisely what Marx stressed when saying that revolutions require a material basis (the contradictions of the economy, politics, ideology and nature that shape an antagonistic society), but that the idea of revolution can only be realized if the contradictions of reality become subjective insights that motivate practices:

"For revolutions require a passive element, a material basis. Theory is fulfilled in a people only insofar as it is the fulfilment of the needs of that people. [. . .] Will the theoretical needs be immediate practical needs? It is not enough for thought to strive for realization, reality must itself strive towards thought" (Marx 1843). Revolution is therefore always a change of society and a change of the human self: "The coincidence of the changing of circumstances and of human activity or self-change can be conceived and rationally understood only as revolutionary practice" (Marx 1845).

The question of which role the Internet and social media play or do not play in spreading outrage and hope is more an empirical question. There is a potential for contagion effects that communicate and intensify emotions of discontent and the desire for collective action, but the Internet certainly is not the only means for communicating the need for protest. Castells says that the Occupy movement "was born on the Internet, diffused by the Internet, and maintained its presence on the Internet" and that its "material form of existence was the *occupation of public space*" (Castells 2012, 168). Social "networks on the Internet allowed the experience to be communicated and amplified, bringing the entire world into the movement" (ibid., 169).

Castells puts a very strong emphasis on the mobilization capacities of the Internet. His argument implies that in the studied cases, Internet communication created street protests, which means that without the Internet there would have been no street protests. In the concluding chapter, Castells generalizes for all analysed movements: "The networked social movements of our time are largely based on the Internet, a necessary though not sufficient component of their collective action. The digital social networks based on the Internet and on wireless platforms are decisive tools for mobilizing, for organizing, for deliberating, for coordinating and for deciding" (ibid., 229).

Jeffrey Juris (2012), a former PhD student of Castells, conducted participant observation at Occupy Boston. He says that whereas the Global Justice Movement primarily used mailing lists and was based on a logic of networking, the Occupy movement is based on a logic of aggregation, in which social media result in "the viral flow of information and subsequent aggregations of large numbers of individuals in concrete physical spaces" (ibid., 266). Individuals would "blast out vast amounts of information", make use of "ego-centered networks" because "the use of Twitter and Facebook [. . .] tends to generate 'crowds of individuals'" (ibid., 267). Like Castells, Juris assumes that social media "generate" protests. He claims that "social media such as Facebook, YouTube, and Twitter became the primary means of communication within #Occupy" (ibid., 266), without empirically validating this claim.

Formulations such as the ones that the Internet resulted in the emergence of movements, that movements were born on the Internet or that movements are based on the Internet convey a logic that is based on overt technological determinism: technology is conceived as an actor that results in certain phenomena with societal characteristics. Movements are not created by the Internet, but from the antagonistic economic, political and ideological structures of society. The Internet is a techno-social system consisting of social networks that make use of a global network of computer networks. It is embedded into the antagonisms of contemporary society and therefore has no inbuilt effects or determinations. Collective social action that makes use of the Internet can have relatively little effect or dampen or intensify existing trends. The actual implications depend on contexts, power relations, mobilization capacities, strategies and tactics as well as the complex and undetermined outcomes of struggles. Castells' model is simplistic: social media results in revolutions and rebellions. He shares the widespread ideological talk about "Twitter revolutions" and "Facebook rebellions" that first became popular with the conservative blogger Andrew Sullivan's claim that the "revolution will be twittered" in the context of the 2009 Iran protests: "You cannot stop people any longer. You cannot control them any longer. They can bypass your established media; they can broadcast to one another; they can organize as never before. It's increasingly clear that Ahmadinejad and the old guard mullahs were caught off-guard by this technology and how it helped galvanize the opposition movement in the last few weeks" (Sullivan 2009).

Castells argues that "the more the movement is able to convey its message over the communication networks, the more citizen consciousness rises, and the more the public sphere of communication becomes a contested terrain" (Castells 2012, 237). He here assumes a linear connection between the technical availability of political information, the change of collective consciousness, and the rise of political protests in an indirect proportional manner. But society's reality is more complex than this simple behaviouristic model (Internet as stimulus, critical consciousness and political action as response) suggests. Information can be online without reaching many citizens, for example, because they do not know of its existence, because the information is structurally kept invisible, because they are not interested in it or do not find it meaningful. The Internet and media in general can also be shut down or censored and those who run them imprisoned, tortured or killed. These are not infrequent practices on the part of states in order to contain protest movements. Castells also underestimates the actual or potential role that ideologies can play in heteronomous societies: the rise of critical consciousness can be forestalled if powerful groups manage to convince the mass of people that the problems in society are different from their actual causes. Historically, ideology has mainly achieved this aim by constructing scapegoats, such as the Jew, the black person, the immigrant, the socialist or the communist, who are blamed for problems in society. Even if alternative information that challenges ideologies is available on media networks, there is no guarantee that ideology is challenged by citizens to a large extent. It is possible to break widespread beliefs in ideologies if struggles not only take on material form, but are also struggles for alternative ideas that become material forces.

12.4.2.2. Position 2—Social Constructivism: We Have Been Witnessing Social Rebellions and Social Revolutions, Where Social Media Have Had Minor Importance; Social Media Are No Relevant Factor in Rebellions

In his book *The Year of Dreaming Dangerously,* Slavoj Žižek (2012) gives an account of the revolutions and social movements that emerged in 2011. Žižek rather focuses on describing contemporary movements' relationship to capitalism. He sees the Occupy movement as a revolt of the "salaried bourgeoisie" (ibid., 12) that is discontent with "capitalism as a system" and with the reduction of democracy to representation (ibid., 87). Alain Badiou (2012) argues that the Occupy movement and other contemporary movements (such as the revolutionary Arab Spring movements in Egypt and Spain) are movements for the commons. For Noam Chomsky (2012), Occupy is a reaction to the "tremendous concentration of wealth" that also yields "concentration of political power" (ibid., 28–29). David Harvey (2012) argues that Occupy is an urban movement that wants to reclaim the urban commons.

For Žižek (2012), Badiou (2012), Chomsky (2012) and Harvey (2012), Occupy and other contemporary rebellions are street protest movements. They consequently do not discuss or mention "social media" such as Facebook, Twitter or the multiple platforms and tools that Occupy has created and uses (such as e.g. TheGlobalSquare, Occupii, Riseup, etc.). Žižek (2012) does not at all mention media, and Badiou (2012, 23) in one sentence says that riots and revolutions have always made use of media and communication: "Moreover, drums, fires, inflammatory leaflets, running through the back streets, circulating words, ringing bells—for centuries these have served their purpose in people suddenly assembling somewhere, just like sheep-like electronics does today". Chomsky (2012, 46) argues that the only way for mobilizing the public is going "out to wherever people are—churches, clubs, schools, unions". He does not consider that a significant share of people are for a significant share of daytime on the Internet and does not discuss if online sociality positively or negatively influences activism. The Arab Spring revolutions and the Occupy movement show for David Harvey (2012, 162) that "it is bodies on the street and in the squares, not the babble of sentiments on Twitter or Facebook, that really matter".

Jodi Dean (2012) gives more attention to the role of social media. She argues that in communicative capitalism, social media would have displaced politics and created the illusion that pointing and clicking are politics, whereas they would in reality be a form of post-politics that is based on "communication without communicability" (ibid., 127). In contrast, the Occupy movement would be "undertaking and supporting actions in the street" (ibid., 216) and would choose inconvenience (217). Thereby it would reverse the post-political ideology of social media and substitute it with real politics. Occupy would have "replaced the ease of MoveOn-style 'clicktivism' with the demanding and time-consuming practice of supporting an occupation" (ibid., 233). Jodi Dean takes the argument that contemporary rebellions are social rebellions and not social media rebellions into a specific direction: She argues that social media are part of an ideology that sees their use as politics, but in reality it is only harmless pseudo-politics, and that the Occupy movement now deconstructs this ideology and replaces it with real politics on the streets.

12.4.2.3. Position 3—Dualism: Social Media Have Been an Important Tool of the Occupy Movement; There Are Technological and Societal Causes of the Movement

The journalist Paul Mason says that the new rebellions, including the Occupy movement, have been "caused by the near collapse of free-market capitalism combined with an upswing in technical innovation, a surge in desire for individual freedom and a change in human consciousness about what freedom means" (Mason 2012, 3). Occupy London has been connected to the UK Uncut protests against increases of university fees, the cut of the Education Maintenance Allowance and other cuts in areas such as housing benefits, disability allowance and child care. The movement, according to Mason, involves students, youth facing poverty and precariousness, and unions. "[I]nstant collaboration" would have extended "Facebook groups and wikis [. . .] into the public squares of major cities" (ibid., 144).

Sam Halvorsen (2012, 431) argues that Occupy is "grounded in place" and uses "online technologies" for facilitating "decentralised communication".

As mentioned earlier, Hardt and Negri (2012, "Opening") argue that there are four causes of contemporary uprisings: finance capitalism's creation of the indebted, IT's creation of the mediatized, the security regime's creation of the securitized, and the corrupt state's creation of the represented (ibid., chapter 1). They see social media as one of four independent causes of the emergence of the Occupy movement and other contemporary rebellions and argue that not only did both online media and face-to-face communication play a role in the Occupy movements, but that the latter were more important: "Facebook, Twitter, the Internet, and other kinds of communications mechanism are useful, but nothing can replace the being together of bodies and the corporeal communication that is the basis of collective political intelligence and action. In all the occupations [. . .], the participants experienced the power of creating new political affects through being together" (ibid.). Activists would have to become "unmediatized" by engaging in "[r]eal communication" that require "an encampment" understood as collective self-learning experience in occupations that creates a new truth by "discussion, conflict, and consensus in assemblies" (ibid., chapter 2).

Hardt and Negri (2012, chapter 3) argue that the regulation and privatization of social networks and the criminalization of users need to be resisted. They say that "[l]iberated network were, in fact, a primary organisational tool in the Spanish encampments as they had been earlier in the countries on the southern coast of the Mediterranean and as they would be later in the British riots and the Occupy movements. [. . .] The constituent power of the common is thus closely interwoven with the themes of constituent power—adopting new media (cellular technologies, Twitter, Facebook, and more generally the Internet) as vehicles of experimentation with democratic and multitudinary governance". Hardt and Negri seem to see mobile phone networks and online social media as inherently democratic and common because of their networked character that enables communication. They forget that mobile phone networks, Twitter and Facebook are not controlled, operated and managed in common, but are rather private property of corporations that are part of the 1% and primarily aim at accumulating money capital. It is difficult to speak of "liberated networks" if the technologies of these networks are private instead of common property. This circumstance also puts the activists at risks: there are multiple stories about how the mobile phone and Internet communication of activists in Bahrain, Egypt, Iran, Libya or Syria was monitored with the help of surveillance technologies produced and sold by Western companies (Fuchs 2012c). As a consequence, state authorities interrogated, tortured, maltreated and killed activists. Capitalist communications companies are not natural allies of movements that struggle for the commons because they see the commons of communications in an instrumental way oriented on profit imperatives and particularistic monetary interests. For communications to become a true realm of the commons, they need to be controlled by the people, not mediated by corporations. Hardt and Negri (2012, chapter 3) are impressed by "techniques for expression and decision making" that contemporary movements use, "such as shaking your hands in the air or following on Twitter", forgetting that the latter technique serves not only internal group purposes, but also the capital interests of Twitter as well as the police's interest in monitoring what movements are doing. The autonomous construction of the commons is also in need of the construction of communications commons that overcome the media's and the Internet's capitalist dimension.

12.4.2.4. Position 4—Social Media and Contradictions: A Dialectical View

A theoretical model I suggest as an alternative to societal holism that ignores media and technology, technological reductionism that ignores society and dualism that ignores causality is to think about the relationship of rebellions and (social) media as dialectical: in the form of contradictions. Figure 12.4 shows a dialectical model of revolts and the media.

Protests have an objective foundation that is grounded in the contradictions of society, that is, forms of domination which cause problems that are economic, political and cultural in nature. Societal problems can result in (economic, political,

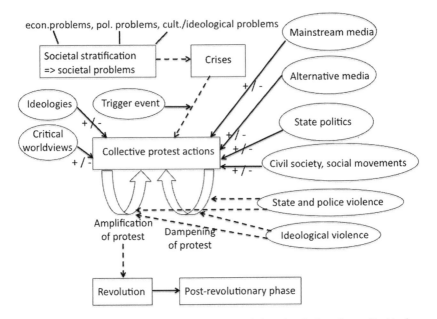

FIGURE 12.4 A model of protests and revolutions and the role of crises, the media, ideology and politics

cultural/ideological) crises[6] if they are temporally persistent and cannot be easily overcome. Crises do not automatically result in protests but are an objective and necessary, although not a sufficient condition of protest. If crisis dimensions converge and interact, then we can speak of a societal crisis. Protests require a mass of people's perception that there are societal problems, that these problems are unbearable and a scandal, and that something needs to be changed. Often actual protests and movements are triggered and continuously intensified by certain events (such as the arrest of Rosa Parks in the US civil rights movement, the public suicide of Mohamed Bouazizi in the 2011 Tunisian revolution, the killing of Khaled Mohamed Saeed by the police in the 2011 Egyptian revolution, the pepper-spraying of activists by NYPD officer Anthony Bologna and the mass arrest of Occupy activists on Brooklyn Bridge in the Occupy Wall Street movement).

It is precisely here that Castells' (2012) focus on the emotions of outrage and hope plays a role—in the potential transition from crises to protests. Subjective perceptions and emotions are, however, not the only factor because they are conditioned and influenced by politics, the media and culture/ideology. The way state politics, mainstream media and ideology on the one hand and oppositional politics/social movements, alternative media and alternative worldviews on the other hand connect to human subjects influences the conditions of protests. They all can have either amplifying or dampening effects on protests. So for example, racist media coverage can advance racist stereotypes and/or the insight that the media and contemporary society are racist in themselves. The media—social media, the Internet and all other media—are contradictory because we live in a society of contradictions. As a consequence, their effects are actually contradictory: they can dampen/forestall or amplify/advance protest or have not much effect at all.

Also different media (e.g. alternative media and commercial media) stand in a contradictory relation and power struggle with each other. And the media are not the only factors that influence the conditions of protest—they stand in contradictory relations with politics and ideology/culture, which also influence the conditions of protest. So whether protest emerges or not is shaped by multiple factors so complex that it cannot be calculated or forecast if protest will emerge as result of a certain crisis or not. Once protests have emerged, media, politics and culture continue to have permanent contradictory influences on them and it is undetermined if these factors have rather neutral, amplifying or dampening effects on protest. Protests in antagonistic societies call forth policing and police action, so the state reacts to social movements with its organized form of violence. State violence against protests and ideological violence against movements (in the forms of delegitimatizing attacks by the media, politicians and others) can again have amplifying, dampening or insignificant effects on protests.

If there is a protest amplification spiral, protest may grow to larger and larger dimensions, which can eventually, but not necessarily, result in a revolution—a breakdown and fundamental reconstitution/renewal of the economy, politics and worldviews caused by an overthrow of society by a social movement that puts the revolutionary forces under the power and control of the major economic, political and moral structures (see Goodwin 2001, 9). Every revolution results in a post-revolutionary phase, in which the reconstruction and renewal of society begins and the legacy of conflict and the old society can pose challenges.

Social media in a contradictory society (made up of class conflicts and other conflicts between dominant and dominated groups) are likely to have a contradictory character: they do not necessarily and automatically support/amplify or dampen/limit rebellions, but rather pose contradictory potentials that stand in contradiction to influences by the state, ideology and capitalism.

12.4.3. A Theoretical Classification of Social Media Use in the Occupy Movement

In the Occupy Research General Survey (http://www.occupyresearch.wikspaces. com/), 74.3% of the respondents indicated that they posted about Occupy on Facebook, Twitter or other social media; 18.3% said that they wrote a blog post about Occupy, 7.9% that they made a video about it; and 72.7% had a face-to-face discussion about Occupy.

TABLE 12.3 Share of survey respondents who used various media for obtaining news about Occupy during a period of one month

Medium	Usage
Word of mouth	76.1%
Facebook	73.2%
Occupy websites	71.2%
e-mail	66.6%
YouTube	62.1%
National or international newspapers	58.7%
Local newspapers	55.3%
Blogs	55.2%
Livestreaming video site	53.6%
Discussions at Occupy camps	46.9%
National or international TV	46.3%
National or international radio	45.1%
Local radio	43.2%
Local TV	38.9%
Twitter	35.0%
Tumblr	19.1%
Chat rooms, Internet relay chat (IRC)	15.7%

Source: Occupy Research General Survey

The following table shows to which degree respondents used certain sources at least once during a period of one month for obtaining news about Occupy. The results show that the Occupy movement makes use of various forms of communication: face-to-face communication, the Internet and traditional mass media. Word of mouth is the most frequently used means for obtaining news about Occupy. Social media and the Internet are more popular news sources for Occupy activists than newspapers, TV and radio. Commercial platforms (especially Facebook and YouTube) are more used as news sources than independent social movement media (Occupy websites, livestreams etc.).

An important theoretical question is how to best classify social movements' media use. For doing so, a theory of information is needed. One can distinguish three basic notions of sociality (Durkheim's social facts, Weber's social actions/relations, Marx's and Ferdinand Tönnies' notions of cooperation) that can be integrated into a model of human social activity and applied to "social media" (Fuchs 2010d). It is based on the assumption that knowledge is a threefold dynamic process of cognition, communication and cooperation (Hofkirchner 2010, Fuchs and Hofkirchner 2005). Cognition is the necessary prerequisite for communication and the precondition for the emergence of cooperation. Or in other words: in order to cooperate you need to communicate and in order to communicate

TABLE 12.4 A classification of the Occupy movement's social media use

	Commercial platforms	*Non-commercial platforms*
Cognition	occupywallstreet page on the social news service reddit (http://www.reddit.com/r/occupywallstreet/) Tumblr blog We are the 99 percent (http://wearethe99percent.tumblr.com/)	Live video streams (http://occupystreams.org); http://occupywallst.org: blog-based news, protest map, how to occupy guide; http://occupylondon.org.uk: blog-based news, live video streams, podcasts (Occupy Radio), newspapers (e.g. Occupied Times, Occupied Wall Street Journal), news services (e.g. Occupy News Network, occupy.com, Occupied Stories), event calendar; live video streams on http://occupii.org/; map-based directory of occupations, map of events, Occupy classifieds, directory of Occupy campaigns on http://www.occupy.net/
Communication	Twitter (e.g. @OccupyWallSt, @OccupyLondon, #OccupyWallstreet, #OWS, #OccupyLSX, #OccupyLondon, #olsx)	Chat (http://occupystreams.org); chat and discussion forum (http://occupywallst.org/), Riseup (http://www.riseup.net; chat, e-mail, mailing lists); InterOccupy teleconferences (http://interoccupy.net), OccupyTalk voice chat (www.occupytalk.org)
Cooperation	Facebook (e.g. Occupy Together: https://www.facebook.com/OccupyWallSt, Occupy the London Stock Exchange: www.facebook.com/occupylondon), Facebook app Occupy Network (http://www.occupynetwork.com/) Occupy Together Meetup (http://www.meetup.com/occupytogether/)	SNS TheGlobalSquare, SNS Occupii (http://occupii.org/), SNS N-1 (https://n-1.cc), SNS Diaspora★ (https://joindiaspora.com/), Occupy wiki (http://wiki.occupy.net), Occupy Pads (http://notes.occupy.net/)

you need to cognize. Cognition involves the knowledge processes of a single individual. These processes are social in the Durkheimian sense of social facts because the existence of humans in society and therefore social relations shape human knowledge (Fuchs 2010d). Humans can only exist by entering social relations with other humans. They exchange symbols in these relations—they communicate. This level corresponds to Weber's notion of social relations (ibid.). A human being externalizes parts of its knowledge in every social relation. As a result, this knowledge influences others, who change part of their knowledge structures and as response externalize parts of their own knowledge, which results in the differentiation of the first individual's knowledge. A certain number of communications is not just sporadic but continuous over time and space. In such cases, there is the potential that communication results in cooperation, the shared production of new qualities, new social systems or new communities with feelings of belonging together. This is the level of cooperative labour and community. It is based on Marx's concept of cooperative labour and Tönnies' notion of community (ibid.).

Information (cognition), communication and cooperation are three nested and integrated modes of sociality. Every medium can be social in one or more of these senses. All media are information technologies. They provide information to humans. This information enters into the human realm of knowledge as social facts that shape thinking. Information media are, for example, books, newspapers, journals, posters, leaflets, films, television, radio, CDs and DVDs. Some media are also media of communication—they enable the recursive exchange of information between humans in social relations. Examples are letters in love relations, the telegraph and the telephone.

Networked computer technologies are technologies that enable cognition, communication and cooperation. The classical notion of this medium was confined to the social activities of cognition and communication, whereas the classical notion of technology was confined to the area of labour and production with the help of machines (such as the conveyor belt). The rise of computer technology and computer networks (such as the Internet) has enabled the convergence of media and machines—the computer supports cognition, communication and cooperative labour (production); it is a classical medium and a classical machine at the same time. Furthermore, it has enabled the convergence of production, distribution (communication) and consumption of information—you use only one tool, the networked computer, for these three processes. In contrast to other media (like the press, broadcasting, the telegraph, the telephone), computer networks are not only media of information and communication, but also enable the cooperative production of information. Social movement media can be classified according to the level of information they make use of. This allows distinguishing between cognitive, communicative and cooperative "cyberprotest" (Fuchs 2008, section 8.5).

The Occupy movement makes use of all three dimensions of cyberprotest. It makes use of both existing commercial media (reddit, Twitter, Facebook, Meetup) and alternative, non-commercial, non-profit media (e.g. TheGlobalSquare, Occupii, Riseup, Diaspora*, N-1). The following table gives an overview classification of online media that Occupy Wall Street and Occupy London link to on their websites.

Occupy Wall Street's website, occupywallst.org, features news in blog format that can be commented on; a collection of live video streams (occupystreams. org) from different countries and regions (Occupy Streams) that are each accompanied by a live chat; a map with links to ongoing occupations; movement media, social media tools, documents, documentaries and other resources; a how-to-occupy guide explaining different movement strategies and practices in multiple languages; a discussion forum; a chat; a global map locating ongoing occupations; a link to the movement's Twitter account, @OccupyWallSt (around 173,000 followers on December 2, 2012), that suggests use of the two hashtags #OccupyWallstreet and #OWS; a link to the page "occupywallstreet" on the social news service reddit; and a link to the Facebook page Occupy Together (www .facebook.com/OccupyWallSt, 412,000 likes on December 2, 2012).

Occupy London's site, occupylondon.org.uk, includes a link to Occupy London's Twitter account, @OccupyLondon (around 36,500 followers on December 2, 2012), a link to the Facebook page Occupy the London Stock Exchange (www .facebook.com/occupylondon, around 45,000 likes on December 2, 2012), an event calendar with the possibility to submit new events, the possibility to submit proposals and raise issues for discussion at the General Assembly, a blog with news postings on which one can comment, a directory of registered users who can connect to each other, links to several live video streams, podcasts of Occupy Radio, the *Occupied Times* (which is a monthly newspaper of the movement inviting contributions that can be submitted online), a link to the Occupy News Network, images and videos, and a directory of various working groups (such as Website Development, Finance, Economics, Internal Communication, Corporations, Press, the Occupied Times, etc.).

There are three dimensions of websites such as Occupy Wall Street and Occupy London and social movement's online media use in general. First, there is the *cognitive dimension* of Occupy's social media use. This includes, for example, online news, blogs, news, images, videos, live video streams, radio streams and podcasts, occupation map, guides, Facebook pages, reddit news, event calendar and the newspaper *Occupied Times*. InterOccupy (interoccupy.net) is a platform where teleconference calls are scheduled and organized that allows activists to discuss and plan protests actions and campaigns. The Occupy.Network (www .occupy.net/) provides a map-based directory of occupations, a map of events, Occupy classifieds, a directory of Occupy campaigns and links to the collaboration tools Occupy Wiki (wiki.occupy.net) and Occupy Notes (notes.occupy.net). The cognitive dimension of Occupy media also includes online newspapers (such as the *Occupied Times,* http://theoccupiedtimes.org/, and the *Occupied Wall Street Journal*) and news services such as the Occupy News Network, Occupied Stories and Occupy.com.

The Occupy News Network (occupynetwork.co.uk) features text-based news, the possibility for online article submission and four live video streams (ONN, OccupyLSX, Global Revolution TV and Timcast) that are partly accompanied by live chats. It describes itself as a "repository for information, news and commentary on the global Occupy movement and counterparts in the worldwide revolution such as the Indignados, Anonymous and the Arab Spring. [. . .] ONN keeps you abreast of developments in the global revolution. Here you can watch livestreams of Occupy protests as they unfold or access archive footage of previous actions. We operate a Criminal Investigations Unit to expose police brutality and abuse of the law; you are invited to upload videos of police brutality and send in your witness statements; our media is our most powerful defence against political repression. We present articles and commentary related to Occupy and the global revolution and we work to hold mainstream media to account by exposing lies and bias" (occupynetwork. co.uk/onn/about-us-2).

Occupied Stories (occupiedstories.com) is another Occupy news service. It describes itself as a "story-sharing platform that recognises the mainstream media's claim to fairness and objectivity as both false and unrealistic—no story is objective, but a point of view. [. . .] Our mission is to encourage critical reflection over blind acceptance and amplify the voices from the front-lines of the occupy movement" (occupiedstories.com/about). Also Occupy.com is a news service: It is "a new media channel that will amplify the voices of Occupy. We use media to call for social, economic and environmental justice. We seek to inspire resistance, engagement and the creation of the new world we imagine". It is also "an open invitation to creators of every stripe: journalists, musicians, photographers, painters, filmmakers, poets, game developers, cartoonists, podcasters—every genre, form and style. We're striving to become an open platform, where everyone can post and everyone can curate" (www.occupy.com/about).

Occupy News Network, Occupied Stories and Occupy.com share the characteristics of being citizens' media, allowing open submission of content, questioning mainstream media, being partial to the oppressed and having a non-commercial and non-profit character, which are typical characteristics of alternative media (Atton 2002; Fuchs 2011a, chapter 8; Sandoval and Fuchs 2010).

Second, there is *the communicative dimension* of cyberprotest in the context of Occupy. It features, for example, blog comments, discussion forum, chats, Twitter profile and hashtags, Facebook pages and reddit news comments. Riseup (www.riseup.net) "provides online communication tools for people and groups working on liberatory social change" (chat, email, mailing lists). The project is funded by donations. The communication is encrypted and does not store IP addresses because Riseup opposes "the rise of a surveillance society" (help.riseup.net/de/security) and thinks "it is vital that essential communication infrastructure be controlled by movement organisations and not corporations or the government" (help.riseup.net/de/about-us). It is a project that wants to "aid in the creation of a free society, a world with freedom from want and freedom of expression, a world without oppression or hierarchy, where power is shared equally", by "providing communication and computer resources to allies engaged in struggles against capitalism and other forms of oppression" (ibid.). OccupyTalk (www.occupytalk.org) uses the open-source voice communication software Mumble in order to enable voice chat of Occupy activists for organizational purposes.

Third, there is the *collaborative/cooperative dimension* of Occupy's cyberprotest. Cooperative comprises collaborative work (Marx) and community (Tönnies). These two dimension are represented in the Occupy movement by wikis (collaborative work) and social networking sites (community).

Tumblr is a commercial photo blog platform. The Tumblr blog "We are the 99 percent" (wearethe99percent.tumblr.com) is a group blog that features images of Occupy movements, on which they show self-written signs that explain the story of why they are part of the 99%. "Let us know who you are. Take a picture of yourself holding a sign that describes your situation—for example, 'I am a student with $25,000 in debt,' or 'I needed surgery and my first thought wasn't if I was going to be okay, it was how I'd afford it.' Below that, write 'I am the 99 percent.' Below that, write 'occupywallst.org'" (wearethe99percent.tumblr.com/submit).

Wiki.occupy.net is a collaboratively edited wiki that presents information about events, projects, campaigns and knowledge related to the Occupy movement. It can be edited by everyone.

Occupy Together Meetup (www.meetup.com/occupytogether) is a domain on the Meetup platform that allows activists to schedule and join local Occupy meetings. The Facebook app Occupy Network (www.occupynetwork.com) is "designed to help connect all the local organising happening on facebook into something bigger". It displays Facebook pages, groups, users and discussions, as well as tweets related to the Occupy movement. It represent the commercial community dimension of Occupy's social media use. But there are also non-commercial platforms associated with Occupy:

The Global Square was a non-commercial, non-profit social networking site that was funded by donations. It "respects privacy for individuals and transparency for public organisations and actions. As a social environment we will facilitate open communication while retaining individual control over privacy. We support the right of individuals to assemble, associate and collaborate and to choose the manner of doing so". "The goal of the Global Square is to perpetuate and spread the creative and cooperative spirit of the occupations and transform this into lasting forms of social organisation, at the global as well as the local level". Facebook and Twitter are perceived as being too limited for the Occupy movement: "Facebook and Twitter have been very helpful for disseminating basic information and aiding mass mobilisation, [but] they do not provide us with the tools for extending our participatory model of decision-making beyond the direct reach of the assemblies and up to the global level. Neither do they provide us with project management tools for our working groups". The site was seen as complimentary tool to meetings that involve physical presence: "The aim of the platform, in this respect, should not be to replace the physical assemblies but rather to empower them by providing the online tools for local and (trans)national organization and collaboration". One basic goal was "news without censorship" by the government.

Occupii (http://occupii.org/) is a non-commercial, non-profit social networking site and live video-streaming platform funded by donations that is associated with the Occupy movement. On October 24, 2012 (07:55, CET) it had 5,294 members. The project is built on the belief that mainstream media manipulate and censor the public sphere: "One person in isolation cannot hope to stand against the behemoths that are the 'Mainstream Media'. But together we can enable those willing and able to be the eyes and ears of the online communities to do so. [. . .] We are already seeing crackdowns on protestors through various means including usage of draconian legislation brought in specifically to create a police state during this year. *We know mainstream media is corrupted.* This will be even more prevalent during 2012. We cannot rely on MSM for any sort of reliable, unbiased reportage. [. . .] We wish to put together a dedicated livestreaming team comprised of 2 elements: one 'on the ground' team of 4 people with 3 independant livestreaming backpacks, allowing us to bring you footage from many events and many angles of same events, creating the link between the events and the online communities. The other element is an 'online' team of producers, editors, graphic designers, writers and 'support' team for the 'ground' crew. [. . .] The total cost of the 3 backpacks is about £1700 ($2740)" (occupii.org/page/donate). The terms of service are relatively short (1,004 words on October 24, 2012) and do not contain any clauses about data use for advertising.

The role of social media in social movements also needs to be studied empirically. I have conducted a survey, in which around 400 Occupy activists shared their views and assessments of the role of social media in the movement and provided information of their media use in protests. The results have been published as book: *OccupyMedia! The Occupy Movement and Social Media in Crisis Capitalism* (Fuchs 2013). The book's basic idea is that there are many claims about social media in revolutions and protests, but that we cannot find out what the real role is without systematically asking activists and studying their experiences and opinions. Such empirical research needs to be grounded in a theory of social media, politics and digital labour.

12.5. Conclusion

David Graeber (2012), who was involved in Occupy Wall Street from the beginning and helped coin the slogan "We are the 99%", describes the origins and development of Occupy Wall Street. He cites an email by Micah White from Adbusters, in which White wrote that Adbusters understood itself as spreading the idea of the occupation, but not as organizer, for which local people would be needed (ibid., 33). Graeber says the local organization work started with a meeting of activists that took place on August 2, 2011, in Bowling Green Park (ibid., 25–32). This shows that Adbusters communicated an idea with visual, textual and online media, but that local organizing was a crucial step in bringing about Occupy Wall Street, which cannot be considered as a movement that was created online. Graeber (2012, 32, 34) describes how working groups were set up, among them a communication group that set up an email mailing list and a public relations group. Graeber's account of the organization of Occupy Wall Street shows that organizing protests requires face-to-face meetings and contacts of activists. Protests are not created online but by the social relations of activists that communicate with each other and connect with others. In this process they especially made use of email lists as a communication tool for staying in touch. For reporting from the protest event on September 17, 2011, live videostreaming and Twitter were especially used (ibid., 43–50).

Graeber's account seems to speak for the theoretical position that was presented in this book: that one should avoid both overstressing and underestimating the role of media technologies in contemporary social movements. Revolutions and rebellions are no "Twitter revolutions" or "Facebook rebellions". Collective political action requires communication. Statistics and observations indicate that face-to-face communication, commercial and non-commercial online social media and mainstream media played a certain role in the Occupy movement.

I suggested one think about the media in social movements in contradictory terms: Media do not have one-dimensional, clear-cut effects on social movements, but rather can have multiple effects that contradict each other. There are both commercial media and alternative media, and one needs to have a look in what relationship these media stand to each other.

Graeber (2012, 55–58) argues that there were two specific roles of the media in reporting on Occupy Wall Street: (a) live video streams, mobile phone cameras, YouTube, Facebook and Twitter were used for spreading images and videos about police violence (such as the video of NYPD officer Anthony Bologna pepper-spraying two young female activists or the video of Lieutenant John Pike pepper-spraying activists who conducted a non-violent sit-in at the University of California campus in Davis; (b) international mass media, especially Al Jazeera and the *Guardian,* reported in a relatively sympathetic manner on Occupy Wall Street. Al Jazeera, for example, broadcast videos about police violence. At the same time, there were attempts by mainstream media, especially Fox, to display Occupy Wall Street as chaotic, violent, criminal and a threat for the public. Online media played a role in documenting police violence but did not suffice for creating a relatively positive public image of the movement, for which the support of mainstream media was needed to reach a broader public. In the case of the Occupy movement, there was a contradiction between right-wing mass media (Fox) and more progressive mainstream media (the *Guardian,* Al Jazeera).

So there are indications that online media stood on the one hand in a friendly relationship with certain mainstream media (Al Jazeera, the *Guardian*) that took up images and videos from social media and broadcast them to a wider audience and on the other hand in a conflicting relationship.

An example: On September 19, 2011, the alternative news service Democracy Now! reported on Occupy Wall Street.[7] The broadcast reports were activist-centred and gave voice to activists such as Mary Ellen Marino, who was interviewed and said, "I came because I'm upset with the fact that the bailout of Wall Street didn't help any of the people holding mortgages. All of the money went to Wall Street, and none of it went to Main Street". The studio guests were David Graeber and Nathan Schneider (editor of the blog *Waging Nonviolence*). On November 18, 2012, policeman John Pike pepper-sprayed non-violent student protestors who conducted a sit-in at the University of California's campus in Davis. This was filmed and uploaded to YouTube. The hacker group Anonymous found out private details of John Pike and posted them online together with the video.[8] YouTube after some time deleted the video, saying, "This video is no longer available due to a copyright claim by Thomas Fowler". Fox also reported about the pepper spray attack on November 21. Bill O'Reilly and Megyn Kelly discussed the attack: "First of all: pepper spray. [. . .] It's a food production essentially. [. . .] They just wanted them to get out of there, stop blocking what they were blocking. [. . .] And it is a crime [. . .] because they were posing, you know, a sit-in, a student protest. [. . .] It looks like the students were failing to disperse. [. . .] The police chief has been placed on administrative leave, right? For obeying orders! Isn't that nice?"[9] Fox News produced a report that presented Occupiers as morons by showing highly edited excerpts from interviews with activists that were interlaced with excerpts from movies and focusing especially on one activist, who said that marijuana should be legalized.[10]

This example shows us several things: Various media relate to social movements in different ways. Alternative media, such as Democracy Now!, tend to share activists' position and give space to the expression of their views. Right-wing mainstream media, such as Fox News, in contrast try to present a very different picture of social movements, presenting them as stupid, violent and plan- and strategy-less and showing sympathy with police violence. Activists hardly get the opportunity to present their views; interviews are manipulated and edited in a manner that allows ridiculing the movement. In the case of Occupy, Democracy Now! and Fox related to the movement in contradictory ways. There are conflicts and contradictions between different type of media and between specific media organizations. These relations are shaped by power: whereas Democracy Now!'s website is the world's 17369th most viewed site, the Fox News site is ranked in position 156 (alexa.com, December 2, 2012). Visibility on the Internet and audience reach are important aspects of communication power and have to do with the budgets and reputation of media. Commercial media that base their revenues on advertisements have advantages, whereas non-commercial media that depend on donations and foundations are facing communicative inequality. The YouTube video that was uploaded on November 18, 2011,[11] received 1,787,720 views until December 2, 2012 (09:05 GMT; = a period of 380 days). These are on average 4,704 viewings per day. In contrast, Fox News' prime-time ratings were around 1.9 million viewers per day.[12] This means that Fox News has the power to reach more viewers in one day than a citizen journalist's clip reaches on YouTube during a year. The net effect is that the right-wing comments and manipulated videos that Fox News showed about Occupy reached a broader viewing than the activist-oriented reporting of Democracy Now! and the uncommented footage available on YouTube. This circumstance shows that how the media relate to social movements is shaped by contradictions that are embedded into power structures and power asymmetries. Alternative media and alternative views are due to the structure of the media landscape in capitalism at a disadvantage and are facing structural communication inequalities.

The classification of Occupy's media use that was developed shows that this movement uses various types of online social media (cognitive, communicative and cooperative cyberprotest-media). They have either corporate or non-commercial character. Examples of established mainstream platforms that are used by Occupy are Facebook, Twitter, reddit, Tumblr and Meetup. These platforms have in common that they use targeted advertising for accumulating capital. They commodify user data and exploit digital labour. Alternative online platforms that Occupy uses include Occupy News Network, InterOccupy, OccupyTalk, The-GlobalSquare, Occupii, N-1 and Diaspora★. These platforms are alternative in the sense that they are non-commercial and non-profit oriented, which means that they are not exposed to the pressures of capital accumulation. *They are working-class social media because they are collectively owned and controlled by the immediate users. Activities on these media are not digital labour (that is exploited), but digital work. The Occupy movement uses both corporate social media and working-class social media.* Occupy's working-class social media are very directly related to the Occupy movement and operated by activists. They define themselves in distinction to and conflict with dominant corporate media. So for example, Occupied Stories describes itself as a "story-sharing platform that recognizes the mainstream media's claim to fairness and objectivity as both false and unrealistic" (occupiedstories.com/about), and the Occupy News Network says it works "to hold mainstream media to account by exposing lies and bias" (occupynewsnetwork.co.uk/onn/about-us-2).

The interviews conducted by Paolo Gerbaudo (2012) indicate that Facebook has been mainly used for reaching the broader public and Twitter as a tool of internal coordination and communication. The first strategy is situated in the context that Facebook has more than a billion users, which Occupy activists seem to find attractive because there is a large public that can potentially reached on Facebook. In respect to internal communication and coordination, there are no evident reasons why Twitter has been used so strongly and not a non-commercial alternative tool.

There are certain risks for a social movement that uses commercial Internet platforms for internal and external communication. In September 2012, Twitter followed a court order and handed over data about Malcom Harris' Twitter use (email address, postings, etc.), who was charged with disorderly conduct and being arrested at an Occupy protest that took place on the Brooklyn Bridge in 2011. "Prosecutors say that messages posted by Harris—who goes by the twitter handle @destructuremal—could show whether the defendant was aware that he was breaking police orders relating to the demo" (*The Guardian Online,* "Twitter Complies with Prosecutors to Surrender Occupy Activist's Tweets", September 14, 2012).

Queen's Counsel John Cooper warns in this context that the police are aiming to monitor activists' social media use: "The police are aware and are getting more aware of powers to force and compel platforms to reveal anonymous sites. [. . .] [A]ctivists are putting themselves at more risk. Police will be following key Twitter sites, not only those of the activists but also other interesting figures. They know how to use them to keep up with rioting and to find alleged rioters. [. . .] In the same way they used to monitor mobile phones when they were trying to police impromptu raves, they are doing the same with Twitter and Facebook, as those who say too much on social media will find" (*The Independent Online,* Activists Warned to Watch What They Say as Social Media Monitoring Becomes "Next Big Thing in Law Enforcement", October 1, 2012). "Prosecutors say the tweets, which are no longer available online, may demonstrate that Harris knew police had told protesters not to walk on the roadway" (*The Huffington Post,* "Twitter Must Produce Occupy Protester Malcom Harris' Tweet or Face Contempt", November 9, 2011). Handing over user data to the police is regulated in both Twitter's and Facebook's terms of use: "we may preserve or disclose your information if we believe that it is reasonably necessary to comply with a law, regulation or legal request" (Twitter Privacy Policy, version from May 17, 2012). "We may access, preserve and share your information in response to a legal request (like a search warrant, court order or subpoena) if we have a good faith belief that the law requires us to do so. [. . .] We may also access, preserve and share information when we have a good faith belief it is necessary to: detect, prevent and address fraud and other illegal activity; to protect ourselves, you and others, including as part of investigations; and to prevent death or imminent bodily harm" (Facebook Data Use Policy, version from June 8, 2012). Activist-controlled platforms have less criminalization risk because they do not lack the distance from activism that the makers of Facebook and Twitter have. One cannot assume that Twitter or Facebook never sees Occupy as dangerous and that it does not give the police access to users' data.

Mark Zuckerberg is the 35th richest person in the world ($17.5 billion; Forbes 2000, 2012). Facebook achieved profits of over US$1 billion in 2011 (Facebook, Form S-1, registration statement). In Occupy's logic, Zuckerberg is clearly part of the "1%". But why should one trust one's own self-defined enemies? Corporate social media use targeted advertising as their capital accumulation model: they commodify data that users generate about themselves (profiles), their social networks, interests and browsing behaviour (Fuchs 2010d). This commodification process is irrespective of content: it does not matter for Facebook, YouTube or Twitter if their users talk about world revolution on the one hand or pop songs, movies and new haircuts on the other hand. All of this information is instrumentalized for selling targeted ad space to advertising clients. The revolution cannot be twittered, but it can certainly be commodified. By using Twitter, Facebook, YouTube and other corporate social media, activists help corporations accumulate capital; they advance the profits of the 1% and thereby contradict their own goal of taking wealth away from the 1%. In the context of socio-economic equality, non-commercial platforms clearly pose advantages for Occupy activists.

In the forefront of the Egyptian revolution, the Facebook group "My name is Khaled Mohamed Said" was blocked by Facebook, which arguing that it infringed on copyrights (Ghonim 2012, 113). Also the Facebook group "We are all Khaled Said", which was managed by social media activist Wael Ghonim, was blocked (ibid., 117). After an inquiry by the admin, Facebook answered that fake accounts had been used for administering the group (ibid., 118). As a result of public and media pressure, the group went up again after 24 hours. In this example, Facebook's argument—that a political Facebook group involved in organizing protests in a country where the opposition is tortured and killed shall not be operated by fake accounts, but only by real-name ones—is particularly striking and odd because it completely ignored the fear of activists, who risk their lives and could be discovered, tortured or even killed, and the resulting need to stay anonymous.

Only relying on the use of alternative media has political and ethical advantages but at the same time disadvantages: in order to reach a broader public that goes beyond the activist community, media are needed that can make content visible to a high number of users/audience members. On the Internet, corporate social media that are based on advertising are better able than non-commercial media to invest money in promoting platform use and developing new features. Therefore, alternative online social media are facing inherent inequalities of visibility: whereas Facebook is the 2nd most accessed website in the world, YouTube the 3rd and Twitter the 10th, Occupii.org is ranked number 795,476, N-1 number 358,909 and Diaspora* number 51,279. Commercial media have an income revenue stream that stems from advertising or the sales of culture, whereas non-commercial media depend on voluntary work or donations. As we live in a capitalist society, alternative media are at a strategic disadvantage. For the Occupy movement this means that its media use is shaped by multiple contradictions that are difficult to navigate and manage.

The role of social media in the Occupy movement is highly contradictory: there are antagonisms between liberal and conservative mass media's reporting;

between the role of face-to-face communication, online media and traditional mass media; and between alternative non-commercial, non-profit social media and commercial, profit-oriented media that employ targeted advertising.

Digital labour is embedded into a global chain of value creation, in which various forms of labour are involved: slave mining labour, highly exploited hardware assemblage labour, highly stressful software engineering, Tayloristic and house-wifized service labour and unpaid prosumer labour. These forms of labour are not visible to ICT users because commodities present themselves as things to consumers and hide and make anonymous the underlying social labour relations. The production of corporate digital media is shaped by a global commodity fetishism and the exploitation of digital labour in various forms. To break up the commodity status and the commodity fetishism of digital media means to construct working-class digital/social media that are based on the logic of the commons created by digital work. The Internet is at a crossroads: it can either develop into an ever more commercial and commodified system that is embedded into the antagonisms of capitalism and advances various forms of exploitation and resulting inequalities, or it can develop into a working-class Internet that is commonly created and controlled by everyday users. Creating such an Internet can only be achieved in struggles. It requires a new working class. A commons-based Internet would be a truly social medium that is not like the corporate Internet, socially produced and privately owned, but is rather produced, reproduced and controlled in common.

Notes

1 "International users may see advertisements on some BBC Online Services. These advertisements are provided and delivered by the BBC's commercial arm, BBC Worldwide Limited" (Terms of Use of BBC Online Services—Personal Use, http://www.bbc.co.uk/terms/personal.shtml, accessed August 8, 2013).
2 https://www.joindiaspora.com/ (accessed November 18, 2012).
3 https://n-1.cc/ (accessed November 18, 2012).
4 Three-month usage access: 43.284% of all Internet users (alexa.com, accessed November 18, 2012). Worldwide Internet users: 2,405,518,376 (http://www.internetworldstats.com/stats.htm, accessed November 18, 2012).
5 Three-month usage access: 0.00376% of all Internet users (alexa.com, accessed November 18, 2012).
6 There are of course also ecological crises that can threaten the existence of humankind. For social theory, the question is how nature relates to society. Humans have to enter into a metabolism with nature in order to survive. They have to appropriate parts of nature and change it with their activities in order to produce use-values that serve needs of society. This means that the process, where the interaction of nature and society is directly established, takes place in the economy. We therefore do not discern ecological crises separately, but see them as one specific subform of economic crises.
7 http://www.democracynow.org/2011/9/19/occupy_wall_street_thousands_march_in (accessed on July 9, 2013).

8　Original URL: http://www.youtube.com/watch?v=BjnR7xET7Uo (no longer online).
9　http://tpmdc.talkingpointsmemo.com/2011/11/fox-news-on-uc-davis-pepper-spraying-its-a-food-product-essentially.php?ref=fpnewsfeed (accessed on July 9, 2013).
10　http://www.youtube.com/watch?v=Zd8o_yqqo9o (accessed on July 9, 2013).
11　http://www.youtube.com/watch?v=6AdDLhPwpp4 (accessed on July 9, 2013).
12　http://stateofthemedia.org/2012/cable-cnn-ends-its-ratings-slide-fox-falls-again/ (accessed August 8, 2013).

13

DIGITAL LABOUR KEYWORDS

Absolute Surplus-Value Production   Absolute surplus-value production is a strategy that capitalists use to make more **profit**: the working hours that employees perform for a certain wage are increased. Marx calls this strategy also the formal subsumption of labour under capital.

Abstract and Concrete Labour   Labour has two dimensions: abstract and concrete labour. Abstract labour creates the **value-dimension** of a **commodity**, concrete labour the **use-value** dimension of a commodity. Concrete labour produces the character of a commodity as a useful good, whereas abstract labour creates the **value** dimension of a good that makes it an economic object that can be exchanged in order to achieve monetary **profit**. In **capitalism**, the value side and abstract labour are the dominant aspect of labour and commodities: capitalism is a system that strives to turn everything into commodities (commodification) so that it is an object of abstract labour and can be exchanged with **money** in order to create profit. Use-values are difficult to obtain in capitalism without being **exchange-values**. There are non-commodified use-values (e.g. many personal relationships with friends), but capitalism strives to turn use-values into values and exchange-values (e.g. by organizing the finding of new friends and partners in the form of for-profit online dating platforms). In the concept of abstract labour, several abstractions from the concrete are involved: (a) an abstraction from the physical properties of goods (their use-values), (b) an abstraction from single products so that social relations between commodities in exchange are established, (c) an abstraction from simple labour activities to more complex tasks, and (d) an abstraction from specific qualities under which specific labour processes took place (such as poor working conditions, low payment, etc.) so that common properties of commodities are foregrounded by the value concept.

Accumulation   See: **capital**

Alienation Louis Althusser argues that alienation is an unscientific and esoteric concept that Marx used in his young years. An analysis of Marx's works shows, however, that he used this term throughout his life, including in later works such as the *Grundrisse* and *Capital*. Alienation means that humans are not in control of fundamental aspects of their lives. In the economy, alienation can refer to the non-control of **labour-power**, the objects of **labour**, the instruments of labour and the products of labour. If these forms of alienation work together, then they constitute exploitation and class relations. Marx argues that alienation is not just non-control, but also the alienation of humans from themselves, from the relations with others, from the entire **work** process and from the economy and from society. This means that in a **class** society, a dominant class controls human minds, bodies, social relations, the work process, the economy and the whole of society.

Audience labour, audience commodity The Marxist political economist Dallas Smythe argued that audiences of commercial, advertising-funded media are workers who create **value** and are sold as **commodity** to advertising clients. Watching commercial television, listening to commercial radio and reading a commercial newspaper is **labour** that is necessary for the realization of the commercial media's **profits**. Dallas Smythe's works have in the **digital labour** debate gained particular importance for understanding how social media's **capital accumulation** models work. Dallas Smythe, just like Autonomist Marxist thinkers like Mario Tronti and Antonio Negri, stressed that **value** creation in capitalism involves not only wage labour but also unpaid labour. Smythe's notion of audience labour has parallels with Negri's concept of the **social worker**, although both ideas were developed independently in the 1970s.

Capital, capitalism Capital is **money** that has to be permanently increased by reinvestments, exploitation of **labour**, new production of **commodities** and more sales that result in an increase of **profits**. Accumulation is an inherent feature of capital: if capital cannot be steadily increased, then bankruptcy of a company is the likely outcome. If capital accumulation stagnates and does not increase at a compound rate that is large enough, an economic crisis is the likely result. Capitalism is an economic **mode of production** that is based on the logic of capital accumulation, which requires class relations, the exploitation of labour and commodity production, sale and consumption. The logic of accumulation is not restricted to the economy, but also impinges other systems of modern society, such as politics (where we find the logic of the accumulation of decision power) and culture (where one encounters the logic of the accumulation of reputation and definition power). Capitalism is therefore also a type of society.

Class society A class society is a society in which one group works and produces goods and other results (such as **money**) that are owned by another group. A certain degree of this **labour** is remunerated or unremunerated. Class societies are based on the exploitation of labour. It can also be completely unremunerated. Examples of class systems are patriarchal forms of work organization in the household, ancient **slavery**, feudalism and **capitalism**. The two basic classes in capitalism are workers, who form a proletariat, and capitalists, who exploit the proletariat. The notion of class is closely connected to the one of **surplus value**.

Collective worker   Marx stresses with the notion of the collective worker that most commodities are produced not by single individuals, but by cooperative work and a combination of the work of many humans. He therefore argues that if one is part of a collective work personnel that together contains many acts of work necessary for creating the **profit** of a company, one is part of the exploited **class** and therefore a member of the working class.

Commodity   A commodity is an object that is sold on the market in a certain quantitative relationship to another commodity: x commodity A = y commodity B (e.g. 1 computer = 1,000£). Marx (1867c) begins *Capital, Volume 1,* by saying that **capitalism** is an "immense collection of commodities" and that the commodity is the "elementary form" of capitalism. The entire first chapter of *Capital 1* is devoted to the discussion of the commodity.

Commodity fetishism   Fetishism is an ideological logic that mistakes social relations for things. It assumes that certain social phenomena are things, which means that it takes them for granted, does not question where they come from and does not see that they have a beginning and an end (a history) and that they can be changed. A typical fetishistic argument is that X (e.g. domination, competition, **capitalism**, egoism, racism, war, violence, etc.) must exist and will always exist because it has always been this way, is typical for human nature, and so on. Alternatives to the way things are today are therefore considered as being impossible. Commodity fetishism is a logic that is immanent to capitalism: the basic elements of capitalism (**commodities, money**, markets, etc.) are the outcome of specific social relations that are not visible in concrete objects (a computer, a printer, a banknote, etc.). These elements therefore tend to create the impression they are natural features of society and of all societies and often deceive humans, who if they are taken in by the logic of fetishism think that there can be no world beyond capitalism and domination.

Communism   Communism is a society of common control and the commons: single individuals or classes do not control society, the economy, politics and culture, but all affected individuals together control society, own the economy, make decisions in the economy and define what is seen as important, good and meaningful in culture. Communism as understood by Marx is a participatory democracy, in which humans are together in control of society.

Concrete labour   See: **abstract and concrete labour**

Constant capital   Constant capital is **capital** that does not create new **value**. It is divided into fixed constant capital (machines, buildings, equipment) and circulating constant capital (raw and auxiliary materials, operating supply items, semi-finished products).

Corvée slavery   Corvée slavery is a form of **slavery** in which slaves for a specific amount of hours per week have to work for the slave master, who owns the output generated in these hours, whereas they own the output of the rest of the worked hours themselves.

Dialectic   The dialectic is one of the most important principles in Hegel's philosophy. It assumes that the world develops in the form of contradictions: one phenomenon never exists in isolation, but can only exist in and through a relationship to another phenomenon. This means that the world is relational. Things have individual qualities and these qualities only exist through the relationships to other things. Individual existence is only enabled by the existence of relations to other things. These relations are not static, but dynamic and productive, and they tend to create new results that emerge from these relationships. A new thing that has emerged from a contradiction is itself not a monad, an isolated thing-in-itself, but stands again in a relationship to something else. The dialectic of things means that they are relational and dynamic: the world is a world in flux, it constantly develops on different levels of organization. Marx used Hegel's dialectical logic for describing how society in general develops as a dialectic of human agency and social structures, how **class societies** develop as dialectical contradictions between an exploiting class and exploited class and how **capitalism** results in crises that are due to the existence of immanent contradictions of the economy and society. Critics of Hegel and Hegelian Marxism have argued that the dialectic constitutes a closed system, in which change is predetermined and there is no space for spontaneity and human agency. Critics of Marx have advanced the point that he conceived the historical process as dialectical natural law and saw **communism** as automatically emanating from **capitalism**. There are different forms of dialectical thinking. Vulgar dialectical thinkers like Stalin argued that the dialectic of society is a natural law and that socialism and communism are natural and inevitable results of history. Humanist Marxists such as Herbert Marcuse or Ernst Bloch have in contrast given a more correct interpretation of Marx's understanding of the dialectic: they argue that capitalism has objective immanent contradictions that result in crises but not automatically in the breakdown of capitalism. The subjective dialectic of society would be constituted by human actions and social struggles. A society could only break down and give rise to a new society if a crisis results in struggles for change. There would be a dialectic of an objective dialectic and a subjective dialectic and no automatic or determined developments of history. This interpretation of the dialectic is a combination of Marx's stress on the contradictions of capitalism (objective dialectic) and social struggles as the driving force of history (subjective dialectic).

See also: **sublation**/*Aufhebung*

Digital labour   Digital labour is alienated **digital work**: it is alienated from itself, from the instruments and objects of labour and from the products of **labour. Alienation** is alienation of the subject from itself (labour-power is put to use for and is controlled by **capital**), alienation from the object (the objects of labour and the instruments of labour) and the subject-object (the products of labour). **Digital work** and digital labour are broad categories that involve all activities in the production of digital media technologies and contents.

This means that in the capitalist media industry, different forms of alienation and exploitation can be encountered. Examples are slave workers in mineral extraction, Taylorist hardware assemblers, software engineers, professional on-line content creators (e.g. online journalists), call centre agents and social media prosumers. In digital labour that is performed on corporate social media, users are objectively alienated because (a) in relation to subjectivity, they are coerced by isolation and social disadvantage if they leave monopoly capital platforms (such as Facebook); (b) in relation to the objects of labour, their human experiences come under the control of capital; (c) in relation to the instruments of labour, the platforms are not owned by users but by private companies that also commodify user data; and (d) in relation to the product of labour, monetary **profit** is individually controlled by the platform's owners. These four forms of alienation constitute together the exploitation of digital labour by capital. Alienation of digital labour concerns **labour-power**, the object and instruments of labour and the created products.

See also: **digital work**

Digital work Digital work is a specific form of work that makes use of the body, mind or machines or a combination of all or some of these elements as an instrument of work in order to organize nature, resources extracted from nature, or culture and human experiences, in such a way that digital media are produced and used. The products of digital work are depending on the type of work: minerals, components, digital media tools or digitally mediated symbolic representations, social relations, artefacts, social systems and communities. Digital work includes all activities that create use-values that are objectified in digital media technologies, contents and products generated by applying digital media.

See also: **digital labour**

Division of labour In a division of labour, various work processes form a specific whole (such as the production of a specific good or service, an organization, a sector of the economy, a part of society, society or the economy as a whole). They are separated parts conducted by specific individuals or groups. Divisions of labour are frequently embedded into class relations, asymmetric power structures and inequalities so that the powerful derive benefits at the expense of workers who are exploited or oppressed. Examples for divisions of labour are: the division of labour between men and women, house workers and wage workers, town and country, different regions, different countries, mental and physical labour, politicians and citizens, legislative and executive power, agriculture and industry, developing and developed countries (global/international division of labour). Marx imagined the abolishment of the division of labour as an important element of a participatory society and formulated in this context the notion of the well-rounded individual: given the abolishment of classes and of the division of labour as well as a high level of productivity, the possibility emerges that everyone becomes a creative cultural worker.

See also: **international division of digital labour**

Double-free labour   By double-free labour, Marx means a characteristic of wage labour in modern society:

(a) workers are "free" owners of their **labour-power**, but they have to sell it on the market in order to be able to survive, and

(b) workers do not own the products of their work; they are "free" of them.

Marx designates with this concept the circumstance that **capitalism** and the Enlightenment estawblished new forms of liberal freedoms that were the privilege of the aristocracy under feudalism, but these freedoms turned into new unfreedoms so that capitalism is itself an unfree **class society**, albeit one that proclaims to be free and to advance freedom.

Exchange-value   Exchange-value is a relationship between **commodities** in which they are exchanged in a certain quantitative relationship: x commodity A = y commodity B. If somebody buys a table for 100€, then the table is exchanged for this sum of **money**. Two commodities (table and money) change owners in the exchange process.

Exploitation   See: **surplus value**, **class society**

Fetishism   See: **commodity fetishism**

Formal subsumption of labour under capital   See: **Absolute surplus-value production**

General Intellect   The general intellect is a category that Marx uses in the *Grundrisse* for arguing that technologies are the outcome of work of the human brain that is organized by the human hand. They are objectified knowledge. The general intellect is general social knowledge that develops with the rising importance of technology (fixed constant **capital**) in production. Marx describes a situation where the general intellect becomes a direct force of production, which is another formulation for the emergence of an information society. Marx was an early information society thinker who saw information technology connected to the development of capitalism and the productive forces.

Housewifization   Housewifization, in contrast to the notion of the feminization of work, does not simply mean that more women work in specific realms of the economy. Housewifization means that jobs take on insecure and precarious traits that have traditionally characterized housework. The Bielefeld school of feminism (Claudia von Werlhof, Maria Mies and Veronika Bennholdt-Thomsen) introduced the term. This school of thought argues that housework is an inner colony of **capitalism** and a form of ongoing **primitive accumulation**, where unpaid labour helps generate capitalist **profits**. It is based on a gender division of labour. In neo-liberal capitalism, more and more people live and work under precarious conditions that have traditionally been characteristic of patriarchal relations. People working under such conditions are, like housewives, a source of uncontrolled and unlimited exploitation. Housewifization is a category that is particularly suited for analysing forms of unpaid and highly exploited **digital labour.**

See also: **reproductive labour**

International division of digital labour The international division of digital labour (IDDL) is a division of labour that involves various forms of labour, exploitation and modes of production that are organized in different parts of the world, are partly anonymously networked with each other and all form necessary elements for the production, usage and application of digital media. The IDDL can involve agricultural, industrial and informational forms of labour, labour that represents various relations of production, such as patriarchy, slavery, feudalism and capitalism, as well as labour that represents specific modes of the organization of capitalism. It often combines forms of labour that represent different modes of production, different class relations, different modes of coercion, different levels of the organization of the productive forces – all under the rule of capital. This circumstance shows that modes of production, class relations, modes of coercion and modes of the productive forces do not develop in a linear manner, where one form substitutes the other, but in a dialectic way so that a new mode of organization incorporates and changes earlier ones.

See also: **division of labour, mode of production, productive forces, relations of production**

Internet prosumer labour, Internet prosumer commodification I have developed these concepts based on Dallas Smythe's notions of **audience labour** and **audience commodification** in order to analyse how corporate social media (Facebook, Twitter, Google, etc.) accumulate **capital** by commodifying the online activities of users. The difference between audience labour and prosumer **labour** is that users of Facebook, Twitter and Google permanently create content and data that is monitored and commodified so that real-time total surveillance of online behaviour enables a data commodity that allows targeting of advertising according to users' interests and activities.

Labour Raymond Williams (1983, 176–179) argues that the word "labour" comes from the French word *labor* and the Latin term *laborem* and appeared in the English language first around 1300. It was associated with hard work, pain and trouble. In the 18th century, it would have attained the meaning of work under capitalist conditions that stands in a class relationship with **capital**. The term "wage labour" is associated with the common usage of the term "labour". In this book, labour designates work that is not controlled by the human subjects engaged in it. Labour is alienated work, where one or several forms of **alienation** are at play: humans do not control their **labour-power**, the objects of work, the instruments of work and the objects of work.

See also: **work**

Labour aristocracy Engels introduced this term for describing a faction of the working class that has higher wages, which enables relatively comfortable lives. Lenin used the term for workers-turned-bourgeois. The notion is related to Marx's concept of **surplus wages**. Today the term can be used in the context of privileged parts of knowledge workers (e.g. management, highly paid software engineers).

Labour-power   Labour-power is the ability and capacity to **work**. It is the subjectivity of the worker, which contains her/his body, knowledge, skills, abilities and so on. Labour-power is developed by education and skills development as well as by activities that reproduce and recreate the ability to work, such as sleep, rest, entertainment, care, love, sexuality, bodily care and communication. In gendered **class societies**, the reproduction of labour-power is organized in the form of a household economy that features a gender division of labour, in which **reproductive labour** that recreates the ability to work is the task and domain that is assigned to specific individuals, namely women in patriarchal societies. The **value** of labour-power is the amount of hours it takes on average to reproduce labour-power. The **price** of labour-power is formed by the wages that capitalists pay in order to control it.

Law of value   The law of **value** says that the higher productivity is, the lower the value of a commodity (i.e. the average amount of hours it takes to produce it). The **value** of a **commodity** is directly proportional to the **labour** objectified in it and indirectly proportional to the level of productivity. Marx argued that historically productivity tends to increase in **capitalism**, which means that the value of commodities decreases. A table that can today be produced in three minutes with the help of advanced machinery could in the 19th century only be produced within several hours. Marx says that the law of value causes a contradiction in capitalism: the time needed for producing goods decreases, but at the same time labour is the only source of value. Whereas the value per commodity tends to be reduced, value is the only source of accumulation and **profit**. This contradiction tends to result in unemployment and the crisis-proneness of capitalism. Marx envisioned a highly productive society, in which the law of value stops operating and the source of wealth is not labour but free time. He argues that this is only possible in a **communist** society, in which production based on **exchange-value** has broken down. In the **digital labour** debate, some people argue that the law of value cannot be applied to phenomena such as Facebook, where social relations, reputation and affects would create value. This however means that the Internet economy is not based on time. Social relations, user-generated content and reputation do not exist outside of time. They are created in time. The more time one has available, the more likely it is that one can create more relations, more content and a higher status and reputation than others. A digital labour theory of value stresses the importance of a time-based theory of the economy for understanding digital media in capitalism.

Mode of production   A mode of production is a historical form of how the unity of **productive forces** and **relations of production** is organized. Marx spoke of patriarchy, ancient **slavery**, feudalism, **capitalism** and **communism** as modes of production. Some observers have claimed that Marx has argued that one mode of production will necessarily result in a new one so that communism is the inevitable outcome of capitalism. The critics say that Marx had a deterministic understanding of history. A close reading of Marx's works shows that there is a **dialectic** of modes of production so that each new mode of production has novel qualities, but also contains specific forms of organization of older modes of production. So for example, there are forms of patriarchy, **slavery** and feudalism at work in capitalism. For Marx, history is the outcome of class struggles. As social struggles are complex aspects of human behaviour, their emergence and result is not determined. This understanding of history therefore invalidates the interpretation that Marx had a deterministic understanding of history, a claim which is often made in order to argue that Marx, and therefore also the criticism of capitalism, is outdated.

See also: **productive forces, relations of production**

Money   Money is a general form of **value** and exchange and the universal **commodity** of **capitalism**. It is general and universal because it is the only commodity that can directly be exchanged with all other commodities. If you have many eggs and want to have a computer, then you first have to sell a lot of eggs in order to buy a computer. Given the form of organization of capitalism, eggs cannot buy you a computer because they are not universal commodities. If you have a lot of money, then in contrast you can directly buy both eggs and computers, which shows that money plays a special role in the organization of the economic exchange of commodities. Money fetishism is a specific form of **commodity fetishism** that can frequently be found in capitalism.

Necessary and surplus labour time   (Socially) necessary labour time is the total labour time that a society needs to expend in order to survive. The necessary labour time of a **commodity** is the time that it takes on average in society to produce this good. Surplus labour time is the amount of labour time that is performed in society beyond necessary labour time. Surplus labour time of a commodity is the labour time that goes beyond the necessary labour time needed for the good's production. Necessary and surplus labour time can be measured in seconds, minutes, hours, days, weeks, months and so on.

New imperialism   "New imperialism" is a term that has been introduced by David Harvey and other Marxist scholars for characterizing transformations of **capitalism** that revisit the old imperialism of the 19th century, which was based on the robbery of resources located in non-Western countries. The new imperialism is based on accumulation by dispossession: the privatization and commodification of public assets and institutions, social welfare, knowledge, nature, cultural forms, histories and intellectual creativity (the enclosure of the commons); financialization that allows the overtaking of assets by speculation, fraud, predation and thievery; the creation, management and manipulation of crises (for example the creation of debt crises that allow the intervention of the International Monetary Fund (IMF) with structural adjustment programs so that new investment opportunities, deregulations, liberalizations and privatizations emerge); and state redistributions that favour **capital** at the expense of **labour**. It also involves a global division of labour, in which capitalism relocates production in such a way that it can highly exploit labour in order to maximize **profits**.

Play labour (playbour)   Play and **labour** have traditionally been two separated spheres of activity, the first taking place during spare time in private and public spaces and the second during working time in factories and offices. Play labour means that the boundaries between play and labour tend to become fuzzy: labour presents itself as play and play becomes a form of **value-generation**. Play is a new management ideology that is, for example, present in Google offices that look like playgrounds but are spaces of highly stressful work with long overtime. The usage of corporate social media (Facebook, Google, Twitter, etc.) is fun, and the playful usage of these platforms hides the circumstance that these platforms are run by companies, make a lot of **profit** and exploit the users' labour.

Price   The price is the **money** form of the appearance of **value** in **capitalism**. One cannot directly observe the value of a **commodity** such as a computer, but one is confronted with its price on the market. The price can be observed and confronts people who are purchasers or sellers on markets. The Hegelian expression of this phenomenon is that value appears in the form of the price in capitalism. Value and prices of commodities are not equivalent. If one knows the value of a certain commodity (i.e. the number of hours needed on average to produce the commodity), then one cannot calculate the commodity's price from it. Marx understood that values and prices do not coincide. This phenomenon came to be known as the transformation problem in Marxist theory. Although commodity values and prices do not coincide, they are also not arbitrary. It is not an accident that a computer mouse is cheaper than a whole computer: it takes more time to produce the computer and its components than it takes to produce a computer mouse. The **law of value** shapes the production of both commodities.

Primitive accumulation   Primitive accumulation is a process in which land, people, knowledge, public services and other goods that are not subject to the logic of **capital** accumulation are expropriated and subjected to the forces of capital. They are commodified. Primitive accumulation often involves physical or other forms of violence. Marx argued that primitive accumulation was the first stage of **capitalism**. Rosa Luxemburg, David Harvey and others, including feminist political economists, have argued that primitive accumulation is a permanent process by which capital creates new milieus of accumulation and exploitation.

Productive forces   Productive forces are phenomena that enable economic production. **Labour-power** is the subjective productive force. Objective productive forces are nature, space-time, resources, infrastructures and technologies. They form objects of work and instruments of work (e.g. buildings, machines). Marx spoke of the antagonism between productive forces and **relations of production** as a specific characteristic of capitalism and one of the causes of capitalist crises.

See also: **relations of production, mode of production**

Profit The profit a company makes in a certain period of time, such as one year, is calculated as total sales minus investment costs.

Rate of profit The rate of profit is the mathematical relationship of profits to investment costs. The lower the investment costs are, the higher is the rate of profit.

Rate of surplus value, rate of exploitation The rate of exploitation is calculated as **profits** divided by wages: the higher the profits and the lower wages, the more exploited is **labour**. Profits can be maximized if wages are minimized. If no wages are paid, then the profits are at highest, which means that labour is exploited to a maximum degree.

Real subsumption of labour under capital See: **Relative surplus-value production**

Relations of production Relations of production are the specific social relations in which production, distribution and consumption are organized. So for example, **capitalism** is based on the social relations of private property, markets and nation-states and on **class** relations between capitalists and workers. Marx argues that capitalism is based on a contradiction of the relations of production and the **productive forces**: Technological progress is required for accumulating ever more **capital**. It advances the social character of production with new forms of collaboration. These social forms of production are incompatible with the private form of ownership, which results in crisis-proneness of the capitalist economy and the phenomenon that germ forms of a communist society, in which wealth is produced and controlled in common, are created by capitalist production.

See also: **productive forces, mode of production**

Relative surplus-value production Relative surplus-value production is a strategy that capitalists use to make more **profit** by increasing the productivity of **labour** so that more **commodities** and more **value** are produced in less time than before. A common way of relative surplus-value production is to use labour-saving technologies that increase the output of labour per hour. Marx terms relative surplus-value production also the real subsumption of labour under capital.

Reproductive labour Reproductive labour is work that recreates the human mind and the human body so that the worker is capable of being economically active day in and day out. It involves activities such as care, love, sexuality, education, child rearing, cleaning, cooking, washing clothes and so on. In patriarchal societies it is typically based on a gendered division of **labour**, where women are assigned to the realm of housework and reproductive labour. This assignment is legitimated by a patriarchal ideology that presents women as social, caring, affective and weak and men as individualistic, labouring, rational and physically strong. Marxist and socialist feminists have stressed that reproductive labour is crucial for the existence of **capitalism**, that it contributes to the production of **value** and that reproductive workers are therefore exploited and part of the working class. Reproductive labour is the foundation of the housework economy that is based on a gendered division of labour.

See also: **housewifization**

Second contradiction of capitalism   James O'Connor has argued that **capitalism** is based on a contradiction between the **productive forces** and the **relations of production** as well as on a contradiction between the capitalist relations of production and the form of the appropriation of nature. The second contradiction would result in environmental degradation and the depletion of nature and would call forth the need for a "red–green socialism" that is based on social and ecological awareness.

Slavery   Slavery is a **mode of production** in which the worker is the private property of a slave owner. As the slave owner owns the slave, s/he is free to do with the slave whatever s/he pleases, which includes the possibility to kill and torture the slave. Slaves therefore face the constant threat of being killed by slave masters, which enables highly exploitative forms of labour. For Marx and Engels, patriarchy is the oldest form of slavery. In it, the wife and the children are the slaves of the husband. Marx describes an ancient form of slavery and feudalism as a specific form of slavery that is based on the labour of peasants who were bondslaves.

Social worker, social factory   These two concepts have been developed in Autonomous Marxism. Mario Tronti introduced the concept of the social factory, Antonio Negri the notion of the social worker. Both concepts designate that **labour** and exploitation reach beyond the factory walls, where wage labour is organized and exploited. They stress that the exploitation of labour includes unpaid forms of labour such as housework and that the working class is larger than the group of wage workers. The factory and the working class tend to extend into society. Antonio Negri and Michael Hardt have further developed the concept of the social worker into the notion of the multitude, a collective workforce that especially uses different forms of knowledge work, which Hardt and Negri improperly term "immaterial labour", and that produces the commons of society. In the context of **digital labour**, the social worker and the social factory are of particular importance because corporate Internet platforms that offer free access and use targeted advertising (e.g. Facebook, Google, Twitter) are based on unpaid user work that is part of the social worker and turns computer and Internet use into a social factory.

Socially necessary labour time   See: **Necessary and surplus labour time**

Species-being   Species-being is a term that Marx used in the *Economic and Philosophic Manuscripts* (1844) in order to argue that it is a fundamental aspect of the human being that it is creative and social. In **class societies**, creativity and sociality would be crippled and limited by the rule of a dominant class that exploits human creativity and sociality and puts it to use for its own benefit at the expense of the exploited class.

Subject/Object   For Hegel, the subjective concept is immanent to human thought. Objectivity is in contrast something outside of human individuals—the objective world that interacts with the human subject. This interaction can result in a product that Hegel calls the subject-object or idea. The world can be described as a **dialectic** of subject and object: a subject interacts with its outside environment in order to exist. The world is fundamentally relational; nothing can exist without relations to something else. These relations can become productive so that a subject–object, something new in the world, emerges that again is a new subject standing in relation to an object. Karl Marx has applied the concepts of subject/object to the economy, where human subjects interact with economic objects (tools of work, object of work) so that a product of work emerges. The concept of subject/object allows describing the work process as dynamic productive process. The dialectic of subject and object is in society not limited to the economy, but a concept that allows understanding the dynamics of all forms of social systems.

Sublation/*Aufhebung*   Sublation is an English translation of the German term *Aufhebung* that Hegel used as a central principle of the **dialectic**. In German the noun *Aufhebung* and the verb *aufheben* have three meanings: to abolish, to preserve and to transcend/lift up. For Hegel, dialectical development means a process of sublation in this threefold meaning of the term: if a new quality of the world emerges from a contradiction, the old status is abolished, qualities of this old status are preserved in the new status and new qualities of the world emerge so that the organization of the specific system being transformed is lifted to a new level. Marx used the notions of *Aufhebung* and *aufheben* for describing how societies develop in the form of contradictions, for describing how the unity of class struggle and class contradictions can result in revolutions that bring about new societies and for analysing crises of **capitalism**.

See also: **dialectic**

Surplus labour time   See: **necessary and surplus labour time**

Surplus value   The working day is in **capitalism** divided into two parts: a paid and an unpaid part. Surplus value is the value that is created in the unpaid part of the working day. It is a specific amount of hours in a specific unit of time (such as a day, a week or a month) that is unremunerated. There are also forms of work that are completely unremunerated. The form of the appearance of surplus value is monetary **profit**. Surplus value is a fundamental feature of **class societies**. It is the heart of the concepts of class and exploitation and for some Marx's most important critical category.

Surplus wage   "Surplus wage" is a term that Marx uses to describe how a group of workers (e.g. managers) receives higher wages than others that are paid out of a specific share of **surplus value/profits**. The task is to buy these workers' agreement to the capitalist system and their support in the execution of exploitation and domination. The notion is related to Engels' and Lenin's notion of the **labour aristocracy**.

Use-value   A use-value is a result of human work that satisfies human needs. Use-values can be physical and non-physical in character. A car is a physical use-value, whereas a social relationship and knowledge are non-physical use-values.

Value, economic value   Value in a Marxist approach (Marx's labour theory of value) is the amount of performed labour hours that are needed for the production of a certain commodity. Each single commodity has an individual value, but what is decisive for the **profits** of a company or industry is the average value (i.e. the average production time per unit) of a specific type of commodity. Specific commodity types have average production times that Marx calls socially **necessary labour time**. The magnitude or size of **value** is measured by the amount of social necessary labour time needed for the production of a specific commodity type. Human labour is the **substance of value**: it is a feature that is common to all commodities; that is, all commodities are the outcome of human **labour** and are objectifications of human labour. **Exchange-value** is the form of the appearance of value in the capitalist economy. **Money** is the common form of the appearance of **value** in capitalism. This means that value cannot easily be observed but is a rather abstract phenomenon. The value of a computer cannot be observed by looking at it or using it. It becomes apparent, however, by the circumstance that one can only own the computer and use it if one pays a certain sum of **money** as prize for it.

Value forms   In *Capital, Volume 1,* Marx explains that there are different forms of economic value:

(a) Simple/isolated/accidental form of value:
x commodity A = y commodity B
(b) Total/expanded form of value
z commodity A = u commodity B = v commodity C = w commodity D = x commodity E = etc.
(c) General form of value
u commodity B = z commodity A, v commodity C = z commodity A, w commodity D = z commodity A, x commodity E = z commodity A, etc.
(d) Money form
a ounces of gold = z commodity A, a ounces of gold = u commodity B, a ounces of gold = v commodity C, a ounces of gold = w commodity D, a ounces of gold = x commodity E, etc.

Variable capital, wages   Variable capital is **capital** that creates new **value**. It is the monetary value of **labour-power** (i.e. the wage). **Labour** is the decisive factor in production: it transfers the value of **constant capital** to the new commodity and adds new value to the commodity. The commodity that is produced in capitalism is therefore more than the sum of its parts (constant and variable capital): it contains a **surplus value** and a surplus product, more value than is contained in the investment goods and new physical and/or symbolic qualities.

Well-rounded individual/development With the notion of the well-rounded individual Marx wants to express that humans only become a complete individual in a **communist** society, whereas they are crippled class individuals in **capitalist** societies: in class societies, human activities are limited to certain activities, important activities are controlled by elites and skills are unequally distributed so that a division of labour is the result. In a classless society, humans have the skills and possibilities to engage in a broad range of activities, human toil is overcome, intellectual and creative work become crucial for all humans and the division of labour is abolished or limited.

Work The term "work" comes from the Old English word *weorc* and is the "most general word for doing something" (Williams 1983, 334). In work, humans make use of their body and brains in order to use tools with which they transform nature (natural resources) and/or culture (experiences) in such a way that something new that satisfies various human needs emerges. If the emerging product is physical in character, then one can speak of physical work; if it is non-physical then one tends to speak of knowledge or information work. All work requires a combination of the power of the human brain and the human body. It is therefore always physical and knowledge work. Each concrete work has, however, varying degrees of the expenditure of physical and psychological power. The category of "immaterial labour" that authors such as Maurizio Lazzarato, Paolo Virno, Toni Negri and Michael Hardt have used is an imprecise category for knowledge work. It is imprecise because it implies that knowledge is immaterial. In a materialist philosophy, the whole world is material; it is created by subjects that interact with their environments in relations that create novelty. Matter is a dynamic process of production that creates and recreates the world. In German, the language in which Marx mostly wrote, there are the terms *Arbeit* and *Werktätigkeit*. The first is a more ambiguous term that Marx used for both work and **labour**. The second is a more general term that means activity that creates works. It can best be translated as "work". The terms "work" and "labour" cannot be clearly separated, for they are dialectically entwined. If work is a general term that applies to all societies, then labour is also a form of work, although necessarily alienated. This means that one can abolish labour, not work, but abolishing labour means abolishing a form of work, so that the historically dominant form of work undergoes **sublation** and is thereby transformed into a different form of work.

See also: **labour**

BIBLIOGRAPHY

Adorno, Theodor W. 1968/2003. Late capitalism or industrial society? The fundamental question of the present structure of society. In *Can one live after Auschwitz?*, ed. Rolf Tiedemann, 111–125. Stanford, CA: Stanford University Press.

Adorno, Theodor W. 1977. *Kulturkritik und Gesellschaft II.* Frankfurt am Main: Suhrkamp.

Adorno, Theodor W. 1996. Chaplin times two. *Yale Journal of Criticism* 9 (1): 57–61.

Adorno, Theodor W. 2000. *Introduction to sociology.* Cambridge, UK: Polity.

Adorno, Theodor W. 2005. Prologue to television. In *Critical models,* 49–57. New York: Columbia University Press.

Adorno, Theodor W., Else Frenkel-Brunswik, Daniel Levinson and Nevitt Sanford. 1950. *The authoritarian personality.* New York: Harper & Row.

Althusser, Louis. 1969. *For Marx.* London: Verso.

Althusser, Louis, and Étienne Balibar. 1970. *Reading Capital.* London: NLB.

Anderson, Chris. 2009. *Free. How today's smartest businesses profit by giving something for nothing.* London: Random House.

Anderson, Kevin B. 2010. *Marx at the margins: On nationalism, ethnicity, and non-Western societies.* Chicago: University of Chicago Press.

Andrejevic, Mark. 2002. The work of being watched: Interactive media and the exploitation of self-disclosure. *Critical Studies in Media Communication* 19 (2): 230–248.

Andrejevic, Mark. 2004. *Reality TV: The work of being watched.* Lanham, MD: Rowman & Littlefield.

Andrejevic, Mark. 2009. *iSpy: Surveillance and power in the interactive era.* Lawrence: University Press of Kansas.

Andrejevic, Mark. 2011. Social network exploitation. In *A networked self,* ed. Zizi Papacharissi, 82–101. New York: Routledge.

Andrejevic, Mark. 2012. Exploitation in the data mine. In *Internet and surveillance: The challenges of Web 2.0 and social media,* ed. Christian Fuchs, Kees Boersma, Anders Albrechtslund and Marisol Sandoval, 71–88. New York: Routledge.

Andrejevic, Mark. 2013. Estranged free labor. In *Digital labor: The Internet as playground and factory,* ed. Trebor Scholz, 149–164. New York: Routledge.

Aneesh, A. 2006. *Virtual migration: The programming of globalization.* Durham, NC: Duke University Press.

Aouragh, Miriyam. 2012. Social media, mediation and the Arab revolutions. *tripleC: Communication, Capitalism & Critique (www.triple-c.at) Journal for a Global Sustainable Information Society* 10 (2): 518–536.

Aouragh, Miriyam, and Anne Alexander. 2011. The Egyptian experience: Sense and nonsense of the Internet revolution. *International Journal of Communication* 5: 1344–1358.

Arora, Ashish, V.S. Arunachalam, Jai Asundi and Ronald Fernandes. 1999. The Indian software industry. Paper presented at the R&D Management Conference in New Delhi. http://www.heinz.cmu.edu/project/india/pubs/rndmgmt.pdf.

Arora, Ashish, V.S. Arunachalam, Jai Asundi and Ronald Fernandes. 2001. The Indian software services industry. *Research Policy* 30 (8): 1267–1287.

Arora, Ashish, Alfonso Gambardella and Salvatore Torrisi. 2001. *In the footsteps of Silicon Valley? Indian and Irish software in the international division of labour.* Stanford Institute for Economic Policy Research Discussion Paper No. 00–41. Stanford, CA: Stanford University.

Arthur, Christopher J. 2004. *The new dialectic and Marx's Capital.* Leiden: Brill.

Artz, Lee. 2008. Media relations and media product: Audience commodity. *Democratic Communiqué* 22 (1): 60–74.

Arvidsson, Adam. 2005. Brands: A critical perspective. *Journal of Consumer Culture* 5 (2): 235–258.

Arvidsson, Adam. 2011. Ethics and value in customer co-production. *Marketing Theory* 11 (3): 261–278.

Arvidsson, Adam, and Elanor Colleoni. 2012. Value in informational capitalism and on the Internet. *The Information Society* 28 (3): 135–150.

Atton, Chris. 2002. *Alternative media.* London: Sage.

Babe, Robert E. 2000. *Canadian communication thought: Ten foundational writers.* Toronto: University of Toronto Press.

Babe, Robert E. 2009. *Cultural studies and political economy: Toward a new integration.* Lanham, MD: Lexington Books.

Backhaus, Hans-Georg. 2011. *Dialektik der Wertform: Untersuchungen zur Marxschen Ökonomiekritik.* 2nd ed. Freiburg, Germany: Ça Ira.

Backhaus, Hans-Georg, and Helmut Reichelt. 1995. Wie ist der Wertbegriff in der Ökonomie zu konzipieren? *Beiträge zur Marx-Engels-Forschung Neue Folge* 1995: 60–94.

Badiou, Alain. 2012. *The rebirth of history: Times of riots and uprisings.* London: Verso.

Bakardjieva, Maria. 2005. *The Internet society: The Internet in everyday life.* London: Sage.

Banaji, Jairus. 2011. *Theory as history: Essays on modes of production and exploitation.* Chicago: Haymarket Books.

Barbrook, Richard, and Andy Cameron. 2001. Californian ideology. In *Crypto anarchy, cyberstates and pirate utopias,* ed. Peter Ludlow, 363–387. Cambridge, MA: MIT Press.

Beck, Ulrich, Anthony Giddens and Scott Lash. 1994. *Reflexive modernization.* Cambridge, UK: Polity.

Beecher, Jonathan F. 1990. *Charles Fourier: The visionary and his world.* Berkeley: University of California Press.

Bell, Daniel. 1974. *The coming of post-industrial society.* London: Heinemann.

Benjamin, Walter. 1934. Der Autor als Produzent. In *Medienästhetische Schriften,* 231–247. Frankfurt am Main: Suhrkamp.

Benjamin, Walter. 1936/1939. The work of art in the age of mechanical reproduction. In *Media and cultural studies: KeyWorks,* ed. Meenakshi Gigi Durham and Douglas M. Kellner, 18–40. Malden, MA: Blackwell.

Benner, Chris. 2002. *Work in the new economy: Flexible labor markets in Silicon Valley.* Malden, MA: Blackwell.

Bennett, W. Lance. 2003. Communicating global activism. *Information, Communication & Society* 6 (2): 143–168.

Bennett, W. Lance. 2005. Social movement beyond borders. In *Transnational protest & global activism,* ed. Donatella della Porta and Sidney Tarrow, 203–226. Boulder, CO: Paradigm.

Bennett, W. Lance, and Robert M. Entman, eds. 2001. *Mediated politics.* Cambridge: Cambridge University Press.

Berardi, Franco "Bifo". 2009a. *Precarious rhapsody.* London: Minor Compositions.

Berardi, Franco "Bifo". 2009b. *The soul at work.* Los Angeles, CA: Semiotext(e).

Bermejo, Fernando. 2009. Audience manufacture in historical perspective: From broadcasting to Google. *New Media & Society* 11 (1–2): 133–154.

Bertin, Imogen, Ursula Huws, Tamás Koltai, Markus Promberger, Nicola Tickner, Peter van der Hallen and Roel Verlinden. 2004. *Opening the black box: Classification and coding of sectors and occupations in the eEconomy.* Leuven: STILE Project.

Bhaskar, Roy. 1993. *Dialectic: The pulse of freedom.* London: Verso.

Biao, Xiang. 2007. *Global body shopping: An Indian labor system in the information technology industry.* Princeton, NJ: Princeton University Press.

Bidet, Jacques. 2007. *A reconstruction project of the Marxian theory: From Exploring Marx's Capital (1985) to Altermarxisme (2007), via Théorie Générale (1999) and Explication et reconstruction du Capital (2004).* http://jacques.bidet.pagesperso-orange.fr/londongla.htm.

Bidet, Jacques. 2009. *Exploring Marx's Capital: Philosophical, economic, and political dimensions.* Chicago: Haymarket Books.

Bigo, Didier. 2010. Delivering liberty and security? The reframing of freedom when associated with security. In *Europe's 21st century challenge: Delivering liberty,* ed. Didier Bigo, Sergio Carrera, Elspeth Guild and R.B.J. Walker, 263–287. Farnham, UK: Ashgate.

Biltereyst, Daniel, and Philippe Meers. 2011. The political economy of audiences. In *The handbook of political economy of communications,* ed. Janet Wasko, Graham Murdock and Helena Sousa, 415–435. Malden, MA: Wiley-Blackwell.

Bolin, Göran. 2005. Notes from inside the factory: The production and consumption of signs and sign value in media industries. *Social Semiotics* 15 (3): 289–306.

Bolin, Göran. 2009. Symbolic production and value in media industries. *Journal of Cultural Economy* 2 (3): 345–361.

Bolin, Göran. 2011. *Value and the media: Cultural production and consumption in digital markets.* Farnham, UK: Ashgate.

Boltanski, Luc, and Ève Chiapello. 2007. *The new spirit of capitalism.* London: Verso.

Bourdieu, Pierre. 1986a. *Distinction: A social critique of the judgement of taste.* London: Routledge.

Bourdieu, Pierre. 1986b. The (three) forms of capital. In *Handbook of theory and research in the sociology of education,* ed. John G. Richardson, 241–258. New York: Greenwood Press.

Brady, Robert A. 1937. *The spirit and structure of German fascism.* New York: Viking.

Bratich, Jack. 2011. User-generated discontent convergence, polemology and dissent. *Cultural Studies* 25 (4–5): 621–640.

Brecht, Bertolt. 1932/2000. The radio as a communications apparatus. In *Bertolt Brecht on film & radio,* ed. Marc Silberman, 41–46. London: Methuen.

Breen, Marcus. 2011. Do the math: Cultural studies into public policy needs a new equation. In *The renewal of cultural studies,* ed. Paul Smith, 207–218. Philadelphia, PA: Temple University Press.

Bruns, Axel. 2008. *Blogs, Wikipedia, Second Life, and beyond: From production to produsage.* New York: Peter Lang.

Bühl, Achim. 2000. *Die virtuelle Gesellschaft des 21: Jahrhunderts.* Opladen, Germany: Westdeutscher Verlag.

Burston, Jonathan, Nick Dyer-Witheford and Alison Hearn, eds. 2010. *Digital labour: Workers, authors, citizens.* Special issue. *Ephemera* 10 (3–4): 214–539.

Butler, Judith, Ernesto Laclau and Slavoj Žižek. 2000. *Contingency, hegemony, universality.* London: Verso.

Caraway, Brett. 2011. Audience labor in the new media environment: A Marxian revisiting of the audience commodity. *Media, Culture & Society* 33 (5): 693–708.

Carnoy, Martin, Manuel Castells and Chris Benner. 1997. Labour markets and employment practices in the age of flexibility: A case study of Silicon Valley. *International Labour Review* 136 (1): 27–48.

Castells, Manuel. 1996. *The rise of the network society.* Volume 1 of *The information age: economy, society and culture.* 2nd ed. Malden, MA: Blackwell.

Castells, Manuel. 1997. *The power of identity.* Volume 2 of *The information age: economy, society and culture.* 2nd ed. Malden, MA: Blackwell.

Castells, Manuel. 2000a. *End of millennium.* Volume 3 of *The information age: economy, society and culture.* 2nd ed. Malden: Blackwell.

Castells, Manuel. 2000b. Materials for an exploratory theory of the network society. *British Journal of Sociology* 51 (1): 5–24.

Castells, Manuel. 2009. *Communication power.* Oxford: Oxford University Press.

Castells, Manuel. 2012. *Networks of outrage and hope: Social movements in the Internet age.* Cambridge, UK: Polity.

Chakravartty, Paula. 2004. Telecom, national development and the Indian state: A postcolonial critique. *Media, Culture & Society* 26 (2): 227–249.

Chakravartty, Paula. 2006. White-collar nationalism. *Social Semiotics* 16 (1): 39–55.

Charusheela, S. 2011. Where is the "economy"? Cultural studies and narratives of capitalism. In *The renewal of cultural studies,* ed. Paul Smith, 177–187. Philadelphia, PA: Temple University Press.

Chen, Chih-hsien. 2003. Is the audience really commodity? An overdetermined Marxist perspective of the television economy. Papers of the International Communication Association Conference 2003. http://citation.allacademic.com/meta/p_mla_apa_research_citation/1/1/2/0/8/pages112086/p112086-1.php.

Chomsky, Noam. 2012. *Occupy.* London: Penguin.

Christensen, Christian. 2008. Uploading dissonance: YouTube and the US occupation of Iraq. *Media, War & Conflict* 1 (2): 155–175.

Cleaver, Harry. 1992. The inversion of class perspective in Marxian Theory: From valorisation to self-valorisation. In *Open Marxism, Vol. 2,* ed. Werner Bonefeld, Richard Gunn and Kosmos Psychopedis, 106–144. London: Pluto.

Cleaver, Harry. 2000. *Reading Capital politically.* Leeds: Anti/Theses.

Cohen, Nicole. 2008. The valorization of surveillance: Towards a political economy of Facebook. *Democratic Communiqué* 22 (1): 5–22.

Cohen, Robert B. 1981. The new international division of labor, multinational corporations and urban hierarchy. In *Urbanization and urban planning in capitalist society,* ed. M. Michael J. Dear and Allen John Scott, 287–317. London: Methuen.

Cohen, Robin. 1987. *The new helots: Migrants in the international division of labour.* London: Avebury.

Commander, Simon, Rupa Chanda, Mari Kangasniemi and L. Alan Winters. 2008. The consequences of globalisation: India's software industry and cross-border labour mobility. *The World Economy* 31 (2): 187–211.

Costanza-Chock, Sasha. 2012. Mic check! Media cultures and the Occupy movement. *Social Movement Studies: Journal of Social, Cultural and Political Protest* 11 (3–4): 375–385.

Coté, Mark, and Jennifer Pybus. 2010. Learning to immaterial labour 2.0: MySpace and social networks. *Ephemera* 7 (1): 88–106.

Couldry, Nick. 2010. *Why voice matters: Culture and politics after neoliberalism.* London: SAGE.

Couldry, Nick. 2011. The project of cultural studies: Heretical doubts, new horizons. In *The renewal of cultural studies,* ed. Paul Smith, 9–16. Philadelphia, PA: Temple University Press.

Couvering, Elizabeth. 2004. New media? The political economy of Internet search engines. IAMCR 2004 Paper. http://citeseerx.ist.psu.edu/viewdoc/summary?doi= 10.1.1.129.1900.

Couvering, Elizabeth. 2011. Navigational media: The political economy of online traffic. In *The political economies of media: The transformation of the global media industries,* ed. Dwayne Winseck and Dal Yong Jin, 183–200. London: Bloomsbury.

Crossley, Nick. 2003. Even newer social movements? Anti-corporate protests, capitalist crises and the remoralization of society. *Organization* 10 (2): 287–305.

Curran, James, Natalie Fenton and Des Freedman. 2012. *Misunderstanding the Internet.* New York: Routledge.

Davis, Angela. 2011. The 99%: A community of resistance. *The Guardian Online,* November 15, 2011.

D'Costa, Anthony. 2002. Uneven and combined development: Understanding India's software exports. *World Development* 31 (1): 211–226.

D'Cruz, Premilla, and Ernesto Noronha. 2009. Experiencing depersonalised bullying: A study of Indian call-centre agents. *Work, Organisation, Labour & Globalisation* 3 (1): 26–46.

D'Mello, Marisa, and Sundeep Sahay. 2007. "I am a kind of nomad where I have to go places and places" . . . Understanding mobility, place and identity in global software work from India. *Information and Organization* 17 (3): 162–192.

Dawson, Michael, and John Bellamy Foster. 1998. Virtual capitalism. In *Capitalism and the information age,* ed. Robert W. McChesney, Eileen Meiksins Wood and John Bellamy Foster, 51–67. New York: Monthly Review Press.

Dean, Jodi. 2005. Communicative capitalism: Circulation and the foreclosure of politics. *Cultural Politics* 1 (1): 51–74.

Dean, Jodi. 2010. *Blog theory.* Cambridge, UK: Polity.

Dean, Jodi. 2012. *The communist horizon.* London: Verso.

Deleuze, Gilles. 1995. Postscript on the societies of control. In *Negotiations,* 177–182. New York: Columbia University Press.

della Porta, Donatella. 2007a. The global justice movement: An introduction. In *The global justice movement: Cross-national and transnational perspectives,* ed. Donatella della Porta, 1–28. Boulder, CO: Paradigm.

della Porta, Donatella. 2007b. The global justice movement in context. In *The global justice movement: Cross-national and transnational perspectives,* ed. Donatella della Porta, 232–251. Boulder, CO: Paradigm.

della Porta, Donatella, and Mario Diani. 2006. *Social movements: An introduction.* Malden, MA: Blackwell.

Deuze, Mark. 2007. *Media work.* Cambridge, UK: Polity.

Diani, Mario. 2003. Networks and social movements: A research programme. In *Social movements and networks,* ed. Mario Diani and Doug McAdam, 298–319. Oxford: Oxford University Press.

Dimitrov, Georgi. 1935. *The fascist offensive and the tasks of the Communist International in the struggle of the working class against fascism.* http://www.marxists.org/reference/archive/dimitrov/works/1935/08_02.htm.

Donk, Wim van de, et al., eds. 2004. *Cyberprotest.* London: Routledge.

Doogan, Kevin. 2009. *New capitalism? The transformation of work.* Cambridge, UK: Polity.

Dossani, Rafiq, and Martin Kenney. 2007. The next wave of globalization. Relocating service provision to India. *World Development* 35 (5): 772–791.

Drucker, Peter. 1969/1992. *The age of discontinuity.* New Brunswick, NJ: Transaction.

Drucker, Peter. 2001. *The essential Drucker.* New York: HarperCollins.

Dussel, Enrique. 2008. The discovery of the category of surplus value. In *Karl Marx's Grundrisse: Foundations of the critique of the political economy 150 years later,* ed. Marcello Musto, 67–78. New York: Routledge.

Dyer-Witheford, Nick. 1999. *Cyber-Marx: Cycles and circuits of struggle in high-technology capitalism.* Urbana: University of Illinois Press.

Dyer-Witheford, Nick. 2002. Global body, global brain/global factory, global war: Revolt of the value-subjects. *The Commoner* 3.

Dyer-Witheford, Nick. 2010. Digital labour, species being and the global worker. *Ephemera* 10 (3–4): 484–503.

Eagleton, Terry. 2011. *Why Marx was right.* London: Yale University Press.

Eatwell, John, Murray Milgate and Peter Newman. 1987. *The new Palgrave: A dictionary of economics,* vol. 3, *K to P.* London: Macmillan Press.

Eder, Klaus. 1993. *New politics of class: Social movements and cultural dynamics in advanced societies.* London: Sage.

Eichstaedt, Peter. 2011. *Consuming the Congo: War and conflict minerals in the world's deadliest place.* Chicago: Lawrence Hill Books.

Eisenstein, Zillah. 1979. Developing a theory of capitalist patriarchy. In *Capitalist patriarchy and the case for socialist feminism,* ed. Zillah Eisenstein, 5–40. New York: Monthly Review Press.

Ekman, Mattias. 2012. Understanding accumulation: The relevance of Marx's theory of primitive accumulation in media and communication studies. *tripleC: Communication, Capitalism & Critique (www.triple-c.at)-Journal for a Global Sustainable Information Society* 10 (2): 156–170.

Engels, Friedrich. 1847. *The principles of communism.* http://www.marxists.org/archive/marx/works/1847/11/prin-com.htm.

Engels, Friedrich. 1884. *The origin of the family, private property and the state.* http://www.marxists.org/archive/marx/works/1884/origin-family/index.htm.

Engels, Friedrich. 1892. *Preface to the English edition of "The condition of the working class in England".* http://www.marxists.org/archive/marx/works/1892/01/11.htm.

Engels, Friedrich. 1895/1896. *The part played by labour in the transition from ape to man.* http://www.marxists.org/archive/marx/works/1876/part-played-labour/index.htm.

Enzensberger, Hans Magnus. 1970. Baukasten zu einer Theorie der Medien. In *Kursbuch Medienkultur,* ed. Lorenz Engell, Oliver Fahle, Britta Neitzel, Josef Vogel and Claus Pias, 264–278. Stuttgart: DVA.

Enzensberger, Hans Magnus. 1974. *The consciousness industry.* New York: Seabury Press.

Erdogan, İrfan. 2012. Missing Marx: The place of Marx in current communication research and the place of communication in Marx's work. *tripleC: Communication, Capitalism & Critique (www.triple-c.at)-Journal for a Global Sustainable Information Society* 10 (2): 349–391.

Ernst, Dieter. 1980. *The new international division of labour, technology and underdevelopment: Consequences for the Third World.* Frankfurt: Campus.

Feagin, Joe R., and Michael P. Smith. 1987. Cities and the new international division of labor: An overview. In *The capitalist city: Global restructuring and community politics,* ed. Joe R. Feagin and Michael P. Smith, 3–34. Oxford: Basil Blackwell.

Ferguson, Marjorie, and Peter Golding. 1997. Cultural studies and changing times: An introduction. In *Cultural studies in question,* ed. Marjorie Ferguson and Peter Golding, xiii–xxvii. London: Sage.

Firer-Blaess, Sylvain, and Christian Fuchs. 2012. Wikipedia: An info-communist manifesto. *Television & New Media,* doi: 10.1177/1527476412450193.

Fisher, Eran. 2010. *Media and new capitalism in the digital age: The spirit of networks.* New York: Palgrave Macmillan.

Fisher, Eran. 2012. How less alienation creates more exploitation? Audience labour on social network sites. *tripleC: Communication, Capitalism & Critique (www.triple-c.at)-Communication, Capitalism & Critique (www.triple-c.at)-Journal for a Global Sustainable Information Society* 10 (2): 171–183.

Fitzpatrick, Tony. 2002. Critical theory, information society and surveillance technologies. *Information, Communication and Society* 5 (3): 357–378.

Flew, Terry. 2007. *Understanding global media.* Basingstoke, UK: Palgrave Macmillan.

Folke, Steen, Niels Fold and Thyge Enevoldsen. 1993. *South-south trade and development: Manufacturers in the new international division of labour.* New York: St. Martin's Press.

Fortunati, Leopoldina. 1995. *The arcane of reproduction.* New York: Autonomedia.

Freud, Sigmund. 1961. *Beyond the pleasure principle.* New York: Norton.

Friedmann, Georges. 1959. *Grenzen der Arbeitsteilung.* Volume 7, *Frankfurter Beiträge zur Soziologie.* Frankfurt am Main: Europäische Verlagsanstalt.

Friedman, Jonathan. 2002. Modernity and other traditions. In *Critically modern,* ed. Bruce M. Knauft, 287–313. Bloomington: Indiana University Press.

Fröbel, Folker, Jürgen Heinrichs and Otto Kreye. 1981. *The new international division of labour.* Cambridge: Cambridge University Press.

Fuchs, Christian. 2003. Globalization and self-organization in the knowledge-based society. *tripleC: Communication, Capitalism & Critique (www.triple-c.at)-Communication, Capitalism & Critique (www.triple-c.at)-Journal for a Global Sustainable Information Society* 1 (2): 105–169.

Fuchs, Christian. 2006. The self-organization of social movements. *Systemic Practice and Action Research* 19 (1): 101–137.

Fuchs, Christian. 2008. *Internet and society: Social theory in the information age.* New York: Routledge.

Fuchs, Christian. 2009. Information and communication technologies and society: A contribution to the critique of the political economy of the Internet. *European Journal of Communication* 24 (1): 69–87.

Fuchs, Christian. 2010a. Critical globalization studies: An empirical and theoretical analysis of the new imperialism. *Science & Society* 74 (2): 215–247.

Fuchs, Christian. 2010b. Labor in informational capitalism and on the Internet. *The Information Society* 26 (3): 179–196.

Fuchs, Christian. 2010c. New imperialism: Information and media imperialism? *Global Media and Communication* 6 (1): 33–60.

Fuchs, Christian. 2010d. Social software and Web 2.0: their sociological foundations and implications. In *Handbook of research on Web 2.0, 3.0, and X.0: Technologies, business, and social applications,* vol. 2, ed. San Murugesan, 764–789. Hershey, PA: IGI-Global.

Fuchs, Christian. 2011a. *Foundations of critical media and information studies.* Abingdon: Routledge.

Fuchs, Christian. 2011b. The contemporary world wide web: Social medium or new space of accumulation? In *The political economies of media: The transformation of the global media industries,* ed. Dwayne Winseck and Dal Yong Jin, 201–220. London: Bloomsbury.

Fuchs, Christian. 2012a. Conference Report: The 4th ICTs and Society Conference: Critique, Democracy and Philosophy in 21st Century Information Society. *Nordicom Information* 34 (3–4): 89–99.

Fuchs, Christian. 2012b. Critique of the political economy of Web 2.0 surveillance. In *Internet and surveillance: The challenges of Web 2.0 and social media,* ed. Christian Fuchs, Kees Boersma, Anders Albrechtslund and Marisol Sandoval, 31–70. New York: Routledge.

Fuchs, Christian. 2012c. Implications of Deep Packet Inspection (DPI) Internet surveillance for society. The Privacy & Security Research Paper Series #1. ISSN 2279–7467. http://www.projectpact.eu/documents-1/%231_Privacy_and_Security_Research_Paper_Series.pdf.

Fuchs, Christian. 2012d. New Marxian Times! Reflections on the 4th ICTs and Society Conference "Critique, Democracy and Philosophy in 21st Century Information Society. Towards Critical Theories of Social Media". *tripleC: Communication, Capitalism & Critique (www.triple-c.at)-Journal for a Global Sustainable Information Society* 10 (1): 114–121.

Fuchs, Christian. 2012e. With or without Marx? With or without capitalism? A rejoinder to Adam Arvidsson and Elanor Colleoni. *tripleC: Communication, Capitalism & Critique (www.triple-c.at)-Open Access Journal for a Global Sustainable Information Society* 10 (2): 633–645.

Fuchs, Christian. 2013. *OccupyMedia! The Occupy movement and social media in crisis capitalism.* Ropley: Zero Books.

Fuchs, Christian. 2014. *Social media: A critical introduction.* London: Sage.

Fuchs, Christian, and Nick Dyer-Witheford. 2013. Karl Marx @ Internet Studies. *New Media & Society,* 15 (5): 782–796.

Fuchs, Christian, and Wolfgang Hofkirchner. 2005. Self-organization, knowledge, and responsibility. *Kybernetes* 34 (1–2): 241–260.

Fuchs, Christian, Wolfgang Hofkirchner, Matthias Schafranek, Celina Raffl, Marisol Sandoval and Robert Bichler. 2010. Theoretical foundations of the web: Cognition, communication, and co-operation: Towards an understanding of Web 1.0, 2.0, 3.0. *Future Internet* 2 (1): 41–59.

Fuchs, Christian, and Vincent Mosco, eds. 2012. Marx is back—The importance of Marxist theory and research for critical communication studies today. *tripleC: Communication, Capitalism & Critique (www.triple-c.at)-Journal for a Global Sustainable Information Society* 10 (2): 127–632.

Fuchs, Christian, and Marisol Sandoval, eds. Forthcoming 2014. *Critique, social media and the information society.* New York: Routledge.

Gaby, Sarah, and Neal Caren. 2012. Occupy online: How cute old men and Malcolm X recruited 400 000 US users to OWS on Facebook. *Social Movement Studies: Journal of Social, Cultural and Political Protest* 11 (3–4): 367–374.

Gamsey, Elizabeth, and Liba Paukert. 1987. *Industrial change and women's employment: Trends in the new international division of labour.* Geneva: International Institute for Labour Studies.

Gandy, Oscar H. 1993. *The panoptic sort: A political economy of personal information.* Boulder, CO: Westview Press.

Gandy, Oscar H. 2009. *Coming to terms with chance: Engaging rational discrimination and cumulative disadvantage.* Farnham, UK: Ashgate.

Gandy, Oscar H. 2011. The political economy of personal information. In *The handbook of political economy of communications,* ed. Janet Wasko, Graham Murdock and Helena Sousa, 436–457. Malden, MA: Wiley-Blackwell.

Garnham, Nicholas. 1990. *Capitalism and communication.* London: Sage.

Garnham, Nicholas. 1995a. Political Economy and cultural studies: Reconciliation or divorce? *Critical Studies in Mass Communication* 12 (1): 62–71.

Garnham, Nicholas. 1995b. Reply to Grossberg and Carey. *Critical Studies in Mass Communication* 12 (1): 95–100.

Garnham, Nicholas. 1998/2004. Information society theory as ideology. In *The information society reader,* ed. Frank Webster, 165–183. New York: Routledge.

Garnham, Nicholas. 2000a. *Emancipation, the media, and modernity.* Oxford: Oxford University Press.

Garnham, Nicholas. 2000b. "Information society" as theory or ideology. *Information, Communication & Society* 3 (2): 139–152.

Garnham, Nicholas. 2004. Class analysis and the information society as mode of production. *Javnost* 11 (3): 93–104.

Gauntlett, David. 2011. *Making is connecting: The social meaning of creativity, from DIY and knitting to YouTube and Web 2.0.* Cambridge, UK: Polity.

Gerbaudo, Paolo. 2012. *Tweets and the streets: Social media and contemporary activism.* London: Pluto Press.

Ghonim, Wael. 2012. *Revolution 2.0.* London: Fourth Estate.

Giddens, Anthony. 1980. *The class structure of the advanced societies.* 2nd ed. London: Hutchinson.

Giddens, Anthony. 1984. *The constitution of society: Outline of the theory of structuration.* Cambridge, UK: Polity.

Giddens, Anthony. 1990. *The consequences of modernity.* Stanford, CA: Stanford University Press.

Gill, Rosalind. 2002. Cool, creative and egalitarian? Exploring gender in project-based new media work in Euro. *Information, Communication & Society* 5 (1): 70–89.

Gill, Rosalind. 2006. *Technobohemians or the new cybertariat?* Amsterdam: Institute of Network Cultures.

Gill, Rosalind, and Andy Pratt. 2008. In the social factory? Immaterial labour, precariousness and cultural work. *Theory, Culture & Society* 25 (7–8): 1–30.

Gillan, Kevin, Jenny Pickerill and Frank Webster. 2008. *Anti-war activism. New media and protest in the information age.* Basingstoke: Palgrave Macmillan.

Glotz, Peter. 1999. *Die beschleunigte Gesellschaft: Kulturkämpfe im digitalen Kapitalismus.* Munich: Kindler.

Göhler, Gerhard. 1980. *Die Reduktion der Dialektik durch Marx: Strukturveränderungen der dialektischen Entwicklung in der Kritik der politischen Ökonomie.* Stuttgart: Klett-Cotta.

Golding, Peter. 2000. Forthcoming features: Information and communications technologies and the sociology of the future. *Sociology* 34 (1): 165–184.

Golding, Peter, and Graham Murdock. 1978. Theories of communication and theories of society. *Communication Research* 5 (3): 339–356.

Goldthorpe, John H. 2000. *On sociology.* Oxford: Oxford University Press.

Goodwin, Jeff. 2001. *No other way out: States and revolutionary movements, 1945–1991.* Cambridge: Cambridge University Press.

Graeber, David. 2011. *Debt: The first 5,000 years.* New York: Melville House.

Graeber, David. 2012. *Inside Occupy.* Frankfurt: Campus.

Gregg, Melissa. 2011. *Work's intimacy.* Cambridge, UK: Polity.

Grossberg, Lawrence. 1995. Cultural studies vs. Political Economy: Is anybody else bored with this debate? *Critical Studies in Mass Communication* 12 (1): 72–81.

Grossberg, Lawrence. 2010. *Cultural studies in the future tense.* Durham, NC: Duke University Press.

Grossman, Rachel. 1980. Women's place in the integrated circuit. *Radical America* 14 (1): 29–50.

Grossmann, Henryk. 1929. *Das Akkumulations-und Zusammenbruchsgesetz des kapitalistischen Systems.* Leipzig: C.L. Hirschfeld.

Gubbay, Jon. 1997. A Marxist critique of Weberian class analysis. *Sociology* 31 (1): 73–89.

Gulias, Max. 2011. A Marxist methodology for cultural studies. In *The renewal of cultural studies,* ed. Paul Smith, 143–151. Philadelphia, PA: Temple University Press.

Habermas, Jürgen. 1984. *The theory of communicative action.* Vol. 1. Boston: Beacon Press.

Habermas, Jürgen. 1987. *The theory of communicative action.* Vol. 2. Boston: Beacon Press.

Hafez, Kai. 2007. *The myth of media globalization.* Cambridge: Polity.

Hall, Stuart. 1981/1988. Notes on deconstructing the popular. In *Cultural theory and popular culture: A reader,* ed. John Storey, 442–453. Hemel Hempstead, UK: Prentice Hall.

Hall, Stuart. 1986. The problem of ideology—Marxism without guarantees. *Journal of Communication Inquiry* 10 (2): 28–44.

Hall, Stuart. 1988. The toad in the garden: Thatcherism among the theorists. In *Marxism and the interpretation of culture,* ed. Cary Nelson and Lawrence Grossberg, 35–73. Urbana: University of Illinois Press.

Hall, Stuart. 1992/1996. Cultural studies and its theoretical legacies. In *Stuart Hall: Critical dialogues in cultural studies,* ed. David Morley and Kuan-Hsing Chen, 262–275. London: Routledge.

Hall, Stuart, et al. 1978. *Policing the crisis.* Basingstoke, UK: Palgrave Macmillan.

Halvorsen, Sam. 2012. Beyond the network? Occupy London and the global movement. *Social Movement Studies: Journal of Social, Cultural and Political Protest* 11 (3–4): 427–433.

Hardt, Michael. 2010. The common in communism. In *The idea of communism,* ed. Costas Douzinas and Slavoj Žižek, 131–144. London: Verso.

Hardt, Michael, and Antonio Negri. 2000. *Empire.* Cambridge, MA: Harvard University Press.

Hardt, Michael, and Antonio Negri. 2005. *Multitude.* London: Penguin.

Hardt, Michael, and Antonio Negri. 2009. *Commonwealth.* Cambridge, MA: Harvard University Press.

Hardt, Michael, and Antonio Negri. 2012. *Declaration.* Kindle edition.

Hartcourt, Wendy. 2011. Using the master's tools. *Media Development* 1 (2011): 19–22.

Hartley, John, ed. 2005. *Creative industries.* Oxford: Blackwell.

Hartley, John. 2012. *Digital futures for cultural and media studies.* Chichester, UK: Wiley-Blackwell.

Harvey, David. 1989. *The condition of postmodernity.* London: Blackwell.

Harvey, David. 2005. *The new imperialism.* Oxford: Oxford University Press.

Harvey, David. 2006. *Spaces of global capitalism: Towards a theory of uneven geographical development.* London: Verso.

Harvey, David. 2007. *A brief history of neoliberalism*. Oxford: Oxford University Press.

Harvey, David. 2012. *Rebel cities: From the right to the city to the urban revolution*. London: Verso.

Harvey, David, Michael Hardt and Antonio Negri. 2009. Commonwealth: An exchange. *Artforum*. http://www.thefreelibrary.com/Commonwealth%3a+an+exchange.-a0211807984.

Haug, Wolfgang Fritz. 1987. *Commodity aesthetics, ideology, and culture*. New York: International General.

Haug, Wolfgang Fritz. 2003a. *High-Tech-Kapitalismus*. Hamburg: Argument.

Haug, Wolfgang Fritz. 2003b. Wachsende Zweifel an der monetären Werttheorie: Antwort auf Heinrich. *Das Argument* 251: 424–437.

Haug, Wolfgang Fritz. 2007. Die "Neue-Kapital-Lektüre" der monetären Werttheorie. *Das Argument* 272: 560–574.

Hebblewhite, William Henning James. 2012. "Means of communication as means of production" revisited. *triubleC: Communication, Capitalism & Critique (www.triple-c.at)-Journal for a Global Sustainable Information Society* 10 (2): 203–213.

Hegel, Georg Wilhelm Friedrich. 1830. *Encyclopaedia of the philosophical sciences*. Part 1: *The Logic*. http://www.marxists.org/reference/archive/hegel/works/sl/slconten.htm.

Hegel, Georg Wilhelm Friedrich. 1991. *The encyclopaedia logic*. Indianapolis, IN: Hackett.

Heinrich, Michael. 1999. *Die Wissenschaft vom Wert: Die Marxsche Kritik der politischen Ökonomie zwischen wissenschaftlicher Revolution und klassischer Tradition*. 2nd ed. Münster, Germany: Westfälisches Dampfboot.

Heinrich, Michael. 2012. *An introduction to the three volumes of Karl Marx's Capital*. New York: Monthly Review Press.

Henderson, Jeff. 1986. The new international division of labour and American semiconductor production in South-East Asia. In *Multinational companies and the Third World*, ed. Chris J. Dixon, David Drakakis-Smith and H. Doug Watts, 91–117. Boulder, CO: Westview Press.

Hesmondhalgh, David. 2010. User-generated content, free labour and the cultural industries. *Ephemera* 10 (3–4): 267–284.

Hesmondhalgh, David, and Sarah Baker. 2011. *Creative labour: Media work in three cultural industries*. London: Routledge.

Hirst, Paul, and Graham Thompson. 1999. *Globalization in question*. Cambridge, UK: Polity.

Hobsbawm, Eric. 2011. *How to change the world: Marx and Marxism 1840–2011*. London: Little, Brown.

Hofkirchner, Wolfgang. 2002. *Projekt Eine Welt: Kognition—Kommunikation—Kooperation*. Münster, Germany: LIT.

Hofkirchner, Wolfgang. 2010. *Twenty questions about a Unified Theory of Information*. Litchfield Park, AZ: ISCE Publishing.

Holman, David, Rosemary Batt and Ursula Holtgrewe. 2007. *The global call centre report: International perspectives on management and employment*. http://www.ilr.cornell.edu/globalcallcenter/upload/GCC-Intl-Rept-UK-Version.pdf, accessed January 5, 2013.

Holtgrewe, Ursula, Jessica Longen, Hannelore Mottweiler and Annika Schönauer. 2009. Global or embedded service work? *Work, Organisation, Labour & Globalisation* 3 (1): 9–25.

Holzer, Horst. 1973. *Kommunikationssoziologie*. Reinbek, Germany: Rowohlt.

Holzer, Horst. 1994. *Medienkommunikation*. Opladen, Germany: Westdeutscher Verlag.

Hong, Yu. 2011. *Labor, class formation, and China's informationized policy and economic development*. Lanham, MD: Rowman & Littlefield.

Horkheimer, Max. 1931. The state of contemporary social philosophy and the tasks of an Institute for Social Research. In *Critical theory and society: A reader,* ed. Stephen E. Bronner and Douglas Kellner, 25–36. New York: Routledge.

Horkheimer, Max. 1947. *Eclipse of reason.* New York: Continuum.

Horkheimer, Max. 2002. *Critical theory.* New York: Continuum.

Horkheimer, Max, and Theodor W. Adorno. 2002. *Dialectic of enlightenment.* Stanford, CA: Stanford University Press.

Howe, Jeff. 2006. *Crowdsourcing: A definition.* http://crowdsourcing.typepad.com/cs/2006/06/crowdsourcing_a.html.

Howe, Jeff. 2008. *Crowdsourcing: Why the power of the crowd is driving the future of business.* New York: Three Rivers Press.

Hund, Wulf D. 1976. *Ware Nachricht und Informationsfetisch: Zur Theorie der gesellschaftlichen Kommunikation.* Darmstadt, Germany: Luchterhand.

Hund, Wulf D., and Bärbel Kirchhoff-Hund. 1980. *Soziologie der Kommunikation: Arbeitsbuch zu Struktur und Funktion der Medien: Grundbegriffe und exemplarische Analysen.* Hamburg: Rowohlt.

Huws, Ursula. 1999. Material world: The myth of the weightless economy. *Socialist Register* 35: 29–55.

Huws, Ursula. 2003. *The making of a cybertariat: Virtual work in a real world.* New York: Monthly Review Press.

Huws, Ursula. 2009. Working at the interface: Call-centre labour in a global economy. *Work, Organisation, Labour & Globalisation* 3 (1): 1–8.

Huws, Ursula, ed. 2011. *Passing the buck: Corporate restructuring and the casualisation of employment. Work, Organisation, Labour & Globalisation* 5 (1).

Huws, Ursula. 2012. The reproduction of difference: Gender and the division of labour. *Work Organisation, Labour & Globalisation* 6 (1): 1–10.

Huws, Ursula, Anneke van Luijken, Swasti Mitter and Annie Phizacklea. 1983. *International division of labour and multi-national strategies.* London: War on Wants.

Ilavarasan, Vigneswara. 2007. Is Indian software workforce a case of uneven and combined development? *Equal Opportunities International* 26 (8): 802–822.

Ilavarasan, Vigneswara. 2008. Software work in India: A labour process view. In *In an outpost of the global economy: Work and workers in India's information technology industry,* ed. Carol Upadhya and A.R. Vasavi, 162–189. New Delhi: Routledge.

James, Al, and Bhaskar Vira. 2010. "Unionising" the new spaces of the new economy? Alternative labour organising in India's IT Enabled Services–Business Process Outsourcing industry. *Geoforum* 41: 364–376.

Jameson, Frederic. 2011. *Representing Capital.* London: Verso.

Jenkins, Henry. 2008. *Convergence culture.* New York: New York University Press.

Jhally, Sut. 1987. *The codes of advertising.* New York: Routledge.

Jhally, Sut, and Bill Livant. 1986/2006. Watching as working: The valorization of audience consciousness. In *The spectacle of accumulation: Essays in culture, media, & politics,* Sut Jhally, 24–43. New York: Peter Lang.

Jones, Steven G., ed. 1998. *CyberSociety 2.0.* London: Sage.

Juris, Jeffrey S. 2012. Reflections on #occupy everywhere: Social media, public space, and emerging logics of aggregation. *American Ethnologist* 39 (2): 259–279.

Kahn, Richard, and Douglas Kellner. 2004. New media and Internet activism: From the "battle of Seattle" to blogging. *New Media & Society* 6 (1): 87–95.

Kang, Hyunjin, and Matthew P. McAllister. 2011. Selling you and your clicks: Examining the audience commodification of Google. *tripleC: Communication, Capitalism & Critique (www.triple-c.at)-Journal for a Global Sustainable Information Society* 9 (2): 141–153.

Kavada, Anastasia. 2012. Engagement, bonding and identity across multiple platforms: Avaaz on Facebook, YouTube, and MySpace. *MedieKultur* 28 (52): 28–48.

Khamis, Sahar, and Katherine Vaughn. 2011. "We are all Khaled Said": The potentials and limitations of cyberactivism in triggering public mobilization and promoting political change. *Journal of Arab & Muslim Media Research* 4 (2–3): 145–163.

Klein, Naomi. 2004. Reclaiming the commons. In *A movement of movements: Is another world really possible?*, ed. Tom Mertes, 219–229. London: Verso.

Knoche, Manfred. 2005. Kommunikationswissenschaftliche Medienökonomie als Kritik der Politischen Ökonomie der Medien. In *Internationale partizipatorische Kommunikationspolitik,* ed. Petra Ahrweiler and Barbara Thomaß, 101–109. Münster, Germany: LIT.

Kolakowski, Leszek. 2005. *Main currents of Marxism: The founders, the golden age, the breakdown.* New York: W.W. Norton.

Kriesi, Hanspeter. 1996. The organizational structure of social movements in a political context. In *Comparative perspectives on social movements,* ed. Doug McAdam, John D. McCarthy and Mayer N. Zald, 152–184. Cambridge: Cambridge University Press.

Kücklich, Julian. 2005. Precarious playbour. *Fibreculture Journal* 5, http://five.fibreculture journal.org/fcj-025-precarious-playbour-modders-and-the-digital-games-industry/ (accessed May 29, 2011).

Kurz, Robert. 2012. *Geld ohne Wert: Grundrisse zu einer Transformation der Kritik der politischen Ökonomie.* Berlin: Horlemann.

Laclau, Ernesto, and Chantal Mouffe. 1985. *Hegemony and socialist strategy: Towards a radical and democratic politics.* London: Verso.

Lakha, Salim. 1994. The new international division of labour and the Indian computer software industry. *Modern Asian Studies* 28 (2): 381–408.

Lauer, Josh. 2008. Alienation in the information economy: Toward a Marxist critique of consumer surveillance. In *Participation and media production,* ed. Nico Carpentier and Benjamin De Cleen, 41–56. Newcastle, UK: Cambridge Scholars.

Lazzarato, Maurizio. 1996. Immaterial labour. In *Radical thought in Italy,* ed. Paolo Virno and Michael Hardt, 133–146. Minneapolis: University of Minnesota Press.

Lebowitz, Michael A. 1986. Too many blindspots on the media. *Studies in Political Economy* 21: 165–173.

Lee, Micky. 2011. Google ads and the blindspot debate. *Media, Culture & Society* 33 (3): 433–447.

Lenin, Vladimir Ilyich. 1917. Imperialism, the highest stage of capitalism. In *Essential works of Lenin,* ed. Henry M. Christman, 177–270. New York: Dover.

Lenin, Vladimir Ilyich. 1920. *Preface to the French and German editions of "Imperialism, the highest stage of capitalism".* http://www.marxists.org/archive/lenin/works/1916/imp-hsc/pref02.htm#fwV22E081 (accessed on July 10, 2013).

Lent, John A., ed. 1995. *A different road taken: Profiles in critical communication.* Boulder, CO: Westview Press.

Livant, Bill. 1979. The audience commodity: On the "blindspot" debate. *Canadian Journal of Political and Social Theory* 3 (1): 91–106.

Lotan, Gilad, Erhardt Graeff, Mike Ananny, Devin Gaffney, Ian Pearce and danah boyd. 2011. The Arab Spring: The revolutions were tweeted: Information flows during the 2011 Tunisian and Egyptian revolutions. *International Journal of Communication* 5: 1375–1405.

Lukács, Georg. 1923/1972. *History and class consciousness.* Cambridge, MA: MIT Press.

Luxemburg, Rosa. 1913/2003. *The accumulation of capital.* New York: Routledge.

Lyon, David. 2003. *Surveillance after September 11.* Cambridge, UK: Polity.

Lyotard, Jean-François. 1979. *The postmodern condition.* Manchester: Manchester University Press.

Machlup, Fritz. 1962. *The production and distribution of knowledge in the United States.* Princeton, NJ: Princeton University Press.

Mansell, Robin. 1995. Against the flow: The peculiar opportunity of social scientists. In *A different road taken: Profiles in critical communication,* ed. John A. Lent, 43–66. Boulder, CO: Westview Press.

Mansour, Essam. 2012. The role of social networking sites (SNS) in the January 25th revolution in Egypt. *Library Review* 61 (2): 128–159.

Manzerolle, Vincent. 2010. Mobilizing the audience commodity: Digital labour in a wireless world. *Ephemera* 10 (3–4): 455–469.

Marcuse, Herbert. 1933. On the philosophical foundations of the concept of labor in economics. In *Heideggerian Marxism,* ed. Richard Wolin and John Abromeit, 122–150. Lincoln: University of Nebraska Press.

Marcuse, Herbert. 1941. *Reason and revolution: Hegel and the rise of social theory.* 2nd ed. London: Routledge.

Marcuse, Herbert. 1955. *Eros and civilization.* Boston: Beacon Press.

Marcuse, Herbert. 1964. *One-dimensional man.* Boston: Beacon Press.

Martin, Randy. 2011. Marxism after cultural studies. In *The renewal of cultural studies,* ed. Paul Smith, 152–159. Philadelphia, PA: Temple University Press.

Marx, Karl. 1843. *Critique of Hegel's philosophy of right.* http://www.marxists.org/archive/marx/works/1843/critique-hpr/index.htm.

Marx, Karl. 1844. Economic and philosophic manuscripts of 1844. In *Economic and philosophic manuscripts of 1844 and the Communist Manifesto,* 13–168. Amherst, NY: Prometheus.

Marx, Karl. 1845. *Theses on Feuerbach.* http://www.marxists.org/archive/marx/works/1845/theses/index.htm.

Marx, Karl. 1849. *Wage labour and capital.* http://www.marxists.org/archive/marx/works/1847/wage-labour/index.htm.

Marx, Karl. 1853a. *The British rule in India.* http://www.marxists.org/archive/marx/works/1853/06/25.htm.

Marx, Karl. 1853b. *The future results of British rule in India.* http://www.marxists.org/archive/marx/works/1853/07/22.htm.

Marx, Karl. 1857/1858a. *Grundrisse der Kritik der politischen Ökonomie: MEW, Band 42.* Berlin: Dietz.

Marx, Karl. 1857/1858b. *Grundrisse.* London: Penguin.

Marx, Karl. 1858. *Fragment des Urtextes von "Zur Kritik der politischen Ökonomie".* http://www.marxists.org/deutsch/archiv/marx-engels/1858/urtext/index.htm.

Marx, Karl. 1859. *A contribution to the critique of political economy.* http://www.marxists.org/archive/marx/works/1859/critique-pol-economy/index.htm.

Marx, Karl. 1861–1863. *Economic manuscripts of 1861–1863.* http://www.marxists.org/archive/marx/works/1861/economic/index.htm.

Marx, Karl. 1865. *Value, price, and profit.* http://www.marxists.org/archive/marx/works/1865/value-price-profit/index.htm.

Marx, Karl. 1867a. *Das Kapital: Band 1.* MEW 23. Berlin: Dietz.

Marx, Karl. 1867b. *Das Kapital: Band 1: Urfassung von 1867.* Hildesheim, Germany: Gerstenberg.

Marx, Karl. 1867c. *Capital, Volume 1.* London: Penguin.

Marx, Karl. 1872. *Das Kapital: Band 1. 2. Auflage* [2nd edition]. MEGA II/6. Berlin: Dietz.

Marx, Karl. 1875. *Critique of the Gotha Programme.* http://www.marxists.org/archive/marx/works/1875/gotha/index.htm.

Marx, Karl. 1885. *Capital: Volume 2.* London: Penguin.

Marx, Karl. 1894. *Capital: Volume 3.* London: Penguin.

Marx, Karl, and Friedrich Engels. 1845/1846. *The German ideology.* Amherst, NY: Prometheus Books.

Marx, Karl, and Friedrich Engels. 1848. Manifest der kommunistischen Partei. In *MEW, Band 3,* 459–493. Berlin: Dietz.

Marx, Karl, and Friedrich Engels. 1848/2004. *The Communist Manifesto.* Peterborough: Broadview.

Marx, Karl, and Friedrich Engels. 1968ff. *Marx Engels Werke* [hereafter *MEW*]. 43 vols. Berlin: Dietz.

Mason, Paul. 2012. *Why it's kicking off everywhere: The new global revolutions.* London: Verso.

Mathew, Jossy, Emmanuel Ogbonna and Lloyd C. Harris. 2012. Culture, employee work outcomes and performance. An empirical analysis of Indian software firms. *Journal of World Business* 47 (2): 194–203.

Mattelart, Armand. 2010. *The globalization of surveillance.* Cambridge, UK: Polity.

Mattoni, Alice. 2012. Beyond celebration: Toward a more nuanced assessment of Facebook's role in Occupy Wall Street. *Cultural Anthropology.* http://www.culanth.org/?q=node/643.

Maxwell, Richard. 1991. The image is gold: Value, the audience commodity, and fetishism. *Journal of Film and Video* 43 (1–2): 29–45.

Maxwell, Richard, ed. 2001a. *Culture works: The political economy of culture.* Minneapolis: University of Minnesota Press.

Maxwell, Richard. 2001b. Why culture works. In *Culture works: The political economy of culture,* ed. Richard Maxwell, 1–21. Minneapolis: University of Minnesota Press.

Maxwell, Richard, and Toby Miller, eds. 2005/2006. Cultural labor. Special issue. *Social Semiotics* 15 (3) and 16 (1).

Maxwell, Richard, and Toby Miller. 2012. *Greening the media.* Oxford: Oxford University Press.

Mayer, Vicki, Miranda J. Banks and John T. Caldwell. 2009. Introduction: Production studies: Roots and routes. In *Production studies: Cultural studies of media industries,* ed. Vicki Mayer, Miranda J. Banks and John Thornton Caldwell, 1–12. New York: Routledge.

McCarthy, John D. 1996. Constraints and opportunities in adopting, adapting, and inventing. In *Comparative perspectives on social movements,* eds. Doug McAdam, John D. McCarthy and Mayer N. Zald, 141–151. Cambridge: Cambridge University Press.

McCarthy, John D. and Mayer N. Zald. 1977. Resource mobilization and social movements. *American Journal of Sociology* 82 (6): 1212–1241.

McCaughey, Martha, and Michael D. Ayers, eds. 2003. *Cyberactivism.* New York: Routledge.

McGuigan, Jim. 2006. Review of John Hartley's "Creative industries". *Global Media and Communication* 2 (3): 372–374.

McGuigan, Jim. 2009. *Cool capitalism.* London: Pluto Press.

McGuigan, Lee. 2012. Consumers: The commodity product of interactive commercial television, or, is Dallas Smythe's thesis more germane than ever? *Journal of Communication Inquiry* (September 17). doi: 10.1177/0196859912459756.

McKercher, Catherine, and Vincent Mosco, eds. 2006. The labouring of communication. Special issue. *Canadian Journal of Communication* 31 (3).

McKercher, Catherine, and Vincent Mosco, eds. 2007. *Knowledge workers in the information economy.* Lanham, MD: Lexington Books.

McLuhan, Marshall. 2001. *Understanding media.* New York: Routledge.

McStay, Andrew. 2011. Profiling phorm: An autopoietic approach to the audience-as-commodity. *Surveillance & Society* 8 (3): 310–322.

Meehan, Eileen. 1984. Ratings and the institutional approach: A third answer to the commodity question. *Critical Studies in Mass Communication* 1 (2): 216–225.

Meehan, Eileen. 1993. Commodity audience, actual audience: The blindspot debate. In *Illuminating the blindspots: Essays honouring Dallas W. Smythe,* ed. Janet Wasko, Vincent Mosco and Manjunath Pendakur, 378–397. Norwood, NJ: Ablex.

Meehan, Eileen. 2002. Gendering the commodity audience: Critical media research, feminism, and political economy. In *Sex & money: Feminism and political economy in the media,* ed. Eileen Meehan and Ellen Riordan, 209–222. Minneapolis: University of Minnesota Press.

Meehan, Eileen. 2007. Understanding how the popular becomes popular: The role of political economy in the study of popular communication. *Popular Communication* 5 (3): 161–170.

Meehan, Eileen, and Ellen Riordan, ed. 2002. *Sex & money: Feminism and political economy in the media.* Minneapolis: University of Minnesota Press.

Mies, Maria. 1986. *Patriarchy & accumulation on a world scale: Women in the international division of labour.* London: Zed Books.

Mies, Maria, Veronika Bennholdt-Thomsen and Claudia von Werlhof. 1988. *Women: The last colony.* London: Zed Books.

Miller, Toby. 2010. Culture + labour = precariat. *Communication and Critical/Cultural Studies* 7 (1): 96–99.

Miller, Toby. 2011. Cultural studies in an indicative mode. *Communication and Critical/Cultural Studies* 8 (3): 319–322.

Miller, Toby, Nitin Govil, John McMurria, Richard Maxwell and Ting Wang. 2004. *Global Hollywood 2.* London: British Film Institute.

Mosco, Vincent. 2004. *The digital sublime.* Cambridge, MA: MIT Press.

Mosco, Vincent. 2009. *The political economy of communication.* 2nd ed. London: Sage.

Mosco, Vincent. 2011. Communication and cultural labour. In *The renewal of cultural studies,* ed. Paul Smith, 230–237. Philadelphia, PA: Temple University Press.

Mosco, Vincent, and Catherine McKercher. 2008. *The labouring of communication: Will knowledge workers of the world unite?* Lanham, MD: Lexington Books.

Mosco, Vincent, Catherine McKercher and Ursula Huws, eds. 2010. Getting the message: Communications workers and global value chains. *Work Organisation, Labour & Globalisation* 4 (2).

Mukherjee, Sanjukta. 2008. Producing the knowledge professional: Gendered geographies of alienation in India's new high-tech workplace. In *In an outpost of the global economy: Work and workers in India's information technology industry,* ed. Carol Upadhya and A.R. Vasavi, 50–75. New Delhi: Routledge.

Murdock, Graham. 1978. Blindspots about Western Marxism: A reply to Dallas Smythe. In *The political economy of the media,* volume 1, ed. Peter Golding and Graham Murdock, 465–474. Cheltenham, UK: Edward Elgar.

Murdock, Graham. 2011. Political economies as moral economies: Commodities, gifts, and public goods. In *The handbook of political economy of communications,* ed. Janet Wasko, Graham Murdock and Helena Sousa, 13–40. Malden, MA: Wiley-Blackwell.

Murdock, Graham, and Peter Golding. 1974. For a political economy of mass communications. In *The political economy of the media I,* ed. Peter Golding and Graham Murdock, 3–32. Cheltenham, UK: Edward Elgar.

Murdock, Graham, and Peter Golding. 2005. Culture, communications and political economy. In *Mass media and society*, ed. James Curran and Michael Gurevitch, 60–83. London: Hodder.

Nanabhay, Mohamed, and Roxane Farmanfarmaian. 2011. From spectacle to spectacular: How physical space, social media and mainstream broadcast amplified the public sphere in Egypt's "revolution". *Journal of North African Studies* 16 (4): 573–603.

Napoli, Philip M. 2010. Revisiting "mass communication" and the "work" of the audience in the new media environment. *Media, Culture & Society* 32 (3): 505–516.

Negri, Antonio. 1971/1988. Crisis of the planner-state: Communism and revolutionary organisation. In *Revolution retrieved: Selected writings on Marx, Keynes, capitalist crisis & new social subjects 1967–83*, 91–148. London: Red Notes.

Negri, Antonio. 1979/1988. Marx beyond Marx: Working notebooks on the "Grundrisse". In *Revolution retrieved: Selected writings on Marx, Keynes, capitalist crisis & new social subjects 1967–83*, 149–176. London: Red Notes.

Negri, Antonio. 1982/1988. Archaeology and project: The mass worker and the social worker. In *Revolution retrieved: Selected writings on Marx, Keynes, capitalist crisis & new social subjects 1967–83*, 199–228. London: Red Notes.

Negri, Antonio. 1991. *Marx beyond Marx*. London: Pluto.

Negri, Antonio. 2008. *Reflections on empire*. Cambridge, UK: Polity.

Nest, Michael. 2011. *Coltan*. Cambridge, UK: Polity.

Neubauer, Robert. 2011. Neoliberalism in the information age, or vice versa? Global citizenship, technology, and hegemonic ideology. *tripleC: Communication, Capitalism & Critique (www.triple-c.at)-Journal for a Global Sustainable Information Society* 9 (2): 195–230.

Neumann, Franz. 1942. *Behemoth: The structure and practice of National Socialism*. London: Gollancz.

Nixon, Brice. 2012. Dialectical method and the critical political economy of culture. *tripleC: Communication, Capitalism & Critique (www.triple-c.at)-Journal for a Global Sustainable Information Society* 10 (2): 439–456.

O'Connor, James. 1998. *Natural causes: Essays in ecological Marxism*. New York: Guilford Press.

O'Reilly, Tim. 2005. *What is Web 2.0?* http://www.oreilly.de/artikel/web20.html.

O'Reilly, Tim, and John Battelle. 2009. *Web squared: Web 2.0 five years on: Special report*. http://assets.en.oreilly.com/1/event/28/web2009_websquared-whitepaper.pdf.

Offe, Claus. 1985. New social movements: Challenging the boundaries of institutional politics. *Social Research* 52 (4): 817–867.

Panitch, Leo, and Sam Gindin. 2004. Global capitalism and American empire. *Socialist Register* 2004: 1–42.

Papacharissi, Zizi. 2009. The virtual sphere 2.0. In *Routledge Handbook of Internet Politics*, ed. Andrew Chadwick and Philip N. Howard, 230–245. New York: Routledge.

Papacharissi, Zizi. 2010. *A private sphere*. Cambridge, UK: Polity.

Pasquinelli, Matteo. 2009. Google's PageRank algorithm: A diagram of cognitive capitalism and the rentier of the common intellect. In *Deep Search*, ed. Konrad Becker and Felix Stalder, 152–162. London: Transaction Publishers.

Pasquinelli, Matteo. 2010. The ideology of free culture and the grammar of sabotage. In *Education in the creative economy: Knowledge and learning in the age of innovation*, ed. Daniel Araya and Michael Peters. New York: Peter Lang.

Paul, Jane, and Ursula Huws. 2002. *How can we help? Good practice in call-centre employment*. Brussels: European Union Trade Union Confederation.

Pellow, David N., and Lisa Sun-Hee Park. 2002. *The Silicon Valley of dreams: Environmental injustice, immigrant workers, and the high-tech global economy*. New York: New York University Press.

Pollock, Friedrich. 1956. *Automation: Materialien zur Beurteilung der ökonomischen und sozialen Folgen.* Vol. 5 of *Frankfurter Beiträge zur Soziologie.* Frankfurt am Main: Europäische Verlagsanstalt.

Porat, Marc Uri. 1977. *The information economy: Definition and measurement.* Washington, DC: Office of Telecommunications.

Porter, Michael. 1985. *Competitive advantage: Creating and sustaining superior performance.* New York: Free Press.

Postone, Moishe. 1993. *Time, labor, and social domination: A reinterpretation of Marx's critical theory.* Cambridge: Cambridge University Press.

Pratt, Andy. 2000. New media, the new economy and new spaces. *Geoforum* 31 (4): 425–436.

Prey, Robert. 2012. The network's blindspot: Exclusion, exploitation and Marx's process-relational ontology. *tripleC: Communication, Capitalism & Critique (www.triple-c.at)-Journal for a Global Sustainable Information Society* 10 (2): 253–273.

Prodnik, Jernej. 2012. A note on the ongoing processes of commodification: From the audience commodity to the social factory. *tripleC: Communication, Capitalism & Critique (www.triple-c.at)-Journal for a Global Sustainable Information Society* 10 (2): 274–301.

Qiu, Jack L. 2009. *Working-class network society: Communication technology and the information have-less in urban China.* Cambridge, MA: MIT Press.

Qiu, Jack L. 2010a. Class, communication, China: A thought piece. *International Journal of Communication* 4: 531–536.

Qiu, Jack L. 2010c. Network labour and non-elite knowledge workers in China. *Work, Organisation, Labour & Globalisation* 4 (2): 83–95.

Ramesh, Bapu P. 2008. Work organisation, control and "empowerment": Managing the contradictions of call centre work. In *In an outpost of the global economy: Work and workers in India's information technology industry,* ed. Carol Upadhya and A.R. Vasavi, 235–262. New Delhi: Routledge.

Reichelt, Helmut. 2001. *Zur logischen Struktur des Kapitalbegriffs bei Karl Marx.* Freiburg, Germany: Ça Ira.

Reichelt, Helmut. 2008. *Neue Marx-Lektüre: Zur Kritik sozialwissenschaftlicher Logik.* Hamburg: VSA.

Rey, PJ. 2012. Alienation, exploitation, and social media. *American Behavioral Scientist* 56 (4): 399–420.

Riethof, Marieke. 2005. Casualization of work. In *Encyclopedia of international development,* ed. Tim Forsyth, 64–65. Oxon: Routledge.

Ritzer, George, and Zeynep Atalay, eds. 2010. *Readings in globalization: Key concepts and major debates.* Malden, MA: Wiley-Blackwell.

Ritzer, George, and Nathan Jurgenson. 2010. Production, consumption, prosumption. *Journal of Consumer Culture* 10 (1): 13–36.

Ross, Andrew. 2001. No-collar labour in America's "new economy". *Socialist Register* 37: 77–87.

Ross, Andrew. 2003. *No-collar: The humane workplace and its hidden costs.* Philadelphia, PA: Temple University Press.

Ross, Andrew. 2008. The new geography of work: Power to the precarious? *Theory, Cul-ture & Society* 25 (7–8): 31–49.

Ross, Andrew. 2009. *Nice work if you can get it: Life and labour in precarious times.* New York: New York University Press.

Ross, Andrew, and Paul Smith. 2011. Cultural studies: A conversation. In *The renewal of cultural studies,* ed. Paul Smith, 245–258. Philadelphia, PA: Temple University Press.

Roth, Karl Heinz. 2005. *Der Zustand der Welt: Gegen-Perspektiven.* Hamburg: VSA.

Roth, Karl Heinz, and Marcel van der Linden. 2009. Ergebnisse und Perspektiven. In *Über Marx hinaus: Arbeitsgeschichte und Arbeitsbegriff in der Konfrontation mit den globalen Arbeitsverhältnissen des 21. Jahrhunderts,* ed. Marcel van der Linden and Karl Heinz Roth, 557–600. Berlin: Assoziation A.

Roth, Roland, and Dieter Rucht, ed. 2008. *Die sozialen Bewegungen in Deutschland seit 1945.* Frankfurt/Main: Campus.

Roy, Arundhati. 2003. Confronting empire. World Social Forum, Porto Alegre, Brazil, on January 27, 2003. http://www.sustecweb.co.uk/past/sustec11-4/following_speech_by_arundhati_ro.htm (accessed January 4, 2013).

Roy, Arundhati. 2012. Capitalism: A ghost story. *Outlook India,* March 26, 2012. http://www.outlookindia.com/article.aspx?280234 (accessed January 4, 2013).

Rubin, Isaak Illich. 2008. *Essays on Marx's theory of value.* Delhi: Aakar.

Rucht, Dieter. 1996. The impact of national context on social movement structures. In *Comparative perspectives on social movements,* ed. Doug McAdam, John D. McCarthy and Mayer N. Zald, 185–204. Cambridge: Cambridge University Press.

Rucht, Dieter. 2004. The quadruple "A". Media strategies of protest movements since the 1960s. In *Cyberprotest,* ed. Wim van de Donk et al., 29–56. London: Routledge.

Runciman, Walter G. 1993. Has British capitalism changed since the First World War? *British Journal of Sociology* 44 (1): 53–67.

Saad-Filho, Alfredo, and Deborah Johnston, ed. 2005. *Neoliberalism: A critical reader.* London: Pluto Press.

Said, Edward. 1978. *Orientalism: Western conceptions of the Orient.* New Delhi: Penguin.

Sandoval, Marisol. 2012. A critical empirical case study of consumer surveillance on Web 2.0. In *Internet and surveillance: The challenges of Web 2.0 and social media,* ed. Christian Fuchs, Kees Boersma, Anders Albrechtslund and Marisol Sandoval, 147–169. New York: Routledge.

Sandoval, Marisol. 2013. Monster media? Critical perspectives on corporate social responsibility in media and communication industries. PhD diss., University of Salzburg.

Sandoval, Marisol, and Christian Fuchs. 2010. Towards a critical theory of alternative media. *Telematics and Informatics* 27 (2): 141–150.

Sayed, Nermeen. 2011. Towards the Egyptian revolution: Activists' perceptions of social media for mobilization. *Journal of Arab & Muslim Media Research* 4 (2–3): 273–298.

Schiller, Dan. 1999. The legacy of Robert A Brady. Antifascist origins of the political economy of communications. *Journal of Media Economics* 12 (2): 89–101.

Schiller, Dan. 2000. *Digital capitalism.* Cambridge, MA: MIT Press.

Scholz, Trebor. 2011. Facebook as playground and factory. In *Facebook and philosophy,* ed. D.E. Wittkower, 241–252. Chicago: Open Court.

Scholz, Trebor, ed. 2013. *Digital labor: The Internet as playground and factory.* New York: Routledge.

Sennett, Richard. 2006. *The culture of the new capitalism.* New Haven, CT: Yale University Press.

Sevignani, Sebastian. 2012. The problem of privacy in capitalism and the alternative social networking site Diaspora*. *tripleC: Communication, Capitalism & Critique (www.triple-c.at)-Open Access Journal for a Global Sustainable Information Society* 10 (2): 600–617.

Shirky, Clay. 2008. *Here comes everybody.* London: Penguin.

Shirky, Clay. 2011. *Cognitive surplus: How technology makes consumers into collaborators.* London: Penguin.

Smith, Paul. 2006. Looking backwards and forwards at cultural studies. In *A companion to cultural studies,* ed. Toby Miller, 331–340. Malden, MA: Blackwell.

Smith, Paul. 2011a. Introduction. In *The renewal of cultural studies,* ed. Paul Smith, 1–8. Philadelphia, PA: Temple University Press.

Smith, Paul, ed. 2011b. *The renewal of cultural studies.* Philadelphia, PA: Temple University Press.

Smythe, Dallas W. 1951. The consumer's stake in radio and television. *The Quarterly of Film, Radio and Television* 6 (2): 109–128.

Smythe, Dallas W. 1960. On the political economy of communications. *Journalism & Mass Communication Quarterly* 37 (4): 563–572.

Smythe, Dallas W. 1977a. Communications: Blindspot of Western Marxism. *Canadian Journal of Political and Social Theory* 1 (3): 1–27.

Smythe, Dallas W. 1977b. Critique of the consciousness industry. *Journal of Communication* 27 (1): 198–202.

Smythe, Dallas W. 1981. *Dependency road.* Norwood, NJ: Ablex.

Smythe, Dallas W. 1984. New directions for critical communications research. *Media, Culture & Society* 6 (3): 205–217.

Smythe, Dallas W. 1994. *Counterclockwise.* Boulder, CO: Westview Press.

Smythe, Dallas W., and Tran Van Dinh. 1983. On critical and administrative research: A new critical analysis. *Journal of Communication* 33 (3): 117–127.

Sparks, Colin. 1996. Stuart Hall, cultural studies and Marxism. In *Stuart Hall: Critical dialogues in cultural studies,* ed. David Morely and Kuan-Hsing Chen, 71–101. London: Routledge.

Steeves, H. Leslie, and Janet Wasko. 2002. Feminist theory and political economy: Toward a friendly alliance. In *Sex & money: Feminism and political economy in the media,* ed. Eileen Meehan and Ellen Riordan, 16–29. Minneapolis: University of Minnesota Press.

Stehr, Nico. 1994. *Knowledge societies.* London: Sage.

Stevens, Andrew, and Vincent Mosco. 2010. Prospects for trade unions and labour organisations in India's IT and ITES industries. *Work, Organisation, Labour & Globalisation* 4 (2): 39–59.

Sullivan, Andrew. 2009. The revolution will be twittered. *The Atlantic.* http://www.theatlantic.com/daily-dish/archive/2009/06/the-revolution-will-be-twittered/200478/.

Tapscott, Don, and Anthony D. Williams. 2006. *Wikinomics: How mass collaboration changes everything.* New York: Penguin.

Terranova, Tiziana. 2000. Free labor: Producing culture for the digital economy. *Social Text* 18 (2): 33–58.

Thompson, Edward P. 1957. Socialist humanism. *The New Reasoner* 1 (2): 105–143.

Thompson, Edward P. 1973. An open letter to Leszek Kolakowski. In *The poverty of theory and other essays* [published 1978], 303–402. New York: Monthly Review Press.

Thompson, Edward P. 1978a. The poverty of theory, or An orrery of errors. In *The poverty of theory and other essays,* 1–210. New York: Monthly Review Press.

Thompson, Edward P. 1978b. *The poverty of theory and other essays.* London: Merlin.

Thorson, Kjerstin, et al. 2010. YouTube and proposition 8. *Information, Communication & Society* 13 (3): 325–349.

Toffler, Alvin. 1980. *The third wave.* New York: Bantam.

Touraine, Alain. 1974. *The post-industrial society: Tomorrow's social history: classes, conflicts and culture in the programmed society.* London: Wildwood House.

Touraine, Alain. 1985. An introduction to the study of social movements. *Social Research* 52 (4): 749–787.

Touraine, Alain. 1988. *Return of the actor.* Minneapolis: University of Minnesota Press.

Tronti, Mario. 1962. *Arbeiter und Kapital,* Frankfurt: Verlag Neue Kritik.

Turner, Graeme. 2012. *What's become of cultural studies?* London: Sage.

Upadhya, Carol, and A.R. Vasavi. 2008. Outposts of the global information economy: Work and workers in India's outsourcing industry. In *In an outpost of the global economy: Work and workers in India's information technology industry,* ed. Carol Upadhya and A.R. Vasavi, 9–49. New Delhi: Routledge.

Valenduc, Gérard. 2007. Occupational monograph: IT professional in software services. In *How restructuring is changing occupations? Case study evidence from knowledge-intensive, manufacturing and service occupations: Final report of WP11,* 71–97. EU FP6 WORKS Project—Work organisation and restructuring in the knowledge society. Leuven: HIVA.

Valk, Reimara, and Vasanthi Srinivasan. 2011. Work-family balance of Indian women software professionals: A qualitative study. *IIMB Management Review* 23 (1): 39–50.

van der Linden, Marcel, and Karl Heinz Roth. 2009. Einleitung. In *Über Marx hinaus: Arbeitsgeschichte und Arbeitsbegriff in der Konfrontation mit den globalen Arbeitsverhältnissen des 21: Jahrhunderts,* ed. Marcel van der Linden and Karl Heinz Roth, 7–28. Berlin: Assoziation A.

van Dijck, José. 2013. *The culture of connectivity: A critical history of social media.* Oxford: Oxford University Press.

van Dijk, Jan. 2006. *The network society.* 2nd ed. London: Sage.

van Dijk, Teun. 1998. *Ideology: A multidisciplinary approach.* London: Sage.

van Dijk, Teun. 2011. Discourse and ideology. In *Discourse studies: A multidisciplinary introduction,* ed. Teun van Dijk, 379–407. London: Sage.

Vercellone, Carlo. 2007. From formal subsumption to general intellect: Elements from a Marxist reading of the thesis of cognitive capitalism. *Historical Materialism* 15 (1): 13–36.

Vercellone, Carlo. 2010. The crisis of the law of value and the becoming-rent of profit. In *Crisis in the global economy,* ed. Andrea Fumagalli and Sandro Mezzadra, 85–118. Los Angeles, CA: Semiotext(e).

Virno, Paolo. 2004. *A grammar of the multitude.* Los Angeles, CA: Semiotext(e).

Wasko, Janet. 1993. Introduction. In *Illuminating the blindspots: Essays honoring Dallas W. Smythe,* ed. Janet Wasko, Vincent Mosco and Manjunath Pendakur, 1–11. Norwood, NJ: Ablex.

Wasko, Janet. 2004. The political economy of communications. In *The SAGE handbook of media studies,* ed. John D.H. Downing, 309–329. Thousand Oaks, CA: SAGE.

Wasko, Janet. 2005. Studying the political economy of media and information. *Comunicação e Sociedade* 7: 25–48.

Webster, Frank. 1995. *Theories of the information society.* London: Routledge.

Webster, Frank. 2002. The information society revisited. In *Handbook of new media,* ed. Sonia Livingstone and Leah Lievrouw, 22–33. London: Sage.

Werlhof, Claudia von. 1991. *Was haben die Hühner mit dem Dollar zu tun? Frauen und Ökonomie.* Munich: Frauenoffensive.

Williams, Raymond. 1958. *Culture & society: 1780–1950.* New York: Columbia University Press.

Williams, Raymond. 1961. *The long revolution.* London: Chatto & Windus.

Williams, Raymond. 1980. *Culture and materialism.* London: Verso.

Williams, Raymond. 1983. *Keywords.* New York: Oxford University Press.

Wolf, Dieter. 2002. *Der dialektische Widerspruch im Kapital: Ein Beitrag zur Marxschen Werttheorie.* Hamburg: VSA.

Wolf, Dieter. 2004. Kritische Theorie und Kritik der Politischen Ökonomie. *Wissenschaftliche Mitteilungen des Berliner Vereins zur Förderung der MEGA-Edition e.V.* 3: 9–190.

Wolf, Dieter. 2008. Zur Methode in Marx' Kapital unter besonderer Berücksichtigung ihres logisch-systematischen Charakters: Zum "Methodenstreit" zwischen Wolfgang Fritz Haug und Michael Heinrich. *Wissenschaftliche Mitteilungen des Berliner Vereins zur Förderung der MEGA-Edition e.V.* 6: 7–186.

Wood, Ellen Meiksins. 2003. *Empire of capital.* London: Verso.

Woolgar, Steve, ed. 2002. *Virtual society?* Oxford: Oxford University Press.

Wright, Erik Olin. 1997. *Class counts: Comparative studies in class analysis.* Cambridge: Cambridge University Press.

Wright, Erik Olin. 2000. *Class counts: Student edition.* Cambridge: Cambridge University Press.

Wright, Erik Olin. 2005. Foundations of a neo-Marxist class analysis. In *Approaches to class analysis,* ed. Erik Olin Wright, 4–30. Cambridge: Cambridge University Press.

Wright, Erik Olin, and Perrone, Luia. 1977. Marxist class categories and income inequality. *American Sociological Review* 42 (1): 32–55.

Yao, Lin. 2010. Revisiting critical scholars' alternative: A case study of Dallas Smythe's praxis. Paper presented at the 2010 Annual Meeting of the International Communication Association. Singapore.

Zhao, Yuezhi. 2007a. After mobile phone, what? Re-embedding the social in China's "digital revolution". *International Journal of Communication* 1: 92–120.

Zhao, Yuezhi. 2007b. Short-circuited? The communication of labor struggles in China. In *Knowledge workers in the information society,* ed. Catherine McKercher and Vincent Mosco, 229–247. Lanham, MD: Lexington Books.

Zhao, Yuezhi. 2008. *Communication in China.* New York: Rowman & Littlefield.

Zhao, Yuezhi. 2010a. China's pursuit of indigenous innovations in information technology developments: Hopes, follies and uncertainties. *Chinese Journal of Communication* 3 (3): 266–289.

Zhao, Yuezhi. 2010b. Directions for research on communication on China: An introductory and overview essay. *International Journal of Communication* 4: 573–583.

Zhao, Yuezhi. 2011. The challenge of China: Contribution to a transcultural political economy of communication for the twenty-first century. In *The handbook of political economy of communications,* ed. Janet Wasko, Graham Murdock and Helena Sousa, 558–582. Malden, MA: Wiley-Blackwell.

Žižek, Slavoj. 2008. *In defense of lost causes.* London: Verso.

Žižek, Slavoj. 2010a. How to begin from the beginning. In *The idea of communism,* ed. Costas Douzinas and Slavoj Žižek, 209–226. London: Verso.

Žižek, Slavoj. 2010b. *Living in the end times.* London: Verso.

Žižek, Slavoj. 2011. Don't fall in love with yourselves. In *Occupy! Scenes from occupied America,* ed. Carla Blumenkranz, Keith Gessen, Mark Greif, Sarah Leonard, Sarah Resnick, Nikil Saval, Eli Schmitt and Astra Taylor., 66–69. London: Verso.

Žižek, Slavoj. 2012. *The year of dreaming dangerously.* London: Verso.

Zoonen, Liesbet van, Farida Vis and Sabina Mihelj. 2010. Performing citizenship on You-Tube. *Critical Discourse Studies* 7 (4): 249–262.

News Articles, Documentaries and Data Sources

Action contre l'Impunité pur les droits humains (ACIDH). 2011. *Unheard voices: Mining activities in the Katanga province and the impact on local communities.* makeITfair Report: http://somo.nl/publications-en/Publication_3727. (accessed August 9, 2013).

Adbusters. 2012. #OCCUPYWALLSTREET. http://www.adbusters.org/blogs/adbusters-blog/occupywallstreet.html. (accessed August 9, 2013).

Apple. 2011. *Apple supplier responsibility: 2011 progress report*. http://images.apple.com/supplierresponsibility/pdf/Apple_SR_2011_Progress_Report.pdf. (accessed August 9, 2013).

Apple. 2012. *Apple supplier responsibility: 2012 progress report*. http://images.apple.com/supplierresponsibility/pdf/Apple_SR_2012_Progress_Report.pdf. (accessed August 9, 2013).

Apple. 2013. *Apple supplier responsibility: 2013 progress report*. http://images.apple.com/supplierresponsibility/pdf/Apple_SR_2013_Progress_Report.pdf. (accessed August 9, 2013).

ARD. 2013. *Ausgeliefert! Leiharbeiter bei Amazon* (At mercy! Contract workers at Amazon) http://mediathek.daserste.de/sendungen_a-z/799280_reportage-dokumentation/13402260_ausgeliefert-leiharbeiter-bei-amazon. (accessed August 9, 2013).

China Labor Watch. 2012a. Eye-witness testimony of worker involved [in] Foxconn's Taiyuan factory riot. http://www.chinalaborwatch.org/news/new-427.html. (accessed August 9, 2013).

China Labor Watch. 2012b. Update: 3000 to 4000 workers strike at Foxconn's China factory. http://www.chinalaborwatch.org/news/new-433.html. (accessed August 9, 2013).

CNN Global 500. 2012. Top companies: Biggest employers. http://money.cnn.com/magazines/fortune/global500/2012/performers/companies/biggest/ (accessed December 27, 2012).

Comscore. 2012. *The power of Like²: How social marketing works*. White Paper. http://www.comscore.com/ger/Press_Events/Presentations_Whitepapers/2012/The_Power_of_Like_2-How_Social_Marketing_Works (accessed June 27, 2012).

Fair Labor Association. 2012. *Independent investigation of Apple supplier, Foxconn*. http://www.fairlabor.org/sites/default/files/documents/reports/foxconn_investigation_report.pdf. (accessed August 9, 2013).

Finnwatch. 2007. *Connecting components, dividing communities: Tin production for consumer electronics in the DR Congo and Indonesia*. makeITfair Report: http://germanwatch.org/corp/it-tin.pdf. (accessed August 9, 2013).

Finnwatch and Swedwatch. 2010. *Voices from the inside: Local views on mining reform in Eastern DRC*. makeITfair Report: http://somo.nl/publications-en/Publication_3586/at_download/fullfile. (accessed August 9, 2013).

Forbes. 2011. AOL-Huffpo suit seeks $105M: "This is about justice". *Forbes Online*, April 12, 2011. http://www.forbes.com/sites/jeffbercovici/2011/04/12/aol-huffpo-suit-seeks-105m-this-is-about-justice/. (accessed August 9, 2013).

Forbes 2000. 2008. *The world's biggest companies 2008*. http://www.forbes.com/2008/04/02/worlds-largest-companies-biz-2000global08-cx_sd_0402global_land.html (accessed August 9, 2013).

Forbes 2000. 2012. *The world's biggest companies 2012*. http://www.forbes.com/global2000/list/ (accessed December 27, 2012).

Forbes: The world's billionaires. 2012. http://www.forbes.com/billionaires/list/ (accessed December 28, 2012).

Forestier, Patrick. 2007. *Blood coltan*. Documentary film. Paris: Java Film. http://www.youtube.com/watch?v=vJ8ZCX4NGHY (accessed December 26, 2012).

Foxconn. 2010. *2010 CSER annual report: Corporate social & environmental responsibility*. Shenzen: Foxconn Global SER Committee.

Foxconn. 2011. *2011 CSER annual report: Corporate social & environmental responsibility*. Shenzen: Foxconn Global SER Committee.

Free the Slaves. 2011. *The Congo report: Slavery in conflict minerals.* http://www.freetheslaves .net/Document.Doc?id=243.

Gootnick, David. 2008. *Testimony before the Congressional Human Rights Caucus: The Democratic Republic of Congo.* March 6, 2008. Washington, DC: US Government Accountability Office.

Greenhouse, Steven. 2012. Early praise in inspection at Foxconn brings doubts. *New York Times Online,* February 16, 2012.

Indian Council of Social Science Research (ICSSR). 2012. *Structural changes, industry and employment in the Indian economy.* http://isid.org.in/pdf/WP1202.pdf (accessed on December 30, 2012).

International Business Times. 2012. Anonymous accused Traxys of "blood trading" in lead ore and coltan with DR Congo. *International Business Times,* June 12, 2012. http://www .ibtimes.co.uk/articles/351164/20120612/anonymous-traxys-dr-congo-coltan-lead-ore.htm. (accessed August 9, 2013).

International Labour Organization (ILO). 1930. Convention C030—Hours of work (commerce and offices) convention, 1930. http://www.ilo.org/dyn/normlex/en/f?p= 1000:12100:0::NO::P12100_ILO_CODE:C030. (accessed August 9, 2013).

International Labour Organization. 2008. *Global Wage Report 2008/2009.* Geneva: International Labour Office.

International Labour Organization. 2010. *Global Wage Report 2010/2011.* Geneva: International Labour Office.

International Standard Classification of Occupations (ISCO-08) ISCO-08 Group definitions—final draft. http://www.ilo.org/public/english/bureau/stat/isco/docs/ gdstruct08.doc (accessed January 5, 2013).

International Standard Industrial Classification of All Economic Activities (ISIC Rev. 4). 2008. *ISIC Revision 4.* New York: United Nations.

ITRI (International Tin Research Institute). 2011. The top tin producers in 2011. https://www.itri.co.uk/index.php?option=com_zoo&task=item&item_id=2361& Itemid=143 (accessed December 25, 2012).

Jobs, Steve. 2010. Interview at the 2010 D8 conference. http://www.youtube.com/ watch?v=KEQEV6r2l2c (accessed December 28, 2012).

Lonmin. 2012. *Statement on Marikana situation.* http://www.lonminmarikanainfo.com/ news_article.php?articleID=1324#.UNc-nBjSF7w (accessed December 23, 2012).

Los Angeles Times. 2011. Arianna Huffington says Huff Po writer's lawsuit is "utterly without merit". *Los Angeles Times,* April 14, 2011.

Meikle, Graham and Sherman Young. 2012. *Media convergence. Networked digital media in everyday life.* Basingstoke: Palagrave Macmillan.

Ministry of Finance. 2011. *Economic survey 2009–2010.* http://indiabudget.nic.in/es2009-10/chapt2010/chapter.zip (accessed January 2, 2013).

MSNBC. 2008. Facebook asks users to translate for free. "Crowdsourcing" aids company's aggressive worldwide expansion. http://www.msnbc.msn.com/id/24205912/ns/ technology_and_science-internet/t/facebook-asks-users-translate-free/#.UP7-ChjSF7w (accessed January 22, 2013).

National Association of Software and Services Companies (NASSCOM). 2012. *The IT-BPO sector in India: Strategic review 2012: Executive summary.* http://www.nasscom.in/ sites/default/files/researchreports/SR_2012_Executive_Summary.pdf (accessed January 3, 2013).

National Bureau of Statistics of China. 2012. *Statistical communiqué of the People's Republic of China on the 2011 national economic and social development.* http://www.stats.gov.cn/english/ newsandcomingevents/t20120222_402786587.htm (accessed December 30, 2012).

National Sample Survey Office (NSSO). 2011. Key indicators of employment and unemployment in India, 2009–2010. NSS 66th round. New Delhi: National Statistical Organisation.

Poulsen, Frank. 2011. *Blood in the mobile*. DVD documentary. Berlin: good!movies.

Qiu, Jack L. 2010b. *Deconstructing Foxconn*. Documentary film. http://vimeo.com/17558439 (accessed December 27, 2012).

Shedd, Kim B. 2012. Cobalt. In *2010 Minerals yearbook*. Reston, VA: US Geological Survey.

SOMO (Centre for Research on Multinational Corporations). 2007. *Capacitating electronics: The corrosive effects of platinum and palladium mining on labour rights and communities*. makeITfair Report: http://somo.nl/publications-nl/Publication_2545-nl/at_download/fullfile. (accessed August 9, 2013).

Special Eurobarometer 359. *Attitudes on data protection and electronic identity in the European Union*. http://ec.europa.eu/public_opinion/archives/ebs/ebs_359_en.pdf. (accessed August 9, 2013).

Statistical Yearbook of the Republic of China. 2010. Nantou, China: Directorate General of Budget, Accounting and Statistics.

Stross, Randall. 2008. *Planet Google*. New York: Free Press.

Students & Scholars against Corporate Misbehaviour (SACOM). 2010. *Workers as machines: Military management in Foxconn*. http://sacom.hk/wp-content/uploads/2010/11/report-on-foxconn-workers-as-machines_sacom.pdf. (accessed August 9, 2013).

Students & Scholars against Corporate Misbehaviour (SACOM). 2011a. *Foxconn and Apple fail to fulfill promises: Predicaments of workers after suicides*. http://sacom.hk/wp-content/uploads/2011/05/2011-05-06_foxconn-and-apple-fail-to-fulfill-promises1.pdf. (accessed August 9, 2013).

Students & Scholars against Corporate Misbehaviour (SACOM). 2011b. *iSlave behind the iPhone: Foxconn workers in Central China*. http://sacom.hk/wp-content/uploads/2011/09/20110924-islave-behind-the-iphone.pdf. (accessed August 9, 2013).

Students & Scholars against Corporate Misbehaviour (SACOM). 2012. *New iPhone, old abuses: Have working conditions at Foxconn in China improved?* http://www.scribd.com/doc/106445655. (accessed August 9, 2013).

Swedwatch. 2007. *Powering the mobile world: Cobalt production for batteries in the DR Congo and Zambia*. makeITfair Report: http://germanwatch.org/corp/it-cob.pdf. (accessed August 9, 2013).

UNHDR. 2009. *Human development report 2009*. Hampshire: Palgrave Macmillan.

UNHDR. 2011. *United Nations Human Development Report 2011*. New York: Palgrave Macmillan.

United Nations. 2002. Final report of the panel of experts on the illegal exploitation of natural resources and other forms of wealth of the Democratic Republic of the Congo. http://www.un.org/news/dh/latest/drcongo.htm (accessed December 26, 2012).

United States District Court Southern District of New York. 2012. *Opinion and order: Jonathan Tasini, Molly Secours, Tara Dublin, Richard Laermer and Billy Altman, individually and on behalf of all others similarly situated, Plaintiffs,—against—Aol, Inc., thehuffingtonpost.com, Inc., Arianna Huffington and Kenneth Lerer, defendants*. Case 1:11-cv-02472-JGK.

US Bureau of the Census. 2012. *Income, poverty, and health insurance coverage in the United States: 2011*. Current Population Reports P60–243. Washington, DC: US Government Printing Office.

US Geological Survey Statistics. 2012. Commodity Statistics and Information. http://minerals.usgs.gov/minerals/pubs/commodity. (accessed August 9, 2013).

Vise, David A. 2005. *The Google story*. London: Macmillan.

Wallraff, Günter. 2009. Undercover. *Die Zeit,* July 2, 2009.

Webster, Juliet. 2011. Doing research, doing politics: ICT research as a form of activism. *tripleC: Communication, Capitalism & Critique (www.triple-c.at)-Journal for a Global Sustainable Information Society* 9 (1): 1–10.

WEED (World Economy, Ecology and Development) and SACOM (Students and Scholars against Corporate Misbehaviour). 2008. *The dark side of cyberspace: Inside the sweatshops of China's hardware production.* http://sacom.hk/wp-content/uploads/2009/01/cyberspace21.pdf. (accessed August 9, 2013).

World Investment Report. 2012. *World investment report 2012.* New York: United Nations.

Yager, Thomas R. 2012. *The mineral industry of Congo (Kinshasa).* In *2010 minerals yearbook.* Reston, VA: US Geological Survey.

Zerdick, Axel, et al. 2000. *E-conomics: Strategies for the digital marketplace.* Berlin: Springer.

INDEX

absolute surplus-value 98, 197, 198, 241, 348

abstract labour 35–6, 41, 46–7, 54, 106–7, 275, 348

accumulation *see* capital accumulation; primitive accumulation

action 253

Adbusters (magazine) 69, 316

administrative ideology 75

Adorno, Theodor W. 78–9, 82–3, 135, 137, 149–50

advertising 98–9; alienation and 255–6; audience commodity and 87–8; audience labour and 91; on Huffington Post 271–3; on Internet 90; price for 117; profit and 80; on social media 101, 116–17, 118, 264–5, 276, 287, 298, 312; statistics for 115; surplus-value of 99

AdWords 117, 118–19

Age of Discontinuity 138

agricultural society, international division of digital labour (IDDL) and 294

alienation 32–3, 95, 349, 351; advertising and 255–6; on Facebook 256–7, 259–63; of labour-power 254–5, 355; on social media 256–7, 259–63

Al Jazeera 341

allocation, mode of 158

altermondialiste movement 311

alternative media 16, 83, 91–4, 332, 342–3, 345

alternative radio 92

Althusser, Louis 32, 62, 164, 349

Amazon 2–3, 7

Amazon Mechanical Turk 2, 7

ancient slavery, as mode of production 162–3, 166–7

Anderson, Kevin 209

Andrejevic, Mark 94–5, 258–9

Aneesh, A. 205

Anglo-American approach, to political economy of communications (PE/C) 79

Anonymous 342

anti-humanism, Karl Marx and 16

Apple 7, 136, 182, 186–93, 287

Aquinas, Thomas 24

Arab Spring 313, 324, 329

Arbeit see labour

Arbeiten (working as a process) 27

aristocracy *see* labour aristocracy

Aristotle 24

Arthur, Christopher J. 47–8

articulation, Stuart Hall and 64

arts, dialectic of 76

Arvidsson, Adam 129, 130–1, 276–7

assembly work 7, 182–99, 293

attention time, on social media 118

audience commodity 93–4, 110–11, 116, 133, 265, 349, 354; advertising and 87–8; social media and 91, 95, 100, 279

audience labour 90, 91, 349, 354; Dallas Smythe and 75–85; exploitation of 76; media and 86